BOULDER BOOK STORE
447-2074 EMAIL BOULDERBK@AOL.COM
HOURS: MON-SAT 9 A.M.--10 P.M.
SUN 10 A.M. -- 8 P.M.
ORDER TOLL FREE 800-244-4651
OR BY FAX 1-303-447-3946

QTY	PRODUCT	DEPT	PRICE
1 @	BOULDER EASYFINDE	350000	6.95
1 @	INSIDERS GT BOULD	116900	16.95

	TOTAL SALE	$23.90
@	@ SALES TAX	$1.76
40294	NET SALE	$25.66

	CASH TENDERED	$30.00
	YOUR CHANGE	$4.34

00001 03-000 ACR 5/18/01 9:55 AM

USED BOOKS ARE NOT RETURNABLE
THANK YOU FOR SHOPPING AT YOUR
LOCALLY OWNED INDEPENDENT BOOKSTORE
VOTE WITH YOUR DOLLARS
PLEASE KEEP YOUR RECEIPT

THE INSIDERS' GUIDE TO

Boulder
& Rocky Mountain National Park

by
Roz Brown
and
Linda Cornett

Insiders' Publishing Inc.

The Insiders' Guide®
An imprint of Falcon® Publishing Inc.
A Landmark Communications company
P.O. Box 1718
Helena, MT 59624
(800) 582-2665
www.insiders.com

•

Sales and Marketing: Falcon Publishing, Inc.
P.O. Box 1718
Helena, MT 59624
(800) 582-2665
www.falcon.com

•

FIFTH EDITION
2nd printing

•

©1999 by Falcon Publishing, Inc.

•

Printed in the United States
of America

•

Publications from *The Insiders' Guide*® series are available at special discounts for bulk
purchases for sales promotions, premiums or fundraisings. Special editions, including personalized covers, can be created in large quantities for special needs.
For more information, please contact Falcon Publishing.

ISBN 1-57380-133-X

Preface

Why visit Boulder? It's not exactly a tourist spot, nor a mountain resort — though it's close to many of Colorado's most popular ones. It takes an hour or a little more to drive to Rocky Mountain National Park, the Indian Peaks Wilderness and many of the ski areas in Summit County, including Winter Park, Breckenridge and Keystone. A couple of hours more takes you to Vail, Aspen and Steamboat Springs. Just up Boulder Canyon, Eldora Mountain Resort, a smaller ski area, is less than an hour away.

Boulder has all the attractions of a big city — art and culture, fine educational institutions, an interesting populace, many excellent restaurants and points of attraction — but without the hassle of a big city.

But Boulder is also an attraction unto itself. It's a national model for municipally owned open space and controlled growth. It's an inspiration for cities that want to preserve and revitalize their historic hearts, while nurturing commerce, the arts and entertainment. It's an outdoor recreation mecca for regular folks and professional athletes alike. Anyone who enjoys hiking, backpacking, bicycling, rock climbing, mountaineering, running and skiing will love Boulder. The annual Bolder Boulder 10-kilometer foot race is one of the nation's largest.

Most visitors to Boulder come to see family and friends — not your typical tourists on a vacation adventure — though adventure possibilities abound in the area. The University of Colorado attracts families for gradua-tion, holidays and ski vacations, with many of the graduates staying in the area. After its early days as a mining supply town — there was no gold discovered right in Boulder, but nearby in the mountains — Boulder's identity became firmly established as a university town in the late 1800s and continues to be so with the university comprising about one quarter of the city's population. With its various scientific institutions, including the National Oceanic and Atmospheric Administration, the National Institute of Standards and Technology and the National Center for Atmospheric Research, Boulder also attracts an international population of scientists and engineers.

Many of us moved to Boulder because it's such a great place to live. It has Colorado's sunny dry climate, is close to the mountains, and is a manageable size. We enjoy the health-promoting attitude, good schools, recreational opportunities and wholesome atmosphere for raising families and living the good life. Athletes from all over the world live and train in Boulder for many of the same reasons, plus the high elevation that gives them the competitive edge.

Boulder also hosts many annual events and festivals such as the Colorado Dance Festival, Colorado Shakespeare Festival and Colorado Music Festival, welcoming a whole entourage of performing artists and audiences each summer.

So read on and explore all of Boulder's fine offerings.

About the Authors

Roz Brown

A South Dakota native, Roz studied close to home before finding the closest thing to nirvana, Boulder, and transferring to the University of Colorado. A transfer student from the University of South Dakota to the CU–Boulder, she was awed by mascot Ralphie the Buffalo, in spite of the Buffs' lack of bragging rights in that decade.

In college she began working in radio and upon graduation in 1979 was hired by Boulder's KBOL. While she was serving as News Director there, the station received the 1983 Colorado Associated Press "News Station of the Year" award.

After the birth of her first child, Roz began freelancing for Denver's KOA as the Boulder Bureau reporter. She has been an adjunct professor for CU's Journalism School, teaching production classes to aspiring broadcasters, and has twice served as president of the Boulder Press Club. She has also written and published newsletters for the City of Boulder since 1982 and has been a contributor to *Nexus, Colorado's Journal of Holistic Health,* since 1992. In 1997 she worked for CBS radio as a correspondent covering the Timothy McVeigh, Oklahoma City bombing trial in Denver and has covered the Boulder murder case of JonBenet Ramsey since it occurred in December 1996.

Roz and her husband David Grimm, communications director for the president of CU, live near downtown Boulder with their daughters, 13-year old Collier and 9-year old Grey. Much to her teenager's mortification, Roz is actively involved at the neighborhood middle school as PTO President. She also enjoys hiking, biking, reading, antique shopping, entertaining and accompanying friends and family at the piano.

Linda Cornett

Born in Oak Ridge, Tenn., Linda Cornett moved with her parents to Idaho Falls, Idaho, when she was three. The family fell in love with the majestic scenery and the outdoor activities of their new home. When a nuclear explosion forced closure of the experimental aircraft site where her father (and many of Idaho Falls' breadwinners) worked, the family moved South again, to Huntsville, Ala., and the NASA facility there.

Alabama never "took," and after graduating from Auburn University with a degree in journalism and working for a year at the local newspaper, Linda packed up books, clothes, a couple of pots, a rocking chair and a waterbed, and headed back West.

Avoiding Denver traffic jams, she saw a road sign to a place with the odd name of Boulder. She stumbled into a town that had shed its rough mining origins to embrace the sophisticated liberalism of a college town. Stopping for supper, she was served black bean soup by a waitress in bare feet and a tie-dyed skirt who casually enlisted the help of the long-haired clientele to suggest a cheap place to stay. For a spot so geographically, socially and politically removed from family and Alabama, it felt a lot like home.

Within a week, she was settled in a house with a group of University of Colorado students and within two weeks she had a job at the Boulder *Daily Camera,* the local newspaper, where she would work on and off for 18 years.

The *Camera* — and a one-year stint at the *Denver Post* — opened the door to the community and the region, as Linda covered everything from public schools and the University of Colorado, city and county government to entertainment, nonprofit agencies, health and minority issues.

She married a native Coloradan whose family is among the German Russians who added their unique culture to the state's rich mix of Mexican, English, French, Italian and native American and Hispanic.

Their two children, now 17 and 20, have the strong sense of place that comes from growing up in a smallish town where a walk down any street turns up a friend or acquaintance.

In 1997, after a total of 20 years in the daily education that is journalism, Linda headed in a new direction, returning to college to work on a master's degree in computer information systems with an emphasis on multimedia. It was a logical choice, since Colorado's Front Range has become a mini-Silicon Valley and the centrally located state is a headquarters for communications giants like TCI.

Linda and her children share their downtown Boulder home with Gloria, the wandering dog; Gloria's dog, Jackson; and Shy, a cat too fat to go far. Artis, 20, is a sophomore at the University of Colorado planning to get a degree in physical therapy, as she recovers from a serious car accident that nearly cost her her right leg. She spends her time with a close group of lifelong friends. Bayard, 17, is a senior at September School, a private high school, and a dedicated otaku (fan of japanimation) who enjoys video games. They're both ready to spread their wings into the wider world, but they will always know where home is.

Acknowledgments

Roz...

Original settlers in Boulder were determined to create an "Athens of the West." With such a lofty goal, you can imagine how challenging it is to "keep up" with this ever-changing community at the close of the 20th century. I have lived in Colorado for 23 years, but updating this *Insiders' Guide* was an educational experience as the state's Front Range continues on a path of rapid change and growth. Thanks first to my best friend and life partner, David Grimm, for constant encouragement, great meals, and sharing my enthusiasm about this special place we call home. To my co-author Linda Cornett, for keeping me on deadline, and to previous authors Reed Glenn, Claire Walter and Shelly D. Schlender for the original text that made my job easier. A special thanks to editor John Harrington for his patience.

To the organizations and individuals who offered me assistance or information: the Boulder Chamber of Commerce, *Boulder Magazine, Nexus,* and the *Daily Camera's* John Lehndorff for keeping track of the constantly changing restaurant scene. To public relations expert Barbara Taylor with the Boulder Valley School District and realtor Irene Shaffer at RE/MAX of Boulder. Also to the many public relations people, communications officers and especially Andrea Robbins, colleague and friend at the city's transportation office. Thanks also to the Boulder Media Women's group for all the "connections" they support. To the late Maria Rogers for instilling an interest in Boulder's history. And to Phyllis Smith for her one-of-a-kind book, *A Look At Boulder; From Settlement to City.* To my friends for their encouragement and my mother, Hope, whose faith in my abilities is essential. And to my daughters, Collier and Grey, who commented only infrequently when trying to locate something on my desk and more regularly encouraged me to "hurry up" so we could find time to take part in Boulder's diverse cultural activities.

Linda...

My heartfelt thanks to:

The people who lived here originally and kept the place so beautiful for the rest of us.

The visionaries who recognized that Boulder had become a town well worth planning and shaping and preserving.

The citizens who agreed, and continue to support that effort.

The residents of 1973, who graciously made room for one more. The visitors who come and appreciate, richen the mix for a while and leave us some of their money.

My dear, old friends, who have shown me so many unsuspected facets of our shared home over the years.

My children and their young friends, who have taught me things I never thought I'd want to know about the younger side of town. My friend Jeannie Vargo, who amused and frustrated and intrigued me for 27 years, and introduced me to the quiet joy of backcountry skiing. Clear trails, Jeannie, fresh powder and blue skies to you.

Table of Contents

Directory of Maps

Boulder & Surrounding Area

Greater Boulder

N

To Lyons and Estes Park
Iris Ave.
Folsom St.
To Boulder Reservoir
Longmont Diagonal
119

28th St.
30th St.
Valmont Rd.

Broadway
Balsam Ave.
9th St.

Sunshine Canyon

Mapleton Ave.

Pearl St.
Pearl St. Mall
Canyon Blvd.
The Village

119
Central Park
Arapahoe Ave.
7

Boulder Creek Path
To Boulder Falls, Nederland, Estes Park & Four Mile Canyon

University Hill
University of Colorado

36
157

Foothills Pkwy.

Baseline Rd.
To Lousville and Lafayette

Flagstaff Rd.
Chautauqua Park

National Institute of Standards and Technology (Atomic Clock)

The Flatirons

U.S. 36 to Denver Int'l Airport and I-25

Table Mesa Dr.

National Center for Atmospheric Research

S. Broadway

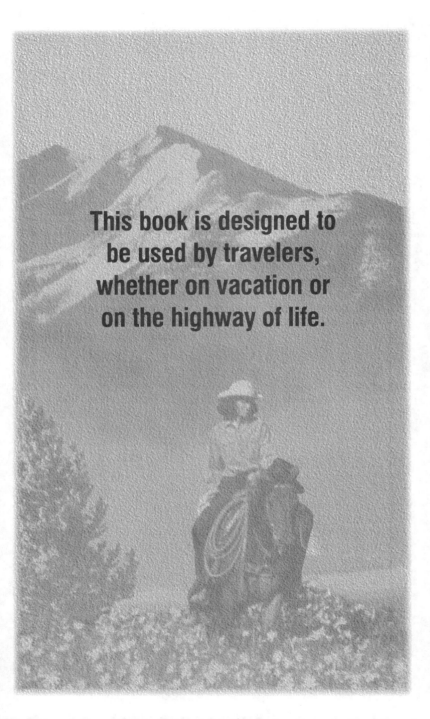

This book is designed to be used by travelers, whether on vacation or on the highway of life.

How To Use This Book

You're not a Coloradan long before you understand the state is divided into two distinct geographical regions, the Western Slope and the Front Range. Most of us live and work in cities along the Front Range, but spend weekends camping, hiking or skiing on the Western Slope. Boulder is one of several mid-sized cities along the Front Range.

Boulder is sometimes mistaken for a suburb of Denver. It's true that development along U.S. 36 has created a commercial corridor between Boulder and Denver, but Boulder residents take great pride in their city's uniqueness. Each year citizens willingly spend thousands of dollars to purchase open space, creating buffer zones around Boulder. What we call unique, however, is sometimes viewed as bizarre and becomes endless fodder for gibes and jokes, especially from those who call us the "People's Republic of Boulder." Others read stories in the paper about Boulder and say they "just don't get it" — usually in reference to our politics, fierce independence, and the egotism that accompanies both. Those of us who've lived here 20 years or more sometimes shake our heads too, but more often wear our city's eccentricity like a badge.

This book is designed to be used by travelers whether on vacation or on the highway of life. All the chapters are independent and can be read in any order. They are cross-referenced where appropriate, so if you find only a sentence in one chapter about something that sounds intriguing it's likely there's an expanded paragraph elsewhere. Check the table of contents, then zip to the chapter you need.

There are Insiders' Tips in each chapter to give you a head start on getting to know Boulder, and the Close-ups offer expanded information on fun stuff like the Molly Brown House.

Like every community there are words in the Boulder lexicon that won't mean much at first — like The Flatirons, Devil's Thumb, Chautauqua, The Rockpile, The Skip and The Hop. Keep reading. They'll soon be familiar.

Boulder is not a large city, just less than 100,000 residents, but the largest city in Boulder County. Still, feeling comfortable in any new community takes time. Remember the city is divided into several distinguishable areas which will be evident as you read the text: the University, the Pearl Street Mall, Crossroads, 28th & 30th Streets, Table Mesa, and north Boulder. Then there are the smaller, nearby communities in Boulder County: Longmont, Louisville, Lafayette, Lyons, Broomfield and the mountain towns. This guide focuses on Boulder County first (and contains chapters on Daytrips and Weekend Getaways less than two hours away). Chapters on Rocky Mountain National Park, Estes Park and Grand Lake follow. Whether you're scouting your next climb or hunting for the perfect martini, you'll find it here. In most cases listings are in alphabetical order, but when they are not, they are not in any order of preference or importance.

We update the guide regularly, so let us know what you like and don't like or if we've missed something. Write us at *The Insiders' Guide® to Boulder*, Insiders' Publishing Inc., P.O. Box 1718, Helena, MT 59624, or visit our website at www.insiders.com.

The *Denver Post* once described Boulder as "The little town nestled between the mountains and reality."

Overview

Cresting the scenic overlook on U.S. Highway 36 from Denver, first-time visitors gaze down upon Boulder and know they've arrived someplace special. Snuggled serenely against the pine-covered foothills, punctuated dramatically with the red Flatirons and crowned with the gleaming white halo of the Continental Divide, Boulder looks like the Promised Land.

That's how it appeared to early settler Capt. Thomas Aikins, who, in 1858, peered at the Boulder Valley through his field glasses and remarked, "The mountains looked right for gold, and the valleys looked rich for grazing." Aikins and his party did find gold in the hills above Boulder, and many have driven the highway over the hill and found their Shangri-La.

A mere 29 miles from Denver, Boulder is sometimes considered part of the Greater Denver Metropolitan Area for statistical purposes. But Boulder considers itself a world apart — and indeed it is.

This green haven at the foot of the Rocky Mountains is a unique enclave of science, education, research, outdoor enthusiasm, elite athletic training, health food, bicycling, recycling, the arts and New Age culture — a kind of Berkeley of the Rockies, sometimes jokingly dubbed "The People's Republic of Boulder."

Boulder is home to Celestial Seasonings tea company, the Naropa Institute (started by Tibetan Buddhists), the Boulder School of Massage Therapy, the Rolf Institute (international headquarters), Ball Aerospace, the National Center for Atmospheric Research, the National Oceanic and Atmospheric Administration, the National Institute of Standards and Technology (home of the atomic clock, by which all U.S. time is set) and the University of Colorado (referred to throughout this book as CU-Boulder), one of CU's four campuses. The university's student and staff population of more than 30,000 (25,125 students and 5,080 employees) makes up more than one-third of Boulder's total population of 94,250, whose median age is 29. (Boulder County's median age is 31.6.)

The Denver Post once described Boulder as "The little town nestled between the mountains and reality."

Boulder People: A Confluence of Cultures

Boulder is full of old and new refugees from congested East and West Coast cities and Chicago — many of them professionals — seeking a better life. And they find it here, along with compatible company and culture in what many longtime residents feel is near-utopia: low crime, high mountains, plentiful blue skies and sunshine, glacial-melt drinking water, good schools, a lively arts scene, an enlightened city government and a wholesome, healthy outlook. In fact, parents often urge their college-age offspring away from Boulder for an eye-opening dip into "the real world." Escapees from the Midwest find the cultural milieu they were missing — and mountains! Boulder natives do exist, but they're rare creatures. (They're usually the ones who don't ski, while almost everyone else in Boulder does.)

Though Boulder has a predominately white, upper-middle-class population, there's a cosmopolitan element provided by the staff and students from foreign countries at the many scientific institutions and the university. Sixty-four percent of Boulder adults attended four years of college; 59 percent have five or more years of college.

Unfortunately, plentiful well-paying jobs and affordable housing are not among

Boulder's amenities. Many local engineers and scientists came to work at IBM or one of the national centers. But most people who live in Boulder have deliberately chosen to do so for the mountains and general ambiance, not necessarily for the job opportunities — and they pay the price in underemployment and a daunting real estate market. Compared to California or Washington, D.C., Boulder's average single-family home price of $274,000 (1998 overall figure from the Boulder County Assessor's Office) might seem affordable. But for those operating within the local economy, surviving in Boulder can be a real challenge. Students vie for all the low-paying jobs and affordable housing, and many CU-Boulder graduates, originally from other states, like it so much that they stay here.

Traditionally, many people, both young and old, have worked for next to nothing just to live in Boulder. But as rents and housing costs continually escalate, it becomes more difficult. Rock-climbing bums, writers, certified massage therapists (there are hundreds), teachers, psychotherapists and scientists are some of the colorful — often unemployed — clients lingering in local coffeehouses. Some of these same folks may deliver your pizza, drive your cab or sell you skis at a local mountain sports shop. Boulder unemployment is only 3.0 percent, but *under*employment is much higher.

Boulderites participate in a number of humanitarian and volunteer efforts including local government, environmental activism and a strong Sister Cities program. Among Boulder's sister cities are Jalapa, Nicaragua; Lhasa, Tibet; Yamagata, Japan; and Dushanbe, Tajikistan, in the former Soviet Union. The Sister Cities programs include cultural exchange as well as humanitarian aid shipments; environmental projects; and exchange of students, doctors and technicians. Boulder families and other organizations host foreign students and sponsor Bosnian refugees and Soviet Jews. In past years many Vietnamese refugees were also brought to Boulder and have succeeded professionally. Habitat for Humanity has a local contingent, and there's a controversial local program to help the trade-embargoed, economically stressed Cubans.

Despite the natural beauty outside their back door, Boulderites do love to travel. Go to a remote island in Fiji, and don't be surprised to bump into someone from Boulder.

Boulder Ethnic Demographics

Note: Based on 1994 data, the most recent available.

White	89.7%
Hispanic	4.8%
Asian	3.8%
Black	1.2%
Native American	0.4%
Other	0.1%

Open Space, Limited Growth and Enlightened Development

Unlike sprawling Greater Denver and other Colorado communities mushrooming to infinity, Boulder is a sort of fixed island surrounded by the protective reefs of open space. In 1967, Boulder became the first city in the United States to tax itself for funds to be used specifically for the acquisition, management and maintenance of open space — an ongoing program. But even earlier, at the turn of the century, Boulder's city government and citizens established a mountain park system by purchasing portions of the city's dramatic mountain backdrop, often called the greenbelt, to protect it from development. (See our History chapter for details.)

Today, Boulder's citizens enjoy almost 29,000 acres of open space in and around the city (another 9,000 acres are planned for purchase in the next few years), 7,000 acres of adjacent city-owned mountain parks, and about 55,000 acres of county open space, some of which is under agricultural lease and is not open to the public. Residents of Greater Denver and nearby communities frequent Boulder's trail-laced, open space too, since their land is largely filled with shopping centers, subdivisions and parking lots. The city of Boulder itself encompasses 27.8 square miles.

Boulder sits in a valley below the Rocky Mountain foothills.

In 1977 Boulder instituted a limited-growth ordinance called the Danish Plan, the brainchild of then-city councilman (now county commissioner) Paul Danish, restricting new building to 2 percent annual growth. In 1985 it was replaced with another growth moratorium, which is still in effect.

There's no getting around the fact that this makes Boulder a more desirable, yet more expensive place to live. Because of limited growth, affordable housing is one of the biggest problems in this small city where the student population occupies most of the lower-priced dwellings. Many people find less-expensive housing in the nearby smaller cities of Louisville and Lafayette, currently bursting at the seams with new development. See our Boulder Neighborhoods and Real Estate chapters for more information.

Because so much natural habitat has been preserved, more than 1,200 deer share the environs with residents. Deer grazing in neighborhood yards is a common sight. Though undeniably picturesque, the deer wreak havoc on local gardens. Gardeners have been distressed to find their tomatoes trampled, peas pilfered and tulips nipped off at the bud. Smart gardeners plant a wildlife garden and build a tall fence around the human garden. Mountain lions and bears occasionally wander into

Those who spend any time in Boulder are bound to hear about Niwot's Curse. There are various versions, though no evidence that Chief Niwot (meaning Left Hand) of the South Arapaho Indian tribe ever said any of them — or even proclaimed a "curse" — according to Boulder's Carnegie Library for local history. Nevertheless, the library's official-unofficial version reads: "The Boulder Valley is so beautiful that people seeing it will want to stay and their staying will be the undoing of the beauty." Another less-official but more common version is: "Once you gaze upon the Flatirons, you will never be happy anywhere else."

town, too. In one case, a concerned citizen fetched his futon to provide a soft landing pad for a treed bear, tranquilized by wildlife officials. Another young bear led police on a chase right down the Pearl Street pedestrian mall. Skunks, raccoons and coyotes are regulars in areas near open space. A city-sponsored backyard wildlife program promotes landscaping that will attract and accommodate songbirds, butterflies and bats.

Outdoor-Sports Capital

Look in any Boulder garage and you're likely to find several bicycles (mountain, touring and racing), several pairs of skis (downhill and cross-country: racing, touring, skating, telemark and mountaineering), snowshoes, perhaps a windsurfer and/or kayak, crampons (climbing spikes), an ice axe and mountaineering gear, rock-climbing ropes and harnesses, backpacks, in-line skates, a fly-fishing rod and a plethora of running shoes. It's no coincidence that *Outside* magazine once named Boulder "the sports town" and in 1999 included it on the "top ten places to live" list.

Residents also engage in more traditional pursuits, such as tennis and golf. Boulder's population of couch potatoes is probably one of the nation's lowest. A 1992 survey by the Centers for Disease Control found that Colorado had fewer fat people per capita and more people who exercise than any other state. Landlocked Colorado ranks second nationally in the number of certified scuba divers per

capita (Florida is No. 1, and California is No. 3). Several years ago, *USA Today* ranked Boulder No. 1 in its rating of the top 50 healthiest places to live in the United States. A *Colorado Daily* (local newspaper) poll found that seven out of 10 Boulderites owned bicycles. According to another guidebook, Boulder's bicycle count is 93,000.

Why Boulder? The mountains seem to attract outdoors-oriented people. Perhaps Boulderites felt obliged to lead the way when citizen Frank Shorter became the first American ever to win an Olympic medal in the marathon — gold in 1972 in Munich, silver in 1976 in Montreal. "When Frank won the gold, everybody in America started running," says Neill Woelk, a veteran sports reporter at Boulder's *Daily Camera* newspaper. Shorter, now a Boulder attorney, also sells a line of athletic wear and is a frequent Olympics commentator. Another famous Boulder runner, Arturo Barrios, held the world record for 10 kilometers until 1993.

Boulder is also known nationwide for its huge bicycling population and local celebrities. Boulder cyclist Connie Carpenter won Olympic gold in 1984 for the road race, and her husband, Davis Phinney, was the first American ever to win a Tour de France stage. Alexi Grewal won an Olympic gold medal in 1984 for the road race. With more than 90 miles of bike lanes and off-street bike paths, citizens can cycle almost everywhere, sometimes faster than by car — and without the parking hassle.

Elite athletes from all over the world move

www.insiders.com

See this and many other Insiders' Guide® destinations online — in their entirety.

Visit us today!

---

to Boulder specifically to train in its health-promoting atmosphere and high altitude. The winners of at least 13 of the last 14 Hawaii Ironman world championships — the world's best triathletes — all live or train in Boulder, among them the 1998 winner, Peter Reid; six-time winner Mark Allen; six-time winner Dave Scott; eight-time women's champion Paula Newby-Fraser (from Zimbabwe); and two-time winner Erin Baker (New Zealand). Olympic ice skater Debi Thomas trained here. Three-time Boston Marathon women's winner Uta Pippig also lives in Boulder. Boulderite Mark Coogan is on the U.S. Olympic team running the marathon. The list goes on and on.

The University of Colorado's football team, the Golden Buffaloes, was the 1990 co-national champion and is considered one of the nation's most successful programs. The women's basketball team is also tops. CU-Boulder's Alpine and Nordic ski teams train at nearby Eldora Mountain Resort, only 21 miles away. The Denver-Boulder Metroplex was recently selected as the No. 1 metropolitan area for sports fans in the nation (ahead of Dallas, Los Angeles, New York and Chicago).

For mere mortals there are health clubs galore, the most popular being the great outdoors. Boulder boasts 100 miles of hiking trails in the mountain parks, literally outside our back doors. One of the world's largest 10-kilometer footraces, the annual Bolder Boulder through the city's streets, attracts more than 40,000 runners. The Flatirons, numerous rock formations and nearby Eldorado Canyon make Boulder a rock-climbing mecca. Read this book's chapter on Boulder Participatory Sports for a full description.

Heart and Soul

Boulder's Pearl Street Mall forms the heart and center of the city. Historic buildings, housing shops, galleries, offices and sidewalk cafes line this photogenic, four-block, open-air walkway — formerly part of Pearl Street. Sadly, since the mall was completed in 1976, constant upscaling and rising rents have driven out many of the older businesses, replacing them with a musical-chairs array of new establishments. But Boulder's downtown mall still lures as many locals as visitors, especially on

summer evenings when string quartets, bagpipers, Peruvian bands and all manner of performers stake out spots by storefronts. One musician hauls his piano in on a wheeled platform. Jugglers, fire and sword swallowers, tightrope walkers and even a Rastafarian contortionist complete the circus-like scene. Lively entertainment, people-watching and the piney aroma of the summer breeze make mall strolling a warm-weather favorite.

The Boulder Creek Path, two short blocks from the Pearl Street Mall, meanders along Boulder Creek as a peaceful but sometimes perilous thoroughfare for bicyclists, in-line skaters, joggers and strollers. Seven-and-a-half miles of scenic path follow the creek as it tumbles down from Boulder Canyon and out onto the plains. Bicycling is so highly regarded in Boulder that sometimes the city plows the snow off the bike path before it plows the streets.

During spring runoff and early summer, kayakers and kids of all ages take tumultuous rides down the creek in boats and innertubes. Also along the path, adjacent to Central Park, the Boulder County Farmers Market operates on Saturdays and Wednesdays from spring through fall, offering local, organically grown vegetables, fruits and flowers as well as crafts and baked goods.

No Boulder summer is complete without a concert and meal at Chautauqua. Chautauqua Park, with its 100-year-old dining hall and barn-like concert hall, houses some of the best music and meals anywhere, including the Colorado Music Festival with artists from around the country. Elsewhere in town, summertime offerings include the Colorado Dance Festival, Colorado Shakespeare Festival, Colorado Lyric Opera, Boulder Creek Festival and, less lofty, the Kinetic Sculpture Challenge — a crazy land and water race along and across Boulder Reservoir in wildly imaginative, but not so navigable, human-powered conveyances.

Industry and Economics

To dispel any notion of Boulder as a bedroom community to Denver, consider this: 78 percent of Boulder County's population works in the county, 45 percent of the City of Boulder's population works in the city, and 45

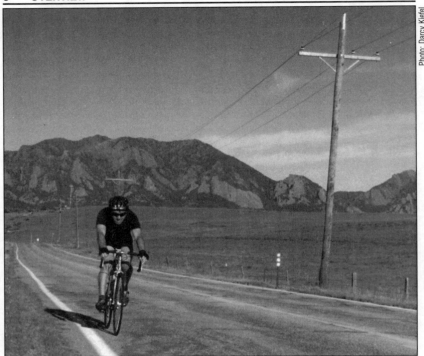

In fitness-crazed Boulder, biking is a popular mode of transportation.

percent of the city's work force commutes in from surrounding communities. Boulder industry focuses on education, scientific research and technology at such places as the University of Colorado at Boulder, the National Oceanic and Atmospheric Administration, the National Center for Atmospheric Research and various other government and university scientific institutes.

Celestial Seasonings tea company, the largest U.S. herb tea manufacturer, makes its home here on Sleepytime Drive. The company revolutionized the tea industry, and founder Mo Siegel picked his way to an herbal tea fortune initially gathering herbs in Boulder's foothills. He is renowned as the hippie who became a millionaire. A bicycling aficionado, Siegel also brought international bicycle competition to Boulder for more than a decade with the Red Zinger Bicycle Classic race in the mid-1970s, which eventually became the now-extinct Coors Classic.

The University of Colorado, IBM Corp. and Storage Technology Corp. are the top three employers in Boulder County, with more than 38,000 employees. Other top county employers are the Boulder Valley School District (3,176 employees), Ball Aerospace (2,500) and Centrobe (2,600). Centrobe's employees are distributed between Boulder, Denver and Colorado Springs, and the company is a nationwide subscription and mailing service for magazine publishers, a products and book distributor. Mountain View, California-based Sun Microsystems plans to relocate from Silicon Valley to Boulder County in the next few years, and will employ 5,000 people here by the year 2002.

The university has in the past housed such scholars as Robert Bakker, a world-renowned paleontologist who transformed the study of dinosaurs with his now widely accepted theory that they were warm-blooded and more closely related to birds than reptiles. Movie mogul Steven Spielberg consulted Bakker during the filming of *Jurassic Park*. CU-Boulder is also currently home to Patricia Nelson Limerick, renowned teacher and historian of the American West and a leader among the "new Western historians." Limerick's ground-breaking work on the roles played by women, Native Americans and other ethnic groups in settling the West won her the 1995 MacArthur Fellowship, a "genius grant" of $275,000 over a five-year period with no strings attached.

Nobel laureate Thomas Cech of CU-Boulder received the prize for his work proving that the genetic messenger RNA can also function as an enzyme, leading to the speculation that RNA could have played a key role in the origin of life. Cech's current work with therapeutic RNA molecules is expected to lead to medical treatments, from attacking viruses to halting infections and alleviating symptoms of genetic disorders like sickle-cell anemia, muscular dystrophy and cystic fibrosis. Nationally recognized as a leader in the field of educational testing, professor of education Robert Linn received the university's highest honor of distinguished professorship in 1996. He is an advisor to key professional and governmental committees as an expert in evaluating test reliability and validity; test comparison, bias and ethics; and the strength and weakness of the mathematical models that define testing. CU physics professor Carl Wieman, was one of two people who created the coldest temperature in 1995. The other scientist was Eric Cornell, a staff physicist with the National Institute of Standards and Technology in Boulder. They led the scientific team that created the long-sought Bose-Einstein condensation — a state that occurs when individual atoms meld into a "superatom" at a few billionths of a degree above absolute zero. Wieman is considered to be one of the premier physicists of his generation and to have achieved some of the most important successes in atomic physics in the past two decades.

CU law professor Charles Wilkinson is a nationally renowned attorney and expert in natural resources management. He has won awards from the National Wildlife Federation and served as Special Counsel to the Department of the Interior in connection with the recent creation of the Grand Staircase-Escalante National Monument in Utah. The author of many books, he is also an expert in Western land and water issues and Native American law and rights.

Atmospheric scientist Walter Orr Roberts, who died in 1990, founded the National Center for Atmospheric Research (NCAR — pronounced "en-car") in Boulder, and his work in solar physics established Boulder as an atmospheric science center, attracting such other scientific facilities as the National Bureau of Standards and Technology (now known as NIST) and Ball Aerospace. He helped found CU-Boulder's Joint Institute for Laboratory Astrophysics and Department of Astrophysical, Planetary and Atmospheric Sciences. Roberts also helped bring Boulder's greatest architectural gem into being: the stunning mesa-top NCAR laboratory, designed by architect I.M. Pei, who also designed the Na-

INSIDERS' TIP

Boulder's backdrop and trademark, the Flatirons, are Pennsylvanian red sandstone and conglomerate that were deposited as alluvial fans and aprons along the edges of the ancestral Rockies. They were dragged upward at their current angle by the rebirth of the Rockies about 65 million years ago. The Third Flatiron (third from the north) is one of Colorado's and the nation's premier, classic rock climbs. It towers 1,400 feet high, a couple hundred feet higher than the Empire State Building, and has been climbed by people without using their hands, on roller skates, naked and in 8 minutes (by separate climbers).

tional Gallery in Washington, D.C., and the pyramid-shaped entrance to the Louvre in Paris. NCAR is also known for being the futuristic setting of Woody Allen's 1970s comedy film *Sleeper*.

Climate

It's no wonder that weather and climate are two big topics of study at local scientific institutes: Boulder's climate is marked by unusual extremes. Foot-deep snow and below-zero temperatures can suddenly transform to breezy 60-degree T-shirt weather by Boulder's capricious Chinook "snow-eater" winds. These warm, dry winds blast down from the eastern slope of the mountains and melt the snow with blinding speed. Boulder's winds have also been known to blow in gusts exceeding 120 miles per hour, removing roofs and toppling telephone poles.

Because of these strong winds, Native Americans chose not to make permanent settlements in the area and mainly visited for summer hunting. The dreaded high winds, Boulder's biggest weather affliction, can come any time but are the worst in winter and can continue for days. It can be so windy that schools won't let young children leave the building without an adult. Safeway supermarket sometimes posts a note on the door asking that carts be returned to the store so errant, wind-blown carts don't damage cars in the parking lot. The winds can make people irritable, and there are tales of pioneer women wandering off onto the prairie or committing suicide, driven insane by the gales. Similar winds (in Europe called the foehn or mistral) are common throughout the world near high mountain ranges.

Sometimes it seems like Boulder has only two seasons: summer and winter. The tulips do bloom in spring, and the leaves change in fall for a brief but spectacular show. But these two fickle seasons are often accompanied by a foot of snow, burying the crocuses and lilacs or blackening fall's golden aspen leaves. Halloween is often one of the most miserable nights of the year with the poor trick-or-treaters braving the freezing rain or snow. Then again, Thanksgiving and Christmas can some-

times be outdoor cafe weather. It rarely rains in Boulder except for summer afternoon thunderstorms and the August monsoon — a week or two of rainy weather.

Boulder's high elevation, 5,430 feet, keeps temperatures cool at night even on the hottest summer days. Mountain breezes and low humidity help too. Tornadoes generally stay well to the east, though hailstorms occasionally shred summer flowers and vegetables.

The record low temperature in the Boulder area is -33 degrees (1930) and the record high is 104 degrees (1954). Boulder has an average of 33 days above 90 degrees and 133 days below freezing. January, the coldest month, averages 21 degrees; July, the warmest, averages 88. Average precipitation is 18.24 inches. The most snow in a season was 142.9 inches; the least, 20.8 inches. Though it may snow or blow, low humidity and a higher-than-California average of sunny days make Boulder's climate one of the most pleasant in the nation.

Area Geography

The foothills of the Rocky Mountains divide Boulder County from north to south. Eastern Boulder County lies on the western edge of the Great Plains with rolling terrain, small ridges and the Davidson Mesa, which runs northeast from south of Boulder to Louisville. Western Boulder County rises from the foothills to the Continental Divide, to a breathless summit of 14,255 feet atop Longs Peak in Rocky Mountain National Park in the extreme northwestern part of the county.

Boulder Environs

Roughly 20 towns dot the mountains and plains of Boulder County, ranging from rustic, high-country settlements like Eldora and Raymond, with only a handful of year-round residents, to sizable burgs like Longmont, second-largest city in Boulder County after Boulder. A former sugar beet and canning capital, Longmont — northeast of Boulder — is now home to Longmont Foods, a turkey-breeding and meat-processing company.

Nothing could be further from Longmont

in both locale and flavor than lofty, funky Ward, former mining boom-and-bust town, now a home for old and young hippies and other escapees from the system. After Longmont, the small plains cities of Broomfield, Lafayette and Louisville are the most populous.

The small towns of Lyons (north of Boulder) and Eldorado Springs (south of Boulder) lie at the mouths of spectacular canyons. Eldorado Springs is also the site of a state park and mineral springs and is a famous rock-climbing area. Hygiene and Allenspark are unincorporated small settlements of a few hundred residents. Jamestown was a former mining boom town with a population of 10,000, now down to less than 300. Its picturesque mercantile cafe is a popular bicycling stop.

Spectacularly sited at the top of Boulder Canyon on Barker Reservoir, Nederland is Boulder County's largest mountain town and an odd mix of eccentric mountain folk, young families, old hippies, conservative Republicans, environmental activists, self-sufficient rugged individualists and a small contingent of out-of-staters who fall in love with it during the summer, move in, and beat a fast trail out after their first winter.

Needless to say, a lot more can be said about each Boulder County town and its unique character and history. See our chapters on Boulder Real Estate and Neighborhoods and Nearby Communities for more information.

Niwot's Curse?

Though Boulder has been utopia for many residents for many years, the city (like the rest of the planet) is currently experiencing an uncomfortable population expansion. Since the late 1970s, the population has increased by about 43 percent, or 28,000 people. Three million people — 75 percent of Colorado's population — live in a 60-mile-wide swath along the Front Range, from Fort Collins to Colorado Springs. By 2020, that number is projected to reach four million. "Too many people and too many cars," is the complaint of residents who remember traffic-free streets and the ability to get anywhere in town in 10 minutes. Gone are those days, and in their place are frustrating waits in traffic jams, rude drivers, nowhere to park and long lines at supermarkets, restaurants and movies.

Unfortunately, Boulder is inheriting some of the problems of a bigger city: increased crime, pollution, traffic and overpopulation. The current challenge is how to deal with them. Growth-cap initiatives on the ballot and emphasis on bicycling and public transportation versus automobile use continue to be some "driving issues" for the future.

Is Arapaho Chief Niwot's curse, "that people seeing the beauty of the Boulder Valley will want to stay, and their staying will be the undoing of the beauty," beginning to come true?

The Number One rule
of thumb to help
newcomers orient
themselves in Boulder
is: The mountains
are to the west.

Getting Here, Getting Around

Before you think about where you're going, it's good to know where you are. Boulder is about 25 miles northwest of Denver, via Interstate 25 and U.S. 36, better known locally as "The Turnpike" because it was once a toll road. The Number One rule of thumb to help newcomers orient themselves in Boulder is: The mountains are to the west. Most of the north/south streets are numbered, starting with Third Street on the west side of town then going beyond 75th Street as you head east. Broadway is a major north-south thoroughfare on a slight diagonal, and Folsom Street is a significant north-south street from North Boulder to the University of Colorado campus. In addition to the city streets and U.S. 36, which becomes 28th Street through Boulder, Foothills Parkway is a divided roadway on the eastern edge of town, but with some traffic lights at major intersections, connecting U.S. 36 and the Longmont Diagonal (Colo. Highway 119). It is a way to bypass Boulder, though we wonder why anyone would wish to bypass our wonderful city.

Baseline Road is a significant east-west route, not just to Boulderites, but also to cartographers, for it marks the 40th parallel on maps of the Earth. If you made a beeline down this road, after a few hundred miles you'd hit the boundary between Kansas and Nebraska. The major east-west cross-streets are Table Mesa Road/South Boulder Road and Baseline Road in the southern part of the city; Arapahoe Avenue in central Boulder (and, to an extent, Canyon Boulevard, a short but important major street); and the Alpine Street/Valmont Road routing and Iris Avenue in the northern part of the city.

North Boulder's alphabetical "tree streets" — Alpine, Balsam, Cedar and so on — are easy to find and remember. Making your way through cul de sac-filled subdivisions, however, requires good directions. Broadway and 28th Street converge in North Boulder, again becoming U.S. 36 toward Lyons.

You'll find basic orientation maps in the front of this book, and more detailed street maps in the front of local phone books. A variety of easier-to-tote maps is available from the city's Transportation Planning Group (formerly GO Boulder), (303) 441-3266, on the second floor of the Park Central Building, 1739 Broadway, including free pocket-size maps for streets, bus and bicycle routes. And remember, it never hurts to ask for directions.

More than most cities, Boulder offers and encourages use of alternative modes of transportation to the car and has a city agency, the Transportation Planning Group, or TPG, to promote, set and achieve such goals. Pay close attention to alternative modes. In 1992, nearly 26 percent of work-related trips within Boulder were made by busing, biking or walking. Among 14 comparable cities, Boulder ranks No. 1 in people who walk to work, work at home and drive with more than one person in the car. It ranks second among those who bike. (the TPG of Boulder says Davis, California, probably ranks first, with Boulder right on its heels.) Alternative modes of transportation can become one of your favorite things about Boulder.

Transportation Issues in Boulder

If you just arrived from a congested metropolitan area on either coast, Boulder might not seem to have much traffic, but if you've been in town a while, you would notice the change over the past few years. Two hundred thousand cars flow through the city itself and people drive a cumulative 2.2 million miles in this little valley every day. That's loads of cars, especially at a higher altitude more prone to air pollution. It's also unsettling to people who don't like the way roads and parking lots eat up land and create canyons clogged with vehicles and the accompanying din and exhaust fumes.

Boulder has given itself a mandate to reduce the car and traffic problem while enhancing our ability to get around. In a classic example of Boulder's foresight and compulsive worrying about quality-of-life issues before they become crises, the city developed its first Transportation Master Plan in 1989, when, believe it or not, the city was still suffering under a regional recession and few people were worrying about too many commuters, too many jobs or too many homes. The Transportation Planning Group tracks traffic patterns, keeps statistics, creates charts and, most important, tries to use these figures to solve the congestion conundrum. Periodic studies confirm that what most people like about downtown Boulder is its atmosphere and pedestrian orientation, and what most people don't like about Boulder is the parking dilemma. The latest version of the Transportation Master Plan, designed to take Boulder through the year 2020, includes a whopping $1 billion worth of projects (including more than $250 million for improved bus service and $30 million for better bike paths), proving that Boulder takes its traffic and growth issues seriously and is willing to back them up with big bucks.

Individuals do their bit too. Some people dream about or design supercars, which would

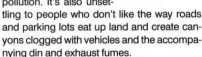

be quieter and safer than current cars and get more than 150 miles to the gallon. Others want better mass transit, including light rail and improved bus service. A few of them serve on the city's Transportation Advisory Board, which studies the issues in depth and makes informed proposals to the city. Planners strive for small-scale neighborhood centers so people don't have to drive as far to reach necessary services. And many people take public transportation whenever possible or get around town on bicycles or on foot whenever they can. A few even put their commitment into action by living carless.

Driving to Boulder

To drive to Boulder from Denver, take I-25 north to U.S. Highway 36 west, better known as the turnpike. The last hill is Davidson Mesa, where you'll get a view of town and find a visitors center kiosk.

If you ask for directions and someone says "Foothills," clarify whether they mean Foothills Highway (U.S. Highway 36), which starts as 28th Street and leads to Estes Park, or Foothills Parkway (Colo. Highway 157), which links U.S. 36 with Colo. Highway 119 and leads to Longmont.

If you are driving to Boulder from the ski areas on I-70, you have two options. The first is to take the Morrison/Golden exit (Exit 259) to U.S. Highway 40. Go north toward U.S. Highway 6, turn left on U.S. 6 then head north on Colo. Highway 93 to Boulder. The second, and to us preferable, option is the Central City/Golden exit (Exit 244) off of I-70. Follow U.S. 6 east for about 15 miles through beautiful Clear Creek Canyon. At the second traffic light, just on the outskirts of Golden, turn left (north) on Colo. Highway 93, which becomes Broadway in Boulder.

Car Rentals

The overwhelming majority of fly-in visitors to Boulder rent cars at Denver International Airport or from agencies near the old

Stapleton Airport and drive to Boulder, but rental cars are also available in town. Locals whose cars are undergoing major repairs, business travelers in the area for several days but only requiring a car for part of the time, CU-Boulder students (25 and older to rent) or visiting academicians and others might wish to rent a car for the short time they really need one.

The Yellow Pages list local and out-of-town agencies under Automobile Renting. Choices include such national firms as Hertz, (303) 413-8023; Avis, (303) 499-1136; National, (303) 442-5110; and Budget, (303) 341-2277. Smaller regional and local companies abound too.

Getting Around Boulder by Car

Plans and dreams aside, the majority of Boulder residents still depend on their cars, even if they secretly wish there were a better way. Don't feel guilty if your car's packed with visiting sightseers or your kids' soccer teammates; you're being a carpool! But if you're all alone, at least try to consolidate your errands so you drive less often.

Boulder has many designated bike lanes, but where there are none, bicyclists may occupy a lane of traffic, just like cars. Pedestrians at crosswalks have the right-of-way, which means you are supposed to stop when you see someone waiting to cross the street.

Except where posted or where there is a red-arrow traffic light, right turns on red are permitted. Wherever the streets are wide enough to make it feasible, which means most arterials, left-turn lanes have been designated. As anyplace else when you're turning left at a green light, pull into the intersection and wait for a gap. Once you are in the intersection, it is still legal to turn on yellow. If you try zip into an intersection after the light turns red, how-ever, you are asking for a stiff ticket, to say nothing of perhaps causing a crash.

Rush Hour

Most cities get only two rush periods. Boulder has three. Morning rush spans 7 to 9 AM. Also, because many of the new commercial and business parks are lacking in restaurants, workers often drive somewhere for lunch, creating a noon mini-rush that starts around 11 AM and lasts until 2 PM. Traffic really swells between 4 and 7 PM. A fourth rush sometimes revolves around CU-Boulder home football games, which jam streets around campus. If you hate traffic, make your trips outside these most popular times, or (hint-hint) consider alternative modes (see this chapter's subsequent "Alternative Modes of Transportation" section).

Weather Hazards

Boulder's normally benign climate often lulls us into thinking that the driving, like the living, is easy. But meteorological aberrations can be hazardous. Summer hailstorms can pock windshields, impair visibility and temporarily cause slippery road surfaces. Snowstorms often start with drizzling rain that freezes before the snow falls, and that snow can undergo several days of melt-to-slush, freeze-to-ice cycles before melting and evaporating completely. Hilly streets and intersections are generally sanded rather than treated with chemicals. Highways and arterials are plowed, but snow on most residential streets is left to be taken care of by the sun. Several years ago, a child walking to an elementary school was killed by a car that had stopped at a red light but was hit from behind by a driver who skidded on the ice. Good snow tires are a must for Colorado winters.

If you drive a camper or sport-utility vehicle or are moving your belongings into town in a rental truck, you'll want to pay attention to high-wind warnings. Colo. Highway 93 between Boulder and Golden is especially vulnerable to wicked crosswinds and is occasionally closed because of them. Mountain driving can be pleasurable or terrifying, depending on individual driver's skill and confidence. Shifting into a lower gear helps save wear and tear on the engine while ascending and on the brakes while going downhill.

Accidents

As elsewhere, serious accidents demand a 911 call to dispatch emergency police, ambulance and even fire units. The Boulder Police accident investigation unit deals with non-injury-producing accidents. For information, call the department's general information line, (303) 441-4444. Vehicle insurance is mandatory in the state of Colorado, with current minimum required coverage of $25,000 for bodily injury, $50,000 per accident and $15,000 property damage. Motorists who leave the scene of an accident without exchanging license, registration and insurance information may have their driver's licenses suspended. (There are other offenses that can result in loss of license too, including driving while intoxicated, reckless driving and possession of certain firearms.)

Emergency Services

You only need to use the American Automobile Association (AAA) once to make it pay off. AAA Colorado, (303) 442-0383, is best known for its emergency road services, such as changing a flat tire, refueling an empty gas tank, pulling vehicles out of snow drifts or mud or towing a broken-down vehicle to a repair center. Because of the distances involved, anyone who drives in the mountains is probably wise to sign up for AAA Plus, offering towing services from as far as 250 miles from home.

In addition to road services, AAA maintains a walk-in center at 1933 28th Street (upstairs from Blockbuster Video), with a travel agency, traveler's check sales, discount luggage, book sales and routing assistance. Many of the services are available for nonmembers as well as members. In addition, AAA sells insurance and provides a locator service for good deals on new cars, bail bonds (not than any Insider would ever need that!) and other services.

Parking

If Boulder accommodated every single driver who wanted a quick trip to a perfect parking space, we would need so many roads and parking spaces that little room would remain for buildings, sidewalks, trees or flowers. On the other hand, for retail and restaurant businesses to remain viable, there must be reasonably convenient customer parking. Periodic studies confirm that what most people like about downtown Boulder is its atmosphere and pedestrian orientation; and what most people don't like about Boulder is the parking dilemma. Four downtown blocks of Pearl Street are pedestrian-only, so there's obviously no parking there, and meters limit parking on adjacent commercial streets. A new parking program was initiated in 1997 on adjacent neighborhood streets to discourage day-long parkers. Two- to three-hour nonresident parking is permitted.

Boulder maintains several staffed parking garages and metered surface lots, which are in great demand. If you get a downtown job, you can get on a waiting list for reserved, long-term parking by checking with the city's Parking Services, (303) 413-7300.

In addition to downtown, another problematic parking area is The Hill, the area around the university. There are metered spaces on retail and commercial streets but long-term parking is also restricted here. Your best bet is to park in the large CU visitor lot on Euclid,

Photo: Darcy Kiefel

The Skip bus runs every 6 to 10 minutes up and down Broadway.

just east of the University Memorial Center (UMC). All other lots on the campus are permit-only parking. CU has its own Parking Services, (303) 492-7384 for students, faculty and staff.

Pathways

Boulder has been ranked among America's most walkable cities by no less an authority than *Walking* magazine. It's also a wonderful city for runners, bikers, in-line skaters and wheelchair users. The most pleasing "roads" are the pedestrian and bicycle paths. They follow streams. They go by parks where you can hear birds sing, and they pass pretty homes with kids playing or adults gardening. Many people along the way smile. The major non-motorized-vehicle thoroughfare is the Boulder Creek Path (see the Boulder Attractions and Boulder Parks and Recreation Centers chapters), which is primarily an east-west route.

Walking some of these pathways to your destination often is faster than driving. Try it with a friend. Eat at some lovely spot on the Pearl Street Mall, then plan to meet on the CU-Boulder campus. You start walking while your friend gets the car. As you head up Broadway look for a little sidewalk just up the hill from Arapahoe Avenue. You'll probably have time to stop at Andrews Arboretum, an area once occupied by train tracks. You can take this pleasant pathway to the university and enjoy the sights on your stroll. You'll get lung-filling exercise and might even have time to read a chapter in your book before your friend gets the car, drives up to the university, parks and finally joins you.

The Transportation Planning Group has several programs designed to increase walking by improving pedestrian facilities. Many neighborhood sidewalks are being replaced for safety reasons and intersections have been made more pedestrian-friendly.

Bicycling

Boulder is one of America's best cycling cities. At this writing, the city boasts more than 90 miles of off-street bike paths, bike lanes on city streets and bike routes. That includes an underpass that allows university students safe biking to outlying dormitories and a climbing lane exclusively for bicyclists on Table Mesa

Drive. Savvy locals know that errands-by-bike sometimes go faster than errands-by-car. The whole idea of the bicycle as transportation is promoted heavily by the TPG, especially during the annual Boulder Walk and BikeWeek in late June.

Boulder Walk & BikeWeek is a major undertaking designed both as an incentive to exercise and to showcase the benefits of the bicycle as transportation. In 1998, about 25 restaurants and bakeries — mostly in Boulder but also one each in Longmont, Louisville, Lafayette and Niwot — offered bicycle commuters free continental breakfasts from 6:30 or 7 to 9 AM. Volunteer mechanics from local bike shops offer $10 tune-ups and bike safety checks. At least one event is held each day, including Walk and Bike to Work Day, Walk and Bike to Ice Cream Day, Walk and Bike to Market Day, Sunrise Breakfast Walk, Walk and Bike to Downtown Day, Intergenerational Walk and, finally, Walk and Bike to Music Day. Clinics covered topics from "Bike Safety for Kids" to "Zen and the Art of Bicycle Maintenance." And of course, there were free gifts and prize drawings to launch the peak summer cycling season. Expect a bigger, better event every year. More than 3,000 residents participate in Walk & BikeWeek.

Spokes for Folks is a program still in transition, but nonetheless a model for city officials from Fort Collins to San Francisco. In 1997, a fleet of more than 150 loaner bikes was launched to provide people with easy pedal power for errands around town. The donated bikes are fixed up by high-school students and painted a rather terrible shade of bright green so they can't possibly be mistaken for anything else. Under Spokes for Folks, people are supposed to pick up a bike, ride it to their destination and leave it for the next person. While 50 percent of the bikes are vandalized in some way, most are fixed and returned to the streets. Spokes for Folks was modeled after a similar program in Portland, Oregon, which because of its size has had less success than Boulder in keeping track of the bikes. Many cities are trying to start their own program based on Boulder's lessons.

Alternative Modes of Transportation

For information about alternative modes of transportation, including pedestrian, bicycle and carpool options, call the Transportation Planning Group, a city agency that offers multiple transportation options. It offers easy-to-read maps of bus routes, bike paths and open-space trails. The pocket-size maps are free, and the larger full-scale ones are a good value at $2. Call the TPG at (303) 441-3266, or stop by its offices on the second floor of the Park Central Building, 1739 Broadway, two blocks south of the Pearl Street Mall. the TPG's Ride Arrangers, (303) 447-2120, can also help you set up carpools and vanpools. Pool drivers can get special training and the option of using city vans.

To encourage bus use, participating businesses and the Downtown Management Commission, (303) 441-4000, provide ECO-Passes so their employees can ride the bus for free. So far more than 12,000 residents have ECO-Passes. One of the great perks is the guaranteed ride program, which uses taxis to take people directly to their door at night. In addition, three Boulder neighborhoods with approximately 3,100 residents have Neighborhood ECO Passes, and new neighborhoods join the program yearly. See the subsequent section for more details on bus service.

Buses, Limos and Taxis

The Regional Transportation District, also known as RTD, is the greater Denver metropolitan area's public transportation agency. RTD recorded-information lines are (303) 299-6000, (800) 366-RIDE or (303) 299-6034 (TDD).

RTD buses are promoted as "The Ride." The main bus station in Boulder, currently the hub of RTD's hub-and-spoke system, is at 14th and Walnut streets. Rides within Boulder cost 75 cents (exact change only), 25 cents for seniors 65 and older (off-peak hours) and 25 cents for disabled individuals with an RTD card; a 10-ride ticket book costs $5.75. Various monthly passes are also available at the bus station and at King Soopers and Safeway grocery markets. Boulder students can buy reduced-rate bus passes, and CU-Boulder students get RTD passes as part of the student activity fee. Seniors are also eligible for discount passes.

RTD buses on Boulder city routes operate every half-hour. Schedules and prices vary for intercity service to Broomfield, Denver, Golden, Lafayette, Longmont, Louisville, Nederland and Westminster. RTD also offers rush-hour express buses to the Denver Tech Center, hourly express buses to Denver International Airport, and special buses to the Eldora ski area via Nederland. Buses for Colorado Rockies and Denver Broncos games depart from the main Boulder terminal and various Park-n-Ride lots for $4 round trip.

Many buses are equipped with wheelchair ramps, and many allow some bicycles on board. Call one of the RTD numbers for details on these amenities or how to reach your destination by bus. Tell the RTD operator where you need to be, when and from where you're starting. To use a bus regularly, pick up a schedule on a bus or downtown at the main Boulder terminal.

The Hop, (303) 441-3266, is a fantastic idea for unclogging travel without greatly inconveniencing people. It uses midsize buses operating frequently instead of infrequent runs by often-empty behemoths. The Hop's circuit has 40 stops including Crossroads Mall, the University Hill shopping area near CU-Boulder and the Pearl Street Mall. Buses drive both clockwise and counterclockwise on the circuit. The Hop runs every 10 minutes Monday through Friday, 7 AM to 7 PM, and every 15 minutes Thursday and Friday, 7 to 10 PM, and Saturday, 9 AM to 7 PM. The University of Colorado Student Union also sponsors Night Hop, which runs a CU-Pearl Street Mall loop Thursday through Saturday from 10:30 pm to 2:30 AM, free to CU students with ID and ECO-pass holders. The fare is 75¢, 25¢ for seniors during off-peak hours or free for folks with a CU ID or any RTD pass. Some merchants also give out Hop tokens to their customers, good for a complimentary ride.

With the success of The Hop, a similar service called The Skip debuted in August 1997. The 22-passenger buses operate every 10 minutes (every six minutes during the rush hours), running north-south on Broadway. The Hop has been so successful, the RTD Board of Directors now wants to introduce the smaller, brightly colored buses in other metropolitan areas. The Jump shuttle will begin service in 2000 on Arapahoe Avenue between Boulder and Lafayette. Should voters approve further funds, the Leap and the Bound will eventually serve Boulder commuters.

Other transportation companies go beyond the RTD network. Estes Park Shuttle, (970) 586-5151, runs year-round shuttle service between any Estes Park location and the Denver International Airport. The ride costs $28 one-way and $50 round trip. Call ahead for a schedule and reservations.

The best way to the ski resorts is via SkiXPress, new weekend service to five ski areas within two hours of metro Denver. The service is being underwritten by the Colorado Department of Transportation and the ski areas. This leaves passengers with a tab of just $15 for round-trip transportation from Boulder (or Denver) to Copper Mountain, Loveland, Keystone, Vail and Winter Park on luxurious buses with reclining seats and restrooms — plus the opportunity to buy discounted lift tickets on board.

Boulder Yellow Cab, (303) 442-2277, can pick up in Lafayette and Louisville as well as Boulder. Drivers charge around $1.60 per mile. Boulder Freedom Cabs, (303) 292-8900, is a new service competing with Yellow Cab. Rates are $1.60 per mile. There are no taxi stands for either company, so call for service. Town and Country Taxi, (303) 776-0496, serves Longmont, Niwot and Lyons. Rates are around $1.50 per mile.

For people with disabilities, life would be

Photo: Daily Camera

With Boulder's traffic congestion, getting around by bus is a good alternative.

all the more challenging without wheelchair-lift-equipped, door-to-door, on-demand transportation service. More than 2,000 use Boulder's Special Transit, (303) 447-2848, which offers low-cost rides to people with disabilities. Call well in advance for reservations and prices. The LIFT, (303) 665-9085, is a Lafayette-based volunteer program for people who have trouble getting around. Call 24 hours ahead.

High-flying Airports

If you have a private plane, you can fly into one of the region's smaller general-aviation airports. Some also have air taxi services that you can book to fly you quickly to a town not on a regular commercial air route.

Boulder Municipal Airport
3300 Airport Rd., Boulder
• (303) 440-7065

Like most airports in Colorado, Boulder's airport is uncontrolled, meaning it has no control tower. Private propeller planes and a few smaller turbojets land here. There is a comfortable lobby where a selection of videos about flying are for sale. A courtesy car will take you to your Boulder destination. To reach the airport, take Valmont Road east to Airport Road.

Flatirons Aviation
3300 Airport Rd. • (303) 440-6522

Located at the Boulder Municipal Airport, this company offers flight instruction ranging from recreational to commercial and is a contact for renting hangars or getting airport information. Depending on the aircraft you choose, lessons range from $42 to $100 per hour plus a $25 per hour instructor fee. The tie-down fee is dropped when fuel is purchased. If needed, hanger space is usually available.

Dakota Ridge Aviation
3300 Airport Rd. • (303) 444-1017

This is another flight school based at the Boulder Municipal Airport. Private, commercial and instructor lessons are all available and start at $40 per hour to as much $152 per hour plus the $26 per hour instructor fee. They don't charge for tie-down if the customer is refueling. Maintenance for all types of planes is ongoing here.

Tri-County Airport/
Crosswind Aviation
395 Airport Dr., Erie • (303) 661-9146

Located in east Boulder County, this airport has a runway big enough for small jets, but most of its air traffic is single- and twin-engine propeller planes. A full range of flight instruction is available. Experimental and unique home-built airplanes occupy many hangars. And the jet-set — that is, the propeller-set — has settled nearby. More than a dozen houses adjacent to the airport sport private hangars with taxi lanes connecting to the runway.

Vance Brand Municipal Airport
10383 N. 85th St., Longmont
• (303) 651-8431

This is an uncontrolled landing field with full services for business and pleasure aircraft. There is a small lobby with snacks available and pilot supplies. They do not have a courtesy car but can arrange for a local rental car company to transport guests to their destination. To reach Vance Brand, take the Diagonal Highway, or U.S. 36, northeast of Boulder to Airport Road and go north 1.5 miles.

Air West Flight Center Inc.
10383 N. 85th St., Longmont
• (303) 776-6266

This is a flight school based at Longmont's Vance Brand Municipal Airport. They have nine planes and teach flying lessons ranging from private pilot to instructor. Depending on the plane you choose, lessons start at $40 per hour and go as high as $160 per hour, plus a $25 per hour instructor fee. Tie-downs are $3 per night or $35 per month.

Twin Peaks Aviation
10383 N. 85th St., Longmont
• (303) 776-8467

This is another flight school based at Longmont's Vance Brand Municipal Airport. Lessons start at $50 per hour and go as high as $135 per hour, plus the $25 per hour instructor fee. They offer scenic rides and rent planes to those who have a license. Tie-down is free with the purchase of fuel, or $35 on a monthly basis.

Jefferson County Airport (Jeffco)
11755 Airport Way, Broomfield
• (303) 466-2314

Located just outside Boulder County, this airfield is nonetheless used by many Boulderites. Also known as Jeffco, it's the fourth-largest airport in the Denver area and can handle corporate jets and aircraft up to 70,000 pounds. No scheduled commercial passenger flights leave Jeffco, but it has plenty of general aviation. The tower is staffed by 10 controllers and has the best navigational landing aids near Boulder. There is a small cafe open to the public.

Denver International Airport (DIA)
8400 Peña Blvd., Denver
• (303) 342-2200, (800) 247-2336

Twenty-three carriers service this 4-year-old airport — the biggest in the nation and one of the biggest in the world. United Airlines dominates, with some 70 percent of the lift out of DIA, but American, American West, Continental, Delta, Frontier, Northwest, TWA and US Airways and Vanguard also serve the airport. DIA is posh with polished granite floors, $7.5 million worth of artwork and an expansive main lobby roofed with 34 translucent, Teflon-coated fiberglass tent canopies designed to invoke snow-covered peaks and cast light like stylized, billowy clouds. Those canopies were canted in different directions for structural efficiency in the wind and heavy weather. Despite its monumental 5 million-square-foot interior, walks are short. The ticket counters are a short way from passenger drop-offs on both sides of the main terminal. Common carriers (i.e., buses and vans) use a separate level, off-limits to private cars. There are three concourses. You have the option of walking to Concourse A via an air bridge over a taxiway, but a swift subway whisks you to all concourses. Stand near the front windows if you want to see the little propellers along the walls whirl as the train passes.

DIA has excellent shops, including some not usually found in airports: Images of Nature, a national wildlife photographer's store; Benjamin Books, a well-stocked bookstore; and Susan Vale Sweaters, offering handmade sweaters from $200 up. You can also find a travel agency and a chiropractor at DIA. An interfaith airport chapel opened in 1996. Fast food includes McDonald's, TCBY and specialty pizza, croissant and espresso shops, all by contract required to sell their goods at prices no more than 10 percent higher than they would sell in a regular mall. Most of these are open daily from 7 AM until 10 PM.

If you need information on Denver International Airport's ground transportation, call (303) 342-4059; for parking (303) 342-4096; for luggage storage and lost and found, call (303) 342-4062.

Driving time to DIA from Boulder is one-hour minimum, and can take longer if traffic is thick. There is currently no direct or easy route from Boulder to the new airport, so allow plenty of time for getting there (see directions below).

Airport Shuttles

There is currently only one van service that offers scheduled airport shuttle service from Boulder. Super Shuttle, (formerly the Airporter)

(303) 444-0808, picks up at Boulder's major hotels, CU-Boulder and your own front door. The hourly service departs the Boulder Broker between 4:30 AM and 9 PM (if you order door-to-door, they'll schedule your pick-up to coincide with a departure from the Broker) and from the airport between 8 AM and 11 PM. Door-to-door service is $22 one-way; hotel service is $18 one-way.

Bus Service

RTD, (303) 299-6000, also operates hourly buses between DIA and Boulder and takes about 90 minutes, with intermediate stops including the Louisville-Superior and Table Mesa Park-n-Ride lots. The fare is $8 one way ($4 for CU-Boulder students), and you can grab advance $13 round-trip tickets at King Soopers or Safeway.

RTD also offers a family plan that allows up to three children 15 and younger to ride free with an adult. Children even get a free set of plastic airline-style wings with each ride.

Taxis and Limos

Boulder Yellow Cab, (303) 442-2277, charges around $50 for one to five people and also picks up in Lafayette and Louisville. If you are feeling flush you can call an on-demand limo service. Airport Luxury Express, (303) 938-1234 or (800) 708-1160, is a new limo service featuring four-wheel-drive Chevrolet Suburbans equipped with cellular phone, television, beverage service and ski and luggage racks. It operates as an on-demand airport charter, particularly for business travelers and groups. By-the-hour rates are $72 during the day and evening and $84 between midnight and 5 AM between Boulder, Denver, Louisville or Lafayette and DIA. Prices are higher to Centennial Airport south of Denver and from Eldorado Springs, Gold Hill, Gold Lake, Lake Valley, Longmont, Pine Brook Hills,

---

INSIDERS' TIP

If you are a pedestrian, cyclist, in-line skater, skateboarder or motorist and have too close a brush with another pedestrian or anyone on wheels who is unmindful of rules of the road, you can report it to the Close Call Hotline, (303) 441-4272. This is a message line, not to be used to report an accident or emergency.

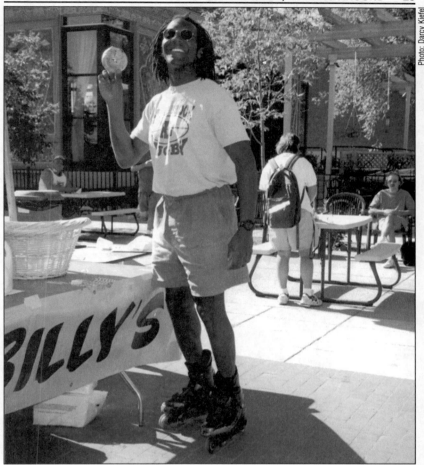

Photo: Darcy Kiefel

Alternative transportation in Boulder includes just about anything on wheels.

Walker Ranch and Ward. Airport Luxury Express also will take you to or pick you up from Colorado Springs, general-aviation airports and mountain towns. Other limo services include Elegante Limousine, (303) 443-7723; Foothills Limousine, (303) 530-0781, or Prestige Transportation Services, (303) 678-8471 or (800) 215-4667.

Car Routes

It's easier to reach the airport with someone else at the wheel, but if you need to drive, here are four options. To choose a route, tune in to KOA radio (850 AM), which has the most frequent traffic-condition reports. The distances listed are based on a *Daily Camera* reporter's story when the airport opened in 1995.

We've found the U.S. Option B to be the fastest from central, north or south Boulder. Once you're on U.S. 36, you won't encounter a single traffic light, and the high-occupancy-vehicle (HOV) lane from Westminster practically to the I-25 interchange speeds things

Photo: Daily Camera

If it's too snowy to drive or bike, some Boulder residents take to their skis.

along even during rush hour. At peak times, you are most likely to encounter congestion on the I-270 leg, and if KOA tells you that route is jammed, your best alternative is Option A. Of course, reverse this to drive from DIA to Boulder. Though driving times vary, allow at least an hour for the trip.

Option A (38.5 miles): Take U.S. Highway 36 to Sheridan Boulevard. Exit at 104th Avenue/

Church Ranch Boulevard and follow 104th Avenue east all the way to Tower Road. Until you get well east of I-25, which is still rural, tremendous growth is happening along this route, which has about two dozen traffic lights. At Tower Road, along the airport's western edge, turn right and take it south to Peña Boulevard, turn left and go east into the airport.

Option B (45 miles): Take U.S. Highway

36 to Denver. Go south briefly on I-25, then I-76 for about a mile to I-270, heading southeast. It merges into I-70 east. Exit at Peña Boulevard and go east into the airport.

Option C (45 miles): This option is best for travel from East Boulder. Take Arapahoe Road (Colo. Highway 7) east to U.S. Highway 85. Take U.S. 85 south to Henderson Road. Go east on Henderson to Tower Road. Take Tower south to Peña Boulevard and go east into the airport.

Option D (42.5 miles): Take U.S. Highway 36 to Broomfield. At Broomfield, take 120th Avenue east to Quebec Street. Jog north on Quebec to Henderson Road. Take Henderson east to Tower Road, turn south to Peña Boulevard and then east on Peña into the airport.

Boulder's dramatic red sandstone slabs, called the Flatirons, trace their true lineage back some 300 million years to the ancestral Rockies.

History

Early Boulder bore little resemblance to today's fair city. For one thing, there were no trees — except cottonwoods and willows along the creeks — since the Boulder Valley is part of the Great Plains grasslands.

Visiting the area in 1873, British travel writer and world traveler Isabella Bird described Boulder as "a hideous collection of frame houses on the burning plain." Those who have viewed early photos of Boulder will indeed agree with Miss Bird.

For another thing, today's pub-filled Boulder was "dry" from 1907 until 1967. Some say the teetotaling history was due to strong religious convictions of the townsfolk, while others cite the need for the state's first university town to remain proper and sober.

Pre- and Early History

Trees or not, geology carved out a special setting for Boulder with its most notable landmark, the Flatirons. The name for these unusual vertical rock formations comes from an old-fashioned clothes iron or "flatiron," standing on end — though some historians say they were named for the Flatiron Building, New York's famous triangular-shaped structure built in 1903 at Broadway and Fifth Avenue.

Regardless of where the name came from, Boulder's dramatic red sandstone slabs trace their true lineage back some 300 million years to the ancestral Rockies. Their sedimentary rock formed by wind and erosion of the mountains, then spent millions more years submerged beneath swamps and shallow seas. These behemoths were then dragged upward to their current arresting angle when the present-day, "new" Rockies formed around 60 million years ago.

Similar formations are found at Colorado Springs' Garden of the Gods and Denver's Red Rocks Park. In her book, *Roadside Geology: Colorado*, Halka Chronic writes, "the tilting of the sedimentary layers has been so extreme that the layers are upside down. Basement rocks may even be thrust out above them."

The reddish color of this upthrust sandstone gave the state its Spanish name.

First Humans

The first humans passed through Colorado about 10,000 years ago and are believed to have descended from Asians who migrated over the Bering Land Bridge as much as 10,000 years earlier. University of Denver scientists found the bones of animals and the spear points used to kill them in northeastern New Mexico. These "Folsom points" are named for the small town of Folsom, New Mexico, near the Colorado border, where they were found along with the first signs of humanity in North America. The ice-age Folsom man was unearthed in 1924. Such early "Westerners" hunted mastodons, woolly mammoths and giant sloths. Folsom and the nearby Capulin Volcano National Monument make for an interesting trip through some unusual volcanic landscape.

Colorado's first-known settlements were those of the Anasazi in southwestern Colorado's Four Corners area around 550 A.D. The Anasazi are known for their basketry and distinctive pottery, but most of all for Mesa Verde, the spectacular series of cliff-side dwellings they built and inhabited around A.D. 1150. It's not known why the Anasazi abandoned their cliff dwellings around 1300 and disappeared, but migration south to the Rio Grande valley because of over-farming is suspected.

Today's Acoma, Sandia, Taos, Zuni and other Pueblo peoples are believed to be descendants of the Anasazi.

During the 16th and 17th centuries, Colorado was home to several tribes descended from the Shoshone and Algonquins. The Utes were Shoshonean mountain-dwellers. Plains tribes included the Cheyenne, Comanche, Arapaho and Kiowa. Other tribes in the area were the Pawnee, Sioux, Navajo, Blackfoot and Crow.

American Indians throughout the Southwest visited Colorado for such things as clay for their pottery, fossil seashells for their medicine men's magic and turquoise for adornment. Bands of Cheyenne and Arapaho visited the Boulder Valley regularly to collect flint for arrowheads and colorful clays for war paint.

By the mid-19th century, the Comanche and Kiowa had been driven out of the Boulder Valley by the Cheyenne and Arapaho, who came originally from the Minnesota-Great Lakes area, where they, in turn, had been driven west by the Sioux. The Arapaho wintered here because the game was plentiful and the winters mild. They also enjoyed and venerated the warm thermal waters at Eldorado Springs. The Utes, enemies of the Cheyenne and Arapaho, still dwelled in the mountains above the Boulder Valley and ranged west to the Salt Lake Basin (thus the name, Utah).

First Europeans and Pioneers

Gold brought the first European explorers to the area. Perhaps the first to venture into Colorado was Francisco Vásquez de Coronado, who arrived in New Mexico in 1541 searching for the mythical Seven Gold Cities of Cibola.

During the 17th and 18th centuries, both the French and Spanish alternately claimed the territory that included all present states on the Mississippi River plus Montana, Wyoming, the Dakotas and part of Colorado. For a while the Territory was called Louisiana after King Louis XIV of France, then New Spain when the Spanish defeated the French in the French and Indian War in 1762. In 1800 Napoleon swapped an Italian kingdom for it with the Spanish, reclaiming it again for France.

American adventurer James Purcell of Kentucky explored the area in the early 1800s before it was U.S. territory and found gold along the Platte River. Then, in 1803, President Thomas Jefferson paid $15 million to France in the famous Louisiana Purchase of some 830,000 square miles — doubling the size of the United States. At the time, Jefferson was maligned for squandering money on questionable, unexplored land.

U.S. Army Lt. Zebulon Pike and Maj. Stephen Long were commissioned to explore the territory, and later, John Fremont came looking for a route across the Rockies. One of Fremont's men, William Gilpin — later to become the first governor of the Colorado Territory — reported that gold could probably be found in the area, stirring some initial interest in what was then considered "the Great American Desert . . . totally unfit for cultivation and, of course, uninhabitable by a people depending upon agriculture for their subsistence," according to Long.

The Gold Rush

Colorado's and Boulder's first permanent white (and a few black) settlers came in 1858

INSIDERS' TIP

Why does Boulder, which is nowhere near the ocean, have a Marine Street? It was named for Marinus Smith, one of Boulder's first citizens and a local farmer.

after gold was discovered in the sands of the South Platte River near present-day Denver. Prospectors worked their way north, panning Cherry Creek (Denver), Clear Creek (Golden), Boulder Creek and others. As these lower "placer deposits" of gold were eventually mined out, prospectors and miners followed the creeks up into the mountains, sometimes finding the "mother lode" in such places as Central City and Black Hawk, then higher to Breckenridge, Gold Hill (above Boulder), Empire, Aspen, Leadville and Cripple Creek. Along with gold, they would also find silver, iron, tungsten, molybdenum and, on the plains, oil and coal. Among the most notable beneficiaries of the mountains' largesse were the unsinkable Titanic passenger Molly Brown and "Baby Doe" Tabor, a wealthy socialite who froze to death, penniless.

First Boulder Settlement

Also in 1858, Capt. Thomas Aikins, a Missouri farmer, led a gold-prospecting group of farmers and merchants to the area. From Fort St. Vrain to the northeast, he peered at the Boulder Valley through his telescope and saw "bands of Indian Ponies and bands of deer and antelope grazing close up to the high foot-hills; . . . and could see that [it] was the loveliest of all the valleys . . . a landscape exceedingly beautiful, those mountains are so high and steep. . . ." In October or November, Aikins and party camped near the mouth of Boulder Canyon beneath the jagged vertical red rocks — an area now designated as Settlers Park. (There's some debate about what Aikins actually viewed through his telescope; the Boulder Valley cannot be seen from Fort St. Vrain because of the topography. There's also "first settler" John Rothrock, about whom less is known.)

According to Aikins, before they had bed-

photo: Linda Cornett

A bust of Chief Niwot, who welcomed the first white settlers in the Boulder Valley with the warning that they would never be able to leave, greets similarly smitten newcomers to the Boulder Courthouse lawn.

ded down for the night, Chief Niwot of the Arapaho paid a visit, saying, "Go away; you come to kill our game, to burn our wood and to destroy our grass." But the miners fed and flattered the tall, handsome Niwot (whose name means Left Hand), who eventually agreed to coexist in peace.

Boulderites love to tell newcomers the story of another comment by the chief which became known as Niwot's Curse. Popular legend has it that Niwot warned the white settlers that they would never be able to leave the Boulder Valley. The number of students who make their lives in Boulder after graduation, the professionals who return after retirement and the vacationers who come back year after year seem to prove the legend true. What Niwot actually said, however, was, "Boulder Valley is so beautiful that people will want to stay, and their staying will be the undoing of the beauty" – a prediction that Boulder policymakers and citizens have been working hard to disprove.

In January of 1859, the Aikins party found gold in a small creek bed between Sunshine and Four Mile canyons. Word got out and within a month there were 2,000 men and 17 women in the Boulder area.

Town Development

Winter closed in, making mining difficult and causing many miners to leave. In February, Aikins called a meeting to form a "Town Company." Later that month, A.A. Brookfield became the first president of the Boulder City Town Company, and 56 shareholders divided 1,280 acres along Boulder Creek into 4,044 lots. Each shareholder received 18 lots; a few lots were given for free to those who promised to provide such services as sawmills. The remaining lots were for sale at $1,000 each. Other homesteading lands at the time cost $1.25 an acre, so the Boulder lots weren't hot sellers, and further settlement was quite slow. Other camps and settlements in the area grew much faster.

Boulder, named after the area's plentiful rocks, began as a raw frontier settlement of tents and crude log cabins along the creek. Roofs and doors were made of split pine, and the floors were dirt.

Originally part of the Nebraska and Kansas territories, Boulder became part of Colorado when Congress established the Colorado Territory in 1861. South of present-day Baseline Road was the Kansas Territory; north was the Nebraska Territory. In 1867, Boulder became the county seat, and the town was incorporated in 1871. Unlike the region's boom-and-bust mining towns, Boulder's economy remained stable because the city functioned mainly as a supply and transportation center for the miners and prospectors — and, later, as a hub for plains farmers. Boulder's population from 1860 to 1870 remained at about 350.

Boulder's first newspaper, the *Boulder Valley News*, began publication in April 1867.

Land Grabs and The Sand Creek Massacre

The technicalities of stealing the land from the Native Americans came from the Pre-emption Law of 1841, stating that a person had prior right to purchase a piece of land if he occupied it and improved it. And next, the Kansas-Nebraska Act of 1853, which referred to preemption of "the public lands to which the Indian title had been at the time of such settlement extinguished." In 1866 Congress validated various settlers' claims to these lands.

Land "ownership" and "improvement" were not understood in the American Indian culture as they were by Europeans. If anything, the American Indians believed the land owned them and didn't need any "improving." This could be the classic clash of cultures, East vs. West — living in harmony with nature vs. controlling it.

But, for the most part, the miners and American Indians coexisted peacefully in the Boulder Valley until the summer of 1864, when there were reports of American Indians attacking some wagon trains and express wagons. The then-anti-Indian (and anti-black) *Rocky Mountain News* (now *Denver Rocky Mountain News*) helped stir up more fear and negativity. That year, the "100 Day Volunteers" were commissioned under Capt. David Nichols with other citizens. Boulder's friends of Chief Left Hand (Niwot) refused to take part in this brigade, which found and attacked peaceful American Indian families camped in accordance with treaties at Sand Creek in eastern Colorado. Thinking the attack was a mistake, the besieged Indians raised the American flag, but were ruthlessly massacred nonetheless. Women and children were scalped, and gentle Chief Niwot, who met with the first settlers, was killed.

Bold Miners, Blizzards, Boom and Bust

The original gold deposit that fueled Boulder's early economy was depleted after about a year. Next, silver from mines in Caribou stimulated Boulder's growth, and some said that Caribou taxes built the Boulder County Courthouse. A wagon road from Boulder to Caribou was completed in 1871, and a stagecoach ride cost $3.50. Mail was delivered by sleigh to Caribou from Nederland in winter.

Four miles from the Continental Divide at 10,500 feet, life was cold and tough at Caribou, but in the early 1870s the lure of silver had drawn nearly 500 residents, who built two-story houses so they could find them in the 25-foot-high snow drifts after storms. The second story also allowed citizens to come and go through their bedroom windows in the deep snow. A rope ran from the mine to the town's center so miners could feel their way home in blizzards. When asked about Caribou's winters, one miner remarked that he did not know how long winter lasted, because he had only been there three years. Caribou was eventually destroyed by fire, diphtheria, scarlet fever and the mining bust over the next few decades.

Mines popped up all over the area: Sunshine, Salina and Magnolia — today, the names of a local canyon, town site and road. Many booming mountain mining towns, such as Ward, soon went bust when the gold ran out. A smelter built at Black Hawk in 1868 renewed interest in deeper mining in the area because ores containing gold could be processed. A few years later a gold-silver ore was found at Gold Hill, and during 1892, the peak year, more than $1 million in gold and silver was produced.

In 1900, ferberite, an ore of tungsten, was identified in Nederland, starting a new rush to the area. (Nederland, meaning "low lands," was named by the Dutchmen who bought the higher Caribou mine.) By 1918, Boulder County had become the main producer of tungsten in the United States, with a total production of 24,000 tons of tungsten trioxide worth $23 million.

By 1910, $20 million in silver had come from Caribou, but it finally ran out. "Caribou, like the reindeer it was named after, pawed its food — silver — from beneath the frozen snow. The lifeblood of its silver veins pinched out, and the town stumbled to a stop, and died," wrote historian John Buchanan.

Trains and Transport

Trains were the lifeblood of the mining industry and early settlement of the area. The first railroad line to Boulder came through in 1879, and narrow-gauge railroad lines were built into the mountains, making it easier to supply mining camps. By 1883 Union Pacific Railroad had 14 miles of narrow-gauge track to Four Mile, Salina, Wallstreet, Sunset and, later, Ward. By 1904 the line went all the way to Eldora and was known as The Switzerland Trail. It became a popular tourist attraction that provided an additional source of revenue to the railroads. But the route had financial problems by 1909, and then-owners Colorado and Northwestern folded. The line continued to operate by the reorganized Denver, Boulder and Northwestern Railroad, which spent the next 10 years debating whether to close The Switzerland Trail line. In 1919 a cloudburst washed out 2,500 feet of track, and the line was never rebuilt.

Colorado's First School and the University

Boulder's identity as a center of education had its beginnings in 1860 with the opening of the state's first schoolhouse. Next, citizens lobbied fiercely to have the city chosen for the territorial (later, state) university. The same Capt. Nichols involved in the Sand Creek Massacre served as a horseback mediator, making an overnight ride from the capital in Denver to secure a pledge of local funds from Boulder businessmen and back again in time to secure the university for Boulder. Boulder's citizens donated land and money to match the $15,000 appropriated by the state legislature for construction of the university on a barren, windswept hill south of town where the Arapaho had hunted.

In 1876, Colorado became a state, at which time the University of Colorado was under construction. Completed in 1877, Old Main, the university's first building, housed the entire university — a few classrooms along with living quarters for the president and janitor and their families. With much ceremony the university opened its doors in September 1877 to 44 students, a president and one instructor.

When Mary Rippon of Detroit was invited to be CU's third faculty member, Ann Sewell, wife of first CU president Joseph A. Sewell, predicted that Rippon "would not stay two days in this lonely place." Rippon decided to come West and give it a try after reading about

Photo: Daily Camera/Karen Toth

Boulder is home to Colorado's flagship university.

Colorado's wildflowers in the *Atlantic Monthly* and hearing that banker Charles Buckingham had donated $2,000 for a university library. She was a French and German professor for 57 years — the first woman in the United States to teach at a state university. She also helped open Boulder's first public library. CU's lovely outdoor theater, site of the Colorado Shakespeare Festival (see our Festivals and Annual Events chapter), is named for her.

To beautify CU's barren, windswept campus, Ann Sewell ordered 50 wagon loads of soil for her landscaping plans. The dirt promptly blew away with the first high wind, but she ordered another 50 wagon loads, and by 1881 had grown 2 acres of lawn with trees and flowers.

Saloons, Red-lights, Religion and Law

Meanwhile, Boulder began to take on the features of a permanent settlement. By 1872, various churches had been built: Presbyterian, Baptist and a Methodist-Episcopalian church. Some citizens became concerned that the town's young men spent too much time in saloons and opened a reading room, where the men could come and peruse the newspapers while inspecting the genteel young ladies occasionally invited as an inducement.

By the 1870s, Boulder men had acquired money and real estate and needed a government and laws to protect their assets. In 1871, Capt. Aikins' son, Lafayette, was appointed town marshal and paid a salary of $72 a year. The only previous law enforcement was the mining district's "club rules," whereby a wrongdoer would have the hair shaved off half his face and head (opposite sides) and be expelled from town.

Liquor licenses costing $100 per saloon were established to raise some revenue for the fledgling town. Loose dogs were a big issue. In 1871 a dog-control program was initiated along with a tree-planting program.

By 1875, local Republican, Democratic and Prohibition parties had formed. Well-educated and feisty, Boulder's women started lobbying for the vote that year. In 1893 Colorado became the second state after Wyoming (then a territory) to grant women the vote.

Less-liberated women (or, perhaps, more — depending upon one's perspective) occupied a red-light district, which stretched from the north side of Boulder Creek at Canyon Boulevard (formerly Water Street) to the present-day library. Pearl Street, Boulder's original main street for commerce, was reportedly named for a well-respected madam. Prostitution and gambling were declared illegal in 1873, but the law was reversed in 1878. Some houses of "ill repute" closed down temporarily and others not at all, and the so-called "brides of the multitude" continued their business.

The increasing number of buildings and fear of fire — a great danger with the high winds — finally brought about the construction of a waterworks in 1874, then the first hook-and-ladder company in 1875. Bucket brigades were the first means of firefighting. The first volunteer firemen were the cream of Boulder society and popular at firemen's balls, parades and firefighting tournaments. So important and highly regarded were the firemen, election of the firemen's officers drew more attention than city elections.

By the late 1870s, increased mining activity was bringing in more crime, and Boulder needed a jail. Prisoners had been kept everywhere from the basement of the fire department to the sheriff's hotel room.

Water also became an issue by the late 1870s, as the population increased and Boulder Creek became polluted with mine tailings. People who didn't have wells had to use the creek water. A reservoir had been built in 1874 at the base of Boulder Canyon, but it too had become increasingly polluted. In 1884 horses were found dead in the creek, and the reservoir was shut down. To avoid the mine-tailing runoff, a new reservoir was built at the mouth of Sunshine Canyon. The Boulder City Improvement Society formed in 1881. By 1882, Boulder's population had reached 3,000. Water had its revenge in the terrifying 100-year flood in 1894 (see details below).

Coal, Oil, Newspapers and an International Population

In the late 1860s, there were 77 buildings in town. Local businesses included sawmills, a brickyard, several blacksmiths and general stores, stables and liveries. Downtown Boulder had a wobbly boardwalk that rose and fell to a different height in front of each different shop — ripping ladies' skirts and gouging shoppers with loose nails.

The business of mining was expanding to other minerals. Coal was discovered east of Boulder on David Kerr's farm. Coal prospector Louis Nawatny bought nearby land, registered a town plat in 1878 and named it Louisville after himself. Two years later, 500 people had settled there. In 1887 a coal mine was dug in Lafayette (named for Lafayette Miller), and by 1892 there were five mines and 200 homes. Polish, Italian, Greek and French immigrants joined the Welsh, Scotch and English miners who had been here since the 1860s. By the 1920s the coal industry would be Boulder County's largest employer with 1,000 men.

Oil was discovered in 1901 near Boulder, and for a while Boulder had its own oil stock exchange and a specialized newspaper, *Oil News*. Wells sprang up all over east of Boulder, and it was predicted that the oil field would stretch to Wyoming. By March of 1902 there were 92 oil companies operating near today's Longmont Diagonal. Natural gas was also discovered along with the oil, but it was considered a nuisance. Ultimately, 183 holes were drilled in Boulder County, but only 81 were functioning. Of these, 76 produced oil; five produced gas.

The weekly *Camera* newspaper, so named because it printed photographs on its front page, became the *Daily Camera* in 1891 and still publishes today (see our Media chapter).

The 100-Year Flood

Just when Boulder was getting its feet on the ground and becoming an established city with various amenities, disaster struck. The winter of 1894 was long, cold and snowy. The heavy snowpack still plastered the Front Range at the end of May. Easterly winds brought a warm spring rain that lasted for 60 hours and melted the snow too quickly. The creeks began to rise in the early morning hours of May 31, soon unleashing an awesome display of nature's power.

"One seething mass of black water, bowlders [sic] and crushed buildings. Nearly every tree has been torn out by the roots and the road bed is entirely destroyed," read the *Daily Camera*, describing the scene at Left Hand Creek near Glendale.

Boulder was experiencing a 100-year flood — one with a 1 percent chance of occurring in any year.

All the mountain roads, bridges, rooming houses and even mines broke apart on Four Mile Creek, Boulder Creek, Jim Creek, Left Hand Creek and the St. Vrain. Buildings washed away at Sunset, Jamestown, Crisman and Ballarat. Jamestown's church floated downstream with its bell ringing. The 2-year-old boom town of Copper Rock was washed off the map. The raging waters destroyed the road at Estes Park and a section of Lyons.

The flood roared down Boulder Creek into town, first wiping out the railroad bridge at Fourth Street then the bridges on Sixth, Ninth, 12th and 17th streets — each piling up on the other in a maelstrom of boulders, buildings, railroad tracks and trees. Witnesses recalled the terrifying sound of the rock- and wreckage-filled water.

"From the Boulder Hotel to University Hill was one vast lake with here and there a small patch of an island," read the *Camera*. After the waters calmed, one resident caught a 7-inch trout on Water Street (now Canyon Boulevard).

For five days, Boulder was cut off from the outside world, and residents on one side of the creek couldn't get to the other side. CU

The Midnight Ride of Capt. David Nichols

A little-known episode in the founding of the University of Colorado became one that sealed Boulder's fate as the chosen site. In 1874 various cities and communities in Colorado were vying for the university, and the situation developed into a bitter rivalry with political intrigues. But the state Territorial House had not yet even passed an appropriation bill for the university, much less decided where it would be.

An 1872 bill for an act appropriating money for a university in Colorado had been defeated. Mountain mining districts opposed the bill saying that Colorado had no use for a university. Republican members of the legislature had agreed in caucus to vote against any but the most necessary appropriations.

Capt. David Nichols of Boulder had been elected Speaker of the Territorial House and put a bill for the university before the legislature again. He got the assembly to approve a bill that said the territory would give $15,000 toward a university on the condition that Boulder contribute an equal amount. In those days $15,000 was a lot of money, and the legislature probably thought that Boulder would be hard put to come up with it. If the bill were tabled again, there would be no telling what would happen to the university.

Nichols jumped on his horse at 6 PM that rainy, late-January night and rode from Denver to Boulder, arriving around 11 PM. He banged on the door until he woke Capt. Frank Tyler, a prominent Boulder citizen, who promised Nichols he would personally take responsibility for raising the funds. Nichols then visited other prominent citizens discussing the situation. Nichols stopped only long enough to change horses, then rode the five hours back to Denver. At 10 AM the next morning he addressed the legislature and announced that he had visited Boulder and obtained promises for the funds.

Capt. David Nichols secured Boulder as the site of the state university. Also shown is a promissory note from a prominent Boulder citizen as backing for the proposed University of Colorado.

With a stronger assurance of monetary backing than the other cities, Boulder got the go-ahead for the university with the passage of the new appropriation bill.

commencement was postponed, and the first mail arrived after five days with news of flooding all over the Front Range. Afterward, miners were out of work because of flooded mines. Amazingly, no one was killed in the flood, and no crimes were committed except the ransacking of someone's trunk. Boulder cleaned up and rebuilt.

A hundred years later, the city is embarked on a campaign to gradually buy buildings in the Boulder Creek floodplain and clear a path for the inevitable next major flood. Pedestrian bridges across the creek are designed to break away and swing to the side so they don't become dams for flood debris. Canyon highways are marked with signs telling motorists to abandon their cars and climb to higher ground in case of flood. In the spring and summer, alarms are tested weekly, reminding residents of the continuing possibility of flood.

Tuberculars, Tourists and Trolleys

As the century came to an end, Boulder was beginning to draw visitors and newcomers other than miners. From its earliest days, Boulder, like other places in the Southwest, attracted people with tuberculosis who hoped the pure air, dry climate and vigorous life would restore their health. In 1895 the Seventh-Day Adventists built the sanitarium (later to become Boulder Memorial Hospital and now the Mapleton Rehab and Sports Medicine Center) for tuberculars. Many eminent CU professors were recovered tuberculars.

Along with the tuberculars came a group of Texas professors in 1897 looking for an airy summer camp and retreat to escape the Texas heat. To the delight of Boulder citizens, the Texans chose Boulder as a site for their proposed Chautauqua — a respected national movement at the time — and the city bought its first park land and named it Texado Park for the Texans. Chautauquas were summer family camps that emphasized culture, nature, recreation and sometimes religion.

The dining hall and auditorium were completed for the grand opening on the Fourth of July in 1898, and the first Chautauquans camped in tents — later replaced by cottages. A 1903 brochure described it as "retirement without loneliness," "not a casino" but "quiet without ennui."

Well-known Boulder photographer Joseph Bevier Sturtevant ("Rocky Mountain Joe") — who produced many memorable photographs of the city's early years — was the official Chautauqua photographer. Chautauqua had a full and varied program, from music and art to political and ethical discussion groups and well-known speakers and performers such as William Jennings Bryan and John Philip Sousa.

Operas, magic shows, military tactics, lace making, baby shows, food booths, fish hatchery exhibits, photo contests, children's races and gypsy camps were but a few of the offerings. Physical health and exercise were emphasized from the start, and the Chautauqua Climbers Club made annual hikes to local landmarks and the higher mountains. Boulder druggist Eben Fine, one of Chautauqua's regular climbers, literally stumbled upon the discovery of Arapaho Glacier in 1900 when he nearly fell into one of its crevasses.

The Switzerland Trail railroad was a popular excursion for Chautauquans, who would ride into the mountains for a picnic and snowball fight. The more adventurous rented handcars and pumped their own way up for a day's outing.

Transportation to and from Chautauqua was difficult, so for the camp's second season, 1899, the city inaugurated its first electric streetcar, which for a nickel "sped" visitors from downtown to Chautauqua gate at 15 miles per hour. A few years later a line was put in to the sanitarium, and others followed.

The railroad brought more tourists to Eldorado Springs, south of Boulder, where a popular resort developed around the area's thermal springs. It attracted such rich or famous — or those soon to be — as young Dwight and Mamie Eisenhower (who honeymooned there), budding musician Glenn Miller (a CU student), actress Mary Pickford and her husband, actor Douglas Fairbanks Sr. (a Jamestown native), writer Damon Runyon, fighter Jack Dempsey and gossip columnist Walter Winchell. From 1907 to 1948, Ivy Baldwin performed his famous high-wire walk 600 feet across the canyon on a steel cable averaging 582 feet high. He made his last trip at age 82.

More Parks and City Planning

Chautauqua began Boulder's golden age of land and park acquisition. The day after Chautauqua opened, the city bought the eastern slope of Flagstaff Mountain from the U.S. Government. Shortly after, the city purchased another 1,800 acres of Flagstaff Mountain west to Four Mile Creek and from Sunshine Canyon south to South Boulder Creek.

The Boulder Women's Club planted trees in town, and in 1907 a parks board became an official city department. Next, the city slowly acquired the land along Boulder Creek from the Colorado and Southern Railway. At the time, the parks board wanted a park along Boulder Creek stretching from the mouth of Boulder Canyon to the eastern edge of town. Central Park land was acquired in 1906 and, steadily, more lots and parcels from the railroad.

Citizens gave gifts of land. Dr. and Mrs. William J. Baird donated 160 acres of their Gregory Canyon holdings in 1911. Hanna Barker and other citizens gave parcels of land. Boulder bought Arapaho Glacier after a battle with U.S. Park Service, which wanted to add it to Rocky Mountain National Park.

A City Vision

In 1908, the Boulder City Improvement Association hired Frederick Law Olmsted Jr., Harvard-educated in the new field of landscape architecture. Olmsted's father had designed New York City's Central Park. The city asked Olmsted how he thought the city could be improved "to help make it increasingly convenient, agreeable and generally satisfactory as a place in which to live and work?"

Olmsted said Boulder should not arrange itself for the benefit of the tourists, "who hastily pass through . . . and often conducting themselves so as to interfere seriously with the comfort and welfare . . . of the permanent residents." Olmsted was suspicious of developers, saying they were usually from out of town. He said that dirty industry only denigrates a community, and to keep it out of Boulder.

On parks, he said, "As with the food we eat and the air we breathe, so the sights habitually before our eyes play an immense part of determining whether we feel cheerful, efficient and fit for life, or the contrary." He was concerned with the "mental and nervous con-

photo: Linda Cornett

The Art Deco-style Boulder County Courthouse on the Downtown Boulder Mall replaced the original courthouse, which burned seven decades ago.

dition of the people." Order was the goal, but "We aim at Order and hope for Beauty," he said.

He envisioned Boulder as a city of homes surrounded by small farms and gardens and advised preserving that feeling of "coziness and quiet attractiveness." He recommended underground wiring and making the Boulder Creek floodplain into a park — "the cheapest way of handling the flood problem." He said the sign of civilized society was the effectiveness of "police" powers to ensure good land use, and he recommended the city manager form of government. Boulderites liked what Olmsted said and, to a large extent, followed his advice.

Slow Growth, Sobering Legislation, War and Depression

Apparently taking Olmsted's advice to heart, Boulder became notable for its lack of industry except for the necessities: sawmills, lumberyards, blacksmith shops, brickyards, flour mills, a brewing company and a foundry. Before World War I, Boulder's biggest industry was Western Cutlery and Manufacturing Company. The CU student population had grown to 6,000, and small businesses began opening in the area around the university known as "The Hill."

By 1908, Boulder's population was 10,000, including enough teetotalers to outlaw liquor 13 years before Prohibition. Boulder remained "dry" from 1907 until 1967. During that period "liquor islands" where people could purchase packaged goods grew up outside the city limits. (Not until 1969 did it become legal to serve liquor in a public establishment; the Catacombs Bar in the Hotel Boulderado was the first to do so.)

Then came World War I in 1917 and, on its heels, the Great Depression in 1929, with not much momentum in Boulder or elsewhere. During the 1930s the Civilian Conservation Corps built and improved trails, made fire lanes in mountain parks, pulled out diseased trees and rebuilt Flagstaff Road up Flagstaff Mountain, overlooking Boulder. They built the Sunrise Amphitheater on Flagstaff, a lodge on Green Mountain and a rock garden at Chautauqua.

The Works Progress Administration built the Mary Rippon Outdoor Theater at the university, a golf course at Flatirons Country Club and other buildings around town.

Small-Town America and the Fabulous '50s

To try to raise Depression-weary spirits, the Boulder Pow Wow was begun on August 1, 1934, to celebrate Colorado's statehood day with a rodeo and various contests, including pie-eating and greased-pole climbing. Ladies had rolling-pin and slipper-throwing contests and needle-threading relays. Men tested their strength and skills at hay-pitching, hog-calling and hard-rock drilling.

In 1937 Boulder High was dedicated, and its "modern" nude sculptures entitled "Strength and Wisdom" caused a brief but heated controversy. The stunted, muscular figures called everything from "powerful and effective" to "wads of chewing gum," but were finally accepted as harmless and have since been nicknamed Minnie and Jake.

By 1945, Boulder was beginning to wake up after the Depression and war. During World War II, 4,077 Boulderites went to war and 77 were killed. The CU campus became a training center for young officers, and their predawn fitness runs were cheered on by coeds from the dormitory windows.

In 1946, 340 parking meters were installed downtown, and a group of young CU graduates founded Arapahoe Chemicals (bought by Syntex in 1965). Chicago-based *Esquire* maga-

---

INSIDERS' TIP

A 100-year flood is defined as a 1 percent chance of a disastrous flood in any one year.

zine moved its subscription operations to Boulder in 1949, the first Eastern business to do so. In 1950 the National Bureau of Standards (NBS) chose Boulder as its main base after considering 26 cities. Boulder's citizens voted to buy 217 acres of land for the bureau and gave it to the United States. Fifteen years later, NBS was a major employer, contributing 10 percent to Boulder's income. Initially at an isolated site south of town, NBS was soon surrounded by small ranch houses in a regular suburbia.

The Boulder-Denver Turnpike (U.S. Highway 36) opened in 1952 and was the first toll road in the nation to pay for itself — 13 years ahead of schedule in 1967.

CU's enrollment increased after World War II as returning military personnel took advantage of the GI Bill. In 1947, someone named "Joe" autographed the northernmost Flatiron formation and began a series of Flatiron-painting pranks, usually by university students painting a giant "C" or "CU" on the First and Third Flatirons. (Look closely at the Third Flatiron and you can still see a faint, slightly orange CU.)

In 1948, an 850-foot ski tow ran up Chautauqua, but it operated only a few seasons due to poor snow.

Industry continued migrating to the area. The Atomic Energy Commission chose an area south of Boulder to install its secret weapons plant, Rocky Flats, in 1951 — despite many misgivings of area residents. In 1955, "Tommy" Thompson of Thompson Engineering Co. — builder of the short-lived Chautauqua ski lift — began building respirators for polio victims. Soon after, Automation Industries moved to town. That same year, Beech Aircraft bought 1,500 acres north of Boulder and started its Aerospace Division there.

The chamber of commerce bought 18 acres east of town for Boulder Industrial Park, and Ball Brothers Research Corp. became the major tenant starting in 1957. The Muncie, Indiana, canning-jar company expanded into aerospace technology in Boulder and designed the Hubble telescope.

With all the new enterprise, Boulder's population shot up in the 1950s, and water became a concern. The population in 1950 was 19,999; by 1960 it was 66,870. In 1959 the Blue Line was established as the first project of the newly formed PLAN-Boulder, an early group of environmentally concerned citizens who wanted to preserve Boulder's unique natural assets. An imaginary boundary line was drawn along the mountain backdrop at an average of 5,750 feet, above which no city water service would be supplied.

The Early 1960s

Young solar physicist Walter Orr Roberts began manning the Harvard-run High Altitude Observatory in Climax, Colorado (near Leadville), in 1940. In 1960 Roberts was offered the directorship of a new National Center for Atmospheric Research (NCAR), and he recommended Boulder as the site. The state donated 530 acres of mesa land south of town for the new laboratory, which was designed by noted architect I.M. Pei. Though controversial at the time, an exception was made to the new Blue Line ruling to give NCAR water. NCAR was to become a jewel in Boulder's crown, and a setting for Woody Allen's futuristic comedy, *Sleeper*.

The U.S. Department of Commerce established its Environmental Sciences Service Administration (ESSA) in Boulder in 1966. ESSA became part of the National Oceanic and Atmospheric Administration (NOAA) in 1970.

Shopping centers began springing up around town, and the Crossroads Shopping Center opened in 1963 outside the city limits with Texas money.

Boulder's water supplies were increased in 1964 and spurred a controlled-growth plan along several "spokes" radiating outward from the city, one east on Arapahoe, one northeast along the Diagonal Highway and one south. In 1969, there was a big controversy over fluoridation of water, a bond issue for a new library and an amendment for liquor-by-the-drink. All three passed. Though citizens rejected a $500,000 parks bond that same year, two years later they passed a $1 million bond to build the north and south recreation centers.

Historically, all sides agreed on greenbelt acquisition — both liberals and conservatives — and wanted to continue to buy land in the mountains and plains to "belt" the city with undeveloped land. To stop the building of a luxury hotel atop Enchanted Mesa, citizens approved the purchase of 155 acres of that land for $105,000. In 1967 a 1 percent sales tax was passed, with 60 percent of revenue to go for street improvements and 40 percent for future purchase of greenbelt lands.

The Turbulent Late '60s and Early '70s

The late '60s brought the hippies, the "transient problem" and general turmoil. The first gentle flower children camped out in Central Park, which had to be closed because it became a health hazard. Later came the more militant anarchists, whose bombs exploded in the Hall of Justice Building, United Bank and Flatirons Elementary School. The Board of Education's auditorium was firebombed. Fortunately, no one was killed in these incidents. Riots in 1971 on University Hill left stores looted and windows broken. Police teargassed the mob and arrested 40 people. In 1972, 3,000 peaceful anti-war demonstrators barricaded the Boulder Turnpike at the Baseline interchange to protest President Nixon's blockade of North Vietnam and the mining of Haiphong Harbor. Mexican-Americans, or Chicanos, were seeking to assert their identity and demand equal treatment, recognition and respect. In 1974, six activists in the Chicano movement were killed in two separate bomb explosions in cars. The explosions were believed by police to be accidental and meant for some other target.

More quietly, the first gay human rights ordinance law was passed by city council in 1973, but when it had its second reading some citizens objected vociferously. Mayor Penfield Tate and Councilman Tim Fuller, the most outspoken supporters, received death threats. Fuller was recalled from office and Tate barely kept his seat. The ordinance was overturned by voters.

New County Clerk and Recorder Clela Rorex attained notoriety after issuing licenses for several same-sex marriages. To express his opinion, one citizen appeared with his horse, Dolly, saying, "If a boy can marry a boy, and a girl can marry a girl, why can't a lonesome old cowboy get hitched to his favorite saddle mare?" He was refused because the horse was under age. Ultimately, same-sex marriage licenses were declared illegal in 1975 by the state attorney general.

PLAN-Boulder County helped write part of Boulder's first Comprehensive Plan in 1970. In 1971 a height-limit ordinance was passed so, in the wave of new construction, residents could keep their mountain views. New buildings could not exceed a height of 55 feet — the height of most mature trees. Voters that year also chose a growth-control study plan to prevent the kind of rapid growth that had occurred in the 1950s.

The "New Wave" Plus Growth and Limitations in the '70s and '80s

The late '70s saw calmer times but also a huge influx of newcomers, particularly from the Northeast, as many young adults tired of life in the drab, polluted, often politically corrupt and overcrowded big cities. Most were well-educated and hopeful of finding jobs in one of Boulder's clean industries. Many had visited the area during vacations and were delighted (or requested) to be transferred here by IBM or Ball Brothers. Many were single parents starting new lives and seeking gold of another sort: good schools and neighborhoods for their children and a happy life.

By word-of-mouth and the "underground" communications network, Boulder had also become known nationwide to neo-Buddhists, bicyclists, runners, the urban disenchanted, spiritual seekers, health food converts and just about every New Age religion as a great place to live. And it's no wonder. Boulderite Frank Shorter became the first American ever to win Olympic gold and silver in the marathon (1972 and 1976); Celestial Seasonings founder Mo Siegel began the international Red Zinger Bicycle Classic; Tibetan Buddhist leader Chögyam Trungpa Rinpoche founded the Naropa Institute in 1974; and the Boulder School of Massage Therapy opened its doors in 1976.

Meanwhile, fearful of urban sprawl and uncontrolled shopping center construction, PLAN-Boulder County campaigned in the late '70s for preservation of open space throughout the county. In 1976, almost $2 million was spent to complete Boulder's downtown pedestrian mall on Pearl Street to draw people back into the city's center. In 1977, the Danish Plan — originated by City Councilman Paul Danish — was approved to limit residential growth to 2 percent annually. To discourage the building of a mega-mall in Louisville (which Danish described as an "environmental pig"), City Council approved a controversial expansion of Crossroads Shopping Mall (now within the Boulder city limits) in 1979.

When a California-based computer software company, System Development Corporation, announced its plans in 1980 to locate on a plateau at the city's southern entrance, on county land designated as open space by the Boulder Valley Comprehensive Plan, city officials nixed it. The company then approached other towns in Boulder County, further infuriating some council members. The City Council ultimately decided to buy the land to put the issue on hold until Boulder residents could vote on it. In the meantime, discouraged by the strong anti-development sentiment, SDC packed up its plans and left Boulder County.

A furious public art debate broke out in 1983 when a New York sculptor, Andrea Blum, was chosen to design an outdoor sculpture at Ninth Street and Canyon Boulevard. Blum's stark, urban-styled white concrete design reminded many citizens of a subway station or public restroom, and it was ultimately rejected as being inappropriate for Boulder's site.

During the 1980s some of Boulder County's plentiful high-tech industries began to falter. Louisville-based Storage Technology Corporation laid off 1,300 people in October 1984, the largest single-day cutback in county history. By the end of the year it had trimmed another 1,290 employees and filed for reorganization under federal bankruptcy law. The ripple effect was felt throughout the high tech industry in Boulder County.

The Boulder Creek Path, which runs from Eben Fine Park at the mouth of Boulder Canyon east to 55th Street, was completed in 1987.

After bitter debate in 1988, Boulder voters approved expansion of Boulder's public library at its current site, a beautiful setting next to Boulder Creek and in the path of a major flood.

Federal agents raided Rocky Flats nuclear weapons plant (8 miles south of Boulder) in 1989 and brought health and safety questions about the plant to local and national attention.

The largest fire in the county burned 2,300 acres and destroyed 44 homes in July 1989 on Sugarloaf Mountain. The fire was believed to have been caused by careless campers, but the cause was never definitely identified.

Shutdowns, the 1990s

By 1991, in the warm glow of glasnost and following several massive demonstrations, the beginning of the end had come for Rocky Flats. The U.S. Energy Secretary eliminated 1,000 jobs at the plant in non-radioactive work and revealed plans to move the whole operation to Kansas City. Many of the plant's employees accepted the government's offer to retrain them at local colleges for new careers.

Neighbors of the National Institute of Standards and Technology (NIST, formerly the Bureau of Standards) were upset with the government facility's plans to expand on 205 acres they had come to think of as permanent open space.

In 1992, a Colorado Springs-based group, Colorado for Family Values, promoted a constitutional amendment that would prohibit state or local governments from passing laws or policies that would allow a claim of discrimination based on homosexual orientation. The amendment was directed at Boulder, Denver and Aspen, which all had approved anti-discrimination laws for homosexuals. Colorado voters passed the amendment, which was overwhelmingly defeated in Boulder. Within days of the election, Boulder, Denver, Aspen, the Boulder Valley School District and individuals including tennis star Martina Navratilova filed a lawsuit challenging the constitutionality of the amendment.

Passage of Amendment 2 initiated a nationwide boycott of Colorado. CU-Boulder football coach Bill McCartney created a statewide furor when, speaking from a University of Colorado podium, he called homosexuality an "abomination of almighty God." McCartney served on the advisory board of Colorado for Family Values and organized the massive Promisekeepers gatherings of Christian men. McCartney was censured by CU-Boulder's president, Judith Albino, for using his position as coach to espouse negative views of homosexuality. McCartney left his coaching position at the end of the 1994 football season.

Rocky Flats operators pleaded guilty to 10 environmental crimes after more than two years' investigation by a grand jury, and the nuclear plant's official work was ended in mid-1992. The building and site are still being decontaminated, and officials are still trying to figure out what to do with it all — plus 14.2 tons of plutonium.

Another building moratorium stunned developers in February 1993 when the Boulder City Council decided it needed time to develop the Integrated Planning Project to determine "what's best for what's left" of developable land in Boulder. County commissioners also initiated a moratorium on mountain building. In September of that year the City Council put a hold on developing large parcels — the so-called last 10 percent of developable land — firmly establishing a population growth cap of 2 percent a year by imposing a limit on the number of building permits issued.

Celestial Seasonings stock sold like hot cakes when 2.1 million shares went on the block in July 1994. Local investors complained that large investors snapped up all the shares before locals had a chance.

Boulder County voters in the November 1993 election passed a .25 percent sales and use tax to buy open space, which could amount to as much as $90 million in the next 16 years. The county purchased 5,000 acres in the Foothills between Left Hand Canyon and Lyons — known as the Heil Ranch.

In mid-December 1993, a Denver district judge ruled the controversial Amendment 2 unconstitutional, and in 1996 the U.S. Supreme Court did the same.

The expansion of NIST was finally approved after three years of controversy and debate.

Schwinn Cycling and Fitness moved to Boulder hoping "to update its stodgy image with a Boulder address and new attitude," according to the *Daily Camera*. Warren Miller Entertainment, a California ski- and sports-movie maker, also put down roots in Boulder — the company already shoots most of its ski footage in Colorado. Two new subsidiaries of IBM set up shop. Centrobe, formerly Neodata, the world's largest magazine subscription fulfillment service (located in Boulder since 1963), moved its corporate headquarters from Dallas to Louisville (Boulder County) in 1993.

In late 1995, Boulder voters made national headlines and created a local uproar by expanding the city's smoking ordinance to ban smoking in all indoor public places except dwellings, sites of private social functions and tobacco stores. Some bars and restaurants have built fully enclosed, separately ventilated rooms for smokers. The Boulder Dinner Theatre had to get special dispensation so an actor could light up on stage, as called for in a play.

The same year, scientists at the University of Colorado and National Institute of Standards and Technology created a form of matter never before seen but predicted by Albert Einstein 70 years ago. Called a superatom, the matter was created by cooling rubidium atoms to within a fraction of a degree above absolute zero, where theoretically all atomic motion ceases. The scientists created the coldest temperature on earth — and possibly the universe — for the experiment. Practical applications are not yet clear.

Bould-ly into the Future

Its destiny dictated by geology — gold, silver and other minerals — Boulder still attracts contemporary settlers because of its spectacular mountain setting. Though settled by miners, farmers and fortune seekers, Boulder somehow identified the importance of education, environmental preservation and quality of life from its earliest days. Holding onto these values, the city has nurtured a major university, internationally known research centers, clean industries and an interesting assortment of citizens who have come from around the country and the world.

Boulder has seen many changes from its rustic and humble beginnings, but then again, the more things change, the more they remain the same.

Boulder leaders today continue to deal with the same issues as the town's founders: dog control, water, the price of land and housing, what to do with all those newcomers "looking for gold." Now, however, the gold newcomers seek is Boulder's special quality of life.

Good Books on Colorado Geology, History and Reference

Geology

Prairie Peak and Plateau by John and Halka Chronic
Roadside Geology of Colorado by Halka Chronic

History and Good Reading

A Colorado History by Carl Ubbelohde, Maxine Benson and Duane A. Smith
A Look at Boulder: From Settlement to City by Phyllis Smith
Stampede to Timberline by Muriel Sibell Wolle (stories and legends of Colorado's gold camps)
A Lady's Life in the Rocky Mountains by Isabella Bird

Other References

The Coloradans by Robert Athern
Glory Colorado! by William Davis (University of Colorado history, 1853-1963)
Our Own Generation by Ron James (CU-Boulder history, 1963-1976)
Colorado Handbook by Stephen Metzger
The Colorado Guide by Bruce Caughey and Dean Winstanley
Colorado: Off the Beaten Path by Curtis Casewit

JOHN'S

**A Charmingly Small
Chef~Owned Restaurant
Opened 1975**

1999
"AMERICA'S TOP RESTAURANTS"
ZAGAT SURVEY

❧

*"Consistently great European & American Cuisine
made with attention to detail"* Daily Camera

❧

*"Needless to say, a dinner at John's takes us on
a tantalizing excursion into delicate flavors
& aromatic pleasures"* Daily Camera

❧

*"John Bizzarro is serious about his cooking and it
shows...the menu is a wonderfully eclectic read,
reflecting Bizzarro's diverse experiences...he's
skilled in many different cooking styles,
and is able to blend them creatively into new
compositions"* Rocky Mountain News

2328 Pearl Street 444-5232
Open 5:30 Tuesday through Saturday

Restaurants

Boulder has earned a nationwide reputation for fine dining. In fact, many of the "best restaurants of Denver" lists include a fair number of Boulder restaurants. Good spots abound in the Pearl Street Mall area, but stupendous possibilities also exist in other shopping areas, the mountains and plains. This chapter is organized by type of restaurant rather than by geographic region, since they're all within an easy drive of Boulder.

You could enjoy a different Boulder eatery every day and not repeat for weeks. Boulder has a stunning variety from rollicking party places to quiet and intimate restaurants for conversation or romance. Basic food, served fast, suits some people, especially families. Others prefer meals custom prepared, and some folks like to linger over a gourmet meal.

In addition to your taste buds, you need to consider your budget. Our price-code key (see subsequent gray box) uses dollar signs to give the range for the likely cost of dinner for two, not including cocktails, beer or wine, appetizer and dessert, tax and tip. Please remember that these symbols provide only a general guide.

Price Code

$	less than $25
$$	$26 to $50
$$$	$51 to $75
$$$$	$75 and more

If you live in Boulder, you've become accustomed to smoke-free dining. If you're new or visiting, Boulder's rigid no-smoking regulations might come as a shock. While all restaurants in the city of Boulder must provide non-smoking areas, none of them accommodate smokers except in a separate (and separately ventilated) room.

Wheelchair accessibility is common but worth checking.

If a restaurant sounds elegant, eclectic or spicy, you can bet your booster chairs that your kids will get a fidget attack unless the restaurant caters to children — or unless your children are used to finer dining than the usual pizza and burger joints that parents often choose in the name of family dining. Many places have special children's menus and entertainment tricks for the kids, so ask about them.

Unless otherwise noted, these restaurants do take Visa and MasterCard. Some also take American Express, Diner's Club and Discover.

For more on takeout or informal food service, or lively nightspots, check our respective Shopping and Nightlife chapters. Our Estes Park and Grand Lake chapters include details on dining and might provide your first excuse to explore those mountain towns.

American

Traditional/Casual

Alleycatz
$$ • 1207 Pearl St., Boulder
• (303) 444-3100

Voted "Best New Restaurant" and "Best American Restaurant" by readers of a local paper, this Boulder institution was, until recently, called Potter's. One of the oldest bars in town, you can choose from more than 15 beers, 300 world-class wines and 12 custom martinis. The restaurant is decorated with the feel of a 1930s speak-easy. The menu includes smoked and grilled New York strip steak with Kentucky sour mash demi-glace, and a rack of Colorado lamb with sautéed cherry tomatoes. The outdoor patio at Alleycatz is by far one of the best spots for people watching on the Pearl Street Mall. Lunch and dinner are served daily with appetizers available until midnight.

Annie's Cafe
$ • 20 Lakeview Dr., Nederland
• (303) 258-3600

Perched atop the Nederland Shopping Center, Annie's is a popular local hangout that serves eggs, pancakes, omelets, sandwiches, salads and homemade soups. It is open for breakfast and lunch daily.

Bart's Restaurant
$ • 585 South Boulder Rd., Louisville
• (303) 665-2060

Sandwiches, steaks and seafood get served here under pictures of WW II airplanes. This spot is especially appealing to families or anyone who loves aviation. The restaurant, which is inexpensive to begin with, offers early-bird specials, with hours varying according to the day of the week. Bart's is open for lunch Monday through Saturday and brunch on Sunday.

Boulder Broker Inn
$$$ • 555 30th St., Boulder
• (303) 449-1752

The English atmosphere, with dark wood and stained glass, is a perfect complement to entrees such as Filet Wellington, prime rib or Alaskan king salmon. A complimentary bowl of in-the-shell Gulf shrimp on ice accompanies each meal, as do a choice of soup or salad plus dessert, often a French pastry or other tempting treat, varying daily. The outstanding Sunday brunch has been a favorite local tradition for 22 years. Reservations are recommended. There is nightly dancing at Bently's. The inn is open for breakfast, lunch and dinner daily.

Boulder Cork
$$ • 3295 30th St., Boulder
• (303) 443-9505

The Cork is Boulder's oldest steak house, specializing in excellently prepared prime rib and steak since 1969. Southwestern dishes including chicken enchiladas and fresh stuffed chiles are complemented by the Southwestern décor. The award winning wine list has been acknowledged with the Wine Spectator Award. The strong presentation of all the meals make it as popular for a business lunch as for a special dinner. You can stop for a sip and a light bite at the bar including angel hair pasta, fresh steamed artichokes, fresh fish, salads and fresh greens and vegetables. The Cork is open for dinner daily and for lunch on weekdays.

Boulder Wrapsody
$ • 1136 Pearl St., Suite 103, on the Pearl Street Mall, Boulder
• (303) 444-1305

If you find yourself hungry but wrapped up in people watching on Boulder's mall, head to Boulder Wrapsody for New Age fast food. Although flatbread has been around for more than 10,000 years, it didn't taste quite like this. Wrapsody infuses its tortillas with flavor and then wraps the world's cuisine inside. Wraps might include marinated chicken, grilled falafel and sun-dried tomatoes, or yellow and zucchini squash. Wrapsody also offers a variety of smoothies like the Top Banana with orange juice, fresh bananas and strawberries. You can eat in or take out. They serve lunch and dinner daily.

The Buff
$ • 1725 28th St., Boulder
• (303) 442-9150

It might be the slogan, "Eat In the Buff," or the unique breakfast items, but either way *Daily Camera* readers voted this restaurant the best breakfast in Boulder in 1998. Frittatas, panini sandwiches, muffalettas, and breakfast chimichangas are offered along with traditional breakfast items. There's a full espresso bar or you can sip a mimosa or bloody Mary with a Denver omelet. A children's menu makes this a great weekend stop for families. A pleasant atmosphere and fast service are the norm. The Buff is open for breakfast and lunch daily.

Chautauqua Dining Hall
$$ • 900 Baseline Rd., Boulder
• (303) 440-3776

This historic 1898 dining hall has been serving summer visitors for more than 100 years in beautiful Chautauqua Park. Since 1997 the restaurant has featured the Rocky Mountain cook-

Chautauqua Dining Hall is very popular during summer.

ing of acclaimed chef Bradford Heap. The interior dining room was beautifully renovated in 1999 and the vistas from the wraparound porch are breathtaking. Fresh soups, salads made with organic Boulder County greens, lamb, griddle-seared ahi tuna, pan-roasted venison, fresh vegetables from local organic farmers and dry-aged New York steak are just a few of the offerings. A children's menu and award-winning fresh fruit pies make this a memorable family dining experience. The Dining Hall expanded its hours in 1999 but days and hours change with the seasons so call ahead.

ChriSar's Grill & Pasta
$$ • 543 Terry St., Longmont
• (303) 651-2772

ChriSar's is mostly American, but with a definite Italian overlay. Dishes like "Sea of Hearts" — shrimp, scallops and artichoke hearts tossed with linguine — are just one of many fine seafood, chicken or pasta meals made from scratch in this quaint and casual 1910 Victorian house with several small dining rooms and a patio full of flowers that is open in summer.

This restaurant is open for breakfast and dinner daily except Monday, for lunch week-days except Monday and for champagne brunch Saturday and Sunday.

Foolish Craig's Café
$ • 1611 Pearl St., Boulder
• (303) 247-9383

This newcomer is just one block east of the Pearl Street Mall and specializes in crepes and omelets. The amazing Homer is a crepe wrapped around onions, Feta cheese, Greek spices, olives, artichokes, mushrooms, tomatoes, spinach and sour cream. The caramelized three-onion soup is too good to miss. Everything is homemade, and the menu items are served throughout the day. Open for breakfast and lunch daily.

Gold Hill Inn
$$$, no credit cards • Gold Hill
• (303) 443-6461

This family-owned restaurant has served six-course dinners in an old-style log inn since 1962. The menu depends on what chef Chris Finn deems good and fresh. One June day, the offerings included hot and sour duck soup or a cold banana bisque, a salmon soufflé appetizer, venison with blackberry sauce and a choice of chocolate torte or apricot-strawberry pie.

The inn opens in May, when the mountain snow flurries abate, and it closes at the end of October, when the snow starts again. During summertime, it's open for dinner all week except on Tuesday. Reservations are recommended. It's a 20-minute drive up the mountains from Boulder, straight up Sunshine Canyon, and about an hour from Estes Park.

JW's Steakhouse
$$ • 2660 Canyon Blvd., Boulder
• (303) 440-8877

The restaurant at the Boulder Marriott in central Boulder has made steak the centerpiece of its menu. The roasted prime rib of beef is a 10- or 16-ounce cut and can be served with a Madeira-laced herb butter sauce. Or try the grilled chicken breast with roasted potatoes and papaya relish. An appetizer could be a meal by itself with escargot, grilled shrimp in garlic butter or crispy onion straws on the menu. Dessert can be accompanied with one of several espresso drinks and a full bar and extensive wine list are available. Breakfast, lunch and dinner are served daily.

Karen's Country Kitchen
$$ • 700 Main St., Louisville
• (303) 666-8020

A historic building with tin walls, cozy rooms and decorative gift items sets the tone for Karen's homestyle cooking. Karen's has won too many baking awards to list here so if you go try the breads, cakes, cookies, pastries and rolls, all of which are baked fresh daily on the premises. And don't leave without a slice of pie, voted "Best" by *Daily Camera* readers in 1998. If you're still hungry, breakfast can include thick-sliced bacon, charbroiled local sausage, hash browns, pancakes and Belgian waffles with fresh fruit. Patrons love the liver and onions so much it has stayed on the menu for 20 years. "Scramlets" are all the ingredients you want folded into eggs.

Karen's is open for breakfast, lunch and dinner weekdays and Saturday and for brunch on Sunday.

Karen's in the Country
$$$ • 1900 Plaza Dr., Louisville
• (303) 666-8503

The country is more elegant than the kitchen, for Karen's second restaurant is in a three-story Victorian house. It offers many of the same baked goods as Karen's Country Kitchen but adds more continental inspirations, including pasta and chicken dishes. With a seat on the enclosed deck, you've got a view of the beautifully landscaped yard with a soothing waterfall and fountain. It's open for breakfast, lunch and dinner weekdays and Saturday and for brunch on Sunday.

Lick Skillet Bakery
$ • 5340 Arapahoe Ave., Boulder
• (303) 449-7775

A big old range is center stage here where you can eat-in or carry-out. The fare demonstrates how innovative chefs can elevate basic ingredients. A descendant of a popular spot in Gold Hill that has since closed, this rendition of the Lick Skillet is an informal cafe. The fresh-baked goods are an excellent way to start the day, washed down with strong coffee or good tea. The muffins and omelets are delicious, as is the chocolate mousse cake — for later, of course. Lick Skillet is open for breakfast and lunch daily.

Limbo
$$ • 2719 Iris Ave., Boulder
• (303) 544-1464

This newcomer transformed your average deli into a bright and friendly eatery with great appeal to the younger crowd. The menu includes 35 different "little plates" — a concept imported from Europe to allow customers to sample the various cuisine including grilled eggplant, grilled asparagus and roasted red peppers. Lunch and dinner are served daily.

Murphy's Bar and Grill
$ • 28th St. and Iris Ave., Willow Springs Shopping Center, Boulder
• (303) 449-4473

Even if it's not your neighborhood, this is has been a favorite neighborhood restaurant for 14 years. A varied menu includes Mexican dishes, fresh salads, pasta and burgers, and appetizers include nachos and hot chicken wings. The walls are covered with nearly every "Murphy's Law" you've ever heard. Murphy's has a full bar and wine list and is open daily for lunch and dinner.

Mustard's Last Stand
$, no credit cards • 1719 Broadway, Boulder • (303) 444-5841

Chicago-style hot dogs, German bratwurst, hamburgers and thick homestyle fries are served in this Boulder institution, and the place provides a funky view of Broadway. OK, they've bowed to popular demand and added veggie-dogs and tempeh burgers, but you don't have to eat them if you don't want to. The "best hot dogs" winner in all the local publications, Mustard's is open for lunch and dinner daily. You can also find a second Mustard's in Denver.

Oliver's Restaurant
$ • 800 28th St., in the Holiday Inn, Boulder • (303) 443-3322

This is a great place to test a wide selection of domestic and imported beers while you chow down on the popular buffalo burger and watch the Broncos. Or try the free appetizers while you play pool during the daily happy hour from 4 to 7 PM. For breakfast the menu offers blueberry pancakes or a breakfast burrito smothered in green chili. Breakfast, lunch and dinner are served daily.

Pioneer Inn
$ • 15 First St., Nederland • (303) 258-7733

Built during Nederland's historical mining days, this landmark offers hearty American fare. Funky and fun, the rustic inn is known for traditional, filling breakfasts, and Mexican-accented favorites, great charcoal-grilled burgers, homemade green chili and varieties of beer.

When you come to the Pioneer, you get to hang out at the big bar with gritty local mountaineers as well as skiers and hikers who stop in to be part of the fun. It's open daily for breakfast, lunch and dinner. The bar's open until 2 AM every night (see our Nightlife chapter for after-hours information).

Pressto Sandwiches
$ • 3960 Broadway, Boulder • (303) 444-0780

This sprightly eatery prepares Boulder's favorite sandwiches. The Pressto concept comes from Tom Kramis, who ate grilled sandwiches in Italy, took the idea to Boulder, reduced the grease by cooking on all nonstick grills and added more interesting and adventurous ingredients. Grilled sandwiches come in 12 varieties and can be mated with salads and desserts. The Sausalito has smoked turkey, sun-dried tomatoes, artichoke hearts, four kinds of cheese and pesto, grilled hot on traditional focaccia bread. Pressto is open weekdays from 10 AM to 7 PM and Saturday from 10 AM to 6 PM.

Red Robin Spirits Emporium
$ • 2580 Arapahoe Ave., Boulder • (303) 442-0320

Enter one of Boulder's major family and teen hangouts. It's a place with high energy, fueled by a variety of burgers, sandwiches and fries. Features include their trademark "smiling" chicken. There's a bar up front and a video game room off to the side. It's open for lunch and dinner daily.

Rev. Taylor's Country Restaurant
$$ • 121 Second Ave., Niwot • (303) 652-2020

Rev. Taylor's looks like a big country store that happens to serve food instead of ingredients to make your own. The restaurant is known for its big filling breakfasts and its good soups, salads and sandwiches for lunch. Dinner gets a little fancier — but not much. Steak, salmon, stew, meat loaf and a few vegetarian offerings comprise the dinner menu. Old-fashioned fountain treats make for traditional American desserts.

Rev. Taylor's booths are so comfortable you could stay put and chat for hours. The place packs with happy families during Sunday brunch. It's open for breakfast, lunch and dinner from 8 AM to 8 PM Monday through Saturday and until 3 PM on Sundays.

The Sink
$ • 1165 13th St., Boulder • (303) 444-7465

This college hangout has been gathering character since the 1930s. But without that college grunge, it just wouldn't be authentic. Self-described "Ugly Crust Pizzas" with various toppings, a huge selection of munchies, including nachos and pizza bread sticks, Sink-

Burgers, soups and salads fill the menu. There's live music, great beer, happy-hour and an unsurpassed youthful exuberance. After all, many of the patrons have recently reached legal drinking age. Organized graffiti comprises the decor. Robert Redford was once the janitor here before he scuttled art at CU-Boulder and went on to make a few major motion pictures. The Sink is open for lunch and dinner daily.

Tom's Tavern
$ • 1047 Pearl St., Boulder
• (303) 442-3893

A perennial "best burger" winner in the *Daily Camera's* Best of Boulder, Tom's has a reputation for the juiciest burger in town. Still, this friendly neighborhood tavern has been around since 1959. Tom Eldridge, a somewhat eccentric City Council member who started the Tavern, says he opened it as a young dreamer of 21 and never got out of it. Tom's is so well-known, some people give directions by using it as a landmark. In addition to its popular burgers, Tom's dishes up steaks, pork tenderloin, ribs and chicken. It's open for lunch and dinner daily.

Turley's
$$ • 2350 Arapahoe Ave., Boulder
• (303) 442-2800

This friendly and unpretentious restaurant is the keeper of the flame of a particular kind of Boulder eating place. Paul Turley has operated three restaurants in Boulder, all of which were immediate hits. Entrees include lots of vegetables, served with a choice of quinoa or brown rice, plus grilled tuna, chicken black bean burrito, scrambled tofu and other Boulderish offerings that eschew red meat or anything resembling gravy. Turley's offers comfort food too, including chicken pot pie and buffalo meat loaf served with knockout mashed potatoes. All entrees come with a choice of soup or salad and a roll or the muffin of the day. There's a good selection of

microbrews and wines as well as full bar service, and the restaurant does fine with smoothies and desserts as well. Turley's is open for breakfast, lunch and dinner daily.

White Buffalo Steakhouse
$$ • 601 S. Main St., Longmont
• (303) 651-0980

Voted "Best of the Best in Longmont" for "Best Steaks," "Best Bartender" and "Best Waitress," many diners agree with the restaurant's claim to have the best beef and buffalo steaks this side of Montana. Prime rib is served nightly, with other selections that include ostrich, buffalo, elk and seafood. The restaurant has a casual western dining atmosphere, and when the weather's nice, you take advantage of northern Colorado's largest patio with beautiful trees, grass and flowers. Live music on the weekends can feature blues, jazz, country swing or light rock. Lunch and dinner are served daily.

Contemporary Cuisine

Alice's Restaurant
$$$ • 3371 Gold Lake Rd., Ward
• (303) 459-3544

This is a romantic, honeymoon kind of place about 35 minutes up the mountain and over a country road. The 100-year-old lodge is charming and rustic, yet it is big enough to hold a private party for 350 people for special occasions such as wedding receptions. Generally, it's a more intimate crowd, with about half the people staying at the Gold Lake Mountain Resort and the other half coming up from Boulder.

The cuisine is innovative American with Pacific Rim overtones, such as Thai crab cakes with lemongrass. Fare includes gourmet vegetarian, seafood, wild game and juicy steaks. The wines are reasonably priced, and the meal is well worth the trip. You have a cocktail before dinner at Karel's Bar or retire there for an after-dinner drink, but the best treat is to retire to your own quaint cabin for the night instead of driving back to town.

Alice's is open for lunch and dinner daily during summer hours, with somewhat shortened winter hours. Reservations are highly recommended.

Dandelion
$$ • 1011 Walnut St., Boulder
• (303) 443-6700

This rather expensive, very stylish restaurant has ratcheted Boulder up another notch on the culinary scale. In a light and airy high-ceilinged room, it draws its stylistic influence from Manhattan's best and most sparkling SoHo restaurants but with a definite Rocky Mountain pedigree. Nationally known chef Kevin Taylor prepares the award-winning cuisine that can be summarized in such clichés as creative and innovative, with fresh ingredients and fine preparation. But the clichés have real meaning in this restaurant, where ordinary ingredients are extraordinarily fresh and given a little twist to elevate the finished product.

Favorites here include shrimp and blue crab cakes with mango orange chutney and a spicy mango sauce, sesame-seared tuna with stir-fried cabbages, wasabi, tobiko and ginger cream, and chipotle-glazed pork chops with roasted corn mashed potatoes and caramelized apples. Beautiful presentation is a hallmark of this excellent restaurant. The wine list is excellent, and the desserts will make you rethink the concept of "sinful." Reservations are recommended for busy times. Dandelion serves lunch and dinner daily.

Dolan's Midtown Restaurant
$–$$ • 2319 Arapahoe Ave., Boulder
• (303) 444-8758

Boulder business people voted Dolan's the best lunch restaurant, with the prime rib special featuring mashed potatoes a sure bet for closing the deal. There's a cozy wood-paneled bar, perfect for watching sporting events in the afternoon and yet elegant enough for appetizers or dinner in the evening. There's also a separate dining room, both serving seafood and steaks, soup and salads. The ahi tuna quesadilla with sliced blackened rare tuna, cilantro, Monterey Jack cheese and pickled ginger is a huge hit. Live Maine lobster is the special every Wednesday and Sunday. Lunch and dinner are served Monday through Friday with dinner only on Saturday and Sunday.

14th St. Bar and Grill
$$ • 1400 Pearl St., Boulder
• (303) 444-5854

See and be seen in this bustling, sunny restaurant with gourmet pizza baked in a wood-burning oven, along with fine salads and rotisserie chicken. Salmon might have a cantaloupe salsa during the summer. The turkey sandwich is like a Thanksgiving meal. The vanilla-bean cheesecake is only one example of the knockout desserts. Overall, everything is consistently good, fresh and innovatively prepared. The patio seating lets you be part of the mall scene. It's open for lunch and dinner daily except Sunday, when it's dinner only.

Jax Fish House
$$ • 928 Pearl St., Boulder
• (303) 444-1811

The winner of several awards, Jax is the place people want to be when they're hungry for fresh seafood. Or is it the martinis? Local newspaper readers say Jax makes the "best" martini in town. Owner/executive chef David Query's restaurant resides on trendy Pearl Street, just west of the Pearl Street Mall. The raw oysters and clams are exceptional. You can doodle on your crisp butcher-paper "tablecloth" while you wait for your spicy gumbo, clam chowder, soft-shelled crab linguine, steamed mussels and vegetarian specials. Save room for the Key lime pie. Jax is open daily for appetizers and dinner only.

Q's Restaurant
$$-$$$ • In the Hotel Boulderado,
2115 13th St., Boulder • (303) 442-4880

From Fred's to the Fleur de Lis to Winston's, one of Boulder's nicest places to dine in downtown Boulder has undergone some diverse changes in the past twenty years. Hotel owner Frank Day ascribes to the belief that a restaurant becomes stale after a few years and has the deep pockets to make a dramatic change that rarely fails to please customers. The *Zagat Survey* rated Q's one of the "top 10 in Colorado for both food and service." Chef John Platt offers changing monthly menus that might include grilled asparagus with arugula, lobster stuffed gold potato, roasted pheasant breast, or chile-crusted Colorado trout, adobe grilled pork loin with peach salsa, or jack cheddar grits and roast zucchini, all presented like a 3-D food sculpture. Organically grown green salads accompany all dinners. A fabulous dessert menu and wine list are standard procedure at the hotel. Breakfast, lunch and dinner are served daily.

Trios Grille and Wine Bar
$$ • 1155 Canyon Blvd., Boulder
• (303) 442-8400

This restaurant is oh-so-sleek and oh-so-delicious. Stylish and contemporary, it enchants both in the way it looks and what it serves. Lunch offers a selection of soups such as yellow lentil and ham, fresh salads and TRIOS Caesar salad, gourmet pizza and pasta. Dinner entrées includes beef tenderloin, salmon with chanterelle mushrooms, and roast pork loin. A jazz trio or blues band might perform, and the sommelier certainly will have some excellent selections from the wine bar to offer, considering the restaurant serves some 170 wines.

Trios has its own private parking lot, a special bonus for a large and lively downtown restaurant. It's open for lunch and dinner Monday through Saturday. Bar hours are later. Trios serves Sunday brunch as well.

Zolo Grill
$ • 2525 Arapahoe Ave., Boulder
• (303) 449-0444

The *Denver Post* in 1999 named Zolo's the "Best Southwestern Restaurant" and raved over the duck tacos and chicken enchiladas. Since opening five years ago, Zolo's has become known for not only its food but its decor, which is eclectic electric, from the copper wires crossing the ceiling to the huge abstract murals on the walls, all with a hip Santa Fe underpinning. The food is spicy and visually exciting, with lots of zigzag saucy accents, sort of like Zorro marks . . . really, we mean Zolo marks. Start with a Zolorita, the bartender's special Margarita version, and finish with a dessert from a list that includes incredible grilled banana cream pie. Zolo is open for lunch and dinner Monday through Saturday and brunch and dinner on Sunday.

Asian

Bangkok Cuisine
$$ • 2017 13th St., Boulder
• (303) 440-4830

This pleasant restaurant off the Pearl Street Mall features fresh food of Thai and Vietnamese origins. Vietnamese spring rolls, vegetarian curries, spicy Dungeness crab, chicken sautéed with lemongrass and an excellent noodle dish called pad Thai are among the best dishes. There's also an interesting Southeast Asian version of stuffed grape leaves. Prices are moderate. There is full bar service, including a new back bar where smoking is permitted — which is newsworthy in Boulder. Bangkok Cuisine is open for lunch Monday, and Wednesday through Friday, and for dinner daily.

Boulder Dushanbe Tea House
$$ • 1770 13th St., Boulder
• (303) 442-4993

If you can take your eyes off the décor you can find a variety of distinctive entrees as well as unique bakery and dessert items here.

Mapo tofu (a spicy Chinese dish), eggplant, wild mushroom pasta, Thai curry noodles, salads and soups are just a few of the items. And don't forget the huge varieties of tea.

The Tea House was a gift from Boulder's sister city of Dushanbe in 1986, but money to erect the elaborate structure was not approved until 1997. The Tea House was an instant hit in part because it's on the Boulder Creek Path, next door to the Museum of Contemporary Art, across from Central Park and adjacent to the Farmer's Market. Artisans from Tajikistan spent most of 1997 living in Boulder to complete the intricate assembly. The Tea House even won an award from readers of Boulder's *Daily Camera* in 1998 as "Best Evidence That Boulder is Different." The creekside patio is a great place to people watch. The Tea House is open daily for breakfast, lunch and dinner.

Chez Thuy
$$ • 2655 28th St., Boulder
• (303) 442-1700

This pretty restaurant, with deep green, brocade booths and a big, carved dragon-and-peacock motif mural, dishes up elegant Vietnamese food so well it regularly makes one of the best lists. Specialties include quail stuffed with seafood served with vegetables and noodles, pork sautéed in a clay hot pot, curried chicken and vegetarian specials, all cooked by owner/chef Thuy Twee. The portions are generous, and you can dine in or take out. It's open for daily for lunch and dinner.

Chinese Dumpling House
$ • WaterStreet Center, Canyon Blvd. and Folsom St., Boulder
• (303) 413-1089

This new, whistle-clean establishment has a limited menu and fast service. Order at the counter, and your food will be brought to your table. The family-owned casual eating spot serves just four varieties of steamed Chinese dumplings, including beef, pork, chicken and vegetarian, plus soups, noodles and salads. There are a few tables inside and a couple more outdoors. Dumpling House is open daily, except Sunday, for lunch and dinner.

Golden Lotus
$ • 1964 28th St., Boulder
• (303) 442-6868

A casually elegant restaurant featuring authentic Chinese cooking including Szechwan, Cantonese and Mandarin cuisines, the Golden Lotus uses the freshest quality ingredients and no MSG. Enjoy the dim sum daily at lunch and Chinese "small bites" on the weekends. This is a large restaurant with plenty of parking just outside the door. It's open daily for lunch and dinner.

Lee Yuan Chinese Cuisine
$ • 4800 Baseline Rd., Boulder
• (303) 494-4210

Boulder has a tremendous selection of good, small, family-owned restaurants. Lee Yuan's is one of them. Two decades ago, this was Lee Yuan's Burger Hut, serving both burgers and carry-out Chinese food. Now the restaurant, in the Meadows shopping center, is a morning-glory-decorated, sit-down establishment that is popular for its less-than-$5 lunch specials as well as its dinner selections. It's very friendly for families. Wine and beer are available. It's open for lunch weekdays and for dinner daily.

Orchid Pavilion Chinese Restaurant & Lounge
$$ • 1050 Walnut St., Boulder
• (303) 449-4353

Voted Best Chinese restaurant in the *Daily Camera*'s reader's poll 10 years in a row, the Orchid Pavilion is staffed by New York-style Chinatown chefs, who cook sesame chicken in huge chunks, crispy whole fish, champagne beef and eggplant in garlic sauce. There is also gourmet seafood and Szechwan vegetables. MSG is never used. You don't even need to ask. The soothing, peach-colored interior includes a huge, genuine Chinese silk-screen and fine reproductions of Tang Dynasty horses. Children are welcome. The restaurant's early-bird specials take the most popular menu items and add a choice of soups, chicken wings, egg roll and fried wonton as well as a choice of steamed or fried rice for one price. Orchid Pavilion is open for lunch and dinner daily.

PanAsia Fusion
$ • 1175 Walnut St., Boulder
• (303) 447-0101

This section of Walnut Street has been

INSIDERS' TIP

If you've been out of New York too long and need a bagel fix you'll find the best bagels at Moe's. *Daily Camera* readers and *Denver Post* critics all agree the homegrown/corporate bagel biz with three Boulder outlets seems to have mastered the bagel for taste and consistency. Not too sweet, not to salty, not too chewy, and there are several Moe's locations in Denver too.

transformed in recent years to include a brewery, an upscale pool hall, a Mexican restaurant and now Asian fare. Here's where East meets West featuring Pacific Rim cuisine with authentic recipes. Favorites include the Korean-style baby back ribs, garlic and soya beef tenderloin, and a salad with spicy tempura prawns and a warm spinach salad with lime vinaigrette and scallion goat cheese. A bonus is the brewed premium loose-leaf teas served in cast-iron pots. Open for lunch and dinner Monday through Friday and for dinner only on the weekend.

Sawaddee
$ • 1401 Pearl St., Boulder
• (303) 447-3321

Voted Best Thai restaurant by *Daily Camera* readers in 1998, the service on this Pearl Street Mall eatery is always appreciated. Garlic pepper shrimp and Thai iced tea, made with spices and sweetened milk, will tempt you. Lemongrass and curried vegetables add to many dishes, characterized by the light flavor of Thai food. It's mildly spicy, and you can ask for hotter or not spicy at all. The chefs will add more vegetables when requested, which is one reason the spot earns high points from Boulder's many health enthusiasts. Sawaddee is open for dinner daily except Monday and for lunch daily except Sunday and Monday.

Siamese Plate & Sumida's Sushi Bar
$$ • 1575 Folsom St., Boulder
• (303) 447-9718

The Siamese Plate gives diners a choice of Western seating or benches with bright cushions. Try the spicy green curry with vegetables and coconut milk, the green-lipped mussels with spicy garlic sauce or the exceptional red curry with chicken, and get an appetizer from Sumida's Sushi Bar one level below. Sumida's also offers happy-hour sushi specials and two-for-one sake midday on weekdays, in the early evening and all evening on Sunday and Monday. If you sit down at Sumida's, you can also order from the Thai menu. Both the Plate and the Sushi Bar are open for lunch Monday through Saturday and for dinner daily.

Silver Palace
$$ • 3100 Arapahoe Rd., Boulder
• (303) 447-3828

The Silver Palace is a fine-dining Chinese restaurant, related to Silver Palaces in, of all places, Vermont and Florida. Boulder's is a lovely and tranquil spot that includes a secluded, romantic patio and service with fine china and silverware on crisp white tablecloths. Signature dishes include Hunan Popcorn, which is very light tempura-style fried calamari with jalapeño peppers and onion; Crispy Pork with Grand Marnier sauce; and Chicken Gwin Jin, pan-seared with a smoky teriyaki flavor. Silver Palace is open for lunch and dinner daily.

Sushi Tora
$$ • 2014 10th St., Boulder
• (303) 444-2280

This is Boulder's most authentic Japanese sushi restaurant, from the low cloth curtains you walk through to enter during good weather to the excellent raw fish, beautifully presented. This quiet restaurant offers the option of tempura, soups and appetizers. It's open weekdays for lunch and daily for dinner.

Sushi Zanmai
$$ • 1221 Spruce St., Boulder
• (303) 440-0733

There is nothing quiet or low-key about this brassy sushi bar and Japanese restaurant. The sushi is first-rate, the owner, chef Nao-San, is a shameless extrovert, and the restaurant is rarely without a line out the door. This most popular Japanese restaurant was voted by *Daily Camera* readers as the best place for karaoke singing in the metro area. One part of the bustling restaurant features the sushi bar and wood-top tables. At the bar, you can watch the flamboyant Japanese chefs prepare miniature boatloads of artistic sushi.

INSIDERS' TIP

Sample local microbrews at the Walnut Brewery and The Oasis — on site where they are made.

Another part of the restaurant features tatami rooms and Benihani-style grill steak tables where the chef performs cooking magic.

Sing-along karaoke nights starting at 10 PM on Saturdays make a noisy place noisier — and that much more fun. Lunch and happy-hour specials bring down the cost of good Japanese food and great Japanese-accented fun. This restaurant is open for lunch weekdays and dinner nightly.

Tra-Ling's Oriental Café
$$ • 1305 Broadway, Boulder • (303) 339-0400

Boulder newspaper readers who don't vote for Orchid Pavillion as best Chinese restaurant are instead voting for Tra-Ling's. The restaurant is nothing special but the food is. The sweet and sour pork is a favorite, as is the Kung Pao Chicken. The egg rolls are always excellent and you can never order enough wontons. It's convenient to the Pearl Street Mall, but with free and reliable delivery why not stay home? Tra-Ling's is open daily for lunch and dinner.

Barbecue

Daddy Bruce's Bar-B-Que and Catering
$, no credit cards • 2000 Arapahoe Ave., Boulder • (303) 449-8890

This place is usually packed with folks, so it's fun to carry-out after sniffing the maple-stoked stove, where ribs get slathered with sauce that's tangy — not sweet. Not exactly health food, but, oh, what a decadent treat. The beef sandwiches are popular with a side of potato salad. Eat a slab of pork ribs and you'll sweat for two hours . . . with a smile on your face. This place is run by Bruce Randolph Jr., an associate minister of Boulder's Second Baptist Church and son of the late and greatly missed Denver philanthropist "Daddy" Bruce Randolph. Daddy Bruce's is open for lunch ever day except Sunday.

KT's Barbecue Outback
$, no credit cards • 2675 13th St., Boulder • (303) 442-3717

Barbecue comes to North Boulder, specifically to one of the new shops on the "backside" of Community Plaza. KT's serves filling hickory-smoked pork and chicken and all the fixin's. It's open for lunch and dinner daily except Sunday.

KT's Barbecue
$, no credit cards • 7464 Arapahoe Rd., Boulder • (303) 786-7608

Hickory-smoked barbecue (fat trimmed) gets served with sweet to spicy sauces rated like ski runs — easy way down, more difficult and double diamond for experts only. This KT's is open for lunch and dinner Monday through Saturday.

Kaddy Shack
$$ • 1000 S. Boulder Rd., Louisville • (303) 661-9896

The Gabby Gourmet, a popular metro area restaurant critic, calls this one of Colorado's top barbecues. A Memphis family has operated Kaddy Shack for more than 15 years in a 100-year-old trio of railroad cars that includes a caboose. Owner Woody Woodard has signed portraits of stars including Elvis and Jay Leno — all people who have eaten his barbecue.

Kaddy Shack's is Southern, hickory-wood barbecue, with a sweet sauce on the baby back loin ribs, served with baked beans, potato salad . . . the works. It's open for lunch and dinner weekdays and dinner only on Saturday; closed Sundays.

Breakfast and Lunch

Dot's Diner
$, no credit cards • 2716 N. 28th St., Boulder • (303) 449-1323
1333 Broadway, Boulder • (303) 447-9184

Dot's was a fixture at 8th and Pearl for 20 years but a developer's offer in 1998 was just too good to refuse. The restaurant has moved to north Broadway with a second location on busy 28th Street. The ambiance doesn't match the old gas station, but the menu is still much the same. It has some of the best buttermilk biscuits in town, along with huevos rancheros and cinnamon rolls. Dot's is open for breakfast and lunch daily.

Marie's Cafe
$, no credit cards • 2660 Broadway, Boulder • (303) 447-0320

Marie's is open through lunch (a hearty Middle European one at that), but it is at breakfast that this cafe really shines. Pancakes, eggs and huge pastries abound. None of the regulars, who include medical professionals from the nearby Boulder Community Hospital and assorted medical groups and support services, seem shy about slathering on the butter or piling on the jam. Maybe they know where to get help if they need it! The atmosphere is luncheonette-basic, with bright lights for perusing the morning paper and suitably efficient service. Marie's is open daily for breakfast and lunch.

Rocky Mountain Joe's Cafe
$ • 1410 Pearl St., Boulder
• (303) 442-3969
$ • 3980 N. Broadway, Boulder
• (303) 444-8510

Breakfast, lunch and Boulder's first espresso bar are here in the Pearl Street upstairs cafe with high ceilings, exposed brick walls and, if you're at a window table, a bird's-eye view of the Pearl Street Mall. Home fries, breakfast burritos with chorizo, huevos and a half-dozen salads are on the menu, along with pancakes. Breakfast dishes are available at lunchtime, as are soups, sandwiches, daytime burritos and salads. There is also a children's menu. The restaurant was named to honor one of Boulder's first photographers, and historic photos line the walls. A second restaurant opened in the North Boulder Village in 1998. It's open for breakfast and lunch daily.

Central and Eastern European

Andrea's Fine Food and Spirits
$$ • 216 E. Main St., Lyons
• (303) 823-5000

Since 1977 German favorites have been offered by Bavarian native Andrea Liermann, one of the bubbliest, most beloved hostesses in the area. Even if you can't spell them, you know the sauerbraten, spatzle, rouladen and Matjesfilet are authentic. There are also steaks, seafood, pasta and vegetarian dishes. Homemade desserts include cinnamon rolls, apple strudel and walnut torte. On weekends accordion and bell musicians play, and dancers perform the "Lederhosen Slapptanz." Andrea's is open for breakfast, lunch and dinner daily except Wednesday.

Black Bear Inn
$$$ • 42 E. Main St., Lyons
• (303) 823-6812

Classic European cuisine with a French touch appears on the menu, which changes seasonally. Wiener schnitzel is especially popular. In the wintertime, patrons with a sweet tooth prefer the chocolate taco. In the summer, they go for homemade ice cream. Black Bear is closed on Monday and Tuesday. It is open Wednesday through Sunday for lunch and dinner.

Copperdale Inn
$$$ • 10 miles up Coal Creek Canyon from Colo. Hwy. 93, Boulder
• (303) 642-3180

Sauerbraten, beef Stroganoff, wiener schnitzel and venison medallions are all real central European dishes, cooked by chefs who love Austrian and German cooking. It's a cozy inn, with red booths and fringed lamps, antler motifs and a family feel. It's open for dinner Wednesday through Saturday and lunch and dinner Sunday.

The Little Russian Cafe
$$ • 1430 Pearl St., Boulder
• (303) 449-7696

Red walls, voluptuous paintings and a weekend mandolin player set the mood for 18 flavors of ice-cold vodka — or is it vice versa? This the place for such hard-to-find classics as hot borscht, beef Stroganoff, stuffed cabbage rolls, shish kebab, salmon steaks, potato cakes, lamb stew and chicken Kiev. This is no place to go for a light bite, but on a chilly winter's evening, when the snow is falling on the bricks and branches outside, you can't find a better match of food, weather and a romantic atmosphere that just makes you want to cuddle up. You can also come here to enjoy the live Russian folk music on weekends.

Little Russian is open for lunch every day but Monday and dinner nightly.

Old Prague Inn
$$$ • 7521 Ute Hwy. (Colo. Hwy. 66), Longmont • (303) 772-6374

Bohemian plates and hand-stenciled walls give this pre-1900 schoolhouse an elegant, homey ambiance. Entrees include roast duck or pork, Czech-style, served with dumplings and sweet-and-sour cabbage. Reservations are recommended. Old Prague is open for dinner daily except Tuesday.

Continental

European Cafe
$$-$$$ • 2460 Arapahoe Ave., Boulder • (303) 938-8250

Epicures and critics usually call this one of the top four restaurants in town — and the only stratospheric one that's in a strip shopping mall. What it lacks in exterior charm is compensated for inside, where the decor is delightful and the food is outstanding.

What's on the menu depends on what's fresh and in season. Appetizers might include smoked salmon roll with crab meat and angel-hair pasta. Imagine this — roasted tenderloin with shallots in a sweet soy sauce and lobster meat garnish, served with a honey-ginger vinaigrette. A popular dessert is the light, cool and refreshing crème brûlée. Beautiful plates and presentation are part of the event, down to the homemade mashed-potato wreaths that frame many entrees. The waiters dote on customers. Even if dinner at the European Cafe is beyond the normal budget, you can get a darned good, dinner-caliber lunch here for about $15; try the fish stew. European Cafe is open for lunch and daily.

The Fancy Moose
$$$ • 1345 28th St., at the Regal Harvest House, Boulder • (303) 545-6485

Enjoy your meal in the elegant dining room decorated in the spirit of a mountain lodge, or dine on the heated outdoor terrace by the waterfall. Rocky Mountain-inspired feasts using Angus beef, cold-water trout, wild game and freshly harvested vegetables. The Sunday brunch features rotisserie roasted Prime Rib, peel-and-eat shrimp and a lavish display of fresh fruit, vegetables, salads, pastries and delicious desserts. After dinner, relax by the pines near the open-pit fire and sip a cappuccino with something delightful from the Chocolate Shoppe. Breakfast, lunch and dinner are served Monday through Saturday, Sunday brunch.

Fawn Brook Inn
$$$$ • Colo. Hwy. 7 Bus., Allenspark • (303) 747-2556

This tiny mountain hamlet isn't where you'd expect fine continental dining, but it's been served here since 1978 by Chef Hermann Groicher and his wife, Mieke, who hail from Austria and Holland, respectively. Secret ingredients include the crisp mountain air and beautiful flower garden, but even if the surroundings weren't so inviting, the Fawn Brook's exquisite homemade fare, from beef vegetable soup through dessert, would be memorable. All that attention to homey mountain detail just makes it better. Venison served with wild berries and mushrooms, and roast duckling are favorite meals.

Hours vary by the season. During summer, it's open Tuesday through Sunday for dinner. During fall and winter, it's open weekends, depending on the weather. Reservations are recommended. Call ahead for directions. It's about 45 minutes from Boulder and a half-hour from Estes Park.

Flagstaff House
$$$$ • 1138 Flagstaff Rd., Boulder • (303) 442-4640

When the Emperor and Empress of Japan came to America in 1994, they dined at only one restaurant on their entire national itinerary: Boulder's Flagstaff House. Chef Mark

Monette offered their entourage pan-smoked salmon salad with caviar, tossed with local greens in wasabi vinaigrette along with lobster consommé with spring vegetables and black truffles. Entrees were Boulder trout from the Cline Trout Farm and rack of Colorado lamb with Provencale vegetables, goat cheese and Japanese eggplant chips. Desserts included Golden Egg Surprise, a cocoa sorbet wrapped with 24-karat gold leaf to make it look like a gold egg.

When legendary French chef Paul Bocuse set up a cooking event with great American chefs from both coasts, he chose the Flagstaff House. *Zagat* calls it one of Colorado's top 20 restaurants and it makes every "best" list that covers the Rocky Mountain dining scene. You get the idea?

The Flagstaff House, perched high on Flagstaff Mountain, has the most romantic, panoramic view of Boulder around. The Monette family has owned it for more than 25 years, and chef Mark Monette has trained in Paris at the Taillevent, the Trogois Brothers in Roanne and La Poularde in southern France, and also trained in Singapore, Tokyo, Thailand and Hong Kong. He has applied a rich blend of culinary knowledge, which has brought the restaurant increasing fame. More than 40 entrees grace the menu, which changes daily, but always includes a commendable selection of meat, seafood and game, and all other courses are comparable. The food is extraordinarily well prepared and artfully presented, and service is excellent too. The wine list is nationally renowned, and the sommeliers are knowledgeable and helpful. The tasting menu with paired wines is a fine way to tap into the best and freshest that have inspired the chef's creativity that very evening.

The Flagstaff is by and large an expense-account restaurant, where a full-course dinner for two will easily run into the three figures but is definitely worth a once-in-a-blue-moon, all-out grand dinner. Wise locals drive up at sunset or after the lights start twinkling in the valley below, order appetizers and wine or dessert and wine or coffee — not as grand as a full-course meal, but easier on the pocketbook. It's open daily for dinner. Reservations are highly recommended, although drop-ins often can be accommodated.

The Greenbriar Inn
$$$ • U.S. Hwy. 36, Boulder
• (303) 440-7979

Picture an English earl strolling home with his spaniel and stopping at The Greenbriar, and you're close to the ambiance of this country inn. It has stained glass, dark wood decor and the vote from one Denver newspaper as the most romantic restaurant in the area. Michael Comstedt, member of the Cordon Bleu Ribbon Escoffier Society, is the award-winning chef. This is lordly traditional fare, great for special occasions. Game is well prepared, but rack of lamb is the signature plate. Among the seafood entrees, the shrimp and scallops ambrosia is divine. Follow with white chocolate cheesecake, or make your own combination for a memorable meal.

The Greenbriar is in the country but only 6.5 miles north of Boulder and about 45 minutes from Estes Park. It's open for dinner Tuesday through Saturday and for Sunday brunch. Reservations are recommended.

John's Restaurant
$$ • 2328 Pearl St., Boulder
• (303) 444-5232

If the Flagstaff is number one, John's is always number two when Boulder voters choose best restaurant or best place for an extravagant dinner. It doesn't have a comparable view, but makes up for it in ambiance and charm. For more than 20 years, chef/owner John Bizarro has garnered Best Chef awards from *Daily Camera* readers. John's has been featured in novels, and national restaurant critics consistently give it top reviews. Take the *Zagat* national restaurant survey, which calls John's "a small, romantically rustic place that's like eating in the chef's living room, always creative, well-prepared New American fare, wonderful service and sophisticated ambiance." The *Daily Camera* calls it "a tranquil eye in the trendy hurricane of food fashions." To quote all the great reviews about John's would fill more than a chapter. John's, in short, is a Boulder institution.

This gem is just a stroll east of the Pearl Street Mall. It is a small house with herbs and flowers grown in back and flowers in front. The atmosphere is elegant but understated. We have never dined there without being delighted with each dish, both in service and superb cooking.

Classic French, Italian and Spanish influences are strong, and so is contemporary American cuisine, which is establishing a culinary tradition of its own. Basque-style seafood stew, with perfectly cooked clams, salmon and shrimp comes in a deliciously sea-flavored broth. If you're feeling more decadent, the creamier and meatier entrees are succulent. The filet mignon is fork-tender and rich, while the wild mushroom ravioli with rosemary porcini is a tender melding of pasta, several species of mushrooms and sun-dried tomatoes under a sprinkling of fresh Parmesan. And from sorbet through cheesecake and the dark chocolate desserts, the final tastes are melt-in-the-mouth good. The wine list is on a par with the cuisine, which is beautifully presented and gracefully served.

There's a magic about John's that can make your spirits glow. Newspaper readers always give John's the award for best restaurant for an intimate dinner. Thanks to the attentive staff, engagement rings have even popped up in desserts. That's what happened to Betsy, now wife of *Daily Camera* food editor John Lehndorff. The dessert was one of the chocolate ones, of course. But this place can elevate any encounter.

Walk-ins can often be seated promptly. John's is open for dinner daily.

Red Lion Inn
$$$ • 38470 Boulder Canyon Rd., Boulder • (303) 442-9368

This Old World inn is just 4 miles up Boulder Canyon. This rambling country inn is popular for family gatherings, business dinners, banquets and weddings. A specialty is wild game, such as venison or pheasant. Much of the menu has become popularized American cuisine, but there are such decided Austro-German influences as red cabbage and spaetzle noodles, a good accompaniment with entrees, followed by a tasty dessert tray. The restaurant offers early-bird specials. It's open for dinner daily.

Photo: Daily Camera/Nico Toutenhoofd

The Sink has been a college hangout since the 1930s.

Creole

Lucile's Creole Cafe
$ • 2124 14th St., Boulder
• (303) 442-4743

Sashay up the porch steps of a side-street Victorian house, open the door, and you're in Cajun country. It's just that easy. Faded calico napkins, tables in every nook and a casual, bustling atmosphere are perfect for the red beans and grits. Try eggs sardou or a lunch of crawfish etouffé. Rice pudding porridge with currants and raspberry sauce is comfort food, Lucile-style. It's open for breakfast and lunch daily.

Redfish New Orleans Brewhouse
$$ • 2027 13th St., Boulder
• (303) 440-5858

Voted the "Best New Restaurant" by *Daily Camera* readers when it opened in 1997, Redfish features Louisiana Creole-influenced cuisine with a menu that changes frequently. Appetizers include seafood gumbo, crawfish Caesar, fresh oysters on the half shell, spiced shrimp and oysters Rockefeller. If there's time for dinner, fresh seafood and house-aged steaks head the list. Desserts include chocolate love and Louisiana bread pudding with bourbon sauce. The on-site brewery turns out six beers, and there's a world-class wine list. This place is popular with the 20-somethings and usually crowded. Those who aren't there for the food are there to play billiards on "red" tables or listen to live jazz. Redfish is open for lunch weekdays and dinner nightly.

Rhumba
$$ • 950 Pearl St., Boulder
• (303) 442-7771

The Rhumba recently took over space where previously two restaurants were located: Abo's Pizza and the Bagel Bakery. Operated by Dave Query and Joe Schneider of Zolo and Jax fame, the eatery serves Caribean-influenced food and beverages. One popular entrée from the dinner menu features snapper roasted in banana leaves with roasted potatoes and a watermelon salsa. It's open for lunch and dinner Tuesday through Sunday and closed on Monday.

French

Bistro St. Tropez
$ • 7960 Niwot Rd., Niwot
• (303) 652-0747

Named after a fishing village in Provence, France, that became the playground of movie stars in the 1950s, Bistro St. Tropez serves a continental menu in an atmosphere where people can socialize with family and friends. The fare is described as contemporary French cuisine with a Mediterranean flair, with entrée selections that include seafood, chicken, beef, pasta, veal and a well-priced bistro wine list and full bar. Bistro St. Tropez is open for lunch weekdays and dinner nightly except Sunday.

Le Français
$ • 2570 Baseline Rd., Boulder
• (303) 499-7429

Real French chefs bake their authentic breads and pastries in stone ovens. The breezy, close-to-CU cafe offers an assortment of croissant sandwiches, French bread and onion soup, spinach salads and those wonderfully decadent French desserts. The ambiance is cafe-casual (after all, the pastry counter is right there), but lunches and especially dinners are restaurant-fine. You can order with beer or wine. Do you like Grand Marnier cake with butter-cream frosting? How about a thick, rich chocolate mousse shaped like a mouse? This restaurant is open for breakfast, lunch and dinner Monday through Saturday.

Indian

Delhi Darbar
$$ • 826 Pearl St., Boulder
• (303) 443-3929

This dimly-lit downstairs restaurant, a branch of a popular Denver establishment, serves aromatic and exquisite Indian specialties, including outstanding tandoori offerings from a special clay oven. Chicken, lamb and vegetarian items grace the huge menu. The inexpensive, all-you-can-eat lunch buffet is a winner with the bottomless-pit crowd. In summer, there is also a pleasant brick patio. Delhi Darbar is open daily for lunch and dinner.

Himalayas Restaurant

$ • 2010 14th St., Boulder
• (303) 442-3230

Authentic Indian, Nepalese and Tibetan cuisine includes tandoori breads and thali, a vegetarian sampler. You can order the chicken and lamb curries milder or hotter. Live Indian music on Sundays includes sitar. This restaurant is open for lunch and dinner daily except on Sunday, when it's dinner only. Reservations are recommended on weekends.

MijBani

$–$$ • 2005 18th St., Boulder
• (303) 442-7000

Voted best Indian restaurant by local newspaper readers in 1998, this small side-street restaurant has a loyal following. The focus here is on meatless meals from southern India, featuring legumes, vegetables and rice. You won't get regular chicken curry in this interesting restaurant, which offers both conventional and futon seating and live or recorded Indian music that simply adds to the ambiance.

The menu is divided into themes. You can order from a selection of thali combination plates, entrees that come paired with suitable side dishes. Exotic varieties of ice cream finish the meal in equal style. Beer and wine are served, but many diners opt for the excellent chai tea, just about Boulder's best. In addition to reasonably complete and á la carte dinners, MijBani also sets out an inexpensive all-you-can-eat buffet lunch. MijBani is open for lunch and dinner daily except Monday.

Narayan's Nepal Restaurant

$ • 1124 Pearl St., Boulder
• (303) 447-2816

Located downstairs on the Pearl Street Mall, Narayan's is back with the distinctive mountain fare that has captivated the many Boulderites who have trekked or climbed in Nepal. Vegetable-stuffed roti (flatbread) comes with lentil or garbanzo soup and is especially good, but the vegetable sampler remains the No. 1 request from the menu. Locals like the bargain prices. Narayan's is open for lunch and dinner daily.

Royal Peacock

$$ • 5290 Arapahoe Ave., Boulder
• (303) 447-1409

Each year, the owners, who are Bombay natives, add yet another peacock motif to their beautiful restaurant. The chai tea with spices and sweetened milk is delicious. Hot curried Indian dishes are served, along with vegetarian choices in rich cream sauces, good basmati rice (order lots for anyone who prefers mild food) and yogurt/cucumber salads. Service is impeccably polite. The staff love kids, although the leisurely pace of the meal can be a bit long for the youngest tykes. Royal Peacock is open for lunch weekdays and daily for dinner.

The Taj

$$ • 2360 Baseline Rd., Boulder
• (303) 494-5216

The sights, sounds, smells and tastes of Boulder's best new Indian restaurant are so genuinely Indian that you have trouble putting it in context with the Basemar shopping center's acres of asphalt just outside the windows. This large space is divided into a rambling procession of dining areas brought to intimate scale by the personal service and excellent food. Note that we said "personal," not "speedy" or "efficient," for The Taj is a place

INSIDERS' TIP

Waiters on Wheels delivers restaurant meals to your door for just $3.50 more than the total meal price (the delivery person also appreciates a tip). Forty restaurants subscribe to this service, ranging from sushi palaces to hot dog joints, including many Boulder favorites, such as Old Chicago, Café Gondolier, Delhi Darbar, Mustard's Last Stand, Nick-N-Willy's, and Mijbani. Meals arrive from 20 minutes to an hour after you call — it's quickest if you order when the restaurant isn't as busy. Call (303) 402-0556 to order or to have a menu delivered.

for dining and lingering. Everything is custom-prepared at dinner. The opulent, inexpensive lunch buffet provides a sampling if you hurry when you eat. There is a full bar. The Taj is open for lunch and dinner.

Italian

Antica Roma
$$ • 1308 Pearl St., Boulder
• (303) 442-0378

This is one of the Pearl Street Mall's most atmospheric restaurants, a stylish trattoria painted and decorated to look like a piazza in a residential quarter of Rome. There's even a fountain in the middle of the room. And with good food, a nice selection of matching wines and knockout atmosphere, it's no wonder Boulderites have flocked there for years.

The selections are a bit overwhelming with panzanella, pizza made fresh and cooked in a wood-burning oven, and of course authentic Italian entrees such as saltimbocca ala Romana. The homemade lasagna, ravioli and tortellini and the rotolo di pasta have received a best of Boulder award. Antica Roma has even made *Wine Spectator* for its award-winning wine list. If you sit on the patio in summer, you can watch the Pearl Street scene to your heart's desire. It is open for lunch and dinner daily.

Attusso's of Brooklyn Italian Cafe
$$ • 1739 Pearl St., Boulder
• (303) 442-2262

This little Italian place just east of the Pearl Street Mall serves traditional manicotti and other dishes whose recipes Italian immigrants brought to New York. "Tradition" is a key word here. This is the place to go for red-sauce Italian favorites, including the aforementioned

manicotti, lasagna and various pastas with assorted toppings. Scaloppini saltimbocca is derived from a phrase that means "to jump in the mouth," and Attuso's version is so good that description is apt. People can sit and relax inside or on the porch. It's open for dinner daily.

Bácaro
$$$ • 921 Pearl St., Boulder
• (303) 444-4888

Boulder's most recent addition to the Italian scene, Bacaro's has a simple décor and a more complicated northern Italian cuisine. A house antipasto specialty is carpaccio, thinly sliced raw meat drizzled with olive oil and lemon juice. Fresh homemade pastas include spinach and ricotta cheese ravioli, angel hair pasta with fresh tomato sauce and black and white tagliolini with mixed seafood in a lightly spiced tomato sauce. Entrée highlights include veal scalloppine topped with prosciutto and sage, served with creamy baked potatoes. The desserts are as extravagant as the pastas and the wine list is comprehensive. The service is also excellent for such a new entry. Open daily for lunch and dinner.

Blue Parrot
$ • 640 Main St., Louisville
• (303) 666-0677

Long before "ethnic" food became trendy, this family-run restaurant was providing locals with informal, inexpensive Italian food. The restaurant opened in 1919, when Louisville's coal mines brought many Italian families into the area. For decades, a special evening in Boulder often would end with a trip to the Blue Parrot for a homestyle Italian meal. Today, the noodles are still homemade, down to the gnocchi, made of mashed potatoes.

The atmosphere here has stayed unpre-

INSIDERS' TIP

For large parties or for special places, dinner reservations are recommended. Reservations matter more in the summer, especially during weekends or events such as CU-Boulder graduation in May. In winter, Valentine's Day and other special evenings book up fast. That doesn't mean you generally need reservations weeks in advance. Even at the finest places, a call just before you leave can mean a table waiting for you when you arrive.

tentious, so it's a good choice for casual family dining, especially for finicky young eaters who prefer bland to zesty. You can even buy Blue Parrot pasta sauce at grocery stores these days. Blue Parrot is open for breakfast, lunch and dinner daily.

Carelli's of Boulder
Ristorante Italiano
$$ • 645 30th St., Boulder
• (303) 938-9300

When this restaurant moved to its new location a few years ago, theater-goers lost a wonderful pre-movie dining spot to south Boulder. But it's worth the drive to sample menu items prepared with the finest imported and domestic ingredients, and all-natural chicken and beef. Carelli's has a cozy fireplace for winter dining or garden patio in the summer. Specialties include pesto di penne, shrimp scampi, chicken picatta and steak pizziola. The restaurant is open for lunch and dinner weekdays, dinner only on Saturday, and is closed Sunday.

15°
$$$-$$$$ • 1965 15th St., Boulder
• (303) 442-4222

Denver Post critics chose 15° as not only the best Italian restaurant for 1998, but also best new restaurant. Executive chef James Mazzio took over the kitchen in 1998. If that's not a familiar name it will be. Mazzio was named one of the 20 best chefs in the country for 1999 by *Food & Wine* magazine. That makes him only one of three Colorado chefs to have been honored with the award. Menus shift seasonally, but the intensely flavored food is year-round. Start with the apple-wood-smoked duck breast with spring greens tossed in a tangerine and rosemary vinaigrette with toasted hazelnuts. A nice entrée might be the basil-crusted salmon served with small beads of pasta with zucchini, yellow squash and peas in a basil nage. Or if it's just dessert and coffee you crave, you've come to the right place. Pastry Chef Vajra Stratigos creates some of cleverest sweets in the state. 15° serves dinner nightly.

D'Napoli Ristorante
$–$$ • 835 Walnut St., Boulder
• (303) 444-8434

Filling Italian fare, mostly of the traditional southern Italian variety, is served in this amiable, casual restaurant. Spaghetti, ziti and fettuccine, the most popular pasta shapes, dominate the menu and are available with an

This Starbucks Coffee shop is in a remodeled gas station on University Hill.

assortment of sauces. Perennial favorites including eggplant parmigiana, lasagna with or without meat and shrimp fra diavolo are also served. Some seafood, some poultry, some meat and pizza are options. D'Napoli is open for dinner 4 to 10 PM nightly except Monday.

Full Moon Grill
$$-$$$ • 2525 Arapahoe Ave., Boulder
• **(303) 938-8800**

If it's Italian food you love, you've come to the right town. Full Moon was listed in the 1998 *Zagat Survey* of America's Top Restaurants. Inspired Northern cuisine is prepared by Chef Brad Heap. Heap trained in top French and Italian restaurants and at the Culinary Institute of America before settling into Boulder, and his artistry shows. Specialties include steamed Prince Edward Island mussels and Maine crab cakes for appetizers. Main courses feature both classic and modern preparations of meat and seafood. Pasta and risotto specials are served and fresh fish is brought in daily for dishes such a pepper-corn-crusted ahi tuna. Great decorative touches are more than merely Italian and include wooden Balinese pigs that decorate the room as visual garnishes to Heap's creations. Full Moon is open for dinner daily and for lunch weekdays.

Laudisio Ristorante Italiano
$$$ • 2785 Iris Ave., Boulder
• **(303) 442-1300**

The *Denver Post* may prefer 15° this year, but Boulderites say Laudisio's is the best Italian restaurant in town. *Zagat* has called it the best Italian restaurant in Colorado and it won *Wine Spectator's* "Best of Award of Excellence" 1993-97. It's one of the most flamboyant dining spots. And why not? The whole Laudisio family is flamboyant, and their namesake restaurant is a metaphor for their passions. They focus on fresh, local ingredients, exquisitely prepared and generously served. The bustling open kitchen puts forth outstanding food as well as a real sense of family celebration. Dining rooms have recently been renovated and there's a stylish new piano lounge. The wine list is extensive, comprehensive and served with knowledge and grace. There's no grace but a lot of potency to the fiery Italian liqueurs called grappas, which seem to come from vi-

als of an ancient laboratory. Yes, the pasta is superb, and so is the risotto, the perfectly cooked seafood and the chicken. And of course, the desserts — tiramisu, champagne zablagioni and innovative glacés. Ask for patio seating under the grapevines or in the quiet dining room with antique Tiffany-style lamps. Laudisio is open for lunch weekdays and for dinner daily.

Modena
$$ • 2690 Baseline Rd., Boulder
• **(303) 554-5644**

This is named after a town in central Italy. Owners plan to open a chain of Modenas if the concept of family-style Italian food, that which is served on large platters for two or more people, is successful in this market. The Modena chef said the concept "is to get everybody at the table tasting everybody's food," for a more enjoyable restaurant experience. The restaurant is open for lunch and dinner daily except on Monday when it's closed.

Millsite Inn
$ • 44365 Peak to Peak Hwy., Ward
• **(303) 459-3308**

They make the dough for their calzones and pizzas fresh here, with a good sauce and anything in them. They have homemade pies and good desserts. Friends give high ratings to their chicken Marsala and other full dinners. The food tends toward Italian-American with a little Mexican, pizza and burgers thrown in. Add to that a comfortably rustic, log-cabin atmosphere. The locals hang out here, meaning residents of the nearby funky town called Ward, skiers and hikers. The guys in the bar have an amiable grubbiness to them and usually pay close attention to the TV broadcasting a game. It is open for lunch and dinner daily, with the bar open until 2 AM when someone's still thirsty.

Neapolitan's
$$ • 1 W. First St., Nederland
• **(303) 258-7313**

There's a variety of Italian food here just 20 minutes west of Boulder in a cozy family-style restaurant. The stuffed shells are delicious, as are the tasty pastas covered in cream or marinara sauces and combination plates.

Homemade garlic rolls are always a nice accompaniment. Neo's serves an outstanding white pizza in addition to red — both available with a variety of toppings. Reservations are taken and carry-out is available. Neapolitan's is open for dinner daily and for lunch and dinner Saturday and Sunday.

Pasta Jay's
$$ • 1001 Pearl St., Boulder
• (303) 444-5800

There was no joy in Boulder when Pour La France Café & Bistro decided the rent at this east Pearl Street location was too high and Pasta Jay's stepped-in to claim the space. But many were just glad it was a popular local eatery and not another chain moving in.

If the atmosphere was perfect for a French restaurant, it suits the Italian food just as well. The exposed brick walls, nooks and crannies for dining, the south facing windows and outdoor patio combine to create a pleasant and lively scene. The menu is constructed on a solid foundation of the most popular Italian dishes: manicotti, spaghetti and various tubular pastas with several flavorful sauces and pizza too. Fans love Pasta Jay's mixed salad, drenched in a flavorful dressing, and warm herb and garlic bread. A decent selection of robust domestic and imported wines is available. Pasta Jay's serves lunch and dinner daily.

Salvaggio's Italian Deli
$, no credit cards • 2609 Pearl St., Boulder • (303) 938-1981

Looking for the best sandwich in town? Boulder newspaper readers say you'll find it here. Whether it's the hot prime rib or pastrami, both are served on freshly baked rolls. Salvaggio's serves special Italian sausages and Boar's Head-brand meats — among the highest quality domestic cold cuts you can buy. Prime rib sandwiches are slow-roasted in the rotisserie oven and, when it comes to popularity, they blow everything else away, hands down. The Cajun roast beef and Mortadella ham are knockouts. Roasted red bell peppers and fresh mozzarella can be added too. The sandwich bread is homemade. It's even better for takeout than for eating in. They are open for lunch and dinner daily.

Mediterranean/African

Falafel Man
$, no credit cards • Crossroads Mall Food Court, Boulder
• (303) 442-2888

This casual eatery serves falafel sandwiches, along with lamb gyros and baklava, an almond-honey-filo dough dessert — all popular foods from the Mediterranean area. Falafels are spicy chick-pea balls, deep-fried, then served in pita pockets along with lots of lettuce and a zesty tahini sauce. Spanakopita is a yummy spinach and feta cheese pastry. It's among the more interesting food that you can grab for mall strolling. Falafel Man is open for lunch and dinner daily.

Mataam Fez Moroccan Restaurant
$$ • 2226 Pearl St., Boulder
• (303) 440-4167

This richly decorated, exotic restaurant is as much about entertainment as fine dining. While sitting on plump pillows under tented ceilings and listening to Moroccan drums, you will eat with your fingers, but you won't be eating what we think of as finger food.

Dine sumptuously on five-course meals such as couscous with vegetables, lamb with artichokes and delicious Moroccan tea and pastries. There is a selection of meat and vegetarian dishes.

But best of all, belly dancers entertain Thursday through Sunday. Belly dancing originated to encourage women through childbirth — hence the focus on strong abdominal movements, which perhaps is why we can say, "Belly dancing and children welcome." But, hey, this is Boulder, so it's not Las Vegas belly dancing for heaven's sake! This restaurant serves dinner daily.

The Mediterranean
$–$$ • 1002 Walnut St., Boulder
• (303) 444-5335

From the bright-red trim to the beautiful iron gate and the avant-garde wood-burning brick oven, this place is stylish and lively. The Mediterranean is another grand restaurant operated by the large Laudisio family. It has been voted best Mediterranean restaurant in the Denver area by *Westword* magazine and Best Appetizers by *Daily Camera* readers. It's what you want it to be: a romantic spot, a congenial gathering place with a good bar and summer patio but also a family spot — kids get kind treatment here.

Spanish tapas, which are small plates of interesting appetizers, include croquetas de gambase y pollo (shrimp and chicken) and lovely mini-pizzas. These are served at the bar or at the table. Light dishes include well-prepared calzones and perfectly dressed salads. Spaghettini di Mare is especially popular. The chefs know how to cook chicken and fish without leaving the heat on a moment too long. Spanish friends say the saffron-gold paella is pretty close to authentic. The Mediterranean is open for dinner daily and for lunch Monday through Saturday.

Ras Kassa's Ethiopian Restaurant
$ • 2111 30th St., Boulder
• (303) 447-2919

A Boulder favorite since 1988, Ras Kassa's recently moved into the city from Eldorado Springs. Meat and vegetarian dishes are served with a big slab of injera, a crepe-like Ethiopian sourdough bread, which you use to scoop up the rest of the food. Use the bread like a spoon to capture every drop of the hot, red sauces or the milder ginger and garlic sauces. Entrees include chicken or lamb, sweet potato stew and butternut squash. Eat in the Ethiopian-decorated interior, with authentic basket-woven tables, or enjoy the creekside patio. It's open for lunch Monday through Friday and dinner daily.

Shishkabob
$, no credit cards • Crossroads Mall Food Court, Boulder
• (303) 443-8844

Enjoy charbroiled kabobs or inexpensive vegetarian dishes such as tofu kabob, spinach delight and eggplant and mixed vegetables. Basmati rice (always fresh and fragrant), cucumber and yogurt salads, vegetarian spinach casseroles and lamb dishes are here. Also some of the best lemonade in town, with rose water adding a special bouquet to the sweet tangy drink. Shishkabob is open for lunch and dinner daily.

Mexican

Casa Alvarez
$ • 3161 Walnut St., Boulder
• (303) 546-0630

No sooner did Casa Alvarez open in a corner of the Walnut Garden shopping center than people started raving about its chili — and the honors started pouring in, including winning the Boulder Chile Olé Contest right out of the blocks. The red and green chili are each just about the best of their type around, but the restaurant has a way with other Mexican specialties too. When it's mild out, the patio is a pleasant place to enjoy your meal. Casa Alvarez makes good Margaritas and sells them two-for-one during happy hour, from 4 to 6 PM every evening. There are also beer and well drink specials. ("Well drink" is the expression for a cocktail made with house-brand spirits.) Takeout is available too. They are open for lunch and dinner daily.

Efrain's
$$ • 101 E. Cleveland St., Lafayette
• (303) 666-7544

Efrain's is in an old farmhouse, where the dining area is relaxed and homey. The great tamales, green chiles and sizzling tostadas make Efrain's one of Boulder County's favorite Mexican restaurants. There are also costillas, which are Mexican ribs in chile verde sauce. Efrain's is open for lunch and dinner daily.

Gustavo's
$ • 357 Main St., Longmont
• (303) 678-8814

Those in the know say that Gustavo Saenz is just a doll, and the fresh-cooked food's a bargain. Gustavo's has homemade guacamole and delicious enchiladas. You can get a tostada for less than $3. The green chile that smothers burritos and tamales is mild and freshly made. Gustavo's is open for lunch and dinner Tuesday through Saturday.

Juanita's Mexican Food
$ • 1043 Pearl St., Boulder
• (303) 449-5273

Juanita's, one of Boulder's favorite Mexican restaurants, is tucked between Tom's and Stage House Books. This place is noisy and usually packed so don't expect a quiet, intimate setting. The front half is slightly more formal, but if you're not distracted by loud music, pool playing or a TV screen in every corner, kids love to sit in the back half of the restaurant where wooden booths make it easier to color the children's menu. Enjoy the traditional Mexican food, which is always hot, fast service, icy, cold Margaritas and a huge selection of beer. Lunch and dinner are served daily.

La Estrellita
$$ • 1718 Broadway, Boulder
• (303) 939-8822

National Hispanic Magazine chose La Estrellita as one of the top 50 Hispanic restaurants in the United States. This "little star" occupies a large, airy space with indoor dining and the loveliest creekside patio around. The beer and Margaritas are very good. La Estrellita's best seller is a combination plate with smothered burrito, relleno and enchilada. Daily specials such as Indian tacos, and a surprise special each Friday keep the menu lively. La Estrellita warns, "Our food may be addictive." They are open daily for lunch and dinner.

Masa Grill Mexican Taqueria
$ • 1265 Alpine Ave., Boulder
• (303) 440-9511

Step up to the counter and order yourself the Burrito Grande, an aptly-named, humongous fresh-made burrito in various combinations, which can be tailored to your liking. Tostadas, fajitas and tacos are also on the menu, and there are daily specials as well. The Taqueria's distinctive cilantro rice is an interesting variation on a common theme. There are also decent fresh lime Margaritas, served at bargain prices during the daily happy hour, plus good beer and soft drinks. This good-sized restaurant is inexpensive and family-friendly, combining the best elements of fast preparation and service with fine, filling food. Olé! It's open for lunch and dinner daily.

Rio Grande Mexican Restaurant
$ • 1101 Walnut St., Boulder
• (303) 444-3690

The old Piccolo's has undergone a huge renovation to become the new Rio Grande, a popular Margarita dispensary and Mexican restaurant. Juanita's may win the best Mexican restaurant contest, but the Rio Grande always wins for the best margarita. Colorful Tex-Mex burritos, enchiladas and fajitas with loads of cheddar cheese, black beans and Spanish rice are featured. The restaurant also offers tortilla chips and pico de gallo, a spicy vegetable relish. The restaurant is open for lunch and dinner daily.

Tia Bennie
$$ • 450 Main St., Lyons
• (303) 823-5014

James Arroyo, a Lyons native, named this casual, family restaurant after his Aunt Bennie. It occupies a 125-year-old flagstone, ranch-style building on the west end of Lyons' main thoroughfare. The cook's combination — cheese enchilada, chile relleno, beans and rice — and the burritos supreme are especially popular. It's open daily for lunch and dinner in summer (closing at 6 PM Sunday), but closed on Sunday during the off-season.

Natural

Boulder Salad Company
$ • 2595 Canyon Blvd., Boulder
• (303) 447-8272

At last something *Denver Post* and *Daily Camera* readers agree on. Sort of. Boulder readers say the Salad Company has the best buffet while the *Post* says it has the best soups. Either way, it's a winner. All-you-can-eat salads, soups and pasta, potatoes, baked goods and fruits are strung along this very popular, very healthy grazing bar. You get in line and choose your items cafeteria-style. It's a super choice for groups who can't agree on what to eat. For all the good eating, you can be rewarded with a big, fresh chocolate chip cookie. They are open for lunch and dinner daily.

Healthy Habits Restaurant
$ • 4760 Baseline Rd., Boulder
• (303) 494-9177

Like the Boulder Salad Company, Healthy Habits is another wholesome restaurant where the grazing is easy. The salad bar is huge, and there are various pastas and soups too. Kids like a slice of pizza, and adults appreciate the cooked vegetables and potatoes at night. It's also great for people attending to their health, for the array of fresh vegetables and low-fat choices is grand. Keep in mind, the chocolate brownie at the dessert counter is still a chocolate brownie, and just because it's called Healthy Habits doesn't mean you can't manufacture an unhealthy meal for yourself by skipping the vegetables and loading up on the buttered bread, cookies and higher-fat items from the salad bar. The restaurant is open for lunch and dinner daily.

Rudi's Restaurant
$$ • 4720 Table Mesa Dr., Boulder • (303) 494-5858

This is a natural-food restaurant that looks and feels like a "normal" place, not like a granola-and-tofu dispensary. Still, the fine dining is based on a variety of influences from all over the world, but with natural and organic ingredients. Samosas, a type of Indian snack food made with mildly spiced vegetables, are a fine starter. Thai vegetable curry and crab-stuffed trout are typical entrees and are served with homemade soup or salad and brown or basmati rice. The tenderloin filet is organically grown. If you come for brunch, try the gingerbread pancakes with whipped cream. Homemade desserts include coffee toffee and Key lime pie. Vegans and people on special diets can get made-to-order food here. Rudi's is open for lunch and dinner daily except Monday and also for weekend brunch.

Pizza

Abo's
$ • 1911 Broadway, Boulder • (303) 443-9113

Abo's has been a Boulder institution for more than 20 years. Stop in for a slice or call ahead for a whole pie. Because of it's great two-for-one plus free drinks special this pizzeria has a huge following with the college crowd. Abo's is open daily for lunch and dinner.

Lefty's Pizzeria
$, no credit cards • 641 Main St., Louisville • (303) 666-6200

The favorite pizzas at this down-home local pizza parlor are the California veggie (artichokes, broccoli, sun-dried tomatoes, spinach, mozzarella, garlic and olive oil) and Craig's Cardiac Arrest (pepperoni, ham, sausage and bacon). But you can also get pineapple, jalapeños and black olives. Best of all, the pizzeria delivers in Niwot and the surrounding 80 square miles, ranging from Longmont to north Lafayette. A percentage of all proceeds goes to Niwot's youth team sports. This little pizza parlor is open for lunch and dinner daily.

Nick-N-Willy's Take-N-Bake Pizza
$ • 801 Pearl St., Boulder • (303) 444-9898
$ • 4800 Baseline Rd., Boulder • (303) 499-9898

Hands down, *Daily Camera* readers favor Nick-N-Willy's pizza to anything else around. Rich in fine cheeses and gourmet touches, Nick-N-Willy's is the pizza version of Alfalfa's. You can buy pizza by the slice and eat it in the store, or call ahead and, 20 minutes later, pick up a whole pizza to take home and bake in your oven. It all started when a friend of Keith McQuillen and Terry Jones opened a great pizza store in California. Keith and Terry found the take-and-bake pizza so delicious, they brought the idea to Boulder. Over the years, different pizzas and toppings have been added and interiors and have expanded into a dozen different Colorado locations. The Aegean vegetarian pizza is one of the most popular, with olive oil, feta, mozzarella, garlic, spinach, sun-dried tomatoes and oregano. There's a big cooler with soft drinks and pre-made salads if you need something to complement your pie. Nick-N-Willy's is open daily for lunch and dinner.

Pubs and Brew Pubs

Bullfrog's
$$ • 1709 Pearl St., Boulder • (303) 442-2542

The owners of The Hungry Toad took their

English pub concept and sort of cloned it on Pearl Street, east of the Mall. The food is similar, the atmosphere is sprightlier (there's even a little outdoor seating area) and the feeling more youthful. In addition to English pub fare, there's live entertainment on Wednesday evenings. The best part, for some downtown workers, is the lunches that sell for $5 or less. Bullfrog's is open for lunch (from 10 AM on weekends) and dinner daily.

The Hungry Toad
$$ • 2543 Broadway, Boulder • (303) 442-5012

This is Boulder's original English pub. Four English beers are on tap, and eight are available by the bottle. Fish and chips, shepherd's pie, salads and burgers are popular. The food's not arty, my lad, but it's hearty, accompanied by comfortable chatter and a pint at your elbow. They're open for lunch and dinner daily.

Mountain Sun Pub and Brewery
$, no credit cards • 1535 Pearl St., Boulder • (303) 546-0886

This bustling place is Boulder's New Age brew pub, with seven made-on-the-premises fresh brews that burst onto the microbrew scene by winning awards. The food is a winner too. Most of it is vegetarian, including meatless salads, chili, soup, garden burgers, burritos and pizzas, so you might call it a health-food brew pub. There are shelves of books patrons can peruse while listening to live folk music on Sundays. They're open for lunch and dinner daily.

Oasis Brewery
$$ • 1095 Canyon Blvd., Boulder • (303) 449-0363

Award-winning ales are brewed fresh on the premises and served from two full bars. Excellent munchies plus commendable ribs, seafood and pasta go with the beer. There are popular chef specials at night or for lunch the "Brew Plate" should fit the bill. There's patio seating, free parking and a pool parlor upstairs. Oasis is open for lunch and dinner through 2 AM daily every night except Sunday, when it closes at midnight.

Old Chicago
$ • 1102 Pearl St., Boulder • (303) 443-5031

It's hard to decide whether to describe this spot on the west end of the Pearl Street Mall as a pub that serves popular Chicago-style pizzas or a pizzeria with a whopping beer selection. More than 110 beers are available from the bar, and the deep-dish pizza is buttery crusted and delicious; whole-wheat crust is also available. The main part of the restaurant truly has a pub feel, while the seating in the back is more spacious. There's also a small patio in the rear. Old Chicago's stout mud pie has layers of coffee and chocolate ice cream, flavored with Australian Sheaf Stout beer. They're open for lunch and dinner through midnight on weekdays and 1 AM on weekends; unlike many brew pubs, the kitchen stays open till Old Chicago's closes.

Rockies Brewing Company
$ • 2880 Wilderness Pl., Boulder • (303) 444-8448

Eight different fresh ales are made on the premises, including the namesake brew, concocted for the Colorado Rockies baseball team. Three are gold-medal winners, pronounced the best beer in the country at the Great American Beer Festival. Sandwiches and salad go with the fresh beer, and if you arrive around 2 PM, you can tour the establishment, see the whole beer-making process and sample the current brews. This was formerly the Boulder Brewery, the first microbrewery in the city. Rockies is open for lunch and dinner daily except Sundays.

Walnut Brewery
$$ • 1123 Walnut St., Boulder • (303) 447-1345

This was Boulder's first true brew pub, and it's still the best. The brewing process is on display here, and you can watch while you drink and dine. The brewmaster concocts six original and seasonal ales, including Buffalo Gold, brewed in small batches to provide a malty, floral happiness . . . we mean, hoppiness. The Walnut Brewery pioneered the practice of donating leftovers from the brewing process to feed happy livestock and to enrich soil in flower beds on the downtown mall. Sometimes, walking the mall is a truly heady experience.

Salads, tenderloin, seafood, pastas and vegetarian entrees help draw the crowds to this distinctive, tall-ceilinged, lively space. Live music on Friday and Saturday can be anything from calypso and reggae to rhythm and blues (see the listing in our Nightlife chapter for details). They are open from lunch through 2 AM every night except Sunday, when it closes at midnight.

West End Tavern
$ • 926 Pearl St., Boulder
• (303) 444-3535

This is more a bar than a pub, for it is really basic and ungentrified — just the way fans like it. It serves good basic salads, soups and plenty of burgers along with 20 different beers and concoctions from the full bar. There's live music or comedy five nights a week and sometimes seven. The rooftop, with the view of the Flatirons, is the most popular summer spot at this friendly neighborhood tavern. Open for lunch and dinner daily, the West End closes at 2 AM.

Cafes/Coffeehouses

Great coffee is everywhere, and Boulder has become a great cafe town. Even food and gourmet stores serve eye-opening, high-caffeine espressos right next to the fresh vegetable juices. There's even an espresso bar in the Boulder Public Library. Boulder's coffee craze is most apparent in the abundance of its coffeehouses.

Most of these places sell only coffee. You can get a cup of coffee for around a dollar at most of these places, while something like a latte can range from $2.25 to around $3.10.

The Bookend Cafe
1115 Pearl St., Boulder • (303) 440-6699

This hip cafe is connected to the Boulder Bookstore. It's a see-and-be-seen place for the cellular-phone set, especially those who want a little lunch with their coffee. The scones, spelt muffins and coffee cake start the day off sweetly, and there's a good selection of mostly salads and light fare for lunch and supper on a daily basis.

The Brewing Market
2525 Arapahoe Ave., Boulder
• (303) 444-4858
1918 13th St., Boulder • (303) 443-2098
Crossroads Mall • (303) 443-2098

This shop has been around for 20 years but only in recent years has an in-house master roasted the beans. The atmosphere's simple, but it opens daily at 6 AM, and the crowds line up because they love the coffee as well as excellent chai — black tea, sweetened milk and spices. Don't be mislead by the Arapahoe address; The Arapahoe Brewing Market is actually a half-block off Arapahoe, next to McGuckin's on the southwest corner facing Folsom.

Buchanan's
1301 Pennsylvania Ave., Boulder
• (303) 440-0222

On the path between student apartments and C.U., this conveniently located shop serves all types of coffee specialties and various pastries from local bakeries. Students in a hurry can even have copies made in Buchanan's copy center downstairs while they wait for the milk to foam. Buchanan's is open daily and stays open late at night with outdoor seating, weather permitting.

Espresso Roma
1101 13th St., Boulder • (303) 442-5011

This is the Hill's version of Cheers — with caffeine. Students hang here for hours in between classes savoring the extensive espresso beverage offerings plus bagels, cake, cookies, biscotti and pastries. Espresso Roma is open daily.

The Foundry
1107 Walnut St., Boulder
• (303) 447-1803

Known for honey-vanilla latte, poppy-seed cookies, sandwiches and cakes, this coffeehouse occupies a small space at the front of Boulder's hippest billiards hall. It has limited seating but adequately serves its pool-playing customers plus the crowd exiting from several new restaurants on Walnut Street.

Javastop
301 Main St., Longmont
• (303) 772-1731

Longmont's answer to Boulder's burgeoning coffeehouse business, this elegant spot is located in the Old Imperial Hotel. They have a wide assortment of coffees and serve fresh pastries daily. They also serve lunch, including soup, sandwiches and salads but have early closing hours on the weekend.

Nederland's Acoustic Coffee
95 E. First St., Nederland
• (303) 258-3209

This quaint coffeehouse is located in a red brick house with a summer patio and decorated rocking chairs on the porch. Inside are tables printed with chess boards where customers can play chess, a sitting area with a tattered Victorian couch and an old wooden ironing board holding the milk and sugar. Used books and new magazines are for sale, and the artwork is both original and daring. In addition to coffee, you can buy herb tea, fresh scones and specials such as mango-apple pie and Italian potato-vegetable soup. Locals come here for poetry readings too.

Peaberry Coffee, Ltd.
2721 Arapahoe Ave., Boulder
• (303) 449-4111
2400 Baseline Rd., Boulder
• (303) 499-7337

Boulder's three locations are among the metro area's growing Peaberry's sites. The owners are from Boulder, but they started their stores in Denver, then expanded to Boulder when it became clear Boulderites love gourmet coffee too. Especially known for their own concoction, Polar Bears, they serve fresh baked goods, bagels, scones, desserts and more daily.

Penny Lane
18th and Pearl Sts., Boulder
• (303) 443-9516

Boulder's historic hippie and teen hang-out offers not just coffee and pastries, but local music and poetry. Also available is a full juice and smoothie bar, bagels and sandwiches and both indoor and outdoor seating.

Starbucks
3033 Arapahoe Ave., Boulder
• (303) 440-5090
1402 Broadway, Boulder
• (303) 442-9199

The Seattle purveyor that launched the craze has two Boulder locations. They are clean-cut stores, for Boulder that is, and serve a full range of coffees plus pastries and bagels. For the coffee lover in your life, Starbucks is sure to please with great gift items.

Trident Booksellers and Cafe
940 Pearl St., Boulder • (303) 443-3133

Regularly voted the best by *Daily Camera* readers, Trident invites endangered bohemians who love to converse over coffee. It's Boulder's answer to Greenwich Village, or as close as you can get here. There's a full range of coffees and pastries with lots of interesting conversation at the next table. Naturally the attached bookstore helps promote the sought-after intellectual feeling.

Vic's
2680 Broadway, Boulder
• (303) 440-8209
3305 30th St., Boulder • (303) 440-2918

Everybody who's anybody knows Vic doesn't exist. But north Boulder baby boomers who frequent Vic's all know the owner, Mike, and he never forgets a name. Vic's serves coffee and pastries with Ella Fitzgerald on the CD player. Local artists show their work here and a Friday open house is common. The new 30th Street store's decor is still more Art Deco/New Age/Retro than the original.

On warm evenings from spring through fall, one of the most popular activities that's unrivaled in entertainment value (not to mention free) is strolling on the Pearl Street Mall.

Nightlife

Boulder isn't particularly known for its wild nightlife — other than the occasional bear or mountain lion paying a nocturnal visit to a residential area — though there's plenty to do and plenty of places to go after dark. The college crowd has its hangouts, as do the single professionals and families. Most residents and visitors looking for a night out go to a restaurant, concert or movie or to one of the many spots listed below.

Because our state is so beautiful and the weather so fine, Boulderites and Coloradans thrive on the out-of-doors. Therefore, many cafes and concert halls are al fresco. On warm evenings from spring through fall, one of the most popular activities that's unrivaled in entertainment value (not to mention free) is strolling on the Pearl Street Mall. During summer weekends the pedestrian mall is transformed into a six-ring circus on every block with jugglers, musicians, magicians, bagpipers, Peruvian bands and the amazing "ZIP code person" (who tells strangers where they live after they tell him their ZIP code — even naming sections of cities and local restaurants). Some of the mall performers have gone on to fame and fortune. One balance and juggling act appeared on the *Tonight Show* with Johnny Carson. Though the mall entertainment is free, performers usually have a donation "hat" and appreciate financial support (they have to pay for permits to perform on the mall).

Another uniquely Boulder form of entertainment is *E-Town*, a locally produced weekly public radio show that focuses on the environment and is recorded live with audience participation at the historic Boulder Theater. It's our own homegrown, eco-version of Garrison Keillor's *A Prairie Home Companion. E-Town* is aired weekly by National Public Radio on various stations across the country and has featured such celebrities as James Taylor, Dan Fogelberg, Dave Barry, Emmylou Harris, Rickie

Lee Jones and The Persuasions. It's quite inexpensive and fun for the audience to play a part in a nationally broadcast radio show.

Those regularly in search of the really bright lights and big names will usually have to travel to the magnificent Red Rocks amphitheater near Golden, or to Denver's park-like Fiddler's Green amphitheater or its Paramount and Ogden theaters and other venues larger than what Boulder has to offer. For a complete Denver listing see *The Insiders' Guide® to Denver,* but some top Denver hot spots regularly frequented by Boulderites are listed subsequently among the Boulder nightspots.

Don't forget that the legal drinking age in Colorado is 21, and that drinking and driving don't mix. Don't jeopardize your life — and ours — by getting behind the wheel after you've been drinking. Make sure your group includes a designated driver.

15°
1965 15ᵗʰ St., Boulder • (303) 442-4222

Just off the east end of the Downtown Mall, 15° offers an ambiance as elegant, crisp and sophisticated as the neon-hued martinis that are the specialty of the bar (recently voted Boulder's "Best Martini" spot with more than 13 varieties on the menu). A limited menu of the excellent, and pricey, continental cuisine served in the restaurant is also available at the bar. The restaurant is open from 5:30 PM to about 11 PM Monday through Saturday and is closed Sunday. (The restaurant will be moving to an undetermined new location in 2000 when the building it is in is refurbished.)

Acoustic Coffee House
95 E. First Street, Nederland
• (303) 258-3209

Folks drive all the way from Denver up to the mountain town of Nederland — even on weeknights . . . in winter — to enjoy various performers at this pleasantly funky little coffeehouse. Performing here are such nationally known musicians as Chuck Pyle, Tim O'Brien, Peter Rowan, Cheryl Wheeler and Catie Curtis. Ticket prices for the bigger names range from $5 to $15, but local performers often play for tips. Microbrews and wine are served in the evenings. The Acoustic is open until 10:30 PM Friday Saturday when there is live music. There's a bluegrass jam Sundays at 3 PM, and other performances generally start around 8. It's also a great stop during the day for fancy coffees, baked goods and tasty sandwiches; open weekdays at 7 AM and weekends at 8 AM. Try a breakfast bagel or one of the delicious scones or brownies. For lunch there's grilled panini sandwiches (focaccia-bread combos grilled in a press). Though the food is a bit Boulder, the atmosphere is definitely Nederland.

Alleycatz
1207 Pearl St. • (303) 444-3100

This longtime Boulder meeting place for the college and 20-something crowd has spruced itself up, changed the menu and decor and switched from a happy-hour-type bar and eatery to casual dining offering the chef's interpretation of American cuisine with an extensive wine list. There's a piano bar from 7 to 10 PM Thursday, Friday and Saturday. Dinner is served until 10 PM and a late-night menu until 11 p.m. Friday and Saturday. Weather permitting, outdoor dining is available on the patio fronting the Downtown Mall. An enclosed garden room with a glass roof and lots of greenery is open year-round. The atmosphere is casual and comfortable but with a new and quieter ambiance. The varied menu includes Caesar salads, gourmet pizzas, fish and chips, Duck Asian and pasta with lobster, shrimp and

scallops and many other tasty-sounding offerings. It's also open daily from 11 AM for lunch.

Bentley's Nightclub
The Broker Inn, 555 30th St., Boulder • (303) 444-3330

Bentley's Nightclub at the Broker (see our Accommodations chapter) is a favorite spot for dancing and meeting interesting people. It attracts an older, more professional baby boomer crowd (versus college kids). Underpaid local professionals, such as writers and teachers, like to frequent the quiet and more sedate "Cabaret" bar to enjoy conversation and nightly drink specials. Dancing is popular Wednesday through Saturday, with salsa Thursdays and swing Saturdays. The bar menu is available every night until 11 PM and the bar closes an hour or two later.

www.insiders.com
See this and many other
Insiders' Guide® destinations
online — in their entirety.
Visit us today!

Boulder Theater
2032 14th St., Boulder • (303) 443-8696, (303) 786-7030 (Boulder Theater Box Office, noon to 6 PM weekdays; noon to 5 PM weekends)

An art deco gem (along with the county courthouse across the street, one of only two in Boulder), the former movie theater has evolved into a lively venue for everything from classical performances by the Colorado Music Festival to world music from Kitaro to former Jefferson Airplane guitarist Jorma Kaukonnen.

The theater is best known, though, as the home of the nationally broadcast radio program *E-Town*. "Live from the historic Boulder Theater in the foothills of the Rocky Mountains, it's *E-Town*," begins radio show that focuses on entertainment and environmental issues — a sometimes difficult twosome. *E-Town* celebrated its eighth year in 1999. The show

---

INSIDERS' TIP

Some of Boulder's best nightlife is along the Pearl Street Mall on warm evenings from spring through fall. String quartets, bagpipers, magicians and other street performers keep the crowd entertained for hours. And it's free (donations are suggested for the performers).

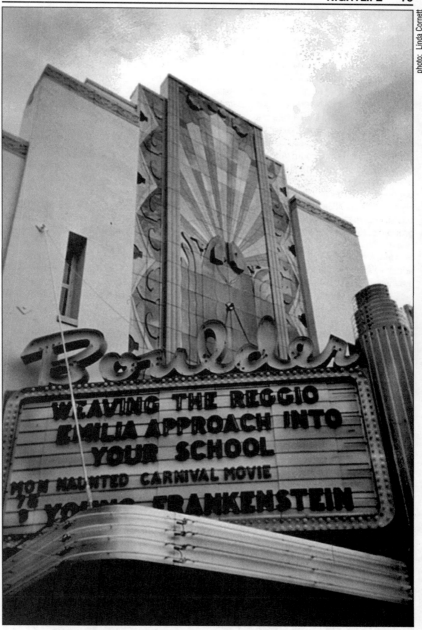

photo: Linda Cornett

The Boulder Theater began life as an Art Deco movie house. After some uncertainty about its fate, the lovely building is now a popular live performance hall and, a return to its roots, has begun showing movies again.

is taped live to be run by National Public Radio and commercial stations. The audience is part of the show, clapping and cheering on cue, sometimes for several takes. It's interesting to see how a radio show works.

E-Town records about 35 shows a year. It features musicians, environmentalists, politicians, authors and others, including James Taylor, Los Lobos, Dan Fogelberg, Sarah McLachlan, cowboy poet Baxter Black, Earth Day founder Denis Hayes, Dennis Weaver, Joan Baez, Bruce Cockburn, Arlo Guthrie, and Leftover Salmon. Run on a shoestring and volunteer efforts, *E-Town* is the brainchild of Boulder husband-and-wife co-producers Nick and Helen Forster. Nick was formerly principal bassist, guitarist and vocalist for the bluegrass group Hot Rize (which still plays reunion concerts).

Drinks and snacks are available, so the audience can sip their favorite beverage while they watch the show. Part of the theater has cafe tables and chairs.

Tickets are available at various locations around town. Ticket prices vary; call the box office for information. Come early for dinner on the Downtown Mall and grab a handy parking space before the crowd arrives.

The Catacombs
Hotel Boulderado, 2115 13th St., Boulder • (303) 443-0486

The appropriately named Catacombs was the first bar in Boulder to legally serve liquor in 1969. It has had several incarnations, including one as an inexpensive Italian restaurant and another as an expensive continental restaurant, but has now resumed its original identity as an easygoing local bar catering to a mixed-age crowd (average age 35). There's live music every night, with an open blues jam on Monday, a '70s an '80s dance mix provided by a DJ on Tuesday, jazz on Sunday and a blues bar the rest of the week. Live music continues from 9 PM to 1:15 AM with no cover charge. Happy hour is daily from 4:30

to 8 PM, and snacks and appetizers are served until midnight. Pool tables are scattered through the underground warren of stone-walled rooms. There is a $1 cover on Fridays and Saturdays, and a smoking section is available – a rarity in Boulder, which allows bars and restaurants to have smoking sections only if they are completely shielded from non-smoking patrons.

Comedy Works
1226 15th St., Denver • (303) 595-3637

"See tomorrow's stars today," is the slogan of this intimate downtown Denver club where Roseanne Barr got her start. Comedy Works regularly runs headliner shows. Tuesday is improv and new-talent night; Wednesday through Sunday are for established performers. Nonsmoking performances are Wednesdays and Fridays at 8 PM and Saturdays at 6:45 PM. Other Saturday shows are at 8:45 and 10:45 PM. Reservations are recommended (only ages 21 and older are admitted). Tickets range from $5 to $25 based on who is performing. Full cocktails and a limited food menu are available during the show.

Conor O'Neill's
(formerly The James Pub & Grille)
1422 13th St., Boulder
• (303) 449-1922

Since 1978, The James Pub & Grille was the closest thing to a real Irish pub in Boulder – red potatoes were a popular dish, live music filled the bar with the trill of traditional folk tunes. Now, the restaurant and bar is a step closer to Tiperary in its new incarnation as Conor O'Neill's Irish Pub and Grill, with an interior created in Ireland and brought to Boulder piece by piece for assembly. There will be two to three fireplaces, a wood burning stove, wooden beams and stonework. The menu will be more authentic, too, with Irish stew and shepherd's pie, teas and 20-ounce English pints of beers from England and Ireland. The James closed in May 1999 and was sched-

---

INSIDERS' TIP

Trios Restaurant offers an inexpensive wine tasting every weekday beginning at 4:30 PM. Learn about wine, and then choose one for dinner at a special discounted price.

Live music is plentiful in Boulder's nightlife scene.

photo: Linda Cornett

uled to re-open as Conor O'Neill's in fall of '99.

Corner Bar
Hotel Boulderado, 2115 13th St., Boulder • (303) 442-4344

An extensive wine list by the glass, specialty drinks and eight microbrewery draft beers (five made in Colorado) are available in this historic bar decorated in dark wood. Upstairs from the Catacombs (see previous entry), the Corner Bar has a casually elegant atmosphere. Food, including snacks from macho nachos to elegant rock shrimp and crab cakes, is served until midnight.

Fiddler's Green
6350 Greenwood Plaza Blvd., Englewood
• (303) 220-7000 (mid-May through mid-September)

About an hour's drive from Boulder, Fiddler's Green, southeast of Denver, offers all types of top nationally known groups, including rock, classical and oldies (the 1999 season included Aerosmith and Shania Twain). Enjoy these summer outdoor events either with reserved seats or a picnic on the lawn. All types of food and drinks are sold in the amphitheater — big picnic spreads from home are not allowed, but backpacks and blankets are. Some folks object that no beverages — including water — can be brought in. No exit is allowed once you enter the concert area; if you forget your I.D. for alcoholic beverages, you can't go out to your car and get it. Concert season is mid-May through mid-September. For tickets call the box office at (303) 770-2222 during the concert season or Ticketmaster, (303) 830-8497.

Flagstaff House
Flagstaff Rd. (west end of Baseline Rd., part way up the mountain), Boulder
• (303) 442-4640

Even those who can't afford dinner at the Flagstaff House — one of Boulder's most elegant and expensive restaurants, perched high on Flagstaff Mountain (see our Restaurants chapter) — can still enjoy the great view and wonderful, outdoor terraced bar for the price of a drink. Overhead heating units are installed for comfort on cool evenings. If you're lucky, you might catch a fantastic summer lightning show out on the plains. For a really romantic drink with someone special, choose this beautiful spot. Flagstaff is open Sunday through Friday from 6 to 10 PM, Saturday from 5 to 10:30 PM.

The Foundry
1109 Walnut St., Boulder
• (303) 447-1803

A full bar with wine, cognacs, beer and mixed drinks, cigars and lots of pool tables make this newer upscale bar a favorite. It's a great place to meet people and mingle in a comfortable, spacious, yet somehow intimate atmosphere. There's live music Fridays and Saturdays with a blues and jazz band starting around 9:30 or 10 PM and playing until closing at 2 AM. Drinks are served until 1:30 AM. An interesting group gathers at the Foundry — people of all types. Light meals such as nachos, sandwiches, pizza, bagels and muffins are served. The Foundry opens daily around noon.

Fox Theatre and Cafe
1135 13th St., Boulder • (303) 447-0095, (303) 443-3399 (box office)

Nominated for club of the year by *Performance Magazine* and several others, the Fox has become one of the top clubs for live music in North America, with acts like Disco Inferno, The David Grisman Quintet, Susan Tedeschi and Run-D.M.C. This cafe/concert hall on University Hill holds more than 600 people and has three full bars and nightly live music by local, national and international performers. People of all ages attend the shows (those over 21 get a bracelet to indicate they can order alcoholic drinks). The cafe is open daily from 9 AM until 2 AM serving casual, gourmet Southwestern fare. Call the box office for ticket prices.

The Grizzly Rose Saloon & Dance Emporium
5450 N. Valley Hwy. (I-25), Denver
• (303) 295-2353, (303) 295-1330 (for concert information)

Voted the nation's No. 1 country music dance hall by the Country Music Association, Grizzly Rose has a 5,000-square-foot dance floor and gets such top names as Merle Haggard and Wynonna. There are free introductory dance lessons Wednesday and Friday at 7 and Sunday at 6. One-dollar longneck beers are available from 7 to 8 PM Monday through Friday (except on concert nights), with various contests and specials other nights. Call (303) 42-DANCE for contest information. Concert tickets are available through Ticketmaster, (303) 830-8497, or at the door; advanced ticketing is necessary for national acts. The Griz-

Nederland's Pioneer Inn offers live music on Friday nights.

zly Rose is open from 11 AM (serving lunch) to 1:30 AM Monday through Friday, from 5 PM until 1:30 AM Saturday and from 3 PM until 1:30 AM Sunday.

Jax Fish House
928 Pearl St., Boulder • (303) 444-1811

Jax is known for its fresh seafood, but savvy Boulderites have latched onto it as a place for a quiet after-dinner drink and plate of raw oysters or shrimp. The full, fishy menu is served in the bar. Jax opens at 4 PM daily, closing at 9 PM Sunday, 10 PM Monday through Thursday and 11 PM Friday and Saturday.

Mercury Cafe
2199 California St., Denver
• (303) 294-9281, (303) 294-9258 (dinner reservations/information)

Dinner, dancing and drinks, you name it, the Mercury Cafe has it. The cafe serves a continental menu on Tuesdays through Sundays from 5:30 to 11 PM, including vegetarian specials, pasta, Mexican food, seafood, steaks and burgers. All the soups, breads and desserts are homemade. The bar is open until 1 AM and serves the Mercury's own microbrewed beers, including Vertigo Lager, Amnesia Blue Ribbon and Bitches Brew Black Bitter Stout. In a separate concert hall, there's nightly dancing. Tuesday nights bring the Lindy Hop, with free classes at 7 PM. Wednesday nights are open stage, with sign-up beginning about 8:30 PM. Swing nights are Thursdays and Sundays, with free swing classes at 6 Thursday and 5 PM Sunday. Open poetry night is every Friday at 10 PM, preceded by Argentine tango with a beginners' class at 7 and intermediate class at 8 PM, each $5. Dances are smoke-free and open to all ages.

Murphy's Bar and Grill
28th Street and the Diagonal Highway (Willow Springs Shopping Center), Boulder • (303) 449-4473

A casual, not-too-expensive restaurant with burgers, salads and nachos and a bar with 36 brands of beer make Murphy's a laid-back destination. Happy hour specials are offered every day. Hours are 11 AM to 2 AM Monday through Saturday, 11 AM to midnight Sundays.

Jose Muldoon's
1600 38th St., Boulder • (303) 449-4543

This popular Mexican restaurant also has a sports bar and claims to serve the "biggest margarita in town" in numerous versions (due, perhaps, to having Boulder's largest selection of tequila). There's an all-you-can-eat tostada bar in the restaurant during the day. The restaurant is open weekends until midnight, and weekdays until 11 (serving meals until 10 PM). Three homemade salsas spice things up, and the restaurant offers asbestos-tongued diners a selection of 250 bottled hot sauces.

Oasis Brewery
1095 Canyon Blvd., Boulder
• (303) 449-0363

Now brewing five of its own beers plus specialties, this large, attractive microbrewery bar and restaurant has Egyptian decor, complete with gently waving papyrus fans over the bar. The Oasis has daily happy hours from 3 to 6 PM and 10 PM until closing, offering discounted beer, wine and mixed drinks made from house liquors. There's free pool during early happy hour every day in the full game room that includes foosball, darts, pool and video games; free pool Monday runs from 3 PM to 2 AM. The restaurant serves all types of dishes and has a late-night menu. The Oasis is open until 2 AM Monday through Saturday and until midnight Sunday. Month-to-month specialty beers are served, such as Belgian Strong Ale and Doppelbock.

Ogden Theatre
935 E. Colfax Ave. (nine blocks east of the State Capitol), Denver
• (303) 830-2525 (box office and recording of upcoming shows)

Big names and performers appear at the Ogden, among them George Clinton, Los Lobos, Great White and The Proclaimers. Call for information on tickets and upcoming shows. Most shows at the Ogden are general admission with no reserved seating necessary. The Ogden box office opens one hour before shows. Ogden tickets are also available in Boulder at the Albums-on-The-Hill ticket counter, (303) 443-3399, 1128 13th Street, and by phone from Ticketweb at (800) 965-4827 or (303) 825-4TIX.

Old Chicago
11th and Pearl streets, Boulder
• **(303) 443-5031**

Known far and wide for its World Beer Tour and Hall of Foam, Old Chicago has more than 110 international and microbrewed beers, with 24 on draft. It's also known for its deep-dish, Chicago-style pizza, its pleasant patio (ask comedian Kevin Nealon, who has been spotted there) and "the big cookie," a delicious, deep-dish, fresh-baked chocolate-chip cookie served hot. Open daily until 1:30 AM, the restaurant serves food until 1 AM on Friday and Saturday and until midnight all other days.

Paramount Theatre
1631 Glenarm Pl., Denver
• **(303) 534-8336 (tickets/information)**

Built in the 1930s by Temple Hoyne Buell, a renowned Colorado architect, this beautiful art deco theater has one of only two Mighty Wurlitzer organs in the country (the other is in New York's Radio City Music Hall). The theater presents comedy, pop music, rock concerts, children's programming, ballet and noted speakers. The box office is open 10 AM to 9 PM the day of events only. Tickets may be purchased through Ticketmaster outlets or charged by phone at (303) 830-8497.

Pearl Street Pub & Cellar
1108 Pearl St., Boulder • (303) 939-9900

Formerly known as Flaps Up & Down, this cozy bar offers one of the few smoking areas in the city. The pub opens daily at noon (11 AM Saturday and Sunday during football season), and is open 'til 2 AM. Food is served until 1:30 AM and Happy Hour runs from noon to 7 PM daily. There are pool tables and eight TVs to keep customers up-to-date on sports and other events.

Penny Lane
1795 Pearl St., Boulder • (303) 443-9516

For 18 years, Isidore Million's coffee shop has been a gathering place for Boulder's avant garde crowd, a warm shelter for kids on the road, a casual venue for local talent and just a place to get a good cup of coffee and a snack. The daunting hours are 6:15 AM to 11 PM weekdays and midnight Friday and Saturday. The menu extends to a juice bar, ice cream, tea, coffee drinks, bagels and scones and other goodies — no alcohol. Tuesday and Thursday from 8 to 10:30 PM is open mike night for whoever has the chutzpah. Mondays, poets share their latest verses. Other nights of the week, Penny Lane offers an eclectic mix of performers, from jazz to folk to African drumming. When it's warm enough — and even when it isn't — the café's outdoor patio offers a view on the passing just-off-the-Mall scene. It's also a good place for a pick-up chess match.

Pioneer Inn
First Street, Nederland • (303) 258-7733

For some entertainment with great mountain atmosphere, stop at the rustic "P.I.," where you can dance to live music Friday nights. The Big Tick — bluegrass acoustic music — is scheduled every Wednesday night, and there's an open mike every Thursday night. The Pioneer also serves great burgers and Mexican food and has a pool table, foosball table and other games. The bar closes at 1:30 AM and the kitchen closes at 10 PM.

The Pub and Cellar
1108 Pearl St., Boulder • (303) 939-9900

The Cellar, right on the Downtown Mall next to Old Chicago, is the only place in Boulder where you can get a late-night snack, according to those who have tried elsewhere to no avail. The Cellar really serves food until 1:30 AM nightly. Tuesday is trivia night, and on Wednesdays there's piano music. Pool tables upstairs, and down, keep patrons busy. A dart room attracts pick-up games.

Red Rocks Amphitheater
Off I-70 W. (north of Denver), Morrison
• **(303) 640-7334,(303) 830-8497 (ticket information)**

This spectacular natural-rock amphitheater

INSIDERS' TIP

Some of Boulder's best nightlife is not in Boulder but in Denver and even the tiny mountain town of Nederland.

is the venue for many top performers (the 1999 summer line-up included Dave Matthews, John Mellencamp and Blues Traveler). Red Rocks information and tickets are available through Ticketmaster, (303) 830-8497. Or check local newspapers for more concert information appearing at Red Rocks.

'Round Midnight
1005 Pearl St., Boulder • (303) 442-2176

This dark, downstairs, nicely urban-feeling nightclub/bar features live music, dancing, pool and good local performers Thursday and Friday and DJ on Wednesday and Saturday from 5 PM to 2 AM. Another feature is more than 50 different varieties of single-malt Scotch. Only drinks (no food) are served, and there are happy-hour specials from 5 to 8 PM daily with $1.50 well drinks, $1.25 domestic beers and 50¢ off everything else. It's one of the few remaining places in Boulder to dance.

The Sink
1165 13th St. • (303) 444-SINK

For a venerable institution (it opened in 1949), The Sink on University Hill is a funky piece of work, with exposed pipes, concrete floors, walls splashed with bright cartoons referring to Boulder institutions and events, and ceilings and bathroom stalls covered with the graffiti greetings of several generations of CU students. In addition to a traditional hungry-student menu of burgers and pizza, The Sink offers beer and potent mixed drinks (limit 2) and historical significance — Robert Redford used to sweep floors there when he was a CU student. Food is served from 11 AM until 9:45 PM and the bar stays open until 2 AM. Beers are $1 on Thursday nights and every night there is a selection of 18 microbrews on tap to choose from.

Sundown Saloon
1136 Pearl St., Boulder • (303) 449-4987

A little off the beaten path in atmosphere but right on the Pearl Street Mall, the Sundown is for those who are sick of the typical Boulder scene. It's a bit more blue collar but has an unlikely mix of clientele. College students might find themselves having a beer with a hard-core Harley Davidson biker in black leather or a lawyer in pinstripes. Despite these "endearing qualities," the bartender assures us that the bar is safe and quiet. There are six pool tables and a big-screen TV, and the bar is open until 2 AM daily.

Tom's Tavern
1047 Pearl St., Boulder • (303) 443-3893

Ask longtime Boulderites where to find the best burger, and they'll usually say Tom's. This unpretentious corner tavern has been a favorite spot for more than 30 years. Besides great burgers, there are great beers on tap including Fat Tire, Raspberry Wheat, Sam Adams, Miller Genuine Draft, Watneys and Coors Light. A full menu is available daily until about 10:30 PM (Tom's closes at 11 PM, 9 PM on Sundays). There's a jukebox back by the kitchen and a television over the bar, but mostly the entertainment is conversation and people-watching.

Trios
1155 Canyon Blvd., Boulder • (303) 442-8400

An elegant, upscale bar, restaurant and home gallery, Trios could be equally at home in Seattle or New York. It attracts an older (than the college kids), more sophisticated professional crowd. There's live jazz on Fridays and Saturdays from 8:30 PM to midnight and other nights (except Monday) from 6 to 10 PM. Monday is blues night starting at 6 PM. Trios also makes good pizza and other light fare for the nightlife patrons. The late night menu is served from 9:30 PM until midnight Sunday through Thursday and 10 PM to 2 AM Friday and Saturday. The wine bar is open the same hours with 60 wines by the glass and more than 300 bottles to choose from.

Tulagi
1129 13th St., Boulder • (303) 938-8090

A recent refurbishing has turned Tulagi into a cozy pool hall and restored it's small stage and dance area into what the owners hope will be a revival of its 1970s popularity. Hours are 4 PM to 2 AM. The cover charge depends on the fame of the performers; some nights are free, when Big Head Todd and the Monsters perform it's $30.

Walnut Brewery
1123 Walnut St., Boulder
• (303) 447-1345

This very popular microbrewery is in a tastefully redecorated old warehouse and makes its own six fresh, delicious beers. Order a sampler and try them all. The complete dinner menu is served until 10:30 PM every night (see our Restaurants chapter for details). The Walnut Brewery is open until 2 AM Thursday through Saturday and until midnight on Sunday through Wednesday. Go early on weekends (before 6 PM) if you don't want to wait in a line that often stretches out the door and down the block. The Walnut Brewery also provides beer to go and catering services.

Walrus
11th and Walnut streets, Boulder
• (303) 443-9902

The Walrus has been around for many years, undergoing various changes of personality and clientele from a fancy restaurant to a neighborhood bar. Currently, the latter is its main identity, with pizza, burgers and appetizers as the favorite fare, along with a full bar, beer and wine. There are six pool tables, air hockey and foosball. Last call every night is 1:15 AM, and food is served until 11 PM on weekdays and 1 AM on weekends.

West End Tavern
926 Pearl St., Boulder • (303) 444-3535

A typical neighborhood tavern and burger restaurant, the West End has one delightful surprise — a rooftop area where diners and drinkers can watch the sun set behind the mountain backdrop or enjoy the coolness of a Colorado summer night under the stars. The West End is open daily from 11 AM to 2 AM.

Wit's End Comedy Club
8861 Harlan St., Westminster (halfway between Boulder and Denver)
• (303) 430-4242

Stand up comedy is offered nightly Wednesday through Sunday, featuring national performers like Fred Anderson and Greg Phelps from shows like Leno, Letterman, A&E and Caroline's. Shows begin at 8 PM, with additional shows at 10:30 PM on Friday and Saturday nights. Ticket prices are $6 on weekdays and $8 on Friday and Saturday.

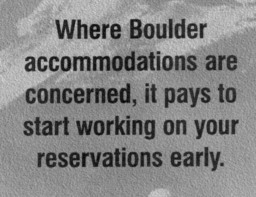

Where Boulder accommodations are concerned, it pays to start working on your reservations early.

Accommodations

Boulder proper offers more than two dozen places to stay, with more than 2,000 rooms ranging from bargain-rate facilities to luxury hotels and romantic bed and breakfast inns. The choices expand when you head for the hills, where country cabins, great adventure ranches and mountain retreats beckon. Many of the accommodations are popular way-stations for travelers planning to continue on to Rocky Mountain National Park and Estes Park (see the chapters on those destinations for more information). In fact, Boulder itself is only 35 miles from Estes Park, which means roughly an hour's drive up, down and around the mountains. Many country places are even closer, so for these, we've listed the approximate driving time to reach both Boulder and Estes Park.

The most recent addition is a Marriott tucked into what had been a parking lot behind McGuckin's Hardware. This astonishingly small lot now accommodates 155 rooms with a magnificent view of the Flatirons. The long-vacant lot at Ninth and Canyon, on the southwestern edge of downtown, has sporadically been proposed as a hotel site; however, every development proposal thus far has been defeated, often by requirements that changed mid-scheme. Don't be surprised to ultimately see a hotel in this convenient spot; then again, don't be surprised if you never do.

Get Your Reservation Early

Where Boulder accommodations are concerned, it pays to start working on your reservations early. From May through October, it's wise to reserve a month in advance. Dates that sell out early include CU-Boulder fall football weekends (especially when the Buffaloes play Nebraska), graduation in mid-May and the Bolder Boulder Memorial Day weekend, all of which pack the town. Since it's not a ski destination, Boulder's slowest season is November through February. Rates are usually lower then too.

Whether you need a room two years from now or right away, the Boulder Chamber of Commerce, (303) 442-2911 or (800) 444-0447, can send you an updated packet of information about Boulder plus the latest hotel/motel rate sheet. The Chamber does not operate a central reservations service. On heavy weekends, the Chamber calls around to see if anyone has canceled, making a room available. So if you're desperate, they sometimes can help.

A Word About Smoking

Boulder policy-makers figured out early the harmful consequences of America's legal drug — tobacco — and established many smoke-free zones. In 1995, smoking was banned in all public places. Many accommodations also prohibit or restrict smoking. Most bed and breakfast inns, for instance, don't allow any smoking indoors. While most hotels provide some smoking rooms, there are fewer and fewer all the time; so if you want the freedom to smoke, be sure to ask for a smoking room.

Price Information

Prices may vary throughout the year, dropping in late fall and winter. Some places offer rooms at various price levels. Some properties also offer discounted business rates for extended stays or discounts for AAA members, senior citizens or others. The accommodation you're seeking can provide more details. Unless indicated otherwise, assume that the property accepts cash, traveler's checks, personal and company checks (both in-state and out-of-state) and major credit cards.

Price Code

Our price-code key, shown in dollar signs ($), is based on average daily summer (peak) rates for a standard room for two adults.

$	Less than $55
$$	$56 to $75
$$$	$76 to $100
$$$$	$101 to $125
$$$$$	$126 and more

Bed and Breakfasts and Country Inns

If you've never stayed at a bed and breakfast or a country inn (though often a distinction is not made between the two, in this area, the difference is that a country inn is considered bigger), try one in Boulder. Each room is individually decorated with special treasures, antique furnishings and paintings. Most rooms have private baths, often lavishly appointed. Many are in former mansions or mountain lodges. No, most Boulderites don't live this way, but plenty of us would like to. These homes are so peaceful and romantic, you may wish you could linger for years. Extra details of decor and service can add immeasurably to the richness of your stay. No wonder these are popular for honeymoons and anniversaries. Keep to yourself or relax in the living room and strike up a conversation with the staff and other travelers. Most bed and breakfasts offer what they now tend to call "continental-plus breakfast," with homemade breads or rolls, a choice of beverage, fresh fruit and perhaps cereal. Some prepare a full breakfast each morning with a hot entree and cereal available too.

Bed and breakfasts rarely permit smoking or pets, and most inns don't allow children younger than 12. If you book your family somewhere that does permit children, make sure the kids are well-behaved — and brace them for the absence of standard hotel offerings such as televisions or indoor heated pools. If you might be arriving during one of Boulder's infrequent hot spells, ask about air conditioning. Some rooms have it, some don't need it, and others do.

Several of Boulder's best bed and breakfasts belong to an association called the Distinctive Inns of Colorado, (800) 866-0621, which can send you a directory including evocative photographs of many member properties.

City of Boulder

Many Boulder bed and breakfasts are near the center of the city, often in mostly residential areas. In a way, they make you an instant resident, for they give you a lovely, distinctive neighborhood to call your own during your stay. A central location means fun just outside your door. It can also mean traffic and other urban noise. Mention a desire for total quiet to the staff if you want a room where you won't notice traffic at all.

The Boulder Victoria Historic Inn
$$$$$ • 1305 Pine St., Boulder
• (303) 938-1300

The Dwight-Nicholson House, one of Boulder's earliest mansions, was renovated in 1889 and turned into a gorgeous bed and breakfast more than a century later. Seven distinctive rooms have queen-size brass beds with down comforters, private baths (three with steam showers) and televisions. This wonderful inn is just a block from the Pearl Street Mall. Here you'll find charming Victorian hospitality and plush comfort. The innkeeper serves a complete breakfast with homemade fruit breads and muffins, afternoon tea and evening port. In summer, the beautiful front garden is ablaze with flowers.

Briar Rose
$$$$$ • 2151 Arapahoe Ave., Boulder
• (303) 442-3007

This was Boulder's first bed and break-

www.insiders.com

See this and many other **Insiders' Guide®** destinations online — in their entirety.

Visit us today!

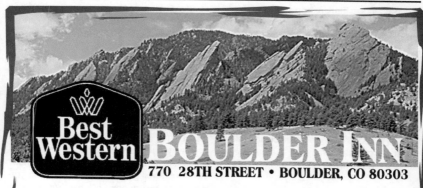

fast, established in 1981, and it remains one of the coziest. This English-style inn has a landscaped courtyard and garden complete with lovely little pond and waterfall. Each of the ten guest rooms has Boulder-made featherbed comforters. Two of the rooms feature wood-burning fireplaces. Tea is served in the afternoon, and a homemade breakfast — delicious baked goods, granola and fresh fruit — greets the morning. The inn is within walking distance of Crossroads Mall, CU-Boulder and downtown.

The Earl House Historic Inn
$$$$$ • 2429 Broadway, Boulder
• (303) 938-1400

The landmark Greene-Earl House is a spectacular 1882 Gothic-style stone mansion. It is also Boulder's newest bed and breakfast, opened in November 1995 with a trellised, wrought iron fence. Original woodwork and tiles handpainted by the original owner's wife make the interior a treasure too. One room has a double bed, and the rest have queens. All the bathrooms have handpainted tiles and either a steam shower or jetted tub. The parlor and dining room seem a million miles from the bustle of Broadway. Under the same ownership as the Boulder Victoria, the Earl House has adopted the practice of serving continental breakfast, afternoon tea and evening port. Two carriage houses on the property each have three bedrooms, two bathrooms, a full kitchen and living room with TV/VCR, stereo and washer/dryer. Each can accommodate up to six people; there is a two-night minimum stay. Carriage house guests are welcome at afternoon tea, but they're on their own for breakfast and evening port.

The Inn on Mapleton Hill
$$$$ • 1001 Spruce St., Boulder
• (303) 449-6528, (800) 276-6528

Five rooms with private baths and two

rooms sharing a bath make up this 1899 home in the Mapleton Hill historic neighborhood. The Inn received the Historic Preservation Award from the Boulder Historical Society in 1992. It's just a minute's walk down tree-lined streets to the Pearl Street Mall. The Inn on Mapleton Hill has a view of both the Flatirons and the downtown area. The Cottonwood Room is romantic with a four-poster bed and a sunroom opening to a south-facing balcony. The comfortable back parlor has a fireplace and television for all guests to enjoy. A generous breakfast is served daily.

Pearl Street Inn
$$$$$ • 1820 Pearl St., Boulder
• (303) 444-5584, (888) 810-1302

Each of the eight Victorian-style rooms here has a wood-burning fireplace. The location is superb, just three blocks east of the Pearl Street Mall, but the inn is tucked behind a high fence and feels private and secluded. There's a lovely garden courtyard for guests to enjoy. Full breakfast, including excellent baked goods and exceptional oatmeal, is served. The innkeeper also puts out afternoon refreshments, which could be hot spiked apple cider, wine and cheese or tea. The Pearl Street Inn's rates are the same year round. The inn, which once had a restaurant, still has wedding, reception and meeting facilities for up to 125 people.

Bed & Breakfast at Sunset House
$$$ • 1740 Sunset Blvd., Boulder
• (303) 444-0801

This is a homestay bed and breakfast, meaning you have your choice of one or two rooms in a private home just north of downtown Boulder. Sunset House is a 1950s ranch, not fancy, but beautifully landscaped, homey and secluded. You'll have your own private entrance to rooms that include a fireplace and television and open to a lovely back patio with views of the city and mountains. To complete the homey picture, owners Phyllis and Roger Olson have a small friendly dog. When the Sunset House is full, Phyllis is happy to refer you to other homestays in the area.

The generous, civic-minded Olsons took out a mortgage on their home to enable Historic Boulder to buy the garden next to the Arnett-Fullen House, the organization's headquarters (see our Attractions chapter). When you stay at Sunset House, you'll indirectly be helping Historic Boulder, and the Olsons might even hand you an application in case you want to join.

The Mountains

The peace and quiet of a mountain lodge can be incredible. Some of these places are just a short drive from Boulder. Others are way, way up where the spring flowers bloom in August. Some locations are even secrets... the owners will give you directions when you inquire. Many are open all year, but check in advance, for some close during winter.

Above Boulder Wildlife Safari Lodge
$$$$, no credit cards • Sugarloaf Mountain, Boulder • (303) 258-7777

Three guest rooms are all you'll find in this very secluded, European-style, big mountain hunting lodge with handmade aspen-log beds, three fireplaces, designer decorations and 300 full-mounted trophies, including grizzly bears, African lions and other wildlife. The owner describes himself as a big-game hunter, professional outdoorsman and environmentalist. Breakfast is continental-plus and often includes wild game sausage. There is a kennel for pets, and children are welcome. It's a five-minute drive from Nederland, 25 minutes from Boulder and 50 minutes from Estes Park.

Allenspark Lodge
$$ • 184 Main St., Allenspark
• (303) 747-2552

Six rooms with private baths, six rooms with shared baths and three cabins with private baths and full kitchens make up this authentic 1933 log lodge. Construction is of ponderosa pine on the first two levels inside and out, with knotty pine inside on the top floor. Many of the furnishings are the same vintage as the buildings. There are hot tubs, a gift shop, a wine and beer bar and a TV in the great room near the flagstone fireplace. Views from this mountain lodge are tremendous, and Wild Basin and its wonderful hiking trails are nearby. Children younger than 14 are welcome in the cabins, and older kids may stay in the

lodge too. It's about a 45-minute drive from Boulder and a 25-minute drive to Estes Park. The lodge includes continental-plus breakfast in its lodge rates.

Alps Boulder Canyon Inn
$$$$$ • 38619 Boulder Canyon Dr., Boulder • (303) 444-5445, (800) 414-2577

When you look at this beautiful inn today, it's hard to imagine that it was once the run-down old lodge that housed the Fraternal Order of the Moose. You enter via a log cabin that was originally a stagecoach stop and bordello during the late 1870s, wander into the lounge that was the old Moose Lodge bar, then head to your room. The inn's 12 enchanting guest rooms are done up with heirloom furnishings. All the rooms are different, as are their private bathrooms: six with jetted tubs, two with claw-foot tubs, one with a soaking tub for two and the others with showers. Each room also has a fireplace, and some feature stained-glass doors. Several rooms are honeymoon-perfect, such as "Wallstreet," which includes that vintage-style tub for two. The inn services a gourmet breakfast, and cheesecake is available in the evening. You can always help yourself to tea and coffee, and hot cider is added in winter. The TV room has a satellite system and VCR with dozens of videos available, and the lounge features a huge stone fireplace, big card table and popular games. There are also fireplaces in the breakfast room and the lobby. The large, rustic dining room has a capacity of 100 people for weddings, receptions and meetings. Children older than 12 are welcome. Hiking and biking trails are close by this inn, which is also close to Boulder Creek. The inn is just a five-minute drive from Boulder and less than an hour from Estes Park.

Boulder Mountain Lodge and Campground
$$ • 91 Fourmile Canyon Dr., Boulder • (303) 444-0882, (800) 458-0882

Twenty-two rooms, many with kitchenettes or full kitchens and all with whirlpool-jetted bathtubs, are available at this rustic motel with homey touches. The campground has 25 first-come, first-served sites with electricity and access to water for 25-foot-maximum RVs or for tent campers. The lodge is in the mountains, and the office is in an old narrow-gauge train depot. There's a private fishing pond for kids, a heated outdoor pool (open seasonally) and hot tubs. Smoking is allowed in some rooms, and pets are welcome with a deposit. The lodge is less than 10 minutes from Boulder and about an hour from Estes Park.

Gold Lake Mountain Resort
$$$$$ • 3371 Gold Lake Rd., Ward • (303) 459-3544, (800) 450-3544

This mountain hideaway is evolving into a wonderful escape for honeymooners (or second honeymooners) or for a pleasant close-by family retreat. Seventeen charming and distinctive cabins are tucked amid the pine trees. Most have new gas stoves, wood floors, antique furnishings and library areas. Bathrooms are being converted into sybaritic playrooms with plumbing. Popular "Victoria's House" features include a velvet fainting couch, and others are . . . well, that Victoria is really something. If Victorian frou-frou is too-too for you-you, you might prefer a cabin done in a Southwestern, cowboy or Native American style. The resort's spa offers massages and facials, and you can book a spa package. The 35-acre lake is beautiful for catamaran sailing, canoeing, kayaking and fly fishing in summer, and ice skating in winter. The lakeside hot tubs are a dreamy treat. Summer brings opportunities for horseback riding on mounts you can rent by the hour or day, great mountain biking on challenging trails, volleyball and hiking. Children are more than welcome. Guests and visitors can dine in the excellent and stylish restaurant called Alice's (see our Restaurants chapter), or enjoy cocktails at Karel's Tavern. Gold Lake Mountain Resort is a 45- to 60-minute drive from either Boulder or Estes Park.

Goldminer Hotel
$$$ • 601 Klondike Ave., Eldora • (303) 258-7770, (800) 422-4629

Three rooms with private baths and four with shared baths are in this historic log hotel from Eldora's mining days. The rooms reflect their original character, with antiques and homemade quilts. There is no smoking in the hotel. There is also one cabin, with a kitchenette, that does allow smoking. This is an away-

A Boulder bed and breakfast may be the perfect site for your wedding.

from-it-all place in a quaint old mining town surrounded by mountains. You can enjoy beautiful views from the hot tub. Pets are only permitted in the cabin; children are accepted. A full breakfast is part of the deal. It's about 30 minutes from Boulder, about an hour from Estes Park and a short drive from the Eldora ski area.

Inn at Rock N River Bed and Breakfast & Trout Pond Fishing
$$$-$$$$ • 16868 N. St. Vrain Dr., northwest of Lyons • (303) 443-4611, (800) 448-4611

This delightful riverside complex has seven rooms near the pond, and The Carriage House, which is a two-story cabin accommodating up to four with a large bedroom, a Jacuzzi tub for two and a fireplace. All units include kitchens. Though it's near busy U.S. Highway 36, the inn is quiet and pretty, with great views of the trout ponds and the St. Vrain River. Full breakfast is included. People stay overnight for the nature and the trout fishing. (You're guaranteed a fish!) Children are welcome. The inn is usually full from May through mid-December, but you can always hope for a cancellation or come in the off-season. It is 3 miles northwest of Lyons (take U.S. 36), 25 minutes from either Boulder or Estes Park.

Best Western Lodge at Nederland
$$$ • 55 Lakeview Dr., Nederland • (303) 258-9463, (800) 279-9463

This oversize log lodge, in the heart of Nederland, is a convenient mountain retreat from Boulder. Accommodations include rooms with king-size beds for couples and rooms with two queen-size beds or a queen and a set of bunk beds for families. All rooms are equipped with hair dryers, coffee makers and small refrigerators; suites also have fireplaces. The spacious lobby has a fireplace, and there's an outdoor hot tub on the deck. There is no restaurant, but Nederland's most popular eating places are within a short walk. In winter, the Lodge at Nederland offers reasonably priced ski packages in cooperation with nearby Eldora Mountain Resort. It is also a great jumping-off place for snowshoeing, backcountry skiing or summer hikes. The activities desk can arrange guided hikes, horseback trail rides and other diversions.

Nederhaus Motel
$$ • 686 Colo. Hwy. 119 S., Nederland • (303) 444-4705, (800) 422-4629

The twelve rooms at Nederhaus are each furnished with antiques. This little hotel with a Swiss-looking facade is within an easy walk of downtown Nederland and is also a short drive to hiking spots and Eldora skiing. Some rooms allow smoking. Pets and children are welcome. The property is about 25 minutes from Boulder and about an hour from Estes Park. There is a coffee shop and a pizza parlor.

Peaceful Valley Ranch
$$$$$ • 475 Peaceful Valley Rd., Lyons • (303) 747-2881, (800) 955-6343

This family-owned, family-run guest ranch, on the site of an old homestead, is a "got everything" facility with 12 cabins, rooms in the main lodge and various other guest buildings as well as a stable and indoor riding arena and other facilities. This is an all-American guest ranch that can house more than 100 people, and newly remodeled conference facilities are available. Staying overnight is dandy, but longer stays are what most seek at Peaceful Valley. Half-week stays are around $565-935 per person, and full-week packages

---

INSIDERS' TIP

If you're traveling to Boulder via Denver International Airport, consider Boulder's shuttle, Super Shuttle Boulder, (formerly the Airporter), as an alternative to renting a car. The shuttle will drop you at nearly all of the city's hotels or motels for $18, or $22 if you want to be delivered directly to your own front door. It's easy to locate at the airport and if you won't be needing a car during you stay, it's mostly hassle-free and extremely time-saving.

begin at $1,270 per person during the summer, including all meals, use of ranch facilities and all recreational programs.

The chef makes ranch-style meals such as prime rib and lemon-flavored catfish. The children's program is extensive. There's an indoor hot tub, indoor swimming pool and children's petting farm as well as activities that include horseback riding, jeep tours and square dancing. The mountainside chapel, with a view of the Indian Peaks behind the altar, is a gorgeous wedding site. In winter, Peaceful Valley offers sleigh rides, stocks cross-country skis, snowshoes and snowmobiles and maintains a small track on the property. The trailhead for extensive marked but ungroomed trails around Camp Dick lies just across the highway. This outstanding resort is just a bit less than an hour from Boulder and about 40 minutes south of Estes Park. No smoking or pets are allowed.

The Eastern Plains

These motels, bed and breakfasts and country inns are open all year and offer good variety and reasonable prices.

Briarwood Inn
$$ • 1228 N. Main St., Longmont • (303) 776-6622

The 17 rooms in this motel include 10 kitchenettes. The owner calls his the best backyard in town, with a quiet patio area, a fish pond and a gazebo. Smoking is allowed. Children are welcome. It's a half-hour drive to Boulder and about 45 minutes to Estes Park.

Ellen's Bed & Breakfast in a Victorian House
$$$, no credit cards • 700 Kimbark St., Longmont • (303) 776-1676

Two guest rooms, each with a private bath, are in this beautifully shaded, quiet, 1910 Victorian-style house, with eclectic furnishings including several interesting art deco pieces collected by the well-traveled owners. Full breakfast is included, there's a hot tub, smoking is allowed, and children and pets are welcome. It's a half-hour drive from Boulder and 45 minutes to Estes Park.

Sandy Point Inn
$$$ • 6485 Twin Lakes Rd., Gunbarrel/ Boulder • (303) 530-2939, (800) 322-2939

With 33 air-conditioned studio suites, each with mini-kitchen and cable TV, this is a great place for people relocating or traveling with families. There's one common kitchen with house-style range, oven and utensils for preparing full-scale meals. A membership at Synergy, a full-service sports club, is complimentary for guests. A complimentary cold breakfast buffet is served in the common kitchen from 6:30 to 10 AM daily and 8 to 10 AM on weekends and holidays. It's a 10-minute drive to Boulder and about an hour from Estes Park. The inn owners also rent one- and two-bedroom condominiums, normally on a monthly basis.

The Victoria Inn
$$$ • 20400 W. 17th Ave., Longmont • (303) 772-4667

Each of this inn's 30 executive suites includes a full kitchen, full bath and a sitting room. These are three-story, blue Victorian-style buildings with contemporary furnishings. There's a heated outdoor pool. Smoking is allowed. Cats are considered with a deposit. Children are welcome. It's a half-hour from Boulder and 45 minutes to Estes Park.

Hotels and Motels

Boulder hotels and motels all include nonsmoking rooms (ask if you need a smoking room). Most have pools; but if it's cold, check when you call to see whether it's a heated indoor pool. The places we've listed have the usual hotel/motel amenities such as televisions and air-conditioning. Some are simple and sweet, others are lavish. Most don't allow pets. Unless noted, all take major credit cards.

Best Western Boulder Inn
$$$ • 770 28th St., Boulder • (303) 449-3800, (800) 233-8469

Around 100 rooms are in this motel, right across the street from the south end of the CU-Boulder campus. Room options include two queen-size beds, one queen-size bed and upgraded kings that have a wet bar area. Admission to the nearby 24 Hour Fitness health club is included during the stay, along with a continental breakfast daily. The motor inn has a hot tub, sauna and outdoor pool (open seasonally). The Fanatics sports bar is also on site.

Best Western Golden Buff Lodge
$$$ • 1725 28th St., Boulder
• (303) 442-7450, (800) 999-BUFF

This comfortable, well-located business and family motel has 112 guest rooms with king- or queen-size beds, some suites and conference/banquet space accommodating up to 40 people. On site is The Buff Restaurant, which is open for breakfast and lunch daily. There is a seasonal outdoor pool and an indoor hot tub. The motel is convenient to Crossroads Mall.

Boulder International Youth Hostel
$ • 1107 12th St., Boulder
• (303) 442-0522

Visitors from all over the world have stayed at this hostel, which is a member of the American Association of International Hostels. Accommodations are scattered among several buildings on University Hill. The hostel has separate dormitories for men and women, at only $15 a night, as well as private rooms for couples and families that go for $40 for two people, and apartments for those wanting longer-term facilities. Each room has a phone, but televisions are located only in common areas. Cable TV hookups are provided but you must bring your own apparatus. Kitchens are also available.

Boulder Marriott
$$$$$ • 2660 Canyon Blvd., Boulder
• (303) 440-8877, (800) 228-9290

This new business and meeting hotel opened in 1997 with 155 deluxe guest rooms and suites. It is tucked into a shopping center in central Boulder with magnificent views of the Flatirons, especially from the rooftop terrace. There is underground parking, an indoor pool, whirlpool, health club and gift shop. JW's Steakhouse and a lounge are inside the hotel with wraparound retail that includes a jewelry store, art gallery and the Essentials Beauty Clinic. It is within walking distance of shopping, restaurants, movie theaters and the CU campus.

The Broker Inn
$$$$$ • 555 30th St., Boulder
• (303) 444-3330, (800) 338-5407

This ornately decorated contemporary hotel has 116 guest rooms and four suites. Rooms feature brass beds, leather recliners and cable TVs with free HBO and Showtime. Services include valet parking, room service and bell staffs. The acclaimed Broker Restaurant and Bentley's nightclub are on site. Amenities include a hot tub, and the hotel is equipped with conference rooms. Full breakfast is included in room rates. Free passes to the nearby 24 Hour Fitness center are part of your stay. Just south of the campus, The Broker Inn is a short walk or a CU-Boulder shuttle bus (take your pick) away from the University. It is also normally the location where passengers leaving and arriving via the Super Shuttle Boulder transportation service switch from smaller city vans to the larger vehicles that run hourly between Denver International Airport and Boulder.

Coburn House
$$$$$ • 2040 16th St., Boulder
• (303) 545-5200, (800) 858-5811

There are 12 rooms in this new boutique-size hotel. Wrought iron and leather furnishings give it a turn-of-the-century elegance. Guest rooms offer fireplaces, Jacuzzis, private balconies, televisions and phones. Continental breakfast is included in all room rates. Stained-glass windows, old City of Boulder renderings, authentic oil paintings and Western prints make the interior a visual delight. The widow's watch on the roof gives you a bird's-eye view of downtown and the Flatirons.

Colorado Chautauqua Cabins
$ • Ninth St. and Baseline Rd., Boulder
• (303) 442-3282

More than two dozen lodge rooms and about 60 cottages are available for rent, with a four-night minimum stay. The one- to three-bedroom cottages offer full kitchens but no telephones, air-conditioning, TVs or swimming pools. What you get here is a great deal on lodgings, one of the most beautiful locations

The famous staircase at the Hotel Boulderado is a favorite spot for weddings. In December, a huge tree stretches to the stained glass dome.

in town, hiking and superb cultural events right outside your door, and a wonderfully nostalgic step back in time. Bookings start in November for the following summer. All but two of the cabins are summer-only rentals. Ask about pets. For more information about Chautauqua Park, see our Attractions chapter.

Comfort Inn
$$$ • 1196 Dillon Rd., Louisville • (303) 604-0181, (800) 228-5150 (nationwide reservations)

The new 68-room Comfort Inn is next to the Mann 12-plex movie theater, just off U.S. 36. Rooms have one or two queen-size beds, and there is also one luxury room with an in-room Jacuzzi and queen-size bed. Continen-

tal breakfast, included in all room rates, is served in the breakfast room. This motor inn also has a meeting room and an exercise facility; for those who want a more aggressive workout, the Louisville Recreation Center is a short drive away.

Courtyard by Marriott
$$$$ • 4710 Pearl E. Cir., Boulder • (303) 440-4700, (800) 321-2211

This business hotel has 12 suites and 137 rooms with either a king-size bed or two doubles, work desks in every room and separate seating areas in the suites. The hotel offers conference rooms, the in-house Courtyard Cafe and Lounge, an indoor pool, whirlpool and workout room. It's right next to the

Boulder Creek Path in a quiet location just east of Foothills Parkway (Colo. Highway 157) on Pearl Street.

Courtyard by Marriott-Louisville
$$$$ • 948 W. Dillon Rd., Louisville
• (303) 604-0007, (800) 321-2211

Just off U.S. 36, this hotel offers 154 guest rooms and suites, a heated indoor pool with a whirlpool, an exercise room and in-room coffee service. There are also numerous banquet and reception facilities. the affordable restaurant features a full breakfast buffet served daily. Accommodations are available for both the physically challenged and for smokers.

Days Inn
$$$ • 5397 South Boulder Rd., Boulder
• (303) 499-4422, (800) 329-7466

This good basic motel is on a main thoroughfare, just off U.S. 36 and near the Table Mesa Park-n-Ride. It is just about the most convenient lodging to the National Center for Atmospheric Research and the National Bureau of Standards and Technology. Some of its 76 rooms have mountain views. Free local phone calls, TV with HBO and complimentary continental breakfast are included.

Econo Lodge
$$ • 2020 Arapahoe Ave., Boulder
• (303) 449-7550, (800) 449-7550

Forty-six rooms comprise this tidy and pleasant family-owned motel. All rooms have king or queen-size beds, cable TV and full bath. Within walking distance of downtown and the University, it features an indoor pool, hot tub and sauna. Coffee and doughnuts are served in the lobby each morning. Refrigerators and microwaves are available.

Foot-of-the-Mountain Motel
$$ • 200 Arapahoe Ave., Boulder
• (303) 442-5688

Each of this motel's 18 rooms is in a red-trimmed log cabin, making this place a quaint and rustic charmer. The mountain against whose foot this motel nestles (hence the name) is Flagstaff. On a quiet street near the pretty Eben Fine Park and the Boulder Creek Path, it is also just nine blocks west of CU-Boulder and the downtown Pearl Street Mall. All rooms have refrigerators and free HBO. Pets are welcome.

Hampton Inn
$$$$ • 912 W. Dillon Rd., Louisville
• (303) 666-7700, (800) HAMPTON (nationwide reservations)

The Hampton Inn is suited for multi-day business or leisure stays. Each of its 80 spacious, traditionally furnished rooms has a king-size bed or two queens, a refrigerator, microwave, coffee maker, hair dryer, two-line speaker phone and television with Nintendo. All rooms feature fine designer furniture and working desks for business travelers. In addition, there is one hospitality suite for small meetings, an indoor swimming pool, hot tub and exercise facility. Continental breakfast is included in all rates. Within walking distance of restaurants, bars and shopping.

Holiday Inn
$$$$ • 800 28th St., Boulder
• (303) 443-3322, (800) HOLIDAY

This well-maintained Holiday Inn features 165 sizable rooms. The major amenity is the Holidome, which features a large indoor pool, hot tub, sauna and exercise room. The motor inn also has a game room and Oliver's casual restaurant and pub. Like all hotels along this strip of 28th Street, it's very close to CU-Boulder.

Holiday Inn Express
$$$ • 4777 N. Broadway, Boulder
• (303) 442-6600, (800) HOLIDAY

This North Boulder motor inn has 62 rooms and will add an additional 44 rooms in 1999, some with microwaves and refrigerators. There is a seasonal outdoor pool, exercise room, guest laundry and complimentary continental breakfast. Free local phone calls also are included. It is a short walk from the intersection of U.S. 36 (28th Street) and Broadway.

Homewood Suites
$$$$$ • Baseline Rd., Boulder
• (303) 499-9922, (800) 225-5466

The 100 apartment-style suites each include a full kitchen and separate living and sleeping areas. There's an outdoor pool, complimentary continental breakfast and a free social hour Monday through Thursday nights including food and drinks. We know one couple who liked the lifestyle so much they went back home, sold their big house and moved into a place about the size of a Homewood Suite! Pets are allowed, and children are welcome. In addition to the fabulous view of the Flatirons, the Flatiron Athletic Club is just next door and Homewood guests pay only $5 per day. The bottom line here is good, basic living for extended-stay guests and mostly business travelers.

Hotel Boulderado
$$$$$ • 2115 13th St., Boulder
• (303) 442-4344, (800) 433-4344

Built in 1909, this is a local landmark as well as the city's finest hotel. It offers old-style grandeur and is famous for the stained-glass canopy in its huge mezzanine. Robert Frost and Louis Armstrong are among its past guests. Its 160 lavishly decorated, Victorian-style rooms are divided between the historic older section of the hotel and the new wing. The VIP suites are the largest and fanciest lodgings. Each has a wrought iron or four-poster bed, its own stereo and a separate living room furnished with Victorian-style desks and sofas. The fanciest, biggest one goes for more than $200 a night, and it's booked almost constantly. The hotel has one of Boulder's best restaurants (see our Restaurants chapter), two bars, a mezzanine entertainment area, lots of conference space, a gift shop and a sensational location just one block from the Pearl Street Mall.

La Quinta Inn & Suites Louisville/Boulder
$$$$ • 902 Dillon Rd., Louisville
• (303) 664-0100, (800) NU-ROOMS

This hotel has three spacious room choices with in-room coffee makers, 25-inch big-screen televisions, over-sized desks, voice mail messaging and data-port phones. There are 120

INSIDERS' TIP

Some Boulder-area motels allow pets in rooms if you check ahead and meet certain requirements, including Boulder Mountain Lodge, Broker Inn, Foot-of-the-Mountain Motel, Homewood Suites. If you're traveling elsewhere in the United States, check out *Pets Are Permitted*, a book listing hotel/motel, kennel and pet-sitting services nationwide.

You won't have any trouble finding ways to enjoy our mountain views.

rooms total, some with microwaves and refrigerators. Summer visitors will enjoy the beautifully landscaped courtyard with gazebo while winter visitors can take advantage of the heated pool and spa.

Raintree Plaza Hotel
$$$$$ • 1900 Ken Pratt Blvd., Longmont
• (303) 776-2000, (800) 843-8240

This is Longmont's only full-service hotel. It housed the Emperor of Japan's entourage during the summer of 1994. There are 295 rooms, of which 86 are extended-stay rooms, each with a full kitchen, fireplace and living room. The hotel also has a 42,000-square-foot conference center, a restaurant and a heated outdoor swimming pool. Guests get free breakfast and evening cocktails. The hotel is popular with business travelers, families and conventions. It's a 15-minute drive to Boulder and an hour to Estes Park.

Regal Harvest House
$$$$$ • 1345 28th St., Boulder
• (303) 443-3850, (800) 545-6285

This is Boulder's biggest hotel, with more than 269 high-quality rooms and great business facilities on 16 acres right next to the Boulder Creek Path. It's an easy walk from CU-Boulder and the Pearl Street Mall. It has resort-type recreation facilities, including indoor and outdoor swimming pools, 15 indoor and outdoor tennis courts, mountain bike rentals and a workout room. The beautifully landscaped inner courtyard is a lively hangout after a Buffs game. Champs lounge and sports bar and The Fancy Moose restaurant are on site.

Residence Inn by Marriott
$$$$$ • 3030 Center Green Dr., Boulder
• (303) 449-5545, (800) 331-3131

This village-like complex has 128 studio

suites, all with full kitchens and fireplaces, designed for extended stays or for families who want a comfortable, relaxing refuge. The Residence Inn provides a complimentary continental breakfast buffet daily and has an outdoor seasonal pool and whirlpool. It has easy access to central Boulder, close to many of the high-tech and other companies there.

Super 8 Motel
$$ • 970 28th St., Boulder
• (303) 443-7800, (800) 525-2149

Seventy-one rooms are in this clean, pleasant motel close to CU-Boulder. Some people have stayed as long as three months in the motel's 12 apartment units, at reduced monthly rates. These relocation units have full kitchens and sitting rooms. Pets are welcome in some rooms, and children 14 and younger stay free in their parents' room.

University Inn
$$$ • 1632 Broadway, Boulder
• (303) 442-3830, (800) 258-7917

This neat little inn at the corner of Broadway and Arapahoe Avenue has 39 rooms with refrigerators, cable TV with free HBO and guest laundry. It's within easy walking distance of both downtown and the University—and right across the street from Alfalfa's Market (see our Shopping chapter). Although close to a busy intersection, with doors and windows shut, the rooms are fairly quiet. A free continental breakfast is provided.

RV Hookups and Campgrounds

If you're planning to stay in your RV or tent in Boulder, check our Sports chapter (see the "Camping" section under Participatory Sports.)

Boulder Mountain Lodge and Campground
91 Fourmile Canyon Dr., Boulder
• (303) 444-0882

This campground has 25 first-come, first-served sites with electricity and access to water for 25-foot-maximum RVs or ten campers. The fee is $14 a night with a two week maximum stay. Shower facilities are available.

The Boulder County Fairgrounds
9595 Nelson Rd., Longmont
• (303) 678-1525

The Fairground site has 92 campsites and can handle nearly 100 RVs. A site for an RV with no hookups or for one tent costs $10 a night. A site with electricity is $12; one with water and electrical hookups is $13. The maximum stay is two weeks. Showers are available free for registered guests. The dump station fee is $2.

The Denver North Campground
Intersection of I-12 and Colo. Hwy. 7, Broomfield • (303) 452-4120

This campground has space for 104 RVs, with 80 full hookups at $25.90 a night for two people, 24 tents at $19.50 a night, a meeting area and hot showers. Call them for reservations.

The Colorado Agency for Campgrounds, Cabins and Lodges
5101 Pennsylvania Ave., Boulder
• (303) 499-9343

This statewide directory service offers free information on camp sites, cabins, lodges, bed and breakfasts and fun things to do.

Meeting Spaces

In addition to the number of hotels, motels and conference centers that offer space for meetings and other get-togethers, these places offer space for rent in and around town.

Boulder Chamber of Commerce
2440 Pearl St., Boulder • (303) 442-2911

A huge family reunion, a big convention or a bonanza of a business meeting should start with a phone call here. Be sure to check on available space as soon as possible. If you're a Chamber member there is meeting space for 50 or more at the Pearl Street location.

CU-Boulder's Glenn Miller Ballroom
CU Campus, Euclid Ave. and Broadway, Boulder • (303) 492-8833

This is a great space for a reunion, reception, or any kind of social gathering, and is therefore usually booked a year in advance. It has room for 1,200 seated theater-style, 800 seated banquet-style with rectangular tables or 450 seated at round tables.

The Boulder Broker Inn
555 30th St., Boulder • (303) 444-3330

There are several rooms on the second floor of the hotel with a maximum capacity of 250. There are also three private rooms.

Broomfield's Interlocken Conference Resort
350 Interlocken Blvd., Broomfield • (303) 466-9799

A newer conference facility between Boulder and Denver, just off U.S. 36, Interlocken can accommodate 1,000.

Hotel Boulderado
2115 13th St., Boulder • (303) 442-4344

A new addition to this historic hotel offers a full-service meeting and conference center with an elegant first-floor space that seats 350 with a separate street entrance from the hotel.

Raintree Plaza Hotel and Conference Center
1900 Ken Pratt Blvd., Longmont • (303) 776-2000

Boasting easy access and plentiful parking, the Raintree offers a 42,000-square-foot conference center with seating for 1,100. There are also several smaller meeting rooms.

The Regal Harvest House
1348 28th St., Boulder • (303) 443-3850

Centrally located, the Harvest's Grand Ballroom can seat 650 theater-style, and there are 10 other conference rooms of varying sizes.

A Place for Your Pet

Most of the accommodations we've listed do not allow pets. Never just leave them in your car. Even with the windows cracked, even on a balmy day, Colorado's strong sun can zoom the temperature in the car to a fatal level within minutes. Check the Yellow Pages under "Kennels" for a complete list of accommodations for your traveling pet.

Cottonwood Kennels
7275 Valmont Rd., Boulder
• **(303) 442-2602**

Cottonwood's motto is "A Bed & Breakfast for Pets." This is one of the largest kennels in Boulder, boarding both dogs and cats. But it's always a busy place. Generally, if you're traveling during the time when the kids are out of school, call six months in advance for kennel reservation. During non-holidays in the winter, give two weeks' notice. When Cottonwood fills, they offer other suggestions.

Shopping

Visitors and residents alike find one of Boulder's delights to be shopping. As in dining, Boulder's retail scene is not yet totally overrun with tedious national chains that substitute themes for individuality and imagination. Except at Crossroads, the big indoor mall, which has its share of clones, very distinctive retail stores dominate the Boulder retail scene. You'll find yourself returning again and again to browse or buy at your favorites, and it isn't unusual to discover a new shop every time you prowl. Note that many of the shops we mention under the information given for the malls are featured later on in the "Specialty Shops" section.

Shopping Areas

Pearl Street Mall
Pearl Street between 11th and 15th streets, Downtown Boulder

Boulder's Pearl Street Mall, the city's original retail area, is still the heart and soul of the city. This photogenic, four-block, open-air walkway is for pedestrians only. It is lined with historic buildings that house numerous shops, galleries, microbreweries, offices and sidewalk cafes as well as newer buildings of a style and scale that harmonize with the old. During the warm months, street entertainers abound, including the ZIP Code Man, who can identify towns and sometimes even describe building styles in your neighborhood, based on your ZIP Code; sword swallower Johnny Fox; contortionists, jugglers, professional musicians and kids with their first violin trying to pick up a few bucks. One shop owner, afraid customers would be driven away by the loud and unharmonic playing of an adult performer outside, paid the man to leave. Fortunately, it's not a recurring problem, as the quality of entertainment generally is quite high. In addition to the buskers who play for the hat, an "out-to-lunch" weekly summer performance series brings formal live entertainment to the mall.

Don't let all the distractions make you forget to shop while you're downtown. Some of Boulder's most popular shoe and clothing shops, cafes, galleries, bookstores and card and gift shops occupy prime spots along the mall and on adjacent blocks. A stroll along the mall will bring you everything from chain stores like Gap Kids, Banana Republic and Nature's Own Imagination to only-in-Boulder shops like the elegant kitchen, bath and bed stock at Peppercorn, charming literary-inspired gifts from The Printed Page, crystals and clogs from El Loro and imported knitted sweaters from Alpaca Connection. Rocky Mountain Chocolate Factory seduces with rich whiffs through the open doors and down the street you can get inspired to work it off with togs and shoes from a shop owned by Boulder's own Olympian, Frank Shorter.

Since the mall was completed in 1976, Pearl Street, both east and west of the mall, has become an increasingly eclectic mix of service and retail businesses plus offices and restaurants. New buildings are going up all around the downtown, new businesses open almost daily and, sadly, some old favorites have closed down.

East, look for the funky, 60-ish Crystal Dragon, the traditional Swiss Chalet for quality watches or H.B. Woodsong's, where you're likely to walk in on an acoustic jam session. There's a fun mix of used bookstores, used clothing and an interesting cluster of craft and gift stores.

The west end is a bibliophile's paradise, from the classy Boulder Bookstore at the end of the mall to the Trident coffeehouse and bookstore and next door the Rue Morgue mystery bookstore, with everything from used paperbacks to signed and rare hard covers. Dozens of top-name mystery writers have spoken and signed their works within the blood red walls of the Rue Morgue. At this writing, creaky-floored, funky old Stage House, packed to the rafters with used books and unusual prints, was going through its death throes with a massive sale. It will exist as a second-floor art books and print shop.

The original Dot's Diner, a friendly, Fifties-style restaurant in a former gas station, has been replaced by a new complex of housing, parking and up-scale shops that include the West End Gardener, 3rd Street Wine Library, Spruce Confections and Bedell and Co. Fine Antiques.

The best parking for the downtown area is in the structures at 14th and Walnut, 11th and Spruce and 11th and Walnut streets. When you park in any of these, ask for validation stickers as you pay for your purchases at downtown stores. Every sticker is good for a half-hour of parking, so you can shop your way to reduced or free parking. The Mall's popularity and the city's general antipathy toward auto traffic and reluctance to build more parking combine to give downtown Boulder a reputation for skimpy parking. Now, however, two new parking structures under construction at the east end of the Mall, due for completion in 1999, will add about 1,000 more parking spaces. To keep the city aesthetically pleasing, a number of small shops will camouflage each structure. The Mall itself is city property, managed by the Downtown Management Commission, (303) 441-4000. Downtown Boulder, Inc., (303) 449-3774, acts as a sort of specialized Chamber of Commerce for businesses in the area.

Crossroads Mall
Between 28th and 30th Sts. and Arapahoe Ave. and Walnut St.
• **(303) 444-0722**

When it was built 30-odd years ago, Crossroads was a traditional small town shopping center, plunked down at the, well, crossroad of what would become two of Boulder's busiest streets (a fact that has frustrated city transportation planners ever since). For years, Boulder was satisfied with its small mall, which drew shoppers from the even smaller towns around. However, in 1979, with the threat of a brand new shopping center in nearby Louisville, city policy makers got busy and encouraged an expansion of Crossroads to keep Boulder's hold on the county's retail economy. Voters approved a public-private partnership with the mall's owners and Crossroads was doubled in size. Now, with increased shopping to the east a reality and a couple of major malls on the horizon, the city and shopping center are once again planning changes to the mall and the surrounding retail area.

Original grand plans, drawn up with the help of citizens attending public work sessions, included an outdoor plaza with skating rink and amphitheater, multi-screen movie theater and an additional floor of retail. Boulder voters in 1998 showed their commitment to the project by giving Crossroads the first ever exemption to the city's 55-foot height limitation, designed to protect views of the mountains. (Yes, there are buildings taller than 55 feet in Boulder, but they were built before the height ordinance was passed.)

That approval appears to be moot, however. As of this writing, that plan is on the shelf; one of the major tenants in the existing mall put the kibosh on plans to bring in a competitor to anchor the expansion. Mall-owner Macerich has proposed a redesign that doesn't expand the size of the mall but would add outdoor promenades, indoor skylights, a play area, several new restaurants and a 16-screen movie theater with stadium seats. The hoped-for completion date is late summer or early fall of 2000, ahead of a mega-mall planned in nearby Broomfield.

But, all of that is in the future. For now, Crossroads is still open for business, with smaller stores and eateries anchored by Foley's, Sears and JC Penney. There has been quite a bit of movement in the mall, as the southern half is cleared out for the renovation. Only Petland, Aladdin's Castle arcade and

Ruby Tuesday's remain open in the echoing area. Space for Dance has taken advantage of the situation to offer dance classes in a former women's clothing store. Periodically, seasonal businesses take over some of the empty space.

Arapahoe Village/The Village/ WaterStreet
Between 28th and Folsom streets, both sides of Arapahoe Avenue and Canyon Boulevard

This excellent shopping area has so many terraced flower beds that some people tell their landscapers, "I want my yard to look like that." In addition to myriad and varied retail shops, this complex of somewhat upscale strip malls has developed into a general entertainment center too, with Boulder's greatest concentration of movie houses and some surprisingly good restaurants. The United Artists Village 4 Theatres and Mann's Arapahoe Village Theatres across the street offer a total of eight screens. Memorable restaurants include the Full Moon Grill, Zolo Grill and the European Cafe. More casual eateries in the area include the Boulder Salad Company, Le Peep, the Noodle Bowl, and several yogurt, soup, ice cream, breakfast and burger spots. Goodies from Great Harvest Bread, Mountain Man Fruit & Nut Co. and The Brewing Market can help keep body and soul together.

This bustling retail area is where you'll find McGuckin Hardware (if they don't have it, you don't need it), Elfriede's Fine Fabrics and Studio Bernina, Rocky Mountain Records and Tapes, Video Station (a locally owned video store whose employees impossibly seem to have seen every movie ever made and remember the details of every one), the addictively aromatic Ead's News & Smoke Shop and Canterbury Oak and Brass furniture. Children's shops clustered near a pleasant child's pocket park include Grand Rabbits toy store, Pour Moi and Rocky Mountain Kids, and nearby is a great kid-clothing store called Zippety Doo-Da.

The newly constructed Marriott Hotel dominates the east end of the Village and offers its own upscale contributions to the shopping, with everything from Essentials Spa to Mustard Seed Gallery and the Buffalo Indian Room

(see our Accommodations chapter for more information).

The WaterStreet shopping complex, on the north side of Canyon Boulevard between Folsom and 27th, features some of Boulder's most luxurious shops. Christina's Lingerie carries expensive underwear, while The Regiment Shops sell quality men's and women's outerwear. Emerson Green is a men's store that prides itself on its "exceptional men's clothing," while J.J. Wells carries equally distinctive women's fashions and accessories. Walters & Hogsett and Meyers Jewelers (see the subsequent "Jewelers" section) offer elegant jewelry. Talbot's is an upscale women's shop.

The little shops in this area are great discoveries. From their names alone, you can guess what fun you'll have at the Colorado Rockies Club, Aspen Eyewear, Time Warp Comics and the Wild Bird Center. Chains include Safeway, Gart Sports, Eastern Mountain Sports and Pier I Imports.

You can reach this area by many transportation modes, for the Boulder Creek Path is on the south edge (making walking and biking easy), auto access is a snap (but the parking lots fill up when hit movies are showing) and it's on major bus routes, including the super-convenient Hop.

28th Street and 30th Street
Between Walnut St. and Iris Ave.

These two major north-south streets bracket Crossroads Mall, and a series of strip malls and freestanding stores stretch northward along these two arteries. Because most of them are fronted by parking lots, it's not easy to wander among them. But if you take the trouble, you can find most of Boulder's discount chains such as Target, Kmart and Marshall's, and interesting specialty shops all strung out along 28th Street.

In the Marshall Plaza Shopping Center you'll find local outposts of nationally known chains such as Toys R Us, Radio Shack, Office Depot and Blockbuster Video. Past Crossroads and Target to the north is a huge Whole Foods market (which introduced Boulder shoppers to the concept of valet parking at a grocery store), a six-plex movie theater, Barnes & Noble books and Video Wherehouse. The charming building just east of the movie theater is the old Boulder Depot, now available for special events and meetings.

Just past Kmart across Valmont is the tiny Willow Springs shopping center, whose shops include Boulder Soccer and Boulder Ink, one of our city's handful of tattoo salons.

Thirtieth Street merchants include Walgreen's, Office Max, Swalley's Music Studio, Cloth Constructions for designer fabrics and wallpaper and Concepts for home furnishings and gifts.

Basemar Shopping Center
Baseline Road and Broadway

Wild Oats health food market is the centerpiece of this L-shape strip mall just south of the CU campus. Next door is Le Français, one of Boulder's most cosmopolitan cafes with a display of desserts to die for. The Basemar Cinema, which shows $2 second-run movies, is just down the strip. This center offers a nice mix of little shops and services, including Buffalo Lock and Key, which is quick at matching keys and getting into locked cars. Herb's Quality Meats boasts a wide variety and does a good business in a town sometimes nicknamed the Tofu Capital of Colorado. The Taj restaurant serves a popular Middle Eastern buffet and Acoma Books has been buying and reselling used scholarly, scientific, technical and general books for 25 years.

The Meadows Shopping Center
Foothills Parkway and Baseline Road

As Boulder has grown eastward, this strip mall has become busier and busier. More than 50 businesses are now part of this large neighborhood shopping complex, located near several retirement and senior-living facilities. It includes the biggest Safeway in town, along with the Photo Finish, Art Cleaners, Runner's Choice and three quick and easy eateries — Nick-N-Willy's Take-N-Bake Pizza, Lee Yuan and Healthy Habits. Michael's Craft Store and Tuesday Morning, a deep-discount store, are two of the anchors. The Pet Ranch has a very helpful owner. Kid-oriented stores cluster in one corner, including fLearn, which stands for "a fun place to learn." It sells educational toys and software and also offers classes taught by qualified teachers who can help kids learn how to type, do Kumon math and program in Lego logic. The Meadows branch library on the south side of the shopping center has a popular meeting room, in addition to the books and other materials of a well-stocked branch.

North Broadway and Community Plaza
Broadway and Alpine Avenue, across from Community Hospital

Metropolitan Home magazine praised the Boulder design group, Communication Arts, for bringing the zip back to these 1960s-era shopping malls sheltered beneath zigzag and loopy roofs. Behind these homey, funky facades, pleasant little shops offer flowers, prescription drugs, haircuts, gifts and more. Ideal is one of Boulder's favorite grocery stores because it combines old-fashioned ambiance with the latest food fashions, a marvelous deli and friendly clerks. Other great shops include the Boulder Wine Merchant, Moe's Broadway Bagels (check out the free samples), European Flower Shop, the Ginger and Pickles toy store, Breadworks (more free samples) the Stage House Too bookstore, Room to Room furnishings and the Jacque Michelle boutique.

North Village Mart
Broadway and Quince Street

This is the low-key, small-scale shopping area that any neighborhood might want. You won't find choices galore here, but you'll notice just how lovely and cozy a small neighborhood shopping center can be. The area fits its neighborhood well. Kids arrive from the bike trails to pick up videos, wander into the pet store and stop for ice cream. Families and friends winding down after work fill the three respectable restaurants, serving Chinese and Italian food and sandwiches. The sandwich store, Pressto, has a Best of Boulder award from *Daily Camera* readers. The Nomad Players, a well-regarded community theater group, performs in the quonset just east of the center. North Boulder Market, which anchors this little shopping center, is a good basic grocery store, with one of the better meat departments in town. A video outlet, liquor store, florist and pet supply store round out the shopping opportunities.

Table Mesa Shopping Center
Broadway and Table Mesa Dr.

In addition to a King Soopers and the usual complement of restaurants and various stores, this South Boulder shopping center has many excellent outdoor stores, including The North Face, Neptune Mountaineering, Play It Again Sports, Doc's Ski & Sports, Active Imprints and Weaver's Dive Center. Weaver's is for divers, but weavers go to Shuttles, Spindles and Skeins. The Cooking School of the Rockies holds classes and has a small retail section with gourmet cookware, and Dragonfire Games invites kids and adults to join in the fun of fantasy card games and model painting.

University Hill
Broadway, north and south of College Ave.

Just west of campus and both affectionately and officially called "The Hill," this area's businesses cater mainly to the university crowd. Named for its location on the side of University Hill, The Hill developed in 1906 as a streetcar stop between the Boulder Depot downtown and Chautauqua Park. In 1928, it received Boulder's first business growth restriction from homeowners who feared their neighbors would eventually sell out to stores, which is the reason that The Hill's retail zone remains so compact. It also explains why many stores look so homey — they actually were homes once. The area underwent a facelift in 1997 with street improvements and the addition of trees and artwork.

An eclectic mix of shoppers frequents this college zone, which ranges from the elegant and ultra-tweedy men's shop called Kinsley & Co. to such grunge-generation services as tattoo and piercing parlors. Coffee is available approximately every 10 feet, as is fast food of one type and another – pizza, bagels, Vietnamese, burgers, Chinese, ice cream. The Colorado Bookstore is the largest business on The Hill, its huge glass windows covered over with brick after anti-war riots (protestors against the war in Vietnam also closed Highway 36 connecting Boulder to Denver) left them in shards. Across the street is the venerable Jones Drug and next door, the Pipefitter offers oddments. Art Hardware provides everything for the budding Picasso and Albums on The Hill has an extensive collection of old and new CDs, tapes and even vinyl records. The Boulder International Hostel is on 12th Street, just one block off The Hill's main drag. If you linger past twilight, the '50s-vintage Flatirons Theatre, Boulder's oldest and largest theater — and the only remaining single-screen theater in town — still shows first run movies, and *Pollstar* magazine rates the Fox Theatre and Cafe the nation's fourth-best concert venue among less-than-800 capacity theaters. No movies in this former movie house; see the Nightlife chapter for more info.

Parking is at a premium on The Hill, but its convenient location on the Hop and Skip routes make it easy to reach from Pearl Street and Crossroads malls, as well as from north and south Boulder. Otherwise, it's best to walk or bicycle to this shopping area. Still, some stores, such as Art Hardware, The Boulder Mountaineer and the Colorado Bookstore, have a few free parking spots for their customers. Also, you can sometimes find metered spaces on campus, a short walk away via a beautiful pedestrian underpass at Broadway and College Avenue that is worth a visit in its own right. If your interests run deeper, you can pick up a free booklet outlining a self-guided walking tour of The Hill at the Hill Annex, a small "city hall" for students and visitors in the 1200 hundred block of 13th Street, behind Buchanan's.

Gunbarrel Square
Gunpark Road and Lookout Road, Gunbarrel

It's not extensive, but for the residents of Gunbarrel who for many years had only a King Soopers grocery and tiny strip mall, the expanded shopping area of Gunbarrel Square is a welcome enhancement. Gunbarrel Square includes the Printed Page, an upscale bookstore with a charming café. Food offerings include Angelo's pizza and subs, a popular Chinese restaurant, a deli and a Southwestern grill, in addition to a Mail Box, flower shop, liquor store, even a private elementary school. Hugh M. Woods is around the corner, with lumber, patio furniture and hardware for the weekend carpenter.

East County

Shopping Areas
Twin Peaks Mall
**Hover Road and Colo. Hwy. 119,
Longmont • (303) 651-6454**

More than 130,000 people each week shop at the 80 stores in this regional, enclosed shopping center, which was renovated and expanded in 1997. (The name refers to the view west to two Rocky Mountain peaks, and not to the tongue-in-cheek rumor that Dolly Parton was to cut the ribbon when the mall opened.) The big draws presently include JCPenney (the original Penney got his start in Longmont), Sears and two Dillard's department stores, featuring higher-end clothing. Another major addition was the United Artists 10-screen movie complex.

At Twin Peaks there's a Victoria's Secret, Roley's, Foot Locker, Gart Sports, Bath and Body Works, Gymboree children's clothing store, Braun's Fashions, Famous Footwear, Kay Bee Toys, Radio Shack and several jewelry and shoe stores. Woodleys Fine Furniture features locally made items, and Colorful Images is an overstock store full of furniture and novelty items. In addition to such sit-down restaurants as the gut-busting Country Buffet and Chelsey London Pub and Grill, there's a food court with burgers, pizza and Chinese food, plus Renzio's dishing up Greek food. In late 1997, Pier I Imports opened a brand new freestanding store next door to the mall.

Lafayette
East on Arapahoe Road, Baseline Road or South Boulder Road

Lafayette's main shopping areas are around the intersection of South Boulder Road and Public Road, which is also U.S. 287. Antique hunters gravitate to West's Antiques, which is a full block long, and nearby Rayburn Antiques and Matthew's Gifts. Lafayette Florists offers the most bedding plants in the county; a visit is a rite of spring for many Boulder County residents. The Lafayette Flea Market is the county's best-known, a rambling series of interconnecting spaces with everything from antiques to unadulterated junk. Take a trip back a few decades by pulling into the Sonic drive-in on Waneka Parkway for a limeade and a chili dog. Country General is still a real country general store, selling farm equipment, dog food, tools and horse halters amid the rapid suburbanization of town. You can get a good bite of Mexican food at Efrain's, which serves the hottest green chili around, or La Familia, which is Spanish for "the family," a good name for this homey eatery.

Louisville
East on South Boulder Road or Louisville exit off U.S. Hwy. 36

Louisville is booming, and its quaint and sleepy downtown is becoming eclipsed by the bright lights of the retail strip along McCaslin Boulevard. While Boulder frets about excessive growth, Louisville welcomes all comers. New big-box retail outlets, fast-food outlets, chain restaurants, a 12-plex theater and hotels have sprung up along what was until recently a relatively sparse roadway. On either side of McCaslin you'll find Home Depot and Eagle Hardware competing across the street from each other, and new chain restaurants that include Applebee's, Chili's and McDonald's. The Village Safeway Shopping Center is at South Boulder Road and Centennial. There's a new Albertson's Food & Store on West Cherry. Louisville Plaza has King Soopers and Kmart at South Boulder Road off of Colo. 42. The Centennial Center, at McCaslin Boulevard and Cherry Street, is near the movie complex and the hotels. In historic downtown, along Main Street, you'll find The Locker Room for personalized sportswear, Wildwood Music and casual, families-welcome eating places including the Marketplace Bakery, The Blue Parrot and Colacci's restaurants and Joe's

---

INSIDERS' TIP

Artwalk is a self-guided tour of a dozen or so galleries on and near Pearl Street that open on the first Friday of every month from 6 to 9 PM. Often, artists are on-hand, and some of the galleries serve complimentary refreshments.

Market for sausage and Italian food, Double Happy Chinese and Tulien's Vietnamese Restaurant. Thunderbird Barbers, complete with an American flag outside, offers a glimpse of Main Street past, as does the ad for 5-cent Coca-Cola painted on the small brick home of the Louisville Historical Society. Close by, the Old Louisville Inn features an antique bar and lots of character. Behind a small retail center along South Boulder Road are the real train cars that house Kaddy Shack World Famous Barbecue.

Specialty Shops

Antiques

Cannon Mine Coffee & Antiques
210 S. Public Rd., Lafayette
• (303) 665-0625

Have a coffee and pastry and try out the ambiance of the antiques available for sale in this unique shop. Like the chair you're sitting in? Make an offer. It's all for sale.

Classic Facets
942 Pearl St., Boulder • (303) 938-8851

This unique little shop specializes in rare antiques — diamonds and colored stones, period jewelery from 1700s to 1950s and vintage designer costume jewelery. Your stuff better be good — consigners from 30 states and nine countries send items to the exclusive shop; 90 percent of the offerings are rejected.

Eighth & Pearl Antiques
740 Pearl St., Boulder • (303) 444-0699

This West Pearl store is actually a consortium of individual dealers, kind of an antiques mini-mall rambling through two commercial buildings. Beautiful old stained-glass windows, lots of furniture and small household objects abound.

Sage Gallery
5360 Arapahoe Ave., Boulder
• (303) 449-6799

Dorothy Sage ran the shop on West Pearl before deciding to offer only the finest-quality antiques at this east Boulder strip mall. Ster-

ling, crystal, porcelain, fine Victoriana and Oriental antiques are among her specialties.

Off Her Rocker Antiques
4 E. First St., Nederland
• (303) 258-7976

This is a funky corner shop that feels like a rustic mountain museum. Old wash basins, oak furniture and nifty used clothes go for bargain prices. On nice days, old rockers bedeck the boardwalk out front, rocking gently in the mountain breeze. The shop is known by watch collectors for its interesting array of old pocket watches in working condition. Local artisans supply such whimsical items to the shop as tinkling wind chimes made from flattened antique spoons and forks.

Paul's Antiques
923 Main St., Longmont
• (303) 776-1866
Days Gone By Antiques
251 Main St., Longmont
• (303) 651-1912
Main Street Antique Mall
370 Main St., Longmont
• (303) 776-8511
Pacific Auction
1270 Boston Ave., Longmont
• (303) 772-7676

Several antique and secondhand stores are strung along Longmont's Main Street. If you're not claustrophobic and don't mind dust, you could spend an afternoon hunting for golden goodies at Paul's, where antiques and junk fill four adjoining buildings with dust and treasures. Days Gone By has a charming collection of toy dishes, linens and old holiday decorations. Pacific Auction specializes in estate sales.

Niwot Antiques
136 2nd Ave., Niwot • (303) 652-2587
Niwot Trading Post
140 2nd Ave., Niwot • (303) 443-0184
Wise Buys Antiques
190 2nd Ave., Niwot • (303) 652-2888
Elysian Fields
7915 Niwot Rd., Niwot • (303) 652-1631

Northeast of Boulder, Niwot has several wonderful antique stores all within a short stroll of each other. Niwot Antiques is the town's giant. This is a cooperative of more than 40 dealers, many with particular specialties that appeal to collectors. One dealer's booth is a riot of brightly colored Fiestaware, another glistens with Depression glass, still another has a good assortment of oak furniture and so on. The Trading Post specializes in estate jewelry and Wise Buys offers fireplace mantels, millwork doors and large pieces of furniture.

Lyons Antique Center
4559 Ute Hwy., Lyons • (303) 545-2266
Left-Hand Trading Company
401 and 405 Main St., Lyons
• (303) 823-6311
and 228 E. Main St., Lyons
• (303) 823-5738
Ralston Brothers Antiques
426 High St., Lyons • (303) 823-6982

Located north of Boulder, Lyons is worth the special trip whether you're in the market for something specific or just browsing. Lyons Antique Center is a barn-like place with a little bit of everything, including furniture, china, glassware, pottery, jewelry and memorabilia, handled by about a dozen dealers. Left-Hand carries antiques with a Western flair, including Indian artifacts. Ralston, in a historic stone building, specializes in vintage radios, phonographs, light fixtures, toys and restored furniture.

Lafayette Flea Market
130 E. Spaulding St., Lafayette
• (303) 665-0433
Lafayette Antiques
611 S. Public Rd., Lafayette
• (303) 665-2212

Good Housekeeping calls Lafayette Flea Market one of the nation's best flea markets. Its 500,000 items include clothes, glassware, pots and pans, dishes and antiques. It's open all year, in a clean, well-organized store with friendly salesclerks.

Art Galleries

Art Affaire
820 Main St., Louisville
• (303) 665-2074

Originals and limited edition prints by artist Tom Kinkade and others is available here. A computerized print-finding service helps buyers track down the piece they've been looking for.

Artcycle
2019 15th St., Boulder • (303) 449-4950

Just north of the Pearl Street Mall, this gallery is such a good idea that's it's gratifying to put it near the top of our listings — alphabetical order being a lucky coincidence. The store is a fine-art consignment shop, where you'll find an ever-changing selection of paintings and quality graphic arts, already framed. It's a great way to change your own style if you're redecorating because you know that someone else will buy and love a painting that's been an old friend of yours. Artcycle is open seven days a week.

Art Source International
1237 Pearl St., Boulder • (303) 444-4080

This store specializes in antique maps and prints, books and vintage Colorado photographs. Many are already framed, some are ready for your choice of frame — all are fascinating. In addition to a great selection of 18th- and 19th-century maps, the gallery displays prints from the same era. Check out the public art just out front – a chess table and two chairs commemorating a Mall frequenter who didn't live to enjoy his dream of playing chess with his grandson on the Mall.

Art Mart
1222 Pearl St., Boulder • (303) 443-8248

This is kind of a crafts supermarket, which bills itself as an "artist outlet store." It overflows with Southwestern objects, including jewelry, pottery, weavings, dream catchers and all manner of other popular items. The large store carries clothing, candles, wood inlays and myriad other crafts. In addition, the outlet has an outlet of its own, Art Mart's Rocky Mountain Factory Outlet, at I-25 and U.S. Highway 34 outside of Loveland.

Artist's Proof NA
5360 Arapahoe Ave., Boulder
• (303) 447-3504

This shop couples fine custom framing, hand-carved matting and dry mounting with

It's xeriscape (ZER-rih-scape), not zero-scape.

It's xeriscape. Not zero-scape. It's beautiful plants that thrive in our dry, windy climate. It's not rocked-over yards or lawns addicted to herbicides, pesticides and fertilizers. Boulder is a center for xeriscaping. At least a half-dozen books have been published by Boulder-area experts on water-wise gardening. And why not? Water use is critical in a climate that gets less than 17 inches of rain a year. What's more, after wandering Boulder's beautiful open space trails, many gardeners grow a liking for this natural style. By comparison, the traditional green lawn is, well, boring.

Close-up

Great garden stores, filled with bedding plants, perennials and ornamentals include Lafayette Florists; The Flower Bin in Longmont; Sturtz and Copeland; and Fruehauf's. McGuckin Hardware has been voted by readers of Boulder's *Daily Camera* as the best place for garden supplies. It's also a good spot for finding plants if you like the flowers you see around the Village shopping center. (For more on marvelous McGuckin's, read this chapter's "Gadgets" section.) Boulder County has its own plant kingdoms. Most are on the way to Longmont, including the GreenSpot Nursery; The Tree Farm; and TreeHouse Nursery. Mikl and Linda Brawner's Harlequin's Market is little but unique, down to the beautiful display of native and/or xeriscape plants in the Brawners' front yard next door. Wander their display garden and point to whatever gorgeous, thriving plant you like. Then ask Mikl or Linda to guide you to the potted version of the plant — small and inexpensive. For more plant stores, check the Yellow Pages under "Nurseries."

— continued on next page

Photo: Daily Camera

Xeriscaping is a popular alternative to traditional landscaping
in environment-conscious Boulder.

If you're shopping for garden space, consider this: 480-square-foot garden plots are available behind the North Boulder Recreation Center. The fee is $45, including water. (Gardeners must provide their own hoses.) Call (303) 441-3400. Or how about a free tree? If you move into a Boulder home with a bare front yard, you can apply to have the city plant a city-owned tree close to the street for you. For information, contact Boulder's forestry division at (303) 441-4406.

Now, about those garden books. Here are gems about Boulder area plants and gardens. *Pieces of Light* by Susan Tweit; *The Xeriscape Flower Gardener: A Waterwise Guide for the Rocky Mountain Region* by Jim Knopf; *Gardening in the Mountain West* by *Daily Camera* columnist Barbara Hyde; *Grow Native: Landscaping With Native and Apt Plants of the Rocky Mountains* by Sam Huddleston and Michael Hussey; *The Shortgrass Prairie* by Ruth Carol Cushman and Stephen R. Jones; *Personal Landscapes* by Jerome Malitz; and *The Undaunted Garden* by Lauren Springer.

unusual art dealership. It specializes in interesting sports memorabilia (especially baseball) and original signed black-and-white photographs and other graphic media.

Boulder Arts & Crafts Cooperative
1421 Pearl St., Boulder
• (303) 443-3683

This is the biggest and most diverse of the city's several crafts co-ops. It shows works of more than 150 artists from Colorado and surrounding mountain states displaying high-quality crafts in all media. Pottery, puppets, jewelry, photographs, weavings, stained glass, woodwork, hand-weaving and other items make great gifts or home decor. The co-op will also ship purchases anywhere in the continental United States. The co-op's best sale is generally in early October.

Busch Gallery
1426 Pearl St., Boulder • (303) 473-9215

Busch Gallery has two floors of contemporary paintings, ceramics, raku, sculpture, bronzes and fine jewelry with space available for community services. Recent shows have included oil paintings by Jim Rabby, jewelry

by Elisa Browsh and watercolors by Monika Pate. Recent collections featured African-American art, custom ceramic art tiles, and hand-blown glass art and decorations from Germany. The Busch Gallery is open daily.

Crystal Galleries Ltd.
1302 Pearl St., Boulder • (303) 444-2277

Museum-quality fossils and shells, rare mineral specimens and exquisite glasswork by René Lalique are found in this gallery. The shop is open limited hours or you can call for an appointment.

Deck the Walls
Crossroads Mall, Boulder
• (303) 443-5795

In addition to custom framing, this shop offers open and limited edition prints and distributes Greenwich Workshop art.

Limited Edition, Inc.
240 2nd Ave., Niwot • (303) 652-2055

Wildlife, Western and maritime limited edition prints are the specialty of this shop in downtown Niwot. The prices make it well worth the drive.

INSIDERS' TIP

The Hop buses run between three of the area's biggest shopping centers — Pearl Street Mall, University Hill and Crossroads Mall. It costs only 75¢, and it comes by every 10 minutes or less. What a speedy, convenient way to explore Boulder's stores. And when you use the Hop, you're helping the environment!

Boulder's Pearl Street Mall is lined with historic buildings.

Mackin-Katz Gallery of Fine Arts
2041 Broadway, Boulder
• (303) 786-7887

This gallery presents several artists but showcases Andy Katz's fine photography, including subjects such as the California wine country, Poland, Israel and Vietnam. Andy started showing locally in a basement gallery of his own under Pour La France and behind a billiards parlor, but this new daylight-filled space is much more conducive to viewing his detailed and delicate works.

MacLaren Markowitz Gallery
1011 Pearl St., Boulder • (303) 449-6807

This is a bright, beguiling gallery showing painting, sculpture, jewelry and imports. Perhaps their best-known artist is Doug West, whose acrylics and serigraphs of Western landscapes have become extremely popular. The gallery sometimes puts on Collectors Evenings, including an opportunity to meet personally with artists. Poster signings, art talks and other special events are occasionally on the agenda too.

Mary Williams Fine Arts
2116 Pearl St., Boulder
• (303) 938-1588

This gallery shows old and new American works, including some with strong Western and Native American orientation. Fine prints and graphics on such themes as botanicals, natural history and architecture from the 17th through 20th centuries abound. If you want a John James Audubon, a Currier & Ives or an Edward S. Curtis on your walls, here's where you'll find one.

Marisol Imports
915 Pearl St., Boulder • (303) 442-3142

West of the Pearl Street Mall, Marisol offers a stunning display of Zapotec and other Mexican rugs, plus Southwestern furniture, Navajo rugs and crafts. The beautiful but expensive rugs become more affordable at Marisol's annual after-Christmas sale. Pottery, woodcarvings and wrought iron are also stocked.

The Middle Fish
1500 Pearl St., Boulder • (303) 443-0835

This gallery honors the childhood nickname of store owner Malinda Fishman. Located next to the Harvest Restaurant, The Middle Fish sells handcrafted items, including ceramic indoor fountains, garden art, handmade dolls, furniture, lighting, jewelry and Judaica. Contemporary rather than classical pieces dominate.

Mustard Seed Gallery
2660 Canyon Blvd., Boulder
• (303) 447-8626

Mustard Seed is one of Boulder's oldest galleries, with a new location at the Marriott Hotel in the Village Shopping Center. The shop showcases contemporary and traditional paintings, jewelry, sculpture, pottery, prints and photography.

Ruth Linton & David Haslam Gallery
1217 Spruce St., Boulder
• (303) 444-9116

Oils, pastels and watercolors featuring such artists as Beatrice Bulteau, Sandra Bierman, Ann Herzog Wright,William Napier and Yan Zhou Xu are shown here.

Smith-Klein Gallery/ Santa Fe Ambiance
1116 Pearl St., Boulder • (303) 444-7200

This gallery houses contemporary art including jewelry, hand-blown glass and folk art animals, by both local and regional artists. A recent show featured a collection of hand-carved Zuni horse fetishes dating to the early 1900s.

Von Eschen Gallery & Frame Shop/ Wing's Gallery
2660 Canyon Blvd., Boulder
• (303) 448-1237/(303) 443-9989

Original art, an eclectic one-of-a-kind jewelery by local artists and limited edition prints from Greenwich Workshop, Mill Pond Press and others are available at these two-in-one shops. Also offered: custom framing, Southwestern pottery by regional artists and decoys and other wood sculpture.

Arts and Crafts Supplies

Art Hardware
1135 Broadway, Boulder
• (303) 444-3063

This is Boulder's top professional (and amateur) artists' supply center, with a full line of art and drafting supplies. The shop also does blue printing, large-format copying for architects and engineers and custom fram-

ing. The store boasts free covered parking for customers, a real rarity on The Hill. It is closed on Sundays.

Promenade's Le Bead Shop
1970 13th St., Boulder • (303) 440-4807

Just off the Pearl Street Mall, this is a small shop with a huge selection of baubles, bangles and bright shiny beads. Glass beads in a stunning variety of hues and sizes, antique beads, African trade beads, sequins, rhinestones, sew-ons, studs, jeweler's string, ear wires, posts, clasps and all the other makings of unique, do-it-yourself jewelry are crammed into Boulder's best beadery. The shop also offers jewelry appraisal by a certified gemologist, and professional pearl stringing.

The Dove's Eye
2425 Canyon Blvd., Boulder
• (303) 443-6031

This is a needleworker's paradise, selling fabrics, yarns, needles and stitching accessories. Custom stitching, classes and unique gifts complete the picture in this special business.

Michael's Arts and Crafts
4800 Baseline Rd., Boulder
• (303) 494-2008

Michael's is a bustling warehouse store packed with craft items, from dried and plastic flowers to the right kind of muslin and paint sets for creating doll faces. Beads, Styrofoam, jewelry findings and all sorts of kits appeal to crafters of all ages and skills. It's a big, reasonably priced place where kids and adults like to wander and take classes. There's a framing shop in the back.

Needlepoint of View Gallery, Ltd.
361 2nd Ave., Niwot • (303) 652-2177

Area needleworkers say its worth the drive to find this small shop, which offers custom designs, patterns by nationally known designers and finishing for a prized piece.

Shuttles, Spindles and Skeins
633 S. Broadway, Boulder
• (303) 494-1071

This store is for anyone who loves a good yarn. The walls and walls of yarn come in a fantastic array of colors for knitting and weaving, and you can find a few handmade items for sale that are masterpieces. Uncarded wool, silk, flax and camel hair are all perfect for making doll hair as well as for spinning. This small, charming store has a cozy atmosphere that just says "welcome." The staff is very knowledgeable, and the shop has a wall of craft books for inspiration and classes to show you how to put the inspiration into action.

Bakeries

Many of our better groceries stock locally produced breads, or you can go straight to the bakeries so you can swim through bread aromas as soon as you open the door. Most have some sort of frequent-buyer program, giving you a free loaf after a dozen or so purchases.

A Taste of Heaven
1918 Pearl St., Boulder • (303) 448-1047

Elegant desserts, breakfast pastries and spectacular wedding cakes are the specialties of this bakery on the east end of downtown Boulder. Lunch includes a variety of sandwiches named for local hot spots and salads that are popular with area businesses and meetings.

Belgian Bakery
3267 28th St., Boulder • (303) 449-7240

You might recognize the owners of this bakery in Tebo Plaza by their European mini car with the (faux) loaf of bread extending from the back. What they're best known for, though, is the sinfully creamy, rich desserts they have brought from their native Belgium.

Brillig Works Bakery
637-G South Broadway in the Table Mesa Shopping Center, • (303) 499-5253

The aroma of fresh-baked muffins, scones, cinnamon rolls and coffee greet shoppers who stop in here. At lunch time Brillig Works offers homemade soups, sandwiches and stews.

Breadworks
2644 Broadway, Boulder
• (303) 444-5667

This shop bakes traditional rustic breads in round loaves and baguettes on a rotating weekly schedule. Focaccia, brownies, cookies, muffins and scones also come out of the huge brick and tile oven. Monday is half-price day for breads left over from the weekend. Breadworks unlocks the door at 7 AM daily.

Great Harvest Bread Company
2525 Arapahoe Ave., Boulder
• (303) 442-3062

This is part of a tightly controlled franchise operation that makes rich, chewy, healthy-feeling breads and rolls. While other bakeries just put out sample bites, if anything, Great Harvest cuts whole slabs and invites you to slather your "taste" with butter.

Le Français
2570 Baseline Rd. in the Base-Mar Shopping Center, Boulder
• (303) 499-7429

This traditional bakery offers almost real French baguettes (French friends say "real" requires French air wafting through the brick ovens), plus decadent French pastries — both savory and sweet. In addition to take-out baked goods, you can eat in at breakfast, lunch or dinner. Le Français, which is owned by a French baker and comes by its authenticity by right, makes the most gorgeous special-occasion cakes. You might want to get married just to have an excuse to order a wedding cake from this wonderful bakery.

Karen's Country Kitchen
700 Main St., Louisville
• (303) 666-8020

Karen's is well known in the county for its prize-winning pies, European-style Danish, wedding cakes and countless desserts, all baked fresh daily on the premises. It's worth the trip to Louisville.

The Lick Skillet Bakery
5340 Arapahoe Ave., Boulder
• (303) 449-7775

It might look like it's part of the neighboring gas station, but folks who live or work in eastern Boulder know that the Lick Skillet is the place to stop for coffee and pastries in the morning. The small shop is popular for raspberry-mousse cake, stuffed focaccia bread and wheat-free fruit muffins.

Bookstores

Not surprisingly, these are among our favorite spots around Boulder. And because we're a college town, there's no shortage of places for bibliophiles to feed their page-turning fever.

Acoma Books
2488 Baseline Rd. in the Base-Mar Shopping Center, Boulder • (303) 494-3309

For 25 years, Acoma has been buying and selling used scholarly, scientific and technical books. Students and professors aren't the only customers, but the shop is conveniently located across the street from the University of Colorado.

Aion Bookshop
1235 Pennsylvania Ave., Boulder • (303) 443-5763

This is a used bookstore with a real antiquarian feeling. The shop rambles through a series of small rooms, which are filled, but not crammed, with a fascinating selection of previously owned and previously loved books. The street level features hardbacks, including many of a serious and scholarly nature, as you might expect from a store on University Hill. Downstairs are more popular books, including paperbacks, sci-fi, mysteries, cookbooks, self-help, sports and such. The selection of science, arts, humanities and great literature is impressive, as is the knowledge of the folks working there.

Barnes & Noble
2915 Pearl St., Boulder • (303) 444-2501

This may be a big chain store, but it's working to offer a more personal touch that's gaining local respect. The store specializes in popular fiction and nonfiction but has a large sampling of more obscure works too. People linger in the in-store coffee shop, and the store is the site of regular meetings of locals interested in both the creative and reading aspects of literature.

Beat Book Shop
1713 Pearl St., Boulder • (303) 444-7111

If you want to turn the calendar back a few decades, check out this quirky store, which specializes in literature, poetry, biography, film, sociology and subculture, with a distinct retro flair. It offers a commendable selection of first editions. The shop also stocks rare records and tapes, some fine art and used CDs.

The Boulder Bookstore
1107 Pearl St., Boulder • (303) 447-2074

This is Boulder's local showpiece, operating since 1993 in the historic Buckingham Building. Bookstore owner David Bolduc and architect Dennis Bloemker received the 1993 award of merit from Historic Boulder for "historic preservation and restoration of the second-floor ballroom." The lovely high-ceilinged room with its antique stained-glass windows is the stage for visiting authors. They have included such famous writers as Barbara Kingsolver, Thomas Moore, William Styron, Amy Tan, Gary Hart, Roger Ebert, Peter Matthiessen, Whitley Strieber, Douglas Coupland and Isabel Allende. The 20,000-square-foot, three-story bookstore offers more than 100,000 titles and also has a large selection of magazines, journals and various book-related items, plus art displays by local artists. The store recently began stocking a small selection of used books, with proceeds going to local charities.

The adjacent, but separately owned, Bookend Cafe, is connected by an open door and makes a nice stop after browsing through the books.

The Colorado Bookstore
1111 Broadway, Boulder • (303) 442-5051

Located next to the big outdoor clock and the pedestrian underpass, this is a classic college bookstore. It sells new textbooks and plenty of used books (they buy and sell) and has a mezzanine devoted to general books. You also can buy CU-Boulder sweatshirts, souvenirs and school supplies. There's a small post office substation, copiers, fax machines, prepaid phone cards, photo processing and other services.

Ead's News & Smoke Shop
1715 28th St., Boulder • (303) 442-5900

Also under an outdoor clock, this is actually a mega-newsstand, with Boulder's best selection of magazines and out-of-town newspapers. It also carries an assortment of travel books, popular paperbacks and adult-only books and magazines and sells cigarettes, cigars and pipe tobacco (but don't light up until you're outside).

Great Horned Owl Children's Bookstore
1075 S. Boulder Rd., Louisville
• **(303) 665-6888**

Books and gifts for little readers, infant to young adult, are found in this Christopher Plaza shop. There's a daily story hour for kids and resources for parents and teachers. Popular Madame Alexander dolls are also on sale here.

Lefthand Book Collective, Inc.
1825 Pearl St., 2nd floor, Boulder
• **(303) 443-8252**

This is Boulder's resource for progressive books on feminism, national and environmental causes, political thought, gay and lesbian studies, Marxism and National Liberation. Periodicals cover political, economic, ecological and third world issues. They also carry gifts, greeting cards, magazines and T-shirts.

Lighthouse Bookstore
1201 Pearl St., Boulder
• **(303) 939-8355**

Below street level on the Pearl Street Mall, this store carries Boulder's largest selection of New Age books dealing with spirituality, self-help, religions from around the world and exploring the inner self. It's well-stocked, and with light filtering in from the streetside windows and the calming music, aroma of in-

cense and music from the store's selection of New Age and traditional music, the atmosphere is conducive to browsing. The staff is especially helpful here too.

Logos of Boulder
2525 Arapahoe Ave., Boulder
• **(303) 449-1919**

This is Boulder's bookstore for historical and contemporary Christian thought. Catering to both Protestant and Catholic readers, the store carries a large and varied selection of Bibles, plus cards, gifts, tapes and CDs.

The Printed Page/Page Two
1219 Pearl St., Boulder
• **(303) 443-8450**
6565 Gunpark Drive, Boulder
• **(303) 530-3339**

The Pearl Street store carries stationery and gifts with a small selection of books, mostly local interest and children's books. Their Christmas and Hanukkah card selection is one of the best in the city. The Gunbarrel store not only carries a similar inventory but houses a pleasant cafe as well.

Red Letter Second Hand Books
1737 Pearl St., Boulder
• **(303) 938-1778**

This store is jammed and crammed with a selection of used books, including classics, travel, biography and all sorts of fiction. It offers classics as well as modern works for buying, selling, trading or simply browsing.

Rue Morgue Mystery Bookshop
946 Pearl St., Boulder • **(303) 443-8346**
This is a mystery lover's paradise for both

INSIDERS' TIP

The best parking for the downtown area is in the structures located at 14th and Walnut, 11th and Spruce, and 11th and Walnut streets. When you're parked in any of these, ask for validation stickers as you pay at downtown stores. Every sticker is good for a half-hour of parking, so you can shop your way to reduced or free parking. Two new parking structures opened in late 1999. A city-owned structure with wrap-around retail opened at 15th and Pearl east of the Pearl Street Mall, and a private structure opened one block north at 15th and Spruce streets.

new and rare used mysteries. This is the oldest — and one of the three biggest — mystery bookstores in the nation. Sisters in Crime, a group of women mystery writers, meets here, and author book-signings are frequent.

Stage House Books and Prints/ Stage House on Broadway
1039 Pearl St., Boulder • (303) 447-1433
2628 Broadway, Boulder
• (303) 545-2330

Sadly, the Pearl Street store is closing out its collection of 100,000 used and rare items, including a huge selection of paperbacks and hardcovers. Stage House will shift focus to carve a niche for itself in Boulder's gallery scene, specializing in graphic art, exotic jewelry, African sculptures, original paintings, posters and an extensive collection of Edward S. Curtis and W.H. Jackson photographs. The new store in Community Plaza has fewer books, but that makes it easier to view the artwork.

Table Mesa Gifts & Books
645 S. Broadway, Boulder
• (303) 499-1269

Table Mesa is a traditional bookstore serving south Boulder, with best sellers, regional books, children's selections and gift books. They gladly help with special orders and carry greeting cards and gift items.

Time Warp Science Fiction and Comics
1631 28th St., Boulder • (303) 443-4500

This is a word-of-mouth favorite among kids and has been nominated as one of the nation's best comic stores. Regionally, it has garnered Best of Boulder and Best of Denver awards from the *Daily Camera* and *Westword*. Time Warp is known for both mainstream and underground comics. If you're a grownup with a secret love of comics, just say you're looking for something for your nephew or niece.

Trident Booksellers & Cafe
940 Pearl St., Boulder • (303) 443-3133

Trident is regularly voted the "Best of Boulder" coffee shop by *Daily Camera* readers. It looks and feels quite European, in the best and most traditional sense, with interesting-looking people huddled over tables, apparently engaged in the most existential of conversations. The adjacent bookstore has a potpourri of used books, new remainders, cards and calendars. The sale table just inside the front door always displays interesting books on history, gardening, cooking, travel, spiritual topics and more.

Troubadour Bookstore
1638 Pearl St., Boulder • (303) 444-0166

A newcomer to Boulder's book scene, Troubadour offers books to the creative souls among us. In addition to books, Troubadour stocks gifts and resources relating to music, dance, theater and writing.

Waldenbooks/Waldenkids
1600 28th St., Crossroads Mall, Boulder
• (303) 442-8557

The Walden chain combined its two stores at the Crossroads Mall a few years ago but kept its huge selection for children. If you're familiar with the chain, you'll recognize this as a traditional store with both hardbacks and paperbacks plus a good selection of magazines. It's a great place to browse while others shop elsewhere.

Word Is Out Women's Bookstore
1731 15th St., Boulder • (303) 449-1415

This section of 15th Street has always had

a collection of eclectic stores, so it's only appropriate a bookstore would eventually locate here. New in 1997, Word Is Out carries a large selection of books on lesbian and gay issues, women's studies, self-development, poetry and criticism. There are also mystery and detective books, gifts, greeting cards, tapes and CDs.

Clothing and Accessories

For Children

Applause
1123 Pearl St. Boulder • (303) 442-7426
This Pearl Street Mall store offers outrageously stylish clothes, endearing baby and toddler duds and enchanting ballerina and princess get-ups for little girls who like to dress up. It's pricey, but if you're looking for something unique, Applause may have it.

Childish Things
2081 30th St., Boulder • (303) 442-2703
Recycled clothing, toys, equipment and nursery furniture for infants, children and maternity fill this friendly consignment shop. It's great for your oldest, who doesn't get the benefit of hand-me-downs.

Feet First
2525 Arapahoe Ave., Boulder
• (303) 939-9618
Feet First has a huge selection of children's shoes in a mind-boggling array of sizes, from "baby's first" to almost-adult. This store claims to be Colorado's largest Stride Rite dealer, and it also carries such name brands as Nike, Keds, Reebok, LA Gear and Skechers.

Gap Kids
2043 Broadway, Boulder
• (303) 473-9891
This chain store just off the Pearl Street Mall is hard to resist, with its constantly changing, colorful window displays. Just like the regular Gap, this store stocks high-fashion clothes with famous names for newborns through preteens. They offer great sales if you happen to wander in on the right day.

Little Mountain Outdoor Gear for Kids
1136 Spruce St., Boulder
• (303) 443-1757
Just around the corner from Gap Kids, this store claims to be the only local outlet specializing exclusively in outdoor clothing gear and accessories for kids. If you're a visitor, Little Mountain offers daily rentals on backpacks and baby joggers.

Pockets Children's and Maternity Consignment
3103 28th St., Boulder • (303) 444-3554
In addition to clothing for infants and children, this store sells used maternity clothes, toys, baby equipment, nursery furniture, car seats, strollers and swings.

Pour Moi?
2525 Arapahoe Ave. in the Village, Boulder • (303) 442-1723
Girls and women will find a wide assortment of clothing here, from reasonably priced casual items to expensive holiday dresses. They start with clothing for 7-year-olds and continue through teens to women's sizes. Lots of unusual accessories and jewelry are also available.

Rocky Mountain Kids
1136 Spruce St., Boulder
• (303) 447-2267
As you might expect from the name, this store sells fleece and other outdoorsy performance clothing but also carries pajamas, holiday outfits and school clothes. There are sizes for infants through about the age of 8, plus backpacks, baby joggers and carriers for sale or rent.

Zippety Doo-Da
2425 Canyon Blvd., Boulder
• (303) 449-2522
"Hot clothes for cool kids" is how this store advertises itself. Recently expanded, this kidswear store has more than a hundred lines of infant and children's clothing including Hartstrings, Guess, Columbia, Flapdoodles and Sweet Potatoes.

For Adults

The closest description we've heard of the "Boulder look" is "always ready for a hike." You could wear out the bottoms of your Vibram-sole boots trekking between all the Boulder stores that have great outdoor gear. See our "Sporting Goods Shops" section later in this chapter for more information.

Alpaca Connection
1326 Pearl St., Boulder • (303) 447-2047

Natural fiber clothing from around the world, including a large selection of hand-knitted wool sweaters from South America, is sold in this former movie theater on the Downtown Mall.

Ann Taylor
2070 Broadway, Boulder
• (303) 449-3971

This is one of Boulder's best centers for women's career clothing, with a good sense of what's casual but elegant, from the blouse to the pumps. Great sale racks are filled with a variety of items year-round.

Applause
1123 Pearl St., Boulder • (303) 442-7426

Applause is in a class by itself, with cutting-edge sportswear and dresses. Applause sometimes sells fabulous suits, other times fabulous pants and shirts. This ahead-of-the-crowd store went through the pleated cowgirl skirt craze years ago. The constant themes are high-quality, moderate-to-expensive clothes to die for, eye-catching shoes and jewelry and sensational kids' clothes that are almost too adorable to get dirty.

Banana Republic Women/Men
1147 Pearl St., Boulder • (303) 442-8250
1142 Pearl St., Boulder • (303) 786-8616

These stores across the street from each other have changed to meet the workplace needs of younger customers, but still sell durable shorts, skirts, pants, blouses and other gear you can wear outdoors and to work, depending on how neatly you tuck things in.

Boulder Bodywear
Crossroads Mall • (303) 447-9100

Clothes cut for comfort but suitable for uptown are found in this shop, whose theme is Unique Street Fashions. Desperately searching for leotard, a body-skimming sheath or a bathing suit in the middle of winter? Here's your source.

Bride's Gallery
4740 Table Mesa Dr., Boulder
• (303) 499-6052

For fancy affairs, this store has tuxes and formal gowns to buy or rent. There are both traditional and contemporary gowns, plus shoes, bras, slips, jewelry and invitations — everything the special bride needs for her special day.

Christina's Lingerie
2425 Canyon Blvd., Boulder
• (303) 443-2421

When you want to fling it all to passion, consider Chistina's, which offers exquisite lingerie and also well-fitting swimsuits, plus a staff that is truly helpful at telling you which styles flatter your figure.

College Corner
1310 College Ave., Boulder
• (303) 786-8243

This store is on the Hill, with CU-Boulder sweatshirts, T-shirts, hats and other memorabilia. Champion reverse-weave sweatshirts and CU-Boulder baseball caps are especially popular; the hats come in a dozen sizes ranging from kids to huge.

C.P. Shades
2098 Broadway, Boulder
• (303) 440-3831

If you want clothing that won't wrinkle — some say it's pre-wrinkled — and that packs like a dream, C.P. Shades is the place to go. The annual New Year's sale is worth waiting for — many garments get marked down to $19.98 from prices exponentially higher.

Fresh Produce Sportswear
1136 Pearl St., Boulder • (303) 444-7573

Located on the Pearl Street Mall, the clothing here is locally manufactured and mostly easy-to-wear knits. People call their neighbors and line up early for biannual sales in April and September.

Get Fleeced
2015 Broadway, Boulder
• (303) 442-6050

Nothing is as beckoning on a chilly Colorado winter day as a fleece jacket or vest. The material breathes well, wicks perspiration away from your body, making it good for active-outdoors types, and provides plenty of warmth for the weight. Here's a colorful collection.

Gioia
1215 Pearl St., Boulder • (303) 440-3979

Sure, you can find seductive stuff in this store for your feminine side, but also flannel

Niwot, northeast of Boulder, is known for its wealth of antique stores.

Photo: Daily Camera/ David P. Gilkey

nightgowns with little roses on them, proper enough for your great-grand-aunt. They have a fine line of hard to find domestics and facial products.

J.J. Wells
2460 Canyon Blvd., Boulder
• **(303) 449-2112**

In a new cluster of shops next to McGuckin's Hardware, J.J. Wells carries a classic collection of women's clothing — classy pants, earth-toned sweaters and dresses that make the transition from office to evening outing. There are accessories, from leather bags to belts to jewelry.

Jacque Michelle Apparel and Home Decor
1118 13th St., Boulder
• **(303) 442-8602**
2670 Broadway, Boulder
• **(303) 786-7628**

This might be called a little "everything shop," selling items from T-shirts to locally made hats, cards and arty things. The new store on Broadway features beautiful seasonal items, many reasonably priced. They will gift-wrap too.

Jila Designs
2041 Broadway, Boulder
• **(303) 442-0130**

Jila's sells original-design women's clothing, in gorgeous silks and rayons. Another Boulder original, Jila is now offering clothes in some national department stores, such as Nordstrom's.

Kinsley & Co.
1155 13th St., Boulder • (303) 442-7260

On The Hill for nearly fifty years, this is Boulder's prime men's clothier (it also carries women's fashions for business, evening and casual). Currently, Kinsley carries Armani and Hugo Boss suits and locally made Carrot & Gibbs bow ties and Ferrell Reed regular neckties, items that unfortunately aren't available directly from the factories.

Knit Wit
2021 Broadway, Boulder
• **(303) 444-6776**

Knit Wit is a cute little store just off the Pearl Street Mall that offers elegant New York and L.A. styles. You can find both casual and dressy clothes and lots of matching accessories.

Plenty
2019 10th St., Boulder • (303) 440-7433

Plenty calls itself "a shop for the heart, home and closet." The two-year-old store just off the Pearl Street Mall carries unique women's clothing, plus a little bit of everything else including jewelry, linens, gifts and handbags..

The Pipefitter
1352 College Ave., Boulder
• **(303) 442-4200**

A throwback to the '60s updated for the '90s, the Pipefitter carries pipes and smoking accessories, ethnic clothing (Pipefitter is the largest seller of reed sandals in the state) and T-shirts, jewelery, candles and incense, posters and cards.

The Regiment Shops
2425 Canyon Blvd., Boulder
• **(303) 443-2713**

Traditional, yet updated, tailored business clothes such as Perry Ellis for men and blazer/skirt combinations for women draw Boulder

---

INSIDERS' TIP

You'll find frazzled and deadline-driven Boulderites at two 24-hour Kinko's copy and computer centers, including a huge new superstore at 28th and Pearl streets. Other useful services are franchises of Mail Boxes Etc., The Mail Station and Pak Mail, which handle packing, shipping and other chores that normally take a couple of stops. And, as a bonus, there rarely are lines. Federal Express has a drop-off at Walnut and 14th streets, while UPS is off East Pearl Street.

professionals to this shop in the up-scale strip mall called Water Street.

Starr's Clothing and Shoe Co. / Starr's — For Her
1712 Pearl St., Boulder
• **(303) 442-3056**
1726 Pearl St., Boulder
• **(303) 447-8740**

Starr's has reasonably priced, rather sporty attire for men, women and children with private parking adjacent. The women's shop next door has beautiful sweaters and a place for children to play while moms shop.

The Studio
2425 Canyon Blvd.,
Boulder • (303) 786-7827

The Studio is a Boulder-inspired idea where you come in, try on the mix-and-match sports and party clothes, then order your favorite in exactly the color and size you want.

Talbot's
2700 Arapahoe Ave., Boulder
• **(303) 449-1556**

Talbot's is back in Boulder, with a large new freestanding store in Arapahoe Village. Women who need professional clothes will find a large selection of suits and blouses with matching accessories.

Timbuktu Station
1035 Pearl St., Boulder • (303) 440-6288

Those whose lifestyle, or at least style, includes lots of traveling love this store, which features fun, casual and professional travel clothes. There's plenty of khaki and other attractive, wrinkle-free options to choose from.

Webb Weaving and Design
189 Spring Lane, Boulder
• **(303) 443-8556**

This out-of-the-way studio offers custom, hand-spun, hand-woven outerwear with painted silk linings. Some silk jackets and tops and pants and skirts to match the linings are also available. Jane Webb is the artist. Make sure you schedule an appointment before visiting so Webb can direct you to the shop about 20 minutes from downtown.

Weekends
1101 Pearl Street, Boulder
• **(303) 444-4231**

For the outdoorswoman or outdoorsman who wants to look very, very good in the wild (or at home in front of the fire), Weekends offers a collection of sturdy trousers, cuddly sweaters and soft-as-butter flannel shirts, all with irresistible style. In summer, there are shorts and T's and jackets for the changeable high-country weather.

Zapa Toes Shoes
2015 10th St., Boulder • (303) 544-6015

This store takes its name from the Spanish word "zapatos," meaning shoes. They carry designer brands that aren't commonly available in Boulder County, such as Fendi, Anne Klein, Donna Karan and Yves St. Laurent. This shop, with buyers in Italy and New York, is determined to make its 10th Street store as hip as any store on the Pearl Street Mall.

Consignment and Resale Shops

While there's plenty of good shopping to be done at our traditional retail outlets, some of the best bargains in Boulder show up on the shelves at these consignment and resale shops. They're the kind of places you want to check back with frequently, for you never know what will have just come in, and the best stuff never lasts long.

The Buffalo Exchange
1717 Walnut St., Boulder
• **(303) 938-1924**

This store specializes in current and retro vintage clothing. If you've got stuff to sell, this place has liberal policies. They buy during all business hours. And rather than taking items on consignment, they buy outright for 40 percent cash or 55 percent credit toward a store trade.

Candy's Vintage Clothing
4483 Broadway, Boulder
• **(303) 442-6186**

People trek far into North Boulder to spend

an hour at Candy's. The selection is large, and the variety astonishing. You might be lucky enough to find a nice Harris tweed jacket or Pendleton shirt. Candy has a huge selection of vintage evening wear, but be forewarned that she drives a hard bargain.

Clothes Encounters of the Second Kind
1622 Pearl St., Boulder • (303) 449-2232

The area east of the Mall has become a real mecca for vintage clothing enthusiasts. This store gets the prize for the best name for a consignment store. The shop specializes in men's and women's apparel from the '70s into the '90s, which may be retro but is certainly not vintage.

Counter Evolution
1628 Pearl St., Boulder • (303) 444-1799

Clothes Encounters spawned a second store nearby that now specializes in true vintage clothing. This shop carries clothing for both men and women mostly from the '20s through the '50s with shoes and accessories to match.

No Place Like Home
3550 Arapahoe Ave., Boulder
• (303) 440-9011

This is one of the cleanest used-furniture stores you'll ever see, with a nice selection of nearly new items. Those with a sharp eye can find some real bargains, but some of the furniture is surprisingly high-priced considering that it's secondhand. Turnover is rapid, so if you're on the lookout for something in particular, it's best to check fairly frequently. The best stuff borders on the antique; less-inspired offerings are simply used. The store also carries some tableware, framed pictures and other small objects. If you consign to them, they'll pick up. If you buy, they'll deliver.

The Ritz
959 Walnut St., Boulder • (303) 443-2850

Around the corner from the Pearl Street Mall, the Ritz inventories a fabulous selection of classic '40s fashions, flouncy prom gowns from the '50s, elegant cocktail attire from various decades and other unusual and vintage clothing. The store also sells and rents great costumes (Halloween and otherwise), including gorilla suits, creepy creatures from horror films and masks of current politicians' faces.

Twice Nice
1646 Pearl St., Boulder • (303) 443-9042

The longest-running resale emporium in this area, Twice Nice sells still-fashionable women's and children's clothing at very reasonable prices. The owner pays cash for quality clothing, jewelry, children's shoes and baby equipment.

Farmers Markets and Food Co-ops

It's not surprising that health-conscious Boulder boasts more than its share of alternatives to the pre-packed, heavily salted fare preferred by the rest of the country. Here are some of our favorite spots for fresh and organic food.

Boulder County Farmers Market
13th Street between Arapahoe Avenue and Canyon Boulevard • (303) 442-1837

As much of a happening and social event as a shopping opportunity, this market operates from 8 AM to 2 PM on Saturdays, and 10 AM to 2 PM on Wednesdays from spring through fall. There's a mouthwatering selection of organically grown vegetables and fruits, baked goods, herbs, bedding plants, fresh flowers, crafts and baked goods. What began as an overflow area on the east side of 13th Street has developed into an al fresco dining experience featuring the best of some of Boulder's best restaurants and bakeries. (See the Attractions chapter for more details.)

Louisville Farmer's Market
At the corner of Spruce and Main streets, Louisville • (303) 666-8747

Louisville's market has 15 to 20 vendors who sell mostly fruits, vegetables and flowers. It is open from 8 AM to noon on Saturdays and runs from late May through early September.

Mountain Peoples Co-op
30 E. First St., Nederland
• (303) 258-7500

This humble food store is a blast from the

past. It is a cooperative, and members pay slightly lower prices. The co-op harkens back to the old-time, small-town neighborhood grocery, but with a New Age twist. They carry a good selection of some of the tastiest organic and locally grown fruits and vegetables. There are also coffee beans, grains, good breads and other wholesome items — no junk food — and most necessities from toilet paper and cat food to Ben & Jerry's ice cream.

Longmont Farmer's Market
Northwest corner of Boulder County Fairgrounds, Hover Rd. and Boston Ave.

As Longmont is still surrounded by farm fields, it makes sense that a farmer's market prospers at the site of the county fairgrounds. Fruits and vegetables are eased out by pumpkins, bales of hay and gourds as the season progresses. It's open on Tuesdays from 3 to 6 PM and Saturdays from 8 AM to 1 PM.

Gadgets

The Better Back Store
3034 Walnut St., Boulder
• **(303) 442-3998**

This store is hardly a frivolity to those in discomfort or pain. The inventory is extensive: back-strengthening exercise equipment, ergonomic office furniture, home furniture such as Ekornes Stressless Chairs from Norway and Backsaver recliners, cervical pillows, Tempur Pedic pillows and mattresses, back cushions, lumbar belts and rolls, seat supports, massage equipment and creams, inversion units and boots, Backsaver snow shovels and other tools, and video and cassette tapes and purses designed to spread the load. All these gadgets aim to help you save your back or just to relax, feel good and even prevent back problems.

Changes in Latitude
2416 Arapahoe Ave., Boulder
• **(303) 786-8406**

This is a nifty shop with nearly everything a traveler could want. High-quality travel luggage and accessories and packs, water purifiers, security gadgets and a snazzy assortment of Ex Officio and Royal Robbins casual wear for men and women will set you off in safety and style. The shop also features a large assortment of books and maps. They'll do passport photos, and they have a travel agency. The online computer travel information center contains State Department reports and files on every country, which they'll print out for you if you need the latest information on necessary inoculations. The store puts on a series of interesting slide presentations, normally on Thursday evenings, which will inspire all but the most home-bound to hit the road, and there are occasional tourist language courses too.

McGuckin Hardware
2525 Arapahoe Ave., Boulder
• **(303) 443-1822**

The slogan here is, "If we don't have it, you don't need it." It's just about true. This gigantic hardware superstore carries a do-it-yourselfer's dream of hand- and power-tools and stuff to do with them. McGuckin's is everything but a lumber yard or plumbing supply house — you won't find plywood, 4-by-6s or miles of piping, but you will find wood trim, door and window hardware, lighting fixtures and accessories, electrical and plumbing supplies and the biggest selection of screws, nuts, bolts, clamps, washers, springs, gaskets and every other gizmo and widget you can imagine. The special-order desk can get items that aren't in stock. In addition, there are high-quality paint and housewares departments. One department makes keys and sells locks, another has video and audio tapes. Christmas decorations abound in winter, and patio furniture moves in with warm weather. Gardening tools and supplies, as well as seeds, annual and perennial plants herald summer. Pet supplies, mailboxes, gas-log fireplaces, fencing materials and more pack into this huge space. McGuckin's also sells sporting equipment, including fishing and hunting supplies, backpacks and camping equipment and some outdoor books.

The spring and fall tent sales are three-day extravaganzas that include closeout and special-purchase merchandise at tremendous savings, as well as a blanket 10 percent off everything in the store. What sets McGuckin's apart from every other hardware store around, especially the big-box chains, is personal service. A veritable army of green-vested salespeople awaits to help, advise, guide and point the way to the department you're looking for.

The Peppercorn
1235 Pearl St., Boulder • (303) 449-5847

This is the queen of Boulder's kitchen stores — and one of the very best in the country. They now have a mail-order catalog, but it's far more fun to personally visit this very pretty, full-to-bursting kitchen store with fine cookware, kitchen gadgets, table linens, a huge assortment of cookbooks and gourmet foods. Need a mushroom brush? A butter mold? A Madeleine pan? A replacement blade for your coffee mill? A spoon rest with a clever design? A set of Calphalon pots? A food processor in Mama Bear, Papa Bear or Baby Bear sizes? Peppercorn has them all — and oh-so-much more. Celebrity author-chefs sometimes do book signings and occasionally put on cooking demonstrations too. Fine china, porcelain, flatware and crystal from the world's best-known makers are what make The Peppercorn a popular spot for bridal registries.

The West End Gardener
805 W. Pearl St., Boulder
• (303) 938-0607

This is a delightful new shop selling top-quality gardening tools, books, fountains, garden signs, wreaths, annuals and bulbs in season, gifts and goodies for plant-lovers. It makes a putterer want to garden seriously, and a serious gardener strive to make the garden more perfect.

Gift and
Specialty-food Shops

The Asian Deli
2829 28th St., Boulder • (303) 541-9377

Need some dried bonito flakes, pickled daikon radishes, lemongrass or divine curries? This store has them all, plus Asian produce and freshly made Vietnamese spring rolls — cilantro and shrimp enclosed in a delicate rice wrapper.

The Cheese Importer's Warehouse
33 S. Pratt Pkwy., Longmont
• (303) 772-4444

The Warehouse is an importer for the Willow River Company and has bargains on wheels of foreign and domestic cheeses and bags of perfect, meltable dark chocolate, all set on industrial-strength shelving in a huge, refrigerated room. A small shop also carries other gourmet foods, coffee, tea and cookware.

Colorado Craft and Cake Supply
1750 30th St., Suite 12, Boulder
• (303) 447-1557

If you are ambitious and want to decorate your own cakes, you can get all the supplies you need here. They sell powdered meringue for frosting and incredible cake decorations.

Herb's Meats & Specialty Foods
2530 Baseline Rd., Boulder
• (303) 499-8166

A Boulder institution, this store is just what the name says. Herb's carries the freshest cuts of meat and a large variety of sauces. If you're particular, the perfect leg of lamb or pork roast can be found here.

International Food Bazaar
2839 28th St., Boulder • (303) 415-1725

Specializing in exotic ethnic foods, this small, convenient store carries everything from tea to spices to olive oil to couscous from the Mediterranean, the Middle East, India and Europe.

The Morocco International Food Market
2690 28th St., Boulder • (303) 444-5587

This small store just down the street from the International Food Bazaar is owned by a Libyan family and carries Middle Eastern and North African specialties.

Mountain Man Nut & Fruit Co.
2525 Arapahoe Ave., Boulder
• (303) 546-0920

A locally owned store that carries gourmet candy such as double-dipped malted-milk balls, all kinds of nuts and dried fruits, trail mixes, peach salsa and dried soups from corn chowder to Circle R Ranch jalapeño black bean, plus teas, coffees, mustards and jellies. They do gift baskets too. In the Village Shopping Center, just around the corner from the movie theater, it's a perfect stop if movie popcorn and candy aren't your thing.

The Oriental Food Market
1750 30th St., No. 84, Boulder
• (303) 422-7830

This market carries all the ingredients you'll need for all manner of Asian cuisine including Chinese, Japanese, Thai, Indian, Cambodian, Laotian, Vietnamese, Malaysian, Philippine and Indonesian. The small deli serves primarily Indonesian specialties.

Salvaggio's Italian Deli
2809 Pearl St., Boulder • (303) 938-1981
1100 28th St., Boulder • (303) 541-9771

If you're a former Easterner, this deli can satisfy your craving for good, New York-style Italian fare. The store carries Italian cold cuts and cheeses, including fresh, water-packed mozzarella and fresh pastas and sauces.

Scoops
Crossroads, Boulder • (303) 447-2826

Soothe your sweet tooth at this sugar showroom. This store has more than 500 kinds of candy, including chocolate-covered gummy bears, gummy spiders and many rows of colorful and sweet-filled bins. It's like landing in Candyland.

Whole Foods Market
2905 Pearl Street, Boulder
• (303) 402-1494

Ever since it opened just off 28th Street, Whole Foods has been the place to be for shoppers who really love food. Past a huge selection of fruits and vegetables there are fish and meat departments that pride themselves on freshness. Aisles are filled with herbs, foods and cosmetics and cleaning supplies with an environmental conscience, bulk supplies of munchies, cereal, honey, oil and nut butters. A deli offers browsers a meal's worth of samples of crackers, cheeses, meat and olives. Among the other stores-within-the-store

are a bread shop, a pizza shop, juice bar and a huge selection of prepared foods, from grilled eggplant to corn cakes to barbecued chicken.

High Spirits

The Boulder Wine Merchant
2690 Broadway, Boulder in Community
Plaza • (303) 443-6761

This store is owned by two of the world's great wine experts, Wayne Belding and Sally Mohr. Both Master Sommeliers, with unerring noses for fine wine, Wayne and Sally can wax poetic about the alkaline soil on a hidden Portuguese mountain and why, after a thunder shower on an afternoon three decades ago, a grape took on overtones of chocolate and black currants. Fewer than 30 Master Sommeliers are active in the United States, and another few dozen have earned the title worldwide. With such expertise, it's no wonder that they team up with the Cooking School of the Rockies to present wonderfully informative wine-tasting classes. The whole staff loves to help customers find a match for both palate and pocketbook. Undiscovered wines at great bargains abound. The Boulder Wine Merchant is also the place to go for unique bottles priced at $500 or more.

The Liquor Mart
Corner of 15th and Canyon Boulevard,
Boulder • (303) 449-3374

This is a supermarket-size liquor store, one of the largest in the United States. The variety is staggering, including hard liquor, beer, ale, wine, champagne, mixers and soft drinks. If you want something exotic, you're as likely to find it here as anywhere in the state. The helpful staff is known for offering informed advice. The store's policy is to grant a 15 percent discount on any unopened case of liquor or wine and 10 percent off a mixed case. If you fax your order to (303) 938-WINE, it will be ready for you to pick up when you get to the store.

For a huge general selection store, The Liquor Mart's wine selection is surprising, both in its depth and its breadth. Dick Fetter, formerly the *Daily Camera* wine columnist, is on hand occasionally as a consultant. He has written extensively about wines and food, and he imports fine wines for a number of Boulder's excellent spirit shops. He and the other wine managers conduct wine-tasting classes, and if you ever can go to one, do. You're in for a treat of fine wines and homey lore about the personalities of great vineyard families. If your taste goes more toward the basic grain, wheel your grocery cart into the refrigerated room full of the world's — and especially Colorado's — great beers. Sometimes, they also stock locally produced mead, a drink made from fermented honey. Single malt scotches include a 25-year-old MacAllan. If you feel like slumming, there's even MD 20/20 and wines flavored with orange and pineapple. On a CU football weekend, the young crowd lines up for cases and kegs.

The Beer Store You Brew It
637 S. Broadway, Boulder
• (303) 494-7000

This is a place where you can enjoy the fun side of brewing your own fresh beer, but a crew handles all the cleanup. If you haven't got your own formula, the store offers dozens of beer recipes and all the equipment and ingredients you need to create your own, personal, absolutely fresh brew. Among the favorites are Beaverstooth Ale, deep amber-colored and hoppy, and Wildfire Red, a robust, slightly sweet red ale. Brewing takes two weeks — just right for the start and end of a nice vacation.

Harvest Wine and Spirits
3075 Arapahoe Ave., Boulder
• (303) 447-9832

Harvest offers outstanding selections of imported and domestic wines, microbrews, spirits and fine cigars. This place is convenient for its location next to the King Soopers grocery store. The friendly, knowledgeable staff is always willing to help.

Home Furnishings

Artesanias
1420 Pearl St., Boulder • (303) 442-3777

Rustic furniture with the flavor of old Mexico shares this Downtown Mall store with ornamental wrought iron and hand-blown glass, candles and other accessories. Furniture, including whimsical, brightly painted items from Texas, is the bulk of the stock, with housewares on the side.

Bartlett Interiors
2020 Pearl St., Boulder • (303) 442-5194

It's a toss-up as to whether clients come here more for the stylish decorating advice or for the elegant and unusual upholstered and wood furniture, lamps, and window treatments. The inventory features many unusual and dramatic pieces to create a distinctive look.

Boulder Creek Furniture
3216 Arapahoe Ave., Boulder
• (303) 415-1201

Rustic furniture, such as peeled-log beds, is the specialty here, including living room, dining room and bedroom furniture hint of a return to summer camp. Materials sound like a forest — aspen, lodgepole, pine and cedar — and the look is attractive and distinctive. It also carries outdoor furniture, entertainment or "home theater" centers as well as furnishings for the home office. Upholstery services are available. Boulder Creek's harmonious "condo packages," composed of living room, dining area and bedroom pieces, are excellent choices for the start-up furniture buyer.

Canterbury Fine Furniture
2480 Canyon Blvd., Boulder
• (303) 442-9049

Plentiful and distinctive, American and English 19th- and 20th-century reproductions can be found in this large store. They carry many pieces that have been redesigned for modern living including computer roll-top desks and hideaway TV cabinets.

Country West Furniture
2525 Arapahoe Ave., Boulder
• (303) 443-2030

In the Village Shopping Center next to McGuckin Hardware, this store has been making country, Southwestern, wrought iron and mountain-log furniture for more than a decade. In addition to thoughtful designs, this store takes pride in its quality items, boasting dovetail drawers and hand-rubbed oil finishes. Country West can also make custom pieces. Armoires, bedroom pieces, dining room sets, entertainment centers, storage units of oak, pine, cherry and maple, and a variety of accessories are available.

Front Range Futons
2125 Pearl St., Boulder • (303) 444-4057

Every college town has at least one futon place, right? The futons here are of various sizes and the store carries futon frames, futon sofas and some accessories. It is, of course, a popular style of furniture in Boulder, and the price is usually right.

Innerspace/Techline
1600 Pearl St., Boulder
• (303) 440-9656

A purveyor of contemporary furniture, this store is known for its inventory of attractive and functional office and home-business pieces. The showroom also offers professional planning and design consultation.

KRJ
2712 28th St., Boulder • (303) 449-3375

Functional and sleek is the theme in this Bluff Plaza shop, specializing in desks and other office furniture and home furnishings in leather. Custom desks are available and there is a broad selection in leather goods with a promise of two-week delivery.

Marisol Imports
915 Pearl St., Boulder • (303) 442-3142

The sprightly showroom features wonderful wood pieces from Mexico, including tables, chairs and hutches plus wrought iron chairs, tables, bar stools and étagères that mesh ideally with either a country or Southwestern look. Zapotec rugs, pottery, large clay jugs, weavings, pillows and all manner of harmonious accessories also are stocked. In the summertime, the rustic rockers set outside the shop beckon footsore shoppers.

Madeiras
30th and Walnut Street, Boulder
• (303) 443-3078

The style here is heavy in Mediterranean influences of Spain, but with a lighter, more contemporary look than traditional Mediterranean. The pieces are rustic handcrafted, solid pine and very affordable.

New Dawn Futon & Furniture
1781 28th St., Boulder • (303) 938-8002

For futon fans who prefer a more traditional look, New Dawn offers classic bed frames designed to accommodate a futon mattress, as well as the usual line of futon sofa-beds.

Room to Room
2624 Broadway, Boulder
• (303) 473-1950

This small shop tucked into the Community Plaza carries reasonably priced, quality furniture and accessories including everything you need to create a unique bathroom, complete with the soap. The store personnel will provide design services on request.

Timberline Studios
2425 Canyon Blvd. in Water Street
• (303) 443-3610

Down upholstery, unique accents, a line of dining and bedroom pieces — Timberline bills its stock as "eclectic furniture for the Colorado lifestyle." Design consultation is also available.

Unpainted Furniture
2034 Pearl St., Boulder
• (303) 443-8229

If you're a do-it-yourselfer, this store carries Colorado's largest unfinished inventory. Hardwood and pine furniture, china and corner cabinets, coffee and end tables, armoires and wardrobes, juvenile furniture, tables and chairs, rockers, chests, dressers, bookcases and toy boxes. The staff has advice and the finishing materials you'll need, or if you want to spend the extra money and wait a few weeks, they'll do the finishing for you.

Jewelers

In addition to dedicated jewelry stores, you'll find jewelry in the Boulder Arts & Crafts Cooperative and other crafts stores, the Crossroads Mall as well as in many of Boulder's art galleries.

J. Anderson Jewelry
3183 Walnut, Boulder• (303) 449-1125

Handmade jewelry is the specialty at Anderson's, which offers custom design and engraving and experienced watch repair. J. Anderson buys and sells gold and silver.

Bill Cronin Goldsmith
1235 Alpine Ave., Boulder
• (303) 440-4222

Since 1979 this shop north of downtown has been manufacturing quality jewelry set with diamonds and other stones. Cronin's specializes in custom goldsmithing, helping local romantics create The Ring to their specifications.

Hurdle's
1402 Pearl St., Boulder
• (303) 443-1084

This is a very traditional jeweler, just what you'd expect to find in a historic downtown like Boulder's. And well it should be, for it was established back in 1947. There's even a little repair booth right in the window, armed with loupes, velvet cushions and the teeny instruments necessary to perform surgery on delicate watches and jewelry. Hurdle's carries estate and new jewelry of all sorts as well as fine watches, including TAGHeuer from Switzerland.

The Little Jewel
1225 Pearl St., Boulder • (303) 443-3353

On the Pearl Street Mall, the Little Jewel crams in a lot of pieces in a lot of styles. There's some Southwestern turquoise and silver. There's some Italian gold. There are chains, earrings, bracelets and wedding sets. And often, there are special sales.

Master Goldsmith
10th and Pearl, Boulder • (303) 443-3424

Since 1971, Master Goldsmiths has been creating unique and custom-designed jewelery in gold and platinum. Ideal Cut diamonds are imported directly to the store.

Meyers Jewelers
1595 Canyon Blvd., Boulder
• (303) 442-2255

Founded in 1960, this store is known for diamond pieces and wedding sets in contemporary and traditional styles. Among its distinctive, exclusive designs are pendants and earrings depicting the Flatirons and, for CU fans, rings and bracelets of nose-to-tail buffaloes marching along in bands of gold or silver. Meyers Jewelers remains a family business, with talented veterans handling on-site jewelry repair and remounts.

Sierra Small Bird
1108 Spruce St., Boulder
• (303) 442-2220

This new business, featuring Native American Fine Art, offers everything from heavy silver jewelery to beaded leather bags, woven rug wall hangings, painted shields, even a finely wrought silver buffalo.

Walters & Hogsett
2425 Canyon Blvd., Boulder
• (303) 449-2626

Gold, silver and gemstones make this a highly regarded jeweler. It stocks fine domestic and imported jewelry, watches, crystal and silver. In addition to repairs, Walters & Hogsett floats an annual fall special on re-plating silver flatware and hollow ware.

Miscellany

Allen Scientific Glass Blowers
1752 55th St., Boulder • (303) 442-2141

The Ph.D. crowd told us that this guide wouldn't be complete without including Ray Allen, called the "God of Scientific Glass." He can make anything out of glass and glass/metal transitions. You know . . . all those things you always wanted for your lab but couldn't find at a really good price.

Blake's Small Car Salvage
2559 Weld County Rd., No. 5, Erie
• (303) 665-4312

This junkyard is so darned pretty it was featured on the *CBS Evening News*. Car parts, fitting everything from a 1959 Anglias to a 1993 Geo Storm, are arranged by country. A Japanese flag flies near the Hondas; a German flag marks the BMWs. Small parts are stored picturesquely in yellow school buses and Chevy vans. The Colorado New Music Association came out here one fall and made, along with other instruments, drums from the hubcaps. What a concert! Talk about heavy metal!

Boulder Early Music Shop
3200 Valmont Rd., Boulder
• (303) 449-9231

The sounds that pluck Boulder's heart strings range from gentle fluty folk stuff to something heavier than grunge metal, and this store has folk instruments such as recorders and hand drums, small, dear items you could pack back home in a suitcase. Hard-to-get sheet music, CDs of early music and learned musicological journals and books are all in stock. The store is a good place to get tickets for local music performances, including those by the excellent Rocky Mountain Chorale as well as events in the Swallow Hill concert series.

Business Express
1904 Pearl St., Boulder • (303) 443-9300

You can't miss the purple palace just east of the Pearl Street Mall. This is a good office, copy and self-service computer store. They also have a large selection of cards and interesting gift items. Not as slick as Kinko's, but a bit friendlier.

Chris Finger Pianos
101 Second St., Niwot • (303) 442-9026

Isn't this simply a grand name for the owner

Boulder's biggest enclosed shopping center is Crossroads Mall.

Photo: Daily Camera/Jay Quadracci

of a piano store? You'll find fine European pianos here, and if you're not sure the piano will get played, rental pianos are available, and financing is an option. The store also sells grandfather clocks.

Dependable Cleaners
2525 Arapahoe Ave., Boulder
• (303) 443-0290

This top-shelf dry-cleaner is located in The Village Shopping Center. Dependable offers same-day service, so you can drop your duds off on the way to work and pick them up on the way home. Located right next to the Men's Wearhouse, Dependable Cleaners is open from 7 AM to 7 PM during the week and 8 AM to 6 PM Saturdays.

Everybody Ltd.
1738 Pearl St., Boulder • (303) 440-0188

After a few years downtown, this store has returned to its original location at the Harvest Commons east of the Pearl Street Mall. It's a smaller shop now but the mail-order service has expanded. Skin Trip body lotion by Mountain Ocean has always been a big seller and the gift baskets never fail to please. They also carry a variety of massage and bath oils.

Old Tibet
948 Pearl Street, Boulder
• (303) 440-0323

Operated by the same family that runs Narayan's restaurant just down Pearl Street to the east, Old Tibet offers an exotic melange of clothing, jewelry, statuary and other unique items imported from Tibet. Sidewalk displays and a jam-packed window draw in strollers heading for the Downtown Mall just one block away.

Paper Doll
1141 Pearl Street, Boulder
• (303) 440-1661
Crossroads Mall, Boulder
• (303) 449-5959

Exquisite is the term that comes to mind when describing the lovely items filling the aisles of the Paper Doll shops on the Downtown Mall and at Crossroads Mall. True to their shared name, the shops stock a wide variety

of stationary and cards, address books, photo albums and other paper goods. In addition, there is a shifting collection of seasonal items like one-of-a-kind Christmas tree baubles, Thanksgiving serving dishes and Valentine's decorations, as well as antique-look jewelry.

Robb's Music
1580 Canyon Blvd., Boulder
• (303) 443-8448

Robb's has digital pianos, electronic keyboards, guitars, drums, band instruments and more. They offer great deals on used instruments and have experts who repair electronic instruments.

Swalley's The Music People
2095 30th St., Boulder • (303) 443-8404

Swalley's is the exclusive home of Baldwin in Boulder, and sells sheet music including that required by local music teachers. They also buy and sell used pianos and have technicians who can come to your home and tune a piano. This is an oldtime music store; it's kept the notes flowing since 1960.

Wildwood Music
804 Main St., Louisville • (303) 776-2366

This store specializes in both acoustic and electric guitars including Fender, Martin, Gibson, Paul Reed Smith, Taylor and Dobro. Wildwood has unbeatable prices.

Nature Stores

Crystal Galleries Ltd.
1302 Pearl St., Boulder • (303) 444-2277

This store features a fine collection of minerals, crystal, fossils and jewelry made from semiprecious gemstones. The glasswork of René Lalique, plus eggs, spheres and bookends are all in the inventory.

Nature's Own Imagination
1133 Pearl St., Boulder • (303) 443-4430
5 E. 1stSt., Nederland • (303) 258-3557

These stores keep shoppers entertained for hours with their unusual items, including minerals, garden items, nature games, gifts and home decor.

Photographic Equipment

Amaranth
2540 Frontier Ave., Boulder
• (303) 443-2550

The pros go here for the full-service custom lab, digital imaging and printing and mounting services. They also have a good selection of frames.

Mike's Camera
2500 Pearl St., Boulder • (303) 443-1715

Like the Boulder Bookstore, this is a local landmark that recently expanded to dazzling proportions. It's Boulder's only complete camera shop dedicated exclusively to photographic equipment, related items and services. Mike's services include camera and video repairs, rentals (full spectrum), used camera sales, digital imaging and photo and video industrial equipment and classes on how to use it all.

Jones Drug & Camera Center
1370 College Ave., Boulder
• (303) 443-4420

More than a drug store, this Hill institution has a very good line of fine cameras, lenses, film and photo accessories, including filters, bags, books, albums and frames. In addition to processing film, Jones has a full selection of darkroom supplies and one of the best offerings of black-and-white enlarging paper in the state. The store also sells high-quality used equipment and has a very knowledgeable and helpful staff.

Moto Photo
2525 Arapahoe Ave., Boulder
• (303) 546-6686

The promise of prints in an hour is what brings customers into this fairly new shop in the Village Shopping Center. Once inside, they find a wide selection of frames and photo albums, as well as a framing department. For $24.95 a year, Club Moto members get a slew of goodies like free film or a free enlargement along with savings on photo developing and merchandise. Oh, and you can make copies for 5 cents a page.

Photo Craft
4335 Arapahoe Rd., Boulder
• (303) 442-6410

This shop is another favorite of the professionals, with custom photographic services, including giant photographic color murals and backlits suitable for trade show and store display. It also offers rush service and custom computer imaging services.

Robert Waxman
2520 Arapahoe Ave. in the Arapahoe Village, Boulder • (303) 544-9842

In addition to full photo finishing services, this chain store offers digital services, photo restoration, classes, consultation on photo presentation, and cameras and accessories.

Sporting Goods Shops

From one end of town to the other, Boulder is speckled with sporting goods shops, including a number of exceptional mountaineering and climbing stores. You don't have to leave Boulder to find such high-country gear as hiking boots, parkas, alpine and Nordic skis, snowboards, snowshoes, in-line skates, rock-climbing, camping and backpacking equipment, clothing and accessories for any terrain or activity. Most stores rent as well as sell clothing, and some of the best deals are end-of-season closeouts on rental equipment.

Bicycle Village
1681 28th St., Boulder • (303) 440-8525

Mountain bikes, road bikes, comfort bikes, clothing, accessories, car racks and bikes for rent — Bicycle Village has it all. This is Colorado's largest Schwinn dealer.

Boulder Army Store
1545 Pearl St., Boulder
• (303) 442-7616

A Boulder favorite, this store is true to its name and features a full array of such army surplus items as ammo cases, camouflage clothing, combat boots and canteens. It's a good place to shop for backpacks, nylon climbing rope, hiking boots, sunglasses, hats and gloves of every description.

The Boulder Mountaineer
1355 Broadway, Boulder
• (303) 442-8355

The Mountaineer offers a great selection of the latest styles of high-tech fabrics in outerwear, hats, gloves, sleeping bags, backpacks, long underwear, all manner of climbing hardware and lots of other outdoor equipment for backcountry skiing and hiking. The store can arrange private guiding and classes in rock and ice climbing.

The Boulder Outdoor Center
2510 47th St., Boulder • (303) 444-8420

Kayaks and canoes are sold or can be rented here, with instruction available and raft trips scheduled. In winter, the center rents snowshoes and avalanche beacons.

Boulder Ski Deals
2404 Pearl St., Boulder • (303) 938-8799

This shop sells equipment and clothing for alpine and Nordic skiing and snowboarding. There's a full-service boot and ski repair shop and custom boot fitting. Mostly new but also some traded-in used equipment is available. The store also sells such accessories as hats, gloves, long johns, socks, sunglasses, goggles and sunscreen. In summer, the shop partially switches over to in-line skating and watersports, including snowboards and kayaking.

Boulder Sports Recycler
1727 15th St., Boulder • (303) 786-9940

This is a great place to pick up used and close-out skis, in-line skates and equipment for racquetball, hockey, baseball, golf, camping, football, watersports, biking, tennis, soccer, fishing and weight-lifting. They also sell used sports clothing.

Doc's Ski & Sports
627 S. Broadway, Boulder
• (303) 499-0963

Voted one of America's top 50 ski shops by *Snow County Magazine* in 1996, Doc's carries equipment and clothing for skiing, skating, snowboarding and biking. They also rent equipment and promise overnight repairs for your skis or snowboard.

Eastern Mountain Sports
2550 Arapahoe Ave., Boulder
• (303) 442-7566

This is a national chain of East Coast origin that also sells North Face clothing and equipment and other top brands, as well as a large number of private-label EMS items. Clothing and equipment are available. It's a great place for fleece items, boots, skis and good service.

Front Range Anglers Inc.
629-B S. Broadway, Boulder
• (303) 494-1375

Fly fishers will find everything they need at this store in the Table Mesa Center, including tackle, rods, reels, waders, classic wool shirts and other gear and garments. The shop conducts beginner and advanced fly-tying and rod-building classes. If you and all that gear have piscatorial wanderlust, you can sign on for a guided trip in United States or to a foreign country. Books, videos, gifts and fish art are also for sale.

Gart Sports
2525 Arapahoe Ave. in The Village, Boulder • (303) 449-6180
3320 28th St., Boulder • (303) 449-9021
1250 S. Hover Rd., Longmont
• (303) 651-9697

Gart's offers a wide assortment of sporting goods from tennis and golf to skiing, fishing and hunting supplies. Gart's is a Colorado-owned company with other stores in Denver and elsewhere in the West. It is ideal for gear for team sports, exercise paraphernalia, logo clothing, athletic shoes and low- to mid-priced sporting goods for skiers and other recreational athletes.

High Gear Cyclery
1834 Main St., Longmont
• (303) 772-4327

Perhaps you've seen them laconically pedaling down a bikepath or city street, bicyclists lounging almost flat with their feet pumping out ahead of them. You are looking at a recumbent and High Gear specializes in the ergonomically correct bicycles, as well as exercise equipment, roof racks, repairs, clothing and traditional bikes.

Louisville Cyclery
1032 S. Boulder Rd., Louisville
• (303) 665-6343

Road- and mountain-bike specialists help here with sales, rental, custom wheels, professional fittings, suspension and repair service. They also carry quality clothing and gear for the whole family.

Mountain Sports
821 Pearl St., Boulder
• (303) 443-6700

As the name implies, this shop focuses on a variety of alpine activities, including climbing, camping, hiking, snowshoeing and Nordic skiing. It offers a fine selection of top-quality equipment and apparel, with friendly, very helpful service. The store sponsors periodic slide shows, lectures and courses. A log book close to the front door enables customers to comment on recent hikes or ski tours they've taken and conditions they've encountered.

Neptune Mountaineering
633 S. Broadway, Boulder
• (303) 499-8866

The first among equals for hard-core climbers and mountaineers is this store in Table Mesa Shopping Center. This huge store is owned by Gary Neptune, a prominent U.S. mountaineer who has reached the summit of Mount Everest and other high peaks. Besides ice axes, ropes, climbing shoes and boots, the store has a good selection of Nordic ski equipment and outdoor clothing. Its book department is one of the best around. Gary's private collection of mountaineering memorabilia, including rarities of immense historic value, is displayed throughout this large store.

The North Face
629-K S. Broadway, Boulder
• (303) 499-1731

Located in the Table Mesa Center, this is a national wholesaler/manufacturer that has established one of its handful of retail stores in Boulder. The Berkeley, California-based company sells its tents, packs, sleeping bags, ski jackets and other products to 800 shops across the country.

Madden Factory Store
2400 Central Ave., Boulder
• (303) 442-5828

For all types of daypacks, backpacks and smaller packs, stop here. For some reason, Madden's packs are more popular in Europe among the outdoor set than in the United States, but this local company makes high-quality, sturdy packs of every description that will last for years, and it's all for sale here at factory outlet prices.

Paddle Shop
1727 15th St., Boulder • **(303) 786-8799**

This shop sells plenty of kayaking equipment, but also rents and sells canoes and rafts. They also carry wet suits and all other related accessories. Kayak instruction and raft trips are available through the shop.

Performance Bicycle Shop
2490 Arapahoe Ave., Boulder
• (303) 444-5044

Performance specializes in everything from service for professionals to periodic pedalers. The USA Cycling Team and Team Mercury get outfitted at Performance.

Play It Again Sports
653 S. Broadway, Boulder
• (303) 499-2011

As its name suggests, this chain store will buy, sell, trade and consign used and new sporting goods. Those goods include equipment for softball, golf, tennis, hockey, skiing, rock climbing, soccer, camping, backpacking, in-line skating and yard games.

Pro Peleton
2615 13th St., Boulder • **(303) 415-1292**

A peleton is the large pack of cyclists riding together in a long road race like the Tour de France. On the backside of the Community Plaza, this new high-end shop specializes in serious road and racing bikes and everything you need to embark on heavy-duty cycling.

Rocky Mountain Diving Center
1737 15th St., Boulder • **(303) 449-8606**

Whether you're a beginner or hope to be an instructor, this store can meet your needs.

There is a complete in-store travel agency that can book escorted or individual diving trips. They also rent and repair diving equipment. Trip veterans participate in an informal dive club with slide shows and periodic potluck dinners.

Rocky Mountain Racquet Specialists
2425 Canyon Blvd., Boulder • (303) 442-1412

This is where Boulder's major tennis, squash and racquetball enthusiasts go for the gear and duds. Racquets and balls, of course, are available, but so is name-brand clothing, footwear and accessories such as eyewear and gloves. This store offers one-day racquet stringing and can also make custom grips.

Rocky Mountain Soccer
2767 Iris Ave. in the Willow Springs Center, Boulder • (303) 938-9166

Soccer is a big deal in Boulder. Apparel and equipment such as shin guards, balls and cleats are available here. It's a real mecca for soccer-holics and has meeting space available for groups who want to plan events centered around this round-ball sport.

Runners Choice
2460 Canyon Blvd., Boulder • (303) 449-8551

This store offers shoes, clothing and friendly advice for athletes at all levels, but it's not just for runners. You'll find equipment and clothing for walkers and swimmers, too, along with free consultations with a podiatrist.

Runners Roost
1129 Pearl St., Boulder • (303) 443-9868

The Roost has full lines of running shoes and accessories, plus books, tapes and magazines. They offer race registration for those who like to do it in packs.

Scuba Joe
3054 28th St., Boulder • (303) 444-7234

Another store with an in-store travel agency, Scuba Joe is a dive and snorkel cen-ter with convenient basic through instructor classes offered on weeknights or weekends.

Sequel Outdoor Clothing
1416 Pearl St., Boulder • (303) 449-4252

This is a Colorado-owned company that manufactures its products in Durango. This store has a storm-test chamber in the front window that simulates rain, wind, hail, lightning and thunder. Enter this chamber and you can experience how the clothes you're planning to buy work in heavy weather. Yes, the water is real — and wet.

Weaver's Dive & Travel Center
637 S. Broadway, Boulder • (303) 499-8500

Weaver's sells dive gear, wetsuits and swimwear. If you don't know how to dive, they'll teach you and help you get certified. If you dive, you can book a group or individual dive trip to some of the world's top underwater destinations. Weaver's has a full-service travel agency on site.

University Bicycles
839 Pearl St., Boulder • (303) 444-4196

You can't miss this shop due to the clever outdoor mural of the bicyclist who appears to be breaking through the shop's exterior wall. This store sells and repairs mountain and road bikes and promises "all the neat stuff you see in bike magazines."

Yard Sales

Lastly, perhaps some of the best shopping in town is at Boulder's yard and garage sales. Check the classified sections of the local newspapers or just drive around town on weekends and keep an eye out for homemade signs on trees and utility poles. Many sales start on Fridays, but Saturdays are the big days — and a few dribble over into Sunday too.

In south Boulder, the bridge across Bear Creek at Table Mesa Drive and the King Soopers entrance is always plastered with yard sale signs around the weekend. Downtown, the corner of Arapahoe Avenue and Ninth Street is often festooned with garage sale signs. With its transient population of students and upwardly mobile adults, Boulder's yard sales offer everything from skis, bicycles, snowboards and windsurfing equipment to violins, art and antiques.

More than 34,000 participants, from the most fleet-footed elite amateur runners to first-time walkers, make the Bolder Boulder 10K Race one of the nation's largest citizen races.

Festivals and Annual Events

Special events make an evening or weekend sparkle. Where possible, our listings include dates, times and prices. Other events bloom with serendipity, so planners can't say exactly when and how much until the event draws near. The chapter ends with "Events Central," mentioning groups that track happenings. You can find even more possibilities by checking our Boulder Attractions and Boulder Arts chapters. Keep in mind, volunteers run many of these festivals, and you're welcome to lend a hand.

January

Polar Bear Club Ice Plunge
Boulder Reservoir 51st St., Boulder
• (303) 441-3461

Pay around $15 to brave ice-crusted water, dance a jig, screech, then hurry to shore (or stay in as long as you wish). Rescue workers stand by in case anyone gets hypothermia from the morning dip. Plungers say, "It's intensely painful, in a pleasurable sort of way." For spectators, admission to this New Year's Day event is free.

Colorado Mahlerfest
Macky Auditorium (on the CU-Boulder campus) and Boulder Public Library (11th St. and Arapahoe Ave.), Boulder
• (303) 447-0513

Mahler fans rave about this one-of-a-kind concertfest during the second week in January. It began in 1988, when enthusiasts played Mahler's Symphony No. 1. Each year, they have played the Bohemian composer's next symphony in line. In 1999 they played Symphony No. 3. The celebration also includes lectures and song recitals. Concert ticket prices range from $9 to $23, with public recitals at the Boulder Public Library free. In 2000 the group plans to branch out by offering a free concert at the Longmont Senior Center.

Boulder Bach Festival
P.O. Box 1896, Boulder, CO
• (303) 494-3159

Only a handful of American festivals play nothing but J.S. Bach. This is one. Local professional musicians and well-known guest artists keep the music lively, playing those hummable tunes you might have thought were modern. The festival is held over the last weekend in January at the downtown Boulder First Presbyterian Church. Additional concerts take place on an irregular schedule from September through May at locations that include the University of Colorado's Grusin Music Hall, University Lutheran Chapel, the Boulder Public Library Auditorium and Denver's St. John's Cathedral. Ticket prices vary.

National Western Stock Show, Rodeo and Horse Show
I-25 on I-70, Denver, CO
• (303) 295-1660

Denver proudly calls itself a "cow town" and proves it during the month of January when the Stock Show comes to town. Since 1906 serious competition combined with showmanship have made this one of the largest stock shows in the world. More than 600,000 people attended in 1998. There were nearly 40 performances including 23 rodeos by the

Professional Rodeo Cowboys Association, two Mexican rodeos, two bull riding events, seven horse shows, three Wild West shows and two evenings of dancing horses. Other events include sheep shearing, mutton busting, barn tours and a children's petting farm. Recent ticket prices were $7 for adults and $2 for children on weekends; $5 and $1 on weekdays. Rodeo and horseshow tickets ranged from $8 to $15 including grounds admission.

Best-of-show steers are often on exhibit in the lobby of the Brown Palace Hotel in downtown Denver.

Old Town Lafayette Oatmeal Festival
100 S. Public Road, Lafayette
• (303) 926-0409

When Lafayette business owners decided to initiate a unique annual festival a few years ago, someone noted that January is "oatmeal month." Not surprisingly, Lafayette now boasts the "world's largest oatmeal breakfast buffet." Quaker Oats was more than happy to participate and the annual festival now includes a 5K health walk, a health fair, art exhibit, kids activities and lots of entertainment. Held on the fourth Saturday in January, the all-you-can eat breakfast costs $3. Event hours are 9 AM until 4 PM.

February

Chocolate Lover's Fling
Glenn Miller Ballroom (on CU-Boulder campus), Boulder • (303) 442-5282

For the price of a good dinner ($20 to $25), eat all the chocolate you want and benefit a good cause on the Friday or Saturday evening before Valentine's Day at the Chocolate Lover's Fling. Feast your eyes on chocolate TV din-

ners, armadillos, cabbages and castles. Boulder's best professional chefs vie with talented amateurs in categories ranging from "Sheer Artistry" to yummy. Enter your creation, or just eat the entries. Profits go to the Boulder County Safehouse, which helps battered families.

www.insiders.com

See this and many other **Insiders' Guide®** destinations online — in their entirety.

Visit us today!

March

4-H Carnival
Boulder County Fairgrounds, 9595 Nelson Rd., Longmont
• (303) 776-4865

This all-day family event on the second Saturday in March has homemade pies and kid-decorated variety booths. Throw shaving-cream pies and walk through a maze of bright-colored calico walls. You might win a T-shirt by launching a stuffed toy lamb into a cute little pen. Admission is free.

Boulder Bach Festival — Kids for Bach/Bach for Kids
Boulder Public Library, 11th St. and Arapahoe Ave., Boulder
• (303) 494-3159

Children audition by tape to perform in this charming, hour-long program. Musicians range from 6 to 17 years old and play a variety of instruments including piano, violin and harp. Admission is free.

April

Conference on World Affairs
CU-Boulder campus, Boulder
• (303) 492-2525

International flags festoon the campus during this week-long series of forums held the

---

INSIDERS' TIP

The Bolder Boulder 10K is a 30,000-plus moving party with some of the world's most fleet runners, thousands of amateur runners, a whole bunch of walkers and live entertainment to cheer people along the way.

week after CU-Boulder's spring semester resumes following spring break. Under new leadership since 1999, Director Jim Palmer has infused new energy and tried to balance forums by offering more that appeal to college students while still drawing the general public. More than 100 speakers jet to Boulder at their own expense to participate. Call ahead for session topics, or just wander into the University Memorial Center to pick up a schedule and slip into one of the many discussions. Admission is free.

Loyalty Parade
Downtown Lafayette • (303) 665-9993

Get ready for fifes, drums, flags and equestrian teams. VFW Post 1771 sponsors this state parade, which was founded to counter communism's May Day celebrations. The "Evil Empire" is no more, but Lafayette's parade remains. It starts at 10 AM on the Saturday closest to May 1, heading south from Public Road to Waneka Parkway.

Kinetic Conveyance Parade
Pearl Street Mall, Boulder
• (303) 444-KBCO

On the last Saturday in April, more than 50 teams enter wild, wacky and wonderful kinetic conveyances — that is, non-motorized contraptions designed to race across water and land. Always imaginative and sometimes even functional during the later challenge portion of the two-pronged competition (see the subsequent listing), kinetic conveyances make a colorful parade. Panache earns points, so the Floating Elvises in a pink "Cadillac," the deliciously tasteless and terminally politically-incorrect Hooters Guys and the Mud Sharks have been favorites. The parade morning starts with "vehicles" on display at 9 AM, followed by a 1 PM parade. At the judging booth, contestants attempt undue influence through skits and bribes . . . the more outrageous, the better. Entrance deadline is mid-April and costs around $15 per craft and $7 for each team member. Watching the parade is, of course, free.

Puttin' on the Leash
Coors Events Center, CU Campus
• (303) 442-4030

The annual fashion show and auction fundraiser for the Boulder Valley Humane Society is held the last weekend in April or the first weekend in May. Auction items have included a trip to swim with the dolphins off the coast of the Bahamas. It starts at 7 PM at the Coors Events Center on the CU campus. Tickets are around $50 per person.

May

Cinco De Mayo Celebration
Clark Centennial Park, Mt. View &
Alpine, Longmont • (303) 772-4358

This cultural celebration offers music, dance, food, singers and much more. A student talent show was new in 1999 with acts related to the Latino culture including dances and storytelling. A salsa contest offered both restaurants and individuals a chance at prizes. Don't, however, expect margaritas on the side — this is a non-alcoholic celebration to honor families and culture. There is no admission charge. Hours are 9 AM to 5 PM.

Kinetic Conveyance Challenge
Boulder Reservoir, 51st St., Boulder
• (303) 444-KBCO

Around 30,000 people attend this race, which begins at 11 AM on the first Saturday in May; but some spectators arrive as early as 6:30 AM to get the best spots and enjoy the balloon festival and pancake breakfast. Some conveyances barely make it more than a few yards from shore before sinking. Especially in the early minutes of the race, rescue craft are busy towing the wrecks back to shore. The race consists of a water leg, an overland stretch and a return across the water. The swiftest contestants finish in 45 minutes, and the lumbering laggards end four hours later. The winners usually have a combination canoe/bicycle thing powered by good-looking legs and shoulders. Entrance fees are roughly $25 for a carload and $5 per pedestrian or cyclist.

Boulder Potters' Guild Show & Sale
2108 55th St., Boulder • (303) 447-0310

Add some color to your home each spring by purchasing reasonably priced handmade clay tiles, sculpture, mugs and more. Typically held at the CU Armory, 4750 N. Broad-

"Paddling ducks" march in the Boulder Creek Festival Parade.

way, admission is free and refreshments are plentiful. Hours are Friday, 10 AM to 8 PM, Saturday from 10 AM to 5 PM and 10 AM to 4 PM on Sunday. A fall sale is held in November.

Strawberry Festival Antiques Show
Boulder County Fairgrounds, 9595 Nelson Rd., Longmont • (303) 776-1870

This is one of three annual antique shows hosted by the St. Vrain Historical Society and held in the exhibit hall at the fairgrounds. (The others are the Heritage Festival in July, and Pumpkin Pie Days in October.) Antiques and collectibles are available but those who aren't buying are usually taste-testing the strawberry shortcake available from the cafeteria. Admission to all three events is $3 per person.

Boulder Creek Festival and Rubber-duckie Race
Boulder Creek, Boulder • (303) 449-3825

This popular rite of spring has been rated the Best Annual Children's Event by *Daily Camera* readers. Throughout Memorial Day weekend, craft booths, music and dance, carnival rides and food stands entertain the throngs who edge their way through the tightly packed venue all the way from Sixth to 13th streets and between Canyon Boulevard and Arapahoe Avenue.

On Sunday, more than 4,000 yellow rubber duckies bobble from the Ninth Street and Canyon Boulevard bridge to the Peace Garden at 11th Street and Arapahoe Avenue — all in the name of fun and charity, benefiting the Boulder Parks and Recreation Department and helping expand its therapeutic program for children and adults with disabilities. It costs $5 to enter a duck, and prizes range from the trivial to major vacations.

Other activities, such as the kids' Fishing Derby, a sports expo, and a huge art and crafts show help to draw approximately 130,000 people to the Central Park area before the fun ends Monday evening.

Bolder Boulder 10K Race
From 30th and Iris Sts. to Folsom Field, Boulder • (303) 444-RACE

This Memorial Day race is rated one of the top road races in the nation and Boulder's Best Annual Event by *Daily Camera* readers. It's amazing how much fun it can be to run or walk more than 6 miles. More than 40,000 participants, from the most fleet-footed elite amateur runners in the A wave to first-time walkers in the ZZ, make this one of the nation's largest citizen races. An international field of celebrity runners and top wheelchair athletes make this an important race on the national 10K calendar too. The Bolder Boulder's nonstop party atmosphere is exhilarating. In addition to aid and water stations, entertainment is provided along the route. All runners finish at CU-Boulder's Folsom Field, where thousands of spectators watch world-class professional racers compete after the amateur races are through.

The 1999 race fee was $24, including a commemorative T-shirt and lunch, or $15 without the shirt. Every runner is timed, so you will get your time and ranking calculated in a variety of ways after the race. You can register at local running stores or at race headquarters in the Crossroads Mall. Try to get your application in by early May. (If the race doesn't fill up, you can register on race morning too, but the price is $10 higher.)

Nearly 40,000 runners make quite a pack, but the race never feels so crowded, for organizers stagger the starting times in successive waves to give everyone room. Along the way, you'll see belly dancers, including the lady with the sword on her head, and high-stepping grandmas, decked out in fringed cowgirl skirts. You'll hear everything from live jazz bands to bagpipers playing rock 'n' roll. Don't fear wimping out. In the ZZ wave, the pace is a pleasant amble, and the cheers from the crowd are just as enthusiastic.

The citizens' race starts at 7:30 AM at 30th and Iris. The elite professionals, among the fastest in the world, start at 11:25 AM so that citizen racers can watch the pros' final laps in Folsom Field. If you decide to watch, pick a spot anywhere along the course or at Folsom Field. Runners have included wedding parties and guys who leapfrog the whole way. Marines usually sign up in the "M" and run in formation entertaining the crowd with military chants along the route. Blind runners and wheelchair racers inspire us all, as do the fleet-footed gazelle types and seniors running with their grandchildren.

June

Artwalk
Pearl St. Mall, Boulder • (303) 444-9116 (Linton-Haslam Gallery)

The Artwalk is an evening open house fea-turing downtown galleries. Some serve refreshments, and many give you the opportunity to meet with the artists and artisans whose works they show. Schedules and maps are available at galleries along the Pearl Street Mall. Artwalk takes place the first weekend in June.

Boulder Outdoor Cinema
Boulder Museum of Contemporary Art
1750 13th St., Boulder • (303) 443-2122

Bring a chair and your own popcorn and be prepared for an informal cinema experience in the museum's parking lot. This outdoor walk-in theater screens "B" movies, cult classics, cartoons and funny short subjects Saturday nights June through August. Prizes are awarded for best costume as it relates to the movie. The film, which starts at dusk, is projected onto an outside wall of the museum. A donation of $5 is requested.

Naropa Summer Institute Performing Arts Series
2130 Arapahoe Ave., Boulder
• (303) 444-0202 or 800-603-3117

Naropa brings dancers, musicians, writers and lecturers from all over the nation. Artists and scholars have included Ram Dass, Maya Angelou, Bernie Siegel, Anne Waldman, Phillip Glass, Cecil Taylor, Meredith Monk and the Gardzienice Theater Group from Poland. Performances are scheduled extensively during June and July. Admission is as varied as the offerings.

The Colorado Shakespeare Festival
CU-Boulder's Mary Rippon Outdoor Theatre • (303) 492-0554

This festival, started in 1958, has presented all the Shakespeare plays. It is now the fifth-largest Shakespeare company in the United States, according to the Shakespeare Theatre Association. The lushly costumed, lavishly acted plays are produced from mid-June through mid-August. In 1999, the three plays scheduled included, *The Comedy of Errors*, *The Merry Wives of Windsor* and *Henry IV*, parts 1 and 2. Because the Rippon's amphitheater-style benches are made of stone, the wise theater-goer brings or rents a soft cushion or a stadium chair. After the sun goes down, the evening can turn cool, so toting a sweater, jacket and even rain gear is smart too. Tickets range from $18 to $35.

Summer Solstice Festival
Pearl Street Mall, Boulder
• (303) 939-8463 (Solstice Institute)

This Native American festival features storytellers, dance and drum presentations. Foods include blue corn and amaranth breads plus Lakota salads with watercress and maple syrup dressing. Arts and crafts by Ute, Arapaho, Cheyenne and Shoshone create visual appeal. Admission to this mid-June weekend event is free.

Walk & BikeWeek
2018 11th St., Boulder
• (303) 441-3266

BikeWeek was a decade old when the city's alternate modes division, added the "Walk" to the title in order to encourage those who don't have a gift for cycling. Scheduled for the third week in June, Walk or Bike to Work Day is held on the Wednesday of that week. Prizes are offered to those who commute the farthest and businesses with the most employees who bike or walk to work. More than 30 breakfast stations offer participants a quick bite to eat before they reach the office.

Boulder County Garden Tour
Various gardens throughout Boulder
• (303) 666-4435

Local gardeners weed and plant like mad for this late June tour, which benefits the Boulder County Mental Health Foundation and features beautiful gardens at private homes. There are also speakers on gardening topics, a plant sale and door prizes. Maps and details are available from local garden centers. Tickets are around $15.

Taste of Louisville
Louisville's shopping districts
• (303) 666-5747

Less-than-a-dollar samples from many Louisville eateries are part of this mid-June celebration, which includes 80 participating businesses. The weekend often includes country-dance lessons, face-painting and shuttle buses, which take revelers between this growing city's shopping areas.

Taste of the Nation
CU-Boulder's Glenn Miller Ballroom, Boulder • (303) 652-3663 (Community Food Share)

More than 40 of Boulder's finest chefs prepare nibble-sized samples, which evening guests quaff with everything from wine and local brewpub beer to mineral water. This mid-June event is one of Boulder's best food festivals. Profits go to Community Food Share, the People's Clinic, International Hunger Relief and rural Colorado communities. In 1998, tickets were $50 in advance and $55 at the door.

Festival of India
Courthouse Plaza, Pearl Street Mall, Boulder • (303) 333-5461

Sponsored by Radha Krishna Temple of Denver, this festival is one of the most colorful annual events all summer. Classical Indian dance, plays, complimentary Indian cuisine and a parade are featured. Held the last weekend in June or July. Hours have been from 10 AM to 10 PM on Saturday and 10 AM to 6 PM on Sunday.

July

The Colorado Music Festival
1525 Spruce St., Boulder
• (303) 449-1397 or (303) 449-2413

Features a first-rate, full orchestra that plays great classical music at the Chautauqua Auditorium throughout the summer. The CMF season starts with a special children's performance and includes a free Fourth of July outdoor concert. You can get a subscription or single tickets to CMF concerts. Insiders often bring a picnic and blanket for a pre-concert dinner on the grassy lawn, and many cluster behind the auditorium and listen to the sounds of brass and strings that waft through the wooden walls. Tickets range from $6 to $35.

CU's Lyric Theatre Festival
CU's Imig Music Building, 18th & Euclid Sts., Boulder • (303) 492-8008

The Lyric Theatre features CU's graduate and undergraduate vocal students from the College of Music. Performances by the musical theater group in 1999 will include *Elixir of*

Photo: Daily Camera

Share a patriotic moment at the Fourth of July picnic at Chautauqua.

Love and *She Loves Me*. Tickets are $18 with discounts for children and senior citizens.

Colorado Dance Festival
2590 Walnut St., Boulder
• (303) 442-7666

This independent dance group presents classes, workshops and performances at the university and other spaces throughout Boulder in the summer. Three hundred students join them, with more than 35 performing and teaching artists. Admission varies with each event.

Colorado Freedom Festival
Central Park and other locations in Boulder • (303) 665-2733

Boulder makes much of multiculturalism throughout the year, but this event, which takes place in Central Park, on the library lawn and in the library auditorium, is where this commitment is put on display. This festival is essentially one big party, celebrating the arts and cultural diversity. The variety offered includes dance, art exhibits, a children's talent show, live music performances, a health expo, ethnic food and more. The festival, often held the weekend preceding the Fourth of July, generally starts early Friday afternoon, runs all day on Saturday and winds down on Sunday.

Fourth of July
An overture of real thunder often ends just before the planned fireworks begin. The public gatherings are grand, but so is a quiet, foothills nook. From a high roost, you can see those giant, bright-colored dandelion puffs all the way from Denver. Once the sun sets, it can get cold. Bring a heavy sweater or blanket. Many other Boulder County communities, such as Longmont, Louisville and Broomfield, have their own fireworks, often with community picnics and concerts.

Boulder Concert in the Park
Chautauqua Park, Ninth St. and Baseline Rd., Boulder • (303) 442-3282

This Fourth of July outdoor concert by the Colorado Music Festival's nationally recognized summer orchestra features pop and sing-along music. Insiders bring picnic baskets and blankets then linger here to watch distant fireworks. The concert starts at 5 PM, and admission is free.

Boulder Fireworks
Folsom Field (on CU-Boulder campus), Boulder • (303) 442-1044

Even without great fireworks, which are launched at dark, this evening extravaganza would be a kick, for the live entertainment is good, and the sing-alongs include popular rock and hokey camp songs. Up With People and other well-known groups have performed in the past. Admission is free, but it's best to get there early, because the place begins to fill up long before the sun sets.

Louisville Fourth of July Picnic and Fireworks
Downtown Louisville and Coal Creek Golf Course • (303) 666-6565

Enjoy a community picnic, art festival, children's games and a band in Memory Square Park, then "Fireworks on the Links," with the couples on the temporary dance floor swinging.

Nederland Fourth of July Parade and Fireworks
Downtown Nederland and Barker Reservoir • (303) 258-3936

A small-town parade and fireworks put a real old-fashioned spin on this most traditional holiday.

Boulder Folk and Bluegrass Festival
Chautauqua Auditorium. Ninth St. and Baseline Rd., Boulder • (303) 443-5858

Local and international performers who have appeared at this popular mid-July event have included stars such as Doc Watson. Since ticket prices vary, it's best to call for complete information.

Rocky Grass Festival
Rocky Grass Hollow, Lyons • (303) 449-6007

In a pretty creekside field, internationally known bluegrass fiddlers and banjo pickers entertain campers and picnickers. Bluegrass workshops, late-night campfires and dips in the St. Vrain River add to the old-time ambiance. In 1998, a three-day pass was $80. Tickets are also available by the day for this weekend event in early August. The producer also presents the famous Telluride Bluegrass Festival in southwestern Colorado.

Boulder Victorian Fair
1206 Euclid Ave., Boulder • (303) 449-3464

Sponsored by the Boulder Museum of History, this festive day, held at adjacent Beach Park in late July, includes military drill re-enactments, carriage rides, blacksmithing and craft demonstrations, children's games and entertainment. Colorado foods, quilts and vintage cars abound. And how about a pie bakeoff? It's a perfect event for Boulder, home of the American Pie Council. There's also a beauty contest for teddy bears and dolls.

Ol' Timers and Miners Days
Throughout Nederland • (303) 258-3936

Head up the canyon to enjoy a pancake breakfast, a barbecue or the festival's Sow-Bellie Lunch. Or join in such contests as the Women's Spike Driving and Men's Hand Mucking competitions. The whole festival harkens back to Nederland's mining history. Admission to this late July event is free.

August

Boulder County Fair
Boulder County Fairgrounds, 9595 Nelson Rd., Longmont • (303) 772-7170

The whole family will love the goats and rabbits at this down-home country fair, which draws more than 100,000 spectators. Sheep yell "Ma-a!" as 4-H parents do the final, pre-show shearing. The harness horses prance, their braided manes decorated with flowers. At the old-timers' rodeo on the last Friday, see

Photo: Roz Brown

The fair comes to town the first week of August each year.

bucking broncos and fancy riding. Admission to the fairgrounds is free, but call ahead to check fees for such events as the rodeo. The fair runs from the first through the second weekend in August.

Chipeta Powwow
Chipeta Park, Nederland
• (303) 258-3936

Local and international dancers join the fun at this event, which features Native American dancing and costumes along with plenty of food, arts and crafts. This mid-August festival is presented by the Nederland Arts and Humanities Council. Admission had not been set at press time, although the fee for past events has been around $5.

Boulder Asian Festival
Pearl Street Mall, Boulder
• (303) 444-1078

The fifth annual Asian Festival was held in mid-August in 1998 and featured Asian food, crafts, arts, performances and children's activities at the courthouse plaza on the Pearl Street Mall. There is no admission fee, but bring some cash if you want to sample the food. Entertainment has included dancers from the Thai Cultural Foundation, Rocky Mountain Chinese School and Philippine-American Dance Troupe.

Old Town Lafayette Antiques & Country Peach Festival
401 S. Public Road, Lafayette
• (303) 666-7200

This annual event in early August features dealers' booths with antiques and crafts all along the Old Town section of Public Road. It features peach cobbler, peach ice cream, peach smoothies as well as other food concessions and entertainment. Hours are 9 AM to 5 PM.

September

Louisville Fall Festival and Labor Day Parade
Downtown, Louisville
• (303) 666-6565

Louisville's Labor Day parade, one of Colorado's largest, attracts more than 25,000 people. The Saturday and Sunday of Labor Day weekend feature an art fair, carnival, music and pancake breakfast. The Monday parade includes pets, the King Soopers Shopping Cart Drill Team, marching bands and antique cars. The parade down Main Street starts at 10 AM.

Boulder Creek Hometown Fair and Harvest Festival
Municipal Building Lawn, Canyon and Broadway • (303) 449-3825

Held for the first time in 1998, this Labor Day weekend event is hosted by the same folks who produce the Boulder Creek Festival in May. Expect a craft fair, garden tent, a dance hall with free dance workshops, a Harvest Moon Sweethearts Dance and Boulder's annual Chili Olé competition. Hours are Saturday 10 AM to 10 PM, Sunday 10 AM to 9 PM and Monday from 10 AM to 7 PM.

Cause for Paws Walk-a-Thon
**Boulder County Humane Society
2323 55th St., Boulder • (303) 442-4030**

In 1998 more than 400 people and their dogs raised $45,000 to help fund the Humane Society's programs. The mid-September event follows the Boulder Creek Path along a four-mile route and returns along the same route to a People and Pet Fair. The $15 registration fee includes a T-shirt.

Dixieland Jazz and Big Band Swing Festival
**1155 Canyon Blvd., Boulder
• (303) 936-3962 or (303) 449-5930**

Boulder Friends of Jazz host this jammin' festival at Trios Grille in mid-September. BFJ solicits grants from enthusiastic arts-funding agencies and private businesses in order to make this a top-notch affair. Admission is $10.

Golden Aspen Trees
Peak to Peak Hwy. (Colo. Hwy. 72) north of Nederland and other locations

The greatest fall festival is the natural one — the annual gilding of the aspen. Mother Nature never calls ahead to reserve a day for the best sight of leaves, so watch local papers for reports of favorable turnings, some time in September or October. The *Daily Camera* runs stories and maps. The aspens east of the Continental Divide generally turn gold, but sometimes pinkish foliage peeks out among the yellow. Often, a whole grove changes at once, for aspen are large, cloned families, connected by their roots. Because "quakies" have loose leaf stems, the shiny leaves really shimmer. The biggest aspen fields are along the Peak to Peak Highway outside of Nederland. Driving is fun. But even better, park at a trailhead and take a stroll. Rocky Mountain National Park boasts several astonishing stands of aspen. The park rangers can direct you to the best. Wherever you hike, the filtered golden light, the tannin scent of fall and the sound of fluttering aspen leaves are unforgettable.

Longs Peak Scottish Highland Festival
Estes Park Fairground, Community Drive, Estes Park • 1-800-90-ESTES

You'll find kilts and caboodles of festivities at this festival, the biggest event of Estes Park's year. It's a celebration of Celtic heritage held the first weekend after Labor Day. The dates for 1999 were September 9th through the 12th. Naturally bagpipes play a large part in the festival and bagpipers take center stage for the weekend parade. (See our Estes Park chapter for more information.)

Walker Ranch Living History
**Walker Ranch, Flagstaff Rd. (west of Chautauqua Park), Boulder
• (303) 441-3950**

The last two weekends in September, blacksmiths pound a ringing "whang" on red-hot iron while the bellows release a throaty sigh. Sunbonnet-clad women prepare victuals at a potbellied stove. They're volunteers, trained by Boulder County Parks and Open

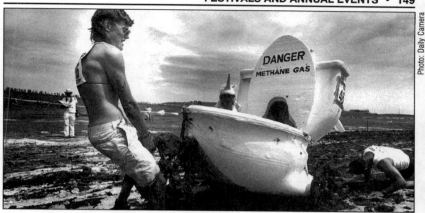

The Kinetic Conveyance Challenge combines creativity, spring wackiness and lots of mud.

Space to live the old-fashioned way for a few days. The ranch is open 10 AM to 2 PM and has free everything, from watching the horses plow to sampling the homemade bread and hand-churned butter. This gorgeous area frequently has brilliant mountain bluebirds. The ranch is on the left, 7.5 miles west of Chautauqua Park, up Flagstaff Road.

Celebrate Lafayette
Old Town Lafayette • (303) 666-9555

Lafayette loves a parade, and this one, held the week after Labor Day, features the Recycled Seniors Umbrella Team, a wild-animal float with real lions and bears and other highlights. The day-long festival also includes a free pancake breakfast, entertainers, bargain hot-air balloon rides, fun booths and a bed race.

Boulder Fall Festival
Pearl Street Mall, Boulder • (303) 449-3774

Loosely styled after a European Oktoberfest, this celebration in late September has become a primo showcase for local and visiting craftsmen. It still includes flowing beer — though now more microbrews than German brews — plus bands, carnival rides, lots of food, and a petting zoo for the kids. It runs 11 AM to 10 PM on Friday and Saturday and 11 AM to 6 PM on Sunday.

October

Band Day
Folsom Field, University of Colorado Campus, Folsom and Colorado Ave. • (303) 492-6584

An autumn regular for more than five decades, Band Day brings stirring high school bands from across the state to compete at Folsom Field. This event is free.

Pumpkin Pie Days Antiques Show
9595 Nelson Rd., Boulder County Fairgrounds, Longmont • (303) 776-1870

More than 80 dealers display antiques and collectibles at the exhibit hall where there is plenty of parking and admission is free. This mid-October event was named for celebrations that brought special trains full of visitors to Longmont from 1899 to 1914. The cafe at the exhibit hall serves the pie and other food delights. Hours are Saturday from 10 AM to 5 PM and Sunday from 11 AM to 5 PM.

Boulder County AIDS Project
2118 14th St., Boulder • (303) 543-0025

A costume contest and prizes highlight the annual BCAP Halloween Bash and Costume Extravaganza. Held the weekend before Halloween, all proceeds benefit BCAP's many programs. The location changes from year to year. Tickets in advance are $10.

Museum in the Dark
University of Colorado Museum, Broadway and 15th St., Boulder
• (303) 492-6892

Bring your flashlight, for tonight the lights are off at the dinosaur museum so that kids discover the real triceratops head and flying pterodactyl with their own, modern torches. This is an educational (rather than a scary) night, and science volunteers bring exhibits such as bats and live snakes. The idea is to take the spooky out of Halloween but keep the delicious sense of discovery. It's also a great chance to get familiar with this excellent, family-oriented museum that always has special exhibits. Call ahead to reserve tickets, which usually sell out by party night. Tickets are $5. Museum in the Dark usually happens the Friday before Halloween.

Munchkin Masquerade, Children's Trick or Treat
Daily Camera, 11ᵗʰ & Pearl St., Bouder
• (303) 449-3774

On the last Sunday in October, approximately 2,000 costumed kids traipse through downtown with their parents plus local performers eager to entertain. The parade runs from 1 to 3 PM.

November

Souper Bowlder Promotion
Boulder Arts & Crafts Cooperative, 1421 Pearl St., Pearl Street Mall
• (303) 443-3683

Hundreds of ceramic soup bowls donated by professional potters sell for $12 each at this benefit for the Boulder County AIDS project and Boulder Shelter for the Homeless. Dried soup mixes from the Women's Bean Project (a work force of otherwise unemployed women) are also offered.

Boulder Potters' Guild Show & Sale
2108 55th St., Boulder • (303) 447-0310

Here's a chance to purchase tasteful, hand-crafted holiday gifts at reasonable prices. This mid-November show and sale runs 10 AM to 8 PM on Thursday and Friday, 10 AM to 5 PM on Saturday and 10 AM to 4 PM on Sunday. There is no admission fee and the kids can snack on delicious treats while you browse.

Nutcracker Ballet
Macky Auditorium (on CU-Boulder campus), Boulder • (303) 449-1343

The Boulder Philharmonic teams up with the Boulder Ballet for four packed performances of this favorite family ballet during Thanksgiving weekend. Everything's magic when local children play the mice, and rising local stars portray Clara and her Prince. During intermission, kids can peek in the orchestra pit, where friendly musicians demonstrate instruments that include the celeste, which makes those little tinkly bell sounds for the Sugar Plum Fairy. Tickets for the 1998 event ranged from $8 to $35 with discounts for students and children.

Hmong New Year
Lafayette Elementary School, 101 N. Bermont Ave., Lafayette
• (303) 665-5046

During this four-day event in late November, coinciding with Thanksgiving weekend, the 700 Hmong who live in Boulder County invite others in Colorado's Laotian refugee (and non-refugee) community to join this celebration, which includes traditional clothing and food. The needlework is stunning. This event is free.

December

Lights of Downtown Parade
Pearl St. Mall, Boulder • (303) 449-3774

This eclectic parade on the first Friday in December launches Boulder's holiday season. Like many parades throughout the year, the route circumnavigates the pedestrian center. The parade is both sweet and hokey. You'll see everything from Boulder's Girl Scout troops with battery-operated Christmas lights in their hair to the local Polar Bear Club members prancing about the cold streets barefoot and bathing-suited, hopping into a hot tub on wheels whenever they need to warm up again. Eco-elves prance by in curled-toe green slippers, passing out information about recycling; local marching bands play; and gleaming antique cars and fire trucks get festooned with ornaments. The parade starts around 7 PM.

Louisville Parade of Lights
Downtown Louisville • (303) 666-6565

Garlands swing from Main Street lamps, and choral groups perform by City Hall. There are open houses and hay rides. More than 20 floats join the parade, which starts at 7 PM on the first Friday in December.

Artwalk
Pearl Street Mall, Boulder
• (303) 444-9116 (Linton-Haslam Gallery)

On the first weekend in December, grab a gallery guide at any local gallery, then enjoy this tour of Boulder's gorgeous arts and crafts purveyors. This self-guided tour of open galleries is free.

Holiday Festival Concert
Macky Auditorium, CU Boulder Campus,
• (303) 492-8008

This early December event is so popular, the auditorium fills up for the dress rehearsal in addition to the actual performance. University of Colorado College of Music students and faculty perform in a festively decorated Macky Auditorium. The program features Christmas favorites and seasonal music from various cultures. There are performances on Friday and Saturday nights and Sunday afternoon. Ticket prices range from $12 to $15.

Historic Homes for the Holidays
Various Boulder homes • (303) 444-5192

Grand homes deck their halls for the holidays, and everyone is invited to have a look during the first weekend in December. Mapleton Hill Victorians and Romanesque Uni-Hill homes are among those that have been on tour in recent years. The decorating by the owners and professionals is spectacular. This fund-raiser for Historic Boulder also includes a gift shop and drawings for door prizes. Ticket prices vary; in 1998, they were $15 for non-members of Historic Boulder and $13.50 for seniors 60 and older.

Celebration of Boulder Ball
Glenn Miller Ballroom, University of Colorado, Broadway & Euclid
• (303) 449-2556

The black-tie holiday ball with silent auction and seated gourmet dinner helps raise money for the Emergency Family Assistance Association (EFAA). The EFAA supports Boulder County families in financial crisis. Tickets have been around $85 per person.

Messiah Sing-along
St. John's Episcopal Church, 14th and Pine Sts., Boulder • (303) 442-5246

Professionals fly in to sing the solos, and the choir practices for weeks to lead a rousing rendition of Handel's *Messiah*. But the passion comes from friends, families and people who just like to sing. Some singers filling the pews are practically pros, while others have never sung before, but they all join in for the rousing "Hallelujah Chorus" which must be audible all the way to the heavens. There are two evening performances and one matinee the weekend before Christmas Eve. Tickets are around $10.

Events Central

Many festivals occur throughout the year. The *Daily Camera*'s "Friday Magazine" is loaded with entertainment information for the upcoming weekend. The chambers of commerce also have information on specific local events, and remember to sample the choices listed in our Boulder Attractions chapter. If you're casting about for something to do, call any (or all) of the following organizations: Boulder Chamber of Commerce, (303) 442-1044; Boulder County Fairgrounds, (303) 678-6235; CU-Boulder Cultural Events/Concert Line, (303) 492-3227; or Chautauqua Association, (303) 442-3282.

Each year, nearly 2 million bicyclists, in-line skaters, walkers, runners — you name it — use the Boulder Creek Path.

Attractions

Boulder's top five, must-see attractions are detailed here, followed by a smorgasbord of other treats if time and taste permit. Also see our chapters on Boulder Festivals and Annual Events, Kidstuff, Sports and Neighborhoods and Nearby Communities.

The Top Five

Pearl Street Mall
Pearl St. from 11th to 15th Sts., Boulder

Business people in the 1970s bit their nails as Boulder plunked down more than a million dollars for a pedestrian mall. How on earth would people shop, some wondered, if they couldn't park in front of a store?

Since then, *The Wall Street Journal* has called the Pearl Street Mall one of the nation's most successful pedestrian malls, and it has won national design awards. It's Boulder's people-watching spot, from kids climbing the bronze frog to college-age lovers buying gauzy new clothes to business people grabbing a savory pie at the Empañadas window. Street musicians embroider the air with a saxophone's blue tones, steel-drum calypso, folk guitar and more. Breathe deeply. The aroma of fresh pretzels might draw you to a kiosk in front of the Courthouse; fresh popcorn or stir-fried something might bring you to a pushcart vendor; or a thick, dark river of perfume might sweep you into the Rocky Mountain Chocolate Factory.

In addition to matchless people-watching, the Pearl Street Mall offers abundant free entertainment — though, of course, the jugglers, clowns and magicians appreciate tips. In the warm months, you can sit to have your portrait painted, your fortune told or get a neck and shoulder massage; or you might pick a ringside seat in one of the many excellent restaurants with patio tables. Thanks to Boulder's clear skies and mild days, people-watchers often sit out even in winter. Some of Boulder's finest restaurants, galleries and shops are found on the Mall. Discover them as you wander, or check our chapters on Boulder Shopping, Arts and Restaurants.

Pearl Street's history does not always reflect such a stylish past. It started Wild West style, with drunks horse racing down the dirt lane that was the main street. And no proper lady walked a white poodle, for these dogs were popular among the "soiled doves" whose creekside homes advertised, "Men Taken In and Done For." To civilize the street, storekeepers built plank walks, but they didn't match sidewalk height between stores, so shoppers bobbed up and down along the way.

By the 1970s, Pearl Street was drearily, Midwestern-y respectable. Aluminum facades hid brick storefronts, cars jammed streets, and "for lease" signs proliferated like mushrooms growing in decay. To halt the decline, planners suggested everything from a covered shopping mall to high-rises. It seemed so risky to restore the original buildings, tweak the Old West character and create strolling space with sculptures, trees and flowers. Now that it's done and has a two-decade track record of success, please exult: "What a great idea!"

If you're a history buff, stop by the Hotel Boulderado, (303) 442-4344, at 2115 13th Street, just north of the mall. This red brick hotel, named after Boulder and Colorado, was built in 1909, the city's pride, with Italianate porch corners, a cherry cantilevered staircase and an Italian stained-glass ceiling. Robert Frost and Louis Armstrong were among the guests. But the Boulderado suffered decline too. The glass ceiling crashed in a 1960s snowstorm; kitchen cooks hung bait over vats to drown rats; and vagrants slept in empty rooms. In the 1980s, Boulderado Concept Ltd. restored the grand old hotel. Wander inside. The

Catacombs Bar in the basement has live blues, reggae and jazz most nights of the week, and there's live music on the mezzanine on Friday evenings; it's reserved for private parties other times.

Another historic area on Pearl Street is the Boulder Courthouse Square, between 13th and 14th streets. The location started as the town's baseball diamond and then was the site of Boulder County's grand Victorian courthouse, which burned down in the 1930s. Local architect Glenn Huntington designed the light-colored stone, art deco courthouse you see today. The lawn, which was extensively redesigned in 1996, is a popular festival spot.

A fountain built in 1935 by the Lions Club began operating again in 1999 after years of disrepair and neglect. It is surrounded by tasteful landscaping and benches, which makes it a wonderful spot to sit and watch Boulder's Summer Concert Band perform Sousa marches on the courthouse plaza.

Just east, at 2032 14th Street, is the Boulder Theater, (303) 786-7030, a turn-of-the-century opera house renovated in the 1930s as the gaudy little sister of the plain blond courthouse. The art deco facade is as lavish as a peacock's tail, and the restored interior has gorgeous, hand-painted, flowery murals. A live music venue to both local and national acts, the former movie house also offers dance, theater and corporate events and can be rented for private parties. The Theater is also home to the weekly E-Town live music/talk performances broadcast by National Public Radio to more than 150 cities.

From the Pearl Street Mall, it's an easy walk to Central Park, between Canyon and Arapahoe streets east of Broadway. An art deco band shell built in 1938 was restored in 1996, and once again hosts concerts and civic events. A steam locomotive and frequent festivals can be found in Central Park.

On Saturday mornings from spring through early fall and on Wednesday afternoons in summer, the Boulder County Farmers Market takes place along 13th Street (see the subsequent Boulder Creek Path entry for details about this market). On the east side of the street is the Boulder Museum of Contemporary Art (see subsequent entry), and the Boulder Creek Path, the next must-see attraction, runs along the south side of the park.

Boulder Creek Path
Throughout Boulder

Boulder's most popular "architecture" is 12 feet wide, 6 miles long and flat on the ground. This 1980s project lets non-car commuters travel the prettiest possible way. The Creek Path dips under 10 major intersections, transforming traffic's roar into a whispered "whoosh." More than a half-dozen wooden pedestrian bridges crisscross the stream, clattering merrily as bicyclists and in-line skaters pass. The bridges are designed to snap to the side and reduce debris if a big flood hits. The whole path was designed with a rising creek in mind. Major flooding is rare, but every few years, some overflow happens. The City's flower plantings along this route are a feast for the eyes.

Each year, nearly 2 million bicyclists, in-line skaters, walkers, runners — you name it — use the Boulder Creek Path. Other non-motor-vehicle routes connect from all over the city, so people can really get around without cars. Be alert, however. Some fierce bicyclists

---

www.insiders.com

See this and many other **Insiders' Guide®** destinations online — in their entirety.

Visit us today!

INSIDERS' TIP

Some of Boulder's most popular stores have become attractions in their own right. Boulderites often take out-of-towners to Alfalfa's Natural Food Market, McGuckin Hardware, The Peppercorn and other distinctive retail establishments just for the fun of it. See our Boulder Shopping chapter for more information.

Photo: Roz Brown

In addition to plenty of artifacts from the city's past, the Boulder Museum of History features a large collection of costumes.

and in-line skaters ignore speed signs and can scare the daylights out of walkers. Especially in busy areas near downtown, keep an eye on kids, your dogs and your own tendency to stray. Choose your chariot — bicycle, feet, in-line skates or wheelchair — and head to the path.

The **Boulder Public Library's** main branch, (303) 441-3100, at 10th Street and Arapahoe Avenue is a good place to start, and in fact, a stop to admire this gleaming facility is worthwhile too. About 3,000 folks use it daily. Look for the dramatic glass entry on the Arapahoe Avenue side. Outside are a Pooh-garden, scent garden and flowers. Inside, the library has approximately 320,000 circulating books, an artists' register showing slides of local artwork and a computerized media/browsing system. Books can be delivered to the homebound who can't get to the library, and another service transcribes text into Braille. Kid-pleasing attractions include a trout habitat, two new multimedia computers with interactive children's software and storytelling hours. The library auditorium on the Canyon Boulevard side is the site of a free

year-round film and concert series. The Learning to Read program provides free, confidential tutoring for everyone from children to adults. There are seven computer terminals with free Internet access, but be prepared to wait as they are extremely popular. The library is open 9 AM to 9 PM Monday through Thursday, 9 AM to 6 PM Friday and Saturday and noon to 6 PM Sunday. There are also three branch libraries in Boulder; their hours vary from each other and the main library.

Just west of the library is the **West Boulder Senior Center** at Ninth Street and Arapahoe Avenue. After passing under Ninth Street, be sure to notice the sculpture of Chief Niwot (Niwot means "left hand") on the left. Continue westward to Sixth Street and Canyon Boulevard, where you'll find the **Children's Fishing Pond**, marked by an abstract metal sculpture that looks like leaping fish. On your right is the **Boulder County Justice Center**, with courts for dreary things from speeding tickets to criminal cases, but also where civil marriage ceremonies are performed. Just beyond, west along the Creek Path, the **Xeriscape Demonstration Garden** displays native plants that make environmentally wise gardening choices for Colorado's arid climate, an herb garden and a "wheel" of lawns comparing bluegrass, two buffalo grasses, fescue and blends.

Continuing westward, the path opens out to **Eben Fine Park** at Fourth Street, a favorite shady picnic and Frisbee-throwing area, with playgrounds and a congenial family atmosphere. At the park, you'll see a tunnel to the north, or right, under Canyon Boulevard. It leads to **Red Rocks/Settlers Park**, site of the 1858 campsite along Boulder Creek by the gold seekers who became Boulder's first citizens. Historical plaques explain some of Boulder's early history. Near more picnic tables, you'll see a steep trail up to the nearly vertical red rocks, naturally called Red Rocks, and a fine hilltop view of the whole area. Take care should you decide to scramble up the rocks for an even better vista.

Back along the creek path and just west of the park is Boulder's kayak course. Even if you're not into whitewater, it's thrilling to watch kayakers and canoeists test their skills in the rapids during spring and early summer. Innertube riders crawl into their black doughnut-shaped vessels here too for a bracing ride down to Broadway. Two historic markers along

the path tell about the **Switzerland Trail** railroad line and **Farmers' Ditch**, two early landmarks in the development of Boulder County.

For a lovely walk into Boulder Canyon, keep going up the hill and to the west along the Creek Path (watch out for speeding downhill cyclists). After a while, the pavement ends, the path dips under the canyon road and deposits you at the base of the **Elephant Buttresses** and the **Dome**, two of Boulder's most popular rock-climbing spots. In one vista, you'll see an old water flume and Lycra-clad rock climbers, a perfect combination on the Boulder firmament. Farther along the path, wild roses and purple asters bloom in summer beside the frothy creek, and wild plums and grapes ripen in the fall. The gravel path continues up along the creekside under the rustling cottonwoods and glinting ponderosa pines to **Four Mile Canyon** about 1.5 miles away. The total distance from Eben Fine Park — the lower bridge at the east end of the park with a boulder marked 0 miles — to the end of the trail is 2.25 miles.

If instead you head east from the Boulder Public Library, you'll soon get to **Central Park** at Broadway. There are small waterfalls, historic railroad cars, a band shell and sometimes an outdoor sculpture exhibit. The Boul-

Boulder Falls is a favorite spot for photographs and recreation.

Photo: Daily Camera/Nico Toutenhoofd

der Museum of Contemporary Art (see subsequent entry) is across the street, east of the park.

On Saturday mornings from spring through fall and Wednesday afternoons during the summer, the **Boulder County Farmers Market** stretches on both sides of 13th Street between Arapahoe Avenue and Canyon Boulevard. This assembly features a colorful parade of produce, flowers, homegrown and homemade goodies and weekly cooking demonstrations by local chefs. This beguiling attraction features a changing cornucopia of produce and related wares and has become Colorado's most successful open-air market. Regulars use it as an opportunity to shop, stroll, nibble and socialize. The location is perfect, close to the Pearl Street Mall and right next to Central Park. During the market's early weeks, vendors specialize in seedlings that you can take home and plant. At summer's peak, the street packs with local fresh tomatoes, Western Slope peaches, Rocky Ford cantaloupe and honeydew melons, green beans, lettuce, fresh herbs and more. Tamales, pirogen and focaccia give the market a true international ambiance. Fresh and dried flowers, lavender water, hot corn on the cob, honey and delicacies from goat cheese to smoked trout tempt from many stands. Don't forget sweet ices, lemonade and fresh-baked pastries, all in a big colorful crowd. The market opens in mid-April and runs through the end of October. Saturday hours are 8 AM to 2 PM. After June 1, a smaller version is also open Wednesday from 11 AM to 4 PM until the weather turns cold in the fall. Downtown workers appreciate the lunch menu at the Wednesday market.

The eclectic atmosphere of the farmers market is a perfect complement to Boulder's unique **Dushanbe Teahouse** located in the center of all this activity. In 1986, the residents of Boulder's sister city of Dushanbe crated and shipped this elegant teahouse to Colorado. Because there was no unanimity on where it should be built or who should foot the bill, the crates remained warehoused for eleven years. Finally in 1997 the city council agreed (the vote was not unanimous) to spend $800,000 for construction of the teahouse at the 13th Street site. The funding helped bring artisans from Tajikistan to Boulder to complete the intricate assembly. The folks who run the cafe at the Naropa Institute now serve daily meals at the teahouse, which is also the venue for a variety of special, community events.

After you enjoy a meal on the Teahouse patio you can return immediately to the Creek Path and continue east, past **Boulder High School** and its athletic fields, to a sunny, stone-bench alcove just west of the 17th Street bridge.

Just beyond is **Scott Carpenter Park**, (303) 441-3427, south of Arapahoe Avenue on 30th Street. Carpenter, a Boulder native who became one of the early astronauts, named his spaceship the *Aurora 7* after a local school. The playground has a spacecraft theme, and the park also has an outdoor swimming pool and a popular skateboard facility. The sledding hill, which once served as the city's landfill many years ago, is one of Boulder's enduring winter meccas.

Farther east, just before Foothills Parkway, you'll pass the **CU-Boulder Research Park**. Landscape designers decided the standard lawn would take too much care, guzzle water and look boring. So, they planted something much better — low-maintenance, drought-tolerant meadows that attract butterflies and birds. The result is so lovely that it's almost too popular.

At the intersection of Arapahoe Avenue and Foothills Parkway is a prairie dog town. Prairie dogs get a bad rap as vermin spreaders, but health officials say it's undeserved, and they are appropriate prey for raptors nesting nearby. Still, don't feed them; they are wild animals and should stay that way. Kids love how they stand like little soldiers, then yip before diving underground. Prairie dogs are a remnant of the shortgrass prairie ecosystem and are food for swooping hawks.

You can take the Creek Path northeast from here, to the tent-roofed stands of the **Stazio Ballfields**, (303) 441-4410, at 2445 Stazio Drive, which are well-lighted and busy well into evening all summer long. Notice that the path veers away from the oldest cottonwood trees. Playing by the creek is fun, but human activity has caused creekside wildlife to decline. By keeping people farther away, critters, such as the red-eyed vireo and yellow warbler, have a better chance. If you ever hear a warbler sing, you'll thank creek planners for giving those birds privacy. As the Creek Path spreads its tentacles, you can take offshoots either to the north or south through residential as well as industrial areas, which is one reason why it is so popular for commuting.

Chautauqua Park
Ninth St. and Baseline Rd., Boulder
• **(303) 442-3282**

At the turn of the century, sites across the nation became gathering spots for summer cultural and educational institutes, all named "Chautauqua" after Chautauqua Lake in upstate New York, where the first such gathering was held. Dozens of Chautauquas once existed, but few remain. Boulder's was one of the rare Western locations. The **Chautauqua Auditorium and Dining Hall**, (303) 440-3776, built in 1898, and a charming nearby colony of wooden cottages comprise the last original site west of the Mississippi.

Chautauqua's main buildings, decked out in crisp gray, would still be a perfect setting for banjo-strumming gallants in flat-brimmed hats, but summer offerings now draw modern crowds with contemporary interests. There's a nod to the past with July's silent films, accompanied by live piano. The Colorado Chautauqua Association Forum is a lecture series dating from 1898, but today's speakers address topics such as health issues, transportation and world affairs.

The **Colorado Music Festival**, (303) 449-1397, has a full orchestra of musicians invited here for the summer and features internationally renowned guest artists as well as rising stars with promising futures. The vast majority of classical performances are instrumental, for the wooden auditorium tends to swallow voices. An orchestra or a powerful soloist can make the wonderful barn resonate with great sound. For ticket events, call the Box Office, (303) 440-7666, between May and September.

Chautauqua Park has 58 cottages for rent from June through August, with a minimum four-night stay. They vary in size, but all have a kitchen, bathroom, living area and one or more bedrooms. For the 1999 season, a four-day stay ranged from $61 to $116 per night depending on the size of the cottage. These fill up fast so make your reservation as soon after November 1 as possible. To rent a cottage for the summer or to learn about the summer programs, call the Chautauqua Association, (303) 442-3282. The Chautauqua Gift Cottage, (303) 443-5839, is open daily in the summer only.

Children like the **Chautauqua Park playground**, especially after they discover low-branched trees for playing hide-and-seek. (Only kids can scamper through. Moms and dads have to hunch.) The **Chautauqua Ranger Cottage**, (303) 441-3408, near the big meadow on the west side of the park, is generally open 8:30 AM to 5:00 PM daily. Its small garden displays native plants, and the rangers dispense plenty of hiking information. The rangers can answer questions, and they're trained to handle emergencies. They also lead free interpretive hikes that depart from the Ranger Cottage at 8 AM Saturday mornings in summer.

Trails lead everywhere. The Boulder Mountain Parks trail system includes everything from short, nearly flat strolls to steep hikes. One of the easiest, and shadiest, is the McClintock Trail, starting southeast of the Chautauqua Auditorium. You can head west on the Chautauqua Trail, cross the big meadow and watch rock climbers. Or head west and south to the Mesa Trail. It's 3 up-and-down miles to the next major attraction, NCAR (see subsequent entry) and twice that far to the Mesa Trail's southern terminus just off the Eldorado Canyon Road.

National Center for Atmospheric Research
West end of Table Mesa Dr., Boulder
• **(303) 497-1000**

Anyone who has ever gazed at the sky can find something of interest at NCAR (pronounced "en-car"). Founded in 1960 to study world climate, NCAR draws scientists from all over the globe to study our wonderful blanket of air. Interesting displays present the fundamentals of their fields of expertise. Sky-watchers can learn about clouds, air currents, lightning, hail, tornadoes and other weather phenomena, including global warming. I.M. Pei designed this mesa-top complex, which helped establish his reputation as a world-class architect. "The mountains," said Pei, "gave us scale trouble from the beginning. We had to return to elemental forms. The Rockies humbled us." Local red limestone was mixed into the concrete so it would blend with the Flatirons. The building's angular forms mimic keyhole doors at the Mesa Verde cliff dwellings. This building is considered one of the nation's finest public structures. Two galleries feature community art. The computers in the basement are some of the world's fastest and largest.

Self-guided tours, with brochures from the lobby, are always available. Guided walking tours take place at noon Mondays and Wednesdays all year, and weekdays and Saturdays during the summer. No reservations are needed for the guided tours, but for information, call (303) 497-1174. If you want to bring a school, scout troop or any other group, tours must be arranged in advance by calling (303) 497-1173. The Walter Orr Roberts Weather Trail at NCAR is the only one of its kind in the country. Just west of the building, the .4-mile trail is not paved but is wheelchair-accessible. There are signs posted at regular intervals along the trail explaining weather patterns that hikers are then able to observe. In addition, there are many short nature trails near NCAR that are spectacular for more ambitious hikers.

The NCAR is open 8 AM to 5 PM Monday through Friday and 9 AM to 4 PM weekends and holidays. Admission is free. The cafeteria is open to the public, weekdays, for lunch.

University of Colorado at Boulder

Intersections of Baseline and Broadway/
Folsom and Colorado/Broadway and
College, Boulder • (303) 492-1411

CU-Boulder's 600-acre campus is one of the nation's most beautiful. The buildings are a visual symphony of red tile roofs and warm, native-stone walls that make the entire campus harmonize, and the landscaping is splendid. Norlin Quadrangle is the three-block-long, tree-lined lawn next to Broadway. Nearby are the oldest buildings on campus, including Macky Auditorium, Old Main, Hale Science Building and the Koenig Alumni Center. Kittredge Pond, near Fleming Law School, and Varsity Pond, just off the intersection of Broadway and College, are "water features" created decades before such amenities got a trendy name. The big old trees, quacking mallards and basking turtles help time stand still — even among the achingly with-it students all around.

For many, the main draw to the campus is the sports teams, and rabid fans might never get past **Folsom Field** or the **Coors Events Center**. Call (303) 492-8337 for information about Big 12 conference games, or see the Sports chapter for more information. For other folks, the campus is fun for exploring. Maps located throughout the campus pinpoint spots of interest, or call (303) 492-6301 for information about campus visits and tours. An hour-long information briefing followed by a one-hour tour is given at 9:30 AM and 1:30 PM Monday through Friday and at 10:30 AM Saturdays from the University Memorial Center in front of Room 235. Go to the main desk for information.

The **University Memorial Center**, known on campus as "the UMC," is at Euclid, just east of Broadway. The **Glenn Miller Lounge and Ballroom** are named after the CU jazz trombone player who popularized Big Band swing. A short walk to the northeast is **Norlin Library**, (303) 492-8705, with more than 10 million books, periodicals, manuscripts, government publications and more — the biggest such collection in the state. The CU-Boulder's public art gallery is in the **Sibell-Wolle Fine Arts Building**, (303) 492-8300. The **Colorado Centennial Foucault Pendulum**, (303) 492-6952, is at Duane Physical Laboratory, inside Gamow Tower, just south of Gate 2 of Folsom Field. It might seem that the 40-meter pendulum changes direction during the day, but it actually stays steady while the earth rotates underneath it. (At the equator, it would swing the same direction all the time.)

INSIDERS' TIP

No summer is complete without a stop at Boulder's Farmers Market. It's on 13th Street, between Arapahoe and Canyon streets, on Saturdays and Wednesday afternoons.

The popular Boulder Creek Path extends the width of Boulder.

The domed **Fiske Planetarium** on Regent Drive is a campus landmark housing a great theater for star shows and featuring one of the finest stargazing machines in the world. Scientists use it to turn the celestial skies back so that they can compare ancient ruins to an ancient sky. Often, they discover important building features align with star patterns that occurred long ago. Regular visitors can enjoy laser light shows and talks — fun in those leaned-back chairs that coddle your neck while you're staring upward. Star shows are normally scheduled on Friday evenings and Saturday afternoons. Adult admission is $3.50, and children and seniors pay $2 for evening shows, including admission to the adjacent **Sommers-Bausch Observatory** afterwards, weather permitting. You can get recorded information on the current week's shows by calling (303) 492-5001. For more detailed information, call (303) 492-5002. At the observatory, the real sky, not a planetarium show, is occasionally open for public viewing. Astronomy students man the telescopes during a special heavenly show, like a spectacular comet, meteor shower or eclipse; but in re-

cent years, clouds have obscured the most heralded events. Still, you can arrange to visit the observatory if you call ahead, (303) 492-5002.

The **Herbarium**, (303) 492-3216, houses nearly a half-million dried plant specimens from Colorado and around the world. It is located in the Claire Small building and is open to the public from 9 AM to 5 PM Monday through Thursday, and 9 AM to 3 PM on Friday.

The **Heritage Center**, a CU-Boulder museum, (303) 492-6329, is in Old Main, which housed the whole university from 1876 through 1884. This authentic Victorian landmark has been renovated, and the beautiful Chapel is an especially cozy area for small performances. The Heritage Center on the top floor is noteworthy for its "Space Room" honoring CU-Boulder's 13 astronauts and for the sensational collection of sports memorabilia. The distinguished alumni gallery in the center includes retired Supreme Court Justice Byron White, Miss America 1958 Marilyn Van Derbur-Atler, Robert Redford (granted an honorary degree), *M*A*S*H* actor Larry Linville and the 1989 Nobel Prize won by CU-Boulder chemist

Tom Cech. An architectural gallery shows the original models for CU, including its rural Italian design. Hours are 10 AM to 4 PM Tuesday through Friday. Summer hours are 9 AM to 4 PM Tuesday through Thursday, May 15 to September 15. Special tours can be arranged, and it's open before and after home football games. Admission is free.

University of Colorado Museum, (303) 492-6892, at Broadway and 15th Street in the Henderson Building, displays dinosaur fossils that include a triceratops head and a pterodactyl, taxidermy specimens and touchable items for kids, including a sea turtle shell you can try on for size. Established in 1902, the museum has grown to include a diversity of displays, notably in paleontology, anthropology and botany. Seasonal programs include a "Museum in the Dark" show for kids just before Halloween, and traveling exhibits are booked into the museum too. It is open 9 AM to 5 PM weekdays, 9 AM to 4 PM Saturdays and 10 AM to 4 PM Sundays. There are occasionally events that interfere with public hours, so call ahead. Admission is free.

For academic information about CU-Boulder, check the chapter on Boulder Child Care and Education.

More Museums, Historic Buildings and Special Places

The Arnett-Fullen House
646 Pearl St., Boulder • (303) 444-5192

This fanciful Victorian landmark is a few blocks west of the Pearl Street Mall. Historic Boulder, a nonprofit group based here, sells a walking-tour guidebook and conducts regular walking summer tours. These inexpensive tours include Pearl Street, the Chautauqua Park area, University Hill and the Whittier and Mapleton Hill neighborhoods. (See our Neighborhoods and Nearby Communities chapter for schedules and rates.) You may also request custom tours, including CU's Norlin Quadrangle. This group also organizes a Christmas house tour and a spring tour of fine local homes in various neighborhoods.

The Arnett-Fullen House is one of the most extreme forms of Gothic gingerbread around, its flamboyance befitting its original owner. Will Arnett was a true 19th-century character. He used $10 gold coins for buttons, built his dream house for twice the $2,000 cost of an average home in those days and died in 1900 while prospecting for gold in Alaska. No wonder his 1877 turreted Pearl Street home is ornate. Arnett also loved his cast-iron fence, which he had shipped from Pittsburgh for $2,000, a fortune back then. Historic Boulder bought the home in 1993 for $329,000. The first floor of the house is open for viewing from 8:30 AM to 4 PM weekdays. If you drop in, be sure to notice the walnut-inlaid spiral staircase.

After much wrangling, Historic Boulder bought the garden just west of the Arnett-Fullen House in 1996. Volunteers will restore it to reflect its true Victorian period. It looks beautiful now, but it will be positively glorious in spring and summer as the "new old" plantings mature.

Boulder County Fairgrounds
9595 Nelson Rd., Longmont
• (303) 441-3927

Anytime you visit, something's happening at the fair. This big, big fairground hosts antique and craft shows, barrel racing (for non-cowboys, that means racing horses in hairpin turns around barrels), national dog shows, bridge tournaments, circuses, motorcycle shows . . . the list goes on. Some events attract more than 100,000, and some are small. To reach the fairgrounds, head north to Longmont on Colo. 119. Turn left at Hover Road, whose intersection is marked with big stoplights. Go north on Hover past the Twin Peaks shopping mall to Nelson Road. The fairground's on your right. Call for an event schedule.

Boulder Museum of Contemporary Art
1750 13th St., Boulder • (303) 443-2122

This not-for-profit museum has three exhibition spaces for rotating shows as well as performing arts and mixed media space. Local, national and international artists and photographers have shown at BMoCA. In 1997 the museum hosted a very successful outdoor cinema program that attracted many first-time museum-goers. The small museum is open Tuesday through Saturday from 11 AM to 5 PM, and Sunday from noon to 5 PM. Admission is $2.

Boulder Museum of History
1206 Euclid Ave., Boulder
• **(303) 449-3464**

The three-story, blond brick Harbeck-Bergheim house, home of the Boulder Museum of History, was built by a New York merchant in 1899 as a summer home. Its most renowned feature is a spectacular 9-foot-tall Tiffany stained-glass window. The museum is an eclectic grandma's attic-type showcase of Boulder County history. Artifacts show how mining, ranching and everyday life affected Boulder. A costume gallery, one of the largest collections in the state, is on the second floor. The museum and gift shop are open 10 AM to 4 PM Tuesday through Friday, and noon to 4 PM weekends. Admission is $2 for adults and $1 for children, seniors and students.

Callahan House
312 Terry St., Longmont
• **(303) 776-5191**

In the early 1900s, a Longmont business-man named T.M. Callahan hired an unemployed Longmont butcher who had gone bankrupt because he refused to pay off the hotel chef with a weekly bottle of bourbon. That butcher, J.C. Penney, went to work for Callahan's chain of "Golden Rule" notion stores, and the Wyoming Golden Rule he and Callahan started became the first store in the Penney chain.

The Callahan home was presented to the city of Longmont in 1938. Each year, it is used for meetings, weddings, showers, receptions, dinners and other social events. The interior is opulently Victorian, with pink tones, ornately carved wood, swirly plaster moldings and exquisite light fixtures.

Callahan House is home to the St. Vrain Historical Society, (303) 776-1870, the Longmont equivalent to Historic Boulder. The society provides brochures for self-guided tours. These are available at the Longmont Museum or the carriage house behind the Callahan House. Group guided tours can be arranged by appointment. Call ahead for reservations and fees. Terry Street, by the way, is just west of Longmont's Old Main downtown.

Collage Children's Museum
2065 30th St., Boulder • (303) 440-9894

The museum's philosophy is: "I hear, I forget; I see, I remember; I touch, I understand." Therefore, dancing with shadows, art and play are major parts of this nonprofit hands-on museum that features changing exhibits and also sponsors community events for children. In late 1997 the *Telling Tales* exhibit opened at Collage. It featured 40 original, framed children's book illustrations. A hands-on project last fall called *Art Express* encouraged children to demonstrate their creativity by decorating barrels for Boulder's annual holiday food drive. The museum is open Monday, 10 AM to 5 PM, Wednesday, 2 PM to 5 PM, Thursday, Friday and Saturday 10 AM to 5 PM and Sunday 1 to 5 PM with extended summer hours. Collage is closed on Tuesday. Story hour is 3:30 to 4:30 PM on Wednesdays. Admission is $3.00 per person; $12 per family; and free for members and children younger than 2.

The Leanin' Tree Museum of Western Art
6055 Longbow Dr., Boulder
• **(303) 530-1442**

Landscapes, bronze sculptures and other original art comprise one of the nation's largest privately owned Western art collections. The artworks, primarily post-Russell and Remington, include paintings and sculpture and are available as a result of Leanin' Tree founder Ed Trumble's 40-year friendship with Western artists. The growing collection keeps expanding into the Leanin' Tree greeting card company's workspace.

Since they opened in 1974, the museum has welcomed more than a quarter-million visitors. The gift shop sells greeting cards, framed art and T-shirts produced at Leanin' Tree. To reach the museum, take the Diagonal Highway (Colo. 119) north to 63rd Street. Turn right on Longbow Drive. The company and museum are the third building on the right. The museum is open 8 AM to 4:30 PM Monday through Friday and 10 AM to 4 PM Saturday and Sunday. Admission is free.

Carnegie Branch Library for Local History
1125 Pine St., Boulder • (303) 441-3110

This small, stately marble-columned building was Boulder's original library. Its original interior has been restored and contains local historic materials including books, diaries, oral histories, tapes, genealogical papers, 200,000 photographs, 700,000 documents and various materials donated by the Boulder Historical Society. If you are researching your house or property, this is the best place to start. Hours are 1 to 9 PM Monday; 11 AM to 5 PM Tuesday, Thursday, Friday and Saturday, with hours extended from 9 AM to 5 PM on Wednesday. Admission is free.

Dougherty Antique Museum
8306 N. 107th St., Longmont
• **(303) 776-2520**

The late Ray Dougherty didn't realize what he was starting when, as a teenager, he bought a reed organ. His wife, Dorothy Dougherty, says the hobby of collecting antique cars, farm equipment and musical instruments just grew and grew (there's also a stagecoach). The antique autos have starred in many parades. That doesn't happen much anymore, because few have the knack for driving them. After all, you don't just turn the key when a car has a steam engine or needs a hand crank.

A mile south of Longmont on U.S. Highway 287 at the family farm, this exhibit is open from 10 AM to 4 PM Friday, Saturday and Sunday, from early June through Labor Day. Admission is $4 for adults, $3 for ages 7 to 12, and free for kids 6 and younger. Large groups are welcome if they call ahead.

Flagstaff Nature Center
Flagstaff Mountain Summit, Boulder
• **(303) 441-3408**

The small log cabin atop Flagstaff Mountain contains interpretive exhibits on Front Range ecology. Its rustic log appearance remains, but the new environmentally sensitive building will have room for more displays and an increased staff. Call the Chautauqua Ranger Cottage at the listed phone number for details on new hours and expanded facilities. Nearby is the landmark Flagstaff Amphitheater, built by the Civilian Conservation Corps, and still the site of evening ranger presentations and, often, weddings. The area affords excellent views of the Boulder Valley and beyond.

To reach the center, follow Baseline Road to Flagstaff Road. The road leading to the large parking lot is well marked and to the right.

Lafayette Miner's Museum
108 E. Simpson St., Lafayette
• (303) 666-6686, (303) 665-7030

This refurbished 1890s coal miner's home was moved into town during the 1910 coal strike. The six-room house, maintained by the Louisville Historical Society, displays clothing, tools and other mining equipment and household items of the time. Hours are 2 to 4 PM Thursday and Saturday and by appointment. Admission is free.

Longmont Museum
375 Kimbark St., Longmont
• (303) 651-8374

This permanent exhibit has earned a national historic award for its Native American beaded buckskin dresses and flint arrows. The museum also displays equipment similar to that used by Major Stephen Long, the namesake of both Longs Peak and Longmont, and his party, who explored the area in the 1820s for the Army. Farming history and large-scale reproductions of early buildings are also on display here. Kidspace includes dress-up, arts and sciences and bubble-blowing. The museum is open 9 AM to 5 PM Monday through Friday; 10 AM to 4 PM Saturdays. On Monday, Wednesday and Friday mornings, 9 to 11:30 AM and afternoons from 12:30 to 2 PM there are staff-supervised discovery programs for children ages two to six. There are extended summer hours. Discovery programs are not available during summer months. Admission is free.

Louisville Historical Museum
1001 Main St., Louisville
• (303) 665-9048

Coal mining gave birth to Louisville, and artifacts from the town's early days plus household and personal items fill this small museum. Hours are 10 AM to 3 PM Tuesday through Thursday, and the first Saturday of each month or by appointment. Admission is free.

Lyons Redstone Museum
340 High St., Lyons • (303) 823-5271

Take a scenic drive from Boulder north to Lyons the town whose sandstone quarries have yielded so much of the building material you see at the University of Colorado and elsewhere in Boulder County. This restored 1881 schoolhouse features displays on the town's history. Hours are 9:30 AM to 4:30 PM Monday through Saturday; 12:30 to 4:30 PM Sunday. Admission is free, but donations are welcome. This museum closes during the winter months.

Old Mill Park
237 Pratt St., Longmont • (303) 776-1870

The oldest log cabin in Boulder County is situated in a privately owned, tree-lined park. A real mill wheel turns at the pond. The park can be reserved through the St. Vrain Historical Society for weddings and meetings. Old Mill Park is open daily to the public for free between 8 AM and dusk, except during private events. Call ahead if you want a tour of the furnished interiors.

Tower of Compassion
Missouri St. and S. Pratt Pkwy.,
Longmont • No phone

This 60-foot-tall pagoda was donated to the city in 1972 by the Kanemoto family, who settled in Longmont in the early 1900s to work in sugar-beet fields. Their family farm later was developed as residences and this city park. The tower was inspired by a family visit to Japan and the Kanemoto's gratitude to the people of Longmont. Its five levels represent love, empathy, understanding, gratitude and giving selflessly of oneself — all elements of true compassion.

Business and Science Attractions

Celestial Seasonings Tour
4600 Sleepytime Dr., Boulder
• (303) 530-5300

Your sinuses will clear as soon as you take a whiff of the 5,000 bales of mint in Celestial Seasoning's peppermint isolation room. Each year, 50,000 people enjoy a 45-minute tour of the nation's largest manufacturer of specialty and herb teas. The tour includes an assembly line where tea gets packed in those pretty little boxes, and there are taste-testing opportunities. Employees' children create safety posters, and the walls are festooned with sayings from the tea boxes. This is a New Age business to its very bones, now with a sleek all-business overlay that belies its counterculture origins in Boulder's haute hippie era.

Free tours are offered daily every hour from 10 AM to 3 PM. Arrive early to get tickets as tours are given on a first come, first served basis. Children must be 5 or older to go on the factory portion of the tour. Groups of eight or more must make reservations. You can also visit the Tea Shop and Emporium, the herb garden and lunchtime cafe whether or not you take the tour. Shop hours are 9 AM to 6 PM Monday through Saturday and 11 AM to 4 PM Sunday. To reach the plant, take the Longmont Diagonal Highway (Colo. 119) to Jay Road. Turn right (east), go a mile to Spine Road, turn left and continue a half-mile to Sleepytime Drive and Celestial Seasonings. Admission is free.

A performer dazzles pedestrians on the Pearl Street Mall.

Photo: Daily Camera

Eco-Cycle
5030 Pearl St., Boulder
• (303) 444-6634

It would be unromantic as well as technically incorrect to describe this as a "trip to the dump," but that's virtually what it is. It is enlightening to see what happens to your recyclables after they leave the curb. Kids love this big, noisy, impressive operation with a magnetic separator, which draws out the steel and leaves aluminum and other nonferrous materials behind. Eco-Cycle is one of the nation's oldest, and still largest, nonprofit recycling companies. Its many honors include a national Excellence Award from the National Recycling Coalition for leadership and environmental protection. Tours are offered Tuesday through Friday from 9:30 AM to 3:30 PM. Children must be 10 years or older to participate in the tour. Admission is free.

Federal Aviation Administration Tours
2211 17th Ave., Longmont
• (303) 651-4315

More than 90 air-traffic controllers watch approximately 40 radarscopes that show the weather and planes moving across nine states. These folks can tell any plane in their area to change routes, altitude and speed because of traffic-on-high or weather. Tours of the FAA facility are available by appointment, and aviators are the most likely to be allowed in the control room. Admission is free.

INSIDERS' TIP

Get your sinuses cleared in a millisecond by the 5,000 bales of mint in Celestial Seasonings' peppermint isolation room. This free tour includes a taste test of new teas.

The Carnegie Branch Library for Local History was Boulder's original library.

Long's Iris Gardens
3240 Broadway, Boulder
• (303) 442-2353

For nearly a century, the Long family has chugged an old tractor out to tend their iris fields. The 2,000 varieties range from pretty mongrels to prize-winning queens. You can go to the big yellow farmhouse in early May to mid-June, depending on the year's weather, or pick your own plants. (The Longs will provide supplies so you can dig your own iris clumps.) The delicate scents and the rows of colorful, fluttering petals can make any day better. Digging-season hours are generally 9 AM to 5 PM daily. An iris clump costs less than $5. The farm is close to town, on Broadway, just south of Iris Avenue (guess how that street got its name). Catalogs come out in April.

National Institute of Standards and Technology
325 Broadway, Boulder • (303) 497-1000

Bring your wristwatch. This 90-minute guided tour takes visitors to the nation's timekeeper, the atomic clock. The leap second gets added here at this very clock. The Solar Forecasting Center is where visitors can watch researchers study the sun. This is the nation's warning system for solar flares. The tour also includes a demonstration in cryogenics, the study of how extremely low temperatures (-320 degrees F) affect various materials. Guided tours are offered Thursdays at 1:30 PM. Summers include an additional tour on Tuesdays at 10:30 AM.

This is a period building, by the way. Built in the 1950s, it has a crew-cut look, from the sparkling pink travertine walls to the shiny terrazzo floors. The building is open 8 AM to 6 PM Monday through Friday. Admission is free.

National Oceanic and Atmospheric Administration/David Skaggs Research Center
325 Broadway, Boulder • (303) 497-3000 or (303) 497-3333 for tour information

Boulder is nowhere near the beach, but it's a center for incredibly sophisticated weather forecasting and oceanic research, thanks to high-powered scientists and their computers that study world weather. Until March of 1999 scientists were spread out over a half-dozen sites in Boulder. The new $60 million building has nearly 400,000-square feet and 1,000 employees. A real coup was securing the National Weather Service, which relocated to Boulder after 100 years in Denver. The National Institute of Standards and Technology is also on this campus. There are exhibits in the lobby, guided tours, school tours and a school classroom. Summer tours in 1999 were held on Tuesday and Thursday afternoons at 1 PM. The tour schedule typically changes after Labor Day. Call the tour information number for a current schedule.

The bike trails in Boulder are so wonderful, wheels can be the highlight of a child's vacation or life in Boulder.

Kidstuff

"**I**'m b-o-o-r-r-e-d!!!"

If you have kids, it's an all-too-familiar refrain. But what to do?

Here are ideas for when you get a little bored with your children's boredom. (Also check the chapters on Boulder Festivals and Annual Events, Attractions and Daytrips.)

Attractions

Butterfly Pavilion & Insect Center
6252 W. 104th Ave., Westminster
• **(303) 469-5441**

No matter how many times children visit, they never tire of the Butterfly Pavilion. After touring the display of living insects, visitors enter a greenhouse for exotic tropical butterflies. The large and colorful butterflies often land on children, producing squeals of delight and a charming sense of awe. In one corner you can watch the last two stages of metamorphosis as butterflies emerge from their chrysalids. A gift shop and cafeteria are adjacent to the Pavilion. Admission is $6.75 for adults, $4.75 for seniors and $3.75 for children. Up to two children ages 3 and under are admitted free with a paying adult. The Pavilion is open everyday from 9 AM to 5 PM.

Pearl Street Mall
On Pearl St. from 11th to 15th Sts.
• **(303) 441-4000**

The gravel-lined pits and small climb-upon boulders (just west of the Courthouse) make the Pearl Street Mall as popular a playground for children as for adults. Permanent climbing sculptures in the 14th Street block feature a snail, beaver and bunny rabbit which never fail to delight toddlers. The well maintained flower gardens are a visual delight.

Gateway Park Fun Center
4800 28th St., Boulder
• **(303) 442-4386**

Newly remodeled and refurbished, there's a new building for the video arcade and snack bar; a restructured go-cart area, miniature golf courses, batting cages and driving range; and added roller hockey and a human maze. Gateway recently added a new play area for children seven and younger.

Laser Storm
700 Ken Pratt Blvd., Longmont
• **(303) 651-6422**

Laser Storm offers Laser Tag, video games and other high-tech diversions. Birthday parties are part of the regular schedule so call ahead to avoid disappointment. If you plan to play laser tag, dress in black for the most enjoyment.

Roll-O-Rena
1201 S. Sunset St., Longmont
• **(303) 651-3720**

At this rink they still do the hokey-pokey and schedule open skate and family skate sessions. It's great fun for a birthday party, although as the parent you'll remember how to skate just about the time the kids get tired. Refreshments are available and the music is lively.

Dexter's Family Farm
95th St. and Valmont Rd., Boulder
• **(303) 604-6426 or (303) 665-3969**

The September/October pumpkin display has been so spectacular, Denver-metro area television stations use it to usher in the fall season. The Dexters usually build a jack-o'-lantern totem pole, straw horses and cheery scarecrows. Dexter's includes a small farm area with cows, chickens, horses and pigs. Children often come on school tours. Bring your camera!

Munson's Family Farm
75th St. and Valmont Rd., Boulder
• (303) 443-5330 or (303) 941-2026

Before frost hits, you and the kids can tromp into the field and twist a pumpkin off the vine. Choose amongst giants and jack-o'-lantern pumpkins, pie pumpkins and winter squash, including Delicata, a sweet, buttery-tasting winter squash that the Munsons say they've made famous. Munson's farm stand at this corner is a great place to let kids help you buy produce all summer.

CU Wizards!
Various locations, CU Campus
• (303) 492-6952

Typically on the last Saturday of the month, September through June, the University of Colorado presents its CU Wizards! program. Wizards (actually, there are 10 Mr. and Ms. Wizards) give free morning lectures that pack science lecture halls with laughing, learning kids. This is a great, informal introduction to astronomy, chemistry, biology and physics for students in grades 5 through 9. Each program lasts about an hour and includes several lively demonstration experiments. The shows begin at 9:30 AM.

Books for the Whole Child
Callahan House, 3rd and Terry Sts.,
Longmont • (303) 776-5191

Ever heard of American Girl dolls? The Callahan House puts on American Girl Victorian tea parties around Christmas time. Be sure to call ahead, for spaces fill quickly.

Lois Lafond and the Rockadiles
Boulder • (303) 444-7095

This group packs the kids in wherever they play with their funky, high-quality songs with kid lyrics. They appear at such events as Halloween parades in the metro area, the Taste of Colorado in Denver, Boulder's Out to Lunch series and others. Watch for them!

Parks

Scott Carpenter Park
30th and Arapahoe Sts., Boulder
• (303) 441-3427

Rated "Boulder's Best Park" by *Daily Camera* readers, this park was named after a local astronaut and features a climbing apparatus resembling a rocket ship. The playground was completely refurbished in 1998 with new equipment to adhere to the "space" theme. The YMCA Skate Park is also here. Open to 8-year-olds and above, its costs between $1 and $5 to test your skills on the 10-foot vertical half-pipe, or you can play it safe on the 6-foot or 4-foot mini-ramps and street course. Helmets and pads are required and can be rented for a small fee. In winter, the park is Boulder's most popular sledding area. After a winter storm, the sledding hill is small enough to be manageable but big enough to be exciting.

Cave Park, also known as Arapahoe Ridge Park
1220 Eisenhower Dr., Boulder
• (303) 413-7200

Cave Park offers the best and most creative array of playground equipment around. It's next door to Eisenhower Elementary but large enough for everyone.

Chautauqua Park
Ninth St. and Baseline Rd., Boulder
• (303) 441-7200

Chautauqua Park boasts a great expanse of lawn, away from traffic, as well as newly installed playground equipment including a child-size playhouse. The huge grassy area is great for kids and Frisbee-chasing dogs and in summer months the Chautauqua Dining Hall is the perfect place to grab a bite to eat, and has convenient restrooms.

INSIDERS' TIP

Grab some wheels and head to the Boulder Creek Path. Don't have wheels? Rent in-line skates or bikes at many bike shops.

Kids and snow are a perfect combination.

Sports

Swimming & Sailing

East Boulder Recreation Center
5660 Sioux Dr., Boulder
• **(303) 441-4400**

The "Lazy River" is very popular with small children and the tall water slide can surprise even the most adult adult. Lap lanes are also available. This center is open Monday through Thursday from 5:30 AM to 9:30 PM; Friday from 5:30 AM to 9 PM; Saturday from 7:30 AM to 7 PM; and Sunday from 8:30 AM to 8:30 PM. At the East, North and South Boulder Recreation Centers, adult city residents pay $4.50; senior citizens 60 and older pay $2.50; teens and children under the age of 18 pay $1.75 per visit. Punch cards purchased in advance will reduce the fee for those who plan to visit regu-

larly. There are also annual passes and a corporate pass program that help reduce costs.

North Boulder Recreation Center
3170 Broadway, Boulder
• **(303) 413-7260**

This is the city's oldest recreation facility. Its family swim on Sunday afternoon is inexpensive and often a lifesaver for parents or children who find themselves winter-weary and/or house-bound. This center is open Monday through Thursday from 6 AM to 9 PM; Friday from 6 AM to 6:30 PM; Saturday from 6:30 AM to 5 PM; and Sunday from 8 AM to 5 PM. The North Recreation Center started a new program in the fall of 1997 for kids 9 through 14. It's called "Boulder Nites," and allows kids to participate in a variety of activities from 7 PM to 11 PM, after parents have registered their children and paid the $8 fee. The Center promises a safe, secure environment with a police officer on the premises. A popular event so far, swimming, laser-tag games, blackout wallyball, alien art, dancing, swimming and diving contests were just a few of the activities offered to kids. For prices, please see the previous listing. The North Center will undergo extensive renovations in 2001.

South Boulder Recreation Center
1360 Gillaspie Dr., Boulder
• **(303) 441-3448**

The South Center was renovated in 1998 to include a new lap pool, new locker rooms, an improved weight room and an elevator. Young runners can take several mostly traffic-free jogging routes from here. This center is open Monday through Thursday from 6:00 AM to 9:00 PM; Friday from 6:00 AM to 9 PM; Saturday from 6:30 AM to 5:00 PM; and Sunday from 8 AM to 9 PM. For prices, please see the previous East Boulder Recreation listing.

Scott Carpenter Pool
30th and Arapahoe Sts., Boulder
• **(303) 441-3427**

This is Boulder's largest public swimming pool, open in summer only, with three wide lap lanes, a 151-foot water slide, snack bar, toddler pool and plenty of space to sunbathe. The pool is open for adult lap swim from 11 AM to 1 PM daily. Open swim is from 1 PM to 5 PM weekdays; 1 PM to 6 PM on Saturday and Sunday. Single-entry admission at all city pools is $4 for adults; $2 for seniors 60 and older; and $1.50 for teens and children 18 and younger. A punch card or an annual pass will reduce the fee. Swimming lessons are offered weekday mornings at both public pools.

Spruce Pool
2102 Spruce St., Boulder
• **(303) 441-3426**

Boulder's oldest public swimming pool, this central Boulder gem was once called the Hygienic Swimming Pool. Open during summer months only, the colorful mural, water slide and grassy sunbathing spot make this a family favorite. The pool is open from 6 AM to 7 PM

for adult lap swim. Open swim is from 1 PM to 5 PM weekdays and from 1 PM to 6 PM on Saturday and Sunday. Single-entry admission at all city pools is $4 for adults; $2 for seniors 60 and older; and $1.50 for teens and children 18 and younger. A punch card or an annual pass will reduce the fee.

Boulder Reservoir
5100 N. 51st St., Boulder
• **(303) 441-3461 or (303) 441-3468**

This is a summer-only magnet for families (see our Parks and Recreation Centers chapter). Sand beach and rentals of non-powered watercraft including canoes, rowboats, paddleboats and Sunfish. The reservoir is open from 6 AM until dusk for sailboarding, sailing, and water skiing. Swimmers are allowed admittance from 9:30 AM until 6:30 PM. Daily admission at the Reservoir is $4.50 for adults; $2.25 for kids 4 through 18; $2.50 for seniors; and free for those over 65 years of age. Resident and nonresidents passes can reduce the summer costs.

Broomfield Recreation Center
280 Lamar St., Broomfield
• **(303) 469-5351**

With a six-lane pool and typical amenities, children find the summer's outdoor aquatics park a real treat. This center is open Monday and Wednesday, 5:30 AM until 10 PM; Tuesday and Thursday, 8 AM to 10 PM; Friday, 5:30 AM to 7 PM; Saturday, 8 AM to 4 PM; and Sunday from noon until 4 PM. Admission for adults is $3; seniors pay $2.50; kids are charged $2 per visit. Annual passes are available.

Louisville Recreation Center
749 Main St., Louisville • **(303) 666-7400**

This center's six-lane pool allows adults to swim while children are entertained in the children's pool that features an impressive water slide. Louisville's center is open Monday through Friday, 6 AM to 10 PM; Saturday, 7 AM to 7 PM, and Sunday from 9 AM until 8 PM. Per visit, adults pay $5; seniors pay $2.75, kids

Children dress as candy canes for the Lights of December Parade.

ages 13 to 17 pay $3.50 and those under 14 pay $2.75.

Lafayette Bob Burger Recreation Center
111 W. Baseline Rd., Lafayette
• (303) 665-0469

This center has it all — a huge water slide, lazy river and children's pool. Even after their fingertips look like prunes and their lips are blue, children beg to visit this one. This center is open from 6 AM until 10 PM, weekdays; 8 AM until 6 PM on Saturday and 10 AM until 6 PM on Sunday. The admission for adults is $3.50; seniors pay $1.75 as do children ages 3 to 12, and the charge for kids 13 to 18 is $2.25.

Viele Lake
1360 Gillaspie Dr., Boulder
• (303) 441-3448

Canoes, paddleboats and lots of Canada geese, this man-made lake is a central feature to this south Boulder neighborhood and a nice place to take a break for students who attend the nearby Fairview High School.

Waneka Lake
1600 Carla Dr., Lafayette
• (303) 673-9124

Lafayette's summer answer to the Boulder reservoir, this lake is open Memorial Day to Labor Day and has a great deal on canoe rentals and a pretty area where the herons hang out. Canoe rental on weekdays during summer months is $3 but increases to $4 for weekends and holidays. The lake is typically open for boat rentals from 1 PM to 8 PM and from 10 AM until 7 PM on weekends and holidays.

Ice Skating

Aspen Lodge
6120 Colorado Hwy. 7, Estes Park
• (303) 440-3371

During the winter this lodge offers free outdoor ice skating during daylight hours and rents skates for adults and children. The Lodge charges $3 for both skating and skate rentals during the daytime, 8 AM until 9 PM.

INSIDERS' TIP

The local recreation centers, which are open to the public for a fee, have great swimming pools, Lazy Rivers and wading areas.

CU Ice Arena and Skate Shop
CU campus, Broadway and College, Boulder • (303) 492-7255

CU-Boulder's indoor ice-skating rink is free to students and members, otherwise the cost is less than $4 plus $1 for skates. You must be a guest of a student or member guest to use this facility. Recreational skating hours vary from day to day.

Gold Lake Mountain Resort
3371 Gold Lake Rd., Ward
• (303) 459-3544

At Gold Lake packages are offered for a day rate that includes not only ice skating, but also a brunch, use of the hot tubs, and availability to other winter sports including snow-shoeing and cross-country skiing. Rental equipment is available. Packages start at $40.

Skiing

Eldora Mountain Resort
2861 Eldora Ski Rd., Nederland
• (303) 440-8700

This resort is tailor-made for family skiing with easy and challenging downhill trails plus lots of ski and snowboarding instructors. This is an excellent learning environment for children. Lessons are available for kids 4 and older. In conjunction with the Mom's Monday, a series of women-only classes on Monday afternoons, Little MAC (an acronym for Monday Afternoon Club) provides two-hour lessons and rental equipment for 4- to 6-year-olds. The Nordic Center is adjacent to the downhill ski areas. In addition to beautiful, wind-sheltered Nordic trails, cross-country instructors set up the lessons so everything's a game, and because there's so much movement, kids tend to stay warmer than they do during downhill skiing.

Team Sports

High school and college sports abound in Boulder, and pro teams are no farther away than Denver. See our Boulder Participatory, Spectator and Professional Sports chapter for further information.

Boulder Junior Soccer
2400 Central Ave., Boulder
• (303) 443-1618

Soccer is a great way for youngsters to learn cooperation and team spirit and for newcomers to make friends. This is the biggest program around, with spring and fall seasons for children as young as kindergartners ranging through Boulder Barrage for strong older players.

YMCA
2850 Mapleton Ave., Boulder
• (303) 442-2778

The "Y" has baseball programs in spring and summer; basketball in winter and spring; and soccer, volleyball, flag football and in-line hockey in fall. Children are grouped according to age. Girls will find as many activities and enthusiastic coaches as the boys.

Hike or Bike

Boulder Creek Path
Broadway and Canyon Blvd., Boulder
• (303) 441-3090

A stroll along the path — keeping mindful of fast-moving cyclists and in-line skaters, please — can take on exploratory aspects with small detours down the creek along the way, to the murky but well-intentioned trout-viewing windows near the Regal Harvest House Bridge or to the duck-pond overlook between Ninth Street and the Justice Center. Freelance musicians might be playing in the park between Broadway and 13th Street. Be sure to read the interpretive signs along the way.

Hiking

For more information on trails in the area, see our Sports chapter.

City Parks and Administration/Open Space
3198 Broadway, Boulder
• (303) 413-7200 or (303) 441-4142;
(303) 441-3440 (Open Space)

After the paved Creek Path, a logical next step might be some of the area's easiest unpaved trails. From the Bobolink trailhead at

Baseline and Cherryvale roads, it's just a little more than .75-mile to the East Boulder Community Center and about 1.3 miles to South Boulder Road. The Baseline-EBCC section features a series of interpretive signs on grasslands, wetlands and river ecology. Short-legged, short-burst-of-energy little hikers often do best with modest walks along relatively flat trails.

The Teller Farm Trail runs 2.2 miles through a picturesque rural area between Arapahoe (the signed trailhead is off a dirt road between 75th and 95th streets) and Valmont Road (the trailhead is near 95th Street). Partway along the trail is a small lake (fishing permitted). The nearby White Rocks Trail, whose trailhead is also near Valmont Road and 95th Street, is about 4 miles long, and its first stretch is really flat. A $7 map is available from the parks department.

With older children who have more stamina, the options multiply. Red Rocks is a good place to start. This short, steep trail, accessible from a well-marked trailhead at the mouth of Boulder Canyon, makes a suitable first challenge with some optional rock scrambling on top. Trails in the Boulder Mountain Parks, Walker Ranch way up Flagstaff Road, Rabbit Mountain open space near Lyons, Brainard Lake and the Indian Peaks Wilderness west of Ward and Rocky Mountain National Park are among the abundant nearby hikes for various levels of stamina and interest. (See our Parks and Recreation chapter and our Rocky Mountain National Park overview.) If it's windy, a trail right against the foothills can provide some shelter from big gusts. If it's snowy, choose a flat one. If it's hot, find a creek with shade, or drive up to the mountains. Remember to watch little ones closely near any creeks with fast-moving waters.

Walden and Sawhill Ponds
75th between Jay St. and Valmont Rd., Boulder • (303) 441-3964

This is a beguiling 113-acre complex of ponds reclaimed from old gravel pits — now an example that demonstrates nature's ability to heal a scarred landscape. The ponds, their aquatic vegetation and fish have become an attractive habitat and breeding area for waterfowl, painted turtles, muskrats and other fauna.

Two miles of ultra-gentle trails, picnic areas and fishing areas make these ponds a fine family destination.

Biking

If your child lacks a bike, isn't it time to buy one? "Pl-e-a-s-e? Pretty please?" The bike trails in Boulder are so wonderful, wheels can be the highlight of a child's vacation or life in Boulder. But make sure children wear helmets. In fact, set a good example and wear one yourself, and ride with them until you're sure they understand trail safety and bicycling rules. Although most riders are polite and considerate of children, paths can get crowded, and a few rude racers are ruthless.

Boulder Creek Path
Throughout Boulder • (303) 441-3090

The path and its tributaries are perfect for in-line skating or bicycling. Many places nearby rent in-line skates and adult bikes.

Boulder Bikesmith
2432 Arapahoe Ave., Boulder
• (303) 443-1132

Should your child's two wheeler "bite the dust" on Boulder's bikepath, this shop is located adjacent to the Boulder Creek Path, with trained experts on staff who can help with bike service, the sale of new or used bicycles, and, as a last resort, in-line skate rental.

University Bicycles
839 Pearl St., Boulder • (303) 444-4196

This is a great downtown location from which you can rent kids' bikes, bike trailers, tandem bikes and trail-a-bikes, a new style of hybrid tandem with an adult-size bike in front and a kid-size one in the rear . . . all good for family wheels.

Libraries

Boulder Public Library (main branch)
1000 Canyon Blvd. at Ninth St. between Canyon Blvd. and Arapahoe St., Boulder
• (303) 441-3100

Most Boulder area libraries offer abundant

reading nooks, computers and storytelling times. This is the city's crown jewel, an eye-popper with an outstanding selection of books, publications, videos and other materials. The espresso shop on the second floor offers a view of the creek that is stunning anytime of year. The main library is open 9 AM to 9 PM, Monday through Thursday; 9 AM to 6 PM, Friday and Saturday; and from noon to 6 PM on Sunday.

George Reynolds Branch Library
3595 Table Mesa Dr., Boulder
• **(303) 441-3120**

A branch library serving south Boulder, there is easy access and an extensive video and audio tape section here. This branch library is open from 9 AM to 9 PM Monday through Thursday; 9 AM to 6 PM on Friday and Saturday; and from 1 to 5 PM on Sunday.

Meadows Branch
4800 Baseline Rd. at Foothills Pkwy., Boulder • (303) 441-4390

This is the newest branch library serving residents who live east of downtown. Adjacent to the Meadows Shopping Center, there is a nice children's section, and with fewer patrons the staff always has time to help. The library is open from 9 AM to 9 PM, Monday through Thursday; 9 AM to 6 PM, Friday and Saturday; and from 1 to 5 PM on Sunday.

Lafayette Public Library
775 W. Baseline Rd., Lafayette
• **(303) 665-5200**

This new and contemporary 30,000-square-foot library opened in October 1997 and is 10 times the size of the original library. The large and knowledgeable staff can help you access books, audio books, computer programs, and the Internet. Lafayette's library is open Monday through Thursday, 10 AM to 9 PM; Friday and Saturday, 10 AM to 5 PM; and on Sunday from 1 to 5 PM.

Longmont Public Library
409 Fourth Ave., Longmont
• **(303) 651-8470**

Longmont's library was built in 1993 on the site of the original Carnegie Library. The city had quite a black eye after it leveled the historic building without public notice. The new library contains a children's section and a separate teen section. There is a large video, CD and audio tape section, periodicals and easy parking. This library is open Monday through Thursday, 10 AM to 9 PM; Friday and Saturday, 9 AM to 5 PM; and Sunday, 1 to 5 PM.

Louisville Public Library
950 Spruce St., Louisville
• **(303) 666-6037**

Louisville's library has a long history, dating back to 1923, when the Chinook Campfire Girls made it their project to collect books that would eventually be housed in the town's library. It wasn't until 1980 that the library had a permanent home, and just 10 years later the collection moved again. It hasn't seemed to bother residents, who visit so often the library has one of the highest circulation statistics for a library of its size in the state! There are children's and young adult sections plus the usual audio and visual offerings. The library is open Monday through Thursday, 10 AM to 8 PM; Friday and Saturday, 10 AM to 6 PM; and Sunday from 1 PM to 6 PM.

Museums

Boulder Collage Children's Museum
2065 30th St., Boulder • (303) 440-9894

The motto here is, "I hear, I forget; I see, I remember; I touch, I understand." Past displays include an interactive computer, dancing with colored shadows and the "Dragons of the Dump" with "recycled" dragons created by kids. If you're not a member there's a nominal admission fee. Collage is open Monday and Wednesday-through-Saturday, 10 AM to 5 PM; Sunday, from 1 PM to 5 PM. They are closed on Tuesday.

KIDSPACE
375 Kimbark St., at the Longmont Museum, Longmont • (303) 651-8374

This museum specializes in self-structured hands-on science, historical and art activities, such as a puppet area, pioneer dress-up theater, reading area and rotating activities including a water table, an electronic board and "Tub-O'Bubbles," where kids can create giant soap bubbles with wands. There is no admission fee but donations are always appreciated. It is open Monday through Friday, 9 AM to 5 PM and Saturday from 10 AM to 4 PM. The museum is closed on Sundays and holidays. A nominal fee is charged for KIDSPACE special events.

University of Colorado Museum
Broadway and 15th St., Boulder
• **(303) 492-6892**

The CU museum has a kids' corner and numerous kids' activities and special events. This place is definitely one of Boulder's best-kept secrets. Find the real Triceratops head, and try on the sea-turtle shell. This museum is open from 9 AM to 5 PM Monday through Friday; Saturday from 9 AM to 4 PM; and Sunday from 10 AM to 4 PM. Admission is free.

WOW! Children's Museum (World of Wonder)
1075 Boulder Road, Louisville
• **(303) 604-2424**

Call it a positive feature of the population growth in eastern Boulder County — a new children's museum! WOW is designed for toddlers and school age children and their families. It offers a variety of interactive and informative educational and creative exhibits and programs that stimulate learning. Opened in 1996, there are both permanent and traveling exhibits. A very clever pirate ship turns out to be a dress-up room. There are three party rooms, a snack area and gift shop. This museum is open from 9 AM to 5 PM Monday through Friday; 10 AM to 6 PM Saturday; and on Sunday from Noon until 4 PM. Parents are admitted free while children pay $6 for all day admission. There are also frequent visitor cards, memberships and group rates.

Denver Children's Museum
2121 Children's Museum Dr. (just off I-25), Denver • (303) 433-7433

If you're up for a drive or heading that direction anyway, this is the biggest, most comprehensive children's museum around. It features a stunning variety of laboratories, interactive displays, a miniature grocery store where youngsters can shop or act as cashiers

and a terrific toddler area. You'll find this museum open from Tuesday through Sunday, 10 AM to 5 PM. It is open late, until 8 PM on Fridays, for Twilight Theater. Admission is $2 for ages 1 to 2; $5 for ages 3 to 59; and $3 for those older than 60.

Classes

Boulder Parks and Recreation Program
5660 Sioux Dr., Boulder
• **(303) 413-7270**

This is the largest program in the city, with children's classes in everything from arts and crafts to yoga. They include one-day workshops, multi-week sessions and options in between. Gymnastics, dancing and swimming are popular. Or try child/parent pottery classes given at the city's Pottery Lab. A new brochure is published four times a year and is available free at all three of the recreation centers. Don't dawdle with the registration — many of these classes are extremely popular and fill up quickly.

Boulder Rock Club
2829 Mapleton St., Boulder
• **(303) 447-2804**

Great practice for eventually scaling the Flatirons, this club has an indoor rock-climbing wall and a variety of children's programs. They start with RockKids — 1½ hours of climbing time for children ages 5 to 9 (available individually or for four lessons). Youth Certification (ages 12 to 17) and Junior Team (ages 10 to 19) are multi-day sessions at various levels.

Flatirons Martial Arts
4770 Pearl St., Boulder • (303) 444-6526

Flatirons Martial Arts specializes in teaching youngsters age 5 and up the skills and self-discipline of karate and other martial arts. The motto here is "the art of peaceful confidence."

American School of Martial Arts
Gunbarrel Square, Boulder
• **(303) 516-1453**

"Karate teaches kids a lot" is the American School's slogan. All ages and abilities are en-

Photo: Daily Camera/K. Schulenberg

Kids can climb a rocket ship at Scott Carpenter Park.

couraged and a flexible class schedule is available.

Northern Colorado Fencers
1725B Walnut St., Boulder
• **(303) 443-6557**

Northern Colorado Fencers boasts nationally and internationally ranked fencers who give good instruction to children, including respect for the rules and safety.

The Cooking School of the Rockies
Broadway and Table Mesa Dr., Boulder
• **(303) 494-7988**

A parent/child Gingerbread House Baking Class is held on four Sundays during November and December. There is also a Cookies 'n Kids class on a Saturday in early December.

Boulder Suzuki Strings
Boulder • (303) 499-2807

This group specializes in string instruction for kids from 4 through high school. Boulder Suzuki Strings offers private and group lessons, note reading, performances, recitals and workshops.

Dance West
1637 Pearl St., Boulder • (303) 545-2252

Dance West offers ballet, jazz, African, hip-hop, techno tap, Latin, modern and family dancing for youngsters of all ages. There are summer camps and lots of great discount rates.

The Studio for Performing Arts
2010 14th St., Boulder • (303) 442-1908

The Studio for Performing Arts offers classes in dance, acting, music, directing and filmmaking. In addition to after-school programs, students put on an annual summer musical performance. In 1999 students performed *Music Man*, *Into the Woods*, and *Darn Yankees*.

The Peanut Butter Players
2475 Mapleton Ave., Boulder
• **(303) 786-8727**

Voted the "Best of Boulder in Kids Entertainment" by *Daily Camera* readers, children delight audiences with musicals several times a year. For a modest fee you can enroll

your child, but be prepared for an extensive rehearsal schedule — the director expects a professional performance and makes kids toe the line. No matter what their experience, every child gets a speaking part, even if it's only one line. Summer programs are on a grand scale.

Summer Camps

A week or more out of the house can go a long way toward relieving the tedium of a bored child's summer. Overnight camps, day camps and camps that provide both options abound in the Boulder area. Camps are great for learning about everything from computers to archery, outdoor skills to swimming. Area newspapers publish special camp issues in spring.

Science Discovery Summer Camp
CU Campus, Regent Dr., Boulder
• **(303) 492-7188**

This camp is cosponsored by CU-Boulder's Science Discovery Program and Experiential Learning Associates. Well-regarded, this camp provides five- or six-day environment-oriented experiences to Colorado wonders such as the Great Sand Dunes and Dinosaur National monuments and Cortez Cultural Center. The program is so popular participants are chosen by a lottery system. There are local programs and overnight options. Activities include hiking, paleontology, river rafting and mountain biking.

Colorado Mountain Ranch
(also known as Trojan Ranch)
10063 Gold Hill Rd., Boulder
• **(303) 442-4557**

The Walkers' family-run mountain ranch is more than 50 years old and includes both week-long overnight sessions and day sessions with Western riding, swimming in a heated pool, Indian lore, archery, gymnastics, drama and confidence-building outdoor adventures.

Boulder Parks and Recreation
5660 Sioux Dr., Boulder
• **(303) 441-4401**

Boulder Parks and Recreation offers many day-camp-type options, from playground pro-

Photo: Roz Brown

The Peanut Butter Players theater company features kids ages 5 to 18.

grams to a Teen Adventure Program with kayaking and overnight camping plus programs for people with disabilities.

YMCA of Boulder Valley
2850 Mapleton Ave., Boulder
• **(303) 442-2778**

The Y offers extensive camps including outdoor nature, sports, teen adventures, teen leadership, "Y-Riders" bicycling, fine arts, making memories and mountain camp. The camps are licensed and staffed by professionals. In addition to excursions to Denver-area fun spots such as Water World, the "Y" staffs daylong summer camps at many schools.

Boulder Valley Community School Program
805 Gillaspie Dr., Boulder
• **(303) 499-1125**

Run by the school district, this program offers all kinds of classes at various locations around town. In 1997, classes included basketball camps for boys and girls, single-track mountain biking and cartooning.

The Front Range Natural Science School, Thorne Ecological Institute
5398 Manhattan Cir., Boulder
• **(303) 499-3647**

This children's environmental education program gets high marks for offering environmental educational classes that include lots of outdoor exploration. Classes are offered year round, but the summer program is the biggest.

Rainbow Valley Farm
10870 N. 49th St., Longmont
• **(303) 651-7222**

Rainbow Valley is a low-key farm school where kids can help gather eggs and handle the sheep. It's quite a drive from Boulder each day but city kids have nothing but good things to say about the experience.

University Of Colorado Basketball School
Colorado Ave., Folsom Stadium
• **(303) 492-6877, (303) 492-6086**

Girls and boys of all ages flock to these camps to work with the head coach of both the CU women's and men's basketball programs. Coaches Ceal Berry and Ricardo Patton and their staff and players hold day and overnight camps, most of them three days long, on the CU campus. There are different levels for children as young as six, as well as elite camps for 15–18-year olds with varsity experience.

Highlands Presbyterian Camp
P.O. Box 66, Allenspark
• **(303) 747-2888**

This mountain setting Christian camp is open to all faiths. Popular with elementary and middle school students, it offers co-ed and day camps for children entering first grade through senior citizens. Specialty camps include horse camps, music, art and drama camps, backpacking, and grandparent/grandchild camps. Traditional camps feature horseback riding, mountain biking, archery, canoeing, crafts, hiking and sports.

Boulder Arts Academy
2590 Walnut St., Boulder
• **(303) 449-9291**

The Academy is the official school of the Boulder Philharmonic and the Boulder Ballet. There are camps for music, theater, dance and art for ages three through adult. In addition to instrument camps that include strings, piano and winds, a 1999 camp offered a chance to appear in the production of *Fiddler on the Roof*. This year the Academy introduced a new opportunity to work with the Colorado Shakespeare Festival at Boulder's Mary Rippon Theater on the CU campus.

Whatever your inclination, the area offers activities that are fun, challenging, inspirational, educational — or perhaps all of the above.

Daytrips and Weekend Getaways

From the mountains to the plains, daytrips from Boulder offer a wealth of activities ranging from culture and history to recreation, shopping, dining and just enjoying the beautiful scenery. Among the places we're sending you in this chapter are the Air Force Academy in Colorado Springs, the gambling casinos of Central City and Black Hawk, the ski resorts of Summit County and Winter Park and the museums and other attractions of Denver. We've given some history and vital information for each, along with special events, dining and shopping opportunities. Among the popular options in the mountains are skiing; Alpine-sliding; and sleigh-, hay- and horseback riding. Disabled folks can learn to ski, rock climb and take on other challenges at Winter Park, site of the National Sports Center for the Disabled. For hiking, backpacking, bicycling and cross-country skiing (and other participatory sports) also see our Participatory, Spectator and Professional Sports chapter.

Denver's Zoo, with its Tropical Discovery exhibit, and the Denver Botanic Gardens, will cheer you with lush greenery and tropical creatures even during the cold winter months. Drive up Pikes Peak in the summer and you can say you've been on top of one of Colorado's "Fourteeners" — the 54 highest mountains that reach 14,000 feet or higher. Or take a leisurely sail across scenic Lake Dillon or Grand Lake.

Whatever your inclination, the area offers activities that are fun, challenging, inspirational, educational — or perhaps all of the above.

Accommodations
Price Code

Accommodation listings include dollar signs ranging from one to five ($-$$$$$) indicating the price range for a one-night stay, double occupancy during the summer season as follows:

$	$55 or less
$$	$55 to $75
$$$	$75 to $100
$$$$	$100 to $125
$$$$$	$125 or more

Restaurants
Price Code

Restaurants are listed with dollar signs ranging from one to five ($-$$$$$) indicating the average cost of dinner for two, excluding appetizer, alcoholic beverages, dessert, tax and tip.

$	$20 or less
$$	$20 to $40
$$$	$40 to $60
$$$$	$60 to $100
$$$$$	$100 or more

Denver

Believe it or not, Denver actually has some attractions that Boulder doesn't, though

Boulderites hate to admit it. Driving time between Boulder and sprawling Greater Denver can vary depending on which part of the city you visit. All the attractions listed here are in the center-city area and an hour's drive or less from Boulder. It's fun to spend a day in the "big city" visiting museums, shops, restaurants or galleries or going to the Colorado Symphony or a show.

Some of Denver's top attractions are the Denver Botanic Gardens, the Denver Zoo, the Museum of Natural History, the elegant Brown Palace hotel (which serves high tea), and the Black American West Museum and Heritage Center. There's also good shopping on Larimer Street, the 16th Street Mall, Cherry Creek at the Tabor Center and the lavish, new Park Meadows Mall — not to mention lots of good restaurants.

If you're a parent, looking for fun activities to do with your children, make sure you see the following "Denver for Kids and the Young at Heart" section. For the complete Insiders' scoop on Denver, check out *The Insiders' Guide® to Denver*.

Getting There

Take US Highway 36 from Boulder to the I-25 Exit. The new, improved I-25, with six lanes in some places, can be a bit intimidating for non-city drivers. It helps to have someone else along for navigation. Once on I-25, stay to the middle/right, because some of the far right lanes are "exit only" to such places as Denver International Airport or Limon in eastern Colorado. Follow I-25 for a few miles as it nears downtown Denver and watch for the sign for the Speer Boulevard S. Exit, which comes up quickly after the sign (not to be confused with the Speer Boulevard N. Exit). Take the exit and head for the tall buildings over Speer Boulevard. There are signs for the Denver Art Museum on Speer past Colfax Avenue.

Or, avoid the hassle of traffic and parking and take the RTD bus, which leaves from the RTD station in Boulder at 14th and Walnut streets (and other stops along Broadway). The bus goes to the Market Street station in downtown Denver, right at the 16th Street Mall. There are numerous trips daily. In Denver, a free shuttle takes riders up and down the 16th Street pedestrian mall. The far end of the mall (and the shuttle stop) is only a few blocks from the State Capitol and art museum. For RTD route and schedule information, call (303) 299-6000. A one-way ticket to Denver is $3. Tickets can be purchased on the bus, but you must have exact change.

In Denver, RTD runs a Cultural Connection Trolley that stops every half-hour at or near Denver's cultural attractions and sights downtown. It runs daily from 9:36 AM to 10:06 PM, from early May until early September. A $3 pass allows riders to get on and off as often as they like. Buy tickets and pick up a map at an RTD station (including Boulder's) or on the bus itself.

To get to the Denver Zoo and the Denver Museum of Natural History by car, take I-25 to I-70 eastbound. Follow I-70 to the Colorado Boulevard exit, then proceed south on Colorado Boulevard for 2 miles to 23rd Avenue and turn right. The zoo is on 23rd Avenue between Colorado Boulevard and York Street (look for signs). The museum is nearby in City Park at Colorado Boulevard and Montview.

To get to the museum from downtown Denver by car, go east on 17th Street (which eventually becomes E. 17th Avenue) and turn left (north) on Colorado Boulevard. Look for signs for the museum and the zoo.

For the Denver Botanic Gardens, from downtown take 14th Street east to York Street, turn right on York (south) and go four blocks; free parking is on the left, and the gardens are on the right.

To reach the Black American West Museum and Heritage Center, go northeast on Stout Street (a block over from California Street) from downtown Denver out to 31st Street.

Attractions

Denver Art Museum
100 W. 14th Ave., Denver
• (303) 640-2793

Denver Art Museum has one of the best and most extensive collections of Native American crafts in the United States plus works of Picasso, Georges Braque, Matisse, Frederic Remington, Winslow Homer, Thomas Hart

Benton and many others. You'll find a cafe and restaurant and gift shop as well. The museum is near the State Capitol. Look for the distinctive castle-like silhouette of cutout geometric shapes. Hours are 10 AM to 5 PM Tuesday through Saturday and noon to 5 PM Sunday (closed Mondays and major holidays). On the first Wednesday of each month the museum stays open until 9 PM. Admission is $4.50 for adults; $2.50 for seniors and students; free for museum members and children younger than 5. Admission is free for everyone on Saturday.

Denver Museum of Natural History and IMAX Theater
2001 Colorado Blvd., Denver
• (303) 370-6357; (303) 322-7009 (reservations); (303) 370-8257 (Hearing-impaired TDD)

Besides dinosaurs, the museum features exhibits of Colorado's birds and animals and a fantastic collection of natural history exhibits and dioramas. From time to time the museum also hosts spectacular world-traveling exhibitions such as "Ramses II" and "Aztec." Prehistoric Journey, an award-winning dinosaur exhibit popular with kids, is a permanent exhibit that includes walk-through "enviroramas." The museum is open daily from 9 AM to 5 PM and until 9 PM on Fridays. Part of the museum, the IMAX Theater, with its four-story screen, shows educational and entertaining movies. Admission to the museum is $6 for adults; $4 for children ages 3 to 12 and seniors older than 60. IMAX shows cost $6 for adults and $4 for children ages 4 through 12 and seniors older than 60. Shows start daily at 11 AM; call for the schedule. There are also combination museum and IMAX tickets available.

Denver Zoo
2300 Steele St., Denver • (303) 376-4800

The "Primate Panorama" exhibit, which opened in 1996, is the zoo's newest attraction. The exhibit re-creates an African village, complete with thatched roofs, and has 29 species of primates from around the world. The gorilla enclosure is one of the largest outdoor gorilla yards in any zoo and is home to Kounda, the largest known gorilla in captivity, weighing 600 pounds. In November 1999 the Komodo Dragon exhibit will open featuring the world's largest lizards. There are only 5,000 of the species left in the wild and zoo officials promise a rich learning experience for visitors. Zoo hours are 9 AM to 6 PM daily in summer, 10 AM to 5 PM daily in winter. Some exhibits close earlier. Admission is $8 for adults; $6 for seniors (62 and older) and $4 for children ages 4 to 12; free for children 3 and younger. Call for free days for Colorado residents. The zoo's cafeteria serves light meals and snacks.

Denver Botanic Gardens
1005 York St., Denver • (303) 331-4000

Enjoy 23 outdoor acres full of beautiful flowers, trees and shrubs, including a Japanese garden and an alpine rock garden just 10 minutes east of downtown Denver. You'll find an indoor conservatory with special tropical and orchid areas plus a library and gift shop. There's increasing focus on Japanese-style designs, native prairie areas and rock gardens. The curator of the Rock Alpine garden, Panayoti Kelaidis, is a Boulder native who has gained a national reputation for his daring eye and superb plant knowledge. For anyone who wants to learn what grows beautifully in this climate, the Botanic Gardens is a required stop. Although most visitors choose the brilliant summer flowers, winter, Colorado's longest season, is a good time to visit — especially to experience the 50-foot-tall tropical forest. For anyone with the winter blues, this lung-full of Hawaii is a sure cure — even if temporary. Hours are 9 AM to 8 PM Saturday through Tuesday; 9 AM to 5 PM Wednesday through Friday. Admission is $5.50 for adults; $3 for students and children ages 6 to 15; and $3.50 for seniors older than 65. Children ages 5 and younger are free.

Black American West Museum and Heritage Center
3091 California St., Denver
• (303) 292-2566

Blacks played an important role in the settling of the West, and documentation at this unique museum shows that roughly a third of the West's cowboys were black. There were also many black businessmen, miners, pioneer doctors, politicians, soldiers and teachers — a fact that historians have generally overlooked. At this museum, numerous photos and displays tell the role of blacks as early settlers in Denver and Colorado. Every six months there's a changing exhibit with such subjects as the history of jazz in Denver or black churches in Denver. Summer hours are from 10 AM to 5 PM daily; winter hours are 10 AM to 2 PM Wednesday through Friday and weekends from noon to 5 PM. Admission is $4 for adults; $3 for seniors and students; (children 3 and younger are free).

Restaurants

On the 1400 block of Larimer Street and along the 16th Street Mall, a potpourri of restaurants offer ethnic foods, sidewalk cafes and lots of ambiance. See the price-code key at the beginning of this chapter. The following are some favorites:

The Little Russian Cafe
$-$$ • 1424 H Larimer Sq., Denver
• (303) 595-8600
Little Russian serves such hearty peasant fare as dumplings, stuffed cabbage, borscht and apple strudel. The cafe is open daily for dinner only. It also offers a great selection of unusual flavored vodka drinks.

The Cadillac Ranch
$$$ • 1400 Larimer St., Denver
• (303) 820-2288
This newcomer of the last few years offers such trendy, tasty fare as chipotle-honey-glazed pork chops and a meat-hater's plate of mashed potatoes topped with applewood-grilled vegetables. Open for lunch and dinner daily, it also serves brunch on weekends.

Josephina's
$$ • 1433 Larimer St., Denver
• (303) 623-0166
A lively, colorful Italian restaurant, Josephina's has been pleasing diners for years with its antipasto, pizza, lasagna, eggplant Parmesan and other Italian favorites. Josephina's is open daily for lunch and dinner.

McCormick's Fish House & Bar
$$ • 1659 Wazee St., Denver
• (303) 825-1107
This popular eatery serves breakfast, lunch and dinner daily, with special weekend brunch on Saturday and Sunday. McCormick's serves all types of American food plus seafood, which is their specialty.

The Wynkoop Brewing Co.
$-$$ • 1634 18th St., Denver
• (303) 297-2700
A few blocks from Larimer Square, the Wynkoop provides an interesting dining and drinking experience. This was Denver's first brewpub, founded in 1988, and it's housed in an historic 19th-century building. Though the Wynkoop can be a bit noisy, crowded and smoky, the choice of ales and pub fare at reasonable prices and the lively atmosphere more than compensate. It's open daily for lunch and dinner.

Racine's
$$ • 850 Bannock St., Denver
• (303) 595-0418
About four or five blocks from the Denver Art Museum (at 13th and Bannock streets), Racine's is a great spot for dessert or an inexpensive meal. Racine's has its own in-house bakery and is known for its great brownies, carrot cake and muffins. Besides sweets, a wide range of meal offerings includes pastas, Mexican entrees and sandwiches. Friendly and inexpensive with a comfortable but interesting ambiance, Racine's offers something for everyone, serving breakfast, lunch and dinner daily. They also have an attractive bar that is a fine place for an after-the-show drink or dessert.

Wazee Supper Club
$$$ • 1600 15th St., Denver
• (303) 623-9518
This is a classic LoDo institution serving up burgers, wonderful pizza, a large beer selection and plenty of neighborhood character

Unsinkable Molly Brown and Her Revived House

A visit to the Molly Brown House is more than a trip into Denver's past. Brown was one of the survivors of the *Titanic*, and a small museum on site tells the story. "Typical Brown luck, we're unsinkable," she proclaimed, after rescue. She had traveled to Europe on the *Titanic's* sister ship, *Olympic*, and spent part of the winter in Egypt with

the Astors, who encouraged her to book first-class return passage on the *Titanic's* maiden voyage. The *Titanic* was the largest ocean liner of its time and was considered to be unsinkable. Its anchor had 1,050 feet of chain. The ship had a gym equipped with stationary weights, a bicycle, rowing machine and an electric camel ride.

On April 14, 1912, at 11:40 PM, the crew of the Titanic spotted an iceberg, which was unavoidable because the ship was too big to maneuver quickly. The ship broadsided the iceberg, broke in two and at 2:20 AM sank to the bottom of the freezing North Atlantic, taking most of its 2,228 passengers — only 705 survived, among them Brown. Most of the survivors were women and children because Victorian ethics demanded that they be saved first. Brown assisted in the rescue efforts in the lifeboat and made the women sing so they would stop crying. After they were rescued she raised more than $10,000 for the survivors. She also submitted an insurance claim against the shipping company for more than $27,000, including a necklace valued at $20,000 and three-dozen gloves at $50.

Molly's real name was Margaret "Maggie" Brown. The name "Molly" was the invention of the 1960s Broadway musical based on the life of Margaret Brown. According to a nine-year guide at the Molly Brown House, the movie version starring Debbie Reynolds — though entertaining — is not very accurate. Brown was born to a Hannibal, Missouri, ditch digger and his wife in 1867. She said Mark Twain inspired her to go west. She went to Leadville, Colorado, and worked as a seamstress at the Daniel and Fisher department store. There, she met her husband-to-be, James Joseph Brown (J.J.), who was from Pennsylvania and working for the Ibex Mining Company. After the 1893 silver crash, J.J. found gold in the Little Johnnie mine and became a millionaire. The Browns then moved to Denver, where Molly was considered by Denver society to have three strikes against her: she was Catholic, Irish and nouveau riche. Nevertheless, the Brown home soon became the focus of Denver society.

She and her husband never got

— continued on next page

The Molly Brown House in Denver is a worthwhile stop.

Photo: Jeff Black

along well, partially due to Molly's unorthodox but charitable behavior. She told impoverished Native Americans to set up their tents on her front lawn after they were driven off the state Capitol grounds. That was the final straw for her husband, who then moved out. Molly continued to live an extravagant life, traveling and circulating in the high society of Denver, Newport and Europe. But she also spent much of her time and money supporting various causes, including women's suffrage, local Catholic charities and the reform of maritime law. She received the French Legion of Honor, with Sarah Bernhardt, for her efforts during World War I. During the 1920s Molly lived at the Brown Palace Hotel, and her lovely home became a boarding house. She died in 1932.

The home fell into ruin, but in 1970 its acquisition and restoration became the first project of Historic Denver, which was created for this purpose. Tour guides wear white Victorian dresses and carry white lace parasols. The dark red stone mansion is a late Victorian Queen Anne-style home, with Romanesque touches. The neighborhood was considered to be upper-middle class when the Browns resided there. Nearby Grant Street was millionaire's row, where cattle barons and railroad magnates lived in rambling mansions.

The Molly Brown house is filled with antiques, many of which are the family's original furniture dredged up from various Denver sources, including thrift shops. The beautiful stained-glass windows and golden oak woodwork are original. More than a half-million dollars in private funds have been raised to restore the Molly Brown House, which is well worth a visit. There's a great gift shop in the old carriage house with a room devoted to the *Titanic*. The Molly Brown House Museum and Gift Shop, (303) 832-4092, 1340 Pennsylvania Street, Denver, is open Monday through Saturday from 10 AM to 4 PM and Sunday from noon to 4 PM (closed Mondays from September through May). The last tour is at 3:30 PM. Admission for adults is $6; seniors 65 and older, $3.50; children ages 6 through 12, $2.00. It's three blocks east of the State Capitol and 1½ blocks south of Colfax Avenue.

---

for over two decades. It's open daily for lunch and dinner.

Accommodations

Since Boulder is so close to Denver, most people just make it a day trip. But should you decide to have a little Denver holiday, many downtown hotels have special weekend-getaway packages. Call the Colorado Hotel and Lodging Association reservations service line at (800) 777-6880 for information. See the price-code key at the beginning of this chapter.

The Brown Palace
$$$$$ • 321 17th St., Denver
• (303) 297-3111
Recently renovated, the Brown Palace is Denver's most famous hotel. It is quite elegant but expensive, starting at $205 for a standard room, $245 for a superior and $265 for deluxe

per night, single or double occupancy. Suites range from $325 to $775. The hotel has three restaurants: Elyngton's and The Ship Tavern are casual; The Palace Arms is an acclaimed formal dining room. Churchill's, a newly opened cigar lounge, serves cocktails. Drinks are also served in the lobby and The Ship Tavern. Lunch and afternoon tea are also served in the beautiful Victorian-style lobby.

The Queen Anne Inn
$$$ • 2147 Tremont Pl., Denver
• (303) 296-6666
Just north of downtown in a historic neighborhood, the Queen Ann occupies two adjacent Victorian buildings, built in 1879 and 1886 in the Queen Anne-style of architecture. Single rooms are in the $85 to $175 range, which includes breakfast. There are 14 rooms, all with private baths. The inn is popular with honeymooners and for weddings.

Shopping

Denver has a number of popular shopping areas, some within walking distance of each other and others not. Downtown in the historic district are Larimer and Writer Squares. Farther afield is Cherry Creek and the new Park Meadows shopping center.

Larimer and Writer Squares
15th and Larimer Sts., Denver
• (no main number)

Historic Larimer Square, at Larimer and 15th streets, is packed full of upscale clothing boutiques, art galleries, cafes and other shops as is Writer Square just across 15th Street from Larimer Square. Looking for antique and estate jewelry? An interesting shop on Writer Square called Victoriana is worth a visit. Find unusual artistic greeting cards at Avant-Card. Anne Taylor, the popular women's clothing and accessory shop, is also in Larimer Square (1421 Larimer).

The Tabor Center
1201 16th St., Denver
• (no main number)

The greenhouse-like Tabor Center at the 16th Street Mall's north end (1201 16th Street) houses such fun places as The Kite Store, Flag World, African House (arts and handicrafts), It's Your Move (game store) and American Sports Classics, a sports memorabilia store — plus miscellaneous clothing and other shops.

The 16th Street Mall
16th Street between Market and Colfax, Denver (no phone)

Along the 16th Street Mall there are lots of inexpensive souvenir-type shops. It's fun to walk up 16th Street or take the shuttle. It's the place for a quick cup of coffee, finding a tacky Denver souvenir or people watching, but not serious shopping.

Cherry Creek Shopping Center
3000 E. 1st Ave., Denver
• (303) 388-3900

With some 160 specialty stores — mostly on the high end — Cherry Creek attracts 16 million visitors annually. Stores include Ann Taylor, Lord & Taylor, Saks Fifth Avenue, Abercrombie & Fitch, Nieman Marcus and Foley's, among others. The center expanded in 1998, adding 30 new stores including Tiffany & Co., Z Gallerie, Eddie Bauer, Banana Republic and the Rainforest Café. North of the mall are several blocks of trendy establishments including art galleries and restaurants. The Tattered Cover Book Store (2955 E. 1st Ave.) is nationally known and has three huge floors of books, easy chairs for reading and a nice restaurant on the top floor with great city and mountain views.

Park Meadows Shopping Center
8401 Park Meadows Center Dr., Littleton
• (303) 792-2533

Denver's newest shopping hot spot is the huge Park Meadows shopping center in Douglas County (and not actually Denver proper). One of the big draws is Nordstrom — it's the only one in Colorado. There's also Denver's first Dillard's department store. Other popular shops are Crate and Barrel and Renovation Hardware with all types of gourmet kitchen, decorating and unusual items. Park Meadows' entertainment section has four virtual theaters at a complex called Starport, where you can do things like virtual hang gliding. There are also movie theaters and a massive food-court area. For those who prefer finer dining, there's the California Cafe with upscale, nouvelle cuisine, Bella Restaurante for Italian food and Alcatraz Brewing Co., brew pub.

Denver for Kids and the Young at Heart

Attractions

On the Road to Denver...

The Butterfly Pavilion & Insect Center
6252 W. 104th Ave., Westminster
• (303) 469-5441

This amazing place is about 20 minutes south of Boulder on the Church Ranch Boulevard Exit off US 36 to Denver. Half of the center is a fascinating display of living insects, the other part is a greenhouse for exotic tropical butterflies. At the insect center, visitors can handle a live tarantula, see scorpions that glow in the dark and exotic cockroaches of the world. In the Butterfly Pavilion, 70 percent humidity and lush tropical foliage simulate the Costa Rican rain forest and butterflies flit around freely, hitchhiking on visitors.

There's also a nifty gift shop full of butterfly-themed items, plus a cafeteria. The center was created by the Rocky Mountain Butterfly Consortium and is a nonprofit organization. Its purchase of the insects from various tropical countries helps create a viable industry for sustaining tropical forests. The Butterfly Pavilion purchases butterfly chrysalises and hatches its own butterflies. Those who visit in the morning can see these beauties emerging from their chrysalids and cocoons. Outside, the facility has butterfly gardens of native wildflowers and prairie grass planted to attract local butterflies, so it's a great place for gardening ideas, too. Open daily, admission is $6.75 for adults, $4.75 for seniors and $3.75 for children. Two children, ages 3 and under are admitted free with a paying adult.

Water World
1800 W. 89th St., Denver
• (303) 427-7873

The 64 acres of water rides and 40 attractions make Water World America's largest family water park. *USA Today* rated its Voyage to the Center of the Earth as one of America's top 10 attractions. To get there, take US 36 to the Pecos exit, close to Denver. Turn north (left) and drive until you see those blue canopies on the hilltop. Water World offers several safe introductions to whitewater rafting. For those missing surf, Water World's big wave pools make plenty. Add an entertaining wading area for tots and grade-schoolers plus many theme rides. Beach Boys music bops from the loudspeakers. A day of splashing costs $19.95 for adults and $18.95 for children ages 4 to 12. Seniors (60 and older) and tots (3 and younger) are free; half-day rates are offered. Water World is open daily in the summer from 10 AM to 6 PM, weather permitting, and accepts major credit cards, but no personal checks.

Lakeside Amusement Park
4601 Sheridan Ave., Denver
• (303) 477-1621

Lakeside opened in 1908. The miniature train still circles the lake, powered by a 1903 steam engine. That tortuous white skeleton marks the 90-foot-tall Cyclone. This ride seems like 3,000 knuckle-white lifetimes, but actually takes only 2½ minutes. The Cyclone's rated one of the top five roller coasters by American Coaster Enthusiasts and is one of the few wooden roller coasters left in the country. Lakeside opens during the week at 1 PM for kiddie rides and the major rides are open from 6 PM to 11 PM. On weekends the whole park is open from noon to 11 PM, from May through Labor Day. Unlimited rides cost $12.50 during the week and $16 on weekends. But if you're just riding the bench, it's $3 (children 2 and younger are free).

The Arvada Center for the Arts and Humanities
6901 Wadsworth Blvd., Denver
• (303) 431-3939

The Arvada Center offers participatory fairy tale theater for children many weekday mornings and some Saturdays. Kids are often invited to come on stage to join the acting. Tickets cost around $4 during the week and $5 on Saturdays; summer shows, $5. The evening adult dramas and concerts, which cost from

---

INSIDERS' TIP

You can still find two funky little places to pan gold, Vick's Gold Panning and The Old Timer Panning (across from the Gold Dust Lodge), about 2 to 5 miles down from Black Hawk on Colorado Highway 119. They don't have phones, so just drive down to see if they're open.

$20 to $26, are excellent, and the free museum has art and cultural displays.

Casa Bonita
6715 W. Colfax Ave., Denver
• (303) 232-5115

For sheer kitsch value, Casa Bonita is an experience not to be missed. It's the favorite dining experience for many youngsters. The Mexican food is passable, the donut-sweet sopapillas are tasty, but the main draw is entertainment. At the indoor lagoon, a dramatic troupe presents plays that usually end with heavily costumed actors splash-landing in the pool. A dark cave maze is popular for hide-and-seek, and troubadours wander among the tables singing "Happy Birthday" when requested. The experience is hokey beyond belief and adored by children. A meal generally costs less than $10; children 12 and younger eat for less than $5.

Rainforest Café
$$ • 3000 East 1ˢᵗ Ave., Cherry Creek Shopping Center, Denver
• (303) 355-8500

More than just a dining experience, the Rainforest Café is an immediate hit with kids of all ages — and that means those well over 40. There's never a dull moment here, where you're greeted by live parrots at the entryway and the phrase, "Your adventure is about to begin." If there's a line, the bar has seats shaped like wild animals and serves exotic alcoholic and non-alcoholic drinks in fanciful glassware. Once you're in line for the main dining room, gigantic saltwater fish tanks make the wait bearable. There are frequent thunderstorms inside the Rainforest which produce showers, all strategically placed to avoid dampening your food. At regular intervals, mechanical elephants, leopards and gorillas put on a show with loud roars and chest pounding. You'll dine under a dense canopy of jungle foliage and watch the stars twinkle under the fiber optic starscape. The extensive menu features the influences of Mexico, Asia, the Caribbean, Italy, the American Southwest and Louisiana. Most entrees have enticing names like Volcanic Cobb Salad, Serengeti Fried Chicken and Jamaica Me Crazy Chops. The crispy fried onions and cranberry relish are clearly signatures, and the children's menu is affordable.

The Rainforest is not just a wild place to eat. A connecting retail store has clothing, toys and kitchenware — all with the exclusive Rainforest logo. While new to Denver, the Rainforest Café has 25 restaurants in the U.S. and 10 international locations. It serves lunch and dinner daily.

Downtown Denver

The Denver Mint
320 W. Colfax Ave., Denver
• (303) 405-4761

Any kid who likes money will love the Denver Mint, between Delaware and Cherokee streets (tour entrance on Cherokee). It began when Coloradans made their own money. In those days, real U.S. currency was hard to find this far west, and locals tired of weighing gold dust to exchange for food. Later, this private enterprise became an official U.S. mint. Teeth-rattlingly loud machines stamp coins from sheet metals. People hush as they pass a safe displaying 27.5 pounds of gold in six 400 Troy-ounce gold bars. The bars are surprisingly small, like $3 bars of good chocolate in shiny yellow wrappers. They're a fraction of Denver's gold, which is one of three stashes nationwide (West Point and Fort Knox are the other two). Twenty-minute tours take place weekdays from 8 AM to 3 PM (9 AM on the last Wednesday of the month) on a first-come, first-served basis. Tours are free but slots fill quickly during the summer, so it's best to get your ticket by mid-morning. The coin sales area operates during the same hours as the tours and is accessible only by taking the tour. The mint is closed on weekends and holidays.

The Molly Brown House
1340 Pennsylvania St., Denver
• (303) 832-4092

Rent the movie *The Unsinkable Molly Brown*, starring Debbie Reynolds, then tour this landmark. It's just a few blocks from Denver's gold-domed Capitol building. Molly Brown was a diamond-in-the-rough whose husband made a gold strike. Denver society snubbed Molly, but she became a heroine when the *Titanic* sank in the freezing North

Atlantic. Molly was on-board that fateful day, and she saved many by pulling them into her lifeboat. Her mansion is 10,000 square feet of Victoriana. It's open from 10 AM to 4 PM Monday through Saturday and noon to 4 PM Sunday (closed Mondays from September through May). The history-filled 45-minute guided tour is $6 for adults, $3.50 for seniors 65 and older and $2 for children ages 6 through 12. The last tour is at 3:30 PM. (See this chapter's Close-up for more information about Molly Brown.)

Denver Art Museum
100 W. 14th Ave., Denver
• **(303) 640-2793**

From the fantasy fortress facade outside to the hands-on displays, kids' corner and videotape nooks inside, kids will particularly enjoy this museum. Count on spending an hour, maybe 90 minutes, with the kids in tow. The museum is open Tuesday through Saturday (closed Mondays) from 10 AM to 5 PM and Sundays from noon to 5 PM. The entrance fee is $4.50 for adults; $2.50 for students and seniors; free for kids younger than 5; and free for everyone on Saturdays.

West of Downtown, Near I-25

Six Flags Elitch Gardens Amusement Park
2000 Elitch Cir. (off Speer Blvd.), Denver
• **(303) 595-4386**

This is Denver's oldest and grandest amusement park, in a brand-new location near lower downtown Denver. Families can enjoy the live restaurant entertainment and the progression from kiddie rides to hair-raising ones. The new location lacks the 100-year-old trees and turn-of-the century elegance of the former park, but with 67 acres, it's more than twice the size of the old park. The 1925 carousel with wooden horses is there. Twister, the famous wooden roller coaster, has been rebuilt, which relieves most parents, because although the old roller coaster was safe, sometimes you wanted to take a hammer on the ride and whack in a few extra nails. Like the old Twister, the new one is listed as one of the top 10 in the country by American Coaster Enthusiasts. The famous landscaping has formal gardens, shaded areas and several thousand young

trees. Elitch's is open 10 AM to 10 PM daily. Unlimited ride admission is $28 for anyone 48 inches or taller and $14 for those 48 inches and shorter. It's free for kids 2 and younger or adults 70 or older.

Elitch Gardens is easy to find. To get there, take I-25 to Speer Boulevard S. and head for the roller coasters.

Children's Museum
2121 Children's Museum Dr., Denver
• **(303) 433-7433**

Near Elitch's, there is a square green building that appears to be wearing a burgundy, pyramid cap. This is the Children's Museum. The hands-on museum offers changing exhibits such as a science lab and King Soopers grocery store. New this year is a Wild Oats Community Market where kids can "play" shopping. Last year marked the opening of an exhibit on water pollution entitled, "We All Live Downstream." The museum is open daily from 10 AM to 5 PM and is closed Mondays September through May. Entry fee is $5 for ages 3 to 59 and $3 for adults 60 and older. Admission is $2 for children 2 and younger. Admission is free the first Friday of every month. Call for show and schedule information for the Children's Theatre.

Forney Transportation Museum
4303 Brighton Blvd., Denver
• **(303) 297-1113**

At press time the Forney Museum was in the process of moving into a larger building. When it opens on Brighton Boulevard in late 1999, it will house the Forney's collection of antique cars, buggies and trains including Big Boy, the largest steam engine in the world. The famous pilot, Amelia Earhart, drove the Gold Bug Kissel roadster. Call for admission prices and hours.

Mile High Stadium
2755 W. 17th Ave., Denver
• **(303) 458-4848**

At Mile High, sports events can make a special occasion, with or without kids. This is where the Broncos battle other National Football League teams, and often practically every seat in the 76,123-seat stadium is occupied. That's part of the reason voters in 1998 agreed to pay additional taxes in order to build the Broncos a new stadium north of downtown near 17th & Bryant. Whether it too will be called Mile High has not been decided. (See our Sports chapter for more information.)

Pepsi Center
1000 Chopper Cir. (tentative), Denver
• **(303) 405-8555 or (303) 405-8546**

The Pepsi Center, located in Denver's central downtown area, officially opened on October 1, 1999. The new arena replaces McNicholls Sports Arena, which was demolished in fall of '99. The Pepsi Center is home to about 160 sporting and entertainment events, including the National Basketball Association's Denver Nuggets and the Colorado Avalanche of the National Hockey League. The Pepsi Center features include two dramatic, six-story atrium entranceways; views of the Central Platte Valley, downtown Denver and the Rocky Mountains; a 236-seat club level restaurant; 95 fully furnished luxury suites; and plenty of parking. The center is easy to reach off I-25; exit South Speer Blvd. to Auraria Pkwy.

Coors Field
20th and Blake Sts., Denver
• **(303) 292-0200**

Home to the Colorado Rockies, this 50,000-seat stadium is extraordinarily detailed, down to 40 plate-size blue columbines on the exterior. (Columbines are Colorado's state flower.) A ball game with kids is delightful here. They'll love the hot dogs, pizza, sodas and snacks. You can find Rocky Mountain Oysters for sale too. (Those are fried bull testicles, in case you're munching one right now and wondering what you just ate.) Rockies Vinny Castilla, Dante Bichette and Larry Walker often hit home runs, and the mascot, Dinger the Purple Dinosaur, is always performing antics somewhere. Obviously, baseball is not just for kids. We know people who take first dates to the ball game. If the chemistry's dynamite, there's plenty of time for getting acquainted. If things just don't click, they can get very, very interested in the game. You get the idea. The Rockies still have the "Rockpile," where you can come on game day and buy tickets for kids or seniors at $1 each or for adults for $4. Tickets in advance are generally $5 to $30;

call (303) ROCKIES (762-5437). From I-25, take the Park Avenue W. Exit to reach the stadium. (See our Sports chapter for more information on the Rockies.)

East of Downtown . . .

In Denver, you'll find many child/adult attractions about 10 minutes east of downtown. We've discussed the addresses, hours and fees of these in the previous section on Denver attractions for adults. Here's some detail about them from a kid's point of view. Please refer to the individual listings of these attractions above for details.

With 23 lovingly landscaped acres, the **Denver Botanic Gardens** has room for serious gardeners and kids who need to frolic.

At the **Denver Zoo**, the Tropical Discovery and Bird World buildings are full of animals that would need overcoats out in a Colorado December. The polar bears and sea lions make any summer day seem cooler. They're most fun to watch from underwater portholes.

Next to the zoo is the huge **Museum of Natural History**. Just follow the crowd toward the Hall of Life and the wonderful mineral displays. They include twinkling gems, gold-filled boulders and a quirky series of statuettes, all made of different colored stones. We grownups talk the kids into lingering in the Explore Colorado Hall, which has beautiful renditions of Colorado's prairie and alpine forest. Changing exhibits always pack in people.

While at the museum, enjoy the IMAX Theater, with 30 speakers to help the sound track thunder into your solar plexus while you watch cliff-hangers about sharks, volcanoes and other wonders.

Shopping and Dining in Denver with Your Kids

Denver's premier shopping area is east on Speer Boulevard at Cherry Creek. Here, you will find a variety of shops and fast food restaurants. Some specific ones are listed below. With kids, downtown shopping is most fun around the Tabor Center, Larimer Square and LoDo (pronounced low-dough) . . . lower downtown. It's not hard to find places to eat with kids. Most shopping areas have casual eateries.

The Wizard's Chest
230 Fillmore St., Denver
• (303) 321-4304
Find all types of magic tricks and toys at this entertaining shop in Cherry Creek.

Warner Bros. Studio Store
3000 E. 1st Ave., Denver
• (303) 321-7747
Look on the second floor of the Cherry Creek Shopping Center for this store with Mickey Mouse, Looney Tunes and all types of cartoon characters on toys and products.

Tattered Cover Book Store
2955 E. 1st Ave., Denver
• (303) 322-7727
1628 16th St., Denver • (303) 436-1070
This is Denver's biggest bookstore, and the lower level has a comfortable reading sofa where older kids can peruse books while you browse. If you're double-teaming your kids, one of you can read with them while the other shops. There is also a new Tattered Cover in lower downtown housed in a rambling old warehouse across from Union Station.

Union Station Gift Shop
170a Wynkoop St., Denver
• (303) 534-1012
The gift shop at the train station provides a chance to look at Union Station and real railroad paraphernalia, and it's open daily from 7:30 AM until the train comes in then closes until the next train arrives.

Healthy Habits
865 S. Colorado Blvd., Denver
• (303) 733-2105
There's a salad bar with 70 items, a pasta and soup bar, plus pizza and a bakery here in a comfortable, casual atmosphere.

The Tabor Center
1201 16th St., Denver • (303) 572-6865
The food court in the Tabor Center, back downtown by Larimer Square, offers pizza, Mexican food, a Vietnamese Kitchen, Burger King, Mrs. Field's cookies, a shop that sells giant cinnamon rolls and many other choices.

Family Accommodations

Holiday Chalet
$$$-$$$$$ • 1820 E. Colfax Ave., Denver
• (303) 321-9975
Originally the home of the Bohm family and built in 1896, this immaculate and friendly hostelry is ideal for families and even accepts pets for $5 per day. It has a unique, historic charm with stained-glass windows and a crystal chandelier to add to the ambiance. The 10 rooms/suites are all sunny and have their own personality with various nooks and crannies. Though Colfax Avenue is a bit noisy, the thick walls of the old mansion provide a quiet refuge. There are three different-sized rooms and all come with a TV, VCR, kitchen and bathroom.

Loew's Giorgio Hotel
$$$-$$$$$ • 4150 E. Mississippi, Denver
• (303) 782-9300
Kids might enjoy the looming *Star Wars* quality of this ultramodern hotel, which has a surprising contrast of northern Italian country-villa decor. This large hotel has 180 rooms and 20 suites and the price includes complimentary continental breakfast and access to a fine Sporting Club. Though the hotel caters more to a business clientele, it offers weekend packages for families.

Denver International Youth Hostel
$ • 630 E. 16th Ave., Denver
• (303) 832-9996
The ultimate bargain accommodation, the youth hostel requires guests to pitch in and do a chore or two here as part of the deal. Like other youth hostels, the doors are locked during the day. Check-in time is between 8 and

---

INSIDERS' TIP

Water World gives you the most splash for your money, and it's only 20 minutes from Boulder.

10 AM and 5 and 10 PM. There are about 30 beds total distributed in various dormitory-style rooms, plus kitchen and bathroom facilities. No frills, but clean and basic accommodations, and you're guaranteed to meet the other guests.

Melbourne International Hostel
$ • 607 22nd St., Denver
• (303) 292-6386

For those seeking a private room at bargain prices, here's the place. Rooms have a refrigerator and some have private baths. Dorm rooms are also available. The hostel has a convenient downtown location and is clean and basic — definitely for the more adventurous and outgoing traveler or family. Check-in is from 7 AM to midnight, but those checking in after 7 PM should call first.

Colorado Springs

Getting There

Just two hours south of Boulder is Colorado Springs. To get there, take I-25 through Denver, and keep going south through the rolling foothills until you're at the foot of Pikes Peak mountain — and Colorado Springs. Try to avoid Denver rush hour, which can add a half-hour to the trip. If you squeak through Denver on weekends or when the traffic is lightest, some commuters who nudge the speed a bit say you can slip into town in less than two hours.

Top attractions in Colorado Springs are the United States Air Force Academy, Cave of the Winds, the Cheyenne Mountain Zoo, Garden of the Gods and the Broadmoor Hotel. For quick, up-to-date information on the area, call Colorado Springs visitors Center at (719) 635-7506 or (800) DOVISIT.

We'll tell you about these many special attractions next. But first, some perspectives from the past.

History

Before 1900, the Denver Rio Grande railroad needed communities near the remote Colorado foothills in order to profit from buying and selling goods along its train route. In 1871, it backed the Fountain Colony, with 150 buildings and 800 residents. The promoter, Gen. William Jackson Palmer, wanted a genteel, well-bred crowd, so he advertised "villa sites" to wealthy English compatriots. Thus began a community that would grow into Colorado's second-largest city, Colorado Springs, with nearly a half-million people.

One Englander said the brand-new community was a "very high-toned sort of new town" run by a "very tony company on teetotal lines." It was a tourist attraction and resort health spa for wealthy tuberculars.

Colorado Springs has gracefully reached much of its potential. But 100 years ago, early settlers who had been assured they were moving to tree-lined avenues and fenced English farmlands got a big surprise when they saw the windswept plain. One irate Englishman, stepping out of his train in a March snowstorm, huffed in a furious, highbrowed Edwardian "haccent," "And h'is this the H'italian climate of H'america?"

The resort town diversified into many other businesses. Tourism, defense and high-tech are big employers. North American Air Defense Command (NORAD) is dug deep into hollowed-out Cheyenne Mountain. South of town is Fort Carson, an active Army base. Colorado Springs is the site of the Winter Olympic Training Center and excellent colleges such as the Air Force Academy, Colorado College and the University of Colorado at Colorado Springs.

Colorado Springs and Boulder share similar aspirations of being well-planned, beautiful, wealthy Utopian communities. But if you could imagine social values as the pendulum of a great clock, then Boulder's liberal outlook would pull the pendulum left. Swing right, and you have the conservative outlook of Colorado Springs. This typecasting isn't clear-cut. But it's a fair comparison that shows over time. For instance, Boulder opposed Amendment 2 that denied special rights for gays, which Boulder residents viewed as a hate vote against homosexuals. A Colorado Springs group called Coloradans for Family Values initiated that amendment. While many of the values they recommend earn praise by focusing attention on family responsibility, this coalition also has raised concerns because of their hostility toward homosexuals and a growing demand to include Christian doctrine in public schools.

Attractions

Air Force Academy
I-25, Exit 156B • (719) 333-2025

Colorado's leading human-made attraction is the Air Force Academy at the base of Rampart Range. The Visitors Center is open 9 AM to 6 PM daily in the summertime. It closes an hour earlier the rest of the year. Four thousand cadets train at the Academy to become astronauts, pilots, engineers, scientists and tactical leaders. The campus includes 143 acres of athletic fields, a 2,500-seat ice rink and a 6,000-seat basketball arena. The Falcon Football team is stiff competition for opponents. What's more, the setting is memorable. More than 18,000 acres of the campus are a wilderness refuge, thick with Colorado's scrubby native oak, Gambel's oak, pine trees and other native plants.

When the campus was established in 1954, 340 architectural firms competed to design the buildings. The Chicago firm Skidmore, Owings and Merrill Architects and Engineers won. Their modern ideas stunned Congress. The chapel was described as an "accordion." That seems funny today, when most people consider that chapel a masterpiece. Overall, the buildings are as crisp as their crew-cut era. But their futuristic tone might make them appropriate for Star Trek's Star Fleet Academy too.

The Visitors Center displays spacesuits of graduates and shows free 14-minute info-movies every half-hour. Cadets lead a free campus tour.

The crown jewel is the chapel, with 17 gleaming aluminum spires that rise 99 feet into the clear blue sky. Ribbons of stained glass separate each spire and create a rainbow of color inside. The arrangement inside says something about the '60s world view of American religion. The Protestant chapel on the main floor seats 1,200. The Catholic chapel, seating 500, is on the lower level, and in the back is a 100-seat Jewish worship area with a

nondenominational area behind. Generally, chapel hours are 9 AM to 5 PM Monday through Saturday and 1 to 5 PM Sundays (in summer, chapel hours are extended to 6 PM daily). You can attend Sunday services at 9 and 11 AM. Jewish services are held on Friday evenings at 7 P M. But it occasionally closes for special services, such as funerals and weddings — and there are a lot of cadet weddings. For an up-to-date schedule, call (719) 333-4515.

Garden of the Gods
I-25, Exit 146 • (719) 634-6666

This drive-through garden has 2½ square miles of eroded red rocks that are remnants of ancient mountain ranges. The highest rock is 350 feet high, and the strange natural "sculptures" include formations known as Kissing Camels and Balancing Rock. To reach these spectacular natural formations take Exit 146 and continue west until it dead-ends. Then take a left on 30th Street. The park is open 5 AM until 11 PM daily May through October and 5 AM to 9 PM November through April. The visitors center is open 8 AM to 8 PM in the summer, with shorter winter hours.

Cave of the Winds
U.S. Hwy. 24 W., Manitou Springs
• (719) 685-5444

Just west of Colorado Springs there are 45-minute guided tours of these caves. It's open 9 AM to 9 PM daily in summer; otherwise, 10 AM to 5 PM. More than 200,000 people a year choose the standard tour, which costs $12 for adults and $6 for kids older than 6. Or, dress in clothing you won't mind getting muddy, bring a flashlight and join the Explorers Trip, where an experienced guide goes climbing and crawling with you into danker, darker, mysterious places. The Explorers Trip lasts three to four hours, costs $70, requires reservations and a $15 per person deposit and depends on a strong confidence that you won't get claustrophobic.

For those who get flutter-nerved just thinking of that Explorers Trip, relax. The regular tour probes caves just deep and narrow enough to feel a little creepy sometimes, but they're perfectly safe. In some areas, tourgoers walk single file, but most corridors open into large cave rooms wondrously lit to show off the stalactites hanging from the ceiling and the stalagmites growing, century by century, from the floor. Hokey lighted areas get dumb names from the guides. In one spot, the crusty gray rock has been rubbed smooth by the oil from millions of human hands, revealing a honeyed glow like alabaster. When you read tales about dwarves, it's easier to imagine that the little folks polished their beloved caves to just such a sheen.

Santa's Workshop
U.S. Hwy. 24, 10 miles west of Colorado Springs • (719) 684-9432.

Another home for dwarves... and elves... and reindeer, is at the North Pole. If you thought the North Pole was a few thousand miles away, here are new directions. It's open in the summer from 9:30 AM to 6 PM daily. Weather permitting, it's open in the fall from 10 AM to 5 PM, except for Wednesdays and Thursdays. Generally, it stays open through Christmas Eve. This sweet little amusement park has 24 safe rides for little kids, a full-size Ferris wheel (the 7,500-foot altitude makes it the highest wheel in the world), and a colorful cottage in which Santa Claus waits in his rocking chair. Kids can have their picture taken with truly plump Santa, whose curly white beard is real. In summer, he often wears knickers with suspenders and a colorful shirt, or red trousers and boots with a colorful shirt. When it gets cold, Santa dons his red jacket. The cost for unlimited rides here is $10.75 per person; $4.95 for seniors; and free for kids younger than 2.

Cheyenne Mountain Zoo
4250 Cheyenne Mountain Zoo Rd. • (719) 475-9555

West of the Broadmoor Hotel, this is one of the largest privately owned zoos in the nation. It started in 1938 as Spencer Penrose's own collection and grew from there (Penrose

Photo: Daily Camera/Jay Quadracci

Denver Botanic Gardens is a short drive from Boulder.

built the Broadmoor Hotel). More than 145 species are at the 75-acre zoo. Perhaps the 6,800-foot altitude invigorates the animals. Maybe it's the generally spacious pens. Whatever, the zoo is known for producing babies, including endangered species, such as tiny, golden tamarind monkeys, black rhinos, red pandas, snow leopards and Andean condors. The most popular animal is the African elephant, followed by the orangutans in their large climbing area. The zoo's open from 9 AM to 5 PM daily in the summer and to 4 PM the rest of the year. Admission is $7.50 for adults; $6.50 for ages 12 to 17 and 64 and older; $4.50 for children ages 3 to 11. The entrance fee also gives you access to the Will Rogers Shrine of the Sun and beautiful vistas. From I-25, take Exit 138 west to the Broadmoor, then turn right and follow the signs.

The Pikes Peak Highway
2 miles west of Colorado Springs on U.S. Hwy. 24

This scenic drive is generally open May through November. It's a long, slow way up, with many hairpin turns to the peak of Pikes, one of Colorado's highest mountains. At 11,578 feet, trees shrink to ground-huggers that might take 100 years to grow an inch. Here, you might spy yellow-bellied marmots. The 14,110-foot Pikes Peak is a boulder-strewn, windswept summit. Take a jacket, even if the temperature in Colorado Springs was more than 90 degrees. And stop at the Summit House, which has been selling delicious donuts and hot chocolate since the turn of the century.

Pikes Peak Cog Railway
515 Ruxton Ave., Manitou Springs
• (719) 685-5401

Since 1891, the bright-red train cars have made the three-hour round trip by following Ruxton Creek through aspen and Englemann spruce forests of Pikes Peak. In addition to wheels and tracks, a cog train has a center cog gear that pulls the train up the mountain, useful against slipping in steep spots. To get there, take U.S. 24 to the Manitou exit. Go west on Manitou Avenue to Ruxton Avenue and turn left. Daily trains in summer depart every hour and 20 minutes with the first at

9:20 AM and the last at 5:20 PM. Tickets cost $22.50 for adults; $11 for children ages 5 to 11 (July 1 to August 15: $23.50 and $11.50). Younger children are free if they ride on your lap.

Cheyenne Mountain Operational Center (NORAD — North American Air Defense Command)
1 NORAD Rd., Stes. 101-215 Alpha Cheyenne Mountain Air Station
• (719) 474-2238 or (719) 474-2239

Tours of NORAD often fill six months ahead of time, so call early for reservations. A bus takes visitors to the mountaintop auditorium for a briefing, slide show and explanation of the mission of Cheyenne Mountain. Then visitors ride a bus through a tunnel to the NORAD Command Center — the entire complex is underground. Inside the facility visitors can walk around in a restricted area. Visitors also see an industrial area with reservoirs and turbines that power the facility. For obvious reasons, this is a high-security tour and you'll be asked for a photo I.D. and Social Security number.

The Winter Olympic Training Center
1 Olympic Plaza, I-25 Uintah Exit 143
• (719) 578-4618.

At the two sports centers here you may see Olympians training — such as Amy Van Dyken, four-time gold medal swimmer, and John McCready, a member of the men's gymnastic team. Free tours are offered daily every hour on the hour from 9 AM to 5 PM daily (during summer every half hour). Sunday tours are 10 AM to 5 PM. Groups of eight or more are asked to make group reservations. Otherwise you can just show up and take the tour, which includes a 15-minute film on the Olympics or the Olympic movement. The best time to see athletes training is on the 9 AM tour or the 4 PM. The center is closed Christmas Eve, Christmas, Thanksgiving, New Year's Day and Easter.

Restaurants

The Broadmoor's many fine restaurants are described under the Broadmoor Hotel, in the next section on accommodations. Other Colorado Springs choices are listed below. See the price-code key at the beginning of this chapter.

The Peppertree
**$$ • 888 W. Moreno Ave.,
Colorado Springs • (719) 471-4888**

Here, the chef will prepare a pepper steak flamed with brandy right at your table — or steak Diane, Châteaubriand and veal sweetbreads. The cuisine is continental and excellent. The atmosphere is very romantic, on top of a hill with a view of the city. Peppertree is open for dinner only.

The Dale Street Cafe
**$ • 115 E. Dale St., Colorado Springs
• (719) 578-9898**

A former Victorian home, this charming cafe offers southern French and northern Italian cooking, including homemade pizzas, pastas, soups, salads and desserts. There are also grilled items and two fresh fish specials daily. Dale Street is open daily for lunch and dinner.

Anthony's
**$$ • 1919 E. Boulder Ave.,
Colorado Springs • (719) 471-3654**

The pasta is made fresh on the premises. You'll be tempted by the veal marsala and seafood pasta. Anthony's is open for lunch and dinner daily.

Giuseppe's Depot
**$ • 10 S. Sierra Madre St.,
Colorado Springs • (719) 635-3111**

Kids especially like Giuseppe's, an old railroad station that has been converted into a restaurant. You can see freight trains go by, and the mountain range too. Ribs, steak, chicken, spaghetti, pizza and a children's menu are here. They serve lunch and dinner daily.

La Casita
**$ • 1331 S. Nevada Ave.,
Colorado Springs • (719) 633-9616**

Right next to I-25 this pink stucco restaurant has great personality, down to the black velvet paintings, metalwork frames and murals of tropical birds. Beer-soaked barracho beans, known as drunken beans, are a house specialty. Try chicken or beef fajitas and menudo. La Casita serves breakfast, lunch and dinner daily.

Manitou Springs

This cute community just west of Colorado Springs offers lots of good restaurants.

The Briarhurst Manor Inn
**$$ • 404 Manitou Ave., Manitou Springs
• (719) 685-1864**

Chef-owned and operated, this inn occupies the landmark home of the founder of Manitou Springs. The varied menu offers rack of lamb, Châteaubriand and trout. The steak tartare and alligator pears (an avocado stuffed with crabmeat and served with a special sauce) are great appetizers. This 123-year-old mansion has seven different dining areas.

The Craftwood Inn
**$$$ • 404 El Paso Blvd.,
Manitou Springs
• (719) 685-9000**

This inn is another mansion, built in 1908. Regional Colorado cuisine includes venison, antelope and wild boar. There's a unique wine list along with views of Pikes Peak in a very romantic atmosphere. There's ostrich and buffalo on the menu, plus vegetarian entrees, seafood and other meats. The seven vegetables served with the meal are cooked separately to perfection then combined in a colorful medley. Entrees usually are served with wild rice or quinoa.

The Mission Bell Inn
**$ • 178 Crystal Park Rd.,
Manitou Springs • (719) 685-9089**

Come here for good Mexican food. The specialty is green chile with pork. Burritos come stuffed with green chile, and flautas are rolled with beef and onions then baked with red chile.

Accommodations

Colorado Springs accommodations are intertwined with attractions. Read this section, even if you're not planning to stay overnight. These places take Visa and MasterCard. See the price-code key at the beginning of this chapter.

The Broadmoor Hotel
$$$$$ • 1 Lake Ave., Colorado Springs
• (719) 634-7711 or (800) 634-7711

For old-world elegance, check the Broadmoor Hotel. With more than 3,000 acres of delights, the Broadmoor, built in 1918, has 700 rooms in four different buildings. The exterior is Italian Renaissance. Authentic Chinese lion statues guard the entry. The renovated interiors have rich hunter green and burgundy tones. Although freshly decorated, it feels straight from the Kennedy Camelot era. You might imagine Jackie, in a pink Chanel suit and pillbox hat, pulling on white gloves as she heads toward the Broadmoor's shops. A beautiful new addition is a bridge across the lake that connects the main hotel with the Broadmoor West for the convenience of the guests. The guests love it and the paddleboats can still glide under it, followed by the Broadmoor's famous white and black swans.

Three 18-hole championship golf courses, 12 tennis courts, a 90,000-square-foot golf/tennis clubhouse and spa, bicycle rentals, horseback riding, fly fishing and hot air balloon rides are all here. The children's program is famous, and hiking trails are right out the door.

Nine restaurants make the dining choices exquisitely difficult. The fanciest is the Penrose Room, with views of both city and mountains. This Edwardian salon offers such continental cuisine as Châteaubriand served on silver place settings by tuxedo-clad waiters. The average price of dinner with wine and dessert is $100 for a couple. Charles Court is casual and contemporary, with one of the best wine lists in the country. Dinner for two here is around $75. Some specialties include baked double Colorado lamb chops with goat cheese and mustard seed crust; Prince Edward Sound grilled salmon; seared Colorado native bass; elk with lingonberry compote; and black-diamond rattlesnake quesadillas. Recently remodeled, The Tavern offers traditional fresh seafood, prime rib and pasta, an assortment of entrees cooked on the new wood-burning open grill over pine, applewood, mesquite and other flavor-enhancing woods. The average

price for two is around $50. Baby-sitting service provides sitters that come to the room. But if you wish to take them along, kids prefer Julie's sidewalk cafe that serves sandwiches, salads and ice cream.

Twenty-five specialty shops include Posh, for women's sportswear and thousand-dollar evening gowns; Broadmoor Kids' Shop for infant and toddler wear; a year-round Christmas store; The Goodnight Trail, for Western wear. The Golf Pro Shop is very popular.

During the summer, the average price for two people staying overnight is $325 for a regular room, with discount rates in the quieter seasons. For $2,415 you can have a night in the Penrose Suite. The sixth-floor suite features a parlor, sun porch, 20-seat dining room and three bedrooms. Julie Penrose, wife of the Broadmoor's builder, Spencer Penrose, lived here in her later years. The furnishings include antiques she collected.

At Christmas, a package deal includes a room, dinner and a show called *Colorado Christmas* at the Broadmoor, with carols sung by talent from Nashville's Opryland. There's also a movie theater on the grounds with first-run movies.

To get there, take Exit 138 off I-25. This is the Circle Avenue exit. Go right (west). Circle Avenue changes into Lake Avenue, and at the end there's the Broadmoor.

The Room at the Inn
$$$ – $$$$$• 618 N. Nevada,
Colorado Springs
• (719) 442-1896 or (800) 579-4621

This is an 1896 Victorian bed and breakfast in the elegant historic district. The seven available rooms range in price from $89 to $140. All have queen size beds, hardwood floors and oriental rugs. A full breakfast and afternoon tea are served. To reach the Inn take exit 143 (Uintah Street). There are phones in each room, but the only TV is located in a common area. Pets are not allowed and children must be 12 or older.

Cripple Creek

About 50 miles southwest of Colorado Springs is the gaming town of Cripple Creek, with gambling, melodrama and more. If you decide to go there, then find you want some peace and quiet to contrast with the hubbub, check out these two places. See our price-code key at the beginning of this chapter.

Hospitality House Travel Park
$ –$$ • 600 N. B St., Cripple Creek
• (719) 689-2513 or (800) 500-2513

Owners Stephen and Bonnie Mackin say you can come and get well — the place used to be a hospital. It has been renovated, then furnished with period furniture and TVs. There's a hot tub, areas for volleyball and horseshoes, and so on. It's very relaxed and has a Victorian feel. There are 50 spots with full hookups for RVs, along with tent spaces. Camping costs around $18; rooms run around $70 with a private bath.

The Victor Hotel
$$$ • 4th and Victor Sts., Victor
• (719) 689-3553 or (800) 748-0870

Near Cripple Creek, consider The Victor Hotel. This recently renovated award-winning Victorian hotel was built in 1899 and includes a new wing. It currently has more than 30 rooms, which generally cost around $99 for two people. Take U.S. 24 southwest of Colorado Springs to Colo. 67 and proceed about 18 miles.

The Gambling Towns: Black Hawk and Central City

Getting There

About an hour southwest of Boulder, on scenic Peak to Peak Highway, you enter tiny Gilpin County. The easiest route is to take Canyon Boulevard west to Nederland, then head south from Nederland on Colorado Highway 119. Enjoy the aspens and great mountain views. Pretty soon, you'll reach the biggest towns in the county — Black Hawk and Central City. These are Boulder's close-in gambling centers, with colorful extras such as brightly painted buildings, historic cemeteries, nearby ghost towns and one of the finest musical theaters in the west — the Central City Opera.

Those coming from Boulder might want to consider taking the Boulder County Express, (303) 829-1966 — an especially good way to travel if you're thinking of drinking while you're up in the mountains. Groups or individuals can go anytime at a cost of $22 per person round trip; seniors and groups of 10 or more pay $17 each. All round trips include casino packages for Colorado Central Station in Black Hawk. These packages consist of $10 in cash, blackjack money, free drink coupons and other extras — making the shuttle trip virtually free. There are daily shuttles normally at 8:30 AM from Boulder or shuttles on demand. Group charters of any size can be arranged in advance. Individuals or small groups should call the night before for a reservation or early on the morning of the trip. Colorado Central Station casino (listed below) offers transportation from Golden and Denver as does Ace Express (303) 433-3613 for various Denver locations.

Love, Hate or Whatever

Depending on your preferences, you'll either love these gambling towns or hate them. If you love them, you'll enjoy the easy entertainment in a beautiful mountain setting, with quaint touches of mining and mountain history.

But if you're after a quaint mountain setting with a bric-a-brac of small mom and pop stores owned by third-generation mountain families, you may hate gambling. This section will describe what the mountain towns offer gamblers. Then it explains what Gilpin County has for those who want something in place of, or in addition to, the one-armed bandits. But first, to understand how legalized gambling has changed the area, consider its history.

History

Placer mining revealed gold south of Boulder, and dozens of mountain towns boomed. Central City and Black Hawk were among them. Up here, the Wild West was not so awfully woolly. Public drunkenness was the biggest crime problem (as it is again today), and miners felt comfortable sleeping in unlocked cabins with their gold dust under their pillows. One congregational preacher reported that, rather than being rude and wicked, a few Central City residents were well-educated and cultivated enough to be among the more pleasant families that "demand and appreciate good preaching."

The pros of a boomtown were showing when Central City built the Teller House Hotel in 1872, one of the most lavish hotels west of the Mississippi at that time. It had a luxurious bar and a tall diamond-dust mirror that was carried over precarious mountain roads by an oxen team. The Teller House drew Mae West and Mark Twain. Sarah Bernhardt and Edwin Booth appeared at the opera house in the 1880s. But the mining operations that fueled these fancy places were not so attractive. Mining sluices ruined the countryside. Trees were toppled to build peaked-roof houses on the sloping hills, leaving the mountains barren for decades.

By the end of World War II, the mother lodes were barren and most Gilpin County mining centers were ghost towns. A few, however, experienced a new boom. "We still get the gold," quipped Central City's mayor in the 1950s. "We get it from some 450,000 tourists a year."

Historian Robert G. Anthearn, author of *The Coloradans*, scorned Central City when he wrote in 1976 that it had become a "classical example of fakery in the world of tourist traps." He lamented, "That once charming little town was turned into the Coney Island of the Rockies."

Well, it was tawdry, but it didn't have gambling then. Before gambling, the colorful little hillside homes sheltered grizzled miners and third-generation families. The area limped downhill on fading tourism. Buildings were condemned, and many residents commuted to Boulder or Denver for work.

Colorado residents voted for gambling in 1990. The measure passed, with limitations. Bets had to stay low, and gambling would be legal in only three places — Black Hawk, Central City and Cripple Creek. Interestingly, the measure was written so that even if one of the towns hated gambling, the state vote could impose it on them. (Since then, the law has been changed so that a town must want gambling before a state vote can bring it into the gaming community. So far, Coloradans have not voted for more gambling.)

Gilpin County voters went along with the state's gambling fever in 1990, hoping to save their towns. Many believed gambling would bring renewed tourism to the little shops and help restore the historic buildings. What they've discovered is that maintaining a community alongside a gambling center is a learning process. Businesses that tried to stick a slot machine next to their gift items couldn't compete with national casino chains that put slot machines wall-to-wall. Expenses such as buying slot machines and paying gambling taxes required deep pockets for getting started, and many local owners went under. People who owned buildings in easy-to-reach areas made good money by selling. Those who lived out of the way had a harder time selling, even though their regular livelihood was being smothered. So, with some people making fortunes and others losing modest savings, many of the pre-gambling residents left. Meanwhile, residents who stayed discovered that gambling profits did not just stay in their towns. The money went to state taxes and out-of-state investors.

As old-timers left, authentic charm left too. Local services dwindled. In Central City and Black Hawk today, don't count on buying gasoline (you can buy gas at the KOA campground on Colorado Highway 46, about 6 miles north, back toward Nederland). And those buildings that locals hoped would be restored often were gutted, with only the facade, or a copy of the facade, remaining.

People who view gambling more positively point out another set of facts. Many old buildings were beyond repair, and re-creating them has given the town a fresh, glitzy kind of charm. Those gutted interiors had been changed many times in the past already. Streets and utilities are in better repair, and the towns are prettier for walking. As for services, there weren't any basic services in Central City at the time gambling came in. Black Hawk had a little grocery store and two gas stations, which are gone. But a small grocery, Annie Oakley's, on Main Street, is now in Central City, and there's another small grocery in the Wild Card Casino on Main Street in Black Hawk. Some people who commuted to Denver for jobs at the supermarkets now can earn more in casinos. Some casinos sponsor local athletic teams and provide matching grants to local schools. Some residents who were struggling before now have nice new homes out of town. Shops can open and close almost weekly, according to Doug Dorsey, chairman of the board of the Black Hawk/Central City Chamber of Commerce, so it's hard to keep track of the businesses in town. Therefore some shops listed in this book at time of publication may no longer exist as you read it now, but new ones may have taken their places.

Without gambling, rural parts of Central City and Black Hawk might have faded into ghost towns. And after the newness of gambling wears off, perhaps diversity will return. Right now, the hunger to build yet another slot palace fuels development. Black Hawk has captured 53 percent of all the gaming revenues in the state. Central City and Cripple Creek fight for the remaining revenues. Central City has been blighted with the "extra-mile" syndrome: People either don't realize it's a mile away from Black Hawk or don't want to drive the extra mile. They see all the casinos in Black Hawk and think they've arrived at both destinations.

Central City has a lot more to offer than just casinos — richer history, the opera house and the Gilpin History Museum (separate listings below) — that gives visitors a good grasp of the colorful past. New in 1996 is a free valet parking system in Central City that solves the former parking problems. Be sure to visit the museum in Central City, especially if the kids are along, to learn about the area's mining history — it's only a block from the gaming area.

A Gambler's View of Black Hawk/Central City

Colorado's limited stakes tend to keep the focus on fun. Bets are $5 and less. Only poker, blackjack and platoons of one-armed bandits are allowed at the nearly 40 parlors, and the maximum hours are 8 AM to 2 AM.

Try setting aside some money — anywhere from $1 to $100 — and see how long you can

play before you lose it. One friend sets the limit at $20 for a night. Another goes for $50. They both recall times when they have played into the wee hours and managed to take home more than they brought, then other days when they have lost all their change in the first half-hour.

Slot machines gulp quarters everywhere. Some casinos offer good deals on food and entertainment. Central City and Black Hawk are less than a mile apart, linked by shuttle buses and plenty of on-the-street attendants. Altogether, the two towns have only six key streets, so it's easy to poke around. In general, Black Hawk gamblers seem more serious, drinking and looking intently at their cards, while Central City is a little more lighthearted. As one gambler puts it, you wander until you find where your luck seems best.

Casinos

Otto's and the Rohling Inn
260 and 160 Gregory St., Black Hawk
• (303) 582-0150

Owners Kay and Bill Lorenz have expanded their operations into two gambling houses with Otto's and the Rohling Inn. There's free parking with validation, and blackjack as well as slot machines. The Lorenzes also operate the Black Forest Inn next door, which is a highly rated German restaurant serving diners for 36 years.

The Gilpin Hotel Casino
111 Main St., Black Hawk
• (303) 582-1133

At the Gilpin the eight poker tables play Texas Hold'em, Omaha and occasionally Stud. There's also off-track betting for dog and horse races. A new Colorado-born poker game called Hold'em 88 is now being offered in at least a half-dozen casinos. It's a simpler version of Texas Hold'em, the most popular form of poker played at casinos. In Hold'em 88 in Colorado, where $5 is the maximum amount allowable for any single bet, the player can lose no more than $10 on a single game. In Texas Hold'em, which has four betting rounds and up to five raises per round, a single game can cost a player more than $100. The Gilpin

Hotel started slot machine tournaments in Colorado, and they still have the biggest. This historic building has the original brickwork facade from 1869. It's Victorian-style adorned with ornate hardwood. The Mineshaft Bar has been a locals hangout for 100 years. It's full of memorabilia and nightly, live entertainment that sometimes includes karaoke singing. There's free valet parking across the street. Lucille Malone's restaurant is named after the hotel's resident ghost. After Lucille's fiance died in a wagon accident, the distraught schoolteacher hurled herself off a balcony. Locals say she's been hanging around ever since.

Colorado Central Station Colo.
Hwy. 119, Black Hawk
• **(303) 279-3000**

The game of Hold'em 88 (explained previously) was invented here. Set in an authentic railroad depot, this casino boasts al least 10 tables of blackjack and seven poker tables, along with 600 slot machines.

Bullwhackers Casinos
101 Gregory St., Black Hawk
• **(303) 271-2733**
Silver Hawk
100 Chase St., Black Hawk
• **(303) 271-2933, or (800) GAMBULL**

Bullwhackers runs two casinos: Bullwhackers and Silver Hawk. These casinos could be described as fancy in a cheesy sort of way. Bullwhackers offers transportation to and from Denver and Westminster (the RTD park and ride at Wadsworth and the Boulder Turnpike, which is Colo. 36).

Teller House
120 Eureka St., Central City
• **(303) 582-3200**

This began as the Teller Hotel, among the finest hotels west of the Mississippi. The famed Face on the Barroom Floor is here plus the Central City Opera. We provide a full description of the hotel in the next section, but for now, be assured that it has slots and turn-of-the-century charm.

You can charter buses for large parties heading to the gambling towns, either through or directly with one of the casinos. This is wise when planning a drinking party. High altitude

makes liquor more potent, and those are winding — and sometimes icy — roads down.

While we hate to end with a caution, here goes. For most people, gambling's plain fun. But Daniel Minerva, Ph.D., a psychologist at Boulder's Addiction Exchange, (303) 442-3110, notes that the tip of the iceberg has grown larger. About six gamblers a year sought his help before 1990. Since legalized gambling, he now works with 30 to 40 people each year who gamble so much they have stopped working, lost their money and started lying. If this ever happens to you, be one of the lucky ones who seek help. Gambler's Anonymous, (303) 754-7119, in Denver is another source.

Black Hawk/Central City When You're Not Gambling

Some gambling friends complain that it gets boring after you've spent all your pocket change and are waiting for your friends to lose theirs. After all, this isn't Vegas. Some slot parlors don't even have a TV ball game. Fortunately, many casinos are catching on. Some places offer sports television and good restaurants, and if you step away from the casinos, you'll find other reasons to see these mountain towns.

Central City Opera House
124 Eureka St. (just west of Main and the Teller House)
For tickets and information contact Central City Opera House Association, 621 17th St., Ste. 1625, Denver
• **(303) 292-6700 or 800-851-8175**

Central City Opera is a beautiful, historic opera house built in 1878. The summer troupe is one of the oldest opera companies in the country, with a distinguished national reputation. All performances are in English, well-sung and wonderfully acted. Everyone stays in historic Victorian character, including the uniformed ushers, who ring brass hand bells when it's time to take your seat. The theater is beautifully decorated, down to the handpainted murals of Pegasus and cafe chairs engraved with the names of famous benefactors. Every seat is good. You're close enough that the actors and actresses come across as real people who feel life so strongly, they've just got to sing about it. See our entry on the Central City Opera in the Boulder Arts chapter for details.

When opera doesn't fit your schedule, sign up for a Festival Extra, (303) 292-6700. There are various choices: At Salon Recitals on weekends, opera stars do short recitals during a gourmet brunch at the Teller House Hotel, next to the opera house at 11:45 AM. Tickets cost around $25. For Opera a la Carte, famous opera scenes are fully staged and cost $5. *Face on the Barroom Floor* is a 30-minute cabaret opera recounting the Teller House's famous legend. These performances are at William's Stable, right across the street, and also cost $5. Seating is general admission.

Teller House
120 Eureka St., Central City
• (303) 582-3200

That Face on the Barroom Floor is painted in the Teller House, right next to the opera. You may expect a colossal face. Well, it's not big, but it's pretty. So are the eight Muses of Central City, originally painted in 1883. Five decades later, a restorer added jokes. You might notice a male figure with two left feet, a swan's head twisted backward and Venus's left nipple on the apple she holds. Take the $3 tour of the Teller House and, when it's not in use, the opera house, (303) 582-3200 (also $3). Tours leave every half-hour daily from 10 AM to 4 PM. Tour departure times are posted on a podium in the lobby.

Gilpin History Museum
228 E. High St., Central City
• (303) 582-5283

Housed in the first stone schoolhouse west of the Mississippi, the museum displays about 10,000 artifacts arranged in places such as the Victorian parlor and kitchen. Business memorabilia dating from mining-days are here, including items from the doctor's office, the law office, bank and more. A general store and hand-drawn firefighting equipment are on display plus an early school room from Russell Gulch. There's also a carriage display, doll collection and mining tools. It's open only from Memorial Day to Labor Day from 11 AM to 4 PM and costs $3 for adults and $1.50 for children 12 and younger.

The Thomas House
209 Eureka St., Central City
• (303) 582-5283,

This is an 1870 Greek-Revival Victorian house. It's mostly yellow with white trim. However, Marsha Thomas was a free thinker, and on a trip back East she brought back a gallon of salmon paint for the porch. During every world war, the government ordered gold mining to stop in an effort to stabilize the economy, so in World War I Central City took a dive. Ben Thomas, vice president of the local mercantile store, no longer had any business. In 1917, the Thomases locked the house and relocated to Denver. Marsha visited for summer operas, but they never moved back. All the furnishings — from spices to fine art to the 13 different varieties of clocks — are intact from 1917. The corset of 4-foot, 11-inch Marsha hangs beside the long johns of 6-foot-plus-tall Ben. Because Marsha was so short, Ben cut the legs off the kitchen's wood-burning stove so it would match her height. It's open 11 AM to 4 PM Thursday through Sunday in summer only, with $3 admission for adults. (If you tour the Gilpin History Museum too, the total cost is only $5 for both.)

St. James Methodist Church
123 Eureka St., Central City
• (303) 582-5882

Founded in 1859, this is the state's oldest church building. The stone church was erected by Cornish masons in 1871. The stained glass is lovely; the pipe organ was installed in 1899; the church seats 350, and it's active today. It's open for free tours 11 AM to 4 PM daily in the summer.

Cemeteries
West on Eureka St., Central City

Ten cemeteries let you glimpse more mining-era history. Was the idea that Woodcutters, Masons and Catholics would go to separate heavens? Judging from the separated plots, it looks that way. Actually, in those days, not everyone could afford a burial. So people were buried in plots bought by their fraternity, charity or lodge. Children's tombstones mark the heartache of the worldwide flu epidemic of 1919 plus smallpox and other diseases that wiped out whole families.

Nevadaville ghost town
1 mile north of Central City

A mile above Central City is a real live . . . well, maybe not live. . . . ghost town. In the 1800s, 4,000 people lived here, operating 20 quartz mills, several stores and hotels. Few historic structures still stand. But nothing's left of many other Gilpin County boomtowns. Lost cities include Deadwood Diggings, Dogtown, Eureka, Gambell Gulch, Gold Dirt, Glory Hole, Hoosier City, Quincy, Springfield, Trail's End and Wide Awake.

Restaurants

Many of the casinos feature only fast food — there's a Burger King in Colorado Central Station. But Jazz Alley across the street offers sit-down dining. Many of the casinos offer very inexpensive buffets. For fine dining, it's wise to get a reservation. Below are a few recommended restaurants. See the price-code key at the beginning of this chapter.

Black Forest Inn
$$ • 260 Gregory St., Black Hawk
• (303) 279-2333

One of the oldest restaurants in Black Hawk, opened in 1958, the Black Forest provides outstanding German cuisine and fine service. The atmosphere is old country with German decor and music — and even a cuckoo clock. In addition to Wiener schnitzel, sauerbraten, game specials and seafood, there's Hungarian goulash, American-type choices, salads, caviar and a Russian-egg appetizer. The German sourdough rye bread is home baked and there's a good wine list. Black Forest is open daily for late breakfast, lunch and dinner.

Fitzgerald's Shamrock Cafe
$$ • 101 Main St., Black Hawk
• (303) 582-3203

This very green Irish-themed restaurant with comfortable booths and tables serves just about everything from corned beef and "shamrock stuffed potatoes" to salads, steaks, prime rib, hamburgers, pork chops, meat loaf, salmon and pasta. It's open daily for breakfast, lunch and dinner.

The Golden Rose Buffet
(Golden Rose Casino)
$ • 102 Main St., Central City
• (303) 825-1413 or (800) 929-0255

Many places offer plenty to fill you up for less than $10 and this casino is one. The Golden Rose Buffet has deals on good meals along with beveled-glass decorations, red valances over white lace curtains and turn-of-the-century photos. The changing buffet ($6.95 during the day and $7.95 at night) includes eight hot items, such as barbecued ribs, hot fresh vegetables and Oriental food. The salad bar greens are romaine and spinach, and the dessert bar includes mousses, parfaits, pastries and ice cream. They serve lunch and dinner daily.

Madeline's (in the Teller House)
$ • 120 Eureka St., Central City
• (303) 582-3200

Next to the Opera House this historic former-hotel-turned casino offers burgers and sandwiches at Madeline's which opens into the historic Face Bar. Other light fare such as soups and salads are available. They serve lunch and dinner daily.

Jazz Alley
$ • 321 Main St., Black Hawk
• (303) 582-1125

If you gamble and win game points, you can get a real bargain dinner. The prime rib special is $5.99, but only $2.99 if you gamble and get 10 points. The restaurant serves a large variety of American-style food including steaks and pasta. It also offers lots of specials such as $1.99 breakfasts. They serve breakfast, lunch and dinner daily.

INSIDERS' TIP

Central City's Thomas House is one of the most well-preserved turn-of-the-century buildings you will ever see. Even the spices in the kitchen are authentic.

A snowboarder gets some air at Copper Mountain.

Accommodations

See our price-key code at the beginning of this chapter.

Harvey's Wagon Ho
$$–$$$$$ • 321 Gregory St., Central City • (303) 582-0800 or (800) 427-8397

Central City's newest casino/hotel has 118 rooms giving a big boost to the accommodations in this little county. It's the only casino/hotel in Central City. Tony Roma's is the on-site restaurant.

The Gold Dust Lodge
$$ • Colo. Hwy. 119, Black Hawk • (303) 582-5415 or 5312

On the main highway in Black Hawk, this lodge offers 24 nicely-decorated, comfortable rooms in a convenient location.

Primrose Inn
$$ • 310 E. First High St., Central City • (303) 582-5808

Jan Ward runs this cute bed and breakfast right next to the Historic Museum, on the northeast side of Central City. Currently open only in the summer, the yellow-and-white Victorian sits high on the hill. Burgundy brocade wallpaper, lace curtains, a brass bed and a 7-foot-tall antique mirror decorate one room. A continental breakfast is included with the room price.

Ski Country
(Both Summer and Winter)

Winter Park and Summit County offer some of the nation's best skiing and summer recreation. Both are within a two-hour drive of Boulder. The individual ski areas, resorts and towns are listed below with separate contact numbers for each. There are also separate listings for getting there, attractions, restaurants, accommodations and recreation.

Please note that we listed prices for accommodations instead of using the price-code key in the Ski Country section. That's because rates are rarely less than $100 per night, especially during ski season, and go can as high as $850 per night at the most luxurious condominiums.

Winter Park

The town of Winter Park, 2 miles north of the Winter Park ski area, offers numerous restaurants and accommodations. It's set in a beautiful valley surrounded by high peaks. Continuing northwest on US 40 brings you to the small towns of Fraser and Tabernash. Fraser often reports the coldest temperatures in the country, so some Coloradans call it "Freezer." But it's a beautiful area with broad open meadows and spectacular views. If you look up toward the Continental Divide to the east, you might be able to spot the jutting rock formation known as the Devil's Thumb, north of Fraser, for which the nearby cross-country ski resort was named. Continuing north will eventually bring you to the towns of Granby and to the intersection of US 34 to Grand Lake on the western boundary of Rocky

The Colorado Avalanche won the National Hockey League's Stanley Cup in 1996.

Mountain National Park. (See our chapter on Grand Lake.)

Getting There

Winter Park is 70 miles west of Denver. From Boulder, drive south on Broadway (Colo. 93) toward Golden and, at the new Golden bypass, follow the signs for I-70 W. or take US 6 up Clear Creek Canyon, which follows the old Colorado Central Railroad bed and deposits you right on I-70 headed west. Follow I-70 and exit onto US 40 W. at Empire and continue over Berthoud Pass, which is well-maintained all winter. There are two entrances to the ski area: Mary Jane offers expert skiing with challenging mogul runs; the main Winter Park base is better for beginners and intermediates. The town of Winter Park is 2 miles farther on US 40. Fraser is 3 miles past Winter Park.

The Ski Train
Union Station, 17th and Wynkoop, Denver • (303) 296-I-SKI

During winter, the Ski Train provides another, more interesting way to get to Winter Park — though it requires going into Denver, making the trip a bit longer than driving directly, but you won't have to deal with traffic or icy mountain roads. The Ski Train departs from Denver's Union Station at 7:15 AM and takes skiers within walking distance of the lifts. It goes through some 30 tunnels, including the 6.2-mile-long Moffat Tunnel, drilled a mile below the Continental Divide — a nifty ride and worth experiencing, especially with children. The Ski Train leaves Winter Park at 4:15 PM, just after the lifts close. The trip takes two hours each way. The adult Coach Car fare is usually $35 for a same-day round trip. It increases to $40 for a round trip on Saturdays during the months of February, March and April. The same trip is $60 in the Club Car including con-

tinental breakfast and aprés-ski refreshments. Discounted lift tickets are available on the train. The Ski Train runs Saturdays and Sundays from mid-December until late March plus additional days during Christmas-New Year's week and on Fridays in March.

Winter Park: The Resort and Area
677 Winter Park Dr.
• (970) 726-5514 or (303) 892-0961

Winter Park operates on U.S. Forest Service land, as do most Western American ski areas, but it is unique in that the city of Denver owns its assets, which are run by a nonprofit corporation. It is Colorado's fifth-largest ski area in terms of skier visits. Skiers and snowboarders can move among four interlinked mountains: the original Winter Park, Mary Jane, Vasquez Ridge and Parsenn Bowl. Twenty lifts, including seven high-speed express quads, access 1,414 acres of skiable terrain. Children's programs are exemplary, including day care for youngsters ages 2 months to 5 years and ski instruction for 3-year-olds to teens.

Downhill Skiing

In winter, skiing and snowboarding, of course, are the main attractions at Winter Park. The 1998-99 price for a one-day lift ticket was $50 for adults. Tickets discounted to $37 are available at Front Range grocery stores and ski shops. The best deal for frequent skiers is the Value Card. It offers adult skiers a 44 percent discount off lift-ticket window rates, two discounted buddy passes, and discounts to the Denver Zoo, the Denver Botanic Gardens and the Ski Train.

If you don't know how to ski or snowboard, January is a good month to learn. Winter Park offers lessons ranging from $20 to $35 per lesson. Discovery Park, a mid-mountain learning area slope with its own slow-moving chairlift, is like a ski area within a ski area, where novices can practice comfortably.

National Sports Center for the Disabled
677 Winter Park Dr., Winter Park
• (970) 726-1540

Winter Park is also well-known for its handicapped ski program and is appropriately the site of the disabled center. Founded in 1970, it has 39 full-time employees, including instructors and coaches, and 1,000 volunteers who work with people with many different types of disabilities — cerebral palsy sufferers, amputees, paraplegics and others — and provide nearly 11,000 private, customized lessons each winter. The center has expanded its scope to include snowboarding and snowshoeing lessons as well as a substantial program of adaptive summer sports.

Cross-country Skiing

Devil's Thumb Cross-Country Center
3530 County Rd. 83, Tabernash
• (970) 726-5632

This center offers 105 kilometers of great groomed trails for beginners to advanced cross-country skiers. There are flat trails for beginners and smooth wide lanes for ski-skaters plus lovely rolling meadows and some steep downhills for thrills. The 1997-98 trail pass was $12 for adults; $10 for children ages 7 to 12 and seniors 60 and older; free for children younger than 6.

Snow Mountain Ranch
1101 County Rd. 53, Granby
• (970) 887-2152 or (303) 443-4743

In addition to its various winter activities for kids and families, Snow Mountain has an additional 100 kilometers of groomed trails, including 3 kilometers illuminated for night skiing. A trail pass is $12 for adults and $5 for

children ages 7 to 12; free for children younger than 6.

Other Winter Activities

Snowcat Tours
Departures from the Balcony House at the base of Winter Park
• (970) 726-5514 or (303) 892-0961

Nonskiers can enjoy the ambiance of the slopes by taking a two-hour mountain tour. They have frequent departures. The cost is $25 for adults, $20 for children and seniors.

Dog Sled Rides of Winter Park
King Crossings Rd. at the Railroad Crossing • (970) 726-8326

Dog sled teams take riders through 1,000 acres of pristine backcountry. Sleds pulled by eight- to 10-dog teams — all purebred Siberian huskies — can attain 30 miles per hour on downhill stretches. The cost for a one-hour ride varies at different times of winter, but figure on more than $140 for two people; reservations are required.

Jim's Sleigh Rides
77849 U.S. Hwy. 40, Winter Park
• (970) 726-9247 or (970) 726-0944

These sleighs take 20 guests in a horse-drawn sleigh past the historic Cozzens Ranch beside the Fraser River. The 70-minute ride includes a bonfire stop with refreshments. The cost — $15 for adults; $12 for ages 3 to 12; free for children 2 and younger — is the same for summer hayrides.

Dinner at the Barn
County Rd. 8, Winter Park
• (970) 726-4923

One of two dinner sleigh rides available in the area, Dinner at the Barn combines a ride through the woods and meadows of an 80-acre ranch with a gourmet dinner served by kerosene lantern light, with Western-style en-

INSIDERS' TIP

Denver Art Museum's newest gallery additions — Art of the American West and European & American Art — opened at the end of 1997.

tertainment following. In summer, horse-drawn wagons replace sleighs. Advance reservations are required. Cost is approximately $40 for adults; $25 for ages 4 to 12; and free for ages 3 and younger.

Dashing Through the Snow
1400 County Rd. 5, Tabernash
• **(970) 726-5376**

This group has one of Colorado's longest sleigh trails — 3 miles — to a secluded and delightful backcountry cabin, where a six-course gourmet feast with a choice of chicken or rib-eye steak is served, with live entertainment as a bonus. The price is $50 for adults, $35 for children or free for those under the age of three. Bonfire/hot chocolate rides are available as well. (Sleigh rides become carriage rides in summer.)

Winter Park Ice Skating Rink
Cooper Creek Sq., Winter Park
• **(970) 726-4118**

Bring the whole family and enjoy free ice skating here with skate rentals nearby at the Ski Broker and SportsStalker.

Call the Winter Park/Fraser Valley Chamber of Commerce, (303) 422-0666 or (970) 726-4118, for information on snowmobile tours and rentals and other winter diversions.

Summer Attractions

Winter Park Resort Mountain Bike Race Series
239 Winter Park Drive, Competition Center • (970) 726-1589

The resort hosts this annual series composed of five events with different formats, including hill climb, circuit racing and point-to-point racing, held from early June to early August. Two hundred-fifty competitors 8 and older take part in each event. The entry fee is $20 in advance or $25 on race day.

Bicycling
Winter Park Chamber of Commerce Visitors' Center
78841 U.S. Hwy. 40, Winter Park
• **(970) 726-4118**

Bicycling is a popular participant sport and

Winter Park accommodates with 600 miles of marked, mapped and maintained trails. There are 10 bike shops in the Fraser Valley, and free town rides every Thursday evening and free women-only rides on Wednesdays throughout summer. Area bike trail maps are available at local bike stores or at the Chamber of Commerce. It is open from 8 AM to 5 PM daily.

Alpine Slide/Zephyr Express/ Music Festivals
Winter Park Resort
677 Winter Park Dr.
• **(970) 726-5514 or (303) 892-0961**

The Alpine is Colorado's longest slide and a big summer attraction for young and old.

With special bike mounts, Winter Park's Zephyr chairlift takes mountain bikers to the top where they can ride 45 miles of steep, exciting single-track trails and gentler jeep roads. Rental bikes are available. Each on-mountain summer activity is assigned a point value, ranging from 10 points for the Alpine Slide to six for mini-golf or the human maze. In 1997, prices ranged from $8 for adults ($7 for children ages 6 to 13 and seniors ages 62 to 69). Full-day park passes for all activities were $40, and morning or afternoon half-day passes were $30. Passes for anyone younger than 5 or older than 70 are free.

Winter Park also hosts two major music events in July: The KBCO World Class Rock Festival and The Winter Park Jazz Festival featuring nationally known bands.

Also at the resort you'll find miniature golf, the human maze, a climbing wall, a zip line, mountain scooters and chairlift rides to the top of the mountain. Summer hours are 10 AM to 6 PM (5 PM in September, weather permitting).

The High Country Stampede Rodeo
John Work Arena, one mile west of Fraser
• **(303) 422-0666 or (970) 726-4118**

The rodeo takes place every Saturday evening from early July to late August. The junior rodeo gets underway at 5:30 PM, followed by the pros. There's bull riding, bronc busting, barrel racing and other popular events. In 1998, admission was $8 for adults and $4 for children. A low-cost barbecue dinner is also available.

The Pole Creek Golf Club
6827 County Rd. 5, Tabernash
• (970) 726-8847

Golf Digest named this the best public course in Colorado. It offers golfers 18 holes of gorgeous greens. In 1999, greens fees were $82 and $50 (for high and low seasons, respectively). Golf carts, which are optional, are $12.50 per rider.

Arapahoe National Forest
Arapahoe National Forest, Ranger District Office • (970) 887-4100

Visitors to the national forest will enjoy fishing, hiking, horseback riding, jeeping and rafting. The Winter Park Chamber of Commerce, (970) 726-4118, has information about outfitters.

Restaurants

The price-code key for restaurants appears at the beginning of this chapter.

Winter Park: The Resort and Area
677 Winter Park Dr.
• (970) 726-5514 or (303) 892-0961

The Winter Park ski area has dining options both at the base and on the mountain. The

Coffee and Tea Market in Winter Park's Balcony House is open for breakfast and lunch, and the nearby West Portal Station day lodge has self-service snack and lunch service as well as the Derailer Bar. The Mary Jane Center features a cafeteria as well as a sit-down restaurant called The Club Car and Pepperoni's Pizza and Sports Bar. The beautiful and monumental Lodge at Sunspot at the top of the Zephyr Express chairlift serves snacks and lunches at The Provisioner, a self-serve facility. Table service is offered in the Dining Room, which is also open for dinner Thursday, Friday and Saturday evenings in winter, with access via gondola. Reservations are recommended. Other on-mountain eating facilities include Snoasis, mid-mountain at Winter Park; Lunch Rock and Sundance Cafe, snack bars atop Mary Jane and Vasquez Ridge respectively.

Gasthaus Eichler
$$ • 78786 U.S. Hwy. 40, Winter Park
• (970) 726-5133

Noted for Austrian and German specialties, try the veal dumplings, bratwurst or goulash. They are open for breakfast, lunch and dinner. Reservations are suggested.

Hernando's Pizza and Pasta Pub
$ • 78199 U.S. Hwy. 40, Winter Park
• (970) 726-5409

This is a local favorite for homemade pastas including delicious lasagna, good pizza and a summer beer garden. Hernando's is open for lunch and dinner during the summer, dinner only during the winter months.

The Shed
$ • 78672 U.S. Hwy. 40, Winter Park
• (970) 726-9912

This is a longtime Winter Park favorite, now serving hearty breakfasts and Southwestern-style dinners. The weekend buffet is popular with hungry skiers. They are closed on both Tuesday and Wednesday.

Carver's
$ • 93 Cooper Creek, Winter Park
• (970) 726-8202

Tucked into a log cabin behind Cooper Creek Square, Carver's offers excellent baked goods and an eclectic menu that includes burgers and pasta, sandwiches and lots of vegetarian fare all moderately priced. Breakfast and lunch are served daily with dinner served Thursday through Sunday.

Crooked Creek Saloon & Eatery
$ • 401 Zerex Ave., Fraser
• (970) 726-9250

This is a family-style Mexican and American restaurant that is best known for giant burgers and fiery wings. There are also steaks and pasta and it's open daily for breakfast, lunch and dinner with the bar open until 2 AM.

Accommodations

Reservations are necessary in this popular area for most accommodations. You can make them through Winter Park Central Reservations, (800) 729-5839 or (970) 726-5587, or by calling individual properties.

Super 8 Motel
78665 U.S. Hwy. 40, Winter Park
• (970) 726-5294 or (800) 541-6130

Right in town, the new Super 8 has 60 rooms, all with two queen-size beds and some with refrigerators. Rooms run to around $135 during winter and $69 in summer. Room rates here increase dramatically depending on the season and certain festival weekends.

Gasthaus Eichler
78786 U.S. Hwy. 40, Winter Park
• (970) 726-5133 or (800) 543-3899

This small, European style hotel offers rooms that are warm and cozy with all of the modern conveniences. The down comforters and lace curtains add to the European flavor. The restaurant serves authentic German cuisine and the guest list often includes many from Europe, creating a lively, international atmosphere. Rates start at around $89 without meals and $108 with meals.

The Iron Horse Retreat
2527 Winter Park Dr., Winter Park
• (303) 573-1545 or (970) 726-8851

This is the resort's only ski-in, ski-out property. It has 130 rooms, all with full amenities. There is a full-service restaurant with room service, heated indoor and outdoor pools and a fireplace in every room. In addition to winter ski packages, golf packages are offered during summer months. Its attractive condos range from $89 to $175 for two during summer and $109 to $600 in winter.

The Grand Victorian
78542 Fraser Valley Pkwy., Winter Park
• (970) 726-5881 or (800) 204-1170

This is the first among equals when it comes to Winter Park's growing selection of charming bed and breakfast inns. Secluded in a grove of lodgepole pines, this romantic neo-Victorian offers lodging in three sumptuous fireplace suites. The rates include a gourmet breakfast and afternoon drinks and hors d'oeuvres. Suites go for about $100 to $145 in summer and $155 to $235 in winter.

Devil's Thumb Ranch Resort
3530 County Rd. 83, Tabernash
• (970) 726-8231 or (800) 933-4339

This is a quiet, beautifully-located retreat ski lodge open year round. It is equally nice for cross-country skiing in winter and horseback riding, hiking and fly fishing and access to mountain biking in summer. Cabin rentals are consistent for both summer and winter months. Three miles north of Fraser, it's 3.5 miles east (right turn off of U.S. Highway 40) on County Road 83 and down the right fork in the road. Cabins rent for $110 to $130 for two people, both summer and winter.

Idlewild Lodge
398 Ski Idlewild Rd. • (970) 726-8352

A great downtown Winter Park location, Idlewild is open year round. A double room at Idlewild costs $170 per night and includes a full buffet breakfast and dinner for two. Summer rates are the same and include three meals plus horseback riding, hayrides, evening entertainment and a children's recreation program. Idlewild is an alcohol- and smoke-free environment (no firearms allowed, either) geared for family vacations.

Summit County

The four ski areas of Breckenridge, Keystone, Arapahoe Basin and Copper Mountain collectively attract more skiers and snowboarders than any other ski destination in North America. They offer an incredible range of great terrain, and for vacationers and weekenders, the towns of Breckenridge, Dillon and Frisco — and the resort developments of Keystone and Copper Mountain — offer outstanding restaurants and accommodations all in proximity to the Greater Denver area and Boulder.

During summer, there's hiking and backpacking in the Arapahoe National Forest; fishing and boating on Lake Dillon; whitewater rafting on the Blue River; and an excellent network of bike trails and several good golf courses in Summit County, as well as a calendar full of special events and festivals. Forest information is available from the Dillon Ranger District Office, (970) 468-5400.

Getting There From Boulder

Road condition or traffic slowdowns excepted, all Summit County ski areas are less than a two-hour drive from Boulder. Drive south on Broadway (Colo. 93) toward Golden and, at the Golden bypass, follow the signs for I-70 W. or take US 6 up Clear Creek Canyon directly to I-70 W. Follow I-70 to the Eisenhower Tunnel. For Arapahoe Basin, exit at US 6 west over Loveland Pass. For all the other resorts, proceed through the tunnel. Keystone is reached by taking the first exit after the tunnel, which is US 6 east. For Breckenridge, take the Frisco exit and drive south on Colo. 9 for about 9 miles. Copper Mountain is directly off I-70, at Exit 195, just before the highway climbs up to Vail Pass.

Breckenridge

Breckenridge, the town, is the oldest and largest of the Summit County communities. It was founded in 1859 when gold was discovered in the area. It remains a picturesque and historic renovated mining town, and the main street is still lined with some of the handsome Victorian homes that housed the first prosperous citizens, and numerous restaurants, cafes, shops and art galleries. Every summer the National Festival of Music at Breckenridge mounts a two-month season of classical music.

Alpine Skiing

Arapahoe Basin Ski Area
U.S. Hwy. 6, Keystone • (970) 496-7077

Arapahoe Basin is America's highest ski area, with a base altitude of 10,800 feet and a summit elevation of 12,450 feet. Rugged terrain, fabled steeps, open bowls and high, tree-free snowfields make it paradise for advanced and expert skiers and snowboarders. The lifts can run into summer, as in 1995, when A-Basin finally closed on August 10.

Both A-basin and Keystone have child-care facilities. Keystone's nursery, which remains open in the evening during night skiing, takes babies as young as 2 months, and parents may use complimentary pagers to stay in touch with the center. Arapahoe Basin's nursery starts at 18 months. Both offer ski lessons from age 3 and snowboarding lessons from age 8.

A-Basin has 61 trails with 490 skiable acres and five lifts. Skiers are 15 percent beginner, 45 percent intermediate, and 40 percent expert. For 1998-99, a one-day pass was $40 for an adult, $12 for children. Tickets can be purchased in advance at King Soopers, Safeway, and Christie Sports.

Breckenridge Ski Resort
1599 C Summit County Rd. 3,
Breckenridge • (303) 573-7350

Breckenridge, the ski area, is huge and wide-ranging. Peak 8 is the original ski area, with a complex network of interlaced trails for all ability levels and access to high, above-the-treeline bowls and chutes as well as Peak 7, a steep mountain that is patrolled but not groomed and has no lift service — extreme terrain by anyone's standards. Peak 9 offers the greatest concentration of beginner and novice terrain and access to Peak 10, fabled for moguls, steeps and open glades. You can ski from mountain to mountain and back again, crisscrossing Breck's 1,600-acre playground via different routes each time. There are excellent children's facilities at both the Peak 8 and Peak 9 bases. Breckenridge has long welcomed snowboarders with a half-pipe, terrain features and just plain good riding.

Breckenridge has 135 trails on 2,031 acres with 20 lifts. In 1998-99, at-the-window tickets were $50 for adults (one-day passes) with tickets available at King Soopers, Safeway and Albertson's supermarkets, Total and Diamond Shamrock gas stations and Gart Sports. Children's rates, ages 5 to 12, are $19. The purchase of multi-day passes can save a skier $5 to $8 dollars per day depending on the number of days purchased.

Copper Mountain Resort
U.S. I-70, Exit 195
• (303) 892-6426 or (800) 458-8386

Copper Mountain, which celebrated its 50th anniversary in 1997, is treasured for its logical, well-laid-out terrain and congenial ambiance. At-the-window, one-day tickets for 1998-99 were $50 for adults and $15 for children ages 6 through 14; kids 5 and younger and seniors 70 and older are admitted free. Discount tickets are available at King Soopers, Safeway, Albertson's, Diamond Shamrock,

Total, Christie Sports and other locations. The Copper Card, which costs $12 to $35, depending on when it's purchased, enables you to buy up to four lift tickets discounted to the lowest available price every time you visit. It also offers additional discounts on food at the resort and on goods and services at Copper and elsewhere in Summit County.

Keystone Resort
U.S. Hwy. 6, Keystone • (800) 842-7415

Keystone is a self-contained resort with skiing on three contiguous mountains: Keystone Mountain, primarily for novice and intermediate skiers; North Peak, with its excellent mogul runs; and The Outback and the Outback Bowl, with powder-holding glades and steeps. Thanks to a huge and efficient snow-making system, Keystone is traditionally the first Colorado ski area to open for the season. Mid-October openings are not uncommon, and Halloween skiing is a tradition. For the 1998-99 season, Keystone also welcomed snowboarders to a sensational snowboarding park in Packsaddle Bowl. It's the only Summit County area (and one of the few in Colorado) to offer night skiing and snowboarding, nightly until 9 PM during most of the season.

Keystone has 91 trails and 21 lifts and offers great deals on night skiing. In 1998-99 a single-day ticket was $50, while a multi-day pass ran around $40. Children ages 5 to 14 ski for $18 per day. Discounts are offered to seniors ages 65-69 and those over 70 ski free. On the Front Range tickets are available at King Soopers, Safeway and Albertson's.

Cross-country Skiing

The Breckenridge and Frisco Nordic Centers are under the same management and share an interchangeable trail pass. Both offer instruction and rentals of cross-country skis and snowshoes.

The Breckenridge Nordic Center
1200 Ski Hill Rd., Breckenridge
• (970) 453-6855

The Breckenridge Center has more than 23 kilometers of groomed track set in the valleys below Peaks 7 and 8.

The Frisco Nordic Center
18454 Colo. Hwy. 9, Frisco
• (970) 668-0866

The Frisco Center has 35 kilometers of trails groomed daily for classical skiing and skate-skiing, with much of the system also offering great views of Lake Dillon and a particularly congenial log day lodge. Both centers offer a lesson guarantee and free afternoon beginner lessons.

Restaurants

The price-code key for restaurants appears at the beginning of this chapter.

Pierre's River Walk Café
$$$ • 1375 Main St., Breckenridge
• (970) 453-0989

Pierre's is a fine French restaurant with lovely atmosphere and outdoor dining available in summer for lunch and dinner. It is closed on Monday during the winter months.

The St. Bernard Inn
$ • 103 S. Main St., Breckenridge
• (970) 453-2572

The St. Bernard specializes in classic Northern Italian food and also offers contemporary cuisine. The Inn is open for lunch and dinner with a lounge available.

The Cafe Alpine
$ • 106 Adams St., Breckenridge
• (970) 453-8218

Charming Victorian setting with an eclectic cuisine including steak and seafood. The Alpine is open for lunch and dinner during the summer, for dinner only during winter months.

Blue Moose Restaurant
$$ • 540 S. Main St., Breckenridge
• (970) 453-4859

The Blue Moose offers a casual atmosphere with a wide range of American-style food served at lunch and dinner.

Mi Casa Mexican Restaurant & Cantina
$ • 600 S. Park Ave., Breckenridge
• (970) 453-2071

Mi Casa has traditional Mexican specialties served for lunch and dinner. Specials also include Mexican-style pork chops and steak.

Mountain Sage Cafe & Gold Pan Saloon
$ • 105 N. Main St., Breckenridge
• (970) 453-5499 or (970) 547-4628

Enjoy a Tex-Mex breakfast as well as cheap pizza and bar food at lunch and dinner. There are also burgers, veggie wraps, game hen and steaks.

The Breckenridge Brewery & Pub
$ • 600 S. Main St., Breckenridge
• (970) 453-1550

This was one of the state's first brewpubs and is still is one of the most popular (there's even a branch near Coors Field in Denver). Avalanche Ale is one of the favorites, and they make their own potent root beer and hearty portions of pub food too.

Accommodations

With lodging for nearly 25,000 visitors, Breckenridge ranks as one of Colorado's major resort towns with all types of overnight options in many price ranges. Call the Breckenridge Resort Chamber of Commerce Central Reservations, (970) 453-2918 or (800) 221-1091, for information or reservations at the town's many condominiums, bed and breakfasts and other accommodations.

William's House Bed & Breakfast
303 N. Main St., Breckenridge
• (800) 795-2975 or (970) 453-2975

This is a lovely 19th-century home in classic Victorian style. Some rooms are wheelchair-accessible. The house has a Jacuzzi, fireplace and sitting area. Rates are from $105 to $185, for rooms or the cottage, depending upon the season. There are five new rooms

Photo: Ski the Summit/Bob Winsett

The classic sights of summer in Summit County are often seen on horseback.

with fireplaces in a new building, The Barn Above the River, overlooking the Blue River.

Beaver Run Resort
620 Village Rd., Breckenridge
• (970) 453-6000

A ski-in/ski-out establishment on Peak 9, this is Breckenridge's largest property with lodging ranging from hotel rooms to three-bedroom suites. The fully equipped resort has indoor and outdoor swimming pools, hot tubs, fitness facilities, shops, restaurants and even an indoor miniature golf course. Winter rates begin at $275; summer rates at $110.

Great Divide Lodge
550 Village Rd., Breckenridge
• (970) 453-4500

Formerly the Hilton, the lodge was renovated in 1998 and roomy rooms now have new furniture, carpet, drapes and artwork. Full hotel services are offered, including complementary van service. Rooms have two queen-size beds, a king-size bed, or a king-size bed with a sleeper sofa. An on-site restaurant provides room service, and a lounge, indoor swimming pool, workout room, sauna and hot tub are available. Prices for rooms begine at $180 per night in winter and $120 in summer.

Summer Activities

National Festival of Music at Breckenridge
150 W. Adams St., Breckenridge
• (970) 453-2918

This festival usually begins in early August and continues through September with clas-sical, jazz and modern music. Visitors are invited to enjoy free, open rehearsals. Concerts are held at the Riverwalk Center, an elegant 750-seat multipurpose facility.

Summit County Historical Society
309 N. Main St., Breckenridge
• (970) 453-9022

The society conducts a variety of walking tours, mainly in summer but also in winter on request.

Washington Gold Mine/ Lomax Placer Gulch
137 S. Main St., Breckenridge
• (970) 453-5579

Ninety-minute tours of Breckenridge's mines are offered Monday through Saturday at 1 PM and 3 PM. The price is $5 for adults, free for children. For directions, call the Breckenridge Guest Services and Activity Center at the number listed.

The Breckenridge Golf Club
200 Clubhouse Dr., Breckenridge
• (970) 453-9104

This club offers outstanding golf at America's only Jack Nicklaus-designed municipal course. High-season green and cart fees in 1998 were $90 for 18 holes.

Breckenridge Stables
1799 Ski Hill Rd. (above the Super Slide on Peak 8), Breckenridge
• (970) 453-4438

This stable offers rides over the Ten Mile Range and prides itself on its gentle horses. One-hour rides are about $18; two hours, $30; half price for children 6 and younger.

INSIDERS' TIP

Those going to Cripple Creek (near Colorado Springs) should go a bit farther to the charming town of Victor — at the end of the same road (Colo. Highway 67). It's only another 6 miles and Victor is where most of the mining in the area took place. It retains the historic character of the times more so than Cripple Creek with its many casinos. Stroll around the small downtown area and enjoy the antique shops — and don't miss the hand-made broom and wax shop.

Frisco, Dillon and Silverthorne

Frisco and Dillon were once mining towns, though the original Dillon is now at the bottom of Lake Dillon, a reservoir, and what you see was either moved before it was filled or rebuilt since then. The reservoir was filled between 1960 and '65. Silverthorne has become known as a major outlet center, with more than 80 manufacturers' outlets. All three now have numerous stores, restaurants and accommodations (including condos) convenient to all the Summit County ski areas.

Cross-country Skiing

The Keystone Cross Country Center
U.S. Hwy. 6, Keystone • (970) 496-4275

Keystone Cross is near the stables on Soda Ridge Road about a mile west of the main lodge. Directed by ebullient former Olympian Jana Hlavaty, it offers outstanding instruction programs and guided ski tours. Nearly 35 kilometers of prepared trails lace through the Snake River Valley and high on the mountain, accessible from North Peak.

White River National Forest
Dillon Ranger District, 680 Blue River Pkwy., Silverthorne • (970) 468-5400

Several Nordic routes are accessible from the road to Montezuma or directly from this old mining camp. Peru Creek is a good trail for novices, while the routes to the St. John and the Wild Irishman Mine trails are popular with intermediate skiers and snowshoers. All are accessed for free.

Restaurants

Alpenglow Stube
$$$$$ • U.S. Hwy. 6, Keystone • (970) 496-4386

In The Outpost at the top of Keystone's North Peak, this restaurant serves elegant, Bavarian-influenced contemporary cuisine for lunch and dinner. Lunch is served only during ski season, dinner is served year round and reservations are required. This is a fixed-price restaurant that includes appetizer and dessert.

Der Fondue Chessel
$$$$ • U.S. Hwy. 6, Keystone • (970) 496-4386

Der Fondue Chessel, in The Outpost, is a self-serve restaurant with Swiss specialties. They serve dinner only, to the oompah of live entertainment. For both options at The Outpost, you can ski in during the day, and in the evening, you ride out on the enclosed gondola from the top of Keystone Mountain. Der Fondue typically closes for month when the ski season ends, from approximately mid-May to mid-June.

Keystone Ranch
$$$$$ • U.S. Hwy. 6, Keystone • (970) 496-4386

Down in the valley, the elegantly rustic Ranch has garnered accolades for its six-course dinners and an outstanding wine list. Only dinner is served and a reservation is recommended. This is a fixed-price restaurant that includes appetizer and dessert. There is year-round dining here.

Ski Tip Lodge
$$$$ • U.S. Hwy. 6, Keystone • (970) 496-4386

Once a stagecoach stop and Summit County's original ski lodge, this restaurant is reminiscent of an Old New England Inn. Its quaint and charming restaurant serves excellent American and continental cuisine. Breakfast is served for guests and the restaurant is open to the public for dinner year round.

Old Dillon Inn
$ • Colo. Hwy. 9 in Silverthorne, north of I-70 • (970) 468-2791

For a great Margarita — though you'll have to fight the crowds — go to the Dillon Inn. The restaurant primarily serves Mexican food at the dinner hour only and has a 19th-century bar and lively music.

The Mint
$ • 341 Blue River Pkwy., Silverthorne
• (970) 468-5247

This restaurant is in one of Summit County's oldest buildings (one of those rescued from the bottom of the lake) and is a good family-dining spot where you cook your own steak or chicken on the grill.

The Arapahoe Cafe
$ • 626 Lake Dillon Dr., Dillon
• (970) 468-0873

Breakfast, lunch and dinner are served in a cozy log cabin. Early in the day you'll find omelets, hamburgers and salads, and by evening steak, seafood and pasta.

The Snake River Saloon
$-$$ • 23074 U.S. Hwy. 6, Dillon
• (970) 468-2788

Open for dinner only, this is a popular spot for aprés-ski, with steak and seafood and not-to-miss late-night entertainment on weekends.

Accommodations

Keystone Lodge
U.S. Hwy. 6, Keystone
• (800) 222-0188

The original Keystone development centered around Keystone Lake and the surrounding woods. The lodge offers luxurious mountain- and lake-view rooms for around $150 per night in low season to $200 in winter high season, double occupancy. Keystone also offers nearby condominium and private home rentals of various sizes, styles and prices. As a rule of thumb, figure on paying from $100 nightly in low season for a one-bedroom unit to $800 in high season, and $500 to $1000 for a two-bedroom.

Chateaux d'Mont
0175 County Rd. 8, Dillon
• (970) 496-4372

Closer to the mountain, the Chateaux costs $650 to $900 per night for a truly deluxe two- or three-bedroom condo within walking distance of the lifts and featuring a private hot tub on a glass-enclosed balcony. Services include a welcome grocery package, fresh flowers,

plush terry-cloth robes, nightly turndown, complimentary newspaper and concierge service.

Keystone Inn
23044 U.S. Hwy. 6, Keystone
• (970) 468-1334

The Inn offers rooms with two double beds, one king, and a few one-bedroom suites. There are also two suites with spas. The restaurant offers room service, and there is a laundry service, ski lockers and three hot tubs. The Inn is within walking distance of the ski lift. Double rooms start at $150 a night and studio condos start at $130. Currently, a pedestrian village is taking shape at the base of the River Run gondola, offering additional lodging options.

Other Winter Activities

Sleigh Rides/Snowmobiling/ Dogsled Rides
Breckenridge Guest Services and Activity Center
150 W. Adams St., Breckenridge
• (970) 453-2918

Skiing is the No. 1 activity in winter in Summit County, but other options, snow-related and otherwise, abound. Winter sleigh rides, snowmobiling, dogsled rides and other activities can be arranged by the Activity Center. In addition to making reservations, these services can also provide information on prices, hours and availability of off-slope activities. Tiger Run, (800) 318-1FUN, is one of the nation's top snowmobile tour operators. Good Times, (800) 477-0144, can arrange snowmobile tours, sleigh rides and dogsledding trips.

Ice Skating
Village of Breckenridge, 535 S. Park Ave., Breckenridge • (970) 453-2000

There's ice skating on Maggie Pond at the village of Breckenridge, behind the Bell Tower Mall. Cost is $8 for adults and $5 for children.

Keystone Lake
Keystone Resort, U.S. Hwy. 6, Keystone
• (970) 496-7103

Keystone Lake is the largest maintained

natural-ice surface in the country. For rink use and rentals the cost is $10 for adults; $8.50 for ages 13 to 17; $5 for 5 to 12; and $1 for those 4 and younger.

Breckenridge's Recreation Center
880 Airport Rd., just off Colo. Hwy. 9, Breckenridge • (970) 453-1734

This outstanding facility offers indoor lap and recreational pools, a kiddie fountain, tennis and racquetball courts, a running track, fitness facilities, a climbing wall and a variety of other programs. There are also outdoor tennis, basketball and volleyball courts; a skateboard park; and a playground. It is open 6 AM to 10 PM on weekdays, 7 AM to 10 PM Saturdays and 8 AM to 10 PM on Sundays. Nonresident adults pay $6.50; youth 13 to 17 and seniors 60 and older, $4; children ages 3 to 12, $3.25; and toddlers get in free.

Summer Activities

Biking
Summit County Chamber of Commerce and Frisco Visitors' Center
• (970) 668-2051 or (970) 668-0376
Dillon Visitors' Center • (970) 262-2866

Mountain biking is king all over Colorado, but in Summit County, riding along the paved Blue River Bikeway connecting Breckenridge and Frisco is a milder option. The route parallels Colo. 9, winding through meadows and forests. If you can handle the uphill, take the paved Ten Mile Canyon National Recreation Trail from Frisco up to Copper Mountain, or put your bike on a free Summit Stage bus and coast down. From Copper Mountain, you can also continue on the Vail Pass Bikeway, a 20-mile route (one-way) that climbs over 10,600-foot Vail Pass and down into Vail Village. These are beautiful rides anytime, but especially in early fall when the aspen trees are turning gold. For trail maps contact either of the above telephone numbers.

Boating on Lake Dillon
300 Marina Dr., Dillon • (970) 468-5100

This is a 3,000-acre reservoir offering opportunities and charters for all types of boating, including fishing and sailboats. The Dillon Marina is open from the end of May through October.

Keystone Golf Course
Keystone Resort Activity Desk
• (970) 496-4386

Designed by Robert Trent Jones Jr., this golf course is known for both scenery and challenge. After exiting onto US 6, look for signs to the golf course (take Soda Ridge Road to the end, then go left on Keystone Ranch Road). The Activity Desk takes tee-time reservations. Greens fees in 1999 were $125 per person, including cart. Keystone lodging guests pay $105 per round, and golf packages are available.

Copper Mountain

Copper Mountain is a self-contained resort that was constructed a quarter of a century ago and has since won kudos for its outstanding trail and slope design as well as its compact and congenial village. It has the distinction of being the site of Club Med's first and only North American ski village.

Alpine Skiing

Copper Mountain Resort
209 Ten Mile Cir., Copper Mountain
• (970) 968-2882 or (800) 458-8386

There are a variety of options for snaring new powder. If you start at the village center you have the choice of two high-speed express lifts, American Flyer or American Eagle, that respectively shuttle skiers toward Copper Peak and Union Peak. These two summits, the snow-kissed slopes cascading down on all sides and the valley between them, offer a sensational array of ski and snowboard terrain for all ability levels. The Union Creek area, with a separate day lodge, is one of Colorado's best novice areas. If you're a new skier who needs practice, you can ride the K and L lifts and ski nearly 1,000 vertical feet of gentle terrain free during part of the ski season.

Copper Mountain is famous for its logical layout. As you are looking at the mountain, with I-70 at your back, most of the easy terrain is in the middle, most of the intermediate runs are in the middle or on the right, and most of the challenging turf is to the left. Copper Peak, 12,441 feet, is (after A-Basin) Colorado's second-highest lift-served summit. Spaulding Bowl, Union Bowl and Resolution Bowl have long been favorites with powder-loving skiers and snowboarders, but in 1995-96, the area built the first of two lifts in Copper Bowl and catapulted into the top rank of Summit County ski areas. All the bowls are steep snow pockets, treasured by advanced skiers and riders. Copper Mountain now boasts 21 lifts (including three high-speed express chairlifts), 2,601 vertical feet and 2,433 acres of skiable terrain — the most in Summit County. You can obtain more information from the resort or call the Copper Mountain Chamber of Commerce at (970)968-6477.

Copper's well-regarded day-care facility is in the Mountain Plaza Building. The children's ski school, which offers ski lessons from age 3 as well as snowboarding instruction for older children, is headquartered in its own building, with ski school desk, kids' rentals and food service under one roof.

Cross-country Skiing

Twenty-five kilometers of machine-set tracks and skating lanes start at Union Creek and wind through the wooded valleys of the Arapahoe National Forest.

Restaurants

The price-code key for restaurants appears at the beginning of this chapter.

Presce Fresco
$ • U.S. I-70, ext. 6505, in the Mountain Plaza Bldg. • (970) 968-2318

This restaurant offers light, contemporary American and continental cuisine at breakfast, lunch and dinner. Open during the ski season.

O'Shea's
$ • U.S. I-70, ext. 6504, in the Copper Junction Bldg. • (970) 968-2882

At the base of the American Eagle lift, O'Shea's has long been popular for ribs, chili, nachos and other popular choices. Lunch and dinner are served during the winter months.

O'Shea's was being remodeled in 1999 and will be open year round upon completion.

Farley's Prime and Chop House
$ • 104 Wheeler Pl., Copper Mountain • (970) 968-2577

After a day of skiing enjoy a leisurely dinner at Farley's, where steaks, ribs and seafood are served hot and in generous portions. Farley's is open during the ski season.

Accommodations

Club Med
50 Beeler Pl., Copper Mountain • (800) CLUB-MED

Geared for week-long ski vacations, the room rate is $980 per wek for adults, $448 for children under 11. There are extra fees for membership and initiation. Club Med offers a basic room without a television or telephone. There are two restaurants on site, a workout room and planned activities for first-time skiers.

Copper Mountain Resort
209 Ten Mile Cir., Copper Mountain • (970) 968-2882 or (800) 458-8386

With the exception of Club Med, all of the overnight lodging at Copper Mountain is in condominiums. Units range from compact studios to luxurious four-bedroom townhomes. Depending on the season, the price for a single room can range from $100 to $250, while a four-bedroom townhome would run $600 to $1,000 per night. Multi-day packages, including excellent family values, are available. All resort guests have free access to the excellent Copper Mountain Racquet & Athletic Club.

Summer Activities

Copper Mountain Resort
209 Ten Mile Cir., Copper Mountain • (970) 968-2882 or (800) 458-8386

During summer months the resort offers golf, horseback riding, mountain biking, paddleboat rides, tennis and free scenic chairlift rides. Over Labor Day weekend, the resort hosts Michael Martin Murphey's

WestFest with three days of country-western music, crafts and food.

Copper Creek Golf Course
104 Wheeler Pl., Copper Mountain
• (970) 968-2339 or (800) 458-8386

At 9,650 feet, this is the highest-altitude 18-hole championship golf course in America. It is said that balls will fly 15 percent to 20 percent farther than at sea level. Greens fees are $42 for 9 holes, $80 for 18. Golf packages are available. Clubs can be rented for $20 for 9 holes or $35 for 18.

The Wheeler-Dillon Pack Trail
Copper Mountain Stables
355 Beeler Pl., Copper Mountain
• (970) 968-2232

This trail begins across the highway from Copper Mountain and climbs steeply into the rugged Gore Range. It offers a challenge for hikers, backpackers and horseback riders. Pack trips can be arranged through the stable.

Summer in Boulder wouldn't truly be summer without the Chautauqua Summer Festival Concerts, a music venue since Boulder's first Chautauqua met in 1898.

Arts

Despite its small-city size, Boulder offers a big-city selection of arts, ranging from local artists with national reputations to the summer Colorado Music Festival with musicians from around the world. The internationally renowned Colorado Dance Festival and the Colorado Shakespeare Festival also attract top talent. The Boulder Museum of Contemporary Art (BMoCA) and the University of Colorado galleries show work by both locally and nationally known artists. In addition to exhibitions, BMoCA and Naropa Institute (see our chapter on Education) hold innovative arts events and community theater, dance and music groups provide a varied mix of entertainment.

Proximity to Denver expands the arts horizon with the Denver Art Museum, Colorado Symphony, Denver Center Theatre Company and a number of small theater companies. Even closer, the Arvada Center for the Arts and Humanities offers theater, music, dance and visual art by Colorado's best and nationally known artists. Other nearby communities of Longmont, Louisville, Lafayette, Lyons, Central City, Golden and Nederland offer their own historical museums, music and theater groups and art exhibitions as well.

Below are the highlights of the area's arts offerings. Note that we have listed museums in our Boulder Attractions chapter.

Dance

Aerial Dance Festival
Dairy Center for the Arts, 2590 Walnut St., Boulder • (303) 444-5569

If dance sometimes resembles floating, flying, swooping through air, Frequent Flyers Productions' Aerial Dance Festival makes it so. The company uses trapezes to set dancers free of gravity. It all began in 1988 with a chilling performance inspired by Anne Rice's vampire novels. Now, the company offers workshops and classes along with periodic performances (the vampire program has become a Boulder staple at Halloween, drawing a repeat audience with many in full white-faced, fanged, black-clad regalia).

Boulder Ballet
**2590 Walnut St., Suite 6
• (303) 442-6944**

Founded in 1984, Boulder Ballet is a company of local professionals and amateurs and visiting professionals. The two annual performances are *The Nutcracker* ballet, which sells out early, with the Boulder Philharmonic Orchestra, and a spring performance (*Cinderella*, over the Easter weekend, in 1999). The ensemble has also performed with Opera Colorado. Performances are held in a variety of places, including Denver's Boettcher Hall and Macky Auditorium in Boulder.

Boulder Jazz Dance Workshop
CU-Boulder Campus • (303) 449-0399

Founded in 1978 by Lara Branen, then a graduate student at CU-Boulder, this August workshop includes performances and returns to Boulder each year, where CU-Boulder's Theatre and Dance Department lends its facilities to this now-independent group. The workshop is open to the public, offering classes in jazz, modern, hip-hop, and street funk; as well as ballet barre and a mat class based on the principles of Joseph Pilates for Dancers 13 and older with intermediate to higher skills.

Following the workshop (the first two weeks in August), there are performances by students, faculty and the company in residence, Interweave Dance Theatre of Boulder, which is composed of some 30 dancers. Thirty to 40 percent of the workshop participants come from other states and countries, including Mexico, Italy and elsewhere. Participants can receive college credit at CU.

Cleo Parker Robinson Dance
119 Park Ave. W., Denver
• (303) 295-1759

This dance company-cum-school and theater is dedicated to providing cross-cultural, African-centered performances and classes. Its fall and holiday performances are at the Denver Center for the Performing Arts. Jazz and modern-dance aficionados will relish this internationally renowned group. Well-known performers from around the world visit the school and theater, and the ensemble goes on extended tours. An annual July event is the International Summer Dance Institute that hosts great master instructors from all over the world. The instructors teach all types of dance, music, theater, storytelling and cultural rituals to children and adults. One of Denver's greatest holiday traditions is the annual December concert, "Granny Dances to a Holiday Drum." There's usually an annual spring performance and Project Self-Discovery, an outreach program for at-risk youth. Call for information and current schedules for these excellent performances, classes and workshops.

Colorado Ballet
1036 14th St. (ticket office),
1278 Lincoln St., Denver (administrative office) • (303) 98-MUSIC (tickets)

In 1993 this Denver-based ensemble debuted nationally at New York's prestigious Brooklyn Center for the Performing Arts. The Colorado Ballet performs such classics as *La Sylphide* and *The Nutcracker* each Christmas season, but also offers more innovative works such as those of George Balanchine. The 1999 season included Martha Graham's *Appalachian Spring*, Alvin Ailey's *The River* and Choo San Goh's *Configurations*. The performance season is from October to May. Series tickets are available.

Colorado Dance Festival
2590 Walnut St. • (303) 442-7666

Now the third-largest dance festival in the nation, the Boulder-based Colorado Dance Festival (CDF) is partially funded by the National Endowment for the Arts. CDF has earned international recognition with its innovative programs and renowned performers, including such top names as Trisha Brown and the late, great tap dancer Honi Coles. The CDF also founded the Boulder-based International Tap Association, (303) 443-7989.

In 1997, CDF embarked on a four-year project: "Let's Dance Together: The Americas," which explores the relationship between social and popular dance of the Americas to concert dance. It includes a multifaceted program of performances, workshops, films, lectures, social dancing and more led by a multicultural team. Call for a performance schedule.

The eclectic 1999 season included performances of flamenco, Haitian dance, an all-woman tango and the athletic movements of David Dorfman Dance. Sunday night "dance parties" invite the audience to snack and dance with performers and lunchtime talks give the community a chance to ask experts questions about the dance. The Colorado Dance Festival is held in the summer only, though it has year-round outreach programs for youth.

University of Colorado Department of Theatre and Dance
CU-Boulder Campus • (303) 492-7355, (303) 492-8181 (tickets)

Throughout the year this talent-filled university department presents a number of innovative performances including ballet, modern, African-American and other dance forms. There are student performances all year-round with the main one presented in late fall and a faculty performance in late spring. Call for a current schedule.

The Naropa Institute Performing Arts Series
2130 Arapahoe Ave. • (303) 546-3538

A private, nonsectarian liberal arts college with roots in Buddhism, Naropa celebrated its 25th year in 1999. Naropa concentrates mainly on avant-garde and new dance, offering classes, workshops and performances. Performances included a concert by composer and Golden Globe winner Philip Glass at the Chautauqua Auditorium.

The Boulder Ballet performs two different ballets each season.

Call the ticket office at (303) 786-7030 for other events and classes.

Boulder Dance Alliance
and Space for Dance
various locations • (303) 444-1357

With a motto of "Dance Is for Every Body," this is your one-stop for dance information. The Boulder Dance Alliance has been a catalyst for the development of dance in Boulder County, and this organization has information on amateur, experimental and professional dance performances, an annual sock hop, lists for teachers and classes for children and adults, plus weekend performances. Space for Dance, which is part of the Boulder Dance Alliance, is searching for a permanent home. For the present it offers a collection of spaces available for rental, including an empty store space at Crossroads Shopping Center. Some of the dance offerings include method demonstrations; The Rocky Mountain Ragtime Festival; a tango and blues soiree; and skiffle, drag and tea dances.

Film

In addition to the special film series listed below, Boulder has some 20 commercial movie theaters, among them United Artists and Mann Theater complexes, Flatirons Theatre on University Hill and the Basemar Cinema Saver Theatres — the best bargain of all. A 12-plex of theaters at the Louisville exit off of U.S. Highway 36 gives moviegoers an even bigger selection, and a 16-plex is planned in a renovation of Crossroads Shopping Center. In the summer, the Almost Free Outdoor Cinema unrolls a screen and turns the parking lot behind BMoCA into an open-air theater featuring everything from classic films like *Easy Rider* to the campy *Rocky Horror Picture Show*. Every Saturday night between early June and early September, fans bring blankets, lawn chairs, even couches and coffee tables and fill in the time during reel changes with costume and trivia contests.

Boulder Public Library
Film Program
Main Branch Auditorium, Ninth St. and
Canyon Blvd., Boulder • (303) 441-3197

This ongoing free film series has everything from Laurel and Hardy and Third World Cinema to special series on science fiction, British classics and other topics not available on video. The library also shows mainstream Hollywood movies. Call for information, or visit the library to pick up the latest schedule. Movies are on Mondays, Thursdays and Fridays at 7 PM.

Chautauqua Summer Film Festival
Ninth St. and Baseline Rd., Boulder
• (303) 440-7666

Moviegoers of all ages will feel like kids at summer camp inside Chautauqua's barn-like auditorium. This summer-only program shows historic silent films from the 1920s and earlier, such William S. Hart's *Straight Shooting* and Max Schreck's *Nosferatu eine Symphonie des Grauens,* with live piano accompaniment by Hank Troy. Prices are $6 for adults and $4 for children (younger than 12). There are special prices for film series.

University of Colorado Program
Council Film Series
CU-Boulder Campus, Forum Rm. (in the
UMC) and Chem. 140 in Chemistry Bldg.
(next building over from UMC), 16th St.
and E. Euclid Ave. • (303) 492-5458

These free and bargain-priced films offer

INSIDERS' TIP

Chautauqua Park's buildings are on the National Register of Historic Places, and the Chautauqua Auditorium was voted by musicians as one of the top-10 places in the country to perform.

Summer in Boulder Means Chautauqua

Black clouds slid down the mountains for the gala opening of the 1996 Colorado Music Festival. As well-dressed attendees sipped wine in white tents on the concert hall lawn, the heavens opened. Soon, drenched waiters in tuxedos were sloshing among the concert patrons offering platters of appetizers. Rivers ran down the nearby sidewalk as people watched in amazement, then suddenly a small river of muddy water rushed through the middle of the tent right under the elegantly set buffet tables, drowning fancy shoes and dampening trouser hems.

The rain stopped long enough for people to move to the concert hall. Giving the season's opening welcome, former Boulder mayor Leslie Durgin lauded Boulder's spirit. "Last year at the Asian Children's Concert when the roof started leaking with a downpour like this one, the audience members offered their umbrellas to the performers. But we have a brand-new roof this year," Durgin proudly announced.

The initial soft rain so pleasantly pattering in the background of the all-Beethoven concert soon became a roar of hail that threatened to drown out the orchestra. Through the new roof, rain began to drip on the audience, and one by one umbrellas opened inside the concert hall. Soon it began dripping on the orchestra onstage. In the middle of the featured concerto, pianist Larry Graham leaned back to dodge dripping water, then looked at the audience and laughed, and the entire concert came to a halt. For about 10 minutes the concert became the sounds of nature's fury and the still-leaking new roof. Finally, the rain lessened and the concert resumed, making it a stormy gala night of music to remember.

At the turn of the century there were 12,000 Chautauquas in the United States. Today there are only three. One of them is in Boulder. Chautauqua is a Native American word that means "two moccasins tied together." It's the name of a lake in New York state that

— continued on next page

Photo: Daily Camera/Lourie Zipf

Flowers and Flatirons frame Chautauqua Concert Hall.

was the birthplace of this former national movement of summer camps/retreats where people went for cultural or spiritual renewal. Boulder's Chautauqua always focused on arts and entertainment while others around the country focused on religion.

Boulder hosted such famous guests as statesman William Jennings Bryant and musician John Philip Sousa. Boulder's Chautauqua has a lovely park setting on the edge of Boulder's Mountain Park system and is a designated national historic district, jointly run by the National Park Service and the City of Boulder. According to *Inside Performance Magazine*, performing artists voted Boulder's Chautauqua one of the top 10 halls in the United States in which they love to perform — even when the roof leaks.

some of the best entertainment around. Catch up on first-run movies you might have missed at the local theater last year. A high-tech Dolby stereo cinema sound processor makes the sound system in the university's Chemistry 140 auditorium one of Boulder's best. Pick up a film schedule at the University Memorial Center (UMC), Boulder Public Libraries, city recreation centers and local supermarkets. The screen is dark during the summer.

International Film Series
Muenzinger Auditorium (CU-Boulder campus), Muenzinger Plaza, west of Folsom Stadium near the corner of Colorado Ave. and 18th St.
• **(303) 492-1531**

Connected with the CU-based Rocky Mountain Film Center, this series is the West's longest-running continuous forum for international and art film screenings and has entertained university and Boulder audiences for more than 50 years. The First Person Cinema is affiliated with the RMFC and features visiting artists throughout the academic year. It includes avant-garde works by independent and personal filmmakers such as Stan Brakhage, Fred Worden and Caroline Leaf, as well as wonderful, entertaining films from all over the world that aren't available in mall theaters or video stores. The spacious, steeply sloping Muenzinger Auditorium offers every moviegoer a perfect view for the right price — $3.50 ($3 for CU students). The 24-hour hotline above lists each week's events.

Ask about the Stan Brakhage Film Forum, a screening of rare and unusual films each Sunday at 7:30 PM in Fine Arts Building N141. The series, named for the renowned filmmaker

and respected CU-Boulder professor, is free and open to the public.

Music

Ars Nova Singers
• **(303) 499-3165**

This group of 40 singers presents music from the Renaissance and 20th century periods, including works by Colorado's finest composers, and performs in churches in Boulder and Denver. Now beginning its 14th season, Ars Nova was one of the first choirs from Colorado funded by the National Endowment for the Arts and the only one to receive funding for three consecutive years. In 1998, the choir performed its first international tour. Ars Nova performs annual Christmas concerts in Boulder and Denver at area churches. The ensemble has performed the complete *Responsoria* by Renaissance composer Carlo Gesualdo, György Ligeti's *Lux Aeterna*, Charles Ives' cantata *The Celestial Country*, and many experimental and avant-garde choral works. The Ars Nova Singers have been heard in radio broadcasts throughout the United States, Canada, South America, and Europe. The group has released six CDs. Ticket prices are $10 and $8 (for students and seniors 60 and older).

Artist Series
CU-Boulder Campus, Macky Auditorium or Grusin Music Hall • **(303) 492-8008**

The University of Colorado-Boulder's Artist Series has been going strong for 60 years with a full season of varied performances. Recent highlights included *Chanticleer,* The

Martha Graham Dance Company and mezzo-soprano Marilyn Horne. The Takâcs String Quartet, the Hungarian artists in residence, also performs. The Artist Series is held in the university's Macky Auditorium, Grusin Music Hall and the Music Theatre in Imig Music Building and includes performance art, jazz, classics, dance, folk and ethnic performances. Tickets prices range from $10 to $30.

Arvada Center for the Arts and Humanities
6901 Wadsworth Blvd., Arvada
• (303) 431-3939

About a 30-minute drive south of Boulder, the Arvada Center is a sophisticated venue for music of all types, from popular to classical, with nationally known groups and performers. During performances, the upper gallery is open for viewing the work of nationally known artists and craftspeople. Summer concerts are in an outdoor amphitheater. The center also offers year-round theater, concerts and dance, a historical museum, and classes in ceramics, dance, writing, acting, visual arts and more.

Boulder Bach Festival
No central address • (303) 494-3159

It began in 1982 as a one-weekend festival; now the Boulder Bach Festival has evolved into a series of concerts year round, highlighting the famous composer's work. The annual three-day Bach festival is in January. The very un-stuffy company performs at Crossroads Shopping Center (a program titled "Bach and Shop"), does a "Blue Jeans Concert" at a farm north of Boulder and a "Turned-On Bach" performance at the Central Park Bandshell. There are also children's concerts in March and May, a fall concert in the 100-year-old Ryssby Church west of Longmont and a New Year's Eve concert.

Boulder Philharmonic Orchestra
2590 Walnut St., Boulder
• (303) 449-1343

Celebrating its 40th season in 1999, the orchestra offered a full season of music with guest performers like Itzhak Perlman and Mstislav Rostropovich. The Sinfonia of Boulder, the state's only professional chamber orchestra, is composed of members of the Boulder Philharmonic led by Phil conductor Theodore Kuchar. The group is performing all of Mozart's symphonies in a three-year series. The Phil also holds an annual Symphony Ball in the spring, sponsored by the volunteer organization, Club Phil, one of the orchestra's greatest assets. The Boulder Arts Academy, (303) 449-9291, with some 700 students, offers group classes and private lessons and has large ensembles. Recently the Boulder Arts Academy collaborated with the Boulder Ballet and offered ballet as well as music classes. Music director Theodore Kuchar from the Ukraine leads the Boulder Phil into its 40th season.

Central City Opera
200 Eureka St., Central City
• (303) 292-6700, (800) 851-8175

One of Colorado's favorite outings, the Central City Opera features operatic works sung in English in this old mining town, recently turned gambling haven. This summer troupe is one of the oldest opera companies in the country, with a distinguished national reputation. The CCO also offers daytime cabaret opera and special youth performances. The opera house was built in 1878 in an effort to bring culture to the formerly rough and rowdy mining town. Performances are frequently sold out, so call ahead for reservations for this summer-only program. Reserved parking is available via a shuttle bus service that takes opera-goers from the parking area (a half-mile away) right to the opera house's front door. The bus leaves about every 10 minutes during the two hours before and after the opera, so there's plenty of time for a meal, gambling or sightseeing in Central City. Tickets range from $5 to $60, depending on the event (the grand ball is $185 and reportedly worth every cent). (Please see the Close-up in this chapter for more information.)

Chautauqua Summer Festival Concerts
Main Office, South of Ninth St. and Baseline Rd. • (303) 440-7666 (summer only), (303) 545-6924, Ext. 18 (otherwise)

Summer in Boulder wouldn't truly be summer without Chautauqua, which features a series of popular-music concerts and performances in addition to the classical Colorado Music Festival (see our subsequent listing and Close-up in this chapter). This historic music venue has been an institution since 1898, when Boulder's Chautauqua first opened as part of a national movement that brought the arts to numerous Chautauqua summer camps around the country. Today, many concertgoers enjoy dinner on the lovely old veranda of the picturesque Chautauqua Dining Hall or bring a picnic to enjoy under the shady trees on the green. The Summer Festival Concerts have featured such groups and performers as Rosanne Cash, Los Lobos, Peter Kater, Michelle Shocked, Richard Thompson, Joan Armatrading, Laurie Anderson, A Gospel Extravaganza with the Persuasions, and the delicately named Mother Folkers. Some folks picnic into the night and enjoy the music (for free) from outside the concert hall. Dance fans can enjoy performances by Cleo Parker Robinson and Danielle Helander. Chautauqua makes it a point to feature quirky concerts such as the Reduced Shakespeare Company, "the Bad Boys of Abridgement" and The Barbershoppers, a large barbershop chorus. The Boulder Folk and Blue Grass Festival is held at Chautauqua along with many other performers and performances, such as Karla Bonoff, Spaulding Gray and Hunter S. Thompson. Tickets range from $8 to $35.

Colorado Symphony
821 17th St., Suite 700 (admin. office) or Boettcher Hall, Performing Arts Complex, 14th and Lawrence Sts. Denver • (303) 98-MUSIC

Many Boulderites gladly make the trek to Denver to enjoy the Colorado Symphony at Denver's delightful Boettcher Hall. The director is Marin Alsop, the highest-placed female conductor in the world, who has been with the CSO for three years. Choices include a regular concert series and special holiday concerts, plus Family, Masterworks and Popular Classics and Pops concert series. The Colorado Christmas concert features the Colorado Children's Chorale and Colorado Symphony Chorus. A New Years' Eve Celebration features a post-concert dinner dance in Boettcher and the Pavilion of the Performing Arts complex. Highlights for the 1999-2000 Masterworks Season include an evening of Copland with pianist mezzo-soprano Marietta Simpson and a program of percussion with Colin Currie.

Family concerts are held in February with such offerings as a Symphony Safari at the Denver Zoo, and an exploration of "What Is Music?" at the Museum of Natural History.

Recent highlights of the Pop series include Maurice Jarre as guest conductor with film clips and musical selections from movies, a gospel choir with the CSO Chorus singing a Handel program titled "Too Hot to Handel" and a "Celtic Soul" program with the Paul Winter Consort and soprano Noirin Ni Riain.

Performances are on Sundays and last 90 minutes. Family series tickets cost $10 for adults and $7 for children.

Colorado Children's Chorale
910 15th St., Denver • (303) 830-8497 (Ticketmaster), (303) 892-5600 (info)

The CCC presents popular and traditional music such as *Beauty and the Beast* and special compositions written for the chorale by resident composers. Children from all over the Denver metro area audition to get into one of the five chorales. There are annual U.S. and

---

INSIDERS' TIP

One of the best local entertainment values is CU-Boulder's Program Council Films and the more art-oriented International Film Series. Both are held on campus. The Program Council features recent first-run movies; the International Film Series has excellent award winners from all over the world that you'll have a hard time finding at a regular theater. Look for a free schedule in the Boulder Public Library and at area bookstores. See the listing in this chapter for more information.

Photo: Linda Cornett

When the private high school, September School, acquired the old Second Baptist Church for classroom and events space, art students wasted no time in making the building uniquely their own.

international choir tours by the group. A December Christmas concert features traditional holiday music, and there's a special spring concert in May. Tickets range from $7 to $22.

Colorado Music Festival
1525 Spruce St., Suite 101, Boulder
• (303) 449-1397 (year round),
(303) 449-2413 (summer tickets)

From late June through mid-August each year, classical musicians from around the country and world come to Boulder to participate in the Colorado Music Festival at Boulder's historic Chautauqua. Now in its 22nd season, the series includes a well-rounded selection of classics, from all-Bach or Beethoven concerts to Mozart, Gershwin, Tchaikovsky, chamber music and much more. There are several children's and family concerts too. The festival chamber orchestra gives Monday night performances at the historic Stanley Hotel Concert Hall in Estes Park. A Boulder Fourth of July tradition is the Colorado Music Festival's free concert on the Chautauqua lawn, highlighted with foot-thumping John Philip Sousa marches. Highlights of the 1999 season include pianist Girvanni Belucci, the St. Petersburg Quartet, guitarist Eliot Fisk and pianist Emma Schmidt. Season tickets are available in advance, or concertgoers can pay at the door. Last-minute tickets are available at the door and range from $12 to $35.

University of Colorado's College of Music
CU-Boulder campus, Boulder
• (303) 492-8008

Another popular tradition is CU's College of Music summer lyric theater, which includes light opera and often a Gilbert & Sullivan production. The Mile High Jazz Camp is always held in the third week of July. Recent concerts included *The Jumping Frog of Calaveras County* and *The Marriage of Figaro*. The internationally renowned artists in residence, the Takâcs String Quartet, are one of the regular pleasures of the College of Music schedule. The annual sellout Festival of Christmas is a scholarship benefit for the College of Music. Most concerts are free; tickets are sold only for major productions.

Fiddler's Green
**6350 Greenwood Plaza Blvd.,
Englewood • (303) 220-7000**

About an hour's drive from Boulder, Fiddler's Green, a popular outdoor concert hall on Denver's south side, offers nationally known groups that aren't likely to visit Boulder. Enjoy these summer-only concerts either with reserved seats or a picnic on the lawn. Tickets are available at the box office or by calling Ticketmaster at (303) 830-8497.

Public Library Concert Series
**1000 Canyon Blvd., Boulder
• (303) 441-3100**

This free series at the Boulder Public Library Auditorium (Canyon Boulevard entrance) offers music lovers a wealth of listening, from Bach to ragtime. Piano and harp soloists, string quartets, members of the Boulder Philharmonic and local musicians are among the varied performers.

Red Rocks
**Morrison St., Morrison • (303) 640-7334
(recorded information and events)**

This spectacular natural-rock open-air amphitheater is the venue for most top performers who come to the Denver area. The 1999 season included performances by Jewel, Motley Crue, Journey, Willie Nelson and Dwight Yoakam, R.E.M., George Thorogood. Red Rocks information and tickets are available through Ticketmaster at (303) 830-8497. Check local newspapers for performers appearing at Red Rocks or call the listed number. Tickets range from $25 to $40 and are available with no service charge at the Pepsi Center and the Denver Performing Arts Complex in downtown Denver (cash only and in person).

Theater

Actors Ensemble Guild Theatre Guild at the Dairy
**2590 Walnut St., Boulder
• (303) 449-3296**

Established in 1987, the Actors Ensemble strives to present award-winning and provocative contemporary theater. The company specializes in contemporary theater, performing two shows a year at the Dairy Center for the Arts. Tickets cost $15.

Arvada Center for the Arts and Humanities
**6901 Wadsworth Blvd., Arvada
• (303) 431-3939**

The Arvada Center opened its stage doors in 1976 and has been an equity theater since 1992, bringing professional talent into an intimate setting. The indoor theater seats 500, and the Ticket prices range from $12 to $28 with discounts for seniors and students. Shows run Tuesday through Sunday with matinees. The Arvada Center also has a huge education program offering more than 100 classes for both children and adults in everything from acting, performing arts and music to ceramics and humanities.

INSIDERS' TIP

Western architecture buffs will love the Boulder Museum of History, which provides exhibits showing the history of Boulder's neighborhoods and gives detailed information on how to tour Boulder, offering several routes and various recommended walks. Be sure to ask about Boulder's two world-class landmarks: the National Center for Atmospheric Research for its building, and the University of Colorado for its landscaping.

Boulder's Dinner Theatre
5501 Arapahoe Ave., Boulder
• (303) 449-6000

From *A Chorus Line* to *Man of La Mancha*, Boulder's Dinner Theatre is the only local venue for popular musicals. This dinner theater has won a number of awards for its professional performances with excellent sets and staging. The food is quite good too. The theater offers cocktails and a choice of delicious dinners — the prime rib is great! — served by its talented singers and performers. Tickets cost $28.50 to $39 per person and are discounted for seniors and children on some performances.

The Boulder Repertory Company
Boulder Public Library, 1000 Canyon Blvd., Boulder • (303) 449-7258

The Boulder Repertory Company presents three shows a year. Lacking a home of its own, this company has performed in approximately 11 different locations since 1975. The Boulder Rep's fine productions are worth seeing. Artistic director Frank Georgianna launched TBRC in 1975, and it has become one of Boulder's most respected companies. Georgianna was a director and actor at the Denver Center Theatre from 1985 to 1994. The performances are usually in the Boulder Public Library auditorium and occasionally in Denver. The company is taking a year off in 1999.

Colorado Shakespeare Festival
Mary Rippon Theatre (CU-Boulder campus) • (303) 492-0554

Film actor Val Kilmer took part in these Shakespeare productions one year, and other top performers, such as TV star Jimmy Smits, have likewise been attracted to this highly regarded annual festival. Held at the outdoor Mary Rippon Theatre, this summer festival is another local institution. It includes both traditional and modern renditions of the bard's work. The 1999 season offered *Henry IV,* parts 1 and 2, *The Comedy of Errors* and *The Merry Wives of Windsor.* Theater-goers can order "Falstaff's Fare," a box dinner made by Traditions Catering, and dine on the green before the show while Shakespeare himself (actor Chuck Wilcox) strolls about chatting with diners. There are evening and Sunday matinee performances.

University of Colorado Department of Theatre and Dance
CU-Boulder Campus • (303) 492-7355

Considered by local critics to present the most consistently good and reliable performances, the CU-Boulder Theatre Department won the 1993 Denver Drama Critics Circle award for Best Season for a Company. Throughout the school year, this university department holds numerous performances at campus theaters. The 1999 season included *Death and the Maiden* and *6 Degrees of Separation.* The department also offers performances by students in the master of fine arts degree program and student dance performances. Call for more information or a complete schedule.

Denver Center Theatre Company
1050 13th St., Denver • (303) 893-4100

The Denver Center for the Performing Arts attracts big Broadway shows with national touring companies, but the Denver Center Theatre Company, now in its 20th season, is the local theater company that performs at the center. Featuring a varied menu of entertainment ranging from works by Dickens and Shakespeare to the life of Janis Joplin, the company has received many awards, including, in 1998, the Tony Award for Outstanding Regional Theatre. The 1999-2000 season includes Richard Hellesen's *Kingdom, The Elevation of Thieves, Gross Indecency: The Three Trials of Oscar Wilde* by Moises Kaufman and *Moon for the Misbegotten.*

Opera Colorado
695 S. Colorado Blvd., Denver
• (303) 98-MUSIC

Opera Colorado's season consists of three operas presented in March, April and May. The 1999 Tickets ranged from $15 to $119, with discounts at selected performances for seniors and students. Some tickets are available at the door if the show is not sold out.

Peanut Butter Players
2475 Mapleton Ave., Boulder
• (303) 786-8PBP

Based in the Toadstool Playhouse, one of Boulder's funky landmark buildings, this theater company of local youngsters ages 5 to 18 offers year-round performances. Luncheon

Central City Opera

Central City's historic opera building, just west of Main and Eureka streets, was built in 1878. The first-rate, sung-in-English performances have entertained even lukewarm opera fans since 1932. Everyone stays in historic Victorian character, including the uniformed ushers, who form a chorus and sing a tune out in the street about a half-hour before the show. Then they ring brass hand bells every 10 minutes or so announcing that the opera will soon begin.

With hand-painted murals of Pegasus and cafe chairs engraved with the names of famous benefactors, the Victorian theater is a treat. Every seat is good. You're close enough that the actors and actresses come across as real people who feel life so strongly, they've just got to sing about it.

And this year, literally, every seat is good, with the installation of new, roomier theater-style and continental seating in front of the orchestra.

The seat renovation project reduced the theater's seating by 27 percent, and more shows are expected to sell out. Get your tickets as early as possible, since some operas sell out weeks or months in advance. (Although on some nights, you can buy tickets at the door.)

Since Colorado voters approved limited stakes gambling in Central City and Black Hawk, getting to the opera is a little more complicated. You can pay $5 for a reserved

Built in 1878, the Central City Opera House features a restored interior with beautiful trompe l'oeil murals by John C. Massman.

spot in the opera house parking lot when you order tickets in advance. Or, try the bus from Denver and Lakewood for every performance and on Fridays from Boulder. Cost is $15 for adults, $13 for seniors 62 and older.

The season kicks off with Opera Pops "Picnic Without Ants" (picnickers $30; patrons $60) in Denver at the Marriott City Center. The price includes an evening of opera pops and an indoor, gourmet picnic.

For something a little more elegant, there is the Opening Night Yellow Rose Ball ($185 per person, including the opera) at The Teller House beside Central City's Opera Building. The eclectic celebration includes presentation of the Central City Flower Girls, a waltz on Eureka Street, ringing bells, a dynamite blast and a sit-down dinner, followed by an opera performance.

Weekend opera dinners, a recent addition created specifically for opera patrons who prefer to avoid the casino atmosphere, begin at 6 PM and are held in a private banquet room in the Teller House. The four-course buffet with dessert, wine and soft music, costs $30 per person and is offered on Friday and Saturday evenings; the price of the opera ticket is extra. Reservations are required; call (303) 292-6700.

If you are on a budget, bring your own picnic dinner, and enjoy it in the little park between the Teller House and the Opera House. It takes about an hour to drive from Boulder to the Opera House parking lot. Try to reach it at least an hour early. This way, a brief traffic jam won't spell trouble, and there will be time for a beverage stop or a stroll around town to enjoy the lovely Victorian houses. Be sure you arrive at the opera house at least 10 minutes before the show. If you're late, you'll be allowed to enter only between acts.

For those who would like just an opera appetizer and not the full course, try the Festival Extra. There are various choices: At weekend Salon Recitals, opera stars do short recitals during a gourmet brunch at the Teller House Hotel, next to the opera house at 11:45 AM. Tickets cost around $25. Opera a la Carte offers fully staged scenes from famous operas Wednesdays and Fridays at 1:15 PM at a cost of just $5. *Face on the Barroom Floor* is a 30-minute cabaret opera recounting the Teller House's famous legend. These performances are at 1:15 PM Saturday and Sunday at William's Stable, right across the street, and cost $5.

Or ask for the Opera Lovers' Guide from the theater for information on places to eat, lodging and background information. The guide is free.

theaters are held on weekends in October and November and from February through April, performed by a small troupe of professional child actors (the $7 ticket includes lunch; the 1999 production is a musical version of *Charlotte's Web*). There are classes during the school year and a day camp in summer that teach such things as music, puppetry, pantomime, dance, makeup, voice dialects, clowning and theater crafts. Each summer PBP puts on a major production at Boulder High School with about 250 children ($5 for adults, $3 for children, $25 for participants). PBP has been in Boulder for six years, after 15 years in Michigan.

Public Theater
Boulder Museum of Contemporary Art
1750 13th St., Boulder • (303) 443-2122

Held at BMoCA, the theater features a One Act Festival of two-person plays. There are dance and new performances four times a year and traditional performances about three times a year. Call or stop by for a current schedule.

Longmont Theatre Company Performing Arts Center
513 Main St., Longmont
• (303) 772-5200

A short drive from Boulder via the Longmont Diagonal Highway (Colo. 119), the

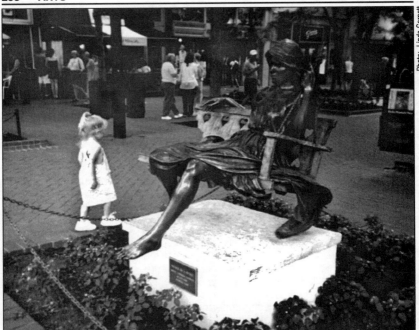

Watching the bustle of the Downtown Boulder Mall with bronze languidness, the sculpture titled Hearts on a Swing reminds the crowd to slow down and enjoy.

40-year-old Longmont Theatre Company offers (annually) two musicals, one drama, comedy, children's performance and Christmas performance. There's also a Shakespeare Festival. The company is celebrating its anniversary in 1999 with a production of *My Fair Lady*. Call for a current schedule of performances.

Naropa Institute Performing Arts Center
2130 Arapahoe Ave., Boulder
• (303) 546-3538

Not limited to theater per se, Naropa has speakers, poetry readings and various performances. In 1994 the institute celebrated its 20th anniversary with a special Allen Ginsberg Tribute in honor of the poet who helped found Naropa. There are student-run theater performances, inter-arts faculty concerts (including music, art, dance and theater), faculty and student readings every semester and annual Balinese and African concerts. Naropa Institute's

center offers music, workshops, dance performances and art exhibits. Call for a schedule of events.

Nomad Playhouse
1410 Quince St., Boulder
• (303) 786-9808

Since 1951, Nomad has been providing community theater in a quonset hut "Just a little off Broadway" — Boulder's Broadway, that is. The theater was completely renovated in 1998. Former Boulderites, now television stars, Joan Van Ark of *Knot's Landing* and Larry Linville of *M*A*S*H* got their acting start with the Nomads, which hosts some excellent serious and not-so-serious drama.

Upstart Crow Guild Theatre
Dairy Center for the Arts, 1590 Walnut St., Boulder • (303) 442-1415

Now celebrating its 20th season with productions of *Major Barbara, The Gates of Sum-*

mer, All's Well that Ends Well and *A View from the Bridge,* this ensemble performs classical plays in their complete and uncut versions, as well as more current productions. Season tickets are $32. Individual productions are $12.

Visual Arts

Admission to the following galleries and shops is free unless otherwise noted.

Artcycle
at 15th St. on the downtown mall, Boulder • (303) 449-4950

Featuring recycled art at its best, this store offers a high-quality selection of pre-owned art in all media and price ranges by successful local and nationally known artists. There are paintings, limited-edition prints, sculptures, photographs and more. Artcycle takes new consignments all the time and also offers custom framing. It is open 10 AM to 6 PM Monday through Saturday, and noon to 6 PM Sunday.

Arvada Center for the Arts and Humanities
6901 Wadsworth Blvd., Arvada • (303) 431-3080

Nationally known artists and Colorado's best artists and craftspeople show their work in the Arvada Center's excellent gallery. There is also a permanent historical exhibit of the area's early days. The gallery is open 9 AM to 5 PM Monday through Saturday, 1 to 5 PM Sunday.

Boulder Museum of Contemporary Art
1750 13th St., Boulder • (303) 443-2122

A nonprofit Boulder institution since 1972, the museum has hosted most established local and area artists over the years as well as regional, national and international visual and performing artists. BMoCA emphasizes contemporary and multicultural exhibitions. Some well-known artists whose works have been shown include photographer Philippe Halsman, painter Beverly Fishman, ceramic sculptor Lynda Benglis and silver printmaker Teun Hocks. The nationally acclaimed exhibition *Animals* by photographers James Balog (who lives in the Boulder area) and Joel Peter Witkin showed a few years ago at BMoCA. Other notable exhibitions have been *Seven Years in Tibet* by Heinrich Harrer and a 40-year retrospective of works on paper by Dorothy Dehner.

The museum also holds popular annual events including the summertime Sculpture in the Park and Art in the Streets, when local artists paint bus benches that are auctioned off to benefit BMoCA, and the Mother's Day exhibition of art by area school children.

BMoCA offers workshops open to the public, including figure-drawing sessions with live models, each Monday from 7 to 10 PM ($4 model fee). The second floor is home to the Public Theater, hosting various performances of dance, music and theater. Admission is $5 for members, $8 for adults, $7 for students and seniors.

The museum is open 11 AM to 5 PM Tuesday through Saturday, 2 to 5 PM Sunday, and is closed Monday. Admission is $2, $1.50 for students and seniors.

Boulder Arts & Crafts Cooperative
1421 Pearl St., Boulder • (303) 443-3683

The co-op has more than 50 members and a total of more than 100 artists, including nationally known artists and participating members and consignees from Colorado and surrounding mountain states. Well-deserved, the co-op won *Westword's* Best Craft gallery in the Denver Metro Area for 1996. Nowhere else in the area will you find such a concentrated collection of top-quality pottery, puppets, jewelry, photographs, fiber art, stained glass, woodwork and other items. Look for Vivian Jean's lovely, pastel-toned majolica pottery and Harriet Peck Taylor's enchanting Southwestern and rain forest batik images made into cards, T-shirts and framed art. Ruth Ann Maze's pottery, Elaine Jackson's dried wildflowers, Bill Ervin's wildlife photography and other outdoor images are top sellers. The co-op has an extensive and spectacular jewelry selection with precious metals and contemporary fashion jewelry. Opened in 1971, the member-directed co-op is currently celebrating its 28th year.

The co-op is open 10 AM to 6 PM Monday through Saturday (until 9 PM in summer and holidays), and 11 AM to 6 PM Sunday.

Boulder Public Library
1000 Canyon Blvd., Boulder
• **(303) 441-4397**

Besides the library's permanent art collection in both wings, there are ongoing exhibitions by contemporary regional artists in various media in an area called The Exhibit Space (entrance on Canyon Boulevard). With a gallery ceiling height of 11 feet, 10 inches and 160 linear feet of exhibition walls, it's one of the largest display spaces in Boulder. Most artists represented are well-known Colorado painters and sculptors, though some national traveling exhibits are also displayed. Another worthwhile stop is at the display cases on the bridge, where all types of interesting exhibits are shown monthly. The Boulder Public Library Meadows Branch, 4800 Baseline Road, also has a display space, featuring such things as raku pottery and the Hawaiian art of leis and ceremonial capes made of feathers. For historic photographs check out the Carnegie Library, 1125 Pine Street, which has digitized about 7,000 of its best photographs so people can view them on a computer screen without touching them and causing possible damage.

The library is open 9 AM to 9 PM Monday through Thursday, 9 AM to 6 PM Friday and Saturday and noon to 6 PM Sunday.

Boulder Stained Glass Studios
1920 Arapahoe Ave., Boulder
• **(303) 449-9030**

Specializing in glass work in Boulder for 24 years, the studio specializes in custom design and fabrication, whether it be architectural or period work. The studio's general approach is architectural, though there's a selection of beautiful glass items ranging from $10 up, including blown-glass vases, jewelry, clocks and imaginative pieces by various Colorado artists. The studio is known for its high-quality contemporary and period leaded, etched and beveled stained glass. It primarily promotes glass crafts by Colorado artisans.

The studio is open 9 AM to 5:30 PM Monday through Friday and by appointment.

CU Art Galleries
Sibell-Wolle Fine Arts Bldg. (east of UMC at Broadway and Euclid), CU-Boulder campus • **(303) 492-8300**

At CU Art Galleries, the large group shows of student work are especially fun and zany — a little bit of New York in Boulder. The recently renovated gallery also hosts exhibitions by nationally known artists like Nene Humphrey and sound artist Bill Fontana. It was voted the best local art gallery in the *Boulder Weekly's* 1999 "Best of Boulder" publication.

Be sure to check out The Sibell-Wolle galleries, which in addition to student work, also regularly feature impressive work by national and international artists. The galleries are open 8 AM to 5 PM Monday through Friday, 8 AM to 8 PM Tuesday, and noon to 5 PM Saturday (summer); call for winter hours. Closed Sunday year round.

Denver Art Museum
100 W. 14th Ave., Denver
• **(303) 640-4433 (hotline)**

Whether you like the architectural style or not, the Denver Art Museum has perhaps the most unusual profile of any building in Denver. With its silhouette of see-through geometric shapes, this modern six-story castle of art resembles a giant paper cutout. Inside is one of the best and most extensive collections of Native American crafts in the United States and an internationally acclaimed pre-Columbian art collection. Enjoy the works of Picasso, Georges Braque, Matisse, Frederic Remington, Winslow Homer, Thomas Hart Benton and two beautiful paintings by Monet: *Waterloo Bridge* and *The Water Lily Pond.* The lower level is dedicated to educational programs with studios, a lecture room, classrooms and a reception area.

The museum has greatly expanded its public programming with a full schedule of classes in studio art and art history classes year-round for adults and children. An underground concourse connects the museum with the public library. Call (303) 640-KIDS for information on family and children's classes and programs; call (303) 640-ARTS for adult classes. In addition, there are free walk-in programs for parents and kids on Saturdays and teacher training. The museum is open 10 AM to 5 PM Tuesday through Saturday (Wednesday until 9 PM), and noon to 5 PM Sunday. Admission is $4.50 for adults; $2.50 for seniors and students; free to members and children younger than 5; and free to Colorado residents on Saturday.

Fiske Planetarium
Regent Dr., CU-Boulder campus
• (303) 492-5001 (star shows),
(303) 492-5002 (administration and information)

Stargazers and sci-fi fans will enjoy the small gallery outside the planetarium's star-show auditorium, which often displays astronomical or futuristic artwork drawing 25,000 visitors a year. Take the kids, and take it all in with both art and a star show, workshop or lab. The planetarium is open 8 AM to 5 PM Monday through Friday and offers public shows on Friday evenings and some Tuesdays and Saturdays. A tour of the gallery is free; starshows are $2 for kids and seniors, $3.50 for adults and laser shows are $5.

Foothills Art Center
809 15th St., Golden • (303) 279-3922

This charming art center is set in an old church in the town of Golden, about a half-hour drive south of Boulder. There's a bian-

nual sculpture exhibit from May through July and a water-media exhibit from September through October. Another annual show is *Colorado Clay* from March through May. The annual Holiday Art Market is in November and December. The art center's church and adjacent buildings are on the National Historic Register. There's a year-round gift gallery too. This spacious art center has five or six galleries all under one roof. Hampton's Cafe, housed in the historic Victorian house next door, makes a nice stop before or after viewing the shows. Art center hours are 9 AM to 4 PM Monday through Saturday, 1 to 4 PM Sunday.

Handmade in Colorado
1426 Pearl St., Boulder • (303) 938-8394

Now in its 10th year, this co-op gallery features the work of 28 Colorado artisans in various media including quilts, photographs, jewelry, stained glass, dried-flower arrangements, wood, blown glass and pottery. The gallery, owned by eight artisans, offers an especially large selection of finely crafted pottery. Some favorite artisans are Jayne Stanley, who won a first place award from the American Indian Art Council for her coiled fiber basketry; stoneware potter Giga Pellouchoud; stained-glass artisan Barbara Marcus and jeweler Lori Llerandi. Gallery hours are 10 AM to 6 PM Monday through Saturday (until 9 PM during summer and holidays), and 11 AM to 5 PM Sunday.

The Leanin' Tree Museum of Western Art
6055 Longbow Dr., Boulder
• (303) 530-1442

This museum houses the nation's largest privately owned Western art collection. The artworks, primarily post-Russell and Remington, include paintings and sculpture and are available as a result of Leanin' Tree founder Ed Trumble's 40-year friendship with Western artists. Admission is free; the museum is open 8 AM to 4:30 PM weekdays, 10 AM to 4 PM Saturday and Sunday. For more information, see our Attractions chapter.

Mackin-Katz Gallery of Fine Art
2041 Broadway, Boulder
• (303) 786-7887

Described by *Town & Country* magazine as having world-class flair, this gallery features the work of Boulder-based photographer Andy Katz and other internationally shown artists, including painters, photographers, potters, furniture makers and glasswork artists. Katz's black-and-white and color photography captures images from around the world, including vanishing Jewish societies, the scenery and people of France, Costa Rica and Japan and a tour of sunny California wineries. His work is also exhibited in museums and galleries throughout the world. The gallery is open 11 AM to 6 PM Monday through Saturday, and noon to 5 PM Sunday.

MacLaren Markowitz Gallery
1011 Pearl St., Boulder • (303) 449-6807

Featuring some of the area's most popular fine artists, MacLaren Markowitz Gallery has a history of top-quality contemporary art in Boulder. Lyrical landscapes by Doug West and the colorful Hispanic-flavored art of Tony Ortega are some of the standard favorites at this attractive downtown gallery. Other popular artists include sculptor Bill Worrell, painters Merrill Mahaffey, Lindsey Leavell, Randy Pijoan, Julia Jordan and Pam Furumo (who also works in pastels). The gallery is open 10 AM to 5:30 PM Monday through Wednesday; 10 AM to 9 PM Thursday, Friday and Saturday; and noon to 5 PM Sunday. Winter hours are abbreviated so call before going.

Mary Williams Fine Arts
2116 Pearl St., Boulder • (303) 938-1588

This gallery specializes in antique prints, original art from the 19th and 20th centuries. You'll find fine prints and graphics with botanical, natural history and architectural themes. If you want a John James Audubon, a Currier & Ives or an Edward S. Curtis on your walls, here's where you'll find one.

The Middle Fish
1738 Pearl St., 18th and Pearl in the Harvest Commons, Boulder
• (303) 443-0835

This venue tucked in the Harvest Commons near the Harvest Restaurant describes itself as a fine craft and gift gallery. There's a mix of local and national artists' work, including folk art, functional and decorative pottery, dolls, mirrors, wood and metal tables, blown glass, fused glass, art jewelry, sculpture and unique smaller gifts. Look here for handcrafted furniture and garden sculpture, including bird baths and bird houses. Middle Fish is open 10 AM to 5 PM Sunday and Monday, and 10 AM to 8 PM Tuesday through Saturday.

Mustard Seed Gallery
Marriott Plaza, 2660 Canyon Blvd., Boulder • (303) 447-8626

Mustard Seed, in business for almost 30 years, has long been a favorite local source for traditional and contemporary paintings, pottery, prints, art glass, jewelry, photography and fine crafts. Mustard Seed is a partnership gallery run by seven artists, and there is a different show each month by members and others. Gallery hours are 10 AM to 7 PM Monday through Saturday, 10 AM to 4 PM Sunday.

Red Canyon Gallery
400 Main St., Lyons • (303) 823-5900

More than 90 Colorado artists show here; 20 are local to Lyons. Red Canyon features an interesting collection of blown glass, stained glass, pottery, fine art, weaving, jewelry, cards, photography and woodworking. This gallery is open daily, year round.

Ruth Linton & David Haslam Gallery
1217 Spruce St., Boulder
• (303) 444-9116

This gallery features fine art from national and regional artists, including classic Impressionistic and realistic works. There's a good selection of oils, pastels, watercolors and fine bronzes, plus jewelry and photography in this attractive gallery a block off the downtown Pearl Street Mall. Nationally recognized artists Sandra Bierman, Elizabeth Black, Ben Galloway, William Napier, Yan Zahu Xu and Lani Vlaanderen are featured. The frame shop staff also provides conservation framing to museum standards.

The gallery is open 11 AM to 5 PM Monday through Saturday, (Friday and Saturday until 9 PM), 1 to 5 PM Sunday. Summer hours are extended daily until 9 PM except for Sunday.

Smith-Klein Gallery
1116 Pearl St., Boulder • (303) 444-7200

This contemporary space offers an extensive collection of old and new jewelry, statues, hand-blown art glass and traditional and contemporary paintings. It also features work by contemporary Native American artists. Smith-Klein is open daily.

UMC Fine Art Gallery
Broadway and Euclid, CU-Boulder campus • (303) 492-6161

Area artists exploring contemporary issues are among those exhibiting at this university gallery, which displays work of both individual artists and groups in various media. Gallery hours are 9 AM to 10 PM Monday through Thursday, and 9 AM to 5 PM Friday. It is closed weekends and holidays.

Village Custom Framing & Art
The Village, 2525 Arapahoe Ave., Boulder • (303) 413-9110

Village Custom Framing & Art is a small but well-stocked gallery with a unique collection of limited-edition art, etchings and antique art, including prints by such well-known artists as Bateman, Brenders, Cole, Larson, Doolittle, Kinkade and Smith. The shop also specializes in quality framing, including conservation framing of all forms of art and memorabilia, plus they have a print-finding service and will restore oil paintings and color photographs. Hours are 9:30 AM to 7:30 PM Monday through Friday, 9:30 AM to 6 PM Saturday and noon to 5 PM Sunday.

Von Eschen Gallery
2660 Canyon Blvd., Boulder • (303) 443-9989

If you're a fan of Western and wildlife art, this is the place to go. There are paintings in all media, bronze sculptures, wood carvings and limited-edition prints. The gallery offers signed and numbered lithographs by such well-known artists as Robert Bateman and Bev Doolittle. Bateman's vivid portrayals of nature have earned national recognition, as have Doolittle's mystifying dual-image watercolors. A new addition is American Indian jewelry and pottery. They also do picture framing. Gallery hours are 9:30 AM to 5:30 PM Monday through Friday, and Saturday 10 AM to 4 PM.

Spectacular rock walls line Eldorado Canyon State Park, making it one of the premier rock-climbing areas in the United States.

Parks and Recreation Centers

From the Boulder Creek Path and mountain parks to the reservoir and recreation centers, our city is rich with recreational facilities, both indoor and out. Boulder offers a total of 54 urban parks and 7,000 acres of mountain parkland, a 1-acre reservoir, a golf course, two outdoor pools, three athletic complexes, a 7.5-mile linear creek-side park, three recreation centers and an extensive program of classes and activities. Following is a description of some of Boulder's most popular parks and their special features. Details on additional outdoor recreational activities can be found in our Boulder Participatory, Spectator and Professional Sports chapter.

Parks

City Parks

Boulder Creek Path
Parallel to Canyon Blvd. and/or Arapahoe Ave. from Four Mile Canyon in Boulder Canyon east to Cherryvale Rd. (approximately 7.5 miles)

Certainly the most popular and accessible "park" — and the best way to see Boulder — is the Boulder Creek Path, which cuts through the heart of the city, following the creek's tumbling path down Boulder Canyon and out to the eastern plains. The Creek Path hugs Canyon Boulevard down to Broadway then veers off south under Arapahoe. It meanders back under Arapahoe after 30th Street. For a close-up look at what goes on inside the creek, from mountains to plains, stop off at the Boulder Public Library and check out the creek fish tank, complete with colorful rainbow trout. You can also take a peek under the water at the observatory on the creek near Folsom Avenue.

Bicyclists, walkers and in-line skaters crowd this scenic path, shaded by some of Boulder's oldest cottonwoods and willows. The path branches off into various other routes and is accessible at sidewalk intersections throughout its length. Many Boulderites use the Creek Path to commute across town, so be sure to stay to the right or you might be run down by those on wheels. Stop and enjoy the scenery, or lunch at one of the many benches.

The Creek Path is described in detail in the Boulder Attractions chapter.

Scott Carpenter Park
Arapahoe Ave. and 30th St., Boulder
• (303) 441-3427 (pool)

Named for Boulder's own astronaut, this is a favorite warm-weather spot for kids, with its outdoor pool and playground featuring a rocket jungle gym commemorating the feats of its namesake. Open swim is from 1 to 5 PM Monday through Friday, 1 to 6 PM Saturday and Sunday between May 29 and Aug. 29. Admission for residents on a per-visit basis is $3.25 for adults, $2 for seniors 60 and older and $1.25 for youth ages 4 through 18; fees for nonresidents on a per-visit basis are $4 for adults, $2.50 for seniors and $1.50 for youth.

Salberg Shelter
19th and Elder Sts., Boulder
• (303) 413-7200

This small park in the north-central part of town has a crafts building, playground and everyone's favorite — a giant, stationary human-propelled barrel. Kids and adults can feel like pet mice in exercise wheels as they run inside the barrel making it spin. The center can be rented out to private groups by calling the Parks and Recreation Department at the listed number.

www.insiders.com
See this and many other **Insiders' Guide®** destinations online — in their entirety.
Visit us today!

Central Park
Broadway and Canyon Blvd., Boulder
• (No phone)

There's always something going on in this pretty park in the heart of downtown, with its historic passenger train, creekside picnic tables and lawns, band shell and plentiful green grass for lounging and watching the passing crowds. Right on the Boulder Creek Path and across from the Boulder Museum of Contemporary Art and the Boulder-Dushanbe Teahouse, the park is also adjacent to the Saturday and Wednesday Farmer's Market along 13th Street.

Spruce Pool
2102 Spruce St., Boulder
• (303) 441-3426

This outdoor pool is a favorite of summer swimmers. Open swims are from 1 to 5 PM Monday through Friday and 1 to 6 PM Saturday and Sunday between June 12 through Sept. 6. There are lap lanes, a kiddie pool and a great slide. Red Cross-certified swim lessons are available. Fees for residents and non-

residents are the same as for the Scott Carpenter Park pool, listed previously.

Eben Fine Park
Third St. and Arapahoe Ave., Boulder
• No phone

This sylvan spot is a favorite for picnics and Frisbee throwing. It's on Boulder Creek and just off the Creek Path. Picnic tables, barbecue grills, big shady cottonwood trees, playground equipment, plenty of room for playing catch or volleyball games and the rippling creek make it a popular summer recreation area. There's also a lovely stone shelter that can be reserved for gatherings.

Mountain Parks

A required experience for all visitors and newcomers to Boulder — and an excellent introduction to the mountain parks — is the drive up Flagstaff Mountain. The hairpin-turn, two-lane drive offers spectacular panoramas along the way as well as pull-offs, trails and picnic spots. Keep your eyes on the road and let your passengers describe the human flies climbing on the rock formations. To get there, take Baseline Road west, follow it's curve to the right and up Flagstaff. (The elegant Flagstaff House restaurant along the way is open for dinner only.)

Boulder's foresight in preserving natural areas while other nearby cities were building housing and more housing resulted in a glut of visitors to Boulder's open space. To reduce that number, and recoup some of the cost of maintaining the area, the city charges cars not registered in Boulder County to park on Flagstaff Mountain or in Gregory Canyon (the area below Flagstaff). Annual permits are $15; daily permits are $3. For permit information call City of Boulder Mountain Parks, (303) 441-3408, or stop along the way to Flagstaff at the Chautauqua Rangers' Cottage at the entrance to Chautauqua Park at the foot of Flagstaff. Self-service stations for the daily permits are available at all the parking areas. Rangers patrol the lots and ticket cars without permits.

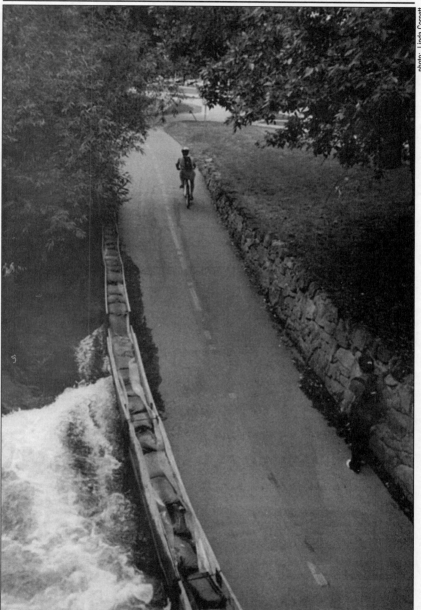

photo: Linda Cornett

Arid Boulder has a love affair with the mountain creek that runs through it, but the town is well aware that water can be treacherous. The Boulder Creek Path serves both as park and clear area for the inevitable major flood. A row of sandbags atop a retaining wall is testimony to the creek's annual spring spillover.

photo: Linda Cornett

So popular has Boulder's aggressive open space and parks program become with residents of neighboring communities that out-of-towners must pay a fee to park in some areas, as here on Flagstaff Mountain.

Rangers also offer a series of free hikes and educational programs in the mountain parks in search of wildflowers, bugs, bats and other wildlife. They even offer an evaluation of canine citizenship to help owners determine if their dogs are well-trained enough to handle the distractions of a hike in the mountain parks. (Dogs may be off-leash but must remain in sight and under voice control in most mountain parks).

More than 100 miles of hiking trails lace Boulder's scenic mountain backdrop. Popular trailheads begin at Chautauqua Park, Flagstaff Mountain, the National Center for Atmospheric Research and Eldorado Springs. You can hike to Bear Peak, Green Mountain, Mount Sanitas and to the Devil's Thumb — all of which are popular, substantial hikes taking from several hours to most of the day, depending upon your level of fitness. (See some specific locations and suggested hikes listed under "Hiking" in the Participatory Sports chapter.)

Boulder Mountain Parks Trail Maps list the length of trails and degree of difficulty and cost $5. Maps are available from the Boulder Chamber of Commerce, (303) 442-1044, 2440

INSIDERS' TIP

On a gloomy winter day, take yourself and/or the kids to the East Boulder Recreation Center where young and old enjoy the leisure pool, spraying mushroom fountain and water slide. If you feel like climbing the wall there's one here you really can climb, or play basketball or racquetball (advance reservations are required). See address and details in this chapter.

Pearl Street; the City of Boulder Parks and Recreation Administration Office, (303) 413-7200, 3198 North Broadway; Boulder Map Gallery, (303) 444-1406, 1708 13th Street; the Chautauqua Rangers' Cottage (303) 441-3408, 850 Kinnikinnick Road (near Eighth Street and Baseline Road in Chautauqua Park), open daily 8 AM to 4 PM; and at City of Boulder Recreation Centers (addresses listed below).

Chautauqua Park
Ninth St. and Baseline Rd., Boulder
• (303) 441-3408 (Rangers' Cottage)

At the base of the Flatirons, Boulder's first park opened as a summer camp and retreat for visitors from Texas in 1898 and was originally called Texado Park. Perched on a hill overlooking the city, today it's the scene of casual summer sports such as Frisbee throwing and badminton. An auditorium hosts a summer concert series, and a dining room serves meals year-round. Many concertgoers bring their own picnics to enjoy under the shady cottonwoods. The Rangers' Cottage at the park entrance has information about the numerous hiking trails that begin at Chautauqua, such as the Royal Arch and the Mesa Trail.

State Parks

Eldorado Canyon State Park
Colo. Hwy. 170, Eldorado Springs
• (303) 494-3943

One of the premier rock-climbing areas in the United States, this canyon is lined with spectacular rock walls. It's a great place to watch some world-class rock climbing or do a bit of hiking. The park is open until dusk. The entrance fee is $1 for walk-ins, $4 per vehicle and $40 for annual state parks pass ($10 for those 62 and older). Check the new maps at the park entrance and ranger station for length and level of difficulty for the various trails.

On the way to the park you'll pass Eldorado Artesian Springs, (303) 499-1316 Ext. 20, a privately owned historic resort (see our History chapter). The thermal pools and snack bar are open from 10 AM to 6 PM daily from Memorial Day through Labor Day; cost per day is $5 for adults, $3 for kids ages 3 through 12 and for seniors 60 and older; children younger than 3 are admitted free.

The park is 8 miles south of Boulder. Take Colorado Highway 93 to Colorado Highway 170 and head west.

Photo: Roz Brown

Kids love the water slide at the East Boulder Recreation Center.

Recreation Centers

The City of Boulder operates three excellent recreation centers. Daily admission for adults is $4.50, children ages 4 to 18, $1.75, seniors over 60, $2.50. Admission is reduced by purchasing a punch card, for which prices vary by age group, number of punches and residency. Sundays from 1 to 5 PM, parents and children pay half price. The centers are open daily; call for specific hours of operation. Reservations must be made two days in advance for the handball, racquetball and tennis courts, and the cost is $8 per court for an hour. Annual passes to the recreation centers are also available.

For just about any sport or activity you might want to pursue, the City of Boulder offers courses and instruction. The city also offers the EXPAND (Exciting Programs, Activities & New Dimensions) for people with dis-abilities. For information on available programs, call the Recreation Department at (303) 413-7200.

North Boulder Recreation Center
3170 N. Broadway, Boulder
• **(303) 441-3444**

Facilities at this center include a 25-yard indoor swimming pool, Jacuzzi and sauna, gymnasium, gymnastics center with a foam pit, dance and yoga classrooms, a handball/racquetball court, two platform tennis courts, four outdoor tennis courts, two outdoor sand volleyball courts, a weight room, locker rooms and showers. Child care is available from 8:30 AM to 1 PM weekdays for $2.50 per hour.

South Boulder Recreation Center
1360 Gillaspie Dr., Boulder
• **(303) 441-3448**

This newly renovated center has a new

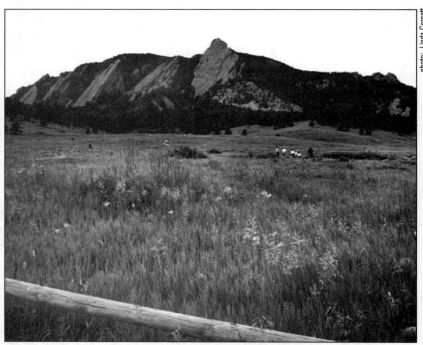

photo: Linda Cornett

The long, lovely slope leading to Bluebell Canyon near Chautauqua lures hikers, backpackers, nature classes and picnickers to explore its charm.

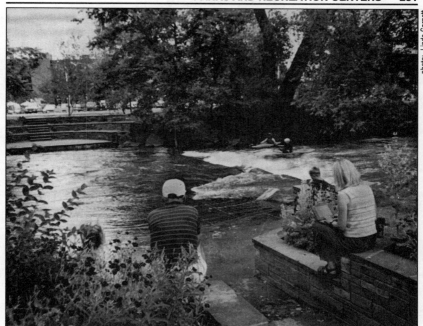

photo: Linda Cornett

The two curved halves of Boulder's Peace Park reach toward each other across Boulder Creek. In between, two kayakers try out the waters.

pool with a wheelchair ramp, hot tub, sauna, locker rooms, showers, classrooms, a gymnasium, expanded weight room, racquetball/handball court, outdoor sand volleyball courts and four outdoor tennis courts. Sundays, a huge inflatable pyramid is put in the pool for kids to play on. Neighboring Viele Lake offers canoeing and paddleboating as well as a fitness course around the lake.

East Boulder Recreation Center
5660 Sioux Dr., Boulder
• **(303) 441-4400**

Boulder's newest recreation center combines a senior center and recreation. The Senior Center wing, (303) 441-4150, includes a cafeteria, common area and an arts and crafts room and computers with Internet access for public use. The recreation facility features a 25-yard indoor lap pool and leisure pool with water slide and children's play area; gymnasium with adjustable basketball hoops; weight rooms with free and body-master weights, rowing machines and stationary cycles; a climbing wall; aerobics room; and dance studio. Outdoors you'll find tennis, basketball and racquetball courts as well as a handicapped-accessible playground. Child care is available from 8:30 AM to 1 PM weekdays and 9 AM to noon Saturdays for $2.50 per hour.

Boulder Reservoir
5100 51st St., off north side of the Diagonal Highway, Boulder
• **(303) 441-3468 (gate),**
(303) 441-3456 (boathouse)

For those craving a beach, this is the closest thing to it in Boulder County. Tons and tons of sand were trucked in to create the beaches for the reservoir, and more is added periodically. Swimmers, sailors, windsurfers, canoeists, kayakers and waterskiers make this a busy place on summer weekends. Various watercraft are for rent, including sailboats and windsurfers; call the boathouse for rates. Grills and picnic tables provide a nice spot for summer barbecues on the swimming beach. The reservoir hosts sailboat races, volleyball tournaments and a national in-line skate series. It's also the scene of the annual Polar Bear Dip on New Year's Day (see our Boulder Festivals and Annual Events chapter) and the Kinetic Conveyance race, in which bizarrely garbed contestants try to muscle homemade vehicles over water, prairie and mud. Waterskiing, sailboat and sailboard classes are available. One-day summer admission to "The Rez" is $4.50 for adults 19 and older; $2.25 for children 4 to 18; $2.50 seniors ages 60 to 64; and free for seniors 65 and older and children younger than 4. Season passes are available; call the gate for information. The one-acre reservoir is open year-round, but services are provided only during the summer — seven days a week between June 12 and Aug. 20, weekends only from May 29 to June 11 and Aug. 21 to Sept. 6. There is no admission charge during the rest of the year.

Boulder Reservoir is 1.5 miles north of Jay Road via the Diagonal Highway (Colo. 119).

Mapleton Center therapy pool
311 Mapleton Ave., Boulder
• (303) 441-0436

If a bathtub-style dip is more your style, try out the therapy pool at the Mapleton Center of Boulder Community Hospital. The indoor pool is kept a balmy 94 degrees. It is used by patients at the rehab hospital, but is also open to the public for open swim — call (303) 441-0542 for hours — and lessons for children through adults. Drop-in fees are $2.75 for kids 1 to 12, $3.50 for ages 13 to 49 and $2.75 for adults over 50. Punch cards are $39 for 15 visits for children and seniors, $49 for ages 13 through 49. 441-0542

YMCA of Boulder County
2850 Mapleton Ave., Boulder
• (303) 442-2778

Boulder's "Y" has a full range of facilities and classes, including racquetball/handball courts; a swimming pool; full gym; indoor running track; Jacuzzi, Cybex, Nautilus and Hydrogym equipment; and single-sex saunas. Admission for non-members is $8 for teens and adults; $4 for kids younger than 13. Adult membership is $50 to join and $35 per month, family membership is $50 to join and $49 per month.

University of Colorado Recreation Center
CU-Boulder campus, Boulder
• **(303) 492-6561**

The CU-Boulder Recreation Center is open only to CU-Boulder students, staff, faculty members, alumni and alumni spouses. Facilities include four pools; the city's only ice rink; handball/racquetball, squash and tennis courts; a gymnasium; fitness system room; weight room; training room; and saunas. Fees vary widely depending on the season and your affiliation with CU-Boulder.

You'll share the trails, routes and roads around Boulder with some of the nation's and world's best athletes who come here to train.

Sports

Many people move to Boulder specifically for what's contained in this chapter: bicycling, hiking, camping, skiing, rock climbing, running and other outdoor sports. As we said in our Area Overview chapter, Boulder has been called "the sports town" by *Outside* magazine, and you'll share the trails, routes and roads with some of the nation's and world's best athletes who come here to train.

Non-Olympians also abound, and you'll find them poking around in sporting goods shops and in the various clubs and organizations for bicycling, skiing, rock climbing and hiking listed in this chapter.

If you're a spectator rather than a participant, you'll be in the minority, but with plenty of exciting entertainment from CU-Boulder's Buffaloes, who are members of the NCAA Division I Big 12 Conference and former national football champions. You can also enjoy professional football with Denver's Broncos or basketball with CU's women and men Buffaloes or Denver's professional Nuggets. Other sports teams in our area include the Colorado Rockies Major League Baseball team, the Colorado Avalanche National Hockey League team (formerly Quebec's Nordiques, the Avalanche have firmly endeared themselves to Coloradans by winning the 1996 Stanley Cup) and various college sports. The Rockies and Avalanche are both based in Denver.

Participatory Sports

Bicycling

Boulder Creek Path
Various locations • no phone

Boulder's plentiful bike paths are the obvious place to start pedaling. Cruise right onto the very popular Boulder Creek Path, the backbone of the bike path network. The Path, which also accommodates pedestrians and rollerbladers, is most easily accessed at Central Park (Broadway and Canyon); Eben Fine Park (Fourth and Arapahoe); the Regal Harvest House Hotel (1345 28th Street, just south of Arapahoe); or Scott Carpenter Park on 30th Street south of Arapahoe Avenue. Most major intersections crossing Arapahoe Avenue have a sidewalk ramp onto the bike path.

Ride east or west — both directions offer a great ride and scenery. Going west, the paved section ends about a half-mile into Boulder Canyon, and a wide packed-gravel path continues a little more than 2 miles (from Eben Fine Park) up to Four Mile Canyon, where the Creek Path ends. It's not a steep or difficult ride to the end of the path, but those new to

INSIDERS' TIP

Though Fido might love to hike, check regulations at the trailheads. Dogs must be on leashes at all times in the Indian Peaks Wilderness Area, with a $50 fine for violators. During winter, for skiing or snowshoeing, take only dogs that truly respond to voice control. Out-of-control dogs on ski trails — especially the downhills — endanger both dogs and skiers.

Boulder's elevation might be a bit breathless as the trail gradually climbs the canyon, paralleling the highway. It's best ridden on a mountain bike, but skinny tires can make it, too, with care on the gravel and "curbs" at the bridges.

For those who prefer no hills, ride east, where the Creek Path sweeps out onto the plains past 30th Street and CU-Boulder's Research Park for a panoramic view of the Front Range, past duck ponds, cottonwoods and prairie dog towns. See the Boulder Attractions chapter for a detailed description of the path.

Bear Creek Greenway
Northeast corner, Broadway and Table Mesa Drive

South Boulderites can enjoy a beautiful bike path that heads northeast from Martin Park on the corner of Broadway and Table Mesa Drive. Access the path at the far northeast end of the park. Called the Bear Creek Greenway, the path winds along Bear Creek under highways and eventually over Foothills Parkway, where cyclists have the choice of heading farther east on the Centennial bike path or heading north across Arapahoe Avenue and connecting with the Boulder Creek Path.

Bike paths weave all around and through Boulder, and a map is a good bet if you don't want to get lost. The transportation department's Bicycle and Pedestrian Map ($2.50) is available at the Boulder Chamber of Commerce, (303) 442-1044, 2440 Pearl Street, and also at the bicycle shops listed below.

Rentals and Information

A delightful symbiosis has developed between the city of Boulder and New Vista High

School. Donated bikes are taken to the school, where students learn to repair and paint them. The bright green bikes are then left at locations around town for use by anyone for free. Just leave the bike in a fairly public place when you're done with it.

Bikes can also be rented at various shops around town, including Doc's Ski and Sports, (303) 499-0963, 627 S. Broadway, south Boulder; University Bicycles, (303) 444-4196, 839 Pearl Street, downtown; the Morgul Bismark, (303) 447-1338, 1221 Pennsylvania Ave., University Hill; The Bikesmith, (303) 443-1132, 2432 Arapahoe Ave., Arapahoe Village Shopping Center; Louisville Cyclery, (303) 665-6343, 1032 S. Boulder Rd., Louisville. Average rates are $12 to $16 for four hours (city or mountain bike); $16 to $21 per full day; and $35 to $50 per weekend.

Other resources for bicycling information are the city's alternative transportation program, 1739 Broadway, second floor, (303) 441-3266; the University of Colorado Bike Office, (303) 492-2322; and the *Colorado Cycling Guide* by Jean and Hartley Alley, two longtime Boulder residents and cyclists. Lights are required for night riding.

Paved Roads
(Skinny Tires)

Niwot

The ride to Niwot is relatively flat and pastoral, winding past ponds and pleasant countryside (16 miles from Broadway and Canyon). Go north on Broadway to Nelson Road and turn right (turn right on Neva Road before Nelson for a shorter ride). Follow Nelson Road to Colo. 73, turn right and go to Niwot Road and turn left; proceed into Niwot and enjoy a meal at historic Rev. Taylor's Country Restaurant, (303) 652-2020.

Lyons

A little more hilly are the rides to Lyons or Louisville. To reach Lyons (16 miles from Broadway and Canyon), ride north on Broadway (U.S. 36), which has a wide shoulder part of the way, all the way to Lyons, and turn left at the railroad track. Andrea's, (303) 823-5000, is a dandy breakfast or lunch pick (closed Wednesdays).

Louisville

To reach Louisville (12 miles from Broadway and Canyon), go south on the bike path along the east side of Broadway to Marshall — south of Boulder — through Marshall and over Colo. 170. Cross U.S. 36, make a right on Dillon Road, a left on 96th Street, then look for nearby Main Street and Karen's Country Kitchen, (303) 666-8020.

Jamestown

For a good mountain ride, head for Jamestown (17 miles from Broadway and Canyon). Take Broadway up Lefthand Canyon (8 miles north of town) and then, after 6 miles, up James Canyon Drive. (Look for mile markers in the canyon.) The picturesque Jamestown Mercantile Cafe, (303) 442-5847, offers breakfast, lunch and snacks.

Ward

The truly tough can ride all the way up Left Hand Canyon to Ward (23 miles one way from Broadway and Canyon) — all steady climbing from the start of Left Hand Canyon. If you can make it over the final hill out of Ward to the Peak-to-Peak Highway (Colo. 72), great meals, homemade pie and local ambiance await you at the Mill Site Inn, (303) 459-3308, just north of Ward.

Flagstaff Mountain

Macho cyclists can also tackle Flagstaff Mountain — a real muscle-buster right in town, due west on Baseline Road. You'll be hunched over the handlebars on the way up, but the zoom down provides some beautiful vistas of the Boulder Valley.

Nederland

Another strenuous ride is the 17 miles up Boulder Canyon to Nederland, but the curving canyon road with its narrow shoulder and speeding cars can be quite hazardous for cyclists. Choose less busy times during midweek and midday for this ride.

Unpaved Roads
(Fat Tires)

Despite all of Boulder's mountain parks, trails and open space, mountain biking on trails is limited to only a few local areas. After the great fat-tire craze began about a decade ago, trails began to erode and hikers complained about speeding cyclists running them off trails. As a result, all of the Boulder Mountain Parks trails are closed to mountain bikes.

Nevertheless, there are a few good off-road trails for mountain bikes on the north, south and east ends of town on city and county open space land and farther afield.

The Boulder Offroad Alliance, a citizen's nonprofit organization formed in 1991 to provide "a positive voice for Mountain Biking," hosts social rides two or three times a week during the summer and encourages riders to volunteer time for trail maintenance. Call (303) 546-2877 for more information.

BOA members also provide descriptions of favorite rides, but the most detailed map available is the Mountain Bike Map: Boulder County ($8), available from Boulder County Parks and Open Space Department in the Courthouse Annex at 2045 13th Street (corner of Spruce and 13th streets). Area bike shops, bookstores and sporting goods shops also sell the map and might charge a bit more for it. A few suggested off-road mountain bike trails follow.

Around Boulder

Greenbelt Plateau Trail

This gentle trail rolls across a mesa top through open grasslands with beautiful views of the foothills. At 1.3 miles, bicyclists may choose to take the dirt path to Community Ditch Trail or continue on the service road to Colo. 93.

This mountain-biker hops down a mountain trail near Boulder.

This trail is ranked as easy and covers 1.6 miles on gravel surface road. The Greenbelt Plateau Trail is south of Boulder, on the north side of Colo. 128, just east of Colo. 93.

Community Ditch Trail

The Community Ditch Trail is a 4-mile dirt service road of moderate difficulty that travels through grasslands, mesas and land with evidence of early farming and mining activity. Taken from the Marshall Mesa Trailhead this ride is a huff and a puff up the mesa, but riders will be rewarded with spectacular views of the mountains and a delightful flat ride along the flower-lined (in spring) mesa and the Community Ditch, which in warm weather invites a swim.

You'll find the trail south of Boulder, at the Doudy Draw Trailhead on the south side of Colo. 170, 1.7 miles west of Colo. 93, or at the Marshall Mesa Trailhead, 0.9 mile east of Colo. 93 on the south side of Marshall Road.

Cross Colo. 93 (Broadway) and continue along the ditch winding back among the cottonwoods. To make a nice loop back to Boulder, head for the Doudy Draw Trailhead at the junction of Community Ditch Bridge. At Doudy Draw Trailhead you can choose between a side trip into Eldorado Springs (turn left on the paved highway) or turn right to return to Colo. 93 to Boulder or the Marshall Mesa Trailhead. Eldorado Springs (about 2 miles) provides a chance to refuel with spring water, swim (in the summer) at Eldorado Springs Resort, graze at the snack bar or gaze at the daring rock climbers in the state park ((303) 494-3943) climbing the impressive Bastille and other formations. To return to Boulder or the Marshall Mesa Trailhead, ride back out to Colo. 93 on the Eldorado Springs road, crossing at the light and continuing straight into the tiny settlement of Marshall. The trailhead is just a little farther east on Marshall Road. If you choose the reverse direction, starting at the Doudy Draw Trailhead, go left (east) at the junction of Community Ditch bridge and the dirt road you're on. The trail crosses Colo. 93 and goes to the Marshall Reservoir inlet and up a steep hill to the Marshall Mesa Trailhead.

East Boulder Trail
Access Teller Farm S. Trailhead, on Arapahoe Rd., 1 mile east of 75th St.

The 7-mile East Boulder Trail has a difficulty ranking of moderate. A 2.2-mile level section of the trail goes through a wildlife preserve and past Teller Lake. Then, a 2.7-mile section climbs a mesa on dirt trails and service roads to the Gunbarrel Farm. The Gunbarrel Farm section travels along a dirt service road with moderate grades and turns east at 1.2 miles into the White Rocks area.

In the Mountains

Mountain bikes are allowed only on certain mountain trails, many of which are shared by four-wheel-drive vehicles or cars. Most mountain biking in the local high country requires an outstanding pair of lungs and legs, since it's mostly uphill and at high altitudes.

Gold Hill

For a ride right out of town, go west on Mapleton Avenue, which becomes unpaved in Sunshine Canyon and continues to the historic mining town of Gold Hill, about 10 miles uphill. From there you can continue to Nederland and return down Boulder Canyon. Or, start the ride at the mouth of Boulder Canyon along the Creek Path, which ends in 2 miles at Four Mile Canyon (County Road 118). Then, proceed up Four Mile Canyon and turn right at the sign for Gold Hill — also about 10 miles uphill from the mouth of Four Mile Canyon.

Switzerland Trail

The historic Switzerland Trail, a former single-gauge railroad track, makes for some scenic riding with spectacular mountain views and reasonable climbing grades. Most riders start at the town of Sunset and go south toward Bald and Sugarloaf mountains. To reach Sunset, head up Four Mile Canyon (above), and stay on County Road 118 past Salina and Wallstreet until you reach Sunset, 17 miles from Boulder. Go right to reach Gold Hill or left to Glacier Lake.

Sourdough Trail

Accessible from the Peak to Peak Highway (Colo. 72) west of Nederland, the Sourdough Trail is 17.5 miles long, but has different segments at various trailheads. The trail was constructed with help from the Colorado Mountain Club mainly for ski touring and mountain biking, and features pleasant rolling terrain through the pines. From Camp Dick Campground to Beaver Reservoir is 2.3 miles. From Beaver Reservoir to Brainard Road, it's 7.4 miles, and from Brainard Road to Rainbow Lakes Road, 7.8 miles. All access to the various connections to the Sourdough Trail is made via the Peak to Peak Highway. Camp Dick Campground is on Middle St. Vrain Road, 5.8 miles north of Ward and 0.5 miles west of Peaceful Valley. One Sourdough Trailhead is on the left-hand side of County Road 96 just east of Beaver Reservoir, 2.5 miles north of Ward and 2 miles west on County Road 96. The Red Rock Trailhead is on the right-hand side of County Road 102, just east of Red Rock Lake, 2.5 miles west on Brainard Lake Road. Another Sourdough Trailhead is on the right-hand side of Rainbow Lakes Road (County Road 116), 4.7 miles south of Ward (7 miles north of Nederland) and 0.4 miles west on County Road 116.

Rollins Pass

For those in really top shape, try Rollins Pass, one of Colorado's premier mountain biking (and four-wheel-drive) routes. This former railroad bed crosses the Continental Divide. Cars used to be able to make this exciting drive over rickety railroad trestles perched above thousand-foot drops, until the Needle's Eye tunnel caved in and was never cleared. Today, the tunnel, 1.5 miles from the Divide, is the end of the road for vehicles, but mountain bikers and hikers can bypass the tunnel and continue on the roadbed over the pass and all the way down the other side to Winter Park, if desired. To reach Rollins Pass Road, drive west up Boulder Canyon (Colo. 119) to Nederland, then south on Colo. 72 to Rollinsville. Turn right (west) on the dirt road marked with signs to Tolland and East Portal and drive 8.5 miles to the East Portal and Moffat Tunnel. The Rollins Pass road begins there, as marked. Bicycling over the pass is an all-day affair requiring another vehicle on the Winter Park side and lodging reservations or plans — not to mention advanced physical fitness.

Camping

Camping beneath the pines in the cool,

clear air of the high country — and perhaps near a gleaming mountain lake or stream — is one of the Rockies' greatest joys. The U.S. Forest Service, State of Colorado and City of Boulder maintain many such sites. (For camping in Rocky Mountain National Park, please see that chapter later in this book.)

Boulder County

Roosevelt National Forest

The following campgrounds are within the national forest. For information about federal regulations within Roosevelt, call (303) 444-6600. Call toll-free, (877) 444-6777, for reservations.

Kelly Dahl
3 miles south of Nederland on Colo. Hwy. 119

This campground offers a scenic view of the Continental Divide and limited hiking. There are 46 sites at an elevation of 8,600 feet. The season lasts from late April or early May through October 31 or the first snow, whichever comes first. The fee is $12 with water ($6 without).

Rainbow Lakes
6.5 miles north of Nederland off Colo. Hwy. 72

Rainbow Lakes is set near several small but lovely lakes. There is no available running water, but good fishing is nearby in the Indian Peaks Wilderness Area. There are 18 sites at an altitude of 10,000 feet; first-come, first-served. The season runs from late April or early May through October 15 or the first snow. The fee is $6.

Pawnee Campground
5 miles west of Colo. Hwys. 119/72 on County Rd. 102 (at Brainard Lake)

This extremely popular (and heavily used) campground offers beautiful views, fishing and non-motorized boating with access to the wilderness area. The 55 sites lie at an elevation of 10,400 feet, and the brief season lasts from July 1 through October 15. The fee is $12 ($6 with no water or trash pickup).

Peaceful Valley and Camp Dick
15 miles west of Lyons on Colo. Hwy. 7, left at the junction with Colo. Hwy. 72, 6 miles farther

Peaceful Valley is a pleasant, pine-shaded campground with 18 sites at an elevation of 8,500 feet. The season is late April or early May through October 31 or the first snow. The fee is $12 ($6 with no water).

To reach Camp Dick campground, located a mile west of Peaceful Valley, follow the dirt road to the 46 sites at an elevation of 8,600 feet. Horses are available for rental nearby. The season is from late April or early May through October 31 or the first snow. The fee is $12 ($6 with no water).

Olive Ridge Campground
15 miles south of Estes Park or 1.5 miles north of Allenspark on Colo. Hwy. 7

Nestled close to lush Rocky Mountain National Park, this campground offers access to the Park as well as horse rentals at nearby stables. There are 56 sites at an elevation of 8,400 feet. The season is late April or early May through Oct. 31 or the first snow. Reservations are required through Destinet, (800) 365-2267, and the fee is $12.

INSIDERS' TIP

Even people who have no intention of ever climbing a rock wall themselves might enjoy watching others do so. A short drive or walk up Boulder Canyon (on foot up the Creek Path from Eben Fine Park, it's less than a mile) takes you to the Elephant Buttresses and the Dome (just past where the Creek Path goes under Canyon Boulevard), two of Boulder's most popular rock-climbing spots. On the Dome, watch climbers tackle a route called the "Disappearing Crack" — you'll see why. A bench along the creek invites spectators.

Mountain Safety and Environment

Colorado's Rocky Mountains can take the unwary and unprepared by surprise. Remember: Going above or near timberline is the same as visiting the Arctic regions of the world. Mountain weather can change from a warm, sunny day to hail, snow, thunder

and lightning in minutes. It can snow at any time of the year. Summer daytime temperatures in Rocky Mountain National Park on Trail Ridge, Fall River and West Slope roads average in the 50s (10 C). The record high temperature in the alpine tundra is 63 (17 C). Wind chill can make these temperatures much lower — and it's usually windy in the mountains.

Visiting the high mountains can be a safe and extremely rewarding experience, as long as people are prepared and aware of the following dangers. As usual, prevention is the best way to make your trip safe and enjoyable.

1. Hypothermia. More of a threat to backpackers, dayhikers and skiers, hypothermia occurs from prolonged exposure to the cold and a resulting drop in body temperature. It's more common among elderly people. Symptoms include a slowed heart rate, puffiness, pale skin, lethargy and confusion. In severe cases, breathing slows and intravenous liquids are required. Hypothermia is a killer and has claimed many victims in the mountains. *always* bring a hat, rain and wind gear and extra warm clothing (layers are best) when going into the mountains. Staying well-hydrated by drinking liquids frequently also helps to prevent hypothermia. Keep a hat on if it's chilly — most body heat is lost from the head.

2. Dehydration. Colorado's dry climate, combined with exertion at high altitudes, can cause dehydration: a drop in the body's water level and often a drop in the body's level of salt. Symptoms include severe thirst, dry lips, increased heart and breathing rate, dizziness and confusion. The skin is dry and stiff. There's little urination, and what is passed is dark. Salt loss causes headaches, cramps (often in the legs), lethargy and pallor. Drink liquids frequently in the mountains. If you're feeling thirsty, your body's telling you that you're already about a quart low on liquids. Take salty snacks such as pretzels, chips and crackers. Rehydration drinks, such as Gatorade, are also good aids to take along.

3. Lightning. Lightning is much more dangerous above timberline. Every year lightning claims a number of lives in Colorado's high country. If a storm develops, stay off ridges and peaks. Keep away from trees, boulders, isolated buildings and metal objects. The safest place is in your car. A tingling sensation at the base of the neck or scalp and hair standing on end with static electricity are both signs that lightning is about to strike near you. Move rapidly to your car. Do not stand still, no matter what. If you are unable to return to your car, squat and wrap your arms around your knees, keeping your head low. Do not lie or sit on the ground (because if lightning strikes you or the ground and travels through your body, you want it to have a way out — an open circuit).

To estimate your distance from a lightning strike, count the seconds between the flash and the accompanying thunder and divide by five to get the distance in miles. It takes five seconds for the sound to travel a mile.

— continued on next page

4. Altitude sickness. Symptoms include headache, dizziness, nausea, shortness of breath and impaired mental abilities. Breathing into a paper or plastic bag for five minutes reduces these symptoms. In severe cases, fluid can build up in the lungs, causing breathlessness, heavy coughing and heavy phlegm. If untreated, these symptoms can lead to seizures, hallucinations, coma, brain damage and death. There is 40 percent less oxygen in the air above 8,000 feet (2,438 meters) than at sea level. To avoid altitude sickness, refrain from strenuous activity for the first few days at high altitude. Move slowly above timberline, eat lightly and drink fluids frequently. Alcoholic beverages may aggravate the symptoms. Move to a lower elevation if symptoms persist. People with respiratory or heart problems should check with a physician before going to high elevations.

5. Sunburn. Sunburn is much more severe at high altitudes because the reduced atmosphere is less able to filter out the sun's harmful ultraviolet radiation. With 5 percent more ultraviolet (light) per 1,000 feet, Colorado has 25 percent more damaging sun rays than Florida's beaches. Skiers and other winter sports enthusiasts need to be especially careful, because reflection from snow can cause severe sunburn. Skiers have been known to get sunburned inside their nostrils. In summer, to avoid burning, wear a long-sleeved shirt and a brimmed hat, and use sunscreen with at least a 15 SPF (sun protection factor) rating.

6. Dangerous currents and floods. Though they look shallow and serene, mountain streams have strong currents, slippery rocks and cold temperatures that have been contributing factors in many drownings. Be especially careful when fishing or allowing children to play near streams. Sudden rains can raise stream levels rapidly and even cause flash floods. If rain continues, move to higher ground.

7. Giardia. Don't drink water from streams and lakes. Tempting though it might be, many mountain streams and lakes contain bacteria and a microscopic organism called *Giardia lamblia*, which can cause long-term intestinal problems. The organism is transmitted into water by cysts in human, domestic animal and wildlife feces. Dogs and cats can catch and transmit Giardia. Symptoms of Giardia include violent diarrhea, gas, cramps, loss of appetite and nausea. Carry your own water bottle filled with tap water. Campers and hikers should boil all stream or lake water for 10 or more minutes, use water-purification kits or the now-popular (and expensive) microfilters (portable pumps that filter water). A microfilter must filter down to four microns to filter out Giardia.

8. Ticks. Not usually a problem in the higher mountains, wood ticks appear in the spring after vegetation begins to leaf in the Lower and Upper Montane zones — the areas below 9,500 feet (2,896 meters). They can appear as early as February in forested and shrubby areas and remain active into late summer. They are rare in the subalpine zone and above the tree line (above 9,500 feet). Applying insect repellent and wearing long pants and long-sleeved shirts help prevent tick bites. The best precaution is to check frequently for ticks on your clothing, hair and body, because it takes several hours for a tick to attach. After being outdoors, undress in a shower or tub or on a ground cloth OUTSIDE your tent. Inspect clothing carefully before putting it back on. Destroy ticks, but do not crunch them with your fingers.

Wood ticks can transmit Colorado tick fever and the more serious (but fairly uncommon) Rocky Mountain fever. Consult a physician if you have localized swelling, a rash, enlarged lymph glands or a fever in the days or weeks after a tick bite. Lyme disease is uncommon in Colorado, but it does occur from non-native ticks that somehow hitch a ride into the state.

To remove an attached tick, disinfect the area. Grasp the tick firmly with tweezers close to its head. Gently remove it by pulling it upward and out from the skin. Never twist or jerk on it. Putting nail polish, cooking oil or petroleum jelly on the tick can make it release its grip more easily.

Golden Gate Canyon State Park
10 miles south of Nederland on Colo. Hwy. 72, 2 miles east on Gap Rd.
• **(303) 582-3707**

Golden Gate offers many miles of hiking plus backpacking, fishing and camping at 7,900 to 10,500 foot elevation. You'll find 165 sites, including some in the backcountry. Fees are $12 per night for RV or motor home sites with electricity, $9 for drive-in tent sites with showers, $7 for walk-in tent sites. There's a one-time reservation fee. Golden Gate is open year round, weather permitting. A day pass costs $4. For reservatons, call (303) 470-1144 from the Denver area or toll-free from elsewhere, (800) 678-2267.

The park is 10 miles south of Nederland on Colo. 72 and 2 miles east on Gap Road for the north entrance. For the south entrance drive 3 more miles, then 4 miles east on Colo. 46.

City of Boulder Mountain Parks

Buckingham Campground
12 miles northwest of Nederland
• **(303) 441-3408**

The campground is at an elevation of 10,160 feet and is accessible to Indian Peaks Wilderness. Buckingham's eight sites, available on a first-come, first-served basis, are heavily used. Camping is allowed only in the designated sites, as the surrounding vegeta-

tion is easily damaged. The season runs from early June until snow season. No ground fires or charcoal fires are permitted; only gas grills or camp stoves may be used for cooking. No reservations are required, and there's no fee charged for camping, but no water is available.

Buckingham Campground is at the Fourth of July Trailhead, 12 miles northwest of Nederland. Take County Road 107 west through Eldora to County Road 130 (a rough road) and proceed to its end.

Climbing

Boulder is internationally known for its great rock climbing areas, particularly the Flatirons and Eldorado Canyon in the state park (see our Boulder Parks and Recreation Centers chapter for more information on these parks). With proper equipment and training, rock climbing can be a relatively safe sport, and rock jocks dancing up the cliffs at Eldorado Canyon might even make it look easy. Tempted as they might be, however, those without proper training and equipment should stay on the ground. Every year Colorado witnesses several fatalities involving inexperienced scramblers without equipment — especially around the Flatirons and Boulder Falls (in the Boulder Canyon). The book *Flatiron Classics* by Gerry Roach, a famous local mountaineer and climber, has detailed route

---

INSIDERS' TIP

Keep track! **Snowshoers sharing trails with cross-country skiers should make their own tracks, wherever possible, because cross-country skis work best in their own tracks and function poorly in snowshoe tracks. People without skis or snowshoes** *should not* **walk in either tracks because it ruins the trail for both skiers and snowshoers, making it frustrating and miserable for both. Please don't ruin someone else's fun.**

information for experienced climbers who want to climb the Flatirons and other popular routes. *Rock Climbing Colorado* by Stewart M. Green is a very thorough book that covers the whole state, describing 1,500 routes.

Those interested in learning to climb have many options, some of which we've listed below.

Colorado Mountain Club
900 Baseline Rd., Boulder
• (303) 554-7688

The CMC, as it is known, holds mountaineering courses in spring and fall. Learn all the basics of rock climbing and mountaineering in these courses. CMC also offers advanced mountaineering courses on a regular basis, as well as many scheduled trips both locally and internationally.

City of Boulder East Boulder Recreation Center
5660 Sioux Dr., Boulder
• (303) 441-4401

The City offers rock-climbing and mountaineering courses as part of its Adventure Program. There's a climbing wall at the East Boulder Community Center.

The Boulder Rock Club
2829 Mapleton Ave., Boulder
• (303) 447-2804, (800) 836-4008

The Boulder Rock Club and Rock School also has an indoor climbing wall and instructions. A full range of lessons and outdoor clinics are available, as is rental equipment. The Boulder Rock Club's 10,000-square-foot Mapleton Avenue facility is open all year.

Colorado Mountain School
351 Moraine Ave., Estes Park
• (970)586-5758

One-day introductory classes prepare people to begin climbing with guides. The school offers guided hikes, climbs (including technical routes of Longs Peak) and equip-

ment rentals. It's open year round; reservations are requested.

Neptune Mountaineering
633 Unit-A, S. Broadway, Table Mesa Center, Boulder • (303) 499-8866

Another excellent resource for climbing and mountaineering information, books and equipment (though no instruction is offered) is this shop owned by Gary Neptune, a prominent U.S. mountaineer who has stood on the top of Mount Everest and many other peaks worldwide. Neptune sometimes teaches and lectures for the Colorado Mountain Club, and his shop hosts guest lecturers like Peter Aschenbrenner, who climbed Nanga Oparbat in the Karakoram in the 1930s and 1953. The museum located in the shop includes boots and crampons from Sir Edmund Hillary's first ascent of Mt. Everest, a Russian oxygen bottle brought back from Everest, antique ice axes, alpenstocks, pitons and carabiners dating back 100 years — the most extensive collection of its kind in the country.

Fishing

Many lakes and streams in the area offer good fishing for both warm- and cold-water species. The Fish Observatory on the Boulder Creek Path just behind the Regal Harvest House Hotel at 1345 28th Street is a fun place to see the local species of Boulder Creek. There are windows built below water level for viewing. Look for brown, brook and cutthroat trout. The Boulder Public Library at 9th Street and Arapahoe Avenue also offers a living stream habitat display showing the fish and plant life found at various levels of the creek.

Some easy-to-reach area streams that offer good trout fishing include the Middle and South forks of St. Vrain Creek; Left Hand Creek between Left Hand Reservoir and Buckingham Park; North Boulder Creek between Colo. 72 and Boulder Falls; Middle Boulder Creek from its headwaters to 28th Street (with special re-

---

INSIDERS' TIP

Boulder's Creek Path is a great place for in-line skating — and the farther east, the flatter the path.

strictions in city limits); and South Boulder Creek from its headwaters to Baseline Road (with special restrictions between Walker Ranch and South Boulder Road). Golden Gate State Park is a good place to take kids fishing, and also offers camping and numerous hiking trails (see details under Hiking). Some favorite spots in and around Boulder are Wonderland and Thunderbird lakes, Walden (there's a special pond for seniors and people with disabilities) and Sawhill ponds. You'll get a detailed map and information on these areas when you buy your fishing license at one of the locations listed below under "Licenses."

Boulder Reservoir
51st St., 1 mile north of Jay Rd.

Out on the eastern plains, with a nice mountain vista, Boulder Reservoir is loaded with crappie, catfish and largemouth bass. It's open year–round. The best place for bank fishing is the deep water near the dam embankment at the eastern end. Boating is prohibited on weekends unless you are a Boulder resident. Please see the subsequent listing under swimming for admission fees. Drive toward Longmont on Colo. 119 to reach 51st Street.

Barker Reservoir
**17 miles up Boulder Canyon,
on Canyon Blvd., Nederland**

Barker Reservoir in Nederland attracts many anglers at its western end, where Boulder Creek empties into this scenic reservoir on the east side of Nederland. Anglers can catch some of the stocked rainbow trout, around a foot long. The water level fluctuates quite a bit, depending on the season and downstream water needs. No boats of any kind are allowed on this reservoir, which is owned by the Public Service Company of Colorado and supplies some of the drinking and irrigation water to towns below.

Gross Reservoir
Flagstaff Rd.

Gross Reservoir is another favorite of local fishermen looking to hook trout and bass. To reach it, drive west on Baseline Road, which becomes Flagstaff Road as it twists and turns up Flagstaff Mountain above Boulder. The Reservoir is a few miles from the top of the road.

Brainard and Red Rocks Lakes
5 miles up Colo. Hwy. 119, Ward

These beautiful mountain lakes attract many anglers looking for rainbow trout, brookies and brown trout. Fishing is permitted with flies and lures only. To reach these lakes, drive up Boulder Canyon to Nederland and head north on Colo. 72; the turnoff is just past Ward, 200 yards on the left. Or, drive up Left Hand Canyon north of Boulder past the Greenbriar Inn. Turn left (west) and proceed up the canyon through Ward and on to Colo. 72. Turn right and look immediately to the left for the Brainard turnoff. Brainard Lake is 5 miles up County Road 102.

Diamond Lake/Indian Peaks

For those who desire more solitude (which you won't find at Brainard Lake), hike up to beautiful Diamond Lake, from the Fourth of July trailhead. To reach Fourth of July trailhead, travel west from Nederland for about 7 miles on County Road 107 — you'll pass through the rustic town of Eldora — then continue up County Road 130 (a rough, dirt road) for about 5 miles. It's about a 2.5-mile hike up to Diamond Lake from the trailhead.

Licenses

Required fishing licenses cost $40.25 for nonresidents, $20.25 for residents, $10.25 for seniors and $1 for kids under 16 and are good for one calendar year. Out-of-staters can also buy licenses for one or five days for $5.25 and $18.25. They are available — along with maps — at McGuckin Hardware, (303) 443-1822, 2525 Arapahoe Avenue in Boulder, and at Nederland's Ace Hardware Store, (303) 258-3132, in the shopping center. For more information contact the City of Boulder Open Space Department (local/Boulder fishing, (303) 441-3440), Boulder County Parks and Open Space (local/county, (303) 441-3950), or the Colorado Division of Wildlife, Department of Natural Resources, (303) 297-1192; fishing report: (303) 291-7535, 6060 Broadway in Denver.

Fitness Centers

Boulder has numerous private health clubs and fitness centers, many of which are open to non-members.

Flatiron Athletic Club
505 Thunderbird Dr., Boulder
• **(303) 499-6590**

Flatiron offers an enormous array of classes and equipment. For $10 you can enjoy all the facilities for the day, including a lap pool and coed hot tub, tennis courts, saunas, a steam room, handball, squash and racquetball courts, a "Treadwall" for rock-climbing, volleyball, aerobics classes, an indoor running track and a complete weight room. There are also Pilates and spinning equipment and classes.

Pulse Fitness Center
2950 Baseline Rd., Boulder
• **(303) 443-2639**
1375 Walnut St., Boulder
• **(303) 447-8545**

For $10 (both locations) nonmembers can have full run of Nautilus equipment, free weights, Step classes, low- and high-impact aerobics classes, physical therapy and massage (when accompanied by a member, the charge is $8).

Boulder Rock Club
2829 Mapleton Ave., Boulder
• **(303) 447-2804**

Boulder Rock Club offers all types of indoor climbing walls for rock climbers (including bouldering, top-roping and lead-climbing) for $14 a day. Lessons (indoor and out), clinics and rental equipment are available here. The Boulder Rock Club's new 10,000-square-foot Mapleton Avenue facility is open all year.

RallySport
2727 29th St., Boulder • (303) 449-4800

Though it's open to members only, RallySport is open to members of other clubs affiliated with IRSHA, the International Racquet, Health and Sports Association, for a fee of $10 a day. This club has a full range of facilities including racquetball, squash, handball, tennis, volleyball and wallyball courts plus all types of classes, weight-training equipment and indoor and outdoor pools.

Golf

Golfers have a reasonable selection of public courses to choose from in Boulder and the surrounding area. Most of the courses listed here have driving ranges, equipment rentals, snack bars, pro shops and lessons.

Coal Creek Golf Course
585 W. Dillon Rd., Louisville
• **(303) 666-7888**

Coal Creek has nine and 18 hole courses, a driving range, snack bar and lounge, golf accessories and rentals. Weekday fees for residents are $14 and $20 ($16 and $27 weekends and holidays) for nine and 18 holes; for non-residents, weekday fees are $18 and $27 ($20 and $32 for weekends). The pars are 36 and 72 for nine and 18 holes. Carts are $10 and $20 but generally are not necessary.

Eagle Golf Club
1200 Club House Dr., Broomfield
• **(303) 466-3322**

Eagle has an 18-hole course, driving range, bar, golf accessories and rentals. Greens fees on weekdays are $20 for nonresidents to walk, $28 with a cart; $30 and $40 on weekends. Residents play for $17 ($25 with cart). The par is 35 or 36 (depending upon from which tees you're playing) on the nine-hole layout and 71.

Flatirons Golf Course
5706 Arapahoe Ave., Boulder
• **(303) 442-7851**

The City of Boulder operates the Flatirons Golf Course. Nonresident player fees are $16.50 for 9 holes, $25.50 for 18. Boulder residents can buy a discount card for $10 and save $4 every time they play. Par is 35 and 70.

Golf Haystack
5877 Niwot Rd., Boulder
• **(303) 530-1400**

The course of choice of "duffers" (according to one self-described local), Haystack is excellent for beginners, and there's no need to reserve a tee time — just show up. The easy nine-hole course is par 32, and greens fees are $10 on weekdays (Monday through Thursday) and $11 on weekends and holidays. No motorized carts are available, only pull-carts.

Wilderness Ethics for Hiking, Camping and Backcountry Travel

Various wilderness areas and national forests have their own sets of use regulations, but the following general guidelines apply to all areas. Remember: Even when we are careful, our presence and actions have an impact on the natural world. As our human population grows, negative impacts become more and more severe.

Close-up

Backcountry Travel
• Travel quietly and in small groups. Avoid disturbing others.
• Spread out impact by exploring less heavily visited areas.
• Leave your pets at home to keep from bothering wildlife and other visitors.
• Stay on maintained trails whenever possible. Do not take shortcuts; doing so destroys vegetation and causes erosion.
• Be especially careful when trails are muddy, and minimize horse use when trails are wet.
• On narrow trails, walk single file rather than several abreast, and try to avoid congregating large groups in sensitive areas.
• Don't pick wildflowers or dig up plants; it's illegal in all parks, and permission is needed on private land. Be judicious in picking fruit so that you leave enough for wildlife.
• Comply with signs regarding vehicles and mountain bikes, which are prohibited on many trails because of erosion problems. Refrain from using bikes on muddy slopes, where deep ruts develop quickly, and yield to other trail users.
• If you are photographing or observing wild animals and they become nervous, you are too close. Back away.
• Give right of way to horses, keeping to the downhill side. The same rule applies to all large mammals, who will become stressed if you remain above them.
• Avoid disturbing nesting birds, and comply with closures designed to protect plants and animals.
• Leave gates as you find them unless signs instruct otherwise.

Campsite Selection
• In heavily visited areas, use existing campsites to confine impact to a small area.
• In less-visited areas, choose a site well away from streams and lakes and out of sight of other users. Eliminate all traces of your camp.
• Carry out all trash. *Do not* bury it.
• If you must use soap for washing or bathing, use biodegradable products, stay at least 150 feet from any water sources, and pour the water into absorbent ground.

Stoves and Fires
• Use a gas stove for all cooking. Wood is scarce in the high country and an essential part of the ecosystem. Gas is quicker, cleaner and won't leave a scar of charred and sterilized soil.
• Campfires are becoming controversial. If you absolutely must build a fire, use only dead and down wood. Use existing fire rings and keep the fire very small. Use only as much wood as will burn completely.

— continued on next page

Photo: Daily Camera

Chautauqua Park is the starting point for many trails in Boulder's open space.

• Never leave fires unattended, even for a moment. When you leave, make certain that the fire is dead and cold. Clean out fire rings so they will be ready for the next visitor.

Sanitation

• Bury human waste in a small cat-hole about 6 inches deep and dug in organic soil (not just leaves or rocks) away from heavy-use areas and at least 150 feet from any water.

• Soiled toilet paper, diapers and sanitary napkins should be carried out.

• Place all trash in trash cans. In Colorado's climate, organic wastes such as orange peels, egg shells and paper can take more than 100 years to decompose if left outside.

• If you feel like doing a good deed, carry out litter left by others.

This safety and environmental information comes from the American Medical Association's *Encyclopedia of Medicine*, *A Roadside Guide to Rocky Mountain National Park* by Beatrice Elizabeth Willard and Susan Quimby Foster, *A Climbing Guide to Colorado's Fourteeners* by Walter Borneman and Lyndon Lampert and the *Boulder County Nature Almanac* by Ruth Carol Cushman, Stephen Jones and Jim Knopf. The latter three are excellent resources for detailed information on these areas of Colorado.

Indian Peaks Golf Course
2300 Indian Peaks Tr., Lafayette
• **(303) 666-4706**

Indian Peaks offers nine and 18 holes, a driving range, snack bar and lounge, golf accessories and rentals. Non-resident fees are $18 and $34 every day. Residents pay $18 and $30. The par is 36 or 72, and golf carts cost $14 or $22.

Lake Valley Golf Club
County Rd. 34, north of Boulder
• **(303) 444-2114**

Also in Boulder, this is an 18-hole championship course. Par is 70. After paying the annual dues, members never pay greens fees. Non-members pay $28 weekdays for 9 holes, including a cart and practice balls, or $45 for 18. On weekends and holidays, they pay $33 for 9 holes with a cart and practice balls, $50 for 18 holes.

Sunset Golf Course
1900 Longs Peak Ave., Longmont
• **(303) 776-3122**

Sunset has both nine- and 18-hole options, a pro shop, instruction and rentals. Fees for Longmont residents are $9 for nine holes and $13 for 18 holes (nonresidents pay $11 and $15). Junior and senior weekday rates are $7 and $10 and are the same on weekends after 2 PM ($12 and $16 for nonresidents). The par is 34 and 68 for nine and 18 holes respectively. Golf carts rent for $12 and $20 but are not usually necessary on this layout that's a pleasure to walk.

Twin Peaks Golf Course
1200 Cornell Dr., Longmont
• **(303) 772-1722**

Twin Peaks offers nine and 18 holes, a driving range, pro shop, snack bar and restaurant. Instruction and rentals are available. Residents pay $13 for 9 holes on weekdays and $19 for 18 holes, $1 more on weekends. Nonresidents pay $15 and $20 on weekdays, $2 more on weekends. Before 1 p.m. on Saturday and Sunday, residents can play 9 or 18 holes for $20, nonresidents for $22. The par is 35 for both the front and back nines. Golf carts ($12 and $20) are generally not necessary because it's so flat.

Hiking and Backpacking

If recreation is Boulder's raison d'Etre, then hiking is, perhaps, the biggest raison. Most people moved to Boulder to be near the mountains, and in Boulder trails are literally out your back door. On the toughest trails and even mountaintops you'll also see lean runners in flimsy nylon shorts and singlets, equipped with only water bottles. Don't mind them, they're probably training for the Leadville Trail 100, a 100-mile race through the mountains, or some other event for super-humans (or super-masochists — whichever you prefer).

There are so many places to hike around here, it's hard to know where to begin. But in town, the logical place to start is the mountain parks. Again, for serious hikers, a map is the best bet for choosing the scenic destination, distance and degree of difficulty accordingly. Maps of the mountain parks are available at the many places listed in the "Mountain Parks" section of our Parks and Recreation Centers chapter. Eldorado Canyon State Park south of Boulder (see the Boulder Parks and Recreation Centers chapter) also has spectacular scenery and good hiking trails. Backpacking and overnight camping are not permitted in Boulder's mountain parks, but they are allowed in nearby national forests. See this chapter's "In the Mountains" (to follow) and "Camping" (previous) sections for more on overnight getaways in the wild. Non-residents' cars parked at the Mesa Trail or Gregory Canyon trailheads must have a $15 annual permit or $3 daily permit. For information on the 45 miles of trails in Boulder Mountain Parks, or information on the mountain trails described, which are in Roosevelt National Forest and the Indian Peaks Wilderness, contact the Boulder Ranger District Office, 2995 Baseline Road, Room 110, (303) 441-3408, or the city's info line at (303) 441-4060, ext. 578.

In Boulder

National Center for Atmospheric Research
1850 Table Mesa Dr., Boulder

For a really short hike, but one with a great view and wheelchair accessibility, stroll out behind the National Center for Atmospheric Research (NCAR — pronounced "en-car"), at the west end of Table Mesa Drive (see our Attractions and Area Overview chapters for details on the research center). The Walter Orr Roberts Nature Trail (0.4 miles round trip), named for NCAR's founder, is perfect for those with limited time or who don't want to walk much. It's also wheelchair-accessible. The drive up the NCAR mesa is beautiful, and you're sure to spot some grazing deer along the way. The nature trail is a pleasant ramble along the mesa top with great views and a fine introduction to the local flora, fauna and terrain.

The NCAR building, known as the Mesa Laboratory, was designed by the internationally acclaimed architect I.M. Pei (who also designed new sections of the Louvre in Paris and National Gallery in Washington, D.C.). It's made of Lyons sandstone mixed with concrete to tint it pink and blend with the Flatirons rock formations. The design is reminiscent of Anasazi ruins like those of Mesa Verde in Southwestern Colorado. If it looks familiar, you may be remembering Woody Allen's comedy, "Sleeper," which was filmed partially at NCAR.

Mallory Cave
NCAR Trailhead

There are various options for longer hikes at the NCAR Trailhead — including a connection to Bear Canyon and the Mesa Trail (description to follow). For an interesting longer hike (3.2 miles round trip), look for the Mallory Cave Trail just south of the NCAR Mesa Trail junction and north of Bear Canyon. This area has been extensively used and is undergoing restoration to prevent more erosion. Please observe the trail closures, which are allowing revegetation as well as protecting endangered wildlife nesting areas. This trail weaves through a forest of ponderosa pines, leading to a meadow of yucca and low shrubs. Follow the small trail to a huge lichen-covered boulder at the entrance to a stone "staircase" between the rock slabs. Look for a sign at the fork indicating a left turn for the cave, which has been notoriously hard to find for many hikers. The final approach is a shimmy up a 50-foot, 40-degree (or so) angle rock chimney with plenty

of hand- and footholds, but challenging nonetheless. The cave is shallow, but the vista is grand. At the age of 18, E.C. Mallory rediscovered this cave, which was known by locals but never recorded. Mallory later graduated from the University of Colorado and worked as a miner and eventually a chemist for the USGS. For many years he kept the cave a secret.

Bear Peak
NCAR Trailhead

For a fairly strenuous hike of four to six hours — or more (depending on your conditioning) — climb Bear Peak (8,461 feet). It's 7 miles round trip with an elevation gain of 2,200 feet and many steep sections of trail. But the view from the top is worth it, and if you're there in the early fall, you'll see tens of thousands of ladybugs clinging to the rocks at the summit, where, amazingly enough, they winter in the rock crevices. Don't disturb them as they prepare for their hibernation. They will emerge in spring to mate and lay eggs. There are several routes up Bear Peak. One good way is from the NCAR Trailhead (described previously) to the Mesa Trail (past the large water tank on the hill and then down the hill). Turn left on the Mesa Trail, which descends and joins Bear Canyon Road below. Turn right on the road and look for the Fern Canyon Trail sign, and follow that trail to the summit of Bear Peak. This is the shortest, but steepest, route. Another alternative is the earlier trail turnoff via Bear Canyon, which affords great views to the west. Just below the summit on the Bear Canyon Trail, a sign points to the Fern Canyon Trail to the northeast. Toward the top, the trail becomes quite steep, and some rock scrambling brings hikers to the summit. A nice loop can be made by going up one trail and down the other.

Royal Arch, Enchanted Mesa, McClintock Nature Trail via Mesa Trail
9th St. and Baseline Rd.
(Chautauqua Park)

The Mesa Trail — also a popular running trail — begins just below the Bluebell Shelter at Chautauqua Park and leads 6 miles south to Eldorado Springs, with close-up views of the Flatirons and Front Range and sweeping vistas of the plains. The steep, strenuous 3-

mile (round trip) hike to the Royal Arch from Chautauqua is a local favorite. Access it south of Bluebell Shelter at the end of Bluebell Road in Chautauqua Park. The trail quickly climbs almost 1,500 feet on the slopes of Green Mountain to this natural sandstone arch that offers superb vistas.

An easier trail, and one suited for young children or tired adults, is Enchanted Mesa and the McClintock Nature Trail (2.5 miles round trip). Begin at the picnic shelter next to Chautauqua Auditorium in Chautauqua Park and descend to cross Bluebell Creek and arrive at a fork. Take the right branch that climbs to intersect the Enchanted Mesa Road at an old apple tree. Cross the road and continue uphill along the creek. Look for interesting interpretive signs on the area's natural history. The trail then reaches the Mesa Trail, where you turn left (south) and continue a third of a mile to a large trail intersection. Take the left fork, passing a covered reservoir to reach the Enchanted Mesa Road, which is closed to traffic. Pines and wildflowers invite a picnic on the mesa top, and this gentle trail also makes a nice moonlight hike. Enchanted Mesa Road intersects McClintock Trail at Bluebell Creek, and this makes a return loop to Chautauqua, downhill all the way back.

Gregory Canyon
West on Baseline Rd. (base of Flagstaff Mtn.)

Several fine hikes start in Gregory Canyon at the base of Flagstaff Mountain, where Baseline Road becomes Flagstaff Road. Catch the Flagstaff Mountain Trail (3 miles round trip, 1,100 feet elevation gain) at the mouth of the dirt road into Gregory Canyon, across from the curving Armstrong Bridge. The trail zigzags back and forth across the paved road to the summit of the mountain. Continue upward, past a fork that leads down to Panorama Point. A small parking lot on the south side of the road from the trail marks a popular bouldering (rock-climbing) area including Monkey Wall, Crown Rock, Alamo Rock, Tree Slab and Pebbles. Though many folks drive up, the hike provides a close-up of rock climbers, wildflowers, native shrubs and wildlife. Flagstaff Summit Nature Center is open weekends in summer from 10 AM to 4

PM. Once you reach the top, look for Boy Scout Trail, which leads a short distance west to May's Point and Artist's Point with fantastic views of the Continental Divide. Another trail at Flagstaff summit called Rangeview leads down to Realization Point, also with spectacular views of the Divide, North and South Arapaho peaks, Mount Audubon, Mount Meeker and Longs Peak.

In the Mountains

Called the Snowy Range by the area's first settlers, the spectacular snow-covered mountains just west of Boulder are part of the Indian Peaks Wilderness Area — among them, skyscraping Mount Audubon, North and South Arapaho Peaks, Mount Toll and others. Many soar above 12,000 feet and several above 13,000 feet. This 73,391-acre area west of Boulder contains some of Colorado's best scenery and highest peaks. The wilderness area, so designated in 1978, encompasses parts of Arapaho and Roosevelt national forests. Indian Peaks shares a boundary with Rocky Mountain National Park to the north and Rollins Pass to the south.

Brainard Lake
Past Ward on Colo. Hwy. 72

The U.S. Forest Service trails throughout the Indian Peaks Wilderness Area are interchangeable as hiking, backpacking and cross-country skiing trails. Some of our favorites are in the Brainard Lake area, just past Ward on Colo. 72. Drive up Boulder Canyon to Nederland and head north on Colo. 72; the turnoff is 200 yards past Ward on the left. Or, drive up Left Hand Canyon, north of Boulder past the Greenbriar Inn. Turn left (west) and proceed up the canyon through Ward and on to Colo. 72. Turn right and look immediately to the left for the Brainard turnoff. Brainard Lake is 5 miles up County Road 102.

Two popular hikes at Brainard Lake are Mount Audubon (13,223 feet, 8 miles round trip and 2,750 feet of elevation gain), an arduous all-day climb, or much easier Long Lake, a 3-mile loop around the lake. Once at Brainard Lake, drive past the lake and look for the Long Lake and Mitchell Lake parking areas for these trailheads. Long Lake is a level stroll around this beautiful lake with spectacular views, colorful wildflowers and wheelchair accessibility. Hikes from this area to Mitchell Lake (1 mile, one way), Blue Lake (2.5 miles, one way) and 12,550-foot Pawnee Pass via Lake Isabelle (4.3 miles, one way) are all spectacular and easy to follow (though not all are easy to ascend) on the well-marked trails. Due to the area's great popularity and heavy use, there is now a $3 per vehicle charge, good for five days, or an annual pass available for $15. The fee goes toward protecting the area.

Hessie and Fourth of July Trailheads
County Rd. 130

South of the Brainard Lake area in the Arapaho peaks area you'll find two very popular trailheads: Hessie and Fourth of July, 8 and 12 miles, respectively, west of Nederland. To reach these trailheads from Boulder, drive to Nederland via Boulder Canyon. From the southwest end of Nederland, follow Colo. 72 to the town of Eldora, where County Road 130 begins at the west end of town. So popular are these trails — and with good reason — that it's hard to find a parking place on weekends, so weekday hiking is recommended. The left fork leads to the old town site of Hessie, 1.5 miles west of Eldora, now just an old cabin or two. The short road to Hessie (and the trailhead) is usually under water and not passable by ordinary passenger cars. So park where permitted along the road. Observe the No Parking signs, because they're strictly enforced, and cars are towed. Reach the Fourth of July Trailhead via the right fork of County Road 130.

Lost Lake (Hessie Trailhead)

The 4-mile round-trip hike to Lost Lake is especially nice in the fall with the changing aspen leaves. The trail is a gravely road that climbs through aspen groves. When it sort of levels out for a bit, listen for the roar of water, take a short detour to the left (not marked) and look for a gorgeous series of cascades culminating in a thundering waterfall. Continue on the trail to a junction sign at a bridge. Don't take the Devil's Thumb Bypass Trail; instead, cross the bridge and continue up the left-hand side of the creek past another beautiful falls.

The trail leads to Woodland Flats, a large, open meadow with fine views of Devil's Thumb and the mountains. Don't miss the sign at this point for Lost Lake to the left, another 0.5 miles up to this pretty, wildflower-lined lake and the site of much early mining activity. Reach the Fourth of July Trailhead via the right fork of County Road 130.

Diamond Lake, North and South Arapaho Peaks and Arapaho Pass (Fourth of July Trailhead)

This trailhead leads to spectacular hikes to Diamond Lake, South Arapaho Peak, Arapaho Pass, Fourth of July Mine and Dorothy Lake. Fourth of July trailhead is just north of Hessie via the same road through the town of Eldora. To reach these trailheads from Boulder, again drive to Nederland via Boulder Canyon. From the southwest end of Nederland, follow Colo. 72 to the town of Eldora, where County Road 130 begins at the west end of town. Follow this dirt road to the Hessie fork and take the right branch, which is a very rocky and bumpy 5-mile ride to Buckingham Campground (also called Fourth of July Campground). From the campground, take the right fork up to the parking lot at the trailhead. From the trailhead (10,121 feet) it's a 3-mile climb to Arapaho Pass at 12,061 feet. One mile from the trailhead is a turnoff to Diamond Lake, another 1.3 miles away at 10,960 feet. The Diamond Lake Trail dips down the valley and crosses the North Fork of Middle Boulder Creek. The trail crosses several small streams and continues upward to a big, wet meadow full of wildflowers. A trail junction sign directs hikers to the left for Devil's Thumb Trail and Jasper Lake, but continue going straight for Diamond Lake, which sparkles like the gem for which it was named. By continuing on the Fourth of July Trail (instead of taking the Diamond Lake Trail), hikers reach the Fourth of July Mine at 1.5 miles, a worthwhile destination in itself, with interesting old mining equipment and a great view of Arapaho Pass on the Continental Divide. At the mine, there's the option of turning right and continuing up the Arapaho Glacier Trail to the glacier overlook and on up South Arapaho Peak (13,397 feet and 3.5 miles one way from the start of the trail). North Arapaho Peak (13,502) is another

.75 miles along a connecting ridge with some exposure.

These peaks should be attempted only by strong, experienced climbers with proper equipment getting an early start to avoid the regular afternoon lightning storms. (The rule of thumb in summer is to be off a peak and headed back down by noon.) By continuing straight up the trail at Fourth of July Mine, hikers can reach Arapaho Pass in another 1.5 miles along a barren, rocky old wagon road. Listen for the whistles of marmots and pikas along the way, and look for these appealing, high-altitude critters. Marmots are similar to groundhogs, and pikas are guinea pig-size creatures related to rabbits, not rodents. Arapaho Pass is usually extremely windy, but the view is sublime, looking over the Continental Divide down the western slope to Caribou Lake and Coyote Park. Another short jaunt of .5 miles to the left leads to scenic, snowfield-crowned Dorothy Lake, at a chill 12,061 feet with usually an iceberg or two. Take care to avoid trampling the tiny tundra flowers around the lake — rock hopping is best.

Backpacking

Hiking trails are interchangeable as backpacking trails, but backpackers will need permits to stay overnight in the Indian Peaks Wilderness Area, which includes many of the trails described above. Certain trails are also off limits for backpacking, so check with the District Ranger Office (see subsequent information) before heading for the hills. Following are various trails in the Indian Peaks and elsewhere that offer access to good backpacking destinations. Also, see the preceding "Camping" section for more details. Information on the Indian Peaks Wilderness is available from the U.S. Forest Service Boulder Ranger District (see below under permits). Entire books have been written just on Boulder-area hiking and backpacking trails with detailed descriptions and interesting historical notes; look for them at local mountain sporting goods shops. An especially good book is *Boulder Hiking Trails* by Ruth Carol Cushman and Glenn Cushman. Another good one is *50 Front Range Hiking Trails* (including Rocky Mountain National Park and the Indian Peaks Wilderness Area) by Richard DuMais.

Hikes in Rocky Mountain National Park are described in that chapter of this book.

Golden Gate Canyon State Park
10 miles south of Nederland on Colo. Hwy. 72 • (303) 582-3707

This state park offers many miles of hiking plus backpacking, fishing and camping at lower altitudes than the Indian Peaks Wilderness Area. It's a lovely spot in the fall with the changing colors. (See admission fees in the preceding "Camping" section.)

Indian Peaks Wilderness

There are numerous backpacking options in the Indian Peaks Wilderness. The Arapaho Pass Area begins at the Fourth of July Trailhead (see above under Hiking) and offers many choices on both sides of the Continental Divide. The trail climbs 3 miles to the 11,900-foot pass and drops down on the other side to Caribou Lake, where it continues southwest over Caribou Pass to Columbine Lake. (See directions above under "Hiking"). To reach Fourth of July Trailhead, travel west from Nederland on Colo. 72 to the town of Eldora. County Road 130 begins at the west end of the town of Eldora. The Fourth of July Trailhead is 5 miles farther (take the right fork at the Hessie intersection).

Pawnee Pass (Indian Peaks)

The climb to Pawnee Pass (12,541 feet) starts at Brainard Lake on the extremely popular Isabelle Lake Trailhead, on the right side of Long Lake, but the crowds thin as the going gets rougher and higher. This 4.5-mile hike is quite steep for the last 2 miles. An interesting backpacking loop leads over the pass to Monarch Lake and returns to the east side of the Divide over Arapaho Pass — you'll need two cars or a drop-off and pickup arrangement to complete this one.

Permits and Regulations

You must have a permit to backpack anywhere in the Indian Peaks Wilderness Area. Permits and detailed maps and routes are available at the Boulder District Ranger Station of the U.S. Forest Service, (303) 444-6600 (recorded information line: (303) 541-2519), at 2995 Baseline Road, Room 110. Permits are not required for individual backpackers, but are required for organized groups. Backpacking group size is limited to 12; permits cost $5 for up to 14 nights. Dogs are allowed in Indian Peaks (but not Rocky Mountain National Park), but must be on a 6-foot (maximum), hand-held leash at all times. (There's a $50 fine for violation of the leash law.) It's important to observe this regulation because the great number of hikers with dogs has caused considerable disturbance to wildlife and other hikers, particularly in recent years. Backpacking permits for Indian Peaks are available on weekends (when the Boulder District Ranger Station is closed) at Nederland's Ace Hardware, 20 Lakeview Drive (in the shopping center). National forest maps of Indian Peaks cost $4 ($6 for waterproof) and are also sold at area climbing, hardware and sporting goods stores.

Horseback Riding

What could be more Western than riding a horse? Most stables are out of town a bit, on the plains or in the mountains.

American Wilderness Experience
2820-A Wilderness Pl., Boulder
• (303) 444-2622

American Wilderness Experience (AWE) is the central reservations service of an adventure-travel company of the same name that offers a variety of eco-activities, including horse-pack trips, sea kayaking in Mexico, dog sledding, hiking, biking and rafting.

Old West Dude Ranch Vacations, (800) 444-DUDE (to request catalog), a division of AWE, offers dude ranch vacations throughout the West.

Bradley Stables
1375 N. 111th Ave., Lafayette
• (303) 665-4637

Bradley Stables offers guided rides, lessons and birthday parties and company picnics year-round, at your place or theirs. The hourly rate is $14 per person. Rides are in the Lafayette and Boulder areas. Trail rides in the flatlands east of Lafayette are $19 each. Lessons cost $18 per person for a 90-minute group

(three or more) lesson, $21 for a semiprivate lesson (two people) and $25 for a private lesson.

Gold Lake Mountain Resort and Spa
Peak to Peak Hwy. (Colo. Hwy. 72), just north of Ward • (303) 459-3544

This resort offers hourly trail rides, wagon rides and customized rides. The hourly rate is $25, $40 for two hours; prices vary for customized rides. Cookout breakfast and picnic lunch rides are $10 more than regular rides. Customized dinner rides are available; again, prices vary. A saddlebag lunch ride lasting three hours with a picnic in a meadow overlooking the Continental Divide is $65. The resort is 15.5 miles north of Nederland (a half-mile north of Ward). The superb view of Longs Peak and the delightful gourmet food at Alice's Restaurant make for a great getaway for a day or longer.

The Lazy H Guest Ranch
Colo. Hwy. 7, about a mile south of Allenspark • (303) 447-1388

Lazy H offers a full dude-ranch program in June, July and August and hourly rides in May, September and October. The cost is $1,185 for a week (including horseback riding, meals and children's program), and hourly rides are $18 an hour per person (children and adults).

Peaceful Valley Lodge and Guest Ranch
Peak to Peak Hwy. (Colo. Hwy. 72), 8 miles north of Ward • (303) 747-2881

Peaceful Valley offers non-guest pack trips, breakfast rides and guided trail rides from mid-May through mid-October, based on availability. Hourly rides cost $20 per person. All-inclusive 4-day packages run $766 to $935 and weekly packages (see our Boulder Accommodations chapter) cost $1,270 to $1,535 per adult, double occupancy.

Hunting

Hunting in Boulder County is tricky business, since public land is so fragmented by private property, where permission to hunt is required. Locations, seasons and regulations for particular animals are complicated (too much so to outline here), so it's necessary to get the appropriate information for elk, deer, bear, mountain lion, grouse, rabbit, squirrel, etc. Pamphlets and information are available wherever hunting licenses are sold, such as Gart Brothers Sporting Goods, (303) 449-9021, 3320 28th Street; McGuckin Hardware, (303) 443-1822, 2525 Arapahoe Avenue; Kmart, (303) 443-7850, 3325 28th Street (small game licenses only); and, of course, the Colorado Division of Wildlife, (303) 291-7227, 6060 Broadway in Denver; call (303) 291-7530 for hunter education and (303) 291-7529 for big-game information.

Just to give you an idea of costs, licenses for Colorado residents cost $20.25 for deer and $30.25 for elk; for nonresidents, licenses cost $150.25 for deer and $250.25 for elk. Costs vary according to which animal is being hunted in which season. (25¢ per license sold goes to search-and-rescue services, if necessary, provided by the state.) Fees may increase pending legislation.

In-line Skating

The Boulder Creek Path is the most popular spot for in-line skating, but any of the city's bike paths are good (check our previous "Bicycling" section). Rates to rent in-line skates are around $5 an hour and $15 to $20 a day. You can rent in-line skating equipment at the following shops:

The Bikesmith
2432 Arapahoe Ave., Boulder
• (303) 443-1132

Look for this bike shop in the Arapahoe Village Shopping Center. All types of bicycling and in-line skating equipment and rentals are available.

Boulder Ski Deals
2404 Pearl St., Boulder
• (303) 938-8799

A large selection of ski and in-line skating equipment is available here for rent or purchase.

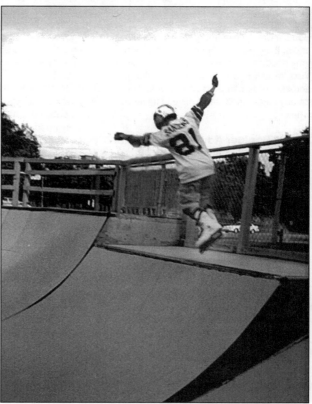

photo: Linda Cornett

Boulder's YMCA spearheaded the effort to provide Boulder's skateboarders a park where they could safely and unharried practice their swooping skills. The skateboard park is next to Scott Carpenter Park on 30th Street, where a graffiti wall has been erected to allow taggers to practice their art legally.

Cutting Edge Sports
2516 Broadway, Boulder
• (303) 413-0228
1387 S. Boulder Rd., Louisville
• (303) 666-4550

Cutting Edge specializes in sales, rental and service on all kinds of bikes, skis and snowboards.

Kayaking, Canoeing and Rafting

Canoeing and kayaking are quite limited in the City of Boulder and mainly done at Boulder Reservoir and Boulder Creek. Boulder kayakers practice at a course set up on Boulder Creek (in memory of an avid kayaker) and at the Reservoir. For extended river trips, they head to the Arkansas River near Buena Vista (a few hours' drive from Boulder), or across the state to Utah and other states. To do any longer trips, you'll have to travel elsewhere.

City of Boulder Adventure Program
East Boulder Community Ctr., 5660 Sioux Dr., Boulder • (303) 441-4401 or (303) 413-7270 (class registration)

The City's Adventure Program offers a variety of river trips plus kayaking and canoeing instruction. Stop by or call for a seasonal schedule of classes and activities.

Boulder Outdoor Center
2510 N. 47th St., Boulder
• (303) 444-8420

An excellent, professional operation dedicated to river preservation, this shop also sells and rents all of the necessary equipment for river outings. Boulder Outdoor Center offers raft trips and resort package trips that include kayaking and canoeing instruction.

Acquired Tastes Inc.
Calls only, no office
• (303) 443-4120 or (800) 888-8582

This reputable Boulder guide service specializes in whitewater excursions on the Arkansas River, with one-, two- and three-day trips available from mid-May through August.

Rugby

Rugby aficionados can contact the Boulder Rugby Club (which currently has no telephone number) through Dave Cunningham at (303) 494-4846.

Running

Anywhere you look in Boulder, you'll see people running. If you're lucky it might be Olympian Frank Shorter, three-time Boston Marathon women's winner Uta Pippig or former world 10K record holder Arturo Barrios. Runners choose just about any location: the Boulder Creek Path (see our Parks chapter), quiet streets through town, the Mesa Trail (see the "Hiking" section in this chapter), various open space trails and even mountains. For more information call the following shops and clubs:

The Boulder Road Runners
P.O. Box 1866, Boulder, CO 80306
• no central phone number

This group offers organized runs and programs for runners of all ages and abilities. For serious runners there are training and running groups and speed workouts; for information, call members Connie Harmon, (303) 499-2061, or Rich Castro, (303) 492-8776.

Runners Roost
1129 Pearl St., Boulder
• (303) 443-9868

Talk to the staff or check the bulletin board at this well-stocked running store for races and running information. Buy shoes, running clothes and other accessories here. (Please refer to our Shopping chapter for more on the Roost.)

Runners Choice
2460 Canyon Blvd. (Village Center near McGuckin's), Boulder • (303) 449-8551

A longtime Boulder running shop, Runners Choice's helpful staff will fit you with shoes or give information on local runs.

Boulder Running Company
2775 Pearl St. (28th and Pearl Sts.), Boulder • (303) 786-9255

This is Boulder's newest running store and

it offers a great selection of running shoes, clothing and other accessories. Talk to the staff about local runs.

Sailing, Sailboarding and Powerboating

With Boulder's capricious chinooks and occasional gale-force winds, sailing and windsurfing can be exciting experiences. The mountains may be our most popular attraction, but water-lovers too can find plenty of places to catch a wave.

Boulder Reservoir
51st St., 1.5 miles north of Jay Rd. via the Diagonal Hwy. (Colo. Hwy. 119)
• (303) 441-3456 (Boathouse)

In the summer sailboats and sailboards can be rented at Boulder Reservoir through the City of Boulder-operated boathouse. The City also offers instruction at Boulder Reservoir. Classes are offered in sailing as well as windsurfing. Daily admission with a sailboard or sailboat (weekdays only) is $15 for city residents, $25 for county residents and $40 for out-of-county residents. For weekends, a season pass is required; cost is $90 for sailboards and for sailboats, $105 for city residents, $175 for county residents and $290 for out-of-county residents. McGuckin Hardware sponsors a wind-conditions hotline at (303) 581-WIND.

Powerboats are permitted at Boulder Reservoir, (303) 441-3468 (administrative office). Admission on weekdays only (Monday through Friday) is $30 for residents and $50 for nonresidents (it's also necessary to have $300,000 watercraft liability insurance). For boats with 49 horsepower or less, admission is $15 for residents and $25 for nonresidents (the same insurance coverage is required). For weekends there are no daily passes; you'll have to purchase a (seven-day) season permit. These cost $165 for city residents, $250 for county residents and $575 for out-of-county residents (for boats with more than 49 horsepower). For boats with less than 49 horsepower, the pass costs $65 for city residents and $100 for both county and out-of-county residents.

Union Reservoir
461 Weld County Rd. 26., Longmont
• (303) 772-1265

Another popular sailing spot (no powerboats) is Union Reservoir. From Boulder, take the Diagonal Highway (Colo. 119) east to Weld County Road 1, and follow the signs. Or, from Longmont take Ninth Avenue east to County Line Road, turn right and follow the signs. The gate fee is $5 on weekends and $4 on weekdays.

Skiing

Since skiing, in all its variations, is so popular with Colorado residents and visitors, we've presented information on the sport in several places in this book. For a brief review, see the subsequent sections. For more information — prices, related activities, lodging — on Ski Country, see our Boulder Attractions and Daytrips chapters.

Downhill skiing

Eldora Mountain Resort
2861 Eldora Ski Rd., Nederland
• (303) 440-8700

It's not Vail or Aspen, but it's only 21 miles from Boulder and there are no mountain passes or giant ski-traffic jams to slow you down. Eldora is a great little ski area right in Boulder County, with nine lifts: three surface, five double chairs and one triple chair. With a top elevation of 10,600 feet, Eldora has 1,400 feet of vertical gain — and beautiful views from the top. You'll probably get more skiing in and less standing in lift lines at Eldora than at the bigger resorts. There's a ski school, rentals, a lodge, races, leagues and even an RTD bus from Boulder that makes numerous daily trips right to the resort.

Other ski areas

Keystone, Loveland, Arapahoe Basin, Breckenridge, Copper Mountain and Winter Park are within a two-hour drive of Boulder (see the "Ski Country" section of our Daytrips and Weekend Getaways chapter). For information on these and other Colorado ski areas, call Colorado Ski Country USA Monday through Friday, (303) 825-SNOW (recorded information) or (303) 837-0793 (administrative office). Discount lift tickets to the aforementioned areas are available at King Soopers and Safeway, among other places.

Rocky Mountain Skiing by Claire Walter, this book's former co-author and contributing editor for *Skiing* magazine, is a great resource book for the entire Rocky Mountain region and is available at local bookstores.

Cross-country skiing

Before you head to the mountains, you can warm up and practice right in Boulder. The Boulder Nordic Club, in cooperation with the Boulder Parks and Recreation Department, sets a nice track around North Boulder Park (Ninth and Dellwood), whenever there's enough snow on the ground. Skiing at the park is free. The Boulder Nordic Club is full of very serious skiers, most of whom compete in the various citizens' races throughout Colorado and beyond. For information about the club, call (303) 530-1253 (no office). Farther away — but still just an hour's drive into the mountains — lie our favorite spots are in the Brainard Lake area: East Portal from Rollinsville (see directions to Rollins Pass Road in this chapter's "Mountain Biking" section), the Hessie and Fourth of July roads at the west end of the town of Eldora and Peaceful Valley (north of Nederland and Ward on Colo. 72). (See the previous "Hiking" section for more directions to these areas.)

The Colorado Mountain Club, (303) 449-1135 (see "Hiking" section), and Flatirons Ski Club, P.O. Box 6120, Boulder 80306 (no official phone number), operate weekly scheduled trips open to the public (membership is eventually expected if you take a number of the trips). They both provide a great way to meet other skiers and explore local ski trails for those new to the area. Ski rentals, books, maps and trail information are available at Mountain Sports, (303) 443-6770; Eastern Mountain Sports, (303) 442-7566; Neptune Mountaineering, (303) 499-8866; Doc's Ski and Sports, (303) 499-0963; Breeze Winter Sport Rentals, (303) 443-9188; and Crystal Ski Rental, (303) 449-7669. (Please refer to this book's Shopping chapter for addresses and other details on these shops.)

Excellent sources for local cross-country skiing are *Peak to Peak Ski Trails of the Colorado Front Range* by Harlan N. Barton and *Backcountry Skiing* by Brian Litz.

For information on snow and avalanche conditions call the U.S. Forest Service hotline, (303) 275-5360.

Eldora Mountain Resort Nordic Center
2861 Eldora Ski Rd., Nederland
• (303) 440-8700

Eldora Mountain Resort's Nordic Center is one of Colorado's largest and most popular cross-country centers, with 45 kilometers of marked and groomed trails. There's a cozy log cabin lodge with refreshments, rentals and lessons. At Eldora, there's also access to the free national forest Jenny Creek Trail. Climb up the Ho-Hum downhill run next to the Little Hawk lift, turn right and look for the trail signs. The trail weaves up and down through the woods and then descends on a narrow trail (which is bad when icy) to the Jenny Creek Road. You can turn around here or follow the creek bed, eventually leading up to Yankee Doodle Lake (9 miles round-trip from the Eldora parking lot). Or, at the Jenny Creek Road, another trail to the right, the Guinn Mountain Trail, leads up a steep, difficult climb to the distant Guinn Mountain cabin (10.5 miles round trip), operated by the Colorado Mountain Club. Skiers can bring camping gear to spend the night; call the subsequently listed CMC number for information.

Brainard Lake

Many national forest summer hiking trails are used for cross-country skiing in the winter.

For absolute beginners who want no hills or spills, the Brainard Lake Road offers nearly level terrain to the lake with no surprises and great scenery. Just follow the road up past the closure — 2.2 miles to the lake.

Left Hand Reservoir at Brainard Lake is more challenging, but the wide trail offers plenty of margin for error. Begin on the south side of the Brainard Road below the gate closure and follow the trail signs up a roadbed

Cross-country skiers enjoy new snow in Chautauqua Park.

Photo: Daily Camera

about 2 miles to the reservoir. There are thrilling downhill runs back on the wide trail.

The Colorado Mountain Club South Trail begins on the south side of Brainard Road 50 yards west of the closure gate and is a bit longer and narrower through wooded areas. Climb a short hill and ski the rolling 2.5 miles to Brainard Lake.

For intermediate to advanced skiers comfortable on narrow, steep hills and turns, there's the Waldrop North Trail, about 5.5 miles round-trip, accessible just north of the closure.

Buchanan Pass Trail begins at the curve on Colo. 72 (5.8 miles north of Ward) at Peaceful Valley. Follow the trail on the north side of the creek west of Camp Dick campground. An 11-mile loop can be made by returning on the Middle St. Vrain four-wheel-drive road (some snowmobiles), but you can ski whatever distance you like.

The Sourdough Trail is 17.5 miles long, but has different segments at various trailheads. From Camp Dick Campground to Beaver Reservoir, it's 2.3 miles. From Beaver Reservoir to Brainard Road, it's 7.4 miles, and from Brainard Road to Rainbow Lakes Road, 7.8 miles. The trail was built mainly for ski touring and mountain biking, and is pleasant rolling terrain though the pines. All accesses to the various connections to the Sourdough Trail are on the Peak to Peak Highway (Colo. 72),

west of Nederland. Camp Dick Campground is on Middle St. Vrain Road, 5.8 miles north of Ward and .5 miles west of Peaceful Valley. One Sourdough Trailhead is on the left-hand side of County Road 96 just east of Beaver Reservoir, 2.5 miles north of Ward and 2 miles west on County Road 96. The Red Rock Trailhead is on the right side of County Road 102, just east of Red Rock Lake, 2.5 miles west on Brainard Lake Road. Another Sourdough Trailhead is on the right side of Rainbow Lakes Road (County Road 116), 4.7 miles south of Ward (7 miles north of Nederland) and .4 miles west on County Road 116.

Snowboarding

All of Colorado's ski areas except Aspen Mountain allow snowboarding, rent the equipment and offer lessons. Snowboards are now generally available for rent at skiing and mountaineering equipment shops, and a whole new genre of snowboard (and skateboard) specialty shops have sprung up to accommodate the popularity of this growing sport. One-day snowboard rentals cost around $20 for the board, boots and bindings on the weekend and $15 during the week. Ask about high-performance equipment. Some shops that rent and demo snowboards include:

• Brothers Boards, 3330 Arapahoe Ave., Boulder, (303) 473-0266.

• University Bicycles, 839 Pearl St., Boulder, (303) 444-4196.

• Boulder Outdoor Center, 2510 N. 47th St., Boulder, (303) 444-8420.

• Twist Snowboard Shop, 1700 Pearl Street, Boulder, (303) 440-6581.

Snowshoeing

The growing popularity of snowshoeing is also evident on all the local trails in winter. One needs no real lessons for this simple sport. Just strap on the snowshoes and start walking. Snowshoes provide the easy ability to leave the crowds on the trails and make your own route — and the cross-country skiers would appreciate it if you did. Snowshoes can be rented at most local mountaineering and ski rental shops (listed in the previous "Skiing" section), at a cost of around $12 a day.

Please note: Snowshoers sharing forest trails with cross-country skiers should make their own tracks, wherever possible, and avoid walking in existing ski tracks. This is because cross-country skis work best in ski tracks and don't work well on snowshoe paths. People without skis or snowshoes should not walk in either tracks — it ruins them both, making it frustrating and miserable for skiers and snowshoers alike.

Soaring and Paragliding

A silent glider ride over the Front Range is an experience of a lifetime. For those who want nothing to stand between them and the great blue sky — other than a chute of sheer nylon — there's paragliding. Local instructors include:

Parasoft Inc. Paragliding School
3232 Redstone Ln., Boulder
• (303) 494-2820

Learn to paraglide at Parasoft, which offers towing — from a truck, paragliders are launched like kites and can fly as much as 135 miles across country out on the plains. Instruction takes place at the north and south ends of Boulder. The school also gives instruction on motorized paragliders (paramotors).

Fly Away Paragliding
Golden • (303) 642-0849

Owner Bill Lawrence, who has competed in two national championships, is a tandem-rated instructor and has been flying for seven years. He originally trained in Switzerland. He runs trips out-of-state but mostly works out of Boulder. His company specializes in pilot training and small classes.

Swimming

Until the really big one hits California and the Pacific Ocean laps the foot of the Rockies, pools and reservoirs are the main swimming options around Boulder. The three City of Boulder-operated recreation centers (see "Recreation Facilities" in our Boulder Parks and Recreation Centers chapter) all have indoor pools. East Boulder Recreation Center has a water slide and Lazy River with innertubes for kids, plus a mushroom waterfall. Outdoor pools are open during summer months only at Scott Carpenter Park and Spruce Pool (also city-operated and in the Parks chapter). Boulder Reservoir's sandy swimming beach helps relieve ocean homesickness a bit (no sharks, only carp).

Eldorado Artesian Springs
Eldorado Springs • (303) 499-1316

Just a few miles south of Boulder in Eldorado Springs, look for the resort in this scenic canyon setting. The pool at the springs of this historic resort offers therapeutic mineral water. The thermal pools and snack bar are open from Memorial Day through Labor Day from 10 AM to 6 PM daily. Rates are $5 for adults, $3 for kids and seniors.

Water World
88th Ave. and Pecos St., Federal Heights
• (303) 427-7873

If you are up for a 30-minute drive, there's a world of water waiting at Water World — a kiddie pool with fountains and slides, a wave pool, massive water slides and a circular Lazy River where you can float peacefully around and around. All-day admission is $19.95

($18.95 for kids under 12, free for tots and seniors 60 and older).

Tennis

Free public tennis courts are usually in great demand and short supply in Boulder. Courts can be reserved for $7.50 for 90 minutes through the city-operated North, South and East Recreation centers, (303) 441-3444, (303) 441-3448 and (303) 441-4400, and the city offers instruction at various levels. The Boulder Tennis Association (no office or address), (303) 449-5984, has tennis ladders and formal and informal tournaments. There's a smattering of free courts around Boulder at various parks and schools including:

• Arapahoe Ridge, 1280 43rd Street (two courts)

• Base Line Middle School, 700 20th Street (two courts)

• Burbank Middle School, 290 Manhattan Drive (four courts)

• Centennial Middle School, 2005 Norwood Avenue (eight courts)

• Fairview High, 1515 Greenbriar Boulevard (eight courts)

• Boulder High, 1604 Arapahoe (three courts)

• Martin Park, 36th Street and Dartmouth Avenue (two courts)

• Chautauqua Park, Ninth Street and Baseline Road (one court)

Spectator Sports

College Sports

Basketball

University of Colorado
Athletic Ticket Office, Folsom Field,
Colorado Ave., Boulder • (303) 492-8337
The women's and men's teams belong to the Big 12 Conference and play home games at the CU Coors Events/Conference Center, Regent Drive in Boulder on the CU campus, capacity 11,198. The regular season runs from December to March. Inividual tickets in 1998

(1999 prices had not been set at press time) were $12 and $8 for reserved seating, depending on location, and $6 for general admission. Students, seniors and children pay half. Call to order tickets, or for season tickets write to the Athletic Ticket Office, Box 372, Boulder, CO 80309.

Football

University of Colorado
Athletic Ticket Office, Folsom Field,
Colorado Ave., Boulder • (303) 492-8337
The Golden Buffaloes belong to the Big 12 Conference in NCAA Division I and play home games at Folsom Field, which seats 51,748. The regular season runs from September through November. For season ticket information call the Athletic Ticket Office, Stadium room 126, (303) 492-8337.

In 1996, the previous Big Eight, of which Colorado was a longtime member, expanded to become the Big 12, adding four teams from the Southwest Conference (the University of Texas, Texas A&M, Baylor and Texas Tech). It's a kind of a super conference like the Southeastern (with 12 teams) conferences. These larger conferences are the current trend in college athletics, primarily to attract a broader-based TV viewing audience (read: as a money-making venture). Unlike the Big Eight, where every team played each other every year, there are two divisions in the Big 12: a north (with Colorado, Nebraska, Missouri, Kansas, Iowa State and Kansas State) and a south (with the four Texas teams plus Oklahoma and Oklahoma State). Each team plays all five opponents in its division plus three from the other division for two years in a row (one year at home, one away). Then, during the next two years, the other three teams in the other division are played. Each team plays eight conference games and three or four games against teams from outside the conference.

Individual game tickets are $36 (the Nebraska game, played here every other year, is $40). Season tickets are available for $220 per seat. Season ticket holders must also contribute $100 to the Golden Buffalo Scholarship Fund. Call the number above for more information.

Volleyball

University of Colorado
Athletic Ticket Office, Folsom Field, Colorado Ave., Boulder • (303) 492-8337

The Buffs belong to the Big 12 Conference and play home games at the CU Coors Events/Conference Center on the CU-Boulder campus. The season runs from September into November. Tickets are $6 for reserved seats, $4 for general admission and $2 for students and children. Call for further ticket information.

Other College Sports

University of Colorado

Other varsity sports teams at CU-Boulder include golf, cross-country, track and field, tennis and skiing, as well as numerous club sports. For information about schedules call (303) 492-7931. For non-varsity club sports, call (303) 492-5471.

Professional Sports

Football

Denver Broncos
Denver Broncos Ticket Office, 1900 Eliot St., Denver • (303) 433-7466

The Broncos belong to the National Football League's American Conference Western Division and play home games at Mile High Stadium, seating capacity 75,103, at 19th and Eliot streets in Denver. The team won consecutive Super Bowls in the late-'90s, making it one of the most popular teams in the Rockies.

The regular season runs from September through December. For ticket information call the listed number. Season tickets are sold out for the foreseeable future, with a waiting list of more than 5,000 names. Single game tickets, if available, are offered the week prior to each game at the Broncos Ticket Office and cost $25 to $56.

Basketball

Denver Nuggets
McNichols Sports Arena, 1635 Clay St., Denver • (303) 893-6700, (303) 893-DUNK for ticket office)

The Nuggets belong to the National Basketball Association's Western Conference and play home games at the Pepsi Center. The regular season runs from November into April. Single game tickets range in price from $10 to $180, season tickets from $441 to $7,560. For season tickets call the listed number or write to 1635 Clay Street, Denver, CO 80204. Some discounts are available.

Ice Hockey

Colorado Avalanche
McNichols Sports Arena, 1635 Clay St., Denver • (303) 893-6700, (303) 575-1900

Yes, Coloradans are nuts about their 1996 Stanley Cup Champions — and rightly so. The Colorado Avalanche (formerly the Quebec Nordiques) belong to the National Hockey League and play home games at the brand new Pepsi Center. The regular season runs from October through April, with the playoffs sometimes lasting into June. Individual tickets cost $20 to $145. Call for more information about ticket prices and game schedules.

Baseball

Colorado Rockies
Coors Field, 2001 Blake St., Denver • (303) 292-0200

The Rockies belong to Major League Baseball's National League West Division and play their home games at the snazzy Coors Field in Denver, seating capacity 50,249. The season runs from April through September. Individual tickets cost $4 to $33. Tickets are available by calling (800) 388-ROCK; for group tickets (25 people or more), and general customer service, call (303) ROCKIES, or write to the Colorado Rockies Baseball Club, P.O. Box 120, Denver, CO 80201.

Soccer

Colorado Rapids
Mile High Stadium, 19th and Eliot Sts., Denver • (303) 299-1599

Members of the new and burgeoning Major League Soccer, the Rapids play home games at Mile High Stadium in Denver, with a seating capacity of 25,000 for soccer. The regular season runs from April to October. Ticket prices range from $12 to $20; tickets are available at Ticketmaster outlets like Foley's department store and Rite-Aid pharmacy. Call for discount and special group rates. Specials include the Family Feast — $49 for four tickets and dinner at the stadium.

Photo: University of Colorado

Sports fans can watch the Colorado Buffaloes in numerous sports throughout the school year.

To keep seeing eagles
flying overhead,
even as these
communities grow, the
citizens of the plains
towns are beginning to
raise more open-space
purchase funds.

Neighborhoods and Nearby Communities

As long as you aren't set on oceanfront property, you just might fall in love with a home in one of Boulder's varied neighborhoods. This chapter is for Looky-Lous who enjoy checking out how other people live. It highlights neighborhoods in Boulder and around the county. Boulder's older (read: pricier) neighborhoods get the spotlight first. We follow with a description of mountain places, then cities on the plains. If you want more practical information on settling down, check our Real Estate chapter.

Historic Boulder Neighborhoods

If you like historic homes the first place to call is Boulder, (303) 444-5192. The organization itself is headquartered in a fanciful turreted gingerbread Victorian at 646 Pearl Street, just a few blocks west of the Pearl Street Mall. From mid-May through September, volunteers lead walking tours of historic areas. The downtown tour starts at 10 AM every Friday. The Mapleton Hill tour starts at 1 PM every Sunday. Both set out from the lobby of the equally historic Hotel Boulderado (enter from 13th Street). The Chautauqua tour meets at the Chautauqua Dining Hall at 10 AM every Sunday (come early and enjoy a wonderful breakfast on the porch). The University Hill tour takes place on the first and third Monday of each month, meeting at

Columbia (Pioneer) Cemetery at Ninth and Pleasant Streets at 10 AM. For a tour of the cemetery itself, meet at the corner at 10 AM on the second Saturday of each month. The tour of the Whittier neighborhood meets at 10 AM every second and fourth Monday in the Hotel Boulderado. Tours cost $4, including a 22-page historic guidebook.

Whittier Historic District

The Whittier Historic District is northeast of the Pearl Street Mall. If you're driving, you may have a first encounter here with the raised pedestrian crossings and traffic circles scattered through Boulder neighborhoods to slow speeders and discourage through traffic in residential areas. The trick with traffic circles is to bear right and yield to other cars and to pedestrians already in the circle.

Many buildings here are as crisp as James Bond's tuxedos, while others are zanier than a television sitcom. *Mork & Mindy's* house, the turreted, gray Victorian at 1619 Pine Street, is a private residence, but you can enjoy it from the sidewalk (the residents lost patience with fame when fans of the show started walking in their front door). At 16th and Spruce streets, a giant owl guards the home of artist Bob Bellows, who creates sculptures from old farm tools. The "feathers" around the owl's beak are spoons. Some homes are painstakingly authentic; others have been altered with abandon. A city policy of "in-fill" development to increase residential density near downtown produced many backyard alley houses in the Whittier neighborhood.

Step inside the Boulder Victoria Bed and Breakfast Inn, then the Hotel Boulderado, catty-corner from each other at 13th and Pine streets, if you like historic interiors. Another to check is the whimsical house at 646 Pearl Street that is now Historic Boulder's home. Among a long line of residents, the Arnett-Fullen house was home to sisters Marion and Ethel Mann, who took their rope twirling expertise to New York City's Vaudeville circuit where they learned a few tricks from fellow performer Will Rogers in the basement of Madison Square Garden. When you visit the gift shop, notice the spiral stairs and other 19th century features.

Mapleton Hill Historic District

Located northwest of Broadway and Pearl Street, Mapleton Hill has both grand old homes and more modest ones. The simple stone house at 1019 Spruce Street is Boulder's oldest surviving house. Mapleton Avenue at the crest of the hill has a distinctive landscaped median, flagstone sidewalks and a canopy of silver maples. Those 100-year-old maples are dear, for this city started as a windblown prairie, and as they age, the city is planting young trees to replace them to maintain the distinctive character of the neighborhood. From stately mansions to just-folks cozies, Mapleton is an eclectic mix of homes. Some have marvelous decorations and superb art. In others, the stereo sits on an orange crate. The area is frequently on Historic Boulder's lavish

fundraising Christmas tour of homes; if you are hoping for a peek inside, that's your best chance.

At the corner of Mapleton and 9th Street is Mapleton Elementary School, the heart of the neighborhood since it opened in 1888. Step inside and check out the photos of student bodies shod in everything from button shoes to Adidas.

www.insiders.com

See this and many other **Insiders' Guide®** destinations online — in their entirety.

Visit us today!

University Hill

This historic area continues to attract many University professors and students. It's walkable from downtown, but keep in mind you're going to put in some distance, uphill. Head south on Ninth Street from Canyon Boulevard, past the grandly conceived and minimally executed sculpture park and cross Boulder Creek and the creek path, where you'll see two interesting buildings. The recently renovated and expanded main Boulder Public Library is on your left, and Highland Office Park, a beautiful renovation of an old school, is on your right. During the '60s and '70s, Highland was the funky home of the Free School, which taught tie-died adult students to throw pots and create stained glass. Today, it's an upscale office building with an old money ambiance. Farther up Ninth Street at Euclid Avenue is an unusual red brick home with the look of a castle, partially obscured by a wood fence. Legend has it two Boulder brothers fell in love with the same woman. They held a house-building contest. The woman chose this octagonal house, which has not a single square room — and the innovative guy who came with it.

Turn left (east) to 1206 Euclid where you'll find the Boulder Museum of History set in a beautifully landscaped park. The museum was built in 1899 as a summer "cottage" for a New

INSIDERS' TIP

Boulder homes show up frequently in decorating and design magazines and in compendiums of fine homes. If you like historic homes, check out *Historic Homes of Boulder County* by Jane Valentine Barker. It sells for less than $30.

A morning glory twines around a stone hitching post in front of a Mapleton Hill home, a charming glimpse into the long history of the downtown neighborhood just north of Pearl Street and west of Broadway.

York stockbroker. If this is a cottage, that New Yorker's regular home must have filled three blocks. It now features a Tiffany window, fascinating snippets of Boulder history and a gift shop. Locals swear the third floor ballroom is periodically frequented by ghostly revelers. One block south, at 12th and Aurora, is the serene white building known as Marpa House. With the look of a foreign embassy, complete with flagpoles, Marpa House is a residence and meditation center for Boulder's Buddhist community.

Three blocks west, at 970 Aurora, is The Academy retirement community, a blend of new and old. The original building on the site was an isolated Catholic girl's school when it was built — the young students fell asleep to the serenade of coyotes and the howl of the unrestrained wind. The building later housed offices and classrooms for the University of Colorado until CU decided to sell. While sitting empty, it lost its roof and upper floors to fire and became a crumbling home to raccoons, squirrels and occasional homeless squatters. In 1998, the building was renovated as the centerpiece of a retirement community aimed at former CU faculty. In this area, you will also encounter sorority and fraternity houses, some stately, some in need of a good spruce-up. To the south, at the northwest corner of 12th Street and Baseline Road is a home designed by local architect Glenn Huntington, whose stately brick buildings set the tone for 1930s University Hill.

Chautauqua Park

Technically, Chautauqua is the name of the historic park and residential area that fills the triangle between Baseline Road, the Flat-

Originally an isolated Catholic girl's school, then a University of Colorado office and classroom building, the Academy at 970 Aurora Ave. on University Hill now houses apartments and bungalows for senior citizens.

irons and a hilly neighborhood of contemporary homes. However, the name Chautauqua has spread to encompass the surrounding neighborhood, as well. In the summertime you can still rent a little old wooden summer cabin at Chautauqua Park, a remnant of the days when Texas school teachers and their families summered in Boulder to escape the heat. Street names honor mountain flowers, such as the daisy-shaped gaillardia and the nodding blue lupine. South of the big Chautauqua auditorium, home to musical and dance concerts and a summer silent movie festival, it's a short hike up Enchanted Mesa. With the purchase of this meadow of grasses and strong-limbed ponderosa pines in the 1960s, Boulder became the first town in the nation to buy open space through a sales-tax bond. Enchanted Mesa is one reason Boulderites can gaze out their windows and see pine forests, rather than houses, in the foothills. Also check the Chautauqua Rangers' Station on Kinnikinick Road, (303) 441-3408, where you can get information on the Boulder Mountain Park system. Displays depict drought-tolerant native plants that thrive in Boulder yards.

Contemporary Boulder Neighborhoods

While you can hoof through Boulder's oldest neighborhoods, you'll probably want to drive to see the newer ones. Many people complain that Boulder is a difficult driving town because it does not always follow a standard grid pattern. If you're lost, remember that if you are facing the mountains, you are facing West. North-south streets are numbered from the mountains, starting with 3rd; Broadway takes the place of 12th Street downtown.

Flagstaff Road

Some of Boulder's most futuristic homes were designed by the late Boulder architect Charles Haertling. The easiest to spot are just up Flagstaff Road. To get there, follow Baseline

Road up Flagstaff Mountain. A tenth of a mile past the fire danger sign is a home of round white towers beside one with sand-colored, pyramidal roofs. These are two of Haertling's 52 creations. Haertling, considered one of America's finest architects, often used drama and fluid forms. If you are ever invited inside a Haertling home, go gladly, for he designed with reverence for Boulder's vistas. If you haven't driven up Flagstaff Road before, by all means, keep going. The panorama of Boulder Valley is gorgeous, and if you've got a map, you can spot most landmarks from up there. If you don't have a Boulder County license plate on your car, you'll have to pay a $3 parking fee at the overlook parking area and elsewhere in the Mountain Parks system. The red roofs you are seeing are the University of Colorado, whose architect imported the red tile roofs of his Italian homeland. The largish bodies of water further to the east are cooling ponds for the coal-fired Valmont Power Plant, where undisturbed fish are said to grow to phenomenal size in the warm water. If you continue up Flagstaff Road past the park boundary, you'll pass widely scattered homes in diverse styles, from one that resembles a French château to monumental log houses.

Return down the mountain to Baseline and turn left on Sixth Street. Then turn left again at Cascade to Willowbrook Road, then left once more. On your right is a white house that some call a spaceship. It's the Volsky house, a 1960s-era Haertling design that earned him a feature in *Life* magazine.

Martin Acres

If you've had your fill of fancy homes, check out Boulder's first tract-home neighborhood, south of Baseline Road, north of Table Mesa Drive and east of Broadway. Most of the homes in Martin Acres were built in 1955, when $13,000 bought a three-bedroom ranch house. They now sell for about 15 times that price, and at that are still among Boulder's most affordable homes. A few droop with neglect, whimpering for someone to fix them up . . . maybe you? Others are so pristine, you can imagine Donna Reed stepping out, finger on chin, to ponder her day's good deeds. The trees are now 40 years old. Some renovations are, well, sort of like a kid's party hat on a businessman. But more and more are enthralling transformations. Martin Acres proves that homes from a plain area, filled with interesting people, add character to a neighborhood. Having said that, there is hope — four decades hence — for some of Boulder's more sterile new subdivisions.

Photo: Daily Camera/Glenn Asakawa

Charles Haertling's Volsky House earned him a feature in *Life* magazine.

Table Mesa

More '70s-vintage, and generally pricier, this is an area of split-levels and raised ranches below the National Center for Atmospheric Research. Table Mesa lies west of Broadway and south of Table Mesa Drive. The Table Mesa Shopping Center is convenient for residents here, as are many mountain trails. The South Boulder Recreation Center on Gillespie Drive butts up against a lovely park encircling what, in the arid West, passes for a lake — Viele Lake. It's an easy, lovely stroll around the lake, particularly if you are fond of geese. One note: don't wear your finest shoes.

If you long for unobstructed views, follow Broadway south to the stoplight at Greenbriar Boulevard. Turn right, and head west past Fairview High School into a neighborhood of earth-toned homes called Shanahan Ridge. Townhomes, condominiums and single-family homes pack the street's north side. The south is open space — a whole valley-full. Residents awaken to meadowlark songs. One of Boulder's finest achievements is leaving open space near residential areas. People pay a premium to live near open, natural areas. Dominating South Boulder is the I.M. Pei-designed National Center for Atmospheric Research. This is one of America's finest public buildings, and in typical Boulder fashion, it is also the gateway to easy and popular nature trails. NCAR is open to the public for free guided tours at noon Monday through Saturday from June to September; winter tours are at noon Mondays and Wednesdays. You can also take a self-guided tour from 8 AM to 5 PM Monday through Friday, 9 AM to 3 PM weekends. The library and cafeteria are also open weekdays. Call (303) 497-1174. To reach it, drive west on Table Mesa Drive and up to the mesa; keep your eyes open for the deer that roam the mesa (and don't forget to rent Woody Allen's *Sleeper* afterward for an I-was-there experience — also check out the Wonderland Hill neighborhood below for another *Sleeper* reference).

Knollwood Neighborhood

This lovely little neighborhood is tucked away so carefully, many longtime Boulder residents don't know it's there. Driving west on Mapleton, cross Fourth Street and find the sign on your left announcing Knollwood Drive. The long building near the entrance, embracing a boulder, is another Haertling home.

Newlands Neighborhood

Ten years ago this now-trendy place to live didn't even have an official name. But the Newland family once owned the land, and what was once just a collection of houses around North Boulder Park is now one of the hottest real estate markets. This neighborhood is west of Broadway from approximately Alpine on the south to Hawthorn Avenue on the north (from Alpine north, east-west street names are pretty much alphabetical). A landscaped island at the intersection of 9th and Evergreen welcomes visitors to the neighborhood. A sculptor resident donated the statue of a crouching, nude woman in the center of the island; his neighbors have had mixed reactions to the public art. Note the bungalows, some original and others spectacular renovations and "scrape-offs," where an owner demolishes the old house and builds a bigger one on the site. There is also a subsidized housing unit in the area but you won't recognize it as such. Approximately 4,899 subsidized units are sprinkled around Boulder, in small, unobtrusive pockets, often close to Boulder's trendiest areas.

Pine Brook Hills

Some of Boulder's grandest modern homes can be found on Linden Avenue in what is called Pine Brook Hills. Back on Broadway, go north past Iris Avenue and turn left (west, toward the mountains) on Linden. These grandiose designer homes can't be missed as many are perched on hillsides with commanding views. Up Linden Avenue is South Cedar Brook Road, and at its very top are the last two homes Haertling designed before he succumbed to cancer in his 50s. You can probably find these homes yourself, but here's a clue. One is round and white. The other's roof mimics an aspen leaf, gently curling upward in the wind.

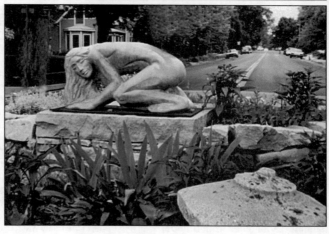

photo: Linda Cornett

Perched in a traffic circle at 9th and Evergreen in north Boulder, this marble statue of a nude woman serves as a somewhat controversial welcome to the Newland neighborhood.

Wonderland Hills

This area was Boulder's first planned multi-unit development and its sense of neighborhood is often appealing to newcomers. To reach the entrance, return to Broadway, going north again, to Poplar Avenue and Wonderland Hills. Several bike paths wind through the neighborhood. In landscaped areas, weeping crab apples, native red-twig dogwood and evergreens make homes seem more secluded than in many areas with much larger yards. Within a two-minute walk of the smallest condo are Boulder-style mansions. Did you spot the white "barnacle" house also featured in Woody Allen's futuristic film, *Sleeper*? It's another Haertling home.

Also clinging to this hillside is the huge structure referred to as "the volcano house." Innocuous on the outside, the bizarre home indulges it's owner's childhood fantasies, from a faux volcano with on-command eruptions into bubbling hot tubs to a fireman's pole connecting the living room with the downstairs

foyer. There's even a mini-movie theater where every seat is a lounger. The owner has been generous about sharing the ambiance with civic groups holding fundraisers, so do good and you may get a chance to try out the "snow room" — walls painted with snow scenes and a snow-maker to shower you with the white stuff in the dead of summer.

Go anywhere you want now, and you'll find a new neighborhood. This "point of interest" tour has focused on the older side of Boulder. East of Broadway are many more homes, generally less than 20 years old and more affordable. Dakota Ridge, north of Wonderland Hill, appeals to young families looking for a newly built home. These new areas are ripe for homeowners eager to add their style to a highly creative town.

Mountain Towns

To get an overview of mountain living, take Canyon Boulevard west out of town and head up Boulder Canyon. Turnoffs to Four Mile Canyon, Magnolia Road and Sugarloaf Road lead to more areas containing mountain homes of various styles. If you continue 17 miles up the canyon, you will reach Nederland and the Peak-to-Peak Highway (Colo. 72), which leads to other mountain communities. Most of them are along this scenic highway, made up of Colo. Highways 119, 72 and 7. These paved roads are beautiful all year, from the sparkling pine-scented days of summer to the shimmering golden world of an aspen grove in fall to a crisp winter day softened with a comforter of snow. These scenic roads can be steep and curvy, so keep your lower gears in tune and don't let the occasional commuter in a hurry rush you along as the views along the way worth the time. Not all mountain towns are listed here, so keep your eyes open to discover one on your own.

Allenspark

8,250 feet • pop. 800 (winter), 3,000 (summer) • 32 miles from Boulder

Founded by Alonzo N. Allen as a mining town, Allenspark was once a stagecoach stop between Ward and Estes Park. Today, Allenspark is a peaceful retirement and vacation community nestled in pine forests on the eastern edge of Rocky Mountain National Park. The style tends to rustic cabins and barns full of trail horses. It has a volunteer fire department, a post office and offers lodges, cabins and restaurants. The Fawn Brook Inn, (303) 747-2556, is a fine dining spot, worth the drive from Boulder. Its hours vary according to the season, so call ahead. To reach Allenspark, go to Ward and Nederland and head north on the Peak-to-Peak Highway (Colo. 72). From Lyons, take Colo. 7.

Eldorado Springs

5,760 feet • pop. 650
• 15 miles from Boulder

This is the closest "mountain" community to Boulder. The gold in these hills comes from the orange and yellow lichens that color the walls of Eldorado Canyon State Park, one of the nation's premier rock-climbing areas. The springs area was winter home for a Ute Indian tribe. In the early 1900s, these same springs sustained a 40-room resort. Trombone player Glenn Miller used to leave studies at CU to play with the Eldorado Springs resort band. Sweet-faced movie star Mary Pickford was a visitor and soon-to-be-president Dwight Eisenhower and his bride Mamie vacationed

here. A quarry once yielded Eldorado Canyon's beautiful red rock. It has closed, but that mining scar remains, a reminder of the trade-offs between promoting industry and natural grandeur.

To see Eldorado Springs, drive south on Broadway. Three miles past Table Mesa Drive, turn west on Colo. 170. After 3 more miles, you'll meet a riffraff of cabins, precariously balanced along a steep mountain stream. Welcome to the bumpy dirt roads that some residents say add character and discourage tourists. Welcome to a town like Li'l Abner's Dogpatch, Colorado, yuppie-style, of course.

Most Eldorado Springs residents are romance-smitten commuters. You can see their influence in the flowers that wink in rock gardens, in the misty wash of rainbow colors on a potter's garage, the blue cow bells cascading near a shake-shingle entry. Drive past the pool and head over the rutted wooden trestles of that one-way bridge. Near a handsome stone lodge called, "The House the Jack Built," do you see the pink trailer home? You took the wrong fork. Go back to the caramel-colored chalet called "L'il' Abner," past the '50s-style, minty green place named "Jitterbug" and by that upscale cottage called "Chelsea Morning." The owner of "Chelsea Morning" recalls how, when she first saw the cabin, she thought, "If my soul could speak, this is where it would want to live." Now along with her husband and young kids, she loves sitting out on their deck, listening to rustling tree leaves and the babbling mountain stream.

Eldorado Springs pool, fed by underground springs, is a favorite summer swimming hole, the warm water delivered from more than a mile below. The springs also provide clear Eldorado Artesian Springs water, available for home delivery or in local grocery stores.

Jamestown

7,000 feet • pop. 277
• 18 miles from Boulder

Gold, silver and fluorspar once brought 10,000 miners to "Jimtown," a town whose name was later "upgraded." Douglas Fairbanks Sr. was born in this shady town. The Jamestown Mercantile Building is a classic false-front store from the mining-town days. The town hall, (303) 449-1806, is open Monday mornings and all day Tuesday. There's a public elementary school and plenty of family values in town, including a desire to keep the children safe. So watch for the speed bumps as you enter and leave. Jamestown is northwest of Boulder. Take U.S. Highway 36 to Left Hand Canyon, turning into the mountains and, at the big fork, jogging right.

Lyons
5,375 feet • pop. 1,227
• 17 miles from Boulder

The red sandstone around Lyons has been the source of much quarry rock, locally called flagstone. Fifteen sandstone buildings, including the Old Stone Congregational Church, are in Lyons' historical district. This dark-brown flagstone church, square with a short steeple, is just north of Main Street, on High Street. The quarries that provided the stone for these buildings still operate around Lyons and are excellent choices if you want flagstone for your patio, classic Colorado stones for your home or beautiful boulders for your garden. Lyons itself has a small-town atmosphere, with cottonwood trees shading the sparkling St. Vrain River, towering blue spruce trees standing beside turn-of-the-century bungalows and plenty of pretty contemporary homes. Vacation cabins and high-tech companies are here plus many good restaurants and antique shops, some decorated to give a Germanic/Slavic feel to the shopping areas.

Bring your swimsuit and make time to visit Meadow Park on the town's western edge; here the St. Vrain accommodates swimmers with an excellent swimmin' hole with overhanging rocks perfect for cannonballing. There are also baseball diamonds, playgrounds, and lots of places to climb, hike and picnic.

The prettiest way to reach Lyons is to take 28th Street or Broadway north from Boulder — the two converge into US 36. The route winds beside the foothills and less than 20 miles from Boulder it deadends into Colo. 66. Turn left here, pass roadside shops and eating places and you're in Lyons, population 1,466. The Town Hall, (303) 823-6622 or (303) 443-3956, is at 432 Fifth Avenue.

Nederland
8,236 feet • pop. 1,750
• 16 miles from Boulder

Nineteen miles up Canyon Boulevard, just past the big blue lake formed by Barker Dam is Nederland, the largest mountain town near Boulder. Here, the aspen trees shimmer next to pretty plots of colorful mountain flowers during the summer, with mountainsides of pine trees and aspen in every direction. Nederland has a good mix of shopping, tourist-oriented businesses and basic services. In fact, you can stretch that "basic services" to include a Laundromat, a video shop, doctors, dentists and vets in a friendly, easygoing community that includes mountain people who wanted to be close to high alpine fields, hippies who came here decades ago to found communes, New Age yuppies and Boulder intellectuals who retreated from the city below. All this makes for an eclectic, worldly, remote but close-enough-to-it-all mountain town. If you want some fun reading about Nederland history, find a copy of local author Marlys Millhiser's *The Mirror*. This fantasy novel describes a Boulder woman who trades places in time with her Nederland grandmother, then discovers the rigors of being a miner's wife, the challenges of driving a wagon team up a treacherous dirt canyon road, and the red light district that even tiny Nederland supported.

Near Nederland are the Indian Peaks Wilderness and the Eldora Mountain Resort, with its downhill and cross-country skiing. Kids love Nederland's local rock store, Nature's Own of Nederland, and the picture of the fierce predatory rabbit at Renee's Bakery. The shops are comfortably close together, picturesque and easy to amble through. It's worth the trip just to hang out at the Acoustic Coffee Shop (see our Nightlife chapter), and Annie's is a good neighborhood restaurant (see Restaurants). All this means that Nederland has settled, by fits and bounds, into the intriguing community its beginnings hinted. Originally a gold-, silver- and tungsten-mining area, Nederland had more than 3,500 residents at the height of the mining boom in 1874. Today, gambling in Blackhawk and Central City, south on Peak-to-Peak Highway, plus Boulder's spillover prosperity, have fueled Nederland's latest boom.

Many residents work in Boulder or elsewhere in the "lowlands" to the east.

Summer events usually include a Kinetic Wind Festival (see our Festivals and Annual Events chapter), a Native American Pow Wow, and a replay of the pioneer days. Check in at the Visitors' Center, on West First Street, where the RTD bus stops. Across from the Visitors' Center is Town Hall, (303) 258-3266.

Pinecliffe

7,960 feet • pop. 475 (winter) 525 (summer) • 20 miles from Boulder

Retired miners and nature lovers live in this enclave southeast of Nederland on Colo. 72. Some are upscale commuters, and some people live "off the grid." That means they're in homes without power, water or sewage hookups. "Off the grid" can mean rough-hewn cabins or a high-tech home complete with photovoltaic cells to provide solar electricity and heat.

Ward

9,253 feet • pop. 166 • 23 miles from Boulder

An 1890s gold strike brought 4,000 people to this greatest gold camp of northern Colorado. Ward merits a footnote to Colorado history, for this is where silver baron (and briefly U.S. Senator) Horace Tabor served as a postmaster toward the end of his life, which he passed in unaccustomed poverty. By 1930, the mines died out, and only three residents stayed behind. Hippies arrived in the 1960s, and many of them have never left; persistent rumors put heiress Patti Hearst in a commune near Ward when she was on the run with the SLA. It's still a place of shaggy hair and beards to match, fringed vests and love beads. On weekends, intrepid Lycra-clad bicyclists perch outside the general store, with great pride, sucking up cold mineral water and swapping stories about their 23-mile ride from Boulder to reach the hilly streets of Ward. Tourists gaze at the rustic buildings, their colors as faded as sand-washed jeans, within the thick mountain forests. The old Ward School, now the town hall and post office, is typical of wood-framed rural schoolhouses.

Ward has an honor-system public library and a general store. The Millsite Inn (see our Restaurants chapter) sits above town on the Peak-to-Peak Highway (Colo. 72), about 8 miles north of Nederland. The beautiful alpine hiking area around Brainard Lake is just west of Ward.

Towns of the Plains

All the towns around Boulder have modern 'burbs, fed by a series of building booms since the 1960s. Here you'll find Boulder County's more affordable housing. Although these towns are more development-friendly and growth-oriented than Boulder, they are beginning to pay more attention to such quality-of-life enhancements as open space. The prosperity of these plains towns is evident in their golf-course competitions and swimming-pool wars. Actually, these aren't wars, but they reflect a trend toward family-oriented community centers. New or remodeled recreation centers have opened in Louisville, Lafayette and Broomfield, and Longmont is still making plans to renovate its center. The water slides and Lazy River pools for kids are great attractions.

Stunned by the rate of growth in their towns, east county residents have been increasingly insistent that natural areas be preserved. To keep seeing eagles flying overhead, even as these communities grow, their citizens are beginning to raise more open-space purchase funds. It might not happen in time to save all the favorite local nature walks, but sentiment is growing to preserve more.

These communities offer many personalities. Rock Creek is nothing but brand-new homes, a huge growth on the side of tiny, historic Superior. Other towns are as old as Boulder, complete with traditional downtowns and beautiful Victorian neighborhoods. Lafayette, Louisville and Longmont offer the contrast between modern developments and older parts of town, known for their quaint atmosphere and lovely trees.

Broomfield

5,200 feet • pop. 37,000 • 8 miles from Boulder

When the Pony Express needed to get overland mail from Julesburg, Scottsbluff or Fort Laramie to Denver, Colorado's Territorial Capital, carriers changed horses at Broomfield.

Travel gave the farming town fame again in 1952, when Broomfield became the site of a toll station on the new Boulder/Denver Turnpike (now known as U.S. 36). The road was especially popular during Saturday CU-Boulder football games. In 1967, it became the nation's first toll road to pay for itself, approximately 13 years ahead of schedule. The Broomfield tollbooth operators had a special friend, a black-and-white dog they named Shep. For more than a dozen years, Shep watched each driver pay 10¢ to stop at Broomfield and 25¢ for the 8-mile drive on to Boulder. His tombstone, near U.S. 36, reads, "Shep. Part Shepherd, Mostly Affection."

Today, residential construction is phenomenal and more businesses are settling in Broomfield around the renovated and expanding central retail center. Southeast of Broomfield is the campus-like Interlocken high-tech office park. The park is home to the Colorado campus for Sun Microsystems, which will incorporate more than a million square feet when completed, and it will house the 800,000-square-foot national headquarters of Level 3. The park is wired with fiberoptic cables to keep the high-tech tenants connected to the world. Interlocken is zoned for at least 25 percent open space including wetlands and natural grasses plus a golf course next to a hotel.

Many of Broomfield's workers commute to Denver and Boulder — the RTD Park-n-Ride facility south of town is the biggest in the Denver/Boulder area. As Boomfield, oops Broomfield, grows it is developing a plan that many hope will preserve open space within the city. A popular bumper sticker reads, "Keep the Field in Broomfield." The Bay, Broomfield's outdoor aquatic park, attracts bathers from around the region. For more information on this growing community, contact the Broomfield Chamber of Commerce, (303) 466-1775, at 741 Burbank Street.

Erie
5,020 feet • pop. 5,000
• 8 miles from Boulder

The town was first settled around 1867 by a Methodist pastor who named it after his hometown of Erie, Penn. Like its namesake, Colorado's Erie is a former coal town. An area of tilled farm fields and new subdivisions, Erie is the site of the 119-acre Tri-County Airport. Some homes near the airport have hangars and taxiways to the airport in their backyards, mirroring the garages and driveways they have in the front. Its current major industries are landfills and junkyards near town. Sound boring? This is Boulder County, remember! Blake's Small Car Salvage has been on national television for being one of the prettiest junkyards around. And a nearby business, Construction Recycling, recycles over 80 percent of the building scraps it receives; see our Boulder Shopping chapter for more details on these two spots.

As housing prices push residential development east from Boulder to Lafayette and Louisville to Superior, Erie is beginning to feel the ripple. The traditionally blue-collar town with dirt streets and funky old homes is beginning to spruce up to welcome newcomers and their tax dollars.

You can reach Erie by taking Arapahoe Road east out of Boulder past U.S. Highway 287. You'll be on a dirt road for a while, which dead-ends. Turn left (north). Go about 1.5 miles and you're in Erie. See the woodworking factory? It welcomes visitors. The Town Hall, (303) 926-2700, is at Lincoln School, 645 Holbrook Street.

Gunbarrel
5,145 feet • pop. 9,006
• 7 miles from Boulder

Great mountain views and fancy homes around a golf course/country club are hallmarks of this large neighborhood of subdivisions. It was first developed in 1963 as a 558-acre subdivision to house the employees of a huge IBM plant across the Diagonal Highway. With Big Blue cutting back on its staff and other high tech firms moving into the area, Gunbarrel has developed into a more varied community.

The commercial part of Gunbarrel, which includes Celestial Seasonings, IBM and Valleylab and a small shopping center, is part of the city of Boulder. Much of the residential area is in unincorporated Boulder County. Even though the City of Boulder has offered to annex twice, residents prefer the autonomy of being in the county.

Take the Diagonal Highway (Colo. 119)

north toward Longmont. Just out of Boulder, turn right on Jay Road. Keep going. To see the fancy houses, turn left on a street such as Carter Road. To get deeper into Gunbarrel, continue on the Diagonal to 63rd Street and turn right (south). The homes and enterprises of Gunbarrel are both to your right and left. The Boulder Country Club, with a golf course backing up against the yards of dozens of homes, is in the heart of Gunbarrel Greens, south off of Lookout Road. Sorry, members only.

Hygiene
5,100 feet • pop. 265
• 14 miles from Boulder

In the 1880s, farmers battled grasshopper plagues and other woes to settle this fertile area. The town earned its name when people suffering from tuberculosis moved to a local sanitarium called Hygiene House. Fresh air and sunshine revived many, as the elements still do today. Hygiene is about a mile west of Longmont in an area full of towering old cottonwoods, Siberian elms, ancient lilac hedges and farm homes with horses mowing the grass. It's at the intersection of North 75th Street and Hygiene Road. A local hangout is Clark's Food Store, the little shop with a rickety, tilting porch awning that hangs like half-closed eyelashes above the front door. Here's a town where the neighbors know each other, so if you decide to hang out for a while, you can be sure they'll talk about you.

Lafayette
5,260 feet • pop. 21,000
• 11 miles from Boulder

Lafayette Miller ran a farm, a stagecoach and a hotel. After he died, Mary Miller discovered coal on their homestead. In 1890, she named a new town after her husband. Coal and farming were the main industries for 50 years. Today, the town is a burgeoning residential community for the high-tech industry and brand-new home tracts, green patches of lawn and hopeful baby trees. To reach Lafayette, head 11 miles east, on either Baseline Road or South Boulder Road through Louisville.

"Old Town" Lafayette has its tidy little bungalows and big street trees. Efrain's is a good Mexican restaurant (see our Restaurants chapter). The city offices, (303) 665-5588, are at 1290 South Public Road, the northeast corner of "Four Corners," a new business district at the intersection of US 287 and South Boulder Road. The Lafayette Chamber of Commerce, (303) 666-9555, is in the old historic district at 309 South Public Road.

Local sentiment favors keeping small-town charm even as affordable and upscale subdivisions boom. There's a move to protect favorite open areas such as Waneka Lake, where people can paddle rented canoes to a blue heron's marshy shallows. You can find a map of these places at the recreation center on 111 West Baseline Road, (303) 665-0469.

The YMCA of Boulder Valley has opened a 55,000-square-foot complex including an ice skating rink, fitness center, gymnasium, indoor running track and other facilities on Arapahoe Road and 95th Street to entertain the burgeoning population. Some residents would like Lafayette to grow no larger than 25,000 people, following the boom-and-balk pattern of Boulder. The population now stands at 21,000. The Indian Peaks Golf Course is within city limits. Several festivals occur in Lafayette each year, including a Loyalty Parade in May and Lafayette Days in the fall; see our Festivals and Annual Events chapter for details.

Lafayette is home to a community of Hmong families, refugees from Laos. It also has one of the nation's few co-housing communities, the Nyland Community Association, (303) 494-2778. It features 42 passive-solar homes built around a common area and the "community house" with guest rooms, activity rooms, a child-care center and dining hall open to residents who don't want to cook evening meals in their homes. Cars are parked outside the community. Only pedestrians are allowed inside.

INSIDERS' TIP

Open space for enjoying nature has proved to be one of the finest assets of Boulder County's communities.

Longmont
4,979 feet • pop. 62,785
• 12 miles from Boulder

Longmont, named after Longs Peak, which in turn was named after Major Stephen Long, started as a 30,000-acre farming community and sugar beet center. The city celebrated its 125th anniversary in 1996. It is the county's second-largest town and is sometimes called Boulder's twin. Sure enough, it offers many services similar to Boulder's, including a hospital, school district, daily newspaper, branch of the County Clerk's Office, state Motor Vehicle Division office and other services. But these twins are not identical. For one thing, Longmont's kind of modest about how pretty it is, and publicity for local events is often low-key. For another, the two towns come from opposite ends of the political spectrum.

From the old Main Street shopping district to the Boulder County Fairgrounds at 9595 Nelson Road, which hosts dog shows, antique shows and the Boulder County Fair in August (see our Festivals and Annual Events chapter), Longmont retains a conservative farming-town hospitality even as it grows and grows. With the exception of far larger Boulder, more homes were sold in Longmont during the first half of 1996 than in any other town in the county, and sometimes it seems that the fields surrounding the town have been planted with house seeds instead of grain. This house crop is sprouting overnight, with townhouses here, single-family homes there and a naked, surprised look to many of these late 20th-century homesteads, as they wait for the saplings in their front yards to catch up and shade their peaked roofs.

To reach Longmont from Boulder, head northeast on Colo. 119 (also called the Diagonal Highway or just the Diagonal for short). Except during rush hour, it's about a 20-minute drive.

To get a feeling for the Victorian houses and tree-canopied streets near Main and Third, check the Callahan House. New houses are in developments all around town. Municipal offices, (303) 776-6050, are at the Civic Center, at Third Avenue and Kimbark Street. The Longmont Chamber of Commerce, (303) 776-5295, is at 528 Main Street.

Louisville
5,350 feet • pop. 19,500
• 11 miles from Boulder

Louis Nawatny founded this town in 1878, after discovering coal 200 feet below a settler's farm. Twelve mines eventually thrived in Louisville, providing high wages for sometimes-dangerous work. In the early 1900s, labor organizer Mother Jones spoke to coal miners in the town. During this time, European miners, who occasionally worked as strikebreakers, came to town. Today, the town takes pride in ethnic, family-style restaurants. Italian eateries include The Blue Parrot and Colacci's, in the Main Street area of Old Town Louisville. The downtown area also has Asian restaurants, Karen's Country Kitchen, The Old Louisville Inn and a host of little shops.

Like Lafayette, Louisville is a coal-mining town that has transformed itself into the epitome of a modern suburb. Two of Boulder County's largest employers, Storage Technology and Neodata, are based here as is the Centura Avista Adventist Hospital, specializing in maternity and neonatal care. The Coal Creek Golf Course was listed by *Golf Digest* magazine as one of the top 25 new golf courses in 1990. When the golf course first went in, next to U.S. Highway 36, there was concern that errant golf balls would hit cars, but it has not been a problem. The highway interchange is booming, with Louisville's first modern hotels, small shops and huge chain outlets, 12-plex theater and practically every chain restaurant you can imagine popping up.

Louisville's population has more than tripled to 19,500 since the 1970s, one of Colorado's fastest growing communities, but the goal is now to stabilize the population around 25,000 and put some effort into preserving open spaces. Newcomers here are legion, and the Community Newcomers Club, (303) 665-9011, meets monthly at Karen's in the Country. Most of the population growth has come from young families, with young kids galore. Still, Louisville strives to maintain small-town charm with events such as a Fourth of July Community Picnic and a Labor Day food celebration (see our Festivals and Annual Events chapter).

Louisville's city offices, (303) 666-6565, are at 749 Main Street. The Louisville Chamber of Commerce, (303) 666-5747, is at 901 Main Street.

Niwot
5,095 feet • pop. 3,700
• 5 miles from Boulder

The unincorporated town is named after Chief Niwot, whose name means "left hand" in the Arapaho language. The original downtown, which was comprised of supply shops

and a school for local farmers, is now filled with antique shops, and surrounded by brand-new housing developments. The old town center also boasts the Niwot Auction, a big bimonthly mecca for antique hounds, and an annual auction festival in the summer. Rev. Taylor's Country Restaurant is a popular hangout.

Niwotians like their left-handed town, leading to Left-Hand Turn, a store for lefties and creative types; Lefty's Pizza Parlor; and the Left Hand Grange. Sometimes Pete Wernick and his Live 5 band rent the Grange Hall for bluegrass concerts. Well, maybe retro-Dixieland is a better description of their music, played on a banjo, bass guitar, drums, clarinet and vibraphone. It's an informal affair on folding chairs, with kids selling cookies during intermission. But the music is excellent — many band members have performed with world-famous Doc Watson.

To reach Niwot, take the Diagonal Highway (Colo. 119) north toward Longmont. One mile after IBM is Niwot Road. Hang a right, and you're there. It's about a 10- to 15-minute drive from Boulder.

Superior
5,400 feet • pop. 6,500 • 9 miles from Boulder

The coal mine closed in 1945 and Superior languished with a rural and remote flavor that belied its location just off the busy highway between Denver and Boulder. But it languishes no more. Superior is in a new boom now because of Rock Creek, a massive development on land annexed by Superior in 1987 and given water rights in 1990. Rock Creek sprawls across more than 3 square miles of rolling grassland. By 2010, it could eventually include up to 8,000 homes and 15 million square feet of commercial space, extending east along U.S. Highway 36 all the way to the Interlocken Office Park at Broomfield and south to Colo. 128. Some large homes stand beside the meticulously landscaped, new wide boulevards, decorated with statuary and leading to tennis courts and a swimming pool. There are also townhomes and an abundance of smaller single-family homes on more modest lots.

Despite the town's fast growth and population of 6,500, the Colorado Department of Highways forgot to show it on their 1994 map. Maybe that's because in the 1990 census, only 208 people lived in Superior. The town is still catching up with much of this growth. Until 1999, Rock Creek's only commercial development was two gas stations. Now, graders are kicking up dust for a discount superstore, grocery, car dealership and other businesses. The Superior Elementary School opened in the fall of 1996, and until then, children were bused to schools in neighboring communities. In 2000, thanks to a bond issue approved by voters, a new school for kindergarten through eighth grade will open in Superior and another in neighboring Louisville. A new high school for the plains towns opened in 1997. The town hall, (303) 499-3675, at 24 E. Coal Creek Drive, is a good information place, as are Rock Creek's real estate offices and show houses. Superior is just south of the Superior/Louisville interchange on US 36.

Real Estate

Colorado generally and Boulder specifically have been among the hottest housing markets in the nation. For a while, the housing market was so hot that Boulder home buyers had a half-hour to run through a home, then sign up before the next buyers beat them to it. Since the fall of 1994, the sizzle has cooled to a normal simmer. People were calling the summer of 1995 "a buyer's market," but now refer to the market as "balanced." That means there are still plenty of buyers and sellers, but sales are slightly slower because buyers can afford to be more discriminating. Prices have leveled off in Boulder, but they have increased dramatically in other county towns — notably Lafayette, Longmont and the mountain towns. For example, some homes on Lafayette's Indian Peaks Golf Course sold for $125,000 a few years ago. The average sale price for a new home in Lafayette by mid-1999 was $365,000. While prices continue to rise in surrounding communities, home buyers have a better inventory from which to select the home of their dreams.

This chapter provides a glimpse of home prices in Boulder County, rental prices and bargain-hunting tips. It gives ideas on what to look for in a Boulder home and neighborhood, and it ends with real estate resources. If you're looking for a Boulder home, happy hunting!

The Homebuyer's Market

Boulder Realtors don't complain that the buying and selling frenzy of the early '90s is over. They say a more "sane" market is better for everyone. But while it's true that prices have leveled off and even eroded slightly, it is still expensive to live in Boulder. Due to strict growth controls few new homes sell in Boulder each month. That means most are single family resales with an average price through April 1999 of $290,000. The majority of new homes are now built in Erie, Lafayette, Longmont and Superior. Nonetheless Boulder is still home to the highest priced homes including the one sold in April 1999 for $1,625,000. Total new home sales in the county were up 12 percent from April '98 to April '99. In addition, the median new home price was up 28 percent during the same period while the median price of resold homes was up a slight 4 percent.

Boulder's Newlands Neighborhood has been "the place to live" the last few years but a 650-square-foot fixer-upper can start at $250,000. If you're willing to live in south Boulder, however, $300,000 will buy a 30-year-old, 2,000-square-foot home with five bedrooms, three baths and a full basement. As the saying goes, it's all relative. Boulder encompasses a wide range of houses and housing styles, from historic cottages, between-the-world-wars Tudor mansions, postwar ranch houses and new subdivisions with contemporary homes. But no matter what you buy, it will cost you. According to the Boulder Chamber of Commerce, a home in Boulder is 44 percent more expensive than the rest of the nation.

Quality of life, the cachet of a Boulder address and the Danish Plan are what have driven local house prices into the stratosphere. Boulder was one of the first cities in the nation to adopt a residential growth-control ordinance (called the Danish Plan after City Councilman Paul Danish), which limits the number of permits for new construction that are issued annually. The law of supply and demand is in effect in Boulder, and with limited new construction coupled with a strong economy, property values have soared, and the issue of "affordable housing" has become a community hot button.

Housing costs considerably less in Boulder County's other communities. During the first half of 1999, the average single-family price for a new home was roughly $273,000 in Louisville, $366,000 in Lafayette, $238,000 in Longmont, $221,000 in Superior, $236,000 in Erie and $503,000 in unincorporated areas. The price for older homes is less, but in new communities such as Superior and Erie older homes don't exist. Generally, rural lots in both the mountains and plains offer good deals, but price swings are enormous. And if you're thinking about building, you need to take into consideration zoning and the cost of water and utilities. When rural sellers put high price tags on agricultural land, most likely, they expect a city to annex the land, and when county land does get annexed, the annexing city can change its zoning to allow much greater density. The market price depends, as always, on location, maintenance and (this being Boulder) the way your horoscope is interacting with current mortgage rates. The Boulder market is softest on the upper end and hottest for condominiums, but no matter what the price, special homes on special lots still sell fast.

Slightly more than half of Boulder's residential real estate buyers are locals who are trading up, and through mid-'99 the number of new sales and resales were identical to those in 1998. Even with the prices leveling off, finding the right place at the right price isn't always easy. Locals, whether tire-kickers or serious buyers, and newcomers alike flock to the open houses (or open homes, as they are pretentiously called these days) held year round, rain or shine, on Sunday afternoons. Check the Saturday and Sunday newspapers, or be alert for "open house" signs if you are out for an afternoon drive to scout neighborhoods. A real estate agent will be on hand to answer questions, often pass out leaflets on the property and perhaps give a very soft sell on the home you're looking at. It's an easy way to comparison shop without the commitment of being taken around by an agent to look at homes by appointment.

www.insiders.com

See this and many other **Insiders' Guide®** destinations online — in their entirety.

Visit us today!

Real Estate Resources

So you're sure you want to move to Boulder County, but where do you start? You can get information on buying or renting in Boulder County from the local chambers of commerce and from the Board of Realtors. The Boulder Chamber of Commerce, for instance, issues a useful relocation packet, as do many real estate agencies. City halls, listed in our Boulder Neighborhoods chapter, can provide general local information. Recreation centers and most grocery stores display free publications about places to live. *Homes & Land of Boulder County* and *Where to Live in Boulder County* are the two biggest and slickest. You can also call one or more of these groups: Boulder Chamber of Commerce, 2440 Pearl Street, Boulder, (303) 442-1044; Boulder Area Board of Realtors, 4885 Riverbend Road, Suite A, Boulder, (303) 442-3585; Office of Human Rights Department of Housing and Human Services, 1101 Arapahoe Avenue, Second Floor, Boulder, (303) 441-3157.

Real Estate Firms

With the booming real estate market, it seems as if there's an agency on every corner. Most of the bigger agencies serving Boulder County provide newcomer relocation services as well as matching you with a place to live. The Boulder Area Board of Realtors (see contact information listed above) can provide you with a list of real estate agencies, and you'll find others in the phone book, the local newspaper and such free periodicals as *Where to Live in Boulder County*.

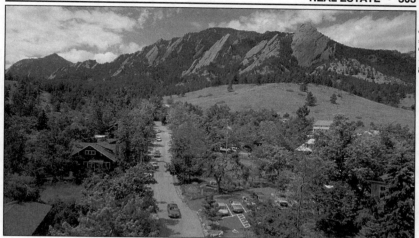

Photo: Daily Camera

The Flatirons serve as the backdrop for many towns and neighborhoods in the Boulder area.

Century 21 — The Bernardi Group
3301 30th St., Boulder
• **(303) 402-6000, (800) 421-2174**

This new agency burst on the Boulder real estate scene in 1996 with the dazzle and flair of a Roman candle when Karen Bernardi left RE/MAX Realty Consultants of Boulder and started her own agency, affiliated with Century 21. The agency has 14 brokers and specializes in single-family homes, condominiums and vacant land in Boulder County.

Buyer Brokers of Boulder
4141 Arapahoe Ave., #101, Boulder
• **(303) 444-6660 (800) 942-8937 (Relocation Hotline)**

After 23 years in the business, Alta Drumm left the traditional real estate industry in 1990 to hire her own brokers. They work exclusively for the buyers of real estate, with no extra fees or retainers charged to buyers. The company works with the sellers, inspectors, lenders and title companies.

Coldwell Banker Colorado Landmark Realtors
2334 Broadway, Boulder
• **(303) 443-3377, (800) 737-6683**

Twenty-five agents work at this downtown Boulder real estate agency which specializes in the upper-end residential and commercial, and vacant land. The 12-year-old firm reported $88 million in sales in 1996.

Colorado Buyer Brokers
4450 Arapahoe Ave., Ste. 100, Boulder
• **(303) 415-2509**

A firm that specializes in working with the buyer rather than the seller. This firm has more than 21 years of experience, although the buyer's broker is still a fairly new concept in real estate. The broker works for the buyer and therefore has no financial stake in selling a particular home.

Fowler Real Estate/Better Homes and Gardens
2970 Wilderness Pl., Boulder
• **(303) 443-6050, (800) 443-6050**

One-hundred thirty agents work here at Boulder's oldest real estate agency. Fowler has grown to be the largest Realtor group in northern Colorado with branch offices in Longmont, (303) 772-9620, 2432 N. Main; in Nederland, (303) 258-7020, 286 N. Bridge Street, and a home information center next to JCPenney's at Crossroads Mall, (303) 442-9141.

RE/MAX of Boulder
2425 Canyon Blvd., Ste. 200, Boulder
• **(303) 449-7000, (800) 825-7000**

In 1999, RE/MAX of Boulder ranked No. 1 among RE/MAX Mountain States agencies in terms of volume per agent, which amounts to a lot of sales since more than 67 agents work out of this office. The agency is particularly strong in relocation services.

RE/MAX Realty Consultants of Boulder
4770 Baseline Rd., Boulder
• **(303) 499-9880, (800) 373-1282 (Relocation Hotline)**

Founded in 1931, this is the county's second-largest realty office, based on volume of sales. This company has more than 62 agents in its own mortgage brokerage service.

Moore and Company Realtors
4875 Pearl E. Cr., Boulder
• **(303) 444-7800, (800) 444-8927**

This 60-plus-year-old, Denver-based business has 13 branches and 1000 agents throughout the state. The Boulder County office has 35 real estate agents handling residential and commercial properties.

Prudential/Wise-McIntire
4710 Table Mesa Dr., Boulder
• **(303) 494-7700, (800) 383-6805**

A worldwide affiliate, this firm has been established in Boulder for 30 years. Twenty-five real estate agents handle both residential and commercial properties.

Walnut Realty
1911 11th St., Ste. 107, Boulder
• **(303) 442-3180, (800) 477-3180**

Broker Tom Kahn describes Walnut Realty as "Boulder's downtown Realtors," and indeed, the office is in a historic building a block from the Pearl Street Mall. However, the firm specializes in a variety of types of property, from ordinary residential to vacant land,

farms, rural and mountain homes and downtown commercial buildings. This company staffs 27 agents.

Wright-Kingdom Realtors Inc.
1844 Folsom Ave., Boulder
• **(303) 443-2240, (800) 343-8885**

Lew Kingdom and Stuart Wright started this real estate company in 1976, when Boulder was a town of around 60,000 people and the average home cost $85,000. This is one of the longer-established agencies in town. It has 30 associates and includes an international relocation service.

Lone Eagles

Boulder County also includes more than 100 single-person realty offices, and some are outstanding. You can check these and other agencies through the Boulder Board of Realtors, although keep in mind that the Board doesn't handle Longmont or Lyons.

Do It Yourself

Some people also try to sell their own homes to avoid paying a commission to a Realtor. For Sale By Owner, (303) 772-1358, puts out a $150 video and manual, and issues a free magazine on available properties. For additional fees, the company also offers various other optional services, including multiple listing, marketing checklists, advertising and representation at closing.

About Home Builders

With boom times come large, California-style subdivisions put up by major developers and builders. Boom times also bring the need for more schools, more utilities, more roads and more services. Communities are leveling "impact fees" at builders, and these fees are built into the price of new construction. Home Builders Association of Metropolitan Denver,

(303) 778-1400, can supply a list of its members, including some large firms building in Boulder County.

Fixer-uppers

If you've bought a house that needs work, or if you are renovating your current home and are having problems finding suitable contractors, Home Improvement Referral Inc., P.O. Box 26012, Colorado Springs 80936, (303) 449-5093 (in Boulder area), provides free information and a referral service that lists 300 Colorado contractors and subcontractors who handle everything from maintenance and repair to custom-built homes.

House-hunting Tips

Whether you plan to be a yuppie commoner living in a simple condominium or the royal owner of a grand mansionette, count on a few rules. Spend time looking, and keep location in mind. The closer to a city center, the more you pay, for it puts you closer to the activities and services that make Boulder and other cities so inviting. The lot itself matters — a good mountain view, a babbling creek, adjacent city open space, a golf course, good entertainment or a public park all add value. So does beautiful, mature landscaping. That's why a tiny Boulder condominium with all these location features might cost more than a spacious single-family home in outlying areas.

On the other hand, Boulder doesn't have many "wrong side of the track" homes, or acres and acres of homogenized housing, although vast housing tracts are blanketing former farmland surrounding outlying communities. One great feature of this city is how mansions can exist right next to apartment buildings, quirky little bungalows and subsidized public housing. This magical mixture happens because many Boulder neighborhoods add diversity in neighbor-friendly ways. Drive with a real estate agent through sought-after Mapleton Hill, Whittier, University Hill or North Boulder neighborhoods. Look closely, and you'll see how diversity can help a neighborhood thrive. Even in developments where every house seems to have been cloned from the one next door, a mix of high and moderately priced housing often develops as the trees have grown and people have renovated their properties, whether in modest areas like Martin Acres or more prepossessing ones like Table Mesa. You can find exclusive "mono-communities" in and around Boulder, but if the only thing stopping you from choosing a more eclectic mix is a fear that it would lower your house value, relax. Diverse neighborhoods that are well-loved in Boulder do just fine.

However, an eclectic neighborhood might not be your cup of tea. Perhaps you prefer a brand-new house in a brand-new neighborhood, where you are no more of a newcomer than anyone else. Area developers and Realtors showcase their offerings through annual tours. In 1999 homes ranged from $87,000 to $1.62 million with varying styles for everyone.

What to Look for in a Boulder House

Boulder has a cool semiarid climate, which means most energy goes into heating, not cooling. Insulation matters. Because it's so sunny, passive solar can do wonders. This doesn't mean you must settle for a '70s-style solar home, with a long wall of south-facing glass and the sun-blasting black-painted oil drums. Energy-efficient homes can blend into any style and still keep January gas bills low. One regular-looking Boulder home earned a national energy efficiency award. Its owner, Craig Cristensen, has no heater at all. He relies on passive solar, super insulation and a 1,000-gallon hot water storage tank, so that even if a rugby team burst in, asking for showers during a cloudy February week, enough solar-heated water would be on hand to douse them all.

Some homes are energy-efficient, but not all. Check winter utility bills before buying. A few summer days get awfully hot (witness the heat wave during the summer of 1995 when temperatures rose to the high 90s), but heat spells tend to be short, and summer nights cool. As long as a home is positioned to keep out the fiercest summer rays, either with deep eaves or shade trees, most residents don't miss air-conditioning.

Keeping the garden green is a problem in

the dry heat of summer. A sprinkler system is a plus, and a modern, water-saving drip system is a super-plus. While some of Boulder's older, most desirable neighborhoods boast the mixed blessing of large, non-indigenous shade trees that provide atmosphere and character but are not really suitable for the region's climate, xeriscaping is a plus in contemporary homes. Xeriscaping is the art and science of landscaping with indigenous drought-tolerant plants that is increasingly popular in the Southwest and Mountain States. See our Shopping chapter's Close-up on Xeriscaping.

Want to Live in the Mountains?

One of Boulder's most distinctive characteristics is that it is a true city with remote mountain living close by. Is a mountain house your dream? Mountain living is not for the fainthearted. Residents keep their snow chains handy. One winter day, the snow on Magnolia Road hid a steeply tilted skating rink. One woman's sporty truck skidded off near the top and plummeted nearly 100 feet. The truck's bed hit first and collapsed like an accordion. Maybe NASA should study the event to improve their hard-landing techniques, for the lucky lady walked out of that truck alive.

Notice a rocky mountainside covered with charred black sticks marking the 1989 Black Tiger Gulch wildfire. As smoke billowed miles away, one mountain couple packed favorite Navajo rugs in the station wagon. They joked that the scare would end in a few hours, and they'd be unpacking. Suddenly they heard a train-like roar and felt blistering heat. The fire had leapt up their ridge. If they had to do it over again, they would have packed the family photo album instead of those rugs. They raced down their bumpy mountain road and will never forget how it felt to breathe searing, hollow air, the oxygen sucked out by the firestorm. That fire caused $10 million in damage and destroyed 39 homes. Another fire in 1990 burned 2,200 acres and 10 homes. Such fires are a natural part of mountain ecosystems. On dry, windy summer days, even the big bomber planes, dropping payloads of slurry, cannot slow the flames.

Icy roads and forest fires are nothing compared to your love of nature? Suppose one dusky evening, a mountain lion eats your dog. The kids are horrified. You're just glad it was the dog. So you build a fence. A mountain lion can jump most fences. And you've blocked land that was open to migrating deer, mountain lions and everything natural up there. Endangered wildlife is one reason Boulder County has decided to slow mountain developments. A mountain home can be wonderful, but unless you're committed to the mountain lifestyle, you can always visit.

On the other hand, if you realize the tradeoffs you're making and the negative impacts you might create, you can do plenty to minimize the problems. Before you build a home, ask your architect about low-impact choices. For instance, architect Dave Barrett of Barrett-Steele, (303) 449-1141, has been written up nationally for his environmentally sensitive homes. If you move into an existing home, you can remodel with attention to fire-fighting materials. Consider replacing cedar shingles with tile, slate, metal or asphalt (if you build new, you won't be permitted to use cedar shakes). Stucco, brick and stone siding do not burn and will protect the interior better than a wood exterior. Be sure dead brush is kept away from your home. Such changes minimize flammability.

Pop into an eco-shop, such as Planetary Solutions, (303) 442-6228, 2030 17th Street, which offers materials and consulting services for environmentally sound building. Jade Mountain, (303) 449-6601, 717 Poplar Avenue, is an appropriate-technology company with solar electric systems and composting toilets. Just being at such a store will give you ideas. Take a course in environmentalism from the University of Colorado, (303) 492-6301, or the Naropa Institute, (303) 444-0202. Check with the Colorado Division of Wildlife, (303) 291-7227, to see how to live with animals. The Thorne Ecological Institute, (303) 499-3647, 5398 Manhattan Circle, is another resource. Train your children about mountain safety, and keep your pets — especially cats — indoors. Mountain lions consider cats tasty tidbits, and cats themselves are miniature mountain lions whose hunting has led to the decline of many rare birds.

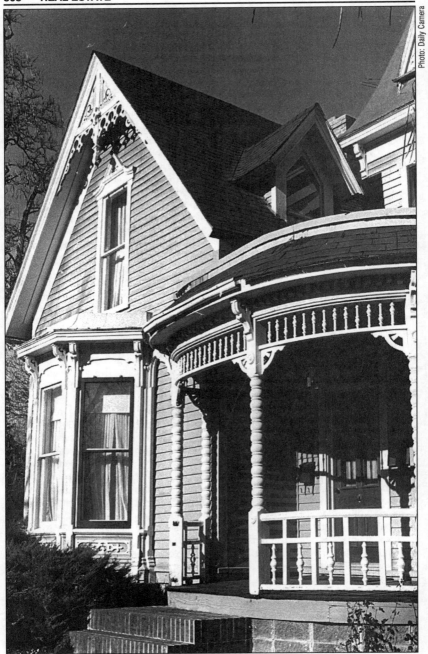

Boulder offers a wide variety of houses, one of which you might call home.

A Few, Few Words About Crime

Some Boulder County residents leave their doors unlocked. Others have security systems on everything except their running shoes. Most people take care walking at night, especially when in deserted areas of CU-Boulder, downtown or the Creek Path. Others head into the dark at 5 AM all by themselves and have a grand time listening to the morning birds. Boulder County's biggest enforcement concerns involve speeding cars and loud parties. Yes, the county has crimes, including murder and abduction. But there are some, well, endearing criminals too.

Take the fleet-footed Gunbarrel burglar. Under cover of night, he slipped into homes along golf course greens. He stole silver; he stole jewels. Fifty officers and a helicopter tried an ambush. The SWAT team's fastest sprinter cornered him, but that burglar leapt the fence like a deer. Finally, in 1992, they nabbed him with a backpack full of jewels. Turns out he was a marathon runner. He had girlfriends around the world. They didn't know about each other but had enjoyed his dazzling gifts. Over seven years, the bold, handsome runner had burglarized 244 homes. Golf course communities sleep better, now that he runs his laps at the jail.

The Renter's Market

Of Boulder's 96,000 residents, 25,000 are CU-Boulder students, and a good majority rent off-campus. They're not the only ones. In the nonstudent population, almost 50 percent of Boulder city residents rent. That's higher than the United States overall, where less than 35 percent of all households live in rented dwellings. Many people moving here rent while searching for something to buy. Others can't afford to buy and remain renters for years. Many who move from Boulder hang onto their homes while they look elsewhere or contemplate returning. Others move up in the market, then use their former digs as an investment.

So brace yourself. Between 1980 and 1990, city rents here went up 40 percent, compared to 20 percent in the United States overall. Much of this was fueled by an extraordinarily low vacancy rate that squeaked down to 1.2 percent in 1992. By the mid-'90s, vacancies hovered around 4 to 5 percent, so rent increases have been easing. Rents tend to be higher near CU and lower in the county. As of summer 1999, prices had stayed near recent levels, meaning you could get a studio or efficiency for about $520 in the city, a one-bedroom apartment for $630, a two-bedroom apartment for about $850, or a five-bedroom house for around $2,000 a month. Reduced rents are available through CU married-student housing and Boulder family assistance programs, but waits for such spaces can run years, so apply early.

Although the real estate market has settled from a sprint to a trot, popping into town and finding a place right away is not a sure thing, except in spring or early summer, when relatively few students are in residence and there are more apartment vacancies. Many rental agencies prefer at least 45 days advance notice, and they can match you with a place best if you visit for a few days so they can show you around.

The city of Boulder has adopted landlord/tenant laws, including such things as handling of security deposits, when a lease is required, when the landlord can raise the rent and so on. Check these laws before you rent, for your own protection. The Community Mediation Service, 2160 Spruce Street, (303) 441-4364, issues a *Handbook of Landlord Tenant Relations* that covers these subjects and also can help resolve disputes including landlord/tenant relations. As for the county, Colorado doesn't have many renter-protection laws, so your lease is where you'll find most of your rights and responsibilities. Read it while wearing your fine-print glasses. Also, some areas allow only three unrelated people per dwelling, and if you're caught cheating, you can be fined until the situation is corrected, so check your tenant responsibilities.

Questions of Affordability

Another dilemma in Boulder is affordability. The effort to preserve open space limits new homes, and people's sentimental attachment to the present character of their block often leads to strong opposition to increased den-

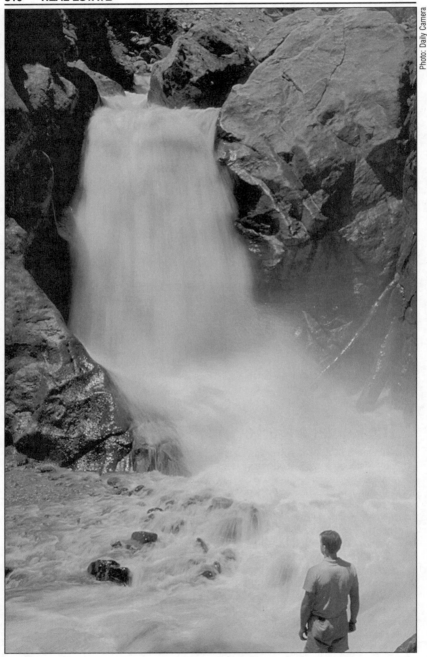

Photo: Daily Camera

Boulder Falls is one of many natural wonders dotting our landscape.

sity. Managing these issues is like squeezing a balloon: locate new housing away from open space and fearful neighborhoods, and housing prices balloon. That's why more and more people with moderate incomes either choose much smaller places than they originally envisioned or buy homes a long drive from their jobs. Some people say, "Big deal. Things always cost more in a city, but it's worth it." Or they say, "Big deal. Commutes of nearly an hour are common near urban centers." Other people fear that our very success will destroy what's best about Boulder. If the topic of affordability interests you, attend one of the frequent city meetings at which planning experts from around the nation share ideas.

Rental Resources

Housing Helpers
2865 Baseline Rd., Boulder
• **(303) 499-4499**

This company offers a number of services, including rental information, the chance to find a roommate or housemate for a modest fee, and help with subleasing. There is also a free referral service that helps you select a Realtor, based on the requirements you outline.

University of Colorado Off-Campus Housing
University Memorial Center, Rm. 336
(CU-Boulder campus), Boulder
• **(303) 492-7053**

This referral service helps students find rooms, apartments, houses and roommate requests. It also provides free copies of Boulder's tenants rights and responsibilities, free model leases and subleases and general information about renting in Boulder.

City of Boulder Housing Authority
3120 Broadway, Boulder
• **(303) 441-3150**

Subsidized housing in the city is available by application to the housing authority. There's a one-year wait for a one-bedroom apartment to a two- to three-year wait for a four-bedroom place. The market, however, is very changeable so it doesn't hurt to call.

Boulder County Housing Authority
2040 14th St., Boulder • (303) 441-3929

In the county, the waiting list for subsidized housing is two to four years, depending on the house size. The wait is shortest for those who are residents of Boulder County, or employed or attend college here.

Retirement for some
might mean their first
backpack trip to Nepal
or that longed-for
second career.

Retirement

In many ways, Boulder so epitomizes the youth culture that many people don't realize it is a splendid place to retire as well. Excellent community services, an increasing commitment to public transportation and a benign four-season climate make it congenial for retirees. But "retirement" doesn't automatically equate with "inactivity," and many so-called "retirees" put working folks to shame when it comes to a range of interests.

A "retired" engineer studies ethics at CU-Boulder and works summers at a greenhouse. When his children were young, this high-level manager left escalating salaries and a thirst for fancier things. He and his wife spend more time with their sons now. The dad loves both his scholarly pursuit and plants. "Retirees" include the fifty-something former satellite communications expert who retired early, moved to Boulder and started hiking, backpacking and knocking off fourteeners (Colorado's 54 peaks that are 14,000 or more feet above sea level); and the eighty-something famous Boulder author who writes less these days because she's so busy managing her very successful stock portfolio. The "Chronologically Gifted" who hike or bike miles might seem intimidating to seniors who plan to age more conventionally. Keep in mind these super seniors impress people a third their age. When we grow up, can we do it too? What's their secret?

About 8 percent of Boulder residents are 65 and older, compared with 12 percent nationwide. (Boulder's large student and early post-grad population explains much of the difference.) Although Boulder offers many retirement complexes aimed at the senior market, most older residents opt for more individuality. Two city-sponsored senior centers and even a community Internet link provide a sense of connection with most recreational opportunities and services.

Long-term older residents have shared ideas for improving Boulder. The saltier ones say, "confine the cats" or "send joggers to South America." They are still nostalgic for 19¢-per-gallon gasoline, passenger trains and manners. But many say the good old days are now, and 78 percent of the seniors who responded to a *Daily Camera* survey said they're happy. In many cases, especially in Boulder's more traditional neighborhoods, seniors mix with other age groups.

Senior Services and Agencies

These are the best one-stop shops for senior-related offerings. People who equate senior centers with "old" tend to avoid them, but the centers provide useful services and opportunities for seniors to connect with their peers. When asked why they use the centers, women report that they're interested in learn-

---

INSIDERS' TIP

CareLink, (303) 441-3905, is an "adult day-care" program at the West Boulder Senior Center that provides companionship, structured activities and medication assistance for Alzheimer's patients and others who are ambulatory but benefit from getting out of the house in a safe, controlled environment.

ing and improving their lives. Men more often list the challenge of staying active. The county has six urban centers with comprehensive resources and three rural centers open for limited hours and with limited on-site staffing. They can connect you with reduced-cost medical, tax and legal aid.

Many of the nearby communities aren't large enough to have their own senior centers, so instead they offer the following resource clearinghouses for seniors in Boulder County:

• Allenspark Aging Services for Boulder County at Allenspark Nursing Clinic, Colo. Highway 7, Allenspark, (303) 747-2592.

• Lyons Aging Services Resources, Bloomfield Community Room, 722 Fifth Avenue, Lyons, (303) 823-9016.

• Niwot Senior Resources (branch of Boulder County Office of the Aging), Eagle Place Community Building, 6790 N. 79th St., Niwot, (303) 652-3850.

Senior Centers

Boulder West Senior Center
909 Arapahoe Ave., Boulder
• **(303) 441-3148**

Centrally located near downtown, just west of the downtown public library, this is Boulder's original senior center. Described as a "traditional" facility, many seniors drop-in here to socialize. Operated by the City of Boulder, hours are 8:30 AM to 4:30 PM on weekdays. Hot lunch is served daily, and dinner is served on Tuesday nights. Information on places to live, medical screenings and assisted-care help is available here. Classes range from watercolor painting to the art of playing snooker.

Boulder East Senior Center
5660 Sioux Dr., Boulder
• **(303) 441-4150**

Located at the East Boulder Recreation Center, this facility also is operated by the City of Boulder. Because of its location, this is the

first choice for seniors who want to combine exercise with socialization and classes. An open floor plan allows the east center to host fairs and art shows and with the adjacent volleyball courts seniors create their own tournaments. Classes include ballroom dancing, tai chi chuan and modern investing. Hours are 8:30 AM to 4:30 PM.

Broomfield Senior Center
280 Lamar St., Broomfield
• **(303) 469-0536**

Hot lunch is served daily and a sunset dinner is scheduled monthly at this center, which is located in the same building as the Broomfield Recreation Center. Hours are 8 AM to 5 PM on Monday, Wednesday and Friday; and 8 AM to 9 PM on Tuesday and Thursday. Fitness classes are available on-site and arts and crafts classes also are offered.

Lafayette Senior Center
103 S. Iowa St., Lafayette
• **(303) 665-9052**

Local entertainers visit this senior social hub regularly and special events are often scheduled on Saturdays. Enjoy the noon hot meail Tuesday through Friday. Open weekdays from 8 AM to 5 PM, the center also offers travel excursions to the mountains, special events, drop-in activities, daily classes and educational seminars.

Longmont Senior Center
910 Longs Peak Ave., Longmont
• **(303) 651-8411**

Longmont is a traditional center offering regular exercise programs, card games, craft workshops, educational programs and daytrips. It is open from 8 AM to 5 PM. Longmont's Meals on Wheels prepares its food at this site and daily lunch service is offered through them.

Louisville Senior Center
900 W. Via Appia, Louisville
• **(303) 666-7400**

Seniors bring their gym clothes to this center, located inside the Louisville Recreation Center. Open from 9 AM to 4 PM Monday through Friday, specialists from the local hospital offer educational courses on staying healthy, and any holiday is an excuse for a special feast. Lunch is served every weekday. Daytrips to wineries, dinner theaters and casinos are scheduled monthly. Classes range from arts and crafts to tax preparation and computer training.

Nutrition

When you're a senior, meal preparation may be a low priority. Perhaps it's the memory of an old stove or the thought of cleaning up afterwards. For those who would rather leave the cooking or shopping to someone else, Boulder has two options.

Meals on Wheels
2355 Canyon Blvd., Boulder
• (303) 441-3907

This is Boulder's most frequently requested senior service. It enables people of all ages to eat regular, nutritious meals, even when they're short on money or are unable to handle food preparation and cleanup. A hot meal is delivered at noon, Monday through Friday, with the cost per meal based on an individual's monthly income. This agency serves the elderly, chronically ill, handicapped and those convalescing from illness, accident or surgery.

ElderShare
6363 Horizon Lane, Longmont
• (303) 652-3663

Operated by Community Food Share, this service delivers basic groceries twice a month to nearly 500 seniors throughout the county.

Resources

Senior Centers in Boulder County offer trips to the Denver Center for the Performing Arts, gambling towns and Denver's Cherry Creek Mall. But it's often the need to get around town that presents the greater challenge. Boulder's commitment to alternative transportation makes it less car-dependent than many Western cities, but there is still plenty of room for improvement. The following services can meet daily transportation needs.

Regional Transportation District (RTD)
14th and Walnut Sts., Boulder
• (303) 299-6000

RTD charges only 25¢ for seniors who ride buses during off-peak hours (not 6 to 9 AM or 4 to 6 PM). An RTD shopping bus goes from the senior housing sites to grocery stores. Most buses accommodate wheelchairs.

Special Transit
4880 Pearl St., Boulder • (303) 447-9636

Special Transit provides handicapped-accessible, door-to-door service. This nonprofit group charges $1.50 each way within the city; $3 between various cities in the county. It's quite a discount — the real cost of this subsidized service is closer to $12 per person. Those using the service must register first, and call a week in advance to schedule a ride.

The Hop and Skip
1739 Broadway, Park Central Building
Boulder • (303) 441-3266

The Hop and Skip are operated jointly by the Regional Transportation District (RTD) and the Transportation Planning Group, the city's alternate modes division. The Hop takes people between major shopping areas and CU-Boulder for 75¢. For the same fee, the Skip, a 22-passenger bus, will take you anywhere along Broadway, operating every 10 minutes and every six minutes during rush hour. The Jump, offering service between Boulder and Lafayette via Arapahoe, will begin operation in the fall of 2000.

See our Boulder Getting Around chapter for more transportation information.

Special Interests

Most Boulder seniors consider retirement a chance to do as they please. For others it might mean their first backpack trip to Nepal or that longed-for second career. Many find retirement lonely or just plain boring. In Boulder there are many work and volunteer opportunities for seniors who want to remain active.

Audubon Society
3109 28th St., Boulder • (800) 274-4201

Community education opportunities are offered through the Society's Human Population and Habitat Program. The Boulder County chapter schedules daily and extended field trips for those interested in birding and offers a list of what birds to look for in this area. A Christmas bird count is held during a 24-hour period in December and enlists more than 100 birders and 30 teams who help conduct the local bird census — part of an annual nationwide effort.

Boulder Rotary
Angle Pines Country Club, 5706 Arapahoe, Boulder • (303) 554-7074

This service organization works to "build a better community" by hosting fund-raising events and distributing the money to local non-profit agencies, including Safehouse and Spe-

cial Transit. The Rotary offers more than $10,000 in scholarships to CU students and funds a study-abroad program for selected CU juniors. Two of the Boulder groups meet weekly for lunch; the third group meets for breakfast.

50+ Employment Opportunities Program
2905 Center Green Ct. S., Ste. C, Boulder • (303) 441-3985

A service of Workforce Boulder County, this program connects people with job-retraining programs and employment possibilities.

Volunteer Connection
1136 Alpine Ave., Boulder • (303) 444-4904

Are you stuck in a life rut? Maybe you're re-entering the work force after an absence or you've been frustrated by "experience only" job ads. Maybe you'd like to consider a career transition, but you're afraid to leave your present job. This service organization has current information on hundreds of volunteer opportunities that could make the difference in your life that allows you to make a difference in the community. The calendar section of the *Sunday Camera* lists current volunteer opportunities available through Volunteer Connection.

Retired and Senior Volunteer Program (R.S.V.P.)
6032 Valmont Rd., Boulder • (303) 443-1933

More than 2,000 registered volunteers in the county participate in this program, both older residents and "junior" volunteers, meaning those younger than 55. One out of every 10 people 60 and older volunteers each year through R.S.V.P., which celebrated its 25th anniversary in September 1997. People join

---

INSIDERS' TIP

By paying $20 to enroll at the 55+ Health Clinic, (303) 441-0444, Boulder County residents can receive 12 months of preventative healthcare, including routine blood-pressure checks, review of prescription medicine, individual wellness counseling and skin-cancer screenings.

because they want to give back to their community while staying active and productive. The Handyman Program, which does fix-it-up jobs for other seniors, attracts seniors as volunteers too.

The Service Exchange
2345 Bent Way, Longmont
• (303) 678-3228

Service Exchange is a volunteer-matching service. Volunteers earn service credits (hours) for their work and then cash them in when they need expertise or assistance from another volunteer.

Education

If you missed out on educational opportunities in your youth, Boulder is the ideal place to be a senior. Many Boulder agencies and private groups offer discounted or age-geared classes to seniors.

CU Seniors Auditors Program
1202 University Ave., Boulder
• (303) 492-8484

With a professor's permission, a senior may audit virtually any class tuition-free (with a small processing charge).

Boulder Parks and Recreation
3198 Broadway, Boulder
• (303) 441-4150

The city's program offers senior yoga, swimming and tennis. The Senior Centers (listed previously) have offerings too. Classes include tai chi for seniors, tennis tournaments and a Boulder Creek walking group. Very popular is the 55/Alive Driving Class — a way to brush up on driving skills, learn new driving laws and, often, get a break on insurance.

Retirement Living

Often Boulder seniors live in single-family homes. Neighborhoods benefit when seniors live near. It helps keep the streets safer when people are in and out during the day, and it can make for great intergenerational interactions. A child's first job might be watering an older neighbor's lawn or shoveling snow, and seniors may be unofficial substitute grandparents when the real ones live far away. When a favorite local retiree broke her hip, kids came by with flowers. Did she flinch at their worried faces? "Guess what!" she said with a grin. "I have metal parts now. That means I'm a bionic woman!" Her humor delighted them, as does seeing her back on morning walks. Another, when asked what's the worst thing about growing old, replied, "Where did I put it?"

When they tire of yard work or keeping up a big house, many seniors do the Boulder yuppie thing and move to a townhouse or condominium. Most housing inquiries at the Senior Centers regard finding affordable independent-living quarters, often with no stairs, and near bus routes and shopping.

Multilevel Facilities

While various specialized levels of senior housing, including independent and assisted living, respite care and nursing homes, are available in Boulder, several multilevel facilities provide a range of options and give people the opportunity to move to increasing levels of care if and as needed.

The Academy
970 Aurora Avenue, Boulder
• (303) 938-1920

Built in 1892, this former private girls school survived the 20th century against all odds. Originally known as Mount St. Gertrude Academy, it was used for classes by the University after the Sisters of Charity closed the school. A fire in 1981 caused severe damage and CU chose not to restore the building. Several proposals for redevelopment were promoted and swiftly rejected by either city planners or the surrounding neighborhood. Finally, in 1996, the plan for a retirement community was approved.

There are three historic buildings on the site including a chapel, conservatory and the Academy, which now houses 18 apartments. There are a total of 33 apartments, 9 assisted living units and 9 bungalows — some still under construction. The buildings are so beautifully restored that when visitors toured the new facility as a stop on Historic Boulder's 1998 Christmas tour, guests of all ages were ready to move in. The rooms are spacious with lots of light and many have beautiful views of the

Flatirons. Colorado Senator Dorothy Rupert and her husband Richard were on the waiting list even before the Academy opened. Monthly fees can range from $2,775 to $4,900, depending on square footage and the view.

Balfour Retirement Community of Boulder County
1855 Plaza Drive, Louisville
• (303) 926-1000

This beautifully landscaped home was designed by award-winning Colorado architects who specialize in retirement housing. In addition to concierge service, the facility offers three meals per day, a private dining room, weekly housekeeping services, scheduled transportation, health promotion and exercise programs, medication management, an in-house beauty salon, massage therapist, a library and internet access. Shopping, restaurants, physician offices, hospitals and cultural events are nearby. Monthly prices for studio apartments begin at $2,150 with one and two-bedroom apartments ranging from $4,100 to $4,850. There is an additional charge for a second person, a move-in fee, pet fee and smoker's fee. Balfour's motto is "Never stop growing," with a goal of building a community that's supportive of people's growth.

Boulder Good Samaritan
2525 Taft Dr., Boulder • (303) 449-6150

Boulder Good Samaritan offers independent- and assisted-living options as well as a nursing home. Taft Towers is Good Samaritan's lowest level of care, with 66 independent-living units as big as 2-bedroom, 2-bathroom apartments that rent for $930 to $1,595 per month. Thirteen assisted-living residents pay $1,675 to $2,175 per month. The nursing home accommodates 60 residents at $121 per day. Good Samaritan has a dining room, transportation services, a full activities program (last winter participants visited the beautiful ice sculptures at Breckenridge), a swimming pool and housekeeping services. The Older Boulder Wellness Center is at Good Samaritan, and was the first nursing home in the nation to equip its facilities with Nautilus equipment. (How Boulder!) For $72 a month,

nonresidents also may use the center three times a week.

Frasier Meadows Manor
350 Ponca Pl., Boulder • (303) 499-4888

A continuing care retirement community since 1960, Frasier offers 200 independent-living units and 15 assisted-living units. There are one- and two-bedroom apartments with a three-month waiting list. This nonprofit facility does not have rental units, but rather requires new residents to choose from three options and sign a binding agreement with a 50 percent refund policy. Amenities include a flexible meal plan, laundry service, housekeeping, transportation, rehabilitation program, a computer center, beauty shop, and recreational opportunities.

Golden West
1055 Adams Cir., Boulder
• (303) 444-3967

Golden West was established by the First Christian Church and has been around for more than 30 years. There are currently 255 senior apartments and 56 assisted-living units in three adjacent, interconnected elevator-equipped buildings. There is a six- to 12-month waiting period for efficiency apartments, which cost $350 to $390 per month, and a 24- to 36-month wait for 1-bedroom apartments, which are $450 per month. A meal plan requires residents to purchase either the noon or evening meal for an additional $160 per month. The assisted-living units are 307 square feet and rent for $2,015 per month. The maximum wait, as of this writing, is about 3 months, and the monthly fee includes 24-hour staffing, 3 meals a day, snacks, medication monitoring, laundry, housekeeping and minimal daily-living assistance. On site are a library, computer center, recreation room, wellness center, beauty salon, sitting and guest rooms, a gift shop and coin laundry facilities. Recreational activities for all residents include exercise classes, educational programs, musical programs (the Kitchen Band is popular), crafts classes, slide presentations and the Residents' Council, which is sort of like a Student Council for seniors living at Golden West.

Independent Living

Some retirees simplify their lives so they can travel and pursue more hobbies while increasing the availability of medical care. Take the woman who moved to one of Boulder County's independent-housing facilities with assisted-care and nursing facilities on the grounds. When she announced that she was renting out the old family home, her children were aghast. She replied, "Well, it's about time. After all, I am going to be 90 this year." She now hosts her women's group in the meeting room of her living center.

Heed this — the independent-living housing market is tight. Although you can get into some places quickly, the waiting list for others is four years long.

The Atrium
3350 30th St., Boulder • (303) 444-0200

The 80 apartments here range from studios to two-bedrooms. Amenities include a craft room, exercise room, beauty parlor and barber shop, underground parking, ice cream parlor, dining room (serving three meals a day) and free laundry facilities. The Atrium frequently schedules special events such as fashion shows, barbecues, a St. Patrick's Day corned beef and cabbage dinner and a New Year's Eve dance that's open to both residents and non-residents (it typically ends at 10 PM). Rates at the Atrium range from $1,350 to $2,750 a month, including weekly housekeeping, linens and linen service.

Presbyterian Manor
1050 Arapahoe Ave., Boulder • (303) 444-0642

Presbyterian Manor is a not-for-profit, independent-living facility with modest costs and a four- to five-year waiting list. The 80 units all have small kitchenettes. The monthly costs are: buffet unit, $285; studio, $320; one-bedroom, $380; and two-bedroom, $440. These rents include utilities. The Boulder West Senior Center and the main branch of the Boulder Public Library are practically across the street, and the YMCA will pick up groups of three or more participating in Y programs, so

residents don't have problems keeping busy, even though the activity schedule is sparse. The manor puts on an annual Christmas dinner and monthly birthday parties, which are held as picnics from June to September and indoors the rest of the year.

Assisted Living

As with independent-living facilities, the waiting list for assisted-living options can be long — six to 12, even 18, months. If you want affordable housing with any assisted-living options, start checking as soon as you can.

The Beatrice Hover Assisted-living Residence
1380 Charles Dr., Longmont • (303) 772-8102

This facility accommodates 55 residents — eight in double suites and the rest in private rooms, all with private baths. The 7-year-old facility provides three meals per day, housekeeping and laundry services, medication assistance and a van to take residents to doctors' appointments and outside activities. The rate structure is complex, based on the accommodation's size and location and the three levels of service (the third, daily assistance with bathing and dressing, is considered the last step before skilled-nursing care is needed); costs range from $1,975 to $2,775 per month. The 121-unit independent-living facility called Hover Manor is nearby. All but 10 percent of these 580-square-foot, one-bedroom apartments are HUD-subsidized and therefore carry strict income guidelines; the 12 non-subsidized units currently rent for $442 per month.

Crossings Ridge Point Assisted Living Inn
3375 34th St., Boulder • (303) 473-0333

Ridge Point, which opened in 1994, is Boulder's newest assisted-living facility. There are 76 apartments with a 24-hour personal-care staff. The monthly costs are studio, $1,895; 1-bedroom, $2,465; and 2-bedroom, $2,935. The rate structure is based on the level of care required. Fees include three meals per

Seniors play shuffleboard near the Boulder Creek Path.

day, housekeeping and laundry services, medication assistance, and transportation to outside appointments and recreational activities. RISE, (Restoring Independence, Strength and Energy) is a physical fitness program that allows residents to work with a personal trainer. The Wellness Spa fee begins at $30. The facility also offers a daily early memory impairment program.

Hawthorn House for Seniors, LLC
3275 23rd St., Boulder • (303) 247-0168

A home with eight private first floor bedrooms with adjacent bathrooms, ranging in cost (depending on need) from $3,500 to $4,500 per month. This facility is nestled in a quiet North Boulder neighborhood next to an open horse pasture and private pond. It offers daily social activities, 24-hour personalized care, live-in staff, home-cooked meals, assistance with medication, dressing, bathing and personal care, housekeeping and laundry service.

The Legacy at Lafayette
225 Waneka Parkway, Lafayette
• (303) 666-0691

Opened in 1997, this 40-room facility offers both a private-pay and Medicaid rate struc-

ture. Services include medication management, twenty-four hour personal care assistance, life enrichment programs, three nutritious meals daily, weekly housekeeping, laundry, transportation, whirlpool and spa. There are four living options; both small and large studios, and small and large one-bedroom apartments. Monthly rates range from $1,950 to $2,575. The Legacy is close to shopping in central Lafayette.

The Mary Sandoe House
1244 Gillaspie Dr., Boulder
• (303) 494-7317

The Mary Sandoe House has 24 assisted-living rooms that residents furnish with their own belongings. The fee, which for private-pay residents is $1,950 per month, includes three meals per day, housekeeping, medication management, laundry service and what is called "minimal assistance" bathing and dressing. The Mary Sandoe House has an activity staff too. There is a waiting list.

Sterling House
7720 Allison St., Longmont
• (303) 682-1066

The new Sterling House opened in 1998. There are studio, and one-bedroom units that look out onto a courtyard. Services include laundry, housekeeping, a twenty-four staff, all meals and special diets, medication assistance, activities, transportation to shopping and medical appointments, and assistance with personal needs. The facility is "committed to quality of life and care while respecting privacy and dignity." Sterling strives to create a sense of family and community by offering a library, living, room, TV room and crafts room. Room rates range from $1,500 to $2,000, depending on level of need.

If you are visiting Boulder and need a sitter, the hotel's front desk or concierge can probably help.

Child Care and Education

Don't you wish someone could hand-hold you into the child-care facility of your dreams? Boulder offers many good options for child care and schools. This chapter starts with the main child-care information centers and reviews how to screen child-care options. It explains how to find a sitter fast, and then goes on to checking out nannies, day care and preschools. The chapter ends with both public and private schools, including universities. For fun with children and summer camps, see the Boulder Kidstuff chapter.

Choosing Child Care

Information Centers

Head to Boulder's **Children's Services**, (303) 441-3180, at the Crossroads Mall, 28th and Canyon streets. Children's Services offers the county's most comprehensive lists of everything: more than 500 family child-care homes, nannies, day care centers, preschools, babysitting co-ops, public and private school information, financial assistance for housing and food, parenting classes and more. It also has a library of helpful books and videos. This city-run agency is open 8 AM to 5 PM, Monday through Friday.

If money's a problem, Children's Services now also runs the reduced-rate child-care program and can also tell you which centers/preschools offer a sliding fee or tuition reduction.

There are also other resources for families with young children. The **Colorado Preschool Program** subsidizes the tuition for kids who

qualify; placement is made through **Child Find**, (303) 447-5078. **Head Start**, (303) 441-3980, operates at two locations in Boulder and two in Lafayette with preschool enrichment for qualifying 3- to 5-year-olds. The **Parenting Place** in Boulder, (303) 449-0177, and Lafayette, (303) 666-4598, offers low-cost centers with support groups, education and play groups. You can bring children as old as 5 with you.

Finding a Sitter

You need a sitter, and Children's Services is closed. If the play starts in five minutes, good luck. Boulder might be a spontaneous kind of town, but good sitters get booked fast. Some services advertise that they can even provide a sitter with at least 24 hours' notice, but don't count on it. It's best to make arrangements for a sitter at least a week in advance.

Before you call a sitter, it's good to prepare a list of questions regarding qualifications. If the sitter you're considering is a teenager or preteen, have they completed the certification course offered by the YMCA? If they are not in the neighborhood, do they drive or will you be responsible for picking them up and getting them home? If your child is a baby, does the sitter have experience with infants? What about rates? Is the sitter prepared to make dinner and play games or help with homework? Does the sitter have references — other families that will vouch for their babysitting skills? A list of questions will make it easier to find a suitable match for your family's needs. **Children's Alley**, (303) 449-

1951, is a YWCA short-term care facility for infants through 12-year-olds. Rates are $1.75 to around $3.75 per hour per child, depending on your income. It's open on weekdays, generally between 7:30 AM and 9:45 PM (it closes at 5:45 PM on Fridays). Call at 4 PM the evening before for reservations—you can't call before then, and the place fills up fast. College students interested in sitting are listed through CU-Boulder's **Student Employment Office**, (303) 492-7349, which takes calls 9 AM to 5 PM Monday through Friday during the school year and until 4:30 PM in the summer.

Workforce, Boulder County's 50+ Program, (303) 441-3985, makes referrals for pre-screened senior sitters, primarily retirees looking for jobs. **Rent-a-Mom**, (303) 322-1399, has a nanny program. Their pre-screened employees can drive and generally are hired for an evening or up to two weeks. The YMCA, (303) 442-2778, offers a list of teenagers who have passed a Red Cross babysitting course. If your child is sick but you still need to go to work, call **Heart of Colorado Caregivers**, (303) 440-0384; **Medix**, (303) 741-2045; and **Take-A-Break**, (303) 665-9741. Rates are generally $8 to $10 an hour. Your employer might even cover part of the cost.

If you are visiting Boulder and need a sitter, the hotel's front desk or concierge can probably help. If you've just moved to town and need to find reliable sitters or child care, ask the mom you see on Pearl Street Mall, call neighborhood churches and schools and talk with workmates. Ask, ask, ask. It's just like home (or your last home). Sometimes, you find a good sitter fast. Sometimes, you've got to keep trying.

Nannies and Au Pairs

A "nanny" can be anyone from a local college student to a grandmother who regularly cares for your child, either live-in or coming to work in your home every day. An "au pair" is a live-in caretaker, often from Europe. Generally between 18 and 25 years old, the au pair lives with you for a year in exchange for child care with modest pay, room and board. One service that has worked successfully for the families enrolled is **AuPairCare**, out of San Francisco, (800) 4AUPAIR. The Yellow Pages and Children's Services both list local referral services.

Day-care Homes and Centers

Every parent wants the best possible environment for their children. Poor-quality child care can harm a child's self-esteem, ability to learn and ability to thrive later in life. *Working Mother* magazine regularly lists Colorado in the top 10 states for the quality of child care, but many experts believe we must set higher standards nationwide. A report by local early childhood expert Mary Culkin recently highlighted infant/toddler care as an area of special concern. She found wide variation in the nurturing and interpersonal interaction at child-care centers, vital indicators of care quality. What's more, just because a center was more expensive did not always correlate with the caregivers being kind to the children. That's why visiting, to check center quality for yourself, is an excellent idea.

Full-time child care in the Boulder area averages more than $150 per week, but cost depends on where you live. Longmont is less; Boulder is more. Smaller caregiver/child ratios, better caregiver training, more nutritious snacks and age-appropriate play materials all add up. Check with Children's Services if you need information about sliding scale fees. And keep your screening questions handy to help narrow your search.

INSIDERS' TIP

Boulder's public schools include magnet schools designed for children with special interests or needs.

Boulder offers a range of child-care options.

We're going to name some accredited day-care centers. Before we do, remember that many excellent, nonaccredited day-care homes provide a warm, safe environment with just a few children. Many top-notch day-care centers and preschools have not gone through the fees, paperwork and visits required for official accreditation. For these reasons, check other places too, and use our short list to compare.

The following 17 centers and preschools are accredited as of 1999 by the National Association for the Education of Young Children or the National Association of Family Childcare Providers. These groups provide the only national, voluntary, professionally-sponsored accreditation system for preschools, kindergartens and child-care centers. They base their decisions on interaction among staff and children, staff and parents, location, staff qualifications, health, safety and physical environment. They are **Sue Stevens**, (303) 666-8774; **The Elm Tree**, (303) 442-7140; **Floc Child Care Center**, (303) 442-6198; **Harmony Preschool**, (303) 444-8452; **Messiah Lutheran Preschool**, (303) 776-2573; **Sunflower Preschool**, (303) 494-2012; **Boulder Day Nursery**, (303) 442-7605; **Mountain View Preschool**, (303) 494-3557; **CU Children's Center**, (303) 492-6185; **Columbine Preschool**,

(303) 443-0792; **Kellog Child Development**, (303) 938-8233; **Peter Pan Cooperative Preschool**, (303) 499-5231; **Children's World on Wedgewood in Longmont**, (303) 776-6118; **Children's World in Broomfield**, (303) 465-2053; **Children's World in Louisville**, (303) 665-7416; **Commerce Children's Center**, (303) 497-5063, and **Children's World South**, (303) 494-3694. The **CU-Boulder Family Housing Children's Center**, (303) 492-6185, also has national accreditation, but it is only available to University of Colorado student, staff and faculty families. Another option is **Town & Country School**, (303) 938-1314, which begins with preschool for kids 2½ and older and continues through kindergarten and elementary school through age 8. The school sits on a big, open play yard on an acre lot, and each preschool class includes a group-certified teacher.

The **Colorado Preschool Program**, (303) 447-5075, conducts development screening and subsidizes the placement of nearly 120 students who can benefit from preschool experience at high-quality, community-based preschools, including **Alicia Sanchez Elementary School**'s bilingual preschool in Lafayette, (303) 665-2044; the **Child Learning Center** at CU-Boulder's Communications Disorders Clinic, (303) 492-5375; **Children's**

House Preschool, (303) 444-6432; Friends'N'Fun Children's Center in Lafayette, (303) 666-5111; Kohl Elementary School's Cottage Preschool in Broomfield, (303) 466-5885; Mountain View Preschool, (303) 494-3557; Nederland Elementary School's Caribou Mountain Preschool, (303) 258-7092; New Horizons Cooperative Preschool, (303) 442-7434; The Family Learning Center's bilingual preschool, (303) 442-8979; and the Rainbow Tree Preschool, (303) 449-4800.

Marcello Games, a volunteer at Our School Pre-School, has produced a film depicting children during a typical school day. He also captured a touching scene of how the children prepared a burial ceremony for an unexpected occurrence, the death of the school's pet guinea pig. You can call Our School to borrow or purchase the video (it sells for around $20), which is an excellent example of top-quality, respectful interactions between two director-certified preschool teachers and their young students.

Extended Care for Older Kids and Other Family Issues

If you can't be there when your kids come home from school but don't want them home alone, you might connect them with employment or volunteer opportunities.

For evening entertainment, keep in mind that many local music clubs and pool halls ban anyone under age, even if they aren't planning to drink. That explains the popularity of places such as Red Robin (see our Restaurants chapter) or Crossroads Mall (see our Shopping chapter) for younger teens and coffeehouses for older teens. Youngsters often plug into programs and facilities available at the YMCA and North, South and East Boulder recreation centers (see our Parks and Recreation Centers chapter), which have excellent swimming programs, gyms and other attractions.

Church groups, Boulder Youth Services, (303) 441-4357, and your local school are other places that can help. In 1996, City on the Hill Ministries, (303) 413-0974, at 7483 Arapahoe

Avenue, built a skateboard park outside the church and welcomes youngsters to use it for free.

Jobs for youngsters, especially those younger than 16, are hard to come by — and vacation periods can stretch interminably for teens with little to do. The three Boulder Recreation Centers offer free access to gymnasiums for teens every weekday afternoon. One of the finest recreation programs, begun in 1966, is the Boulder Junior Rangers. Since then, some 4,000 teens ages 14 to 17 have undertaken a variety of construction and maintenance projects in the Boulder Mountain Park System. Digging, hauling, planting and cleaning have not only provided teens with a modest summer income, but also have given them insight into conservation and ecology. At age 18, Junior Rangers may graduate to assistant Senior Rangers and at 21 to Senior Rangers, supervising teams of 10 to 12 Juniors. The YMCA's Youth Employment Center, (303) 442-2778 ext. 218, operates as a clearinghouse for jobs from lawn-mowing and babysitting to tutoring younger children. They've helped find work for teens as young as 13.

If a family is in real trouble, Children's Services (see "Information Centers" in this chapter) is a source for information about other organizations, classes, counseling and further options to help resolve ongoing family conflicts and even abuse issues that can be damaging. Boulder County's Family Preservation Program, (303) 441-1000, funded by the Boulder County Department of Social Services, Medicaid and the state's juvenile justice system, draws on the expertise of several agencies to offer intensive short-term intervention techniques to stabilize families in crisis.

Schools

Public Schools

Two school districts serve Boulder County — Boulder Valley and St. Vrain.

The Boulder Valley District, (303) 447-1010, includes Boulder, Broomfield, Gold Hill, Jamestown, Lafayette, Louisville and Nederland. Nearly 26,950 students attend 32 elementary schools including one K-8, twelve middle schools, one middle-senior high, seven high schools, three charter schools and one technical education center. Average class size is 25. Most teachers have more than 10 years of teaching experience and hold master's degrees. Some schools offer before- and after-school meals and care, enrichment programs and summer sessions. The annual budgeted operating expenditure per pupil is $4,800.

The **St. Vrain District**, (303) 776-6200, serves Dacono, Erie, Firestone, Federick, Hygiene, Longmont, Lyons, Mead, Niwot, Peaceful Valley and Raymond. It has around 18,300 students in 32 different schools, including elementary schools including one K-8 charter school, five middle schools, three middle/senior high schools, three senior high schools, one alternative high school and one career development center. It employs 1,050 teachers. Average child/teacher ratio is 24-to-1, and the annual expenditure per pupil is $4,700. Some schools offer before- and after-school meals and care and enrichment programs.

Even though Boulder public schools place quite high in national and statewide rankings (and were rated by *Money* magazine as one of the top 100 school districts in the nation in 1996), controversies have stirred the system in recent years. Such issues as middle school versus junior high school, individualized learning versus back-to-basics, phonics versus whole language for beginner readers, a disquieting pattern of threatened and rescinded teacher layoffs and other thorny problems have taken an inordinate amount of community energy. On top of what appears to be chronic district-wide dissension, the Boulder Valley Schools' "site-based management" approach means that each school sets its own policies within the framework of district goals. Hoping to get back on course, voters in 1997 drummed out a "back to basics" school board majority and overwhelmingly supported four new members seen as being friendly to teachers, whole-language reading curriculum and middle schools. While voters appeared to be in agreement with many of the previous board's goals, the polarized, divisive, "televised" interactions were a turnoff. Many in the community are still unhappy with the previous board's decision to hire a retired naval commander as the new superintendent — a man with much experience but none in early childhood education. Superintendent Tom Seigel agreed he was in an awkward position following the election, but the new board hadn't yet issued him a pink slip when this book went to press.

Boulder's Open Enrollment policy means that you have a choice between sending your child to your neighborhood school, a different neighborhood's school or one of the focus or alternative schools popping up around Boulder. So check around to see which suits you and your youngster.

Boulder students do much better than those in the rest of Colorado — also not surprising considering that Boulder parents are among the most well-educated in the nation. Boulder's college-bound students had an average SAT score 54 points higher than the nation for verbal and 62 points higher for math. The ACT scores are comparable. St. Vrain's SAT and ACT scores are also higher than the state and national averages.

But what do those scores mean? Back-to-basics proponents say they test firm knowledge and are necessary to get into a good college. Others believe that worshipping the Dow Kid Instructional Average can skew education into nothing but a testing drill. When choosing a school, there are other important matters. What's the school's curriculum? How many children will be in your child's class? What's the ratio of adults to kids? Are parents encouraged to help in the classroom? What's the school's teaching style? Do the desks face forward and do the teachers fill the walls with chemical element charts, or do kids study in a reading nook with old sofas and decorate the walls with their own creations? Testing scores won't tell you which schools are as homogenous as Wonder Bread and which have a richer cultural diversity. Test scores won't tell you what it's like to be at the school. Visits and talks are crucial, for your school is a community, where you and your children can make friends, build memories and learn about life.

Here's one warning: Boulder County has grown fast. That can mean overcrowding. This was a winning theme in a student editorial cartoon contest. In the cartoon, one adult says, "I feel sorry for those goof-offs at our school. They're not getting the education they need." The other adult replies, "I agree. But it's a good thing they ditch class, or we'd have to hold class on the football field." Since 1996, more than 2,000 students have been added to classrooms. Budget constraints mean facilities and staff haven't kept up with increased enrollment, and some new communities are catching up on building schools nearby, forcing children from those communities to face busing to more distant schools or overcrowding. So ask about this "growing" issue.

Public Focus Schools

Some children thrive in any situation, like hardy garden plants. Others need a special environment before they bloom. If you've got a unique bloomer, check the focus and alternative schools, often called "magnet" schools. Some provide more structure than a traditional classroom. Others offer more open-ended explorations. There are programs with specially trained staff for bilingual children or children with unusual developmental needs. A few include Family Resource Schools, outreach programs as good as having a wonderful aunt or uncle around, ready to help plan after-school activities and improve the school's community.

You'll get the best information about magnet schools if you visit. Here are some teasers: See the beautiful rain forest mural kids designed at **University Hill Elementary**, (303) 442-6735. Also check out Uni Hill's Rainbow Press, where kids edit and publish real books, in languages including English, Spanish and Asian dialects. **Washington Bilingual School**, (303) 449-6618, has a goal of 50 percent English-dominant and 50 percent Spanish-dominant children. Platt Middle School's **Choice Program**, (303) 499-6800, boasts one of the most interesting science rooms around. Even in politically correct Boulder, **Casey Middle School**, (303) 442-5235, stands out with its emphasis on multiculturalism and a motto of

"Pride in Diversity." **Horizons K-8 School**, (303) 447-5580, is one of three charter schools in the Boulder Valley district. The school maintains high academic and behavioral expectations, offering mixed-age classes and individualized goal setting. Two additional charter schools will be operating by 2000.

Fairview High School, (303) 499-7600, has added an International Baccalaureate program for juniors and seniors. It is designed with more rigorous, internationally academic regarded standards. There were 976 students enrolled in IB in 1998-99, and more than half took at least three of these challenging courses. **New Vista High School**, (303) 447-5401, is designed to cultivate students' unique talents and gifts, as well as their ability to be responsible for their own learning. It graduated its first class in 1996, sending 50 percent of its students on to college and boasting one National Merit Scholar.

Passages, (303) 447-5573, is a dropout prevention program for high school students.

Now in its fourth year of operation, Boulder's **Summit Middle School** was founded by parents but operates under the auspices of the school system. This is a tuition-free, public charter school offering grades 6-8 a rigorous, academic curriculum designed to meet the needs of students wanting greater challenges. Call Boulder Valley School District for more information, and when you do, perhaps you'll learn about even more new focus schools (schools that offer a special, non-typical way of teaching, operated by the school district) or charter schools (schools that offer a special, non-typical way of teaching, funded by the school district but managed by the citizens forming the school) in the works. On one hand, the diversity such schools offer gives people more choices and helps teachers learn from a rich variety of styles. However, there are fears that too much diversity could spread resources thin and create factions that turn attention toward bitter arguments on style rather than letting teaching occur in a nonpolitical, caring environment.

The **Boulder Valley's Arapahoe Campus**, (303) 447-5220, offers high school students education in trade skill programs.

This one isn't such a fun teaser, but it's worth knowing: **Halcyon**, (303) 499-1121, is a day-treatment program for troubled adolescents. It includes around 30 staff people working with 20 students.

In 1997, St. Vrain opened a charter school, **Twin Peaks Charter Academy**, (303) 682-9377, for elementary students, grades K-8. An alternative high school program is offered at **Olde Columbine High School**, (303) 772-6363. The **Career Development Center**, (303) 772-3333, is at the same location, 1200 South Sunset. This vocational school is for adults and high school students who take electives in the CDC building. Courses include welding, automotive and building trades, health and dental, agriculture, horticulture, accounting, office systems and other specialties. The **Adult Education Center** at 619 Bowen, (303) 678-5662, offers adult diploma courses including classes in citizenship.

Private Schools

You can find private schools run by religious organizations and schools as nondenominational as a pin-striped suit. At some, kids aren't expected to read until they're past 3rd grade. At others, the academic drills start in preschool. Boulder's Children's Services lists private schools in Boulder County. In addition to the local schools below, some students commute to schools in Denver.

Jarrow Montessori
3900 Orange Ct., Boulder
• **(303) 443-0511**

Class sizes are generally small (between 16 and 20) in this school, which has a total enrollment of 210. Located on 3 acres in a pretty, quiet part of North Boulder, Jarrow Montessori offers a toddler program for kids 18 months to 3 years, a primary program for 3- to 6-year-olds, then an elementary program through 6th grade. Different age groups are blended in each classroom. This is a certified American Montessori Society school, with child-guided education. Teachers gather the interest of the student, and with the teacher's help, children guide their own learning. Education goes from concrete, hands-on experiences to abstract associations.

Friends School
5465 Pennsylvania Ave., Boulder
• **(303) 499-1999**

About 140 kids attend, ranging from 2 years 9 months through 11 years old (preschool through 5th grade). The average class size for preschool is 14 and for elementary about 20, with two teachers per classroom. Lots of hands-on materials, a custom curriculum for each student, and a caring atmosphere characterize Friends School.

Boulder Country Day School
3800 Kalmia Ave., Boulder
• **(303) 444-3603**

Preschool through 5th grade are taught at this very traditional, academically oriented program for 250 students. French and Latin are part of the curriculum. Computers, art, music and drama are taught here too. Class sizes are no bigger than 10 in the preschool and no larger than 15 in the elementary grades. Students wear uniforms and the principal greets them by name as they arrive each morning, holding an umbrella for them if it's raining. The 4th- and 5th-grade teachers send home biweekly progress reports about how each child is doing. In late 1996, Boulder Country Day bought a large tract of land in Gunbarrel on which it plans to relocate, eventually adding middle and high schools.

Shining Mountain Waldorf School
987 Locust Ave., Boulder
• **(303) 444-7697**

From preschool through high school, this school offers a rich blend of arts, music and drama interwoven with academic curriculum. There are 360 students and 50 faculty. For a chemistry experiment, students might draw what they observe as well as describe it in words. Primary class lessons can include lore about traditional fairy tales, folk stories and weaving. People who are not familiar with a Waldorf School should give it a visit to observe the warm, comfortable pace at which children learn and the richness of materials available. The philosophy behind Waldorf is more than 75 years old, and in addition to regular accreditation, teachers receive two years of training in Waldorf methods.

Shepherd Valley Waldorf School & Garden
6500 W. Dry Creek Parkway, Longmont
• **(303) 530-2644**

Boulder's second Waldorf School opened when the demand exceeded space available. This Gunbarrel-area school has preschool through 8th grade. The school will relocate in 1999 after construction of a new building on a 38-acre farm site. This will allow for a farm and garden atmosphere, making it unique in Boulder for those seeking Waldorf instruction. Class sizes are 15 to 20 students. And if you're not familiar with Waldorf schools, check the previous entry.

Sacred Heart of Jesus School
1317 Mapleton Ave., Boulder
• **(303) 447-2362**

This Catholic school has a preschool childcare program then a school from kindergarten through 8th grade. It's well-regarded for its traditional academic program and religious coursework. Lots of parents volunteer here, helping to add to the community atmosphere. Nearly 400 children attend.

September School
1902 Walnut Ave., Boulder
• **(303) 443-9933**

Hands-on learning and creativity distinguish this grade 9 through 12 high school of about 100 students. Classes average 8 to 10 students. The teaching staff is dedicated and excellent, including professional scientists and musicians with a knack for communicating with students as peers. The four-building campus

includes a small, former church at Canyon and 19th streets.

Alexander Dawson School
4801 N. 107th St., Lafayette
• **(303) 665-6679**

Alexander Dawson offers a tried-and-true basics academic approach for K through 12. More than 375 students were enrolled for the 1998 fall term. The sprawling campus east of Boulder includes tennis courts, art rooms, a pottery studio and a theater. The buildings look as clean as new pennies, and the staff takes a rigorous, academic approach, from Latin through Advanced Placement Biology plus interscholastic sports and a creative-writing magazine.

Bridge School
The Abbey, 6717 S. Boulder Rd., Boulder
• **(303) 494-7551**

One of Boulder's newest private secondary schools for grades 6 through 12 is the Bridge School, designed for motivated, intellectually curious learners. The school also seeks youngsters with good character and a willingness to take risks and challenge themselves. High school includes computer competency, an interdisciplinary approach to science, senior seminars in English (including one on literature written before 1914), foreign languages, art and physical education. Community service is also part of the graduation requirement. Founded with just a handful of students, 105 students were enrolled for the 1998 fall term.

The Final Decision

If only Boulder had just one little red schoolhouse, you wouldn't have to agonize over what will be best for your child. Here's a comforting story: One teacher, substituting throughout Boulder County, wore jeans to a school where the children called her by her first name and she read story books to them from a rocking chair. She loved the friendly environment but worried that its open-ended structure let some kids slide. At another school, she wore a business suit, the kids called her "Mrs." and she lectured from a desk. While academic performance was more easily measured here, she worried that creativity was stifled. Which school was better? She rated them equally good. But at the more casual school, she wove in more structure. At the more traditional school, she slipped in creative moments. If you know a school's program and your child's needs, the fit doesn't have to be exactly, always perfect. You're a parent. You're a wonderful part of your child's life. You can help provide balance, just as this excellent teacher does.

Extra Help

Boulder also has resources for children who need assistance in boosting study skills. fLearn, (303) 499-4386, 4800 Baseline Road, No. B-102, offers tutoring and sells educational materials to classroom teachers, homeschoolers and parents. A certified teacher oversees the program. Other options include **Sylvan Leaning Center**, 1600 38th Street, (303) 449-1700, and **Huntington Learning Center**, (303) 545-2100, 1722 14th Street, both offering help with general study skills, reading, writing and math, motivation and other issues designed to lead to better grades and enhanced self-esteem.

School officials also can refer you to private tutors for your child. Some tutors advertise in the local classifieds, and the university is also a reservoir of older students, education majors and specialists in other disciplines.

Colleges and Universities

Boulder students can choose from a wealth of higher education opportunities. Before discussing the colleges and university in Boulder, consider other schools near enough to Boulder to commute to Denver, site of the **University of Denver**, (303) 871-2000; the **University of Colorado at Denver**, (303) 556-3287; **Regis University**, (303) 458-4100; and **Metropolitan State College**, (303) 556-3058.

Colorado State University, (970) 491-1101, is in Fort Collins, roughly an hour north of Boulder. The **Colorado School of Mines**, (303) 273-3000, and **Red Rocks Community College**, (303) 988-6160, are in Golden, about a half-hour's drive south of Boulder.

Higher education centers in Boulder itself include:

University of Colorado at Boulder
Office of Admissions, Regent Administrative Ctr. 125, Campus Box 6, Boulder • (303) 492-6301

With all those red-roofed buildings, CU-Boulder is known as one of the nation's prettiest campuses. It's also close to recreational activities that make attending CU-Boulder lots of fun, including watching top teams such as the CU Buffs football team and CU women's basketball. But for academics, it offers excellent opportunities too.

CU-Boulder is most renowned for its science programs. Psychology, biology and English are among the most popular undergraduate majors. Classics and dance are among the smallest. CU professor Thomas Cech won the 1989 Nobel Prize in chemistry. In 1995 professors Carl Wieman and Eric Cornell were awarded the Fritz London Award for their work in low temperature physics. Also that year, history professor Patricia Nelson Limerick was awarded a prestigious McArthur Foundation grant, given for intellectual creativity. More CU undergraduate and grad-school alumni have become astronauts than graduates of any other school, including the service academies. With such a history, it's no surprise that CU-Boulder got more than $174 million in outside research funds in 1996.

Boulder is the largest campus in a four-campus system. Other campuses are CU-Denver on the three-college Auraria campus; CU-Colorado Springs; and the Health Sciences Center, including the University Hospital, in Denver. Approximately 25,000 students attend CU-Boulder, with 20,000 undergraduates and 5,000 graduates. As a state school, it gives tuition breaks to in-state residents, who make up nearly 70 percent of the student population. Non-degree candidates may pay to attend university classes as part of the university's continuing education program.

People older than 55 can audit classes for a nominal fee, (303) 492-8484, with the professor's permission.

The Naropa Institute
2130 Arapahoe Ave., Boulder
• (303) 444-0202 • (800) 772-6951

Celebrating 25 years in Boulder in 1999, Naropa is an accredited college offering undergraduate and graduate programs in the arts, social sciences and humanities. The school was founded in 1974 by Chogyam Trungpa Rinpoche, and its educational philosophy is rooted in the Buddhist contemplative tradition. Approximately 800 degree-seeking students attend Naropa. Students can earn bachelor's degrees in music, psychology, dance/movement studies, dance therapy, religious studies, writing and literature, environmental studies, early childhood education and interdisciplinary studies. Master's degrees are available in psychology, dance therapy, gerontology, art therapy, and writing and poetics. The institute also offers a performing arts series and many workshops and annually holds the Naropa Summer Institute, drawing faculty and students from around the world. Naropa also offers ongoing courses and workshops to the community at-large.

Boulder College of Massage Therapy
6255 Longbow Dr., Boulder
• (303) 530-2100

The Boulder School of Massage Therapy is a leading massage therapy education center. In 2000 the school will celebrate its twenty-fifth year as a non-profit institution. BCMT's diploma program includes in-depth training in a variety of approaches to massage therapy. The program includes human sciences, ethics, movement studies, career development and professional internships. Over 2,500 students have graduated from BCMT, with average enrollment each year at 250.

Front Range Community College
5490 Spine Rd., Gunbarrel
• (303) 447-5220
2255 N. Main St., Ste. 118, Longmont
• (303) 516-8999

Two-year degree and certificate programs are available at both locations in a variety of subjects. Some programs are specifically designed for students who intend to continue their education at a four-year college or university. Tuition is about half the cost of a four-year college.

Continuing Education

One of the most valuable lessons an educated person can learn is to keep on learning. If you have that attitude, you're going to love Boulder. Young and old, dabblers and those intent on gaining a specific new skill take courses from time to time. To get one of the enticing catalogs for these offerings, call or write the phone numbers below. Or, if you're already in Boulder, head to the library, a recreation center or a major grocery store, where these catalogs are usually available for free.

Boulder Parks and Recreation
3170 Broadway, Boulder
• (303) 441-3412

All three of Boulder's recreation centers offer skill-building courses. Gymnastics for kids and pottery for adults are very popular. The dance classes for both are very popular. Then there's yoga, martial arts, guitar, cooking, sign language, investing and whitewater kayaking. Most of these classes take place at the recreation centers. When the Parks and Recreation

---

INSIDERS' TIP

If you have chosen a child-care center but want to make one final check on its reputation, ask the State Department's Office of Child Care Services in Denver, (303) 866-5958, to share their licensing files. These files reveal complaints and reviews about the center. To see a file, make an appointment, or you can order copies of file information at 50 cents per page.

offerings first get published each season, the registration phones can be busy for a long time. Then, it's quicker to come to any of Boulder's three recreation centers and register in person.

CU-Boulder Continuing Education
1221 University Ave., Boulder
• **492-5148 or (800) 331-2801 (out-of-state), (800) 332-5839 (in-state)**

This fabulous catalog offers 300 courses each semester including everything from full-credit, college-level courses taught by CU-Boulder professors to noncredit pursuits such as beginning computer courses and art/poetry workshops. Noncredit classes often are taught by professionals — some just starting out in their fields and willing to share boundless enthusiasm, others nationally famous who will always love teaching. Classes usually take place right on the CU-Boulder campus, in the evenings and on weekends.

Regis University Boulder Campus
6235 Lookout Road, Suite H, Boulder
• **(303)-530-9514**

Through the School for Professional Studies, adults can complete bachelor of science degrees in business administration, computer information systems, religious studies and many more subjects by taking accelerated evening classes. A master's degree is offered in science and management and in computer information science.

Alternative Schools

In addition to schools offering continuing education classes for adults, there are more than 30 schools in Boulder offering training and certification in holistic and spiritual fields. A list of some of the most established schools follows.

BMS Center for Clinical Hypnotherapy
75 Manhattan Drive, Ste. 103, Boulder
• **(303) 494-111 • (303) 494-1001**

BMS offers courses to become a nationally certified clinical hypnotherapist. Advanced courses also are available to psychologists, social workers and other licensed professionals. The Center is authorized and certified by the National Guild of Hypnotists and the American Association of Professional Hypnotherapists.

Colorado Cranial Institute
1080 Hawthorn Ave., Boulder
• **(303) 449-0322**

The institute offers private, individual training sessions in craniosacral work to teach the proper treatment for a wide range of common health problems ranging from back pain to migraine headaches to head, jaw, neck, pelvis and diaphragm pain.

Colorado Institute for Classical Homeopathy
2299 Pearl St., Ste. 401, Boulder
• **(303) 440-3717**

The Colorado Institute offers a two-year program of in-depth homeopathic study. The curriculum is designed to prepare participants for a professional career and the national exam with the Council for Classical Homeopathy. CICH is a nonprofit organization and its program is approved and regulated by the Division of Private Occupational Schools, Colorado Department of Higher Education.

The Cooking School of the Rockies
637 S. Broadway, Ste. H
• **(303) 494-7988**

The Cooking School has a big kitchen area and store that's open 10 AM to 5 PM Monday through Saturday. In the cooking school, students can refine their wine-tasting skills, watch famous chefs from around the world demonstrate their favorite techniques, or learn hands-on everything, from professional French cooking to sushi rolling and gingerbread house baking. A professional chef's course includes a trip to France.

Guild for Structural Integration
3107 28th St., Boulder
• **(303) 447-0122 • (800) 447-0150**

Dedicated to the traditional teaching of Dr. Ida P. Rolf, GSI offers basic training in the Rolf method of structural integration, continuing education, advanced training and introductory courses in anatomy and physiology and massage.

Hakomi Institute
1800 30th St., Ste. 201, Boulder
• (303) 447-3290

Hakomi Integrative Somatics (HIS) is a body-centered psychotherapy influenced by the techniques of Gestalt, bioenergetics, Feldenkrais and by the spiritual principles of Taoism and Buddhism. The institute offers training in healing developmental and traumatic wounds.

International Breath Institute
2525 Arapahoe Ave., Ste. E4-287, Boulder • (303) 444-8615

Founded in 1991, The IBI is a holistic wellness educational organization emphasizing personal and professional development through instruction in the TransformBreathing Energy System (TEMS).

Polarity Center of Colorado
1721 Redwood Ave., Boulder
• (303) 443-9847

This Center offers professional training and is accredited by the American Polarity Therapy Association. Polarity therapy is a comprehensive health system based on understanding the human energy field founded on the work of Dr. Randolph Stone.

Rocky Mountain Center for Botanical Studies
2639 Spruce St., Boulder
• (303) 442-6861

A ten-month Western program includes the study of herbal therapeutics, botany, physiology, earth-centered herbalism, field identification, clinical work and medicine-making field trips. The center is devoted to in-depth exploration of plants as healing allies.

Rolf Institute
205 Canyon Blvd., Boulder
• (303) 449-5903

The Rolf Institute was founded in 1971 and graduates about 75-100 students each year from its Boulder school. Developed by Dr. Ida P. Rolf in the 1940s, Rolfing is a series of 10 specific and individualized hands-on sessions designed to realign the body's structure.

The School of Natural Cookery
P.O. Box 19466, Boulder
• (303) 444-8068

Established in 1983, this vegetarian cooking school is internationally recognized for both its nonprofessional and professional students. A strong curriculum in the art of preparing whole grains, beans and vegetables include the techniques of meal composition and improvisation.

School of Natural Medicine
2888 Bluff St. Ste. 403 • (303) 443-4882

The School of Natural Medicine was established in 1977 by Director Sharan, also a founder of the British School of Iridology in Cambridge, England. SNM offers natural physician training in iridology, herbal medicine, naturopathy, and transcenDance natural medicine. An extensive summer program in Boulder supplements correspondence courses.

After hello, a new neighbor's first question is usually about a doctor, dentist or orthodontist.

Healthcare and Wellness

Many people come to Boulder for the inherently healthful and congenial lifestyle, but even happy people have babies and sometimes get sick or hurt. This section lists referral services, then describes major medical facilities to assist you with your healthcare needs. We also give you an Insiders' look at how to choose from Boulder's large selection of alternative care providers — in case you're in Boulder County partly because you want to get even healthier.

In Boulder, however, it's not only people who have medical alternatives, but also their furry friends. Boulder's love affair with pets is evidenced by the many options for animal health care listed at the end of this chapter.

Emergency

Call 911 if you are any place in Boulder County and need help fast. Not only can you get help, but our 911 is designed to automatically locate you unless you're calling from a party line.

Physician and Dentist Referral Services

After hello, a new neighbor's first question is usually about a doctor, dentist or orthodontist. Once you know what kind of physician you need, word of mouth is often a good bet for finding someone you're comfortable with. If you don't have a neighbor, friend or coworker to ask, start by checking the Yellow Pages under "Physicians" or "Dentists" or call

one of the area's referral services. The **Boulder County Medical Society**, (303) 545-6178, lists around 400 doctors; and (800) DOCTORS, operated by **Community Health**, has a local phone number, (303) 443-2584, which provides referrals to about 300 Boulder-area doctors, dentists, counselors, chiropractors, midwives and other licensed healthcare professionals. Four of the larger medical clinics also offer referrals. The **Boulder Medical Center's Patient Services**, (303) 440-3000, lists more than 50 physicians and has two satellite clinics in Louisville, including one at Centura Avista Hospital. **Centura's Health Advisor**, (303) 777-6877, is a 24-hour phone line providing referrals, healthcare information and community information. **Longmont Clinic**, (303) 776-1234, lists around 40 local physicians. **Kaiser Permanente**, (303) 440-0884, is a large health maintenance organization, which can also refer its own patients to more than 450 of its associated physicians in the Denver/Boulder area.

Hospitals

Boulder Community Hospital
1100 Balsam St., Boulder
• **(303) 440-2273 (general),**
(303) 440-2037 (emergency)

With 265 beds, Community is the largest full-service hospital in Boulder County. It takes pride in its emergency, maternity, cancer (full radiation service) and open-heart surgery centers, among other specialties. It emphasizes high-quality and family-centered care. For inpatient care, the Colorado Hospital Association's data indicate Community is one of the state's best hospitals for success rate, short length of stay and low-cost service.

The care is first-rate here, and the atmosphere tends toward the friendly and relaxed. Labor and delivery rooms might include old-fashioned rocking chairs and other homey touches, with lots of encouragement for family and new baby to happily bond. A friend who's had surgery in the cancer care center reports that her room's stereo system was top-notch. She's a professional hospital worker from out of state, and she gives the cancer unit an "A+" for the personal attention she received. With advance notice, pet visitation is allowed (be sure the pet's with a trained handler and you have a recent copy of vaccinations). While there are sort of official visiting hours, the staff tends to be pretty relaxed about visitors if you would like them more often.

A satellite clinic in Lafayette is Community Medical Center, (303) 666-4345, at 2000 South Boulder Road.

Mapleton Center
311 Mapleton Ave., Boulder
• (303) 443-0230

The Seventh-Day Adventists built their tuberculosis sanitarium here nearly a century ago. The location is beautiful, near Mount Sanitas Trail and the peace of the foothills. Today the hospital is a division of Boulder Community, offering rehabilitation services for victims of strokes, accidents, brain injuries, developmental disabilities and more, and behavioral health services for people suffering from psychiatric disorders, chemical dependency, alcoholism, depression, drug abuse, eating disorders and teen behavior problems.

"Easy Street," a special part of the rehabilitation facilities, has stores, curbs, cars and restaurants so patients can practice real-world situations again. For patients working on balance, there is equestrian therapy and a low-ropes course. In past years therapy for head-injury patients has included a hike up 14,000-foot Pikes Peak to improve physical coordination and self-confidence. A warm-water, non-chlorinated therapy pool is open to anyone; call for hours and fees. A new satellite facility, (303) 530-4675, at 6685 Gunpark Drive, Suite 130, in Gunbarrel, offers physical therapy, speed and occupational therapy and pediatric rehabilitation.

Behavioral-health services at Mapleton include inpatient psychiatric care and day-treatment programs for adults and adolescents. The hotline for emergency evaluation is (303) 440-5656.

Centura Health
Avista Adventist Hospital
100 Health Park Dr., Louisville
• (303) 673-1000 (general),
(303) 673-1111 (emergency)

This hospital, commonly referred to simply as Avista Hospital, was built in 1990 in booming Louisville and has beds for 58 patients. This well-regarded, full-service hospital offers 24-hour emergency service, single-room family-centered maternity, a nursery, a pediatric unit, a cardiac unit, inpatient and outpatient rehabilitation services and diagnostic services including whole-body MRI and CAT scan . . . the works.

INSIDERS' TIP

Boulder County is home to two yoga ashrams or resident communities: the Eldorado Mountain Yoga Ashram in Eldorado Springs and the Shoshoni Yoga Retreat south of Rollinsville. Both communities share the same Hindu- and Buddhist-derived spiritual lineage.

Charter Centennial Peaks Behavioral Health Systems
2255 S. 88th St., Louisville
• **(303) 673-9990, (800) 242-7837**

Centennial has facilities and programs for children, adolescents, adults and seniors. There are 72 beds for inpatient care and day-treatment and outpatient programs for anyone with emotional, behavioral or substance-abuse problems. The Counseling and Assessment Center, a free consultation service, can help determine whether someone needs therapy and suggests where to get assistance, for instance, from counselors, social workers, support groups or psychiatrists.

Longmont United Hospital
1950 Mountain View Ave., Longmont
• **(303) 651-5111 (general),**
(303) 651-5000 (emergency)

This 142-bed hospital has a full range of services, from a whole-body CAT scanner to emergency services, home healthcare, a therapy pool, maternity, psychiatric services and an adult day-care program. In 1996, the hospital built a medical office building next door and leases space to physicians and other medical providers.

The Mapleton/LUH Rehab is on the hospital grounds. Patients who need minimal rehabilitation as they head home can get transitional care. Longmont United added a cancer care unit in 1995, with full chemo- and radiation-therapy services.

A satellite clinic in Niwot is United Medical Center of Niwot, (303) 652-9135, at 6857 Paiute Avenue. A second satellite, United Medical Center of Lyons, (303) 823-6535, is located at 303 Main Street, Unit C. Both offer urgent care and family practice.

Hospice

Hospice of Boulder County
2825 Marine St., Boulder
• **(303) 449-7740**

This hospice, established in 1978 and one of the first in the nation, offers an interdisciplinary program of home care, counseling, educational services and bereavement support to meet the needs of terminally ill patients and their family members. Services are provided in patients' homes and in nursing homes; there's no inpatient facility, and care for the terminally ill is provided regardless of a person's ability to pay. The hospice also has a volunteer training program.

County Health Department Clinics

Boulder County residents come to clinics for low-cost immunizations, well-child care, confidential HIV testing, senior clinics, environmental health screening and more. There's a free directory of services available through the **Boulder County Health Department**, (303) 441-1100. Clinics are located in Boulder at 3305 N. Broadway, (303) 413-7500; in Longmont at 529 Coffman St., Suite 200, (303) 678-6166; and in Lafayette at 1345 Plaza Court, (303) 666-0515. The Arc (as it's informally called) is the county's **Addiction Recovery Center**, (303) 441-1275, at 3470 N. Broadway, offering detox and treating substance abuse and co-dependency. The center also operates an impaired-driver prevention program, (303) 441-1279.

The **Boulder County AIDS Project**, (303) 444-6121, at 2118 14th Street in Boulder, offers information about prevention and treatment along with a food bank, counseling and buddy systems for clients with HIV. The **Mental Health Center of Boulder County**, 1333 Iris Avenue, Boulder, has a crisis line, (303) 447-1665, and a general line, (303) 443-8500. The **Rape Crisis Team**'s 24-hour crisis line is (303) 443-7300.

The **Boulder Heart Institute**, (303) 440-3222, at 2750 Broadway in Boulder, offers services ranging from a basic cardiac risk-factor screening to various types of cardiac wellness programs and state-of-the-art exercise testing to assess athletes' fitness levels.

The **People's Clinic** is a healthcare clinic offering comprehensive adult, pediatric and prenatal care for low-income residents. Clinics are in Boulder at 3303 N. Broadway, (303) 449-6050, and 3100 34th Street, (303) 449-5988.

Finding Holistic Healthcare

As early as 1896, patients admitted to Boulder's Colorado Sanitarium were given Swedish massage, hydrotherapy treatments and a vegetarian diet as a cure for illness. Advertised as a resort, the sanitarium encouraged people to come for "refreshment of the mind, body, and spirit," and to that end operators offered their own line of whole-grain cereals and health foods. Many tubercular patients were drawn West to such facilities and soon recovered from what was believed a fatal condition. What was then viewed as radical medical treatment is now tame by comparison to other offerings from Boulder's holistic health community. In Boulder the word "wellness" is used as much or more than "healthcare" or "medicine," and the line between conventional medicine and alternative approaches is blurred.

Holistic doctors believe in treating the whole person, rather than the symptoms of illness. Naturally there is some skepticism about alternative therapies from those who practice traditional medicine, but unless an illness is life-threatening, exploring options can be a first step toward taking control of your health.

Selecting the right therapy and a suitable practitioner can be overwhelming without a few basic guidelines. Holistic medicine defines "complete therapeutic systems" as those based on a philosophy or set of beliefs which include a comprehensive range of treatments. Some examples are Ayurvedic medicine, Chinese medicine, herbal medicine, homeopathy, indigenous medicine, naturopathic medicine and nutritional therapy. (Chiropractic and osteopathy are sometimes called complete systems but just as often fall under the physical or bodywork category.)

Ayurvedic medicine is central to the culture of India and dates back to 3000 B.C. A variety of healing and prevention techniques fall under Chinese medicine, including the use of herbs, acupuncture and t'ai chi ch'uan. Once the only source of medicine for ancient cultures, herbal medicine dates back to ancient Egypt but has only recently regained credibility in Western cultures. Homeopathy is based on the 19th century "Law of Similars" and uses the substance causing an illness in minute quantities to cure that same illness. Indigenous medicine, or shamanism, employs a variety of healing techniques found in most tribal communities. Naturopathic medicine is sometimes called "common sense" medicine because it relies primarily on four components for good health: fresh air and clean water, balanced diet, exercise and "right living." Finally, nutritional therapy originates from naturopathic medicine, where diet is emphasized as the key to good health.

Not all people seeking a more holistic approach to health want to embrace a complete system of therapy. Perhaps you're suffering from chronic tension or lack of vitality and just want to try a new bodywork therapy. In that case, Boulder is the right place to be. Acupressure, aikido, Alexander technique, Breema, dance therapy, Feldenkrais, Hellerwork, massage, neuro-muscular therapy, polarity therapy, reflexology, Reiki, Rolfing, yoga, and Zen shiatsu are just a few of the offerings available.

Unlike "systems" of healing, there are techniques often, but not always, used in conjunction with the larger complete therapies. Practitioners of these techniques also abound in Boulder. They include applied kinesiology, aromatherapy, biofeedback, color therapy, crystal and gem therapy, flower essences, hydrotherapy, hypnotherapy, iridology, magnetic therapy, sound therapy and visualization therapy, to name a few.

If you feel like an oddball for choosing alternative health options, consider this: Nearly half the population is said to use at least one remedy not prescribed by a doctor; over one-

---

fifth have visited a complementary practitioner. It's predicted that the number of adults using some form of alternative therapy will rise to one in two by the millennium. The reason was outlined in a 1995 survey in the *British Journal of Clinical Psychology* that showed many people turn to alternative therapies when they see signs of improvement that conventional medicine failed to provide.

If you decide it's worth your money to seek alternative healthcare, you're not alone, but it will take some research. Finding the right practitioner is complicated by Colorado's vague licensing requirements, which might someday change. For the uninitiated, it's easy to confuse a certified dietitian with one who has one or two years of non-federally certified training with a registered dietitian who has several years of university training. The same is true with naturopathic physicians. Some have attended federally accredited, four-year programs that have the same basics as medical school, then specialize in the science and counseling skills that can help a person stick with a good diet, exercise and weight reduction stress. Others who call themselves naturopathic physicians have taken a correspondence course for six months through the mail. Clearly, screening and getting as much information as possible about a practitioner's competence is recommended. Don't be afraid to ask the healthcare provider about qualifications. Which program did they attend? What was the program's accreditation — for instance, federal or state? How many years of study did they undertake, and what are they qualified to do? Can they provide references?

If you are seeking an expert in wellness counseling, choose carefully. Listen for word-of-mouth recommendations. *The Daily Camera*'s Monday "FIT" magazine includes a regular weekly column featuring three healers (usually an M.D. and two alternative professionals) discussing a health question from different perspectives. It's a great way to compare treatment philosophies and glean names of reputable professionals. Read the local holistic journals such as *Nexus,* which is available at many grocery stores, especially the health-food stores.

Here's the most important aspect of choosing alternative care: Patients of holistic doctors are required to take responsibility for their own wellness, an uncomfortable role for many of us raised on conventional medicine. Don't expect a magical quick fix for improving your health through lifestyle changes, but be aware that confidence in a practitioner is intrinsic to the success of their work.

Interdisciplinary groups and practitioners, as well as specialists, abound. For instance, naturopathic physician Charley Cropley, (303) 554-9000, is the director of **The Center for Radiant Aliveness** and specializes in nutrition counseling. Chiropractor Jay Wilson, (303) 449-7414, also is an expert on nutritional issues. Nancy Rao, (303) 545-2021, and JoHanna Reilly, (303) 541-9600, are among Boulder's half-dozen naturopathic physicians with excellent reputations in the alternative health community.

Medical doctor Bob Rountree of the **Helios Health Center**, (303) 499-9224, co-authored an excellent reference book, *Smart Medicine for a Healthier Child*, for those wanting to compare conventional and alternative therapies. Co-author Rachel Walton is a Boulder pediatric nurse who teaches classes to new mothers on using natural medicine to care for babies and young children. Helios is an example of physicians and health professionals teaming up because they appreciate the way conventional and alternative healthcare can complement each other. In fact, one of Helios' doctors is a board-certified acupuncturist and homeopath, as well as an M.D.

Similarly, **Wellspring for Women**, (303) 443-0321, is a group of women nurse practitioners, acupuncturists and homeopaths who have designed a practice focusing on the health needs of women. Check out these professionals and clinics, and ask them for referrals to other qualified professionals. Naturopathic physician Todd Nelson, (303) 449-1330, and chiropractor Darryl Hobson, (303) 449-4498, each offer Vital Health Through Wellness seminars, which include fasting and cleansing.

For a sampling of schools offering training and certification in holistic and spiritual fields in Boulder, see our Child Care and Education chapter.

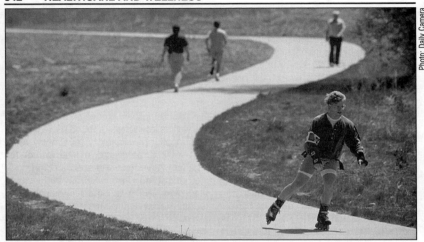

An in-line skater navigates an S-turn out east on the Boulder Creek Path.

Photo: Daily Camera

Wellness for Pets

Boulderites love their pets. Owners regularly bring their dogs along to outdoor cafes and especially while running or hiking. In fact, residents feel so strongly about "pet rights" they approved a ballot measure in 1996 to exempt certain park and open-space areas from a city ordinance that required dog owners to keep their pets on a leash.

It's no surprise then that so many options exist for keeping pets healthy. **Allpets Clinic**, (303) 499-5335, at 5290 Manhattan Circle, stands out because it offers 24-hour veterinary care. This pet clinic has a welcoming fire hydrant out front for the dogs and separate entrances and waiting areas for clients with dogs and cats. In 1992, Allpets received the veterinary economics hospital design award, and in 1993 it was chosen as Boulder's small business of the year. For those in central or north Boulder, the **Boulder Emergency Pet Clinic**, (303) 440-7722, at 1658 30th Street, may be more convenient. This critical care and trauma center has a doctor on duty all night, every night, and no appointment is necessary.

Other vets specialize. The **Boulder Valley Cat Clinic**, (303) 444-6369, at 2825 Wilderness Place, deals with feline medical and behavioral problems, offers a low-cost vaccination clinic and boasts of "no barking dogs." **Centennial Valley Animal Hospital**, (303) 666-9363, at 259 Century Circle in Louisville, handles cats, dogs and exotics. **Dr. Nancy Loving**, (303) 444-9494, at 2160 James Canyon Drive, specializes in performance and sport horse care.

In Boulder there are also holistic veterinarians who treat sick pets with such techniques as chiropractic, osteopathy or acupuncture.

INSIDERS' TIP

Practitioners of alternative medicine are regularly listed or advertise with *Nexus*, Colorado's holistic health, metaphysics and natural lifestyles directory and magazine. The bimonthly publication is free at health food stores and is supplied to 300 outlets in Boulder and Denver.

Holistic veterinarians believe in the animal's ability to heal itself and almost never use antibiotics when confronting illness. While the holistic movement in veterinary medicine is still small you can locate a holistic veterinarian in the Denver-Boulder metro area, by calling (303) 733-2728 or the **Rocky Mountain Holistic Veterinary Medical Association** at (303) 693-9314.

Boulder supports one daily, one semi-daily, two general-interest weeklies and a number of special-interest newspapers.

Media

The story goes that when one of Boulder's early citizens decided the rough mining town needed a newspaper to encourage a sense of community, he simply drove his wagon to a nearby town, loaded up that town's newspaper press, and Boulder had its newspaper. Apparently the notion took and Boulder has been blessed (or cursed, depending upon your perspective) with a wealth of newspapers ever since. Currently, the town supports one daily, one semi-daily, two general-interest weeklies and a number of special-interest newspapers. Boulder was one of the first cities in the nation where *The New York Times* became available for home delivery. And, the Denver dailies show periodic fascination with the odd little town to the north.

In addition to four local radio stations, the city also has cable television channels for city information, citizen input and CU programming. Denver's four local television stations also include Boulder in their coverage area.

Newspapers

Boulder has one complete daily newspaper, the *Daily Camera*, which was recently sold to Scripps-Howard after many years in the Knight-Ridder newspaper chain. The *Colorado Daily,* a give-away that isn't technically daily, focuses more on University of Colorado news and readers. The free *Boulder Planet* provides an all-local news package and the give-away *Boulder Weekly* digs for local scandal and investigative stories. Specialty papers focus on topics from business to natural healing to women.

Dailies

Colorado Daily
5505 Central Ave., Boulder
• (303) 443-6272

Published since 1897, this free and informative independent paper serves the university community and Boulder. It's published five days a week. Friday is an extra-large weekend edition. In summer, it cuts back to two days a week. The paper covers local, regional and national news plus sports and entertainment, and has a very vocal editorial and letters to the editor section. There are also classified advertisements. It's available on campus and at drop sites around town.

Daily Camera
1048 Pearl St., Boulder • (303) 442-1202

The *Camera*, Boulder's only complete daily newspaper, covers the people, issues and events of Boulder, CU-Boulder, neighboring towns and Boulder County. Regular daily sections and pages present local, national and international news, business news and entertainment news. The *Camera's* award-winning sports section is competitive with Denver dailies and covers local preps, CU and Denver's professional teams and features special sections on skiing and the Bolder Boulder 10k race.

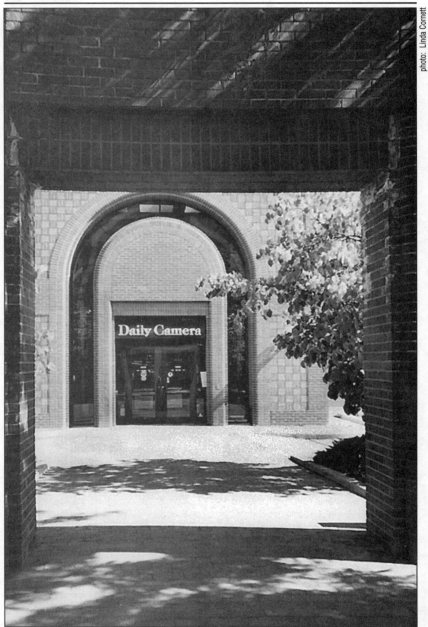

photo: Linda Cornett

The Daily Camera, Boulder's oldest newspaper, fills the corner of 11th and Pearl streets. The newspaper periodically flirts with the idea of moving part of its operation out of bustling downtown, but so far has stayed put.

The larger *Sunday Camera* includes separate sections for business, lifestyles, entertainment, a TV guide, color comics, news-focus stories, local guest opinions and *The New York Times* crossword puzzle. Among the weekday special-interest sections are "FIT," a weekly health and fitness tabloid; "Business Plus"; a food section; "Discovery," a science and technology section; "Get Out" for local recreation; and "Friday Magazine" for entertainment in Boulder, Denver and along the Front Range. Weekly tabloids cover the Boulder County towns of Lafayette, Louisville, Superior and Erie.

Special sections throughout the year include the "Boulder County Almanac," "Best of Boulder," back to school and college sections, a "Holiday Guide" and "Memories," a monthly tabloid of engagement, wedding and anniversary announcements.

Camera writers, photographers, ads, sections and the whole paper have won awards from various state and national organizations.

Weeklies

Boulder Planet
**New Hope Group Publications,
2028 14th St., Boulder • (303) 444-5761**

From news to arts to sports to astrological readings, this three-year-old free weekly paper prides itself on being completely local, a direct challenge to the old-timer *Daily Camera,* which has added more countywide and national and international coverage. The *Planet* specializes in obituaries and lots of other items not usually included in a weekly paper. The coverage is lively and well written. The *Planet* (known affectionately as "the Peanut" to staffers) is available at drop sites and in boxes around town and is delivered free in limited areas.

Boulder Weekly
**690 S. Lashley Ln., Boulder
• (303) 494-5511**

Specializing in news, arts and entertainment, this 5-year-old weekly was possibly the first paper in the country to break the news of the militia connection to the Oklahoma City bombing. It has columns, investigative articles

and interviews with local people plus entertainment, a classified section and other special sections. The paper is free at numerous local drop sites.

Monthly

Boulder County Business Report
**4865 Sterling Dr., Ste. 200, Boulder
• (303) 440-4950**

This monthly newspaper is a leading information source on trends in real estate, high technology, finance, tourism and business. A subscription is $25 per year, or the paper is free at 250 local drop sites.

Magazines

Boulder County Guide
**P.O. Box 1075, Boulder, CO 80306
• (303) 449-7433**

Published annually, this free guide has numerous local restaurant menus completely reproduced plus shopping, services and recreation and a professional directory. Look for it in local shops, bookstores, supermarkets and other drop sites.

Boulder Magazine
**1919 14th St., Ste. 709, Boulder
• (303) 443-0600**

Published three times a year — summer, fall and winter/spring — this handy guide has all kinds of local information and interesting articles on local people, places and things to do. Subscriptions are $15 per year, or specific issues are available for $5. The magazine is free at numerous local drop sites.

Nexus: Colorado's Holistic Journal
**1680 Sixth St., Suite 6, Boulder
• (303) 442-6662, (888) 644-6662**

Celebrating its 18th anniversary, *Nexus* describes itself as a holistic health and natural lifestyles directory and magazine for Boulder, Denver and the whole of Colorado. Readers will be amazed at the variety of therapies available locally. *Nexus* is published in a newspaper tabloid-type format. Subscriptions are $21 per year (six issues), or pick up *Nexus* for free at health-food stores, bookstores, restaurants, shops and universities around Boulder and the state.

Radio Stations

The numerous Front Range radio stations whose broadcasts are received in Boulder are listed here along with the more popular local stations. See this chapter's Close-up for details on Boulder's local radio favorites.

Adult Alternative

KBVI 1490 AM (Boulder Valley news and music)

KTCL 93.3 FM (Modern rock and new music)

KXPK 96.5 FM (Alternative and retro)

KBCO 97.3 FM Boulder and 1190 AM (Adult album alternative)

Adult Contemporary

KOSI 101.1 FM

Big Band

KEZW 1430 AM (Nostalgia, Big Band and easy listening)

Christian

KRKS 990 AM and 94.7 FM (Christian/talk)

Classical

KVOD 92.5 FM (Classical, public radio news)

Community

KGNU 88.5 FM in Boulder/Denver; 93.7 in Ward and the mountain regions (Pacifica, ethnic and world music, much attention to local affairs)

Country

KYGO 98.5 FM

KLMO 1060 AM (Country, Paul Harvey and ABC News)

KCKK 104.3 FM

Jazz

KHIH 95.7 FM (Jazz, other music, news)

KUVO 89.3 FM

News/Talk

KHOW 630 AM (News, talk and popular morning show)

KTLK 760 AM (Business and talk)

KVCU 1190 AM (student-run University of Colorado station)

Oldies

KXKL (KOOL) 105.1 FM

Public Radio

KCFR 90.1 FM (Colorado Public Radio, classical, National Public Radio and local news)

KUNC 91.5 FM (Classical, jazz, oldies, new and alternative)

Rock

KKHK 99.5 FM (Classic rock)

KIMN 100.3 FM (Classic rock)

KRFX 103.5 (Classic rock)

KBPI 106.7 FM (Classic and progressive rock)

Sports

KOA 850 AM (News, talk, sports)

KKFN 950 AM (Sports/talk)

Top-40

KALC 105.9 FM

Television Stations

Depending on the location in Boulder, TV reception can be a bit fuzzy to completely nonexistent because of the mountains. Reception without cable is even worse in mountain towns such as Nederland. For this reason most area residents have cable.

Besides the broadcast stations listed below, there are more than 30 cable stations, including Channel 8, the City of Boulder station, which is available only on Boulder Cable. The city channel has all types of programs on local issues, such as the environment, seniors, arts, city council meetings, sports and leisure and information programs on science, travel and much more. TCI cable Channel 54 is Community Access TV of Boulder with talk shows, performance, community interest and even local cooking programs. CATV offers inexpensive classes to train citizens to produce and edit their own videotapes for presentation on Channel 54. It also provides the audio for Radio Reading Services of the Rockies, a program for the blind with reading of the *Daily Camera*, *Rocky Mountain News*, *Denver Post* and *Colorado Daily* newspapers plus BBC News and local weather. The University of Colorado has channel 55, used primarily for foreign news programs and CU events.

Broadcast Television Stations

KWGN Channel 2 (Independent/WB)
KCNC Channel 4 (CBS)
KRMA Channel 6 (PBS)
KMGH Channel 7 (ABC)
KUSA Channel 9 (NBC)
KBDI Channel 11/12 (Community/PBS)
KTVD Channel 20 (Independent/UPN)
KVDR Channel 31 (Independent Fox)

Cable Television

There is only one cable supplier for Boulder: Boulder Cable (owned by TCI Cablevision of Colorado Inc.), (303) 930-2000. In eastern Boulder County, cable is provided by TCI, (303) 466-7376, and Comcast Communications, (303) 443-5005. For mountain communities, there is Pagosa Vision, (303) 258-0304 or (800) 222-1332, or Galaxy Cablevision (800) 365-6988.

Boulder is known as much for its eclectic spirituality as its traditional offerings.

Worship

In the early part of this century, Boulderites often referred to their growing community as "the Athens of the West," and the city's willingness to embrace religious diversity is reflected in that lofty motto.

The Presbyterians were the first to bring worship services to what we now call the Boulder Valley, followed quickly by the Congregationalists, the Baptists, the Episcopalians, the Methodists and followers of the Catholic faith. The church sanctuaries seemed large enough when built in the late 1800s, but with the country moving West, nearly all of the faiths quickly outgrew their modest worship halls and built larger churches. Architecturally impressive, many of the truly beautiful downtown Boulder churches were built with local materials.

Boulder is known, however, as much for its eclectic spirituality as its traditional offerings. An annual listing compiled by *Nexus*, Colorado's holistic journal, shows more than two dozen "unconventional" spiritual groups meet regularly. This metaphysical emphasis alongside the time-honored religious faiths is one of the best aspects of Boulder.

This chapter provides some history and current events involving Boulder's religious community. It then describes worship centers located downtown — easy for both tourists and newcomers to reach. It ends by describing other groups that are part of the rich texture of Boulder worship.

From Pioneer Churches to the Gay-rights Debates

In 1859 a Methodist circuit preacher delivered Boulder's first sermon to 50 people. Churches of other denominations followed, their spires leading pioneers across the prairie. The First Congregational Church, now site of the Carnegie Library on Pine Street, had Boulder's first full-time pastor, building and church bell. A few churches of historical significance still stand. Longmont's **St. Stephen's Episcopal Church**, (303) 776-1072, 470 Main Street, was built in 1881. The building now houses the Polar Bear Art Gallery, and worship services are held at a newer and larger sanctuary, at 1303 S. Bross Lane, that is also called St. Stephen's Episcopal Church. That same year, Colorado's first Swedish community built the **Swedish Evangelical Lutheran Church of Ryssby**, (303) 776-2704, on 63rd Street south of Nelson Road. They styled it after Swedish churches but built it with local sandstone. Members hold special midsummer and Christmas ceremonies that include Scandinavian traditions. For the winter service, they decorate the simple chapel with evergreen boughs and candles that make halos on winter-frosted panes. The church is very popular for weddings, and the bride and groom often leave in a horse-drawn buggy. Another church still standing is the **Lafayette Congregational Church**, (303) 665-4206. The plain, white church at 300 E. Simpson Street is currently home to the Mary Miller Theater.

If you enjoy religious history, check with **Historic Boulder**, (303) 444-5192, at 646 Pearl Street. This nonprofit group occasionally conducts tours of sacred places and has a self-guided tour for sale (see our Attractions chapter for details). They also keep lists of historic buildings in which people may hold weddings. The vista from the Flagstaff Mountain Amphitheater makes it a favored wedding site. Boulder's proximity to the foothills, with easy access to nature trails, has created many special places to seek spirituality, without man-made structures or traditional ceremonies.

But worship is about more than creating, or finding, special places. The **First Congre-**

gational Church was Boulder's first church. At the dedication ceremony in 1870, the minister encouraged his parishioners to attend every Sunday, but admonished them to "leave the tobacco at home!" Church members helped raise funds to bring CU to town, and for many years, its ministers taught philosophy at the new university. Grandma Dartt was a Seventh-day Adventist who trudged through young Boulder's saloons, offering temperance and religious information. In 1895, the Seventh-day Adventists began building a tuberculosis sanatorium where Mapleton Avenue heads up Sunshine Canyon. A popular hiking trail, Mount Sanitas Trail, is named after the health center, and the Mapleton Rehabilitation Clinic stands there today. (The **Seventh-day Adventist Church**, (303) 442-1522, is nearby at 345 Mapleton Avenue.)

If many of Boulder's worship halls were built with sandstone, then their souls are built of wood, tin, lead and iron. The pipe organs at many of the downtown churches were crafted with loving care and pinched pennies. The three manual Casavant organ at First Presbyterian is often played for Bach concerts. The Roosevelt organ at First United Methodist sat unused at a Denver church before it was moved to Boulder. By far the largest church organ is enjoyed by parishioners at the First Congregational Church, but even this instrument pales in comparison to the giant at Macky Auditorium on the CU campus. Built in 1923 from contributions by Boulder citizens, the 100-rank organ is housed under the stage and would cost at least $1.5 million to replace. Other notable downtown church organs include the Austin at St. John's Episcopal Church, the hand-built pipe organ at Trinity Lutheran and the three manual McManis organ at the First Baptist Church.

The issue of separation of church and state crops up periodically. During the 1960s the State Board of Education backed religious and civic groups that asked that schools refrain from Christmas pageants. These days, school kids may sing songs from many religions at "winter festivals," and the focus is on informing people about various faiths. Still, seemingly small events create a large furor where issues of separation of church and state are concerned. Before Christmas 1995, a big fuss developed after people started hanging little angel ornaments from a tree on public land, and the following spring, law enforcement officials were taken to task for marking sites of fatal vehicular accidents with white crosses as part of a safety awareness campaign.

The **Interfaith Council**, (303) 666-9415, embodies Boulder's egalitarianism. Its members represent many of the world's major religions. The group includes approximately 40 of Boulder's hundreds of religious communities — mainstream Protestant and Catholic churches, synagogues, Buddhists, Baha'i, Islam and some evangelical churches. The Interfaith Council has helped establish the Boulder Shelter for the Homeless, Share-a-Gift and the Community Table. The council also grapples with social issues such as giving women more choices in church leadership and alleviating hunger. Various members share religious perspectives. The Muslims have given talks about Islam. Michael Medved, a nationally known movie reviewer who is Jewish, talked before the council on violence in the media.

Although no longer based in Boulder, another group with a controversial history is the **Promise Keepers**, (303) 964-7600, in Denver, founded in 1990 by former CU-Boulder football coach Bill McCartney. With friends, he organized the Promise Keepers as a "Christ-

---

INSIDERS' TIP

Karma Dzong Shambhala Center is one of the largest communities of practicing Tibetan Buddhists in the West.

centered ministry, dedicated to uniting men through vital relationships to become Godly influences in their world." Members follow conservative evangelical and Catholic teachings. Gatherings initially held on the CU-Boulder campus are now held nationwide. In 1997 more than 600,000 men gathered on the Mall in Washington, D.C., for a Promise Keepers' rally that was one of the largest religious gatherings in U.S. history. In 1999 there were 14 gatherings scheduled including one in Denver, July 16-17.

Worship Centers

Newcomers should check the *Daily Camera's* Saturday religion calendar. The variety of offerings will meet nearly everyone's spiritual needs or desire for spiritual exploration.

Near the Pearl Street Mall

Located near the University of Colorado campus, it's no surprise that most of Boulder's oldest — and many of the largest — houses of worship are downtown, within walking distance of the Pearl Street Mall, which has been the civic center of town for a long time.

First Presbyterian, (303) 402-6400, at 1820 15th Street, has an estimated 2,400 members, with 2,000 attending Sunday services. The original sanctuary celebrated its 100th year in 1995. A major remodel in 1998 added nearly three hundred new seats in the main chapel and a 30,000 square foot children's wing. Members describe it as a reformed, evangelical church with a big, warm congregation. It has large teen, singles and college groups plus other smaller groups so people can become affiliated. The church provides space for performances by local music groups, such as the Boulder Bach Festival, the Boulder Chorale and for recitals by student groups. It offers a weekly preschool, summer camps, snow camps and weekly school programs in every-

thing from crafts and cooking to family conflict resolution.

Sacred Heart of Jesus, (303) 442-6158, at 2312 14th Street, is a Roman Catholic church with more than 1,200 registered households and lots of people who drop in. Sacred Heart School, across the street, is affiliated with the parish (see our Child Care and Education chapter). The large community outreach program includes a lunch program for transients and distribution of food baskets. The church offers daily masses in English and a weekly Spanish mass.

Karma Dzong Shambhala Center, (303) 444-0190, at 1345 Spruce Street, is a center for Tibetan Buddhism called "Vajrayana," which translates as "diamond vehicle." The center includes 600 adult members, making it one of the largest communities of practicing Tibetan Buddhists in the West. The top floor, a shrine room, is full of traditional Tibetan red and gold. People are welcome to drop by in the afternoon. Every Sunday morning, there's a 10:30 open house that includes a talk on Buddhism, meditation and a question-and-answer session. Members say that although Buddhism may sound exotic, it's very ordinary; it's about living your life well, with compassion and wisdom.

St. John's, (303) 442-5246, at 1419 Pine Street, is a traditional Episcopal Church with very contemporary sensibilities. Among Boulder Episcopalian churches, it's the only "AIDS-aware faith community" — and is one of the few such of any denomination. The congregation, which now numbers about 1,000, was founded in 1873 and is one of the oldest in town. The present church, where the big Messiah Sing-along happens each December (see our Festivals and Annual Events chapter), dates back to 1902.

The **First Baptist Church**, (303) 442-6530, at 1237 Pine Street, was founded in 1872, making it another one of the oldest churches in town. With more than 250 members, its Chancel Choir and the Handbell Choir are well-known for concerts and cantatas.

First United Methodist Church, (303) 442-3770, is at 1421 Spruce Street. The **Christian Science Reading Room**, (303) 442-0335, is at 1434 Pearl Street, on the Pearl Street Mall. It is an extension of the **Church of Christ Science**, (303) 444-1770, nearby at 2243 13th Street. The **First Congregational Church**, (303) 442-1787, at 1128 Pine Street, across from the original Congregational church site, is a medium-size, liberal church with about 850 members. On the opposite corner is **Trinity Lutheran Church-ELCA**, (303) 442-2300, at 2200 Broadway.

That's just a sampling of the worship centers downtown.

Around the County

The **Unitarian Universalist Church**, (303) 494-0195, at 5001 Pennsylvania Avenue, mirrors Boulder's liberalism. The church welcomes diversity of race, age, abilities, sexual orientation, culture and religious backgrounds to its adult services and children's classes.

VineLife Community Church, (303) 449-3330, at 7845 Lookout Road in Niwot, is a nondenominational/evangelical/charismatic church started in 1982. More than 1,000 people attend Sunday services, which often include contemporary Christian music, lively sermons and homey, inspirational stories. Teaching Biblical insights and positive family-raising skills are important parts of the ministry, and the church prides itself on its active and involved children's and youth ministry as well.

The **Boulder Valley Christian Church**, (303) 494-7768, at 7100 South Boulder Road, is an independent evangelical Christian church with 500 members. Christmas and Easter music programs are popular events.

Unity of Boulder, (303) 442-1411, at 2855 Folsom Avenue, is a New Age, Christian church. It has grown considerably since 1975, when minister Jack Groverland came to town. He's a dynamic speaker, and sermons are full of both laughter and seriousness. The Unity newsletter goes out to 2,600 people, and 1,000 people attend two different Sunday services. Nearly 3,000 people have taken the church's Course in Miracles, a year-long course that starts each quarter. Unity puts on a professional-quality Christmas play that ends up being both entertaining and enlightening, thanks to the great singing, music, philosophical religious themes and humor. The church offers both Sunday school and a summer day camp called Angel Camp. The church houses a metaphysical bookstore and gift shop.

Camp St. Malo, (303) 444-5177, a Catholic conference facility at 10758 Colo. 7, near Allenspark, is where Pope John Paul II rested on his 1993 trip through Colorado. **St. Catherine's**, better known as the "Chapel on the Rock," is at the same location. During the summer, it is open to the public, with Sunday masses occasionally held from Memorial Day to Labor Day.

The **Sacred Heart of Mary**, (303) 494-7572, at 6739 South Boulder Road, was built in 1873 and is the oldest Catholic church in Boulder County. It started as a Prairie Church and still has an old cemetery in the back. Its priest describes it as a progressive, medium-size congregation with about 700 families, meeting in a beautiful church. The church offers classes in adult education and centering prayer. Drop-ins are welcome at daily mass.

For many years the **Benedictine Catholic Abbey of St. Walburga**, (970) 472-0612, 32109 N. U.S. 287, Virginia Dale, was located next door to Sacred Heart of Mary. Due to growing development and traffic in this once-tranquil area, the Abbey moved in 1996 to a

---

INSIDERS' TIP

The **Swedish Evangelical Lutheran Church** is all that's left in what was once the town of Ryssby, founded in 1869 by settlers from Ryssby, Sweden. The name refers to a clearing in a forest. The small chapel is now popular for weddings and is decorated for Christmas services.

quieter location in Larimer County. The Abbey is now home to a private secondary school.

Around eight percent of the Boulder population is Jewish, according to Allied Jewish Federation surveys. The Jewish community is very active in civic and local affairs. Area synagogues include **Bonai Shalom**, (303) 442-6605, 1527 Cherryvale Road, a conservative synagogue of nearly 150 households, nestled near a pretty stream, and **Har Hashem**, (303) 499-7077, 3950 Baseline Road, a reform congregation with more than 400 families. Both offer programs for youths, singles and families, and Hebrew school education. In 1998, Har Hashem built a beautiful new sanctuary and seven new children's classrooms to accommodate its growing membership. The **Jewish Renewal Community of Boulder**, (303) 271-3540, is part of an international cross-denominational movement. Approximately 150 members meet for services in members' homes and also hold monthly community Shabbats.

The **Second Baptist Church of Boulder**, (303) 499-4668, 5300 Baseline Road, has 300 members and a great musical presence. The Community Choir is open to any church member who likes to sing; the Men's Chorus, to males who like to do so; and Angels Without Wings is a chorus for children ages 3 to 13. The Shekinah Glory Choir is a young adult choir of superb voices that has performed all around the Denver area. **Boulder Meeting of Friends**, (303) 447-2168, a Quaker group, gathers at 1825 Upland Avenue for Sunday morning meetings. The **Boulder Mennonite Church**, (303) 443-3889, at 1520 Euclid Avenue, has a strong emphasis on family, service and faithful daily living. It founded the Victim-Offender Reconciliation Program, in which volunteers are trained to mediate in the community court system in property-related teen offenses. The **Islamic Center of Boulder**, (303) 444-6345, is at 1530 Culver Court. The Jesusonian Foundation, (303) 581-0456, at 4699 Nautilus Court S., #304, sells Urantia Books and secondary works. Urantia study groups have approximately 100 members. Mo

Seigel, president of Celestial Seasonings, was instrumental in forming the **Jesusonian Foundation**, which is not a religion, but rather "encourages individuals to live the gospel of Jesus through service."

In Boulder many choices are also available for exploring spirituality either through self-examination or meditation. The **Shoshoni Yoga Retreat**, (303) 642-0116, 21614 Colo. 119, has log cabins, massage and health therapy rooms and hiking trails. Many come to practice yoga or meditation or for spiritual renewal. Shoshoni members who founded Rudi's Restaurant, a well-regarded natural-food restaurant, have published a vegetarian cookbook, The Shoshoni Cookbook. **Dances of Universal Peace**, (303) 440-5714, offers attendees a chance to learn key phrases and gestures from many different religions through participatory song and dance. **Followers of Bahai'**, (303) 443-6422, 437 Pine Street, have been meeting in Boulder for more than 20 years. The **Ridhwan Foundation**, (303) 447-0025, 5869 Marshall Drive, teaches the "Diamond Approach" and has 250 local members. Members of the **Gurdjieff Foundation**, (303) 554-8120, meet regularly to study and practice the teachings of G.I. Gurdjieff. **Followers of Eckankar** (303) 443-1610, 1800 30th Street, Ste. 208, meet monthly for classes and book discussions. The **Church of Gaia**, (303) 443-1096, 8563 Flagstaff Road, is an Earth-centered church offering training in such Native American ceremonies as sweat lodges, pipe circles, vision quests and other ceremonies. Those interested in learning more about Native American worship also find programs at the 20-year-old **Naropa Institute**, (303) 444-0202, 2130 Arapahoe Avenue (see our Child Care and Education chapter). The **Society for the Greater Community Way of Knowledge**, (303) 938-8401, teaches how to live with certainty, strength and wisdom in an emerging world.

CU-Boulder also has a department of religious studies, (303) 492-8041, and ethics classes through the Philosophy Department, (303) 492-6132.

From spectacular vistas of seemingly endless snowy peaks to tiny, gem-like flowers that grow high above the tree line, Rocky Mountain National Park is without a doubt one of the world's treasures.

Rocky Mountain National Park

A trip over Trail Ridge Road in Rocky Mountain National Park is a peak experience, literally. The nation's highest mountains, sparkling lakes and streams, abundant wildlife and stunning wildflowers will leave visitors breathless from both the beauty and the altitude.

Trail Ridge Road transports visitors to a world of different life zones, climates and vegetation that would take thousands of "horizontal" miles to reach — a trip comparable to driving more than 2,500 miles from Denver to Fairbanks, Alaska. But this world is compressed "vertically" in just a 50-mile drive over Trail Ridge Road, the highest continuous highway in the United States, following the path etched by generations of Native Americans. Every 300 feet of elevation equals one degree of latitude or 70 statute miles north. The road provides stunning views of peaks with memorable names — Never Summer Mountains, Mummy Mountain, Lumpy Ridge, Storm Peak, Chief's Head Peak, Isolation Peak, Twin Sisters. Keep your camera handy for the many scenic pull-outs. If you ever contemplated investing in a wide-angle lens, this is the trip to make it worthwhile.

From spectacular vistas of seemingly endless snowy peaks to tiny, gem-like flowers that grow high above the tree line (one-third of the Park's 415 square miles is above this level), Rocky Mountain National Park is without a doubt one of the nation's — and the world's — treasures.

You're almost sure to see grazing deer and elk and, if you're lucky, maybe some Rocky Mountain bighorn sheep, the Park's symbol. Above timberline by boulder fields, listen for the whistle of the pikas — cute, furry animals that look like rodents but are related to rabbits. You may spot a yellow-bellied marmot, a large rodent similar to a groundhog, sunning on a rock. Gray jays or spiffy black-trimmed Clark's nutcracker birds will swoop down looking for handouts (but don't feed them, it's illegal and unnatural for them). It is rare to encounter bears and mountain lions since they are wary of humans; if such a meeting should occur, remember to stand tall, back away slowly and whatever you do, don't turn and run.

Leave the crowded roadsides, walk a mile or two along one of the park's 355 miles of trails, and you'll begin to feel like one of the first humans ever to set eyes on this beautiful wilderness area.

History

As with the rest of Colorado, the first humans wandered through the area that is now Rocky Mountain National Park some 10,000 to 12,000 years ago. Part of what is now the Park's Trail Ridge Road was once part of the Ute Trail, a major route across the mountains for American Indians.

The first Europeans who visited the area were French fur traders collecting animal pelts. The area became U.S. territory in 1803 as part of the Louisiana Purchase. Mineral deposits in the area proved unproductive, so there was never great mining activity.

Because of the astounding beauty, the area was destined to be a tourist attraction from its earliest days. For centuries, American Indians had visited the area and considered it sacred. Braves visited the area west of present-day

Estes Park for vision quests and supposedly climbed Longs Peak to trap bald eagles for their feathers. By the time the settlers arrived, the Utes, having driven out the Arapaho, occupied the area.

After chasing the California Gold Rush in 1849, Joel Estes came looking for Colorado gold in 1859. Estes and his family homesteaded a beautiful parklike valley in 1860. Other settlers arrived slowly to try ranching and farming at elevations below 9,000 feet. Indian agent and soldier Kit Carson built a cabin on the eastern edge of the Park in Tahosa Valley.

More visitors began arriving in 1864, determined to meet the challenge of climbing Longs Peak, northern Colorado's highest mountain. William Byers, who was editor of the *Rocky Mountain News* in Denver, was one of the early climbers. He and two friends stayed with the Estes family when they made their attempt at the climb. Although they were unsuccessful, Byers went back to Denver and wrote glowing accounts of the area, calling it Estes Park after his host. In 1868 Byers returned with Major John Wesley Powell (the renowned one-armed explorer of the Colorado River and Grand Canyon), and the two made the first recorded climb to the summit of Longs Peak. Byers wrote another story about Longs Peak and Estes Park, attracting more tourists, hunters and adventure seekers. Around the area, settlers were finding a good income by housing the increasing number of tourists in their cabins. Later they began building rustic lodges (and even a nine-hole golf course). These lodges eventually evolved into dude ranches, which were popular in the early 20th century.

Had he stayed, Joel Estes might have become one of the richest men in the area, but the long, snowy winter of 1866 did him in. Later that year Estes sold off his claim and cattle for a yoke of oxen and headed south. Griffith Evans bought the Estes homestead, which he operated as a makeshift hostel until he added some cabins and opened a full-scale dude ranch in 1871.

By the 1870s, the area was becoming known around the world for its spectacular scenery. British writer and world traveler Isabella Bird visited the area in 1873 and stayed at Evans' ranch. Her adventures and travels in the area were published in 1879 in the extremely popular book, *A Lady's Life in the Rocky Mountains*, and by 1882 the book was in its seventh edition; it's still a best seller at the park gift shops.

Lord Dunraven (the Fourth Earl of Dunraven, Viscount of Mount Earl and Adare) also visited the Evans ranch. It was common for European gentry to visit the United States, and this Irish nobleman and avid hunter liked Estes Park so much that he secretly acquired more than 15,000 acres through third-party purchases and other under-the-table deals, as it was illegal for foreigners to homestead. He then created a private hunting sanctuary for himself and his European hunting cronies. The earl even announced in the *Rocky Mountain News* that "admission to Estes Park, his game preserve, was by invitation only." But eventually the area's beauty defeated even the earl, because it attracted many others who disputed the legality of his claims.

Meanwhile, in 1876, Lord Dunraven invited Western landscape painter Albert Bierstadt to Estes Park to capture its beauty on canvas and help the earl select a spot for his English Hotel. A lake and moraine in the park are named for the painter, whose exhibited works attracted even more attention — and tourists — to the area.

At his English Hotel near Lake Estes, Dunraven entertained such guests as Buffalo Bill Cody, Kit Carson, Gen. William Tecumseh Sherman and other notables in the early 1880s. Initially it catered mainly to foreign clientele — the earl's hunting buddies. Its name was later changed to the Estes Park Hotel, which operated until it burned to the ground in 1911.

Settlers continued to homestead and began contesting the earl's land claims. Dunraven eventually leased the land to ranchers and left. Failing to establish exclusive rights to the preserve and challenged about the legality of his claim, Dunraven stopped visiting Estes Park in 1881. He leased his land and hotel to Theodore Whyte, his property manager, and in 1904 the land was purchased by well-known inventor Freelan O. Stanley (inventor of the Stanley Steamer). Diagnosed with tuberculosis, Stanley, like many of his time, came to be cured in the dry mountain air (and eventually was cured).

In 1905 the town of Estes Park was platted at the confluence of the Fall and Big Thompson rivers on land sold by John Cleave. Like many locals, Cleave said he "couldn't stand to see the danged place overrun by tenderfeet tourists," so he moved away.

Construction in Estes Park came from logging operations in Hidden Valley, Hollowell Park and Wild Basin. On the western side of the park, the Kawuneeche Valley, other logging operations provided materials to build dude ranches and develop Grand Lake village, west of the Continental Divide from Estes Park.

Designation of Rocky Mountain National Park

The ever-growing tourism prevalent by the early 1900s and use of the area by individuals and businesses raised concern among residents about preserving the area's pristine beauty.

In 1905 President Theodore Roosevelt had added the area as part of the new national forest system, but many felt that greater protection and preservation were needed, among them H.M. Wheeler, who had opened a national forest office in Estes Park in 1907. Wheeler suggested creating a "wildlife reserve" in the nearby mountains. Enos A. Mills, a 20-year resident of Estes Park and a naturalist, writer, conservationist and innkeeper, helped promote the park even further. Around 1909 Mills began campaigning to preserve the area.

Other citizens joined Mills, among them the well-known Stanley. The group formed the Estes Park Protective and Improvement Association to protect and preserve the area's scenery and wildlife.

Mills was so eloquent that President Roosevelt commissioned him to tour the country promoting the preservation of wild lands. The national park concept had begun with an act of Congress in 1872 designating Yellowstone as the first national park. The stated objectives of national parks were first to preserve natural and historical objects including wildlife, scenery and ecosystems, and second to promote the enjoyment of these resources by the public.

Finally, in 1915, after years of debate on the size and boundaries of the Park, President Woodrow Wilson signed a bill passed by Congress making Rocky Mountain National Park the nation's 10th national park. The new park encompassed 415 square miles of forest, aspen groves, alpine tundra, rich wetlands and 76 peaks soaring above 12,000 feet. Soon after, the first Park superintendent was installed, and rangers were hired to enforce the new restrictions on hunting and cattle grazing.

During the next decades, evidence of human settlement in the Park, such as the briefly booming silver mining town called Lulu City in the late 1870s, was removed, and natural vegetation was painstakingly restored.

In 1975 Rocky Mountain National Park was named the 21st biosphere reserve in the world. The biosphere reserve system was established by the United Nations Man and Biosphere Programme to observe and monitor changes in natural ecosystems, especially those resulting from human activities. There are more than 320 biosphere reserves worldwide in 80 countries.

Since 1974, Congress has been pondering a recommendation from then-President

---

INSIDERS' TIP

Rocky Mountain National Park has one of the nation's highest paved roads, Trail Ridge Road, which traverses miles of tundra similar to what you'd find above the Arctic Circle. Look for elk, deer and birds not found elsewhere. (But don't feed the wildlife — it makes it more difficult for them to survive in the wild.)

Richard Nixon that 239,835 acres of the Park be designated as Wilderness, prohibiting expansion of roads and buildings in that area; the designation would not effect current activities in the Park. Although the designation has not yet been made, National Park Service policy requires that the Park be managed as a wilderness until Congress takes action. In 1980, 2,917 acres of the Indian Peaks Wilderness Area were added to Rocky Mountain National Park. Meanwhile, a backcountry/wilderness plan is being prepared to guide Park staff in protecting the Park from human impact. For more information, write to Wilderness Planning, Rocky Mountain National Park, Estes Park, CO 80517.

Visitors' Centers

Perhaps the Park's early promoters and protectors realized how popular it would become. Today, more than 3 million visitors come to Rocky Mountain National Park every year. Five Visitors' Centers at the Park accommodate this yearly crush of humanity.

The main Visitors' Center is 2.5 miles west of Estes Park on U.S. Highway 36 and is open daily year round. Call the staff at (970) 586-1206 for weather, camping and other specific information, (970) 586-1333 for a recorded message, and (970) 586-1319 for the hearing-impaired.

On the west entrance to the Park, the Kawuneeche Visitors' Center, (970) 627-3471, sits 1.3 miles north of Grand Lake on U.S. Highway 34, and is also open daily year round.

The Moraine Park Museum lies 5 miles west of Estes Park on Bear Lake Road and is open daily from May to mid-October. The museum is open weekends beginning in mid-April.

Most spectacularly situated of all, the Alpine Visitors' Center, at 11,796 feet atop Trail Ridge Road, is 25 miles west of Estes Park and is open daily from June to September, weather permitting. Next door, a park concessionaire operates Trail Ridge Store and a snack bar, where diners can enjoy a simple meal along with a panoramic view. Call the main park number, (970) 586-1206, for information about the Alpine Visitors' Center.

Lily Lake Visitors' Center, 6 miles south of Estes Park on Colo. 7, is open daily from June to Labor Day, depending upon snow conditions, and open weekends during May and September.

Besides providing education about the Park's different ecosystems, plus maps and directions, the centers remind visitors of the Park's regulations:

1.   No pets are allowed on trails or away from roadways. Pets must be leashed at all times.

2.   Feeding or touching wild animals is prohibited, along with hunting or harassment of wildlife. This includes stalking wild animals for photographs, which frightens them and makes them less viewable for other visitors.

3.   Picking wildflowers or plants is prohibited. Removing, disturbing, damaging or destroying natural features, including rocks and pine cones, is illegal.

4.   Fishing requires a valid Colorado state fishing license. Only artificial lures may be used (but children 12 years of age and younger may use bait, in open waters only).

5.   Camping is restricted to designated areas.

6.   A permit is required for all overnight stays in the backcountry. There are restrictions on the use of pack animals.

7.   Gathering firewood is prohibited. Fires may be built only in picnic areas and campsites with grates. Either bring your own wood or ask at the ranger stations or park headquarters about purchasing some.

8.   Vehicles must remain on roads or in parking areas. Parking any vehicle or leaving property unattended for more than 24 hours without prior permission is prohibited.

9.   Hitchhiking is permitted from road shoulders only.

10.   Trail bikes, snowmobiles and all other vehicles are restricted to roads. Snowmobiles are permitted only on the west side of the park.

11.   Firearms are to be kept unloaded.

12.   All your own trash must be removed from picnic areas and campsites and disposed of in trash cans and recycling receptacles.

13.   Having open alcoholic beverages in a vehicle on Park roads and in parking areas is illegal.

Entrance to the park is $10 per vehicle and $5 for walk-ins and bicyclists; passes are good for a week. An annual pass to Rocky

A tourist enjoys the view from Trail Ridge Road.

Photo: Daily Camera/Crissy Pascual

Mountain National Park costs $20 and an annual pass to all national parks is $50. People 62 and older can get a national pass for $10 and those with disabilities can receive a lifetime national pass for free.

Recreation

Bicycling

Bicycling in the Park is allowed only on roads, and these are heavily used by cars. Since the roads climb from about 9,000 feet to more than 12,000 feet, riding is quite strenuous throughout. No off-road or mountain biking is allowed on any of the trails.

For a challenging ride on a dirt road, follow Old Fall River Road, the first auto route over the Continental Divide, which is described by Park officials as a "motor nature trail." You'll be sharing the road with vehicles as it climbs 9.4 miles before joining Trail Ridge Road at the summit of 11,796-foot Old Fall River Pass (see more information under the section on Driving, below). Old Fall River Road is one-way uphill — for cars and bicycles. Plan to ride down Trail Ridge Road.

Bicycling over 50-mile-long Trail Ridge Road is only for the fittest of the fit, and even

they will want to spend the night on the other side at Grand Lake before returning. Trail Ridge Road crosses the Continental Divide, and at its highest point is 12,183 feet, making it one of the world's most spectacular bike rides. But this road, too, is heavily traveled by cars.

Bear Lake Road is a strenuous 10-mile climb of 1,500 feet from the Beaver Meadows Entrance Station to Bear Lake at 9,475 feet.

Remember that you will be riding at high altitude and be prepared for early afternoon thunderstorms, cold temperatures, icy roads and thin, thin air.

Camping

To reduce the impact on the park, car camping is allowed only in five roadside campgrounds. Camping reservations can be made five months in advance for individuals and groups at three of the campgrounds, and campgrounds are frequently packed full from mid-June to mid-August so plan ahead. The maximum stay in the Park is seven days during summer and 14 days during winter (only Moraine Park, Timber Creek and Longs Peak campgrounds are open year-round). At Longs Peak Campground, the limit is three days, and only tents are allowed. Although they can't go on trails with you, pets are allowed in campgrounds (leashed at all times). Reservations can be made through Destinet at (800) 365-2267 using Visa or MasterCard.

Permits are required for all backcountry camping; call the Backcountry Office at (970) 586-1242; there is a $15 fee Memorial Day through Labor Day.

Remember, you are bedding down in someone else's home; make sure all food is stored in airtight containers in the trunk of your car, or suspended high in a tree if you are in the backcountry to avoid a mid-night visit from a black bear.

The campgrounds listed below offer a great way to enjoy the Park at close range. There are no electrical, water or sewer connections in any of the campgrounds. Sewer dumping stations are located at Moraine Park, Glacier Basin and Timber Creek campgrounds. Public telephones are located at Moraine Park, Glacier Basin, Timber Creek and Aspen Glen. For general information about the Park and specific information on recreation, rentals, campgrounds or even ticks, call the public information office at (970) 586-1206. For emergencies, call (970) 586-1399 or 911.

Glacier Basin: Located 9 miles from Park Headquarters off U.S. Highway 36 on Bear Lake Road, this campground has 152 sites. Reservations are required. The site accommodates tents and recreational vehicles (it has dump stations, but, like all the Park's campgrounds, no hookups). The season is from early June through Labor Day. The fee is $16 per night.

Moraine Park: The Park's largest campground, Moraine Park has 250 sites and is located 3 miles west of Park Headquarters off Bear Lake Road. It's open all year and accommodates recreational vehicles and tents. Water is turned on mid-May and turned off mid-September. The fee is $10 per night in the winter and $16 per night in the summer; reservations are required Memorial Day through Labor Day.

Longs Peak: This smaller campground is 11 miles south of Estes Park and a mile west on Colo. 7. It offers 26 tent campsites (no RVs or motor homes) on a first-come basis. The fee is $10 per night in the winter, $16 in summer. It's open all year with water turned on in mid-May and turned off mid-September.

Timber Creek: Also open all year, Timber Creek is 10 miles north of the Grand Lake entrance to the Park and has 100 sites accommodating tents and recreational vehicles. The fee is $10 per night in winter, $16 in summer, and water is turned on in early June and off in mid-September. The campground operates on a first-come, first-served basis with no reservations.

Aspenglen: Aspenglen is open mid-May through late September on a first-come, first-served basis. It is located immediately inside the Fall River entrance of the Park and has 54 sites for tents, motor homes or recreational vehicles. The water is turned on in mid-May and turned off in late September. The fee is $16.

Group Sites: The Park has 15 group sites in Glacier Basin (see the individual entry for location) that accommodate groups of 10 to 50 people. They are open early June through Labor Day with water turned on and off the same times. Dump stations are provided and there is a public phone. The fees range from $30 to $60, depending on the size of the group. Reservations are required and made through Destinet at (800) 365-2267. All other times, sites are available on a first-come basis at Moraine Park Campground.

Sprague Lake Handicamp: This campsite is designed to accommodate all visitors with disabilities. From the campsite parking area 7 miles from Park Headquarters, a half-mile wheelchair accessible nature trail leads to the tent campground for a maximum of 10 people/5 wheelchairs. There is a three-night limit. For reservations, contact the Park, (970) 586-1242.

Climbing

Whether you want to do a technical rock climb of the famous east face of Longs Peak, known as the Diamond, or hike to the top of Longs Peak, the Park's climbing challenges are renowned and unlimited. Technical climbers should familiarize themselves with the Park's climbing regulations at Park Headquarters. Colorado Mountain School is the Park concessionaire, offering mountaineering and technical climbing instruction and a guide service. For those who'd like to learn call (970)

586-5758. As with other activities in the park, low-impact techniques are emphasized — motorized drills are prohibited and climbers are urged to use brown chalk, neutral-colored webbing and to follow established routes. Registration is not required for technical climbers, but be sure to tell a reliable friend or relative of your climbing plans, should you be overdue. If you prefer both feet on the ground, you might catch a glimpse of technical climbers practicing their skills on Lumpy Ridge just north of Estes Park.

Registration is required for overnight bivouacs, and $15 permits are available at Park Headquarters, the West Unit Office and at most Rangers' Stations. To obtain a permit, call the Backcountry Office at (970) 586-1242. A permit cannot be obtained in advance, although a reservation can be made in advance by phone until May, then by writing during summer months to Superintendent, Rocky Mountain National Park, Estes Park, CO 80517.

Driving

The main park drive, Trail Ridge Road, is the highest continuous highway in the United States. It runs 50 miles from Estes Park to Grand Lake over the Continental Divide and was built in 1932. This spectacular trip through the Park should be taken by anyone who visits. The road climbs through the evergreen forests amidst the eerie, gnarled krummholz — wind-sculpted trees — and up to the alpine tundra above the tree line, comparable to being in the Arctic Circle. Krummholz means "crooked wood" in German.

Depending upon weather conditions, the road is generally open from Memorial Day until mid-October. Allow three or four hours for this scenic drive, with stops at the numerous overlooks for stupendous vistas of glacier-carved peaks, snowfields and cirques, and perhaps a snack at the Alpine Visitors' Center

on top. Take the short half-hour round-trip Tundra Walk to see the tiny delicate flowers that have adapted to this harsh environment, some of the 900 species of flora found in the park. Be sure to stay on paths because the alpine tundra is fragile and some of the flora is extinct outside the Park.

The Bear Lake Road makes another scenic drive, leading to a lovely high mountain basin. Traffic during summer months through the Park is quite heavy. In some areas, shuttle buses take visitors to certain trailheads, such as Bear Lake, where there's a choice of trails. A shuttle runs from Glacier Basin to Bear Lake. Parking lots at Bear Lake and Glacier Gorge Junction will be full between 10 AM and 3 PM on summer days, so plan accordingly.

Old Fall River Road runs from Horseshoe Park Junction to Fall River Pass. Expect a leisurely pace on the 15-mile-per-hour road as it runs one-way uphill west of Endovalley Picnic Area. A gravel road with many switchbacks, it gives visitors an idea of early travel across the mountains since it was the first road over the Divide in northern Colorado. A guide booklet is available at the Visitors' Centers describing interesting sights along the way. You can make a loop up Old Fall River Road and return on Trail Ridge Road. Old Fall River Road is west of Estes Park on U.S. Highway 34 at the Fall River Entrance Station. The road is paved for the first 2 miles from the entrance. Take note of the alluvial fan along the way, caused by a flood in 1982. RVs and trailers are not allowed on Fall River Road because of the narrow switchbacks. The road opens July 4th and is closed in winter.

Driving Tips

1. There are no service stations in the Park. Enter with a full tank of gas.
2. Observe posted speed limits — roads are narrow, winding and heavily used.
3. Travel in early morning or late after-

noon. Wildlife is more active at these times, and the light is more beautiful. During mid-day, traffic can be bumper to bumper.

4. Downshift to lower gears when going up or down steep grades. This will reduce engine stress and keep your brakes from burning out. Manually downshift automatic transmissions. Go down hills in a lower gear than you use to go up.

5. Tap brakes gently and repeatedly on downhills to reduce brake wear and possible overheating (or failure).

6. Be sure to look first and signal at turnouts and parking areas. Watch for oncoming traffic. Sound the horn on blind corners to alert oncoming drivers, if necessary.

7. When you stop, always set the emergency brake, and park in gear if you have manual transmission.

8. Lock your car when unattended, place valuables out of sight or take them with you.

9. Stay in your own lane. Don't drive in the middle to avoid being near the edge. The roads were designed with plenty of room, and you'll only cause an accident by driving down the center.

10. Don't be surprised if your car doesn't perform normally at high altitudes. Cars tuned for lower elevations may overheat or act as though they're not getting enough gas. Drive in a lower-than-usual gear to keep RPMs up and to avoid overheating. Don't pump the accelerator, as it will cause flooding and make matters worse. On warm days some cars may get vapor lock in the fuel line. If this occurs, try to get the car off the road at the nearest pullout. Stop the engine and allow it to cool. If there is snow or cold water nearby, put it on the fuel pump and the line leading to the carburetor. Let the car cool for 15 minutes before trying to start it again.

Fishing

Fly fishers will find four species of trout in the mountain streams and lakes of the Park: German brown, rainbow, brook and cutthroat. Valid Colorado fishing licenses are required for all fishing in the Park; use of live bait is prohibited except for children 12 and younger. See the fishing regulations at Park Headquar-

ters, one of the Rangers' Stations or the "Fishing" section in our Boulder Sports chapter. No fishing is allowed in Bear Lake, and some lakes and streams on the east side of the Park are closed to protect the greenback cutthroat trout, which is being reintroduced to its native habitat.

Sprague Lake at the east edge of the Park is good for catching pan-sized brook trout; however, it's right next to the road and is heavily used. From Estes Park, drive west on U.S. Highway 36 to the Beaver Meadows Entrance Station. Turn left (south) at the first intersection after the entrance, and continue on the Bear Lake Road for about 6 miles.

For a day's outing — a combination hiking and fishing trip — go to Peacock Pool. Begin at the East Longs Peak Trailhead and hike about 4 miles up the trail to a spur that leads to Peacock Pool, 11,360 feet high. This is a hard hike but offers spectacular views. Another 1.5 miles from Peacock Pool is Chasm Lake with deep water, but according to latest reports, no fish, though it's a scenic spot right under the spectacular diamond east face of Longs Peak. The Longs Peak Trailhead is 9.2 miles south of Estes Park on Colo. 7; turn right at the sign.

Hiking and Backpacking

With 355 miles of trails, Rocky Mountain National Park is prime hiking and backpacking country. There's something for everyone, from the wheelchair users to backpackers. Below are some day hikes, rated accordingly. It's best to get a map at one of the Visitors' Centers for detailed descriptions, including distance, elevation and type of terrain.

Very Easy

The Bear Lake Nature Trail is a half-mile paved path circling Bear Lake. A brochure available at the trailhead describes the subalpine landscape. Elevation is 9,475 feet. Leave from the Bear Lake parking area.

The Sprague Lake Nature Trail, known as the Five Senses Trail, is a half-mile trail around Sprague Lake, at 8,710 feet in altitude, and is wheelchair accessible. Take the road to Bear Lake, and turn off at the sign for Sprague Lake.

Easy

Trails from Bear Lake to Nymph, Dream or Emerald lakes present a little more challenge, at 3.6 miles round trip.

The Gem Lake, a round trip hike, makes for a pleasant walk and begins outside the Park on Devil's Gulch Road.

Moderate

Bear Lake or Glacier Gorge to Mills Pond or Black Lake is a good 6- to 10-mile round-trip hike that takes a few hours, as does Bear Lake or Glacier Gorge to Sky Pond.

Chasm Lake is a bit more strenuous at 4.2 miles one-way but well worth the gorgeous view of the Diamond on Longs Peak and the beautiful lake. Start at the Longs Peak Trailhead, off Colo. 7, north of Meeker.

Long or Difficult

Bear Lake to the top of Flattop Mountain is a little more difficult. The hike to Thunder Lake starts at Wild Basin off Colo. 7 between Allenspark and Meeker, and you should plan on it taking most of the day.

For Ypsilon Lake, start at the Lawn Lake Trailhead at Horseshoe Park on Fall River Road. Don't forget your lunch or rain gear.

A Classic

Longs Peak has always been considered America's Matterhorn. At 14,255 feet high, it is the highest peak in the Park and the northernmost "fourteener" in the Rockies (these are the highest peaks, of at least 14,000 feet). The dramatic peak has fascinated writers, artists, climbers and explorers since the first recorded American sighting in 1820 by Stephen Long. The Arapaho are believed to have climbed Longs to obtain eagle feathers on its summit. In 1868 two famed non-natives made it to the top: one-armed Colorado River explorer John Wesley Powell and Denver newspaperman William Byers.

Climbing Longs is still an exciting accomplishment today and an all-day affair — usually taking about 14 hours round-trip. It should be attempted only by strong hikers who are already acclimated to the altitude. The climb should not be attempted by novices. It's crucial to be off the peak and on the way back down by noon to avoid the daily summer thunderstorms and dangerous lightning, which has claimed the lives of many hikers. Remember that fresh snow is possible any day of the year.

The most popular (and only non-technical) route is the East Longs Peak Trail, usually called the Keyhole Route, which starts at the Longs Peak Trailhead and climbs 8 miles and 4,855 vertical feet to the top. The first 6 miles are the easiest and follow an ever-climbing trail through beautiful forests of pine and aspen up to timberline with fantastic views. Those who want to bail out before this point can take the well-marked turnoff to Chasm Lake, at around 4 miles, to a gorgeous lake right beneath the 1,000-foot vertical diamond on Longs' sheer, spectacular 1,675-foot east face (a popular world-class technical climbing route). Chasm Lake is 4.2 miles from the trailhead.

But, continuing on the Keyhole Route, at mile 6 you reach the Boulderfield and hop from boulder to boulder for one mile up to the Keyhole, a prominent rock formation. To the left of the Keyhole is the chilly-looking Agnes Vaille Shelter Cabin. Vaille made the first successful winter ascent of the east face with Walter Kiener in 1925 but collapsed from exhaustion on her way back and froze to death while Kiener went for help.

After passing through the Keyhole, at 13,100 feet, the hard part begins. The route is marked by red and yellow paint circles over the rocky Ledges, which have intimidating drop-offs. The Ledges lead to a 600-foot steep couloir of loose gravel and running rivulets called the Trough. After climbing the Trough

INSIDERS' TIP

Ptarmigan are birds found only in the Arctic regions or the high mountains such as those in Colorado. They are nearly impossible to spot even when they are right in front of you because they have perfectly camouflage-colored feathers that match the rocks. They are the size of pigeons and look something like a quail.

and negotiating the huge boulder at the top, you pass through the notch and cross the Narrows — more rock ledges with even more dizzying exposure. The Narrows lead to the Homestretch, a short, steep couloir to the top, not really difficult, but at this point in the game a bit much. The Homestretch requires some hand-holds but has solid footing. At the top of Homestretch, you have reached the huge summit of Longs, which encompasses four acres. Enjoy the view, do a few push-ups to show how really tough you are and take a look down the diamond, but don't stay too long if noon is approaching. If there is any snow — possible well into July — ice axes are necessary for safely climbing the Ledges, Trough, Narrows and Homestretch.

The Longs Peak Trailhead is 9.2 miles south of Estes Park on Colo. 7; turn right at the sign. Those who don't want to do it all in one day can backpack part of the way up Longs and camp in the Boulderfield, a spectacular but rather inhospitable campground — cold and windy and around 12,000 feet in elevation — among the boulders. But you'll need to reserve your permit well in advance by writing the Backcountry Office, Rocky Mountain National Park, Estes Park, CO 80517. There are numerous backcountry sites and zones for individuals and groups throughout the Park. For more information, maps or reservations, call the Backcountry Office at (970) 586-1242, write to the address above, or just show up.

Horseback Riding

Horses are not allowed to travel cross-country in the Park, but there are more than 260 miles of trails for horseback riders. Horses and guides can be hired at a number of liveries outside the park and **Hi Country Stables** has two locations inside the Park at Moraine Park and Glacier Basin. Reservations are sug-

gested, (970) 586-2327 or (970) 586-3244 (open only in summer months).

Skiing and Snowshoeing

Though most visitors to the Park come in summer, winter offers great cross-country skiing and snowshoeing opportunities. January and February offer the best conditions, sandwiched between the spotty coverage of early winter and the avalanche danger of late winter. Bear Lake and Wild Basin are the Park's most popular cross-country areas. The Visitors' Center on U.S. Highway 36, 2.5 miles west of Estes Park, is staffed daily from 8 AM to 5 PM except Christmas Day. Rangers lead cross-country tours from Kawuneeche Visitor Center on Saturday afternoons and snowshoe hikes are offered Saturday and Sunday at Bear Lake. Rangers can answer questions and provide trail maps detailing 40 miles of marked trails around Bear Lake and 88 miles of mainly unmarked trails around Wild Basin. There's a $10 entrance fee per vehicle (don't forget your chains if you don't have snow tires) and $5 for skiers, walkers or cyclists at all times. For more information call the Park at (970) 586-1206.

Equipment can be rented in Estes Park (see cross-country rentals under the Estes Park chapter of this book). Precautions to take to heart: don't ski or snowshoe alone; return to the trailhead well before dark; pack in extra food and water to keep your hardworking body fueled, extra clothing, a map and compass, flashlight, waterproof matches, space blanket and a first aid kit.

Here are a few of our favorite sites:

Glacier Basin Campground: (Easy) Drive 5 miles up Bear Lake Road. Park on the west side of the road at the large parking area (which is the shuttle bus parking area during summer months) and walk across to the east side to begin skiing on the main trail from the campground, which heads southwest for a mile on

---

INSIDERS' TIP

Pikas are small gerbil-sized creatures found only near the tree line. Though they look like rodents, they are actually related to rabbits. Look for them in rock piles around or above Timberline in Rocky Mountain National Park.

At 14,246 feet, Longs Peak towers over Bear Lake in Rocky Mountain National Park.

level terrain to Sprague Lake. There are many trails in and around the campground as well.

Black Lake: (Intermediate to Difficult) Begin at the Glacier Gorge Junction parking lot, which is about 11 miles up Bear Lake Road. Follow the signs southwest toward Alberta Falls and The Loch. After the intersection of Icy Brook and Glacier Creek, turn south and follow Glacier Creek to Mills Lake. Continue past Mills and Jewel lakes along the creek. When you leave the trees, continue up the open slope to Black Lake and enjoy the spectacular view of Longs Peak to the east, McHenrys to the west and Chief's Head Peak to the south.

Wild Basin Trailhead: (Difficult) Drive 13 miles south from Estes Park on Colo. Highway 7 (past the Longs Peak trail at 9.2 miles) to the Sandbeach Lake Trailhead. Turn right and drive another mile to the National Park Service parking lot. The Sandbeach Lake Trail starts at the large sign in the parking area and climbs northeast through the pines 4.2 miles to Sandbeach Lake.

Programs and Tours

Park rangers offer a variety of fun and educational programs and guided tours throughout the year. Among our favorites are the full moon walks in early spring. Reservations are required at (970) 586-1223. For bird lovers there is a spring migration bird walk (bring your binoculars and field guide).

The nonprofit Rocky Mountain Nature Association, created in 1931 to encourage the use of Rocky Mountain National Park as an outdoor classroom and research area, offers almost 100 classes in the Park. Classes range from Nature Sketchbooks and Animals Inside and Out for kids to adult classes on Spring Raptor Migration, "Uppity" Women of the Rockies, Intro to Mushrooming and Weather, Climate and Stars. Fees are quite reasonable and teachers can earn recertification units. Call (800) 816-7662 or (970) 586-0108 for more information.

Charles Tour & Travel Services in Estes

Park offers scenic tours of Trail Ridge Road, Fall Foliage/Elk Bugling tours and arranges horseback riding trips in the Park and Bear Lake hikes: (800) 586-5009 (metro Denver area only) or (970) 586-5151.

Auto Tape Tours are cassette tapes that narrate the drive over Trail Ridge Road. The tapes give highlights of history, facts, legends and nature and cost $9.95 at all of the park visitors' centers. The tapes are available starting from either the Estes Park or Grand Lake side of Trail Ridge Road.

Safety

A visit to Rocky Mountain National Park can be the experience of a lifetime, but don't ever forget that this is not a climate-controlled theme park — it is the real, wild world with unaccustomed dangers. Don't be afraid to enjoy it, but do use some foresight and diligence.

Altitude sickness: The flu-like symptoms of altitude sickness — nausea, headache, dizziness, rapid heartbeat, breathlessness — may be your body's way of telling you to head to lower ground. Follow its advice. To minimize the effects of altitude, avoid alcohol and tobacco, drink lots of fluids, eat frequently and lightly and rest.

Animals: The Park is richly inhabited. As guests here, human visitors must learn the acceptable rules of behavior. Never feed the wildlife; a human diet is not suitable for them and making beggars of them is dangerous for both species. Photographers should take a long lens and shoot from inside a car or from the roadside; aggressive photographers who approach animals may be fined $50. Keep food locked away in airtight containers in your car trunk when in bear country. If you encounter a black bear, stand still or slowly back away; never approach a bear, particularly a female with cubs. If you encounter a mountain lion, stop, pick up small children, stand tall, back away, yell. *do not* run (running is your signal to the lion that you are game).

Avalanche: Open slopes, particularly after a recent wind or snow storm, can be triggered by as little as a footfall into a massive avalanche. Visitors traveling in such areas should travel in groups, wear electronic transceivers and carry shovels and poles to use as probes. If you are swept up in an avalanche, discard equipment and swim toward the top of the moving snow.

Giardia: No, it's not just from bad restaurants. Giardia, a microscopic organism that can cause diarrhea, cramps, weight loss (the bad kind) and bloating, lives in the digestive systems of humans and wildlife. It can also flourish in that crystal stream, mountain lake or enticing snow field. If you must drink the water, boil it for at least five minutes, or use a filtration system capable of removing microorganisms.

Hypothermia: There's a saying in the Rockies — If you don't like the weather, wait five minutes. A sunny day can turn suddenly to overcast, wind, cold, even snow. Exposure to wet and cold can lead to hypothermia, a lowering of the body's core temperature. Symptoms are confusion, drowsiness, shivering and slurred speech. A warm, non-alcoholic drink and warm, dry clothing are the treatment; coming prepared for any weather is the prevention.

Snowfields: There's nothing more thrilling than zipping down the slick face of a snowfield or glacier in the middle of summer, on a tube or sled, or by the seat of your pants — particularly when you discover just how difficult it can be to stop. For safety and preservation reasons, snow play and sledding are permitted only at Bear Lake and Hidden Valley, but look for warning signs in those areas, as well.

Storms: The high peaks of Rocky Mountain National Park are a favorite target when Thor starts practicing his aim with lightning bolts. Thunderstorms are frequent in early to mid-afternoon. If you're up top when a storm begins, get off ridges or peaks and avoid exposed rocks and trees. If you're on horseback, dismount and put a little distance between you and your horse. Better yet, start out early in the morning so you're down well before practice time.

Sunburn: Elevation also means that you are less protected than normal from ultraviolet radiation and that dazzling snow increases the risk of a severe burn. UV-protectant sunglasses, a hat and covering clothing are a good idea, with heavy-duty sunscreen on exposed skin. Don't forget to slather the kids.

Ticks: Visitors are warned not to take anything from the park, but sometimes it's difficult not to. Ticks, tenacious members of the spider family, love nothing more than hitching a ride on a warm, blood-pumping body passing by. They are plentiful in early spring and summer. To discourage the hangers-on, spray on insect repellent before setting out, keep your ankles covered with thick socks and if you are wearing pants, tuck them into your boots or socks. Check for ticks periodically throughout your visit to the park, especially in places where your clothing ends, such as your neck, the end of your sleeves and your pants or shorts legs. If you find one, carefully remove it with tweezers, being sure to get the whole body; remaining embedded parts can cause infection or serious illness like Rocky Mountain Spotted Fever and Colorado Tick Fever (fortunately, no cases of Lyme Disease have been reported in the Park).

Water: A beautiful mountain stream can sweep you off your feet — literally. Keep in mind that during spring runoff, even a shallow stream can pick up enough force to knock down adults and carry them away.

Watermelon snow: You know not to eat the yellow snow, but did you know that pink snow is bad news, too? This snow, called watermelon snow because of it's color and taste, is actually a colony of algae that can send you running for the nearest port-a-potty.

The history of Estes Park and Rocky Mountain National Park are so deeply intertwined that one would probably not exist without the other.

Estes Park

Estes Park (elevation 7,522 feet) lies 63 miles northwest of Denver and 34 miles northwest of Boulder at the eastern entrance to Rocky Mountain National Park and is the year-round home of almost 5,000 hardy souls (swelling to 15,000 in summer). It exists primarily as a base camp and service area for visitors to the Park, offering hotels, restaurants, shopping, equipment rentals, tours and other diversions for tourists — with a nearly endless choice during the summer months. Since more than three million visitors come to Rocky Mountain National Park every year — and most of them during summer — things can get a bit hectic along Estes Park's main drag.

In winter, some of the shops close, with their owners heading south, but many shops stay open, particularly the art galleries. Some restaurants have abbreviated hours during winter. But winter and other "low-season" months may be the best time to get the flavor of this small town beautifully situated at the base of spectacular Longs Peak and Rocky Mountain National Park, with quite an interesting history all its own.

Among the most notable newcomers attracted by the beauty of the mountain valley was Windham Thomas Wyndam-Quin, fourth Earl of Dunraven. Following a series of hunting trips, the Earl in 1874 began acquiring land, through means legal and otherwise, with the intention of creating a grand estate.

In 1877, Dunraven built a hunting lodge in a beautiful setting, calling it the Estes Park Hotel. Locals, who resented the acquisitive foreigner, referred to it as the "English Hotel."

Estes Park homesteaders began to join forces against the Earl's purchases and eventually Dunraven moved on to more hospitable areas.

The remains of the buildings he left behind have been removed from the park as it is returned to its natural state.

Victorian traveler and writer Isabella Bird wrote extensively and lovingly about the scenic beauty of Estes Park in the fall of 1873. For those interested in the area's history and a fascinating glimpse of life for the first settlers, her book *A Lady's Life in the Rocky Mountains* is required and entertaining reading.

Stephen King wrote more horrifyingly about the malevolent spirits inhabiting the fictional Overlook Hotel (actually the Stanley Hotel, where King lived when he wrote the novel) and their effect on a family hired to "winter over" in the empty hotel. King was so unhappy about the movie version of *The Shining*, starring Jack Nicholson, that he returned to the Stanley to film a television series closer to the novel.

On July 31, 1976, real horror came to Estes Park when the burbling Big Thompson River was transformed by mountain storms into a deadly gusher powerful enough to pick up and carry cars, boulders, homes, bridges and trees as it crashed down on the tourist-packed town. At least 139 people were killed (7 were listed as missing), and 88 people were injured, making it the largest natural disaster in Colorado history. The flood destroyed 361 homes and 52 businesses. Estes Park has rebuilt but the flood left as its legacy a heightened awareness of the inextricable connections between humans and the land on which they perch.

Indeed, the history of Estes Park and Rocky Mountain National Park are so deeply intertwined that one would probably not exist without the other. Even the Estes Park Chamber of Commerce brochure begins with "The Park." The main employers in Estes Park are the school district, medical center, Town of Estes Park, Holiday Inn, Estes Park Center/YMCA of the Rockies, Harmony Foundation (a drug and alcohol rehabilitation center), Rocky Mountain National Park, Michael Ricker Pewter Casting Studio and the Estes Valley

Recreation and Park District. The town receives all Denver TV stations through a TV translator or cable and has one radio station, KRKI 1470 AM. The *Trail Gazette* newspaper is published twice weekly.

Visitor Information

For information about almost anything in the area, call the Estes Park Chamber Resort Association (800) 443-7837 or (800) 44-ESTES. The area code for Estes Park is 970 and calls from Boulder are long distance.

For reservations and other businesses in the area call (970) 586-4402 or (800) ROCKY MT. This number is for Estes Park Central Reservations, which provides information on participating, but not all, properties.

Community Information

Some tourists enjoy connecting with the quieter, community side of an area. Others suddenly need a community service. These days, many visitors stand transfixed by the beautiful surroundings and decide to make Estes Park their permanent home. This chapter provides information for all three, starting with medical care and worship, moving on to real estate and retirement, then ending with schools and child care.

The Chamber's Resort Association (see above) offers a free Relocation Package. It has an area overview plus demographics and real estate information. The Community Development Department in the town Administrator's Office also may have helpful information; call (970) 586-5331.

Medical Care, Dental Care . . . Even Pet Care

Estes Park Medical Center
555 Prospect Ave., Estes Park
• **(970) 586-2317**

This facility has a staff of 10 full-time doc-

tors, plus 20 specialists who visit weekly or monthly. The center includes 24-hour emergency care, radiology and 16 inpatient rooms. Emergency helicopter service can transport patients to specialized hospitals. Also see the Boulder chapter on Healthcare and Wellness.

Timberline Medical
131 Stanley Ave., Suite 202, Estes Park
• **(970) 586-2343**

This family practice also operates an urgent care center for treatment of injuries and illnesses that require immediate care but don't call for hospitalization. It is open 8 AM to 8 PM Weekdays, 9 AM TO 5 PM Saturdays and noon to 6 PM Sundays.

Estes Park Dental
343 S. St. Vrain Ave., Estes Park
• **(970) 586-9330**

For a toothache, this clinic has Saturday and evening hours plus same-day emergency care. Other possibilities appear in the Yellow Pages under "Dentists."

Boarding House for Dogs and Cats
863 Dry Gulch Rd., Estes Park
• **(970) 586-6606**

This is a good place if you're thinking of leaving your furry friend shut in the car while you wander the lovely local shops (don't!). Colorado's intense sun can turn a car into an oven within minutes. This can happen even on a cool day — even with a window partially rolled down. On weekends, the Boarding House books fast, but generally a few days' notice works for short-term boarding. Reservations a few weeks in advance work best.

Worship

Estes Park has more than a dozen churches, with an average church membership around 300. Many offer Bible School, evening programs and summer camps. Check the Yellow Pages under "Churches" for details. Every Friday, the local newspaper, the *Trail Gazette*, lists services and church news. Then there's the Estes Park Center/YMCA of

The Stanley Hotel, inspiration for Stephen King's *The Shining*, has hosted the rich and famous since 1906.

the Rockies, (970) 586-3341 (see listing under accommodations), with a fulltime pastor on staff plus programs and facilities for church-related (and secular) events.

It's less than an hour's trip to Boulder as the angel flies. Some Boulder County churches actually are closer to Estes Park than to the City of Boulder. So, you can broaden your choices by also checking the Boulder Worship chapter.

Real Estate

Estes Park is becoming a more year-round community. While it has always drawn retirees, lately there's a new demographic in town — computer commuters. As the Front Range booms, industries needing highly skilled workers move closer to Estes Park, increasing its draw as a bedroom community to Boulder. All this means Estes Park is getting younger, drawing families and a wider range of business skills.

In the good old days, you could find a rental when everyone left for the summer, but people aren't leaving so often anymore. For a summer rental, start checking six months in advance. For a long-term rental, get your name in six months early, then check monthly.

Homes to purchase are more available than homes for rent, but prices are not cheap. Something for less than $100,000 is unusual; the average price of a three-bedroom home in 1998 was $221,289 — up from $141,000 in 1994 — so the real estate market has been booming. The pop of air-gun hammers is more common around town these days and condominiums are springing up all around town. The valley is still a long way from expected build-out of 22,000 (valley winter population now is about 9,000), but builders are booked a year in advance. Investors are holding their income properties, and just a few timeshare opportunities are available. All of this information is not meant to discourage you, but rather remind you to start looking.

The Estes Park Chamber Resort Association provides a list of local Realtors.

Retirement

Some locals estimate that more than half the full-time residents of the Estes Valley are retired. That doesn't mean non-working or seniors — many people have jobs because they enjoy keeping busy, and many others have taken early retirement from big companies. Whatever age they are and whatever "work" residents do, it's true that many people look all over the nation then choose to retire in Estes Valley. If you're among them, visit the Estes Park Senior Center.

Regarding transportation, one local senior warns that you shouldn't come up here without your own, since there is no public bus system.

Estes Park Senior Center
220 Fourth St., Estes Park
• **(970) 586-2996**

The center is open from 9 AM to 3 PM Monday through Friday. The Senior Center serves meals five days a week. In the summertime, approximately 40 people enjoy dining here every day. During the winter, the number is in the 30s. About 25 meals a day are transported to seniors' homes. There's a blood pressure clinic once a month. Exercise classes happen three times a week. The Senior Center is also a good place to connect with town activities, including book groups, lectures, art classes, pinochle and bridge clubs. It hosts card games twice a week and a weekly oil-painting class. For the Retired and Senior Volunteer Program (RSVP), call (970) 586-9486. The local quilt guild and the rock and mineral club hold meetings here too.

Education and Child Care

Public Schools

The Park School District R-3, (970) 586-2361, includes almost 450 square miles and the towns of Estes Park, Allenspark, Glen Haven, Pinewood Springs and the eastern slope of Rocky Mountain National Park. The district employs around 200 people, serving the more than 700 school-age children in the valley.

Though small, Park School District R-3 includes art, music, gifted and talented programs, special education, reading and sports programs. Volunteers contribute nearly 150 hours each month. The district runs an Aquatic Center, open to the community during non-school periods. Computer and industrial technologies are part of many classrooms. Around 40 percent of teachers have master's degrees. The pupil/teacher ratio is 16.5-to-1. Nearly 95 percent of Park District children graduate from

high school, and 80 percent of these go on to higher education.

For more information write or visit the following schools:

• Park School District R-3 (administrative office), 1501 Brodie Avenue, (970) 586-2361

• Estes Park High School, 1600 Manford Avenue, (970) 586-5321

• Estes Park Middle School, 1500 Manford Avenue, (970) 586-4439

• Estes Park Intermediate School, 1505 Brodie Ave., Estes Park, (970) 586-7406

• Estes Park Elementary School, 650 Community Drive, (970) 586-9529

Private Schools

Eagle Rock School and Professional Development Center
2750 Notaiah Rd., Estes Park
• **(303) 442-7655**

This is a year-round, tuition-free, ungraded residential high school. It has been developed and funded by the American Honda Corporation as a public service. A beautiful setting, excellent staff and facilities for science, arts and physical education are here. It focuses on young people who are not experiencing success in their current school settings and are willing to commit to growth and change. Individualized learning opportunities are offered to 100 students, who are accepted through a careful application process.

Preschools and Child-care Centers

During the winter, it's easier to find child care. But as summer brings wildflowers to the mountains, it brings visitors into Estes Park Valley. If you might need summer child care, even for a week or a few days, day-care centers recommend you start looking at least by midwinter.

To connect with child-related programs in the valley, visit the Estes Park Public Library, (970) 586-8116, 335 E. Elkhorn Avenue. Parents can check out stuffed animals for their children there, and it also offers a list of babysitters who can come to your home or hotel room. Most are teenagers who have gone through a Red Cross Training Program for first aid and CPR. Summer reading programs for children also are there. Call the Larimer County Social Services Program in Estes Park, (970) 577-2150, to request a list of licensed day-care centers and homes plus applications for reduced fee services.

Mountain Top Preschool
1250 Woodstock, Estes Park
• (970) 586-6489

About 60 kids attend the preschool and child care center at this facility, which is the largest in Estes Park. Drop-ins are not accepted and there is a short waiting list.

Kreative Kids
650 Community Dr., Estes Park
• (970) 586-6727

This is a private, nonprofit kindergarten/day-care learning center for children ages 5 to 12, located next to the elementary school. It leases space from the school district and has a good relationship with the schools. It's $2.50 per hour for each child. Drop-ins are considered if there is space after the regularly enrolled children arrive.

Circle of Friends Montessori Preschool
2515 Tunnel Rd., Estes Park
• (970) 586-3341 ext. 1137

Located in the Estes Park Center/YMCA of the Rockies, this school has 20 to 30 children, 20 of whom attend full time. There's a parent-toddler program offered in spring for children ages 18 months to 3 years. There is also a kindergarten program.

Eateries

Estes Park has a large number of restaurants and casual cafes to choose from, ranging from doughnut shops and pizzerias to fine French restaurants and gourmet Italian inns. Italian and Mexican food seem to predominate, but steaks, burgers and trout are ubiquitous as well. Watch out for "Rocky Mountain Oysters," they're not seafood; in fact they come from a part of the bull that you might not want to consume. Fans say they taste a little like liver.

Even if you can't afford a meal at the historic Stanley Hotel, it's worth a visit for its landmark status, lovely setting and to see the shiny green Stanley Steamer automobile parked in the lobby. Those on a budget can still enjoy coffee or afternoon tea at the Stanley on the front veranda or a snack from the Dunraven Grill's bar menu. The Stanley also hosts free classical concerts on Sunday afternoons.

Reservations are not required at most Estes Park restaurants but are accepted and recommended at some of the more popular spots, particularly for groups during the crowded summer season. Almost all restaurants of any size beyond a hole in the wall accept major credit cards.

Price Code

The key below shows the price range for an average dinner for two excluding beverages, appetizers, desserts or tip.

$	Less than $25
$$	$25 to $50
$$$	$50 to $75
$$$$$	$75 and more

Lazy B Ranch
$–$$ • 1915 Dry Gulch Rd., Estes Park
• (970) 586-5371

For a family night out and a taste of the old West, sidle up to the chuckwagon where wranglers are dishing out barbecued beef, baked potatoes, beans and biscuits with coffee or lemonade (no alcohol allowed on the trail, partner). After dinner, there's a live stage show with western music, stories and jokes. Souvenir and gift shops are open before dinner and after the show. The Lazy B is open summers only, seven days a week.

The Baldpate Inn
$–$$ • 4900 Colo. Hwy. 7 S., south of Estes Park • (970) 586-6151

You'll get a lot more than lunch or dinner if you visit the Baldpate Inn. This classic mountain inn and historic local landmark was placed on the National Register of Historic Places in 1996. The inn, which is open Memorial Day until mid- to late October, is 7 miles south of Estes Park at 9,000 feet altitude, across from the Rocky Mountain National Park Visitors' Center at Lily Lake and serves lunch and dinner daily. There's a unique salad bar set in an old claw-foot bathtub plus delectable home-made soups, breads and pastries. Dinner is equally charming and delicious; reservations are a must. Mae West, Jack Dempsey and Rin Tin Tin stayed here, and you'll see their photos — along with opera singer Tetrazinni and world leaders — in the amazing collection in the dining room assembled by the two original owners. The inn has the world's largest key collection, which is open to the public.

Donut Haus
$ • 342 Moraine Ave., Estes Park
• (970) 586-2988

If it's just a doughnut you're craving, line up at the Donut Haus — there usually is a line stretching out the door of this tiny doughnut bakery that also has a large variety of other fresh-baked items. It's right beside the multi-colored giant slides.

Estes Park Brewery
$–$$ • 470 Prospect Village Dr., Estes Park • (970) 586-5421

The brewery has a pub, family restaurant and outdoor deck, serving pizza, sandwiches, burgers and salads. During summer it's open from 11 AM to midnight daily. (Check for winter hours, which may vary.) There are free brewery tours with free samples of the nine microbrews sold on tap and by the bottle. The Renegade Red has won a gold medal at the Great American Beer Festival.

Safeway
$ • Stanley Village North of the intersection of U.S. Hwys. 34 and 36, Estes Park • (970) 586-4447

For picnic or camping supplies on the way to Rocky Mountain National Park, look for the big Safeway supermarket up on the hill above the downtown area. There's also a salad bar and deli in the store.

Ed's Cantina and Grill
$ • 362 E. Elkhorn Ave., Estes Park
• (970) 586-2919

In addition to all the Mexican favorites plus barbecued ribs and sandwiches for lunch and dinner, this comfortable South-of-the-Border spot serves the local microbrew from Estes Park Brewery. Ed's is open for breakfast, too.

Mountain Home Cafe
$ • Stanley Village, intersection of U.S. Hwys. 34 and 36, Estes Park
• (970) 586-6624

Formerly known as Johnson's and right in the shopping center, this little cafe isn't glamorous. But the food is quite good, especially the Swedish potato pancakes with sour cream and applesauce and the baked Alaska oatmeal. It's a favorite of area residents for the breakfasts served all day. You can also get lunch here Monday through Saturday, and the cafe is open Sundays for breakfast from 8 AM until 1 PM (closed afterward).

Laura's Fine Candies
$ • 129 E. Elkhorn Ave., Estes Park
• (970) 586-4004

Though it's not exactly a meal, for some it's considered daily bread. Of all the cotton candy and caramel apple stores, Laura's really stands out. There are 16 flavors of this delicious fudge that's made with whipping cream. Locals have braved the summer weekend crowds packed on Elkhorn Avenue just for a piece of this stuff. Laura's also has homemade cookies, soft pretzels and ice cream.

Notchtop Baked Goods & Natural Foods Cafe and Pub
$ • Upper Stanley Village, intersection of U.S. Hwys. 34 and 36 • (970) 586-0272

This local favorite has a pub with its own microbrew — Notchtop, of course. Stop here for delicious pastries or an inexpensive lunch. Very casual, with newspapers and magazines to read (such as *Mother Earth News*), this little cafe is a nice break from the tourist scene and serves nutritious food and natural beverages, plus great locally roasted Silver Canyon coffees. The cafe is open daily from breakfast through dinner. There's live music (no cover) Friday through Sunday nights from Memorial Day until Labor Day.

The Other Side
$ • 900 Moraine Ave., Estes Park
• (970) 586-2171

Specializing in an "all-American" menu, this restaurant at the entrance to Rocky Mountain National Park at Mary's Lake Road has a pleasant view of a little duck pond. The menu offers seafood, steaks, prime rib, burgers and a Sunday champagne brunch. Lunch and dinner are served daily, while breakfast is served Thursday through Sunday.

The Mountaineer
$ • 540 S. St. Vrain Rd., Estes Park
• (970) 586-9001

Fast and friendly service is the hallmark of this unpretentious little cafe, with lots of granny-type knickknacks and corny paintings on the wall. But it's quite cozy and out of the hustle-bustle of downtown Estes Park. It's about a half-mile south on Colo. Highway 7 across the street from the Diamond Shamrock gas station and Estes Park Rehabilitation Center. Open daily for an early breakfast (at 6 AM), the restaurant features lots of morning food choices, including homemade biscuits and gravy and cinnamon rolls, and is quite inexpensive. Local climbers and mountaineers (and tourists) like to stop here for a tasty and inexpensive breakfast, lunch or dinner.

Molly B Restaurant
$ • 200 Moraine Ave., Estes Park
• (970) 586-2766

For coffee, a light breakfast or a big meal, try this casual cafe that's open year round. Along with the usual breakfast foods, you'll also find great choices for lunch or dinner, including seafood, vegetarian dishes and burgers and homemade desserts. It's another favorite stop of local mountaineers for an early breakfast or a late snack. Note that the restaurant takes a brief break daily between 3 and 5 PM.

Nicky's Restaurant and Resort
$-$$ • 1350 Fall River Rd., Estes Park
• (970) 586-5376

Nicky's claim to fame is the delicious prime rib roasted in rock salt. Out a few miles on Fall River Road (a pleasant drive), this large, attractive restaurant has a huge menu with lots of variety, including Italian and Greek special-ties, steaks and a salad bar. It's open year-round, for breakfast, lunch and dinner daily from June to September and for lunch and dinner, with breakfasts on weekends only the rest of the year.

Poppy's Pizza & Grill
$ • 342 E. Elkhorn Ave., Estes Park
• (970) 586-8282

In the spiffy Barlow Plaza, this pleasant pizzeria has all types of pizza — pesto, Polynesian, Mexican, to name a few — for reasonable prices. Some of the individual pizzas are around $3. There are also homemade soups, salads, desserts and sandwiches. When the weather cooperates, you can sit outside on the nice patio overlooking the river. Poppy's is open for lunch and dinner year round, but closes for a time during January.

Mama Rose's
$ • Barlow Plaza, 338 E. Elkhorn Ave., Estes Park • (970) 586-3330

This tidy Italian restaurant in a pretty reproduction of an old Victorian home has a large selection of dishes. It offers a very pleasant veranda overlooking the river for dining. Choose from chicken Parmesan in wine sauce, seafood fettuccine, fresh basil pesto, baked pasta and other Italian dishes. The restaurant serves lunch and dinner daily and Sunday breakfast buffets during the summer. The restaurant closes from January through March.

Wild Basin Lodge & Smorgasbord
$ • Off Colo. Hwy. 7, 13 mi. south of Estes Park • (303) 747-2545

Casual, come-as-you-are dining with lots of food and a great view of a rushing river are the highlights of this landmark lodge. The all-you-can-eat smorgasbord is a daily dinner occurrence during summer Monday through Saturday, and for lunch and dinner on Sunday. After summer the restaurant is open weekends until November 1 and reopens weekends on Palm

---

INSIDERS' TIP

Well before he became a famous author, a teenage Stephen King applied for a writing position at Boulder's *Daily Camera* newspaper. He was rejected.

Sunday. During July and early August, the lodge is sometimes the scene of the Allenspark Melodrama performances (see the "Tours, Attractions and Festivals" section subsequently in this chapter). Wild Basin is at the south entrance to Rocky Mountain National Park.

Black Canyon Inn
$$–$$$ • 800 MacGregor Ave. (Devil's Gulch Rd.), Estes Park • (970) 586-9344

This historic mountain lodge offers a romantic fireside atmosphere to complement the fine dining. Seafood specials with pasta include salmon fettuccine or tomato fettuccine with fresh sea scallops. The restaurant also offers some wild game selections, including elk, plus duck and prawns. Black Canyon serves dinner only every day, and reservations are required.

Dunraven Inn
$–$$ • 2470 Colo. Hwy. 66, Estes Park • (970) 586-6409

Probably not quite what Lord Dunraven had in mind, the Dunraven Inn calls itself the "Rome of the Rockies" and specializes in Italian food. (Lord Dunraven was the Irish nobleman who bought all of Estes Park in the 19th century to create his own private hunting reserve, but was eventually ousted by locals.) The Dunraven Inn has long been a favorite stop for steak and Italian dishes, including shrimp scampi, lasagna, eggplant Parmesan and chicken cacciatore plus a large selection of Italian wines. Be sure to make reservations during the summer months when the restaurant is packed. Dinner is served daily.

The Stanley Hotel
$$–$$$ • 333 Wonderview Ave., Estes Park • (970) 586-3371, (800) 976-1377

For a special treat, try the Stanley's Sunday champagne brunch, served year round from 10 AM to 2 PM in the hotel's MacGregor ballroom. Unlimited champagne or mimosas accompany an unbelievable spread — every pastry you can imagine and every breakfast dish plus seafood, prime rib and much, much more. An eclectic mix of live music adds to the atmosphere (get dressed up if you want to, but casual is fine, too). For those with time

and a hearty appetite, it's a real bargain for the $21.95-per-person price. Dinners at the Stanley are served in the Dunraven Grille, which was just completely renovated and has a brand-new bar. Choices include teriyaki ahi, chorizo-smoked chili rellenos, prime rib and elk with such side dishes as ahi or duck salad and spicy red bean or beer-cheese soup. The Dunraven Grille also offers a bar menu from 11:30 AM until 3 PM Mondays through Saturdays. During summer there's usually a long waiting list for tables on the hotel's lovely front veranda with its spectacular mountain view, and where breakfast, lunch and dinner are also served. The Stanley serves breakfast, lunch and dinner daily year round.

La Casa and La Casa Grande
$ • El Centro Mall, 222 E. Elkhorn Ave., Estes Park • (970) 586-2807

La Casa is a Mexican restaurant with some extra spice — Cajun. If there's a difference of opinion on what spicy cuisine to have, La Casa restaurant offers the perfect alternative with its traditional Mexican and Cajun favorites, including blackened redfish, burritos and fizzy Margaritas. There are also choices on La Casa's international menu for those who don't like it hot. La Casa Grande on the riverside is used for receptions and special parties. It's open for lunch and dinner daily.

La Chaumiere
$$–$$$ • U.S. Hwy. 36, Pinewood Springs • (303) 823-6521

Those with sophisticated palates who savor sautéed sweetbreads say La Chaumiere offers the best around. Another popular item is the duck liver paté. Classic French dining in a serene setting with its own deer park is what La Chaumiere has used for years to draw its faithful patrons. Though a bit out of the way (12 miles southeast of Estes Park), French food lovers don't mind the extra drive for the diverse, changing menu, including specialty game meats, lamb, beef and seafood. The restaurant has its own smokehouse and organic garden and makes its own ice cream. A six-course, $21.50 dinner special is served Sunday. The restaurant is open for dinner daily, but is closed Mondays.

Summertime Horse Shows

This n-e-e-e-i-i-i-g-h-borly valley is full of summer horse shows. Each event brings around 250 sleek beauties to the Estes Park Fairground, (970) 586-6104, on the east side of town near Lake Estes. Admission is free for all shows except the Westernaires. Here's a general calendar:

Around the third week in June, the quarter horses show off their spin-on-a-dime and quarter-mile sprinting skills in barrel racing, roping, pole bending and riding displays.

Close-up

The fourth week in June features miniature horses. Some baby miniatures stand only a foot tall, and even adults are less than three feet. These knee-high horses dance to music and can pull a little surrey. Hitch six to a buckboard wagon, and you've got a team. Sometimes, a contestant brings a miniature stagecoach with a team of eight. While miniatures may seem just right for tucking in with a child's toy animals, experts say they act like regular horses. Only cuter.

As June ends and July begins, in thunder the Arabians. The International Arabian Show started here more than 40 years ago then outgrew little Estes Valley. But many of the nation's best Arabians still come here. Two days feature Arabian cattle-cutting championships. It's the second-largest such event in the United States. We promised not to print this but couldn't help ourselves — some local experts say Arabians can be as good or better at cutting cattle as quarter horses. The costume class is the favorite spectator event. Watch for Arabian sheiks and princesses and even horses in flowing capes.

When July ends and August begins, as many as 500 horses leap to the Hunter-Jumper events. They keep three show rings hopping, we mean, jumping.

Westernaires normally take on the town during the second weekend in August. The precision riders are dazzling, dedicated, Denver-area teens. In past years, they've done some routines in black lights so their costumes glow, and their lively, Old West skits are always popular. The fee is usually $5 per person for the Friday and Saturday shows, which start around 7:30 PM.

Photo: Town of Estes Park

Don't miss Estes Park's annual Hunter-Jumper horse shows in July and August.

Nightlife

Estes Park isn't big on nightlife, but there are a few choices for not-too-weary travelers or residents.

The Old Gaslight Pub
246 Moraine Ave., Estes Park
• (970) 586-0994

DJ's provide the varied mix of music on weekends, with plenty of room for dancing. There are dinner specials such as fish and chips, Italian dishes and other favorites. The bar has some British beers on tap and local microbrews.

Park Village Playhouse
900 Moraine Ave., Estes Park
• (970) 586-2885

Visit this playhouse to enjoy good, old-fashioned melodrama. The curtain goes up at 8 PM, doors open at 7 PM; reservations are suggested.

Park Theatre
Corner of Moraine Ave. and Rockwell St., Estes Park • (970) 586-8904

Enjoy first-run movies every night from May through September here. The cafe is open until 6 or 7 PM during summer.

Wheel Bar
132 E. Elkhorn Ave., Estes Park
• (970) 586-9381

Now celebrating 54 years of operation, this local landmark has been owned and operated by the same family since 1945. This comfortable neighborhood bar offers beers, microbrews on tap and cocktails at happy-hour prices. Upstairs there's Orlando's steak house for a full meal.

The Stanley Hotel
333 Wonderview Ave., Estes Park
• (970) 586-3371, (800) 976-1377

The Stanley presents theater and fine arts performances and claims to put on more performances than any other private property in the West. Performances vary with the season and include free concerts, Big Band dancing during the summer and holiday galas like "The Shining" Halloween Ball and a popular New Year's Eve party. There's a year-round jazz series and a Friday-night dance program. Call for the current schedule of events and ask about special honeymoon and "romance" packages.

Estes Park Brewery
470 Prospect Village Dr., Estes Park
• (970) 586-5421

The brewery has a pub, family restaurant and outdoor deck, and serves pizza, sandwiches, burgers and salads. During summer it's open from 11 AM to midnight daily. (Check for winter hours, which may vary.) There are free samples of the nine microbrews sold on tap and by the bottle. The Renegade Red has won a gold medal at the Great American Beer Festival.

Accommodations

Estes Park has so many motels, bed and breakfast inns, lodges and cabins, visitors will have a large choice and range in quality and atmosphere. But reservations are a good idea during the crowded summer months and a must over holiday weekends. Choose a modern motel, a rustic lodge or cabin or a place right out of history. All of these accommodations accept major credit cards, with the exception of the cabins at Estes Park Center/ YMCA of the Rockies. Pets are not allowed at any of these properties, except for the cabins at Estes Park Center/YMCA of the Rockies.

Price Code

Our code reflects what you'll pay on average for a double room.

$	Less than $30
$$	$30 to $50
$$$	$50 to $75
$$$$	$75 to $90
$$$$$	$90 and more

Alpine Trail Ridge Inn
$$$–$$$$ • 927 Moraine Ave., Estes Park • (970) 586-4585

This tidy blue-trimmed white motel is right on the highway, but its clean and pleasant rooms are a good value. There's a heated swimming pool, and family and kitchen units are available. You can request either smoking or nonsmoking rooms. Enjoy good meals at the Sundeck Restaurant right on the property.

Aspen Lodge at Estes Park
$$$$$ • 6120 Colo. Hwy. 7, Estes Park • (970) 586-8133, (800) 332-6867

Located 7.5 miles south of Estes Park, this beautiful 3,000-acre ranch is a full resort offering hayrides, swimming, fishing, tennis, racquetball, horseback riding, wildlife van tours, mountain biking, hikes and a great children's program for kids 5 to 12 that includes Indian lore and nature rambles. It's the largest log lodge in the state, according to the owners. There are cozy cabins, a hot tub, saunas and winter sleigh rides. Three-, four- and seven-day packages make this all-inclusive resort quite affordable, with all meals and activities (except horseback riding) included. Smoking is prohibited at this property.

The Baldpate Inn
$$$$$ • 4900 Colo. Hwy. 7 S., Estes Park • (970) 586-6151

In January 1996, the Baldpate was placed on the National Register of Historic Places. Family-owned and operated as a bed and breakfast, this classic mountain inn and historic local landmark is unsurpassed in charm and history. Built from local wood and stone in 1917, it's the quintessential rustic mountain getaway. The inn is 7 miles south of Estes Park across from the Rocky Mountain National Park Visitors' Center at Lily Lake. Guests can stay in the Mae West and Jack Dempsey rooms, where these and many other stars stayed. The Baldpate Inn has 12 rustic rooms and three cabins with colorful homemade quilts, calicos, gingham and alluring log-cabin decor. One cabin is a newly redecorated honeymoon suite. There are five massive stone fireplaces and a library.

A three-course breakfast is included in the room rate. The inn has the world's largest key collection and an amazing photograph collection. Breakfast is included in the room rate and the dining room serves delicious meals with homemade pies, pastries, breads and soups. Smoking is not allowed. The Baldpate Inn is open Memorial Day until October, weather permitting.

Estes Park Center/YMCA of the Rockies
$–$$$, no credit cards • 2515 Tunnel Rd., Estes Park • (970) 586-3341

There's something for almost everyone (except maybe honeymooners) at the Y. This enormous facility, just outside Estes Park, can accommodate 3,469 and runs numerous camps and programs. The Y is the place for families or other groups and offers everything from rustic cabins that sleep four to ten lodge rooms that sleep four to six. There's a miniature golf course, tennis courts, livery, craft shop, library, museum, post office and theater. Concerts are given regularly. It's open year round. Pets and smoking are allowed in the cabins but not in the rooms.

Romantic River Song Bed & Breakfast Inn
$$$$$ • Lower Broadview Rd. (off Mary's Lake Rd.), Estes Park • (970) 586-4666

Reservations are a good idea at this lovely, secluded bed and breakfast set on 27 acres right along the Big Thompson River. Guests like it so much they return from year to year, often booking a year in advance. During the high season reservations need to be made about 15 weeks in advance. During the rest of the year it's not nearly as busy. Each of the rooms is custom-decorated either with lovely antiques or whimsical handmade furniture. One room has the beautiful 200-year-old bed of the owner's grandmother; another has a delightful bed made of gracefully arching willow twigs complete with (decorative) nesting birds. There's a river stone-faced Jacuzzi in one room and fireplaces in most rooms. The list of amenities goes on and on at this lovely old home. Gourmet breakfast comes with the price of the room. This is a no-smoking inn.

Fawn Valley Inn
$$$$$ • 2760 Fall River Rd., Estes Park • (970) 586-2388, (800) 525-2961

Only a half-mile from Rocky Mountain National Park, these year-round condominiums are set on more than 8 acres along the Fall River. They feature complete kitchens and fireplaces, and there's a heated outdoor pool. Bruce's Dark Horse Restaurant & Lounge offers fine and casual dining and is popular for its weekend dining specials. There are facilities for reunions and conferences. Smoking is allowed in some of the units.

Streamside Cabins
$$$$–$$$$$ • 1260 Fall River Rd., Estes Park • (970) 586-6464, (800) 321-3303

Describing itself as a "Village of Cabin Suites," these cabins are for those who want to "rough it" in luxury. They have skylights, fireplaces, wall-to-wall carpeting, private decks, gas grills, steam rooms and jetted tubs. The cabins are on a wooded hillside on Fall River about a mile from Estes Park. The 16-acre site offers fishing and solitude. The cabins are listed among the 19 "Best of Estes," by an Estes Park *Trail Gazette* survey. Special packages are available. Smoking is permitted.

Misty Mountain Lodge
$$$–$$$$$ • 232 E. Riverside Dr., Estes Park • (970) 586-4100

This attractive and very reasonably priced lodge is a great value right in town. It's set against a hillside, away from the crowd across the river. There are multi-room suites, kitchens and fireplaces, a hot tub and great off-season rates. Smoking is allowed.

Eagle Manor Bed and Breakfast
$$$$$ • 441 Chiquita Lane, Estes Park • (970) 586-8482

Bed down in the home of Estes Valley pioneer Frank Bond (as in Bond Park) for a quiet stay. The Tudor-style home, built in 1917, has just four guest rooms (each with cable, two with private baths). Lovely oak floors, two fireplaces and antique furniture remind visitors they are staying in a gracious old home; an indoor swimming pool and sauna and outdoor hot tub satisfy their itch for 20th century amenities.

Sunnyside Knoll Resort
$$$$$ • 1675 Fall River Rd., Estes Park • (970) 586-5759

This is a resort for couples committed to romance. Each unit has a fireplace, cable television and VCR and many have jacuzzis for two situated with a fireplace view. There is also a heated outdoor pool and two outdoor hot tubs.

H-Bar-G Ranch Hostel
$ • 3500 H-Bar-G Rd., Estes Park • (970) 586-3688

If you don't mind some togetherness in exchange for very low rates, the H-Bar-G, in it's twenty-sixth year of operation, offers cabins, family accommodations and separate buildings for men and women. There is a tennis court, volleyball court, game room, barbecue pit and fireplaces to cozy the place up. Guests are expected to bring their own sleeping bags and to contribute a clean-up chore or two. A shared kitchen is available. Visits are limited to three days. The H-Bar-G is a member of Hostelling International and a membership card gets you a $10 bunk. Memberships are $25 and only members can stay.

The Stanley Hotel & Conference Center: A Grand Heritage Hotel
$$$$$ • 333 Wonderview Ave., Estes Park • (970) 586-3371, (800) 976-1377

The stately queen of the area's hotels, the Stanley is truly a classic and on the National Register of Historic Places. The inspiration for Stephen King's book, *The Shining*, the Stanley was also the scene for shooting the 1997 TV miniseries of the same name. King returned in 1996 as screenwriter and executive producer and stayed six months for the shooting. During the filming for the new version, the hotel lobby and MacGregor room were restored to

---

INSIDERS' TIP

Those who would like to rub shoulders with the daring rock jocks who climb the "Diamond" face of Longs Peak (a world-renowned climb) should try an early breakfast at either The Mountaineer or Molly B's. Climbers reputedly have their pre-climb breakfasts at these cafes.

a more authentic turn-of-the-century look by the film directors and Grand Heritage (the company that owns the Stanley), going from white walls back to natural woods and patterned wallpapers.

The hotel was purchased recently by Grand Heritage, which owns and operates castles and historic buildings around the world. Grand Heritage financed a $3.6 million restoration of the Stanley completed in spring of 1997, maintaining the hotel's turn-of-the-century decor. Rooms have canopy beds, Victorian wallpaper and other period details. Those feeling extravagant should ask for the Stephen King suite. Though there are no skeletons in the closet, it's where the Emperor and Empress of Japan stayed during their visit a few years ago as well as other VIPs over the years.

Historic tours of the hotel are offered year round, five times a day (see the "Attractions" section of this chapter for more information). The Stanley also hosts free concerts every Sunday, "fairy tale weddings," dinner theater, holiday galas, Big Band dancing, the Colorado Music Festival during summer and the famous "The Shining" Halloween Ball. Smoking is allowed at the Stanley.

Arts

Estes Park offers the full range of choices for quality art. Shops, galleries and boutiques dot the main streets with a plethora of Native American art and representations of Rocky Mountain National Park in every medium. Besides visual arts, performing arts include theater and classical concerts, jazz and contemporary music. Larger performing-arts events and festivals generally take place during the summer.

Visual Arts

Charles Eagle Plume Gallery
9853 Hwy. 7, Allenspark
• (303) 747-2861

The Charles Eagle Plume Gallery and Museum of Native American Arts has been a local landmark since 1917 and is a favorite stop. Located 10 miles south of Estes Park on Colo.

7, it has a huge collection of art and artifacts, including rugs, jewelry, pottery, baskets and beautiful beadwork of the Plains Indians. Active in the Native American rights movement, founder Charles Eagle Plume graduated from the University of Colorado in 1932 and was later awarded an honorary Doctorate of Humanities from CU-Boulder. The gallery is open daily April through December, weekends or by appointment January through March.

Sundance Center for the Arts
150 E. Riverside Dr., Estes Park
• (970) 586-6353, (970) 586-0832

This complex of galleries and frame shops specializing in Western and nature art includes Impressions Ltd., and Colorado Essence, which are the biggest galleries in town with regular programs of shows and openings. Look for animals and other woodcarvings at the Mountain Wood Carvers, located at the same address in the complex, (970) 586-8678.

The Glassworks Studio and Gallery
323 W. Elkhorn Ave., Estes Park
• (970) 586-8619

This is the only hot glass studio and gallery in the area. There are free public glass blowing demonstrations daily, year round, by owner Garth Mudge, who displays the delicate art.

The Michael Ricker Pewter Museum, Gallery and Casting Studio
2 miles east of town on U.S. Hwy. 34, Estes Park • (970) 586-2030

Ricker claims to have the world's largest pewter-casting studio, where more than 25,000 pewter sculptures are cast each month, and also the world's largest pewter sculpture (10 feet by 30 feet). Ricker's presentations and commissions include The White House, the U.S. Olympic Committee, Disney World and Pope John Paul II. Several of Ricker's works are on display in the Smithsonian Institution. Children will enjoy the re-creation of a turn-of-the-century American town. The museum, gallery and casting studio are open seven days a week year-round. There's also a Ricker Pewter retail shop in town at 167 E. Elkhorn Ave.

Galleries of Estes Park Association
P.O. Box 987, Estes Park, CO 80517
• (no phone)

The association publishes the Estes Park Gallery Guide, listing the town's shops and galleries. For information write to the association or call the Cultural Arts Council, P.O. Box 4135, 160 Moraine Ave., Estes Park, CO 80517, (970) 586-9203. For other information try the Resort Chamber at (970) 586-4431 or (800) 44-ESTES.

Performing Arts

Chamber Music Society of Estes Park
P.O. Box 1331, Estes Park, CO 80517
• (970) 586-9203

This society of some 100 chamber-music-loving members sponsors concerts all year in the Estes Park area, inviting different musicians from around the state and nation. The society also sponsors an annual Chamber Music Festival, held over a weekend in fall. Past festivals have featured the American Chamber Players and The Mendelssohn Trio. Information is available on concert locations, dates and prices from the Cultural Arts Council at the number listed above or from artistic director Louise Dickey in Boulder, (303) 494-8934.

The Estes Park Music Festival
Stanley Concert Hall, Stanley Hotel, Estes Park • (970) 586-9203

Boulder's nationally acclaimed Colorado Music Festival Orchestra comes to Estes Park on Monday evenings during the summer from late June through early August. For more information about this better-than-the-best orchestra, see our Boulder Arts chapter. Ticket prices vary.

Music in the Mountains
Rocky Ridge Music Center, Colo. Hwy. 7, 12 miles south of Estes Park
• (970) 586-4031, (402) 486-4363 (in winter)

Rocky Ridge offers chamber music and opera. Student and faculty recitals take place here on Fridays and Sundays around 3 PM

from late June until the end of August. Call for current ticket prices.

The Stanley Hotel
333 Wonderview Ave., Estes Park
• (970) 586-3371, (800) 976-1377

For year-round entertainment check the Stanley Hotel, which presents theater and fine arts performances and claims to put on more performances than any other private property in the West. The Stanley also hosts free concerts on Sundays. There's a year-round jazz series and a Friday-night dance program. Call for the current schedule of events.

Shopping

Estes Park's shopping area is an attractive but bewildering sort of gingerbread glitz with a theme and style somewhere between Switzerland and Coney Island. Saltwater taffy in the Rocky Mountains? Unfortunately, some of the clothing, jewelry, knickknacks, "art" and other items found in the shops have nothing to do with Estes Park, Colorado or the Rocky Mountains. Other offerings are more Southwestern and related to Native American tribes nowhere near the area.

Despite this, a really nice feature of the Estes Park shopping area is the riverside walkway called Confluence Park behind the main street shops and right on the Big Thompson River. Lots of little wooden bridges provide access across the river to free parking lots all around. Almost all of the shops along the south side of Elkhorn Avenue go through to this very pleasant and relaxing walkway beside the tumbling river, with shade trees, flowers and lots of benches to rest on.

MacDonald Book Shop
152 E. Elkhorn Ave., Estes Park
• (970) 586-3450

Established in 1928, this large bookstore in an old log cabin was originally the home of turn-of-the-century residents. The owners of the bookstore and adjacent coffee shop (below) have had the bookstore for four generations. Out-of-town newspapers, including *The New York Times*, are available along with a wide selection of hardbacks, paperback children's books, books on cassette, magazines and calendars. Be sure to read the history plaque out front explaining how the first bookstore on the site was opened in the owners' living room. Colorful Scottish plaid carpet and exposed log beams set the interior mood.

MacDonald Paper & Coffee House
150 E. Elkhorn Ave., Estes Park
• (970) 586-3451

Right behind the bookstore of the same name, this cozy coffeehouse has a casual relaxing atmosphere that invites visitors to stay for a while. The shop has a great selection of stationery, greeting cards, gift wrap and posters and also offers espresso, cappuccino, a wide variety of teas, tempting pastries, fresh-squeezed orange juice, Italian fruit drinks and other beverages. Tables are sprinkled around upstairs and down among the cards. It's light, bright and pleasant, decorated throughout in blond wood. Sit down with a cappuccino and write a card or letter. The coffeehouse opens daily at 8 AM.

Craftsmen in Leather
135 W. Elkhorn Ave., Estes Park
• (970) 586-2400

"Come in and smell the leather," invites this 26-year-old store. You can take a self-guided tour of the shop, try on some of the hats in the huge inventory — which includes everything from fur felt and suede to wool and straw — and learn how to care for leather goods. The store also sells belts and buckles, handbags and luggage, wallets, moccasins and jewelry.

Rocky Mountain Knife Company
125 Moraine Ave., Estes Park
• (970) 586-8419

This tiny shop bills itself as the Biggest Little Knife Store West of the Mississippi. It's not just knives, though. The walls and shelves are covered with everything from kitchen cutlery to crossbows, swords and battle axes,

tomahawks, blow guns and sling shots, water balloons and martial arts supplies. Oh, and they sharpen knives, too.

Common Scents
205A Park Lane, Estes Park
• (970) 586-5665

The smell is enough to bring you in the front door of this little shop, selling wax potpourri handmade in Estes Park. This is a mix-your-own store — make yourself an olfactory apple pie by combining apple, cinnamon, clove and vanilla. Or, buy one of the ready mixed blends like Long's Peak Trail — pine, blue spruce, cedar, blue columbine and lavender. The potpourri can be stored in a ventilated basket to scent a room for weeks, or melted in a potpourri pot to spread aroma through the whole house.

Outdoor World
156 E. Elkhorn Ave., Estes Park
• (970) 586-2114

Shop here for a great selection of high-quality boots, backpacks, jackets, water bottles and everything you need for the outdoors.

Glass Blowers
126 E. Elkhorn Ave., Estes Park
• (970) 586-5963

Those who would like a blown-glass hummingbird can find one of the best selections in the area at this shop. Most of the blown glass is made at the shop's other studio in Manitou Springs, Colorado. You'll find hummingbirds in every color of the rainbow here, from red and green ruby throats to copper rufous hummers. All types of other miniature figures are represented in glass as well.

The Hiking Hut
110 E. Elkhorn Ave., Estes Park
• (970) 586-0708

This shop offers a nice selection of backpacks, jackets, sunglasses and other acces-

---

INSIDERS' TIP

For those who want a quiet and more authentic experience with some local people, small inns and bed and breakfasts are good alternatives to the motel scene.

sories for hiking and camping in the mountains.

The Talking Teddy
521 Lone Pine Dr., Estes Park
• (970) 586-6483

Visit this fun shop for a mind-boggling assortment of teddy bears in all sizes and styles, teddy bear-related items such as Smokey Bear hats, teddy bear-decorated T-shirts and individual bears made by various "teddy bear artists." The shop also sells various plush animals and other collectibles.

Western Brands
141 E. Elkhorn Ave., Estes Park
• (970) 586-3361

If it's a hat you need, stop here. There's a great selection of cowboy hats plus wonderful felt bowlers, top hats and more. Western Brands also carries lots of Levi's, T-shirts, jackets, blankets, "cattle drover" coats and other items to make you feel at home on the range.

Park Theatre
Moraine Ave. and Rockwell St.,
Estes Park • (970) 586-8904

A sprinkling of small shops are nestled around the historic Park Theatre, which was built in 1913. The theatre's impressive white tower — Estes Park's tallest structure — was added to the building by a former owner as a monument to a woman who left him at the altar. The Park Theatre's cafe and snack shops — open from 8 AM until 9 PM daily — are a good place to stop in summer. Down the lane next to a little shopping mall is Ye Old Tin Shop, at No. 134, (970) 586-5129, with a charming collection of reproductions of antique metal tins, including Morton Salt, Lipton Tea and Hershey's Kisses tins, and many more unusual antique signs and metal plaques — all quite inexpensive.

Stanley Village
Intersection of U.S. Hwys. 34 and 36,
Estes Park • (970) 586-6114

This shopping center is located directly below the imposing, white Stanley Hotel, which is perched on a hillside above town — you can't miss it. Slightly to the east are a Safeway

and a shopping area that offers visitors lots of necessary services. To the east of Safeway is a Coast to Coast Hardware store, (970) 586-3496, for those little gadgets you always end up needing on a trip. There's also the Notchtop Baked Goods & Natural Foods Cafe and Pub and Mountain Home Cafe (see the previous "Restaurants" section of this chapter for details on each) as well as many other shops and a movie theater.

Winona Knits
344 E. Elkhorn Ave., Barlow Plaza, Estes Park • (970) 586-0947

Winona Knits offers an attractive and affordable selection of sportswear with golf, fishing and tennis themes and other nice casual clothing for the family. Winona's motto: "Life should be comfortable."

Canyonlands Indian Arts
146 W. Elkhorn Ave., Estes Park
• (970) 577-0479

This shop features top-quality Indian and Southwest jewelry, authentic pottery, kachinas, carvings and Navajo rugs.

Moses Street Photography
157 W. Elkhorn, Estes Park
• (970) 586-7221, (888) 315-1125,
(800) 634-8401

OK, it's not exactly shopping, but we thought you might want to know about this service. Moses Street specializes in portraits, but we're not talking about a stool in front of a fake bookcase. In addition to glamour portraits and family reunions captured on film, Moses will actually capture your image at the top of a mountain or canoeing across a crystal lake, if that's where you want to go. "We travel anywhere in the world to do any type of people photography," Moses promises.

Tours, Attractions and Festivals

All of these beautiful mountains could keep you happy for years. But even the most dedicated nature lover sometimes needs a change. There's a lot to see in Estes Park, since much

Photo: Longs Peak Scottish Festival

The Longs Peak Scottish Festival is held each year in early September.

of the early Colorado history was made here by settlers such as Alexander MacGregor and F.O. Stanley — not to mention 19th-century writer Isabella Bird and Enos Mills, the "Father of Rocky Mountain National Park."

This section begins with fun tours that you can take, followed by the main year-round attractions you'll want to be sure to see. Then there's information on festivals, both big and homespun — Estes Park diversions that happen around the same time each year.

Estes is such a family-oriented place, you'll notice many of these diversions are perfect for kids. Summer camp programs follow — definitely kidstuff. The section ends with Events Central, including event addresses and how to find them. Most of these events can use volunteers. It's a great way to get acquainted, so don't be shy about lending a hand.

By the way, Boulder County is just a stone's throw from the Estes Valley. Some Boulder County attractions are closer to Estes than they are to the city of Boulder. Even events

smack on Boulder's Pearl Street Mall are less than an hour away, making them fair game for your fun. See the Boulder Festivals and Annual Events and Attractions chapters.

Estes Park Shuttle and Tours
429 W. Elkhorn Ave., Estes Park
• (970) 586-5151

This company offers summertime tours over Trail Ridge Road, a Grand Lake Tour, horseback riding trips in the park, Bear Lake hikes and Fall Foliage/Elk Bugling tours, and year-round shuttle service from Denver International Airport. Call for current rates.

American Wilderness Tours
875 Moraine Ave., Estes Park
• (970) 586-1626

Six-wheeled vehicles take you off the beaten path and into the backcountry. Some tours include steak dinners and sing-alongs. Tours for private groups are available. Call for prices.

Aerial Tramway
420 E. Riverside Dr., Estes Park
• (970) 586-3675

Right in town, this three- to five-minute ride overlooks the town with great views of Longs Peak and the Continental Divide. The tram takes you to the summit of Prospect Mountain where you can take your time hiking, picnicking, and photographing the spectacular vista from the observation platform.

Attractions

Estes Park Area Historical Museum
200 Fourth St., Estes Park
• (970) 586-6256

This interesting museum shows the history and heritage of the area's first settlers, including an 1859 photograph of just-arrived first settler Joel Estes and six of his 13 children. Look for the original National Park Headquarters building out back next to an old homestead cabin. The museum includes a Stanley Steamer, pioneer artifacts, historical photos and documentation of the founding of Rocky Mountain National Park. Open May through October from 10 AM to 5 PM Monday through Saturday, and from 1 to 5 PM Sunday. Open in March and December from 10 AM to 5 PM Tuesday to Saturday, and from 1 to 5 PM Sunday. Open by appointment only during the rest of the year. Admission is $2.50 for adults, $2 for seniors (60 and older) and $1 for children ages 5 to 12.

MacGregor Ranch Museum and Education Center
180 MacGregor Ln., 0.5 mile north of
Estes Park • (970) 586-3749

The MacGregor Ranch Museum and Education Center is a working ranch commemorating the Alexander Q. MacGregor family, one of the valley's largest and most influential ranching families. MacGregor battled the infamous Lord Dunraven over an illegal land claim at Estes Park. Dunraven had bought up all the land for his private hunting reserve. The museum displays domestic items, furniture, silver mining and ranching equipment plus photos of life in the area in the 1870s through the mid-20th century. Historical photos and docu-

ments of MacGregor's battle with Dunraven are on display. Admission is free, but donations are encouraged. Open Tuesday through Friday from June through August (closed weekends). The facility is open to school groups year round. It's a half-mile north of Estes Park off Devil's Gulch Road.

Enos Mills Cabin
At the base of Twin Sisters Mountain,
Estes Park • (970) 586-4706

The Enos Mills Cabin operates as a nature center and museum today, but it was the home of the well-known "Father of Rocky Mountain National Park." Mills campaigned nationally for the establishment of the national parks in general and specifically for Rocky Mountain National Park. A naturalist, writer and inn owner in Estes Park, his cabin, built in 1885, is at the base of Twin Sisters Mountain and has several nature trails on the property. His daughter, Enda Mills Kiley (yes, it's Enda, not Edna), and others offer tours of the house, which also has Mills' books, photos and other memorabilia on display. Copies of his books are for sale. Admission is free. The cabin is open from 11 AM to 4 PM Tuesday through Sunday, Memorial Day through Labor Day, and other times by appointment only.

Estes Park Brewery
470 Prospect Village Dr., Estes Park
• (970) 586-5421

Open summers from 11 AM until midnight, with shorter hours off-season, the brewery with its pub and restaurant offers a free video tour and samples of the nine microbrews. See the "Nightlife" section of this chapter for details.

Estes Park Public Library
335 E. Elkhorn Ave., Estes Park
• (970) 586-8116

Looking for Internet access? The library has it, plus CD-ROMs that can be checked out. This library is also kid-friendly. It loans toys in addition to books and has a parent-child center with educational activities that change monthly. Librarian Kerry Aiken is a local puppeteer and performer. She does a children's story hour on Thursdays and Saturdays and also works with the parent-child center. The library is open 9 AM to 9 PM summer weekdays, 9 AM to 5 PM Fridays and Saturdays, and 1 to 5 PM Sundays. During winter the library opens at 10 AM Monday through Saturday.

The Stanley Hotel
333 Wonderview Ave., Estes Park
• (970) 586-3371, (800) 976-1377

The inspiration for Stephen King's *The Shining* (see the "Hotels" section of this chapter), the Stanley continues to be a testament to a grand era. Ghosts aside, the Stanley stands on its own as a show-stopper and has hosted the rich and famous since its construction in 1906 by F.O. Stanley, inventor of the Stanley Steamer automobile. Diagnosed with tuberculosis and given little time to live, Stanley came to Colorado for the curative value of the pure mountain air and lived another 30 years. During those years he built his classic hotel and helped promote the establishment of Rocky Mountain National Park.

Among the Stanley's treasures are a 1909 Steinway piano in the music room and a shiny, green Stanley Steamer with brass trim and wooden fenders in the hotel lobby. Stanley proclaimed it was an excellent mountain car because it didn't stall, and to prove his point he once drove the car up the steps of the U.S. Capitol.

Tourists are welcome to visit, and historic tours are offered year round five times daily; participants are asked for a $5 donation. The tours go through all of the public rooms and down into the tunnel underneath the hotel, which is built on solid rock. Visitors will see fool's gold glittering in the rock that supports the original hotel beams. There's a small museum on the ground level. Many community events take place at the Stanley. You can also stay as a guest.

Estes Park Center/YMCA of the Rockies
2515 Tunnel Rd., Estes Park
• (970) 586-3341

The YMCA of the Rockies is a huge facility with log cabins, lodges and a leisurely pace that makes you automatically switch to strolling gear. It offers loads of family-oriented activities. During the winter, when the town is quieter, you can purchase a day pass to use the YMCA's facilities. The pass lets you have fun at the indoor gym and roller rink. There's an indoor swimming pool plus outdoor volleyball, basketball and tennis, There's also a library and museum.

During the summer, more than 4,000 people stay at the YMCA of the Rockies. (If you'd like to be one or stay during the winter, check the previous "Accommodations" section of this chapter.) Using the facilities in this busy season is limited to those staying as guests or those with proof of membership in a hometown YMCA. Once you've shown that proof, a number of programs are open for your enjoyment. In addition to winter offerings, there's an outdoor mini-golf course here. Complimentary family programs usually give you six options each day, ranging from survival classes and Indian lore to games of water balloon volleyball and campfire songs. For a fee, YMCA registered guests and hometown YMCA members can also enjoy Y-organized horseback riding, mountain bike rentals (including kids' sizes) and whitewater rafting.

The Lulu W. Dorsey Museum, (970) 586-4331, on the YMCA grounds, explores the history of the facility, which has buildings dating to the early 1900s.

Dick's Rock Museum
490 Moraine Route, Estes Park
• (970) 586-4180

Dick's has been in the same location for 30 years, celebrating the varieties and uses of rock from the region. The free museum displays jewelry, fossils, crystals, slabs of rock waiting for shaping and a 24-inch diamond saw hefty enough to do the job. There are pictures of a bunny, a kissing couple and others formed in the natural swirls of rock, a rock farm where everything is carved from rock and rock "butterflies." Hours vary; call ahead.

Summer Camps

Many accommodations around Estes Park offer special programs for children. Check the previous "Accommodations" section in this chapter for possibilities. Summer camps around Estes Park are also organized by church groups, so check the Worship section of the Estes Park Community chapter for some phone numbers you can call for more information. For instance, Covenant Heights, (970) 586-2900, is a conference center with facilities for up to 200 people that is used for a number of children's programs. The programs must be church-related, educational or nonprofit.

Cheley Camp
(In winter) P.O. Box 6525, Denver, CO 80206 • (800) 226-7386
(In summer) 3960 Fish Creek Rd., Estes Park • (970) 586-4244

Cheley's summer camp program has been featured in national magazines such as *Country Living*. It's probably the largest privately owned camp west of the Mississippi and has been around since 1921. Nearly 500 kids enjoy the fun, in camps of 60 each, grouped by age and sex. The camps are four weeks or eight weeks. Mountaineering, with fabulous vistas everywhere, and horseback riding on nearly 150 camp-owned horses are especially popular activities. And with hiking right out the back door, it's easy to guess that the children get to know the Rocky Mountains. Cheley starts filling up by January, so apply early.

Estes Park Center/YMCA of the Rockies
2515 Tunnel Rd., Estes Park • (970) 586-3341

The YMCA has a summer day-camp program for potty-trained 2-year-olds through high-schoolers. It's from 8:30 AM to 3:30 PM and programs are grouped according to age. The older kids can be in leadership programs and adventure hikes. The youngest kids are more likely to stay close by. Pre-registration is required and parents must either be staying at the Y or be Y members.

Festivals and Annual Events

January

Frost Giant 5K or 10K Race
Municipal Building, 170 MacGregor Ave., Estes Park • (970) 586-8191

You might be a mild-mannered human, but you'll become an Estes Park frost giant if there's a little humidity and freezing weather, for your breath will add lacy frozen filigrees to your eyebrows and hair. If you join the 200 or so runners and walkers who participate, you'll puff up a scenic road to MacGregor Ranch and circle back for a total of either 5 or 10 kilometers (roughly 3 to 6 miles). The 5K race starts around 11 AM; the 10K starts at noon. Entrance fees are roughly $18 and include a Frost Giant T-shirt. It costs less without the T-shirt, more if you register late.

February

Romance of the Rockies
Downtown Estes Park • (970) 586-6641

Simple pleasures bless the 100 or so sweethearts who arrive this weekend to tie the knot. You have two chances to marry or renew wedding vows on Valentine's Saturday or Sunday. The group ceremonies generally are at a nice restaurant or the municipal building. Saying "I do," the sheet wedding cake and glass of punch are $5 per couple. Pay extra for champagne and photographs. Then tour the town in antique Stanley Steamer cars, limousines or hay-rack rides for a small price. Some years a Valentine's Dance is featured too. Local hotels and motels offer special sweetheart packages. Call ahead.

Imagine This!
Estes Park High School, 1600 Manford Ave., Estes Park • (970) 586-9203

The rest of this event's title is See It! Hear It! Do It! Be It! This is the single biggest arts event of the year sponsored by the Cultural Arts Council of Estes Park, which represents all the arts in the area. Artists, musicians, jugglers and actors give youngsters and adults a chance to create art at more than 26 hands-on activities areas. There's also a silent auction of original art work, gift certificates and merchandise. In the evening a benefit performance of dancers, musicians and other artists from the Estes Valley keeps the entertainment going. Dubbed as the main "friend-" and fundraiser of the year for the nonprofit Arts Council, a small donation is requested at the door.

Dog Weight Pull
Estes Valley • (800) 44-ESTES

In Jack London's *Call of the Wild*, Buck pulls a 1,000-pound sled over a wager of gold. This isn't quite as dramatic, but it's more the real thing — a four-state, regional dog-pull contest held the last weekend in February. Dogs wear special harnesses to prevent injury, and weights are added incrementally. Dogs pull weighted sleds and wagons; winners are those who pull the most weight over the course in a minute. Small challengers have included a 10-pound poodle mix. A 200-pound Irish Wolfhound was among the largest. The little guy and the bruiser don't face off; they're in different classes and compete against dogs their own size.

Fine Arts Guild of the Rockies Annual Musical
Stanley Concert Hall and various locations, Estes Park • (970) 586-9203

Generally during two weekends in late February or early March, a guest director works with the community to present a favorite musical, such as *Mame*, *Brigadoon* or *The King and I*. Local guild members star in this community-theater event. The curtain rises at 7 PM for the Thursday through Saturday performances, and there's also a 2 PM Sunday matinee. Call for exact dates and location.

March

Women's History Month
Various locations, Estes Park
• (970) 586-9203

The Cultural Arts Council of Estes Park celebrates female artists and performers with a series of exhibits and programs that run into April. Call for a schedule.

April

Estes Park Oratorio and Chamber Concert
Stanley Concert Hall, Stanley Hotel, 333 Wonderview Ave., Estes Park
• (970) 586-9203

This free Sunday concert offers a special way to celebrate Easter with music for the season. Call for the exact date.

May

Duck Fest
Downtown Estes Park
• (970) 586-4431, (800) 443-7837

On the first Saturday in May, thousands of floating yellow plastic ducks, each tagged with a sponsor and charity choice, raise more than $20,000 at this annual event. To help you remember the date, the Rotary Club sponsors it on Kentucky Derby Day. But ducks aren't as quick as a thoroughbred. They start at Nicky's Restaurant, 1350 Fall River Road, and depending on the runoff, bobble downtown on the Fall, then, nearly two hours later, reach the Wheel Bar, 132 E. Elkhorn Avenue. The mayor and police chief pull out the winning duck and distribute great prizes, such as trips to Disneyland and Hawaii. Sponsoring a duck costs around $20. Watching is free. Proceeds go to local charities.

Art Walk and Jazz Festival
Downtown Estes Park
• (970) 586-9203, (970) 586-6104

More than 20 galleries feature special exhibits and artists' demonstrations on this self-guided studio and gallery tour Friday through Sunday. Children's art activities are offered,

---

INSIDERS' TIP

In the fall one of the area's top evening attractions is the eerie but beautiful mating call of the elk. (The elk bugle at dawn and dusk.) To discourage individual drivers and traffic jams at Horseshoe Park and other popular listening spots, Rocky Mountain National Park offers bus trips for the public to listen to these impressive animals bugle. Call the Estes Park Chamber of Commerce, (800) 443-7837, or park headquarters, (970) 586-1206.

and from 1 to 5 PM, live jazz concerts put an extra spring in the step of revelers in downtown Estes Park. This festival usually happens the second weekend in May.

Dance Fest
YMCA of the Rockies, Estes Park
• (970) 586-3341

This annual celebration of dance is for all ages, with a Saturday night and Sunday afternoon performance early in May. Dancers are chosen from local dance studios and donations are collected at the door. The program includes tap, jazz, ballet, Middle Eastern and hula.

Parade of the Years Old-time Car Rally
Estes Park Historical Museum, 200 Fourth St., Estes Park • (970) 586-6256

Estes Park is a center for old-time cars, partly because Freelan Oscar Stanley, who built that big white hotel, invented Stanley Steamer Mountain Wagons. This rally is sponsored by the Estes Park Historical Museum, where around 25 cars in the Estes Park Historical Automobile and Touring Society are displayed Saturday and Sunday. Meanwhile, around 40 or 50 old-time cars drive up from Loveland, re-enacting Stanley's historic arrival in his Stanley Steamer. You'll see them around town all weekend. Stanley Steamers, by the way, are huge touring cars with steam engines, similar to the engines in steam locomotives but smaller. Other wonderful cars you may see during the weekend include Ford Model A's, 1930 Ford Roadsters and Pierce Arrows plus '60s vintage Jaguars, Mustangs and Corvettes. The rally is held in late May, usually during Memorial Day weekend.

June

Lake Estes Fishing Derby
Lake Estes Marina, U.S. Hwy. 36, near Lake Estes • (970) 586-2011

Every three weeks during summer, the Division of Wildlife drops 400 fish at many points along the Estes Valley river system, making trout plentiful. They double-stock the rivers and lake for this event, and the town buys some

extra-big fish to tempt anglers. What's more, the Cline Trout Farm in Boulder donates some fish for the weekend (the first one in June). All this means contestants in the 8 AM to noon fishing derby are likely to pull in fine catches. Entrance fees are around $2.50 in advance, $3.50 on the day of the event (with a T-shirt, admission is $12 and $14). Proceeds go to the fire department and local youth programs.

Wool Market
Estes Park Fairground, Community Dr., Estes Park • (970) 586-6104

Tourists are welcome to enjoy this working wool market, the largest natural fiber show in the country. Around 10,000 wander among the market's animal shows. Events start the Thursday prior to the second weekend in June with workshops and seminars on spinning, weaving, dyeing, raising animals, tax laws, shearing and grading wool. Throughout the weekend, enjoy spinning and weaving contests and a children's tent. See llamas, angora rabbits, alpacas and sheep, or consider buying one of the beautiful sweaters, yarns or other wool-related items. Admission is free.

Teddy Bear Picnic
YMCA of the Rockies, 2515 Tunnel Rd., Estes Park • (970) 586-6483

The Talking Teddy Store has sponsored this picnic since 1983. Cute silly events may include a dentist who talks to children about care of their bear's teeth (and children's teeth). Cele-bear-ties, such as Smokey Bear and Celestial Seasoning's Sleepytime Bear, have appeared. There are prizes for the largest bear family, biggest bear and cutest bear costume. Sandwiches, cake and beverages might be on hand for nibbling. The picnic starts mid-morning and lasts until the teddies get tired. Admission is free to this Father's Day weekend event.

Scandinavian Midsummer Festival
Bond Park, Downtown Estes Park
• (970) 586-9203

The local Scandinavian Club's festival honors traditional celebrations for the year's longest day in late June. Friday, they erect a maypole ("May" is a Swedish word for dressing in green), and onlookers decorate it with greens and live flowers. Norwegians, Danes and Finns used to start a bonfire in a Viking longboat to scare away the evil spirits on this long, long day. The Scandinavian Club hasn't found any people in Estes willing to burn up boats. So enterprising club members hammer one together and launch it near the Lake Estes Marina. The fire reflects on the water, reminding celebrants of Norwegian fiords brooding under tall mountains. Revelers then dance into the evening. All weekend, professional dancers in bright-colored folk costumes invite onlookers to learn new steps. You also can attend workshops, where sages share Scandinavian history. Food booths offer Swedish pancakes with bright red lingonberries. Or nibble potatas korv — a beef, pork and potato sausage. Crafts for sale include wheat-weaving items, painted-wood folk paintings and rosemaling items, which are paintings of traditional flower designs. Proceeds go to pay the dancers, who often come from around the world.

July

Estes Park Fireworks Display
Lake Estes, Estes Park • (970) 586-6104

Locals arrive around 8 PM on the Fourth of July, generally gathering in the Stanley Village Shopping Center or near Lake Estes. Outdoor bands entertain the crowds. Around 9:15 PM, the fireworks shoot up at the edge of the lake, so the reflections bloom in the water below. If you position yourself well, you get to see all this drama with the mountains as a backdrop. The event is free.

Western and Wildlife Art Show
Call for location • (970) 586-9203

Sponsored by the Fine Arts Guild of the Rockies, this annual late-July favorite features more than 30 participating artists from Colorado and the West with work in a variety of media including painting, sculpture, prints and more. Western landscapes and characters from the Old West are the main subject matter. There's a "quick draw" and auction of original works.

Rooftop Rodeo
Estes Park Fairground, Community Dr., Estes Park • (970) 586-6104

The rodeo started in 1923 as the Estes Park Stampede, stopped during WWII, but revived right afterward and has been galloping ever since, hanging onto its designation as one of the country's oldest rodeos. A parade through downtown starts it off. Team roping, bulldogging, broncos and steer wrestling are part of the week's events, which are sanctioned by the Professional Rodeo Cowboys Association. A carnival offers plenty of rides. Cowboy poets read on a stage with a campfire scene. Sometimes, the poet brings his harmonica or strums a guitar. Then there's country-western music, with the likes of Sweethearts of the Rodeo and the Darn Thirsty Cowboys.

Prices vary depending on who's in the main corral. By the way, it's not called "Rooftop Rodeo" because you have to watch from a roof. The name is to remind people of the 7,200-foot elevation and the United States' highest paved highway, Trail Ridge Road.

Fiber Celebration
Call for location
• (970) 586-5882

This juried show gives artists who work in fiber their moment in the sun. It's sponsored by the Art Center of Estes Park.

August

Best of the West Estes Brewfest
Estes Park Brewery, Prospect Village Dr., Estes Park • (970) 586-5421

Eight kinds of locally brewed beer, brats

and hotdogs and live music under a late summer sun draw an enthusiastic crowd to this annual event, now in its seventh year.

Throughout the Summer

Cowboy sing-alongs
Downtown Estes Park
• **(970) 586-4431, (800) 44-ESTES**
This fun chance to yodel your love for the sagebrush is held Thursdays, Fridays, Saturdays and Sundays from mid-June through mid-August at 7:30 PM in Bond Park.

Music in the Mountains
Rocky Ridge Music Center, Colo. Hwy. 7, 12 miles south of Estes Park
• **(970) 586-4031**
Locals call Rocky Ridge a real educated, into-classical-music group that does chamber music and opera. Student and faculty recitals take place here on Sundays around 3 PM from late June until the end of August. Call for current ticket prices.

The Estes Park Music Festival
Stanley Concert Hall, Stanley Hotel, 333 Wonderview Ave., Estes Park
• **(970) 586-9203**
Boulder's nationally acclaimed Colorado Music Festival Orchestra comes to Estes Park on Monday evenings during the summer from late June through early August. For more about this better-than-the-best orchestra, see the Boulder chapter on Arts. Ticket prices vary.

Summerfest
YMCA of the Rockies • (970) 586-3341
The YMCA of the Rockies sponsors this free summer series that includes everything from classical to jazz to bluegrass to Dixieland. The series runs from mid-June through mid-August.

September

Labor Day Crafts Show
Bond Park, Estes Park
• **(970) 586-9203, (800) 443-7837**
On Labor Day weekend, craftspeople from all over the state set up about 100 booths with

pottery, bronze and wood sculpture, sewing, jewelry, photography and oil painting. The local volunteer fire department puts on this event, and it benefits the Muscular Dystrophy Association and the fire department.

Longs Peak Scottish Highland Festival
Estes Park Fairground, Community Dr., Estes Park
• **(970) 586-6308, (800) 443-7837**
This four-day festival in early September is a 10-ring circus. It's so grand, *USA Today* has listed it as one of the nation's top 10 things to do. At least two and sometimes three top ceremonial bands come to play in the tattoo concerts, which include drums, bugles and bagpipes. The White House Drum and Bugle Corps has performed here, as have the Governor General's Foot Guard from Canada and the Royal Highlands Scot Guards. Celtic folk musicians arrive for competitions. Irish stepdancers display their dazzling footwork. Evening concerts thrill Celtic hearts all over town. There's always at least one chance to sing *Auld Lang Syne*.

Music isn't the only drawing card at this festival. There's jousting, dancing, a dog show, whiskey tasting and seminars on topics Scottish. Highland games include tossing a stone the size of a shot put, throwing a caber, which is a large log roughly shaped like a telephone pole, and other heavy athletics. Highlanders demonstrate how to shoot antique cannon, and how to fly fish with lures. Dr. James Durward, founder of this festival, points out that lure fishing had to start in Scotland. After all, a thrifty Scot isn't going to dig up a new worm every time he casts his line!

Altogether, about 3,000 performers come to this event, and approximately 30,000 people come to see it. Those wanting products can buy quilts, sweaters and other crafts related to these island peoples. Hungry revelers can buy scones, which are slightly sweet biscuits; Scotch eggs, hard-boiled then rolled in bacon crumbs; sausages; hot dogs; and pastie, sort of a non-flaking turnover with hamburger inside. Don't forget the shortbread. When you're full, you can quaff it down with Scotch or Irish libations. There's plenty of soda on hand for the lads and lassies.

Ticket prices are around $15 for a one-day field pass and $25 for a two-day pass. Children younger than 15 can get in one day for $7, and the wee bairns who have not yet reached the tender age of 5 get in free. All the money earned by the festival goes back into the festival and other local nonprofits.

Fine Arts and Crafts Show
Bond Park, Estes Park • (970) 586-9203

Sponsored by the Fine Arts Guild of the Rockies, this mid-September event is a juried, national art show. More than 80 booths display everything from pottery and small items to paintings and photography. Estes Park is working to become more of an art community, for instance bringing in national traveling art shows. This show has been going on for more than 19 years and is a pleasant way to pass the afternoon.

Kids and Folks March
Stanley Park Ballfields, 380 Community Dr., Estes Park • (970) 586-8191

This 10K (6.2 miles) walk goes through downtown Estes along the Fall River's pedestrian walks to the Donut Haus, 342 Moraine Avenue, and back. Check-in is at 8 AM, but you can start as late as noon. Some people stop and shop or eat along the way. It's free, but many locals march with pledges to support community projects. The march takes place in mid-September.

Chamber Music Festival
Call for location • (970) 586-9203

Sponsored by the Chamber Music Society of Estes Park, here's a special weekend (in late September or early October) for Chamber music aficionados. There's a variety of concerts with local and Colorado performers presenting an entertaining program. Call for ticket prices.

October

"The Shining" Costume Ball
Stanley Hotel, 333 Wonderview Ave., Estes Park
• (970) 586-3371, (800) 976-1377

Stephen King wrote his horror classic, *The Shining*, after being inspired by a stay at the Stanley Hotel. Once you see what a lovely, elegant place the Stanley is, you'll be even more impressed by how creepily King remade it in his pull-up-the-covers-and-keep-the-lights-on story. You can make a similar transformation by dressing up for the Stanley's annual costume ball, held Halloween night. You don't have to be horrible and ghoulish. Just be sure whatever you wear is good for dancing and easy to sit in for dinner.

Throughout the Fall

Bull Elk Bugling
Rocky Mountain National Park
• (970) 586-1206

Anyone who expects the bull elk's mating call to sound like a royal French horn is in for a surprise. These huge animals belt out a whistling squeal. It might strike you as wimpy, but, boy, does it ever carry! The haunting call can carry across valleys and reach high mountain meadows. Forest rangers say the best time to witness (and hear) elk bugling is throughout the fall in the morning, from sunrise to an hour after, and then at dusk, starting about an hour before sunset. Three areas tend to provide good viewing: Moraine Park, Horseshoe Park and Upper Beaver Meadows. To view wildlife, don't leave the designated trails and roadways. While bull elks rarely charge tourists, there are incidents of rangers charging visitors . . . and the fine they charge for harassing wildlife can be stiff. The Bighorn Brigade will be around to answer questions and remind you to stay out of the meadows. If you prefer smaller crowds, come on a weekday.

You can also find seminars on helpful subjects like photography. Call for a schedule.

Quaking Aspen
Rocky Mountain National Park
• (970) 586-1206

Mother Nature gives us hot dry years when the leaves turn gold early, and she also bestows cool, moist summers when the green leaves never quite believe it's time to change. Because the golden aspen season varies, call the Park's information office to learn the best time (generally mid-September through mid-

October) and places, which tend to be around Bear Lake Road and Moraine Park. Park officials say aspen stands outside the Park can be even more spectacular. The highway to Allenspark is designated a scenic byway, with huge aspen stands. Colorado highways 119 and 72, heading south to Nederland and Central City, are good too. Wherever you drive, find a chance to step out on a trail and walk. Get the aspens between you and the sunlight to take in their luminescence and brilliant color. Listen to the fluttering leaves. Smell the tannin. While strolling, you may notice elk coming down from the high country to beat the winter snows. Rangers request that you don't pick any aspen leaves, since our thin mountain soil needs their nutrients. To preserve the Park's beauty for the future, remember to leave with only your memories and photographs.

November

A Christmas Memory
Stanley Hotel, 333 Wonderview Ave., Estes Park
• **(970) 586-3371, (800) 976-1377**

This annual dinner theater is a family-oriented, funny account for the holidays. Tickets to the play alone are around $10, and for the play and dinner, they're closer to $30. Performances are generally Friday and Saturday from the weekend following Thanksgiving until Christmas.

Christmas Parade
Estes Park Fairground, Community Dr., Estes Park

When the downtown Christmas lights come on, the parade begins. It starts around 5:30 PM the Friday after Thanksgiving, heads through the main shopping district and ends at the Chamber of Commerce around 7 PM. Bruiser, a wonderfully dog-like puppeteer, sits atop his dog house performing tricks. Santa's sleigh is always the last float in line. Onlookers dress in winter woolens, parkas and blankets. On a mild evening, a jacket will do. If it's cold, some people wear everything they've got. No matter what the thermometer says, the sight is heartwarm-

ing — and free. Stores downtown stay open to sell Christmas goods and warm refreshments.

Oratorio Concert
Community Church of the Rockies, 1700 Brodie Ave., Estes Park
• **(970) 586-4404**

The Oratorio Society and Estes Park Chamber Orchestra perform portions of the *Messiah* in a concert where it's obvious that the performers have practiced and practiced. When you just come for the performance, you can hum along with "The Hallelujah Chorus" if you must, but do it softly — this is a performance, not a sing-along. The concert usually starts around 7 PM the Sunday after Thanksgiving. Donations are appreciated.

December

Round the Table Sing-Along
Stanley Concert Hall, Stanley Hotel, 333 Wonderview Ave., Estes Park
• **(970) 586-3371, (800) 976-1377**

Generally during the first weekend in December the Estes Park Chorale sings traditional and contemporary songs of the season, and the audience is invited to join in. The sing-along starts around 7 PM. Contributions are welcomed.

Holiday Home Tour
Throughout Estes Park Valley
• **(970) 586-4644**

Proud owners of six fine Estes Park homes decorate for Christmas, then open their doors on a Saturday in mid-December so you can wander inside. The Quota Club, a local businesswomen's group, sponsors the event, and profits go to local health and social needs. Usually the tour is from 11 AM to 4 PM.

A Christmas Memory
Stanley Hotel Theatre, Stanley Hotel, 333 Wonderview Ave., Estes Park
• **(970) 586-3371, (800) 976-1377**

A Stanley tradition, this dinner-theater production is a funny, tearjerker, family classic about Truman Capote's boyhood with a wise but dotty aunt who makes holiday fruitcakes. The run of the play usually begins the day after Thanksgiving and continues on weekdays and weekends until just before Christmas. Check with the hotel for show times and ticket prices, which are generally $10 for the evening show and around $30 for dinner and the show. Also making a visit to the Stanley a treat is an annual Christmas tree show sponsored by the Estes Park Women's Club with about 50 dazzling, decorated tabletop trees in the main lobby contributed by different local groups. Visitors can buy a raffle ticket and perhaps win a tree. The trees are displayed the Monday after Thanksgiving until Dec. 21.

Events Central

Here are the phone numbers and locations of the main event centers in town.

Estes Park Chamber Resort Association and Visitor Information Center
500 Big Thompson Ave., Estes Park
• (970) 586-4431, (800) 44-ESTES

Stop here for local information. To reach the center, coming from Boulder on U.S. Highway 36, go to the second stoplight and make a right. The center is right across from the Taco Bell on U.S. Highway 34. It's open from 8 AM to 8 PM Monday through Saturday, then from 9 AM to 6 PM on Sunday.

Cultural Arts Council
P.O. Box 4135, 160 Moraine Ave.,
Estes Park, CO 80517 • (970) 586-9203

The CAC represents all the arts in the area with the broad goal of enhancing the quality and accessibility of the arts in the Estes Valley. Call or write to these folks for music, art or theater events and programs.

Estes Park Fairground
Community Dr., Estes Park
• (970) 586-6104

The fairground is near Lake Estes. To get there, you take either U.S. Highway 34 or 36 to the east side of town. The fairground is on US 36. Right after you pass Lake Estes, turn south onto Community Drive. You'll see arenas, the stables, the covered building for special events and ballfields. You're at the fairground now!

The Stanley Hotel
333 Wonderview Ave., Estes Park
• (970) 586-3371, (800) 976-1377

Once you're in downtown, you'll see the big white Stanley Hotel on a hill northeast of town. The Stanley Concert Hall is up there too. You can't miss it; but if you do, just pull over anywhere and ask for directions. Everybody knows the Stanley. Call to check on the schedule of events.

Estes Park Center/YMCA of the Rockies
2515 Tunnel Rd., Estes Park
• (970) 586-3341

To reach the YMCA, take U.S. Highway 36 to the second stoplight. Take a left at Elkhorn Avenue. At the second stoplight, turn left on Moraine Avenue. Follow the signs to the YMCA. The tree-lined road winds through a lot of countryside, but you'll soon be there.

Even if you're not staying at the YMCA, it can be a good place to call. They don't publicize their events very much, because they've got a built-in audience. But they often welcome non-guests. For instance, the public is welcome to attend the Christian Artists Music Seminar Concerts held from June through August with all types of music.

Participatory Sports

Most people visit Estes Park to see Rocky Mountain National Park and go camping, hiking or fishing. Yet in addition to these activities, you can participate in everything from windsurfing on Lake Estes to golf and tennis in Estes Park. Horseback riding is a popular activity in the area, with trails leading into the Park or the surrounding national forest. Several rafting companies take thrill-seekers to such frothy rivers outside the immediate area as the Poudre and Arkansas. The following are some of the town's many options.

Bicycling

Colorado Bicycling Adventures
184 E. Elkhorn Ave., Estes Park
• (970) 586-4241

For information about where to bicycle or to rent a bike, stop here — the only bike shop in town. It's a full-service bike shop offering sales and shipping. This shop not only rents brand-new mountain bikes in different models, but also offers several different guided bicycle tours, including a downhill ride from the top of Trail Ridge Road in Rocky Mountain National Park. Cost is $68 per person and includes bike, helmet and souvenir water bottle plus a continental breakfast. It's about a four-hour trip, from Estes Park and back again. No riders under 12 allowed.

There's also a downhill tour in the North Fork Canyon ($45 per person), better suited to riders of all ages — they've taken bicyclists ages 4 to 90. Another tour is Johnny Park, in Roosevelt National Forest, for more aggressive riders who don't mind a few hills and want to get off-road ($50 per person). Bicycle rentals are $5 per hour up to $21 for a full day. Performance models with shock absorbers cost slightly more.

The shop also rents all types of bike accessories, including trailers to pull children, locks, packs and car racks. The shop sells a guidebook of all off-road areas in Roosevelt National Forest and has free maps that show cyclists where to ride right from the store on their own.

Camping

(See the Rocky Mountain National Park chapter for information on camping in the national park.) Two campgrounds are run by the Estes Valley Recreation and Park District: Mary's Lake Campground and Estes Park Campground, but there are also a number of privately owned campgrounds in the area.

Mary's Lake Campground
Mary's Lake Rd. (directions below)
• (970) 586-4411

Though not exactly remote or secluded, Mary's Lake has great views by a pleasant lake plus a heated swimming pool, hot showers, 30- or 50-amp service, a playground, store and laundry. Drive south of town on U.S. Highway 36 and turn left on Mary's Lake Road. The campground is 3 miles from town and the national park, and is open mid-May through September. Prices to camp range from $20 for tent camping to $24 or $26 per night for RVs, depending upon services chosen. For more than two people there's a $2.50 charge per person.

Estes Park Campground
Hwy. 66 (Tunnel Rd.) a mile past the
Estes Park Center/YMCA of the Rockies
• (970) 586-4188

More peaceful and secluded is the Estes Park Campground which has 65 tent sites and 12 RV sites (no hookups). Head west on U.S. Highway 36 and then left for 3 miles on Colo. Highway 66 (which becomes Tunnel Road) a mile past the Estes Park Center/YMCA of the Rockies at the end of a paved road and adjacent to the Park. The campground is open late May through early September. Cost is $20 per tent and $24 to $26 for RVs; amenities include showers and rest rooms, a playground and public phone and firewood and ice for sale. Pets are permitted on a leash.

National Park Resort Campground
2501 Fall River Rd. • (970) 586-4563

Right at the Park's Fall River entrance, this campground is AAA-approved and adjacent to the national park. It has hot showers, hookups, cable TV, a livery and secluded, terraced sites. It's open May through September. Charges for two people range from $17 to $23 per night for tent camping and $20 to $26 for RV's. There's a charge of $2.50 for each additional person. The campground is open all year and pets and children are welcome.

Jellystone Park
5495 U.S. Hwy. 36
• (970) 586-4230, (800) 722-2928

In addition to tent, camper and RV sites there are housekeeping and camping cabins; it's 5 miles southeast of Estes Park on US 36. The wooded sites are pleasant and quiet. It's open May through September and charges from $20 to $26 per night for two people and

$2 for each extra person. Pets and children are welcome.

Paradise RV & Travel Park
1836 Colo. Hwy. 66 • (970) 586-5513

Near the YMCA along the Big Thompson River, this adult-oriented park offers RV hookups, bathrooms and a laundry. It's open May through September and charges from $18 to $22 per night for two people and $2 for each extra person.

Elkhorn Lodge Wilderness Camping
600 W. Elkhorn Ave., Estes Park • (970) 586-4416

A 10-minute hike from the Elkhorn Lodge is the opportunity to experience Indian and old-West camping in your own tent or a rented tipi. Transportation to the campground, water and portable toilet are provided. There are no other amenities but you live surrounded by wildlife and rugged trails leading through wilderness. If you decide to wimp out, there's a restaurant, saloon, swimming pool and bathing facilities available at the lodge.

Blue Arrow RV Park and Campground
Colo. Highway 66, adjacent to the south entrance to Rocky Mountain National Park • (970) 586-5342

This is Estes Park's largest RV park and campground. With 170 sites, Blue Arrow offers history along with its views and amenities like a country store, laundry, playgrounds and nondenominational church services. The 30-acre site was originally a camping ground for Arapahoe and Ute living in the area. In the 1960s, historical buildings were hauled to the site to create a "frontier town" for moviemakers. Still remaining, and in use, are the original Bear Lake Lodge, built in 1919 and later removed from the Park, and a Central City brothel, now used as the camp's recreation hall.

KOA Campground
One mile east of Estes Park on Hwy 34 • (970) 586-2888

Try out a rented tipi or set up your own tent or RV in this campground with showers, a grocery and gift store, fishing equipment, game room, mini-golf and laundry facilities. A tipi that will sleep two to four (mattresses are provided, bring your own linens) is $30 a night tent sites are $22 and RV sites with hook-ups are $26 to $28.

Climbing

Colorado Mountain School
P.O. Box 2062, 351 Moraine Ave., Estes Park, CO 80517 • (970) 586-5758, (800) 444-0730 (outside Colorado)

Learn rock climbing or mountaineering at this highly regarded school. One-day introductory classes prepare people to begin climbing with guides. The school offers guided hikes, climbs (including technical routes of Longs Peak) and equipment rentals. The school is open year round and reservations are requested.

Colorado Wilderness Sports
358 E. Elkhorn Ave., Estes Park • (970) 586-6548, (800) 369-4165

This shop offers instruction and guiding both indoors and out. Learn to climb on the indoor rock-climbing wall and practice these skills on guided field trips.

Fishing

Some local spots include the Big Thompson River, Lake Estes and Mary's Lake. The best spot on the Big Thompson River is said to be the stretch 8 miles downstream from Lake Estes called Grandpa's Retreat (flies and lures only), where the Colorado Division of Wildlife and the National Forest Service have created several deep holes. The Big Thompson runs along U.S. Highway 34; there are small parking areas along the shoulder. You'll also find several handicapped-accessible fishing ramps along this stretch.

Lake Estes, on the east side of town between U.S. Highways 34 and 36, is stocked by the Colorado Division of Wildlife with rainbow trout and also has a few German brown trout.

Mary's Lake inlet is another good spot to

try. Follow US 36 to the east end of town to Mary's Lake Road at the traffic light, turn left and drive 1.5 miles.

You can fish in Colorado without a license only on the first full weekend in June. Otherwise, you must have a license. One-day licenses are available for $5.25; a five-day license is $18.25. Colorado residents can get an annual pass for $20.25 and non-residents must pay almost twice that. Fishing licenses are available at the following locations: Do It Best in Upper Stanley Village, (970) 586-3496; Estes Angler in Picadilly Square, (970) 586-2110; Late Estes Marina on US 34, (970) 586-2011; Mary's Lake Campground, 2120 Mary's Lake Road, (970) 586-4411; Scot's Sporting Goods, Moraine Avenue at US 36 West, (970) 586-2877.

Scot's Sporting Goods
870 Moraine Ave., Estes Park
• **(970) 586-2877**

Stop by and ask owner Scot Richie — the local fishing authority — where to catch the big ones. He can also recommend and sell the best things to catch them with, including a selection of flies tied by local anglers who know what Estes Park fish like best. The shop also offers fly-fishing lessons and guided trips on the Big Thompson River and rents fishing equipment.

Estes Angler
338 W. Riverside Dr., Estes Park
• **(970) 586-2110, (800) 586-2110**

Here's another good outfitter. Inquire about the best places and flies to use and pick up everything you need to tie them, plus all types of clothing and equipment. Guided fishing trips and instruction for beginners are also available.

Rocky Mountain Adventures
1360 Big Thompson Rd., Estes Park
• **(970) 586-6191 or (970) 493-4005 or (800) 858-6808 in Fort Collins**

This company offers year-round guided fly-fishing day trips on Big Thompson River a few miles from Estes Park and overnights on the Poudre, Upper Colorado and North Platte rivers. The company is permitted by the forest service in those locations and licensed by the State of Colorado. The main office in Fort Collins is open year round. The Estes Park office is open Memorial Day to Labor Day.

Colorado Wilderness Sports
358 E. Elkhorn Ave., Estes Park
• **(970) 586-6548, (800) 504-6642**

In addition to a complete fly shop and outdoor equipment and clothing, this shop offers rental equipment and instruction and guided trips in and around Rocky Mountain National Park.

Trout Haven
810 Moraine Ave., Estes Park
• **(970) 586-5525**

For the angler who doesn't want a wilderness experience but rather a guaranteed catch, there's Trout Haven. No license is required and everything is provided — including the cleaning. You pay 50 cents an inch for whatever you catch. It's located a little more than a mile west of downtown on US 36 behind Kentucky Fried Chicken. They'll cook your catch on the spot at the on-site restaurant, or you can trade it in for smoked trout and take it with you or have it packed in ice to go.

Golf

Lake Estes Executive Course
690 Big Thompson Ave.
• **(970) 586-8176**

This nine-hole course along the banks of the Big Thompson River provides a good game and view to go with it. Cost is $11 daily; $7 after 3 PM.

Estes Park Golf Club
1080 S. St. Vrain Rd. • (970) 586-8146

This 18-hole course is one of the oldest golf courses in the state, dating from 1912. In early fall elk wander onto the course — watch out for their divots. Cost is $33 daily; $20 after 2 PM.

Miniature Golf

Miniature golf may be little, but in Estes it's big. Courses are all mini-amusement parks, where it's easy to spend money on silly activities. The cost is usually fairly reasonable. You might pay as little as $1.50 for a game, but you're likely to want to stay and spend more if your party is having fun. During the summer, these places often stay open from early morning until 10 at night.

Estes Park Ride-A-Kart
2250 Big Thompson Ave., Estes Park
• (970) 586-6495

This mini-amusement park has 36 holes of miniature golf, go-karts, bumper boats and a miniature train.

Fun City
375 Moraine Ave., Estes Park
• (970) 586-2070

Kids will enjoy the 36-hole miniature golf course, bumper cars, video arcade and two slides at Fun City, which is open every day in the summer, and on weekends only in the spring and fall.

Tiny Town Miniature Golf
840 Moraine Ave., Estes Park
• (970) 586-6333

Tiny Town features a 19-hole miniature golf course with lots of challenging and entertaining features.

Hiking and Backpacking

Most hikers head to Rocky Mountain National Park, but the nearby Roosevelt National Forest also offers excellent backcountry trails. Stop at the Estes Park Office of Roosevelt National Forest for maps and information about hiking trails: (970) 586-3440, 161 Second Street, P.O. Box 2747, Estes Park, CO 80517. See "Hiking" in our Rocky Mountain National Park chapter for other hiking opportunities. You can also stroll along the Big Thompson River corridor from Lake Estes all the way to the YMCA Camp, or get sidetracked by the shop windows downtown and call it a hike, or follow Highway 7 on a pleasant separated trail.

Lily Mountain Trail
Colo. Hwy. 7 (directions below)

An easy 1.5-mile hike, this trail begins near Estes Park and climbs to 8,800 feet with fantastic summit views of Estes Park, Longs Peak to the south and the Continental Divide to the west. The trailhead is 6 miles south of Estes Park on Colo. Highway 7. Just before the 6-mile marker look for a small turnoff on the right and a parking area and trailhead sign.

Crosier Mountain Trail
Devil's Gulch Rd. (directions below)

A harder 8-mile round trip that climbs to the top of Crosier Mountain (elevation 9,250 feet), this trail runs through lush meadows and aspen groves past ruins of old homesteads. You'll have superb views from the summit. The trailhead is about 8 miles northeast of Estes Park on Devil's Gulch Road, a mile past Glen Haven. Look for a large gravel cut on the south side of the road to the right.

Lion Gulch
U.S. Hwy. 36 (directions below)

Another pleasant trail of moderate difficulty, Lion Gulch leads to an area of old homesteads and is about 3 miles one way. The trailhead is at mile marker 8 from Estes Park on US 36.

Fish Creek Trail
U.S. Hwy. 36 at Lake Estes

This unpaved 6-mile (one way) hike starts out easy, but becomes moderately difficult when you reach the final two miles. It follows Fish Creek from its mouth at Lake Estes to its intersection with Colo. Highway 7 south of Mary's Lake.

Horseback Riding

Estes Park has numerous stables and outfitters offering everything from kids' pony rides to trail rides and pack trips into the mountains. Most rides head into Rocky Mountain National Park.

Elkhorn Stables
600 W. Elkhorn Ave., Estes Park
• (970) 586-5225

This stable offers breakfast rides, rides ending with a steak dinner, country music and dance, hourly rides and ponies for children. Open year round, it guides trips into the national park for $27 for a two-hour trip. Take time to tour the 120-year-old lodge and stables.

Sombrero Ranch on the Dam on Lake Estes
U.S. Hwy. 34 E. • (970) 586-4577

Offering rides into the national forest (not the Park) Sombrero charges $17 an hour or $28 for two hours. There's a breakfast ride, a steak-fry evening ride and an overnight pack trip or fishing trips.

Aspen Lodge
6120 Colo. Hwy. 7, Estes Park
• (970) 586-8133, (800) 332-6867

A 3,000-acre ranch resort, Aspen Lodge offers rides into both Rocky Mountain National Park and Roosevelt National Forest. It's south of Estes Park on Colo. Highway 7. Rides cost $18 an hour or $35 for a longer "ranch ride," meadow ride or steak dinner ride. A two-hour breakfast ride costs $28.

Miscellaneous Sports

Stanley Park
380 Community Dr., Estes Park
• (970) 586-8189

Run by the Estes Valley Recreation and Park District, Stanley Park has a playground, basketball, volleyball and tennis courts, baseball/softball and soccer fields, shelters and a picnic area.

Lake Estes Marina
Lake Estes on U.S. Hwy. 34
• (970) 586-2011

This public facility offers fishing access, picnic areas, a hike and bike trail, bike rentals and fishing, sport, pontoon, canoe and paddle boat rental. There's also a marina store that sells fishing licenses, bait and tackle, snacks and clothing.

Rocky Mountain Athletic Club
1230 Big Thompson Road, Estes Park
• (970) 586-8418

With all of the options in the surrounding outdoors to keep fit in, you might not think there's anything to be added by an indoor facility. Well, how about racquetball, handball

and squash, free weights and resistance equipment with a view of the mountains, aerobics classes, a therapeutic massage and whirlpools and saunas? The Athletic Club offers all that plus a treadwall that gives a taste of rock climbing and an aerobic workout at the same time. There's also a reaction time workout station — wield a staff at randomly flashing targets a la Luke Skywalker. The guest fee is $10 per visit.

Off-Road Rentals
401 Lakefront St., Estes Park
• (970) 586-6371

Some historic sites are so remote that it's hard to imagine the original inhabitants getting there without a four-wheel-drive vehicle. Current-day visitors don't have to wonder. Vehicles rented from Off-Road come equipped with maps and historical information to lure you into unpaved territory. Off-Road will also design a trip to suit your specific interests, as well. Drivers must be 25; Jeeps rent for $89 a day.

Rafting

There's no rafting to speak of right in the Estes Park area, but there are numerous outfitters that will take you on full- or half-day trips on the Poudre or Arkansas rivers and rather far afield to the Dolores and Colorado rivers.

Colorado Wilderness Sports
358 E. Elkhorn Ave., Estes Park
• (970) 586-6548, (800) 369-4165

Inquire here about a variety of raft trips on different Colorado rivers offered — full- or half-day. Colorado Wilderness Sports also offers rock-climbing instruction and has an indoor rock-climbing wall.

Rocky Mountain Adventures
1360 Big Thompson Rd., Estes Park
• (970) 586-6191 or (970) 493-4005 or (800) 858-6808 in Fort Collins

Half- and full-day and overnight trips are offered for white water rafting from beginner to advanced levels. The company also provides kayak instruction and lake touring in sea kayaks on Lake Estes. Trips are on the Big

Thompson, Poudre and North Platte rivers. All the necessary equipment, plus lunch and snacks are provided, along with licensed guides. The Fort Collins office is open year round, and the Estes Park location is open Memorial Day to Labor Day.

Rapid Transit Rafting Ltd.
161 Virginia Dr., Estes Park
• **(970) 586-8852, (800) 367-8523**

Whitewater adventures include full day trips on the Colorado River or half-day trips on the Poudre River leaving from Estes Park. There's a variety of rafting, from exciting deep canyon rapids to relaxing float water stretches. Trips are suitable for beginners as well as experienced rafters. All the necessary rafting gear, experienced licensed guides and lunch or snacks are provided. Reservations are recommended.

Wanderlust
3500 Bingham Hill, Ft. Collins
• **(970) 484-1219**

The Cache La Poudre River (apparently named by a French trapper who had left his hunting supplies stored nearby) is the highway for Wanderlust rafting trips, leaving from Estes Park, Ft. Collins and Loveland. Trips range from the Taste Trip (6 miles for rafting newbies) to a full-day of white water stretching 18 miles and requiring that rafters be in good physical condition. Wanderlust's guides can be seen on reruns of the TV show "Walker – Texas Ranger" involving white water rafting. Reservations are required.

Cross-country Skiing

See the Rocky Mountain National Park chapter for ski trails in the national park. Rental equipment is available in the following outdoor shops in Estes Park.

Estes Park Ski Shop
184 E. Elkhorn Ave., Estes Park
• **(970) 586-4241**

Rental cross-country ski packages (skis,

boots, poles) average about $10 (downhill skis $14; snowshoes $10, snowboards $14).

Colorado Wilderness Sports
358 E. Elkhorn Ave., Estes Park
• **(970) 586-6548, (800) 369-4165**

Stop here for ski and snowshoe rentals, plus a range of other outdoor equipment, clothing and accessories. Rentals average $10 for cross-country packages.

The Colorado Mountain School
351 Moraine Ave., Estes Park
• **(970) 586-5758 or (800) 444-0730 (outside Colorado)**

This revered climbing and mountaineering school also rents skis. Rental cross-country ski packages (skis, boots, poles) average about $10 (snowshoes $10).

Swimming

Estes Park Aquatic Center
660 Community Dr., Estes Park
• **(970) 586-2340**

Just south of Lake Estes, the center has an indoor/outdoor pool. Admission for a swim is about $5 and includes a locker and towel.

Lake Estes Marina
1770 Big Thompson Ave., Estes Park
• **(970) 586-2011**

The waters of Lake Estes are too chilly for swimming unless you like wearing a wet suit, which can be rented here, along with windsurfing equipment and other small craft. The marina, which has beaches and picnic areas, is east of town on U.S. Highway 34.

Tennis

Stanley Park
380 Community Dr., Estes Park
• **(970) 586-8191**

Just south of Lake Estes and operated by the Estes Valley Recreation and Park District, Stanley Park has six courts, which are free.

Beauty is the main attraction in Grand Lake, which prides itself on being a family town.

Grand Lake

For those who want to visit Rocky Mountain National Park but also want to avoid the crush and hustle of Estes Park, Grand Lake is an amiable alternative. A little more than a mile from the western entrance to the Park and on Colorado's largest natural lake, Grand Lake offers a quieter experience. One of the oldest settlements on the Western Slope, this six-block town is a rustic community of some 320 permanent residents, with picturesque false-front buildings with split lodgepole pine facades, wooden boardwalks and a bar with a hitching post where local cowboys sometimes ride up on horses to have a cold one.

Grand Lake's main attraction is the area's beauty, and it prides itself on being a family town. There's no nightlife to speak of, other than a few bars with music in summer and on weekends in spring and fall. There's no movie theater, but in summer there's live professional theater and a good children's recreation program. The town has two tennis courts, a town park and a beautiful beach on the lake. The Grand Lake Golf Course is one of the top 10 in the state.

The area offers access to some of the state's best hiking, fishing and other outdoor activities. The trio of large lakes — Grand Lake, Lake Granby and Shadow Mountain Reservoir — offer a variety of water sports, including boating, water skiing, windsurfing and fishing. Routt and Arapaho National Forests offer great hiking and backpacking, as does the western side of the Indian Peaks Wilderness Area.

In summer, Grand Lake's population swells to about 4,000, with many tourists coming through daily on their way to Rocky Mountain National Park or for various outdoor pursuits. In winter, there's excellent cross-country skiing at Grand Lake Ski Touring Center and national forest trails and downhill skiing nearby at Winter Park and Silver Creek. The town also boasts an ice skating rink and many sites for ice fishing and sledding.

The Rocky Mountain Repertory Theatre draws young actors from across the country every summer to a professional season of performances.

Because of its more isolated location — literally at the end of the road — Grand Lake never experienced the development of Estes Park, and residents consider this a blessing. Nevertheless, the town and area offer the necessary amenities for visitors, including guest ranches, cabins, motels and lodges along with gift shops, galleries, cafes and fine-dining establishments. Abundant camping, fishing, hiking and natural beauty lure nature lovers to the area.

History

Grand Lake's name comes from the early name for the Colorado River, the "Grand," with headwaters beginning on the Continental Divide just north of the lake. Ute Indians frequented the area for hunting expeditions over the Continental Divide, following trails along Grand Lake's North Inlet and Tonahutu Creek up into the mountains. Arapaho and Cheyenne also visited the area to hunt the plentiful game and fish in the large lake, but relations were not peaceful.

Grand Lake was known as Spirit Lake by the Utes after a particularly tragic incident. During an attack by the Cheyenne and Arapaho, the Utes put their women and children on a makeshift raft and sent them out to the middle of the lake to escape harm. But a storm came up and the raft capsized in the deepest part of the lake, drowning all aboard. Back on land, most of the Ute warriors died in the battle. After this, the Utes never camped near the lake again and believed that the early morning mists and fogs rising from the lake were the spirits of their dead.

The area was settled in 1867 by homesteader Joseph "Judge" Westcott, who supported himself by trapping and fishing and selling the live, boxed fish to hotel restaurants around the region. In the next decade, other families began arriving, and there was a short-lived gold boom.

But it was the area's natural beauty and abundant fishing and hunting that brought other settlers. Wealthy families built summer homes on the beautiful lake in the late 1800s. In 1905, the Grand Lake Yacht Club was registered as the world's highest at 8,369 feet.

The biggest tourist boom started in 1952 when the Colorado-Big Thompson Project was completed, bringing irrigation to the eastern slope through a series of dams, reservoirs, channels and a 13-mile tunnel under the Continental Divide. The project created Shadow Mountain Lake and Lake Granby, greatly enlarging the area's water recreation opportunities.

The town's history is reflected in the Kauffman House, a former stage stop and hotel built in 1892 and operating today as a history museum.

Getting Around

Grand Lake is 102 miles northwest of Denver, via Interstate 70 west to U.S. Highway 40 (Exit 232). Follow US 40 over Berthoud Pass (11,315 feet and well-maintained year round) and through Winter Park, Fraser and Granby. Grand Lake is 40 miles north of Winter Park. Just past Granby, follow U.S. Highway 34 (and signs to Rocky Mountain National Park) 16 miles north.

Coming from Boulder or Estes Park during the summer, just cross Trail Ridge Road (closed in winter, 44 miles from east to west) through Rocky Mountain National Park to the other side. Grand Lake is 1.3 miles south of the Kawuneeche Visitors Center at the west entrance of Rocky Mountain National Park.

Recreation

Bicycling

A map of the area's mountain biking trails can be found at Rocky Mountain Sports (970) 627-8327, 1137 Grand Avenue, Grand Lake. The shop is open year round and offers information on local mountain biking. The folks here also rent bikes and other equipment, along with sleds and show shoes in winter.

Camping

There's abundant camping in the area in the National Park, forest and recreation area. The Kawuneeche Visitors Center of Rocky Mountain National Park is 1.3 miles north of Grand Lake and is open daily year round. For information, call (970) 627-3471.

Sites in Rocky Mountain National Park

Permits are required for all backcountry camping. Permits are limited in number and are available year round at the West Unit Office at the western entrance of the park on US 34. Permits are available on a first-come basis but may also be obtained in advance by writing to Backcountry Office, Rocky Mountain National Park, Estes Park, CO 80517 or (970) 586-1242; there is a $15 fee Memorial Day through Labor Day.

Timber Creek Campground, 10 miles north of Grand Lake, is the closest developed campsite to Grand Lake. It has 100 sites accommodating tents and recreational vehicles. The fee is $10 per night in winter, $16 in summer, and water is turned on in early June and off in mid-September. The campground operates on a first-come basis with no reservations.

Sites in Arapaho National Recreation Area

This area has 350 campsites in four campgrounds. About 3 miles south on US 34, turn left on County Road 66 and go a mile to **Green Ridge Campground** on Shadow Mountain Lake. (80 sites) ($12 per night, limit 7 nights). Six miles south of Grand Lake on US 34 is **Stillwater Campground** on Lake Granby (145 sites) ($15-20, limit 7 nights).

To reach **Arapahoe Bay Campground** continue a mile south of Stillwater Lake Campground, turn left on County Road 66, and go 10 miles (77 sites) ($12 per night, limit 7 nights).

For **Willow Creek Campground** go south 8 miles on US 34, turn right on US 40 and go 3 miles to this campground on Willow Creek Reservoir. (35 sites) ($8 per night, limit 7 nights).

For more information, call the **Arapaho National Forest**, Sulphur Ranger District Office, at (970) 887-4100; for reservations call toll-free (877) 444-6777.

Sites in Arapaho National Forest

To reach **Sawmill Gulch Campground** go 3 miles northwest of Granby on US 40, turn right on Colo. 125 and go 10 miles. Five sites are available at $7 per night with a 14-night limit. **Denver Creek Campground**, with 25 sites, is 2 more miles up Colo. 125 and charges no fee.

A combination campground, bed and breakfast and recreation park, privately owned **Winding River Resort Village**, (970) 627-3215, has more than 160 campsites adjacent to Rocky Mountain National Park with hot showers, RV hookups, a store and laundry — plus luxurious bed and breakfast rooms. Continental breakfast is included. There's a huge list of activities, including hayrides, horseback riding, a Frisbee golf course, mountain biking and much more. Drive a mile north of Grand Lake on US 34 and turn left across from the National Park Visitors' Center. Follow the signs for 1.5 miles. Tents cost $18 per night for two and $3 for each additional person. RV sites cost $11 to $24 per night for two people and $3 for each additional person.

Fishing

Fishing is great in Grand Lake, Lake Granby, Shadow Mountain Reservoir, the Colorado River, Willow Creek and Monarch Lake. **Budget Tackle** shop owner Bill Leach, (970) 887-9344, is a good local source of information and has a shop about 3 miles from Grand Lake on US 34 and another in Granby. Check the *Daily Tribune* or the weekly *The Prospectus* for his weekly fishing report. Colorado fishing licenses are required for anyone 15 or older. See the "Fishing" section of our Sports chapter for information on fishing licenses.

Golf and Tennis

Grand Lake Golf Course, (970) 627-8008, is one of Colorado's most challenging and beautiful, set among the aspen and pines with gorgeous views of the Continental Divide (it doubles in winter as a cross-country ski area). If your ball goes astray on a narrow fairway, it's likely to winter over in the forest — you'll never find it. At an altitude of 8,420 feet, it can be chilly, and afternoon showers are common, so bring a jacket and rain gear. To reach the course go a quarter-mile north of town on US 34, turn left on County Road 48, and drive another mile. It's walking only and the fee is $50 per person for 18 holes.

There are public tennis courts at Grand Lake Golf Course and at the park in the center of town (maintained by the Grand Lake Metropolitan Recreation District, (970) 627-8328); both are free.

Hiking and Backpacking

It's best to pay a visit to the local forest service office or the National Park for detailed maps and information about local trails. Maps are available at the Sulphur Ranger District Office, 9 Ten-Mile Drive, Granby, CO 80447, (970) 887-4100. Grand County also publishes an excellent recreation guide, which is available from the Chamber of Commerce, visitors' centers or the forest service office. Another good source of information for both hiking and backpacking is **Never Summer Mountain Products**, (970) 627-3642, 919 Grand Avenue, Grand Lake, CO 80447.

Sites in Rocky Mountain National Park

Numerous trailheads, including Green Mountain, Onahu Creek, Timber Lake and the Colorado River Trail are just inside the park. The first two can be short day hikes of a mile or so to the intersection with the Tonahutu Creek Trail, which ventures ever farther into more remote areas of the park. The latter two are more challenging. The **Colorado River Trail** — the easier of the two — goes a scenic 2 miles to Shipler Park and 4 miles to Lulu City, an early mining town site, where all vestiges of civilization were removed when the park was created. The more difficult **Timber Lake Trail** winds 5.5 miles up to a lovely, high, tree-lined lake surrounded by wildflowers with a view of 12,000-foot Mount Ida on the Continental Divide. From Grand Lake there are two nearby trails: the 27-mile, three-day Tonahutu Creek/North Inlet Loop and the easier, shorter East Inlet Trail, which is better for day hikes. The former is a spectacular trip that crosses Andrews Pass and penetrates the heart of the national park — for experienced backpackers only.

The latter offers several alternatives with a short trip to beautiful Adams Falls (0.75 miles each way) or a bit farther to a lovely high meadow perfect for lunch. Lone Pine Lake and Lake Verna are another 4.5 and 5.25 miles respectively. To reach the East Inlet Trailhead, follow W. Portal Road 1.5 miles from Grand Avenue to the end. The Tonahutu Creek/North Inlet Loop begins at the north end of the town at the Park boundary.

Sites in Indian Peaks Wilderness Area

Permits are required for overnight camping in the wilderness area and are available at the Sulphur Ranger District Office, 9 Ten-Mile Drive, Granby, CO, 80446. Call (970) 887-4100 for more information. Permits cost $5 for a limit of 14 nights. Group size is limited to 12 (including pack animals). Advance reservations are required for Crater, Jasper, Diamond and Caribou lakes. **Arapaho Pass Trail** follows Arapaho Creek 10 miles to the top of the pass at 11,900 feet. The first 8 miles are an easy, gradual climb; the last two are tougher and steeper. The trail begins at Monarch Lake, as does the **Buchanan Creek Trail**, a more difficult hike along Buchanan and Cascade creeks to Crater Lake, a good spot for camping and fishing. For an alternative and longer trip that climbs the divide, follow the Pawnee Pass Trail east instead of turning south to Crater Lake. It's a difficult 3-mile climb to the top of the 12,541-foot pass. (Also see Pawnee Pass Trail in our Boulder Sports chapter in the "Hiking" and "Backpacking" sections.) To reach Monarch Lake and the trailhead for these routes, take US 34 south to County Road 6, turn left and go 10 miles to Monarch Lake.

Horseback Riding

Sombrero Stables, (970) 627-3514, 304 W. Portal Road, Grand Lake, CO 80447, offers everything from pony rides for kids to breakfast and steak-fry rides for Mom and Dad to pack trips into the Park for several days for the more adventurous. Rides are $20 an hour. Prices vary for rides with meals. Call for reservations. **Winding River Resort Village**, (970) 627-3215, P.O. Box 629, Grand Lake, CO 80447, also offers hourly guided rides for around $18 an hour.

Llama Trekking

It's hard to picture John Wayne hitting the trail on a llama, but the sure-footed imports are a natural for Colorado's mountain trails. Groups from **Nature Valley Ranch**, (970) 627-3425, about 10 miles north of Granby (157 County Road 4480, Grand Lake, CO 80447) sets out daily on hiking treks with doe-eyed llamas doing the heavy hauling. Treks are daily during the summer, by arrangement at other times of the year. Reservations are required and parties must include six or more participants.

Snowmobiling and Skiing

Grand Lake is the "Official Snowmobiling Capital of Colorado," according to *Snow West* magazine, with more than 300 miles of groomed and ungroomed trails. It's also one of the few places where you can snowmobile right from your front door, out of town and into white solitude. Many local shops rent snowmobiles, among them **Spirit Lake Rentals**, 347 W. Portal Road, (970) 627-9208, and 801

Photo: Daily Camera

Grand Lake lies on the western side of Rocky Mountain National Park.

Grand Avenue, and **Catride**, (970) 627-8866, 724 Grand Avenue — both in town. Another rental shop is **On the Trail**, P.O. Box 1675, Grand Lake, CO 80447 (970) 627-2429.

Cross-country Skiing

Green Mountain Trail, a one-way trail in the national park, makes a nice tour if you have two cars: Leave one car at Green Mountain Trailhead and the other at the Tonahutu Creek/ North Inlet Trailhead. Starting at Green Mountain Trail, 3 miles north of Grand Lake on US 34, the trail goes uphill for 2 miles then turns right on Tonahutu Creek Trail. It's a pleasant 4-mile downhill run to your waiting second car.

During ski season, the Grand Lake Golf Course becomes the **Grand Lake Touring Center**, (970) 627-8008, with 25 kilometers of groomed ski trails around the course and a connecting trail to Soda Springs Ranch and other trails. (Directions are given under Golf.)

At Tabernash, 12 miles north of Winter Park, the **YMCA Snow Mountain Ranch Nordic Center**, (970) 887-2152, offers many kilometers of groomed trails, lighted night skiing and a whole range of facilities including lodging, pools and a roller-skating rink.

Farther down the road toward Winter Park in Fraser is **Devil's Thumb Ranch**, (970) 726-8231, which offers more than 100 kilometers of trails including some nice meadows and rolling terrain as well as more challenging tracks.

All the touring centers above rent ski equipment as well as Grand Lake's **Never Summer Mountain Products**, (970) 627-3642, 919 Grand Avenue, which also sells ski and other outdoor equipment.

Downhill Skiing

Winter Park Ski Resort is 40 miles south of Grand Lake (central reservations: (970) 726-5514 or (800) 453-2525) and offers some of the state's best skiing. Smaller and quieter, **Silver Creek Resort**, (970) 887-3384 or (800) 448-9458, is 15 miles south of Grand Lake and a great family resort for beginning to intermediate skiers (17 miles north of Winter Park on US 40). Please refer to our Sports chapter for more information.

Watersports

This area is known for watersports and there are rental shops galore — especially along the shores of Lake Granby and Shadow Mountain Lake. **Spirit Lake Marina**, (970) 627-8158, 1030 Lake Avenue, offers boat rentals and lake tours from mid-May through mid-October. Bumper boats (like bumper cars) are also available to rent. Grand Lake Marina, (970) 627-9273, 11246 Lake Avenue, rents a variety of watercraft, including motorboats, fishing boats, canoes and paddleboats, as does Highland Marina at 7878 U.S. Highway 34, (970) 887-3341.

Annual Events

Western Week Buffalo BBQ
(mid-July) Grand Lake • (970) 627-3402

This event takes place in mid-July and is an old-time celebration. Included in the week of events is the Spirit Lake Mountain Men Rendezvous, a parade down Grand Avenue and, of course, a grand barbecue with all the fixin's.

Lipton Cup Regatta
(early August)

Named for English tea baron Sir Thomas Lipton, who was wined and dined by early members of Grand Lake's Yacht Club, this race is not open to the public. Spectators, however, can watch the yacht club sailors compete for the prestigious sterling silver Lipton Cup.

Then there are the Memorial Day weekend auction and parade, the grand scale Fourth of July fireworks display, turtle races and the Grand Festival of the Arts in August. For the more sedate, there's Bingo Friday and Saturday nights at the Town Park.

Grand Lake is alive and well in the winter months as well with ice fishing derbies, snowmobile drag races, an ice golf tournament, ice/snow sculpture competition, concerts, sled-dog races and other events. Call the Chamber of Commerce, (970) 627-3402 or (970) 627-3372, for a complete schedule, dates and details.

Restaurants

Grand Lake's six-block main street, Grand Avenue, is lined with numerous small eateries with a variety of offerings, from beer and burgers to cappuccino and pastries. There are also a few fine dining establishments tucked away at both ends of town and a little ways

out of town. For a tasty treat, stop in at the Rocky Mountain Chocolate Factory about midway down Grand Avenue.

Most restaurants have sections for smokers and nonsmokers, and the ones we've noted here accept major credit cards.

Price Code

The price code is based on dinner for two people, excluding cocktails, beer or wine, appetizer, dessert, tax and tip.

$	Less than $25
$$	$25 to $50
$$$	$50 to $75
$$$$	$75 and more

Chuckhole Cafe
$ • 1131 Grand Ave., Grand Lake • (970) 627-3509

Choose the Chuckhole for a hearty breakfast, featuring a full breakfast menu, plus lunch choices of burgers, chili, sandwiches, salads, homemade pies and cappuccino. The Chuckhole serves breakfast and lunch daily.

Pancho & Lefty's
$ • 1101 Grand Ave., Grand Lake • (970) 627-8773

No Colorado town is complete without a Mexican cafe, and here it is. The Pancho & Lefty combo means both Mexican and American dishes. Have a tasty taco, burrito, burger or steak, and there's a full bar too. The cafe is open daily for lunch and dinner.

Caroline's Cuisine
$$ • 9921 U.S. Hwy. 34 (Soda Springs Ranch), Grand Lake • (970) 627-9404

For quite a reasonable price, enjoy French-American cuisine and an extensive wine list at this attractive restaurant. There's a children's menu and a full bar. Caroline's is open for dinner daily except Mondays.

The Mountain Inn
$ • 612 Grand Ave., Grand Lake • (970) 627-3385

A crowded parking lot is usually a good sign and so are the full tables inside this cozy restaurant, specializing in "Grandma's cooking." The catch of the day complements the menu, which features homemade chicken pot pie, old-fashioned stews, real mashed potatoes (which seem to be a big item in Grand Lake) and Mexican food. The restaurant is open year round.

The Rapids Lodge and Restaurant
$-$$ • East end of town; turn left at the end of Grand Ave., Grand Lake
• (970) 627-3707

Ask for a table by the window here to enjoy the beautiful, rushing Tonahutu River. And why not celebrate with a $200 bottle of 1979 Chateau Haut Brion Graves (first growth) or a slightly less expensive Dom Perignon in an atmosphere worthy of such grand libation. Those on a budget needn't be dissuaded; there are less expensive drink and food offerings, including pasta dishes for less than $10 and children's dinners. The meal includes an extensive hors d'oeuvres tray with shrimp, two delicious patés and sorbet. Dinner offerings include Alaska king crab legs, trout stuffed with crab, filet mignon and other delectable choices. Steamy espresso or cappuccino can accompany the dessert of the evening. The serene dining room offers a rustically elegant Victorian atmosphere. Rapids is open year round for dinner only.

Grand Lake Lodge Restaurant
$$ • 0.25 mile north of Grand Lake off U.S. Hwy. 34, Grand Lake
• (970) 627-3967

Enjoy an evening cocktail or full meal on the lodge's open porch, or enjoy the same grand view inside the comfortably rustic dining room. Either way, you'll have a glorious view of the lake and surrounding area. The restaurant specializes in Continental cuisine with open grill. There are full breakfasts and a spectacular Sunday champagne brunch. There's weekly entertainment in the bar. The dining room serves breakfast, lunch and dinner and is open daily from Memorial Day through the week after Labor Day.

Marie's Grand Lake Cafe
$ • 938 Grand Ave., Grand Lake
• (970) 627-9475

Slept in? No problem — Marie serves breakfast all day, along with a selection of American and Mexican food, for reasonable prices. The restaurant and bar is closed Tuesdays.

Rocky Mountain Coffee Company
$ • 915 Grand Ave., Grand Lake
• (970) 627-5005

True to it's name, the Coffee Company offers rich coffee and espresso, along with tea, homemade soup, sandwiches and some sinful pastries. It's open at 7 AM for folks eager to hit the slopes or the trails or the lakes or the shops.

E.G.'s Garden Grill
$$ • 1000 Grand Ave., Grand Lake
• (970) 627-8404

Sit outside and watch the Grand Lake scene pass while chowing down on everything from light fare like salads and sandwiches to gourmet burgers and ribs.

Daven Haven Lodge
$$ • 604 Marina Drive, Grand Lake
• (970) 627-8144

Dinner is served daily at 5 PM at this hearty restaurant on the lake. Steaks, seafood and pasta are the specialties. There's a menu for kids and seniors can split entrees.

Terrace Inn
$$$ • 813 Grand Lake Ave., Grand Lake
• (970) 627-3000

It's about ambiance in this charming 1920s

INSIDERS' TIP

Grand Lake is considered to be on the "western slope." Estes Park and Boulder are on the "eastern slope" (almost always referred to as the Front Range). The Continental Divide that runs along the spine of the Rocky Mountains in Colorado is the dividing line between east and west as far as slopes and river drainages go.

circa inn on Grand Lake's main street. Breakfast, lunch and dinner are served in the upscale dining room.

Accommodations

Grand Lake has a large selection of lodges, motels and cabins. Many are right on the lake; others are along scenic creeks tumbling down from the mountains. It's always a good idea to ask to see a room before you put your money down, should you decide to strike out on your own, but below are some recommended places to stay.

All the accommodations listed accept major credit cards, but leave Spot or Fluffy behind — no pets are allowed in any of these properties.

Price Code

Our price code is based on the average cost of a double occupancy room.

$	Less than $30
$$	$31 to $50
$$$	$51 to $75
$$$$	$76 to $90
$$$$$	$91 and more

Columbine Creek Ranch Bed and Breakfast
$$ • 14814 U.S. Hwy. 34, Grand Lake • (970) 627-2429

This early 20th-century lodge with its own trout ponds once hosted Lucille Ball and Desi Arnaz. There are seven unique rooms and four cabins. The ranch specializes in family reunions, and for groups of 30 or more, a pig roast is included. There's a fireplace and big-screen TV in the family living area and a hot tub nearby. Smoking is not allowed. Fishing equipment is furnished free, but there's a fee for each fish caught. Gas grills are available for guests wishing to cook their own trout.

The Rapids Lodge
$$-$$$ • East end of town; turn left at end of Grand Avenue, Grand Lake • (970) 627-3707

The oldest lodge in Grand Lake, built in the early 1900s, the Rapids Lodge looks quite rustic from the outside. But once inside, guests will be charmed by the lovely restored Victorian decor and antiques. The dining room looks out on the rushing Tonahutu River — a feast for the eyes with its frothy water spraying over large boulders. It was the river that powered a generator, making the Rapids the first electrified building in Grand Lake. Carpeted and comfortable, the rooms in the lodge are a nostalgic combination with lace curtains and hearts-and-flowers wallpaper. Each room has a big brass bed or a four-poster wooden one, mounded with fluffy quilts. You can easily imagine yourself back at the turn of the century in this delightful retreat. Those who relish the sight and sound of the rushing water should ask for a room on the creek side. Nonsmoking rooms are available in the adjacent Rapids Chalet; there are also individual cabins and bright, modern condominiums along the creek that sleep up to 12 people. The lodge is open year round.

Lemmon Lodge
$$ • East end of town behind yacht club; turn right at the end of Grand Avenue, Grand Lake • (970) 627-3314 (summer), (970) 725-3511 (winter)

Situated right on Grand Lake's lapping edge, Lemmon Lodge offers a variety of small and large (up to 12 persons) cabins in a pleasant, wooded area of five private acres. There are kitchens in all but one of the cabins, barbecue grills and picnic tables on the grounds and a children's playground right on the beach. The lodge's location on the North Inlet of the lake offers great fishing and a private boat slip, so bring your rod and boat. Cabins are often reserved a year in advance, and there's a four-day minimum stay required from late June to early September (three-day minimum over Memorial and Labor Day weekends). Smoking is allowed in some of the cabins; pets are not.

Grand Lake Lodge
$$ • 0.25 mile north of Grand Lake; look for the sign, and turn on U.S. Hwy. 34, Grand Lake • (970) 627-3967 (in-season), (970) 759-5848 (off-season)

Perched on a hilltop overlooking the lake,

the historic, log-beamed main lodge is very inviting. This classic mountain lodge lies on the boundary of Rocky Mountain National Park with an inviting heated swimming pool right in front. The lodge's window-lined dining room sprawls out onto a front porch affording a grand view for an alfresco meal. In the evenings, guests gather in the lodge's friendly, relaxed atmosphere to watch a movie, play cards or warm their toes around the big circular freestanding fireplace. A 14-person hot tub has been added. The cabins, tucked away in a lodgepole pine forest up the hillside, don't share the lodge's grand view. The comfortable, austere (no phones or TV) cabins range from two-person modern duplexes to the Ford Cabin (where Henry Ford stayed in 1927), which sleeps 10 people. The lodge opens the first weekend in June and stays open through the second weekend in September (minimum stays of two and three days are required on weekends and holidays, respectively). Smoking is allowed; pets are not.

Trail Mountain Bed & Breakfast
$$$ • 4850 County Rd. 41 (6 miles south of Grand Lake or 8.4 miles north of Granby on U.S. 34)
• (970) 887-3944

Ideal for adult couples or small groups looking for privacy in a pristine setting with a taste of luxury, this bed and breakfast inn is close to lots of area activities such as golf and skiing. Each of the three large guest rooms has a private bath, shower, gas fireplace and two-person Jacuzzi tub. Each room has a deck, and two rooms have private entrances. There's a big fireplace in the great room, near the dining area, plus a wet bar. Smoking and pets are not allowed.

Columbine Creek Ranch
$$$ • 14814 U.S. Highway 34
• (970) 887-2429

There's a catch-and-release

pond right outside the five cabins and one apartment that make up the Ranch; if you can't give up your catch, you can keep it for a fee. Cabins all have gas grills and there's a hot tub for guests. Minimum stay is two nights, three nights over holidays.

Mountain Lakes Lodge
$$$ • 10480 Highway 34
• (970) 887-8448

Dogs are welcome at this hewn log lodge, built in 1955 on the waterway between Lake Granby and Shadow Mountain Reservoir. Ten cabins and a log house have private decks and barbecues, color TV and kitchenettes. There's a two-night minimum on summer weekends and a three night minimum on holidays.

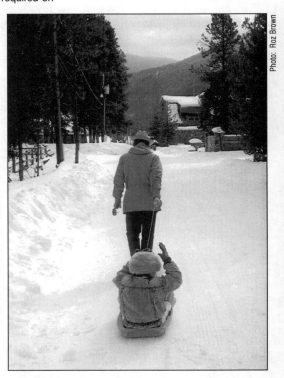

Photo: Roz Brown

Winter in Grand Lake — a perfect time to hitch a ride.

Index of Advertisers

Index